WITHDRAWN

# Sport in the Global Society

General Editor: J.A. Mangan

SPORT IN ASIAN SOCIETY

SPORT IN THE GLOBAL SOCIETY
General Editor: J.A. Mangan

The interest in sports studies around the world is growing and will continue to do so. This unique series combines aspects of the expanding study of *sport in the global society*, providing comprehensiveness and comparison under one editorial umbrella. It is particularly timely, with studies in the cultural, economic, ethnographic, geographical, political, social, anthropological, sociological and aesthetic elements of sport proliferating in institutions of higher education.

Eric Hobsbawm once called sport one of the most significant practices of the late nineteenth century. Its significance was even more marked in the late twentieth century and will continue to grow in importance into the new millennium as the world develops into a 'global village' sharing the English language, technology and sport.

Other Titles in the Series

Women, Sport and Society in Modern China
Holding Up *More* than Half the Sky
Dong Jinxia

Sport in Latin American Society
Past and Present
Edited by J.A. Mangan and Lamartine P. DaCosta

Sport in Australasian Society
Past and Present
Edited by J.A. Mangan and John Nauright

Sporting Nationalisms
Identity, Ethnicity, Immigration and Assimilation
Edited by Mike Cronin and David Mayall

The Commercialization of Sport
Edited by Trevor Slack

The Future of Football
Challenges for the Twenty-First Century
Edited by Jon Garland, Dominic Malcolm and Michael Rowe

Football Culture
Local Contests, Global Visions
Edited by Gerry P.T. Finn and Richard Giulianotti

France and the 1998 World Cup
The National Impact of a World Sporting Event
Edited by Hugh Dauncey and Geoff Hare

The First Black Footballer
Arthur Wharton 1865–1930:
An Absence of Memory
Phil Vasili

Scoring for Britain
International Football and International Politics, 1900–1939
Peter J. Beck

Shaping the Superman
Fascist Body as Political Icon: Aryan Fascism
Edited by J.A. Mangan

Superman Supreme
Fascist Body as Political Icon: Global Fascism
Edited by J.A. Mangan

Making the Rugby World
Race, Gender, Commerce
Edited by Timothy J.L Chandler and John Nauright

Rugby's Great Split
Class, Culture and the Origins of Rugby League Football
Tony Collins

The Race Game
Sport and Politics in South Africa
Douglas Booth

Cricket and England
A Cultural and Social History of the Inter-war Years
Jack Williams

The Games Ethic and Imperialism
Aspects of the Diffusion of an Ideal
J.A. Mangan

Sport, Media, Culture
Global and Local Dimensions
Edited by Alina Bernstein and Neil Blain

SPORT IN ASIAN SOCIETY

Past and Present

Editors

J.A. MANGAN
University of Strathclyde

FAN HONG
De Montfort University

FRANK CASS
LONDON • PORTLAND, OR

First published in 2003 in Great Britain by
FRANK CASS PUBLISHERS
Crown House, 47 Chase Side, Southgate,
London, N14 5BP

and in the United States of America by
FRANK CASS PUBLISHERS
c/o ISBS, 5824 N.E. Hassalo Street
Portland, Oregon 97213-3644

Copyright © 2003 Frank Cass & Co. Ltd.

Website: www.frankcass.com

British Library Cataloguing in Publication Data

Sport in Asian society : past and present. – (Sport in the global society)
1. Sports – Asia – History 2. Sports – Social aspects – Asia
I. Mangan, J. A. (James Anthony), 1939– II. Hong, Fan
306.4'83'095

ISBN 0-7146-5342-X (cloth)
ISBN 0-7146-8330-2 (paper)
ISSN 1368-9789

Library of Congress Cataloging-in-Publication Data

Sports in Asian society : past and present / editors, J.A. Mangan, Fan Hong.
  p. cm.
Includes bibliographical references (p.) and index.
  ISBN 0-7146-5342-X (cloth) – ISBN 0-7146-8330-2 (paper)
  1. Sports – Asia – History. 2. Sports – Social aspects – Asia. I. Mangan, J. A. II. Hong, Fan.
  GV649 .S69 2003
  796'.095–dc21   2002151405

This group of studies first appeared as a special issue of
The International Journal of the History of Sport (ISSN 0952-3367),
Vol.19, Nos.2, 3, June–September 2002, published by Frank Cass

All rights reserved. No part of this publication may be reproduced, stored in or introduced into a retrieval system, or transmitted, in any form or by any means, electronic, mechanical, photocopying, recording or otherwise, without the prior written permission of the publisher of this book.

Printed in Great Britain by Antony Rowe Ltd., Chippenham, Wilts

Contents

List of Tables and Figures   vii

Foreword   **Bi Shiming**   ix

Series Editor's Foreword   xi

Prologue – Asian Sport:
From the Recent Past   J.A. Mangan   1

1. Imperial Origins: Christian Manliness,
   Moral Imperatives and Pre-Sri Lankan
   Playing Fields – Beginnings   J.A. Mangan   11

2. Imperial Origins: Christian Manliness,
   Moral Imperatives and Pre-Sri Lankan
   Playing Fields – Consolidation   J.A. Mangan   35

3. Celestials in Touch: Sport and the   N.G. Aplin
   Chinese in Colonial Singapore   and Quek Jin Jong   67

4. 'Sportsmanship' – English Inspiration and
   Japanese Response: F.W. Strange and   Ikuo Abe
   Chiyosaburo Takeda.   and J.A. Mangan   99

5. 'Healthy Bodies, Healthy Minds':
   Sport and Society in Colonial Malaya   Janice N. Brownfoot   129

6. Cricket in Colonial India:
   The Bombay Pentangular, 1892–1946   Boria Majumdar   157

7. Sport in China: Conflict between Tradition   Fan Hong
   and Modernity, 1840s to 1930s   and Tan Hua   189

8. Ideology, Politics, Power: Korean Sport — Transformation, 1945–92   Ha Nam-Gil and J.A. Mangan 213

9. Shackling the Lion: Sport and Modern Singapore   Peter A. Horton 243

10. The Juggernaut of Globalization: Sport and Modernization in Iran   H.E. Chehabi 275

11. *Pancasila*: Sport and the Building of Indonesia — Ambitions and Obstacles   Iain Adams 295

12. Communist China: Sport, Politics and Diplomacy   Fan Hong and Xiong Xiaozheng 319

13. The Road to Modernization: Sport in Taiwan   Trevor Slack, Hsu Yuan-min, Tsai Chiung-tzu and Fan Hong 343

14. Sport in Modern India: Policies, Practices and Problems   Packianathan Chelladurai, D. Shanmuganathan, Jaihind Jothikaran and A.S. Nageswaran 366

15. From Iran to All of Asia: The Origin and Diffusion of Polo   H.E. Chehabi and Allen Guttmann 384

Epilogue – Into the Future: Asian Sport and Globalization   Fan Hong 401

Select Bibliography 408

Notes on Contributors 417

Index 421

Tables and Figures

Figure 4.1　Categorical phases of athletic exercise　127

Figure 4.2　Kinds of athletic exercise　127

Table　4.1　Virtues of *Kyogido*　128

Table　8.1　An abbreviated history of the Korean sports movement　219

Table　8.2　Olympic medal results at the Olympic (summer) Games　222

Table　8.3a　Korean economic growth, 1956–95　234

Table　8.3b　Changes in Korean per capita gross national product (US$), 1960–95　234

Table　13.1　Results of Taiwan's participation in the Asian Games, 1954–98　364

Table　13.2　Results of Taiwan's participation in the Olympic Games, 1960–2000　364

Table　14.1　Pension rates for sportspersons in India　377

Table　14.2　National Welfare Fund rates for Indian sportspersons　378

Foreword

I greatly enjoyed *Sport in Asian Society: Past and Present*. Its coverage of so many Asian nations in one volume is impressive. It discusses aspects of the origins of modern sport in Sri Lanka, Japan and India, recounts the fascinating story of 'ping-pong diplomacy' in China, covers politics and sport in South Korea, India and Indonesia, fills a historical gap with its discussion of the evolution of sport in Taiwan, provides a novel perspective on sport in Malaysia and deals with the cultural diffusion of polo in Asia. Above all, it analyzes the evolutionary process of modernization in sport in Asia.

As an Asian, and as a Chinese, I am delighted to see this publication of a collection on Asian sport in English. Although it does not cover all the countries in Asia (that would require a volume of encyclopaedic proportions) it is an impressive pioneering work. It has brought the works of Asian scholars, especially indigenous Asian scholars, to the attention of the international community. (I would add here a special note of appreciation to my Chinese colleagues, Fan Hong, Tan Hua and Xiong Xiaozheng, whose academic work in China and Chinese, I know and respect.)

Sport in Asian Society amply fulfils the laudable ambition of J.A. Mangan, Series Editor of Sport in the Global Society, to bring the voices of Asia to the world through the medium of the English language. It provides a fine example of intellectual liaison between countries and continents and will help an international audience comprehend the significance of Asian sport in different political, cultural and historical settings. Best of all, it will overcome the traditional domination of Anglo-American historical studies and sociological theories in sports studies. Academic works like this will advance theoretical and empirical studies in Asia. I sincerely thank the contributors to the book for the quality of their essays; the editors, J.A. Mangan and Fan Hong, for their intelligent action in bringing Asian scholars to the fore and the publisher, Frank Cass, for making it happen.

Final thoughts: Asian is a continent with a rich history. However, in the eighteenth and nineteenth centuries Asia fell behind Europe and

North America. After more than 100 years in the doldrums, Asia is experiencing the fresh winds of progress once again. Asian sport, for example, has become fully respected in the 'global village'. I am sure the readers of *Sport in Asian Society* will read it, like I have, with great pleasure. It is well researched and well written. It will enhance their knowledge of Asian culture and society in general and sport in particular. Enjoy it as I did.

BI SHIMING
former President, Chinese Society for the History of Sport
Beijing
October 2002

Series Editor's Foreword

Asian sport is certainly on the map. Japan and Korea have recently hosted, to thunderous international applause, the FIFA Football World Championships (men); Korea will shortly host the Asian Games in Pusan. In 2003 China hosts the FIFA Football World Championships (women) and not too far ahead is the long-awaited Beijing Olympics.[1] This volume is published in celebration of the 2002 Asian Games in Pusan. It is by way of an acknowledgement that in the twentieth century Asia made notable contributions to modern sport.

While congratulations for their enthusiastic involvement in modern sport are extended to all the Asian countries, perhaps special mention should be made of China. What a cornucopia of talent has emerged from that great nation in recent years. It is no longer a 'sleeping dragon'; it is wide-awake. Joseph Stiglitz wrote recently that he had been involved for nearly 20 years in discussions with Chinese leaders regarding the transition from communist to market economies and added that he had been 'a strong advocate of the gradualist policies adopted by the Chinese, policies that have proven their merit over the past two decades'.[2] Other policies, especially regarding sport, incidentally described comprehensively and cogently in a forthcoming volume in the Sport in the Global Society series, in many if not all regards, also elicit admiration.[3]

In sport, as in other things, all is not perfect in China, but where is it perfect? International performances by Chinese in recent decades have much to commend them. Arguably, they inspire Asia to emulation, not necessarily to exact organizational imitation, but to future achievement. As Stiglitz has remarked in another context: 'For Asians, a variety of Asian models has worked well, and this is true for Malaysia and Korea as well as China and Taiwan'[4] and, it must surely be added, other nations of that vast continent.

The twenty-first century may well see the global consolidation of the market-state, which, as Phillip Bobbit has suggested, is emerging from 'the *relationship* between strategy and the legal order as this relationship has shaped and transformed the modern state'.[5] Bobbit's dense and subtle work, in some respects threateningly apocalyptic, deals with survival not sport, yet it offers some insights sanguine in prospect and of particular interest to those who track global sport into the future. Bobbit writes:

The central point in recognizing the emergence of the market-state is not simply to slough off the decayed nation-state. It is also to emphasize the importance of developing 'public goods' – such as loyalty, civility, trust in authority, respect for family life, reverence for sacrifice, regard for privacy, admiration for political competence – that the market, unaided, is not very well adapted to creating and maintaining. The market-state has to produce public goods because that is precisely what the market will not do.[6]

Unquestionably sport can also be a 'public good': the market alone cannot, or more pointedly will not, develop and sustain it if it fails to deliver financial profit. If the nation's ambitions are mass health, mass pleasure and positive international image, clearly all 'public goods', sport is ruthlessly reduced to a system of exclusive control by market forces, but then none of these things will come to full fruition. In pursuit of sport as a public good, as *Sport in Asian Society* demonstrates, in some respects some nations in Asia have been ahead of much of the world.

J.A. MANGAN
International Research Centre for Sport,
Socialisation and Society
University of Strathclyde
October 2002

NOTES

1. Dong Jinxia, *Women and Elite Sport in Modern China: Holding Up* More *than Half the Sky* (London and Portland, OR: Frank Cass, 2002).
2. Joseph E. Stiglitz, *Globalization and its Discontents* (London: Allen Lane, 2002), pp.x–xi.
3. Ibid., p.218.
4. Ibid.
5. Phillip Bobbit, *The Shield of Achilles: War and Peace and the Course of History* (London: Allen Lane, 2002), p.xxi.
6. Ibid., p.814.

PROLOGUE

Asian Sport: From the Recent Past

J.A. MANGAN

Sport in Asian Society: Past and Present is concerned with the arrival, spread and advance of modern sport in Asia. Of necessity, it cannot be comprehensive in its coverage of happenings, issues and practices, but it is one of the first attempts to cover these happenings, issues and practices in Asia. More attempts in the series Sport in the Global Society are not far behind.[1]

One thing should be made quite clear. There is no procrustean effort to crush contributions into a spurious thematic 'coherence'; the virtue of this collection is in its demonstration of the eclectic role of modern sport in modern society. Thus a variety of themes, related and unrelated, are deliberately made available. They illustrate the conceptual, empirical and analytical subtlety of studies of modern sport. *Sport in Asian Society* aspires simply to be what it is – an exercise in eclecticism.

An eclectic approach is wise:

> Asia is the largest continent in the world. It is almost five times the size of the United States. Yet the name is no more than a geographic expression. The continent has no racial, political, cultural, religious, or historical unity. Its countries and its peoples are of seemingly infinite variety. The word Asia is derived from *asu*, an early Greek word for sunrise, although some scholars trace its roots to the second millennium BC Hittites, who applied the term to what is now Turkey, where they resided. In the course of the Christian millennia, the Europeans used the term to include all the countries to their east. They also coined other designations for Asian subregions, such as the Near East, the Middle East, and the Far East, depending on their distance from Europe. The Americans, facing Asia across the Pacific, quite logically in reverse order could have advanced the notions of the Near West, Middle

West, and Far West. Asians of course had indigenous names for their own and neighboring lands.[2]

Furthermore: 'Asia is a geographic vastness and variety. It comprises one-fifth of the world's total land area. It embraces an extreme of topographical features: deserts, forests, mountains, plants ... and extremes climates are registered.'[3] Not only this, but the recognized boundaries of Asia

> embrace some 17 million square miles of continental landmasses, main lands, and outlying archipelagos. Overall, they range 5,000 miles north to south and 6,000 miles east to west. Asia is separated from Europe by the Ural Mountains and the Caspian and Black Seas, and from Africa by the Suez Isthmus.[4]

This is the Asia of this volume (with the single exception of Siberia). Thus it covers the Middle East, South and South-East Asia, East and Central Asia and North-East Asia.

Finally, this Asia consists of peoples of racial, linguistic and cultural complexity, and their histories – secular and religious:

> More than half of the world's population lives on the continent. China, with over a billion inhabitants, is the world's most populous. India follows not far behind. Four countries – Bangladesh, Indonesia, Japan and Pakistan – each have over one hundred million people ... of the world's largest eight cities, six are in Asia: Beijing, Bombay, Calcutta, Seoul, Shanghai, and Tokyo. Yet almost three-fourths of the continent's inhabitants are overwhelmingly rural.[5]

In summary, Asia is the largest and most diverse continent on earth, with the greatest range of land elevation of any continent, the longest coastline, the most extremes of climate and the most varied forms of vegetation and animal life on earth; and the peoples of Asia have established the broadest pattern of human adaptation of any of the continents.[6] Needless to say, generalizations about Asia must be made with extreme caution. Nevertheless, it is widely accepted that this Asia, 'drawing on indigenous traditions and adapting Western skills to express them, emerged as the world's most dynamic continent by the end of the twentieth century'.[7] Among the adapted western skills has been modern sport.

In view of what has been written above, it is easy to see that a single volume, for all the increasing importance of modern sport to Asia, can only skim the surface.

Central to the contributions of *Sport in Asian Society* is a subscription to the triadic approach discussed in the series editor's foreword to an earlier volume on Asia in the series *Sport in the Global Society*.[8] There I wrote, with regard to studies of sport in Asian culture: 'A triadic approach is overdue: Western voices on Asia, Asian voices on Asia, Eastern and Western voices on Asia.'[9] The metaphoric gathering of corn in foreign fields, I suggested, was a thing of the past. I remarked additionally that in sports studies in the West, 'which have come late to the Asian historical field, this radicalism *should* be built on'.[10] This is the intention of *Sport in Asian Society* and the series Sport in the Global Society. I have stated that the series would ensure 'that Asian academics will be encouraged not only to contribute to but to edit and author books on history, sociology and other disciplines, in the series in the future – to the benefit of East and West'.[11] The reason is self-evident: they possess 'the cultural and linguistic tools to ensure a valuable balance to European perspectives'.[12] I have begun to keep my promise with *Sport in Asian Society*. And shortly in the series, the East will continue to speak to the West, and Asians speak for themselves: 'Eastern commentators will [thus] advance Western perspectives on Asia.'[13]

On a personal but relevant level, few things have given me more professional pleasure in my years in academia than to have been able to encourage, sustain, and see to completion the work of my Asian research students. Their courage in bringing views and visions of the Orient to the English-language reader, by way of (for them) a difficult foreign language and different academic customs and traditions, is nothing short of remarkable. Their talent, revealed in their speedily published monographs, speaks for itself. I have learnt much from them. They have educated me. I see Asia with new eyes. If I do not fully comprehend their cultures, then I comprehend more of their cultures than before.

It is with pleasure then that I edit this volume with an Asian former research student of mine, now an English university academic, Dr Fan Hong.

In the twentieth century, claims D.A. Low, the colonized nations of Monsoon Asia went through three successive stages: the Groping, the Great Achievement and the Rectification.[14] The first occurred spasmodically until the Second World War. Its aims were the eradication of imperial political domination and the search for a new social order. A first set of Gropings were undertaken by the early western-educated elites.[15] Most of them were 'good at making speeches, passing resolutions, fashioning the fundamental trends of Asia's rising nationalism'.[16] Progress was slow but confidence was boosted by the defeat of a European nation in the Russo-Japanese War of 1904–5; encouraged further by the collapse of the Russian, Austro-Hungarian and Ottoman empires, a new spirit of assertion gradually characterized Monsoon Asia.[17] Out of such beginnings, after much conflict and many setbacks, this Asia, set slowly on fire by secular nationalists and 'spiritual' communists, transformed its political structures. Monsoon Asia entered the era of the Great Achievement.[18] The post-war years saw a widespread transference of power. Imperialism steadily retreated and a variety of political configurations replaced it.

While close scrutiny of regions, groups of nations and individual nations is necessary to comprehend distinct patterns and variations of these patterns, the general picture with respect to imperialism in the Great Achievement period was much the same – replacement and then the period of the Rectification in three successive phrases: the Renovations, the Second Starts and the Conservative Outcome[19] in the pursuit of modern nation states and more equitable and appropriate social orders.[20] The Renovations, dramatic as they were and involving considerable change, stimulated a desire for more complete change. This in turn produced a rejection of 'long-evolving revolutionary propensities'[21] and then came the period of Conservative Outcomes – the product of fear of irreparable social damage.[22] Support for revolutionary action had begun to wear thin – 'a widespread change of temper was now taking place in much of Monsoon Asia'[23] – and by the 1980s pragmatic, growth-orientated and often authoritarian regimes prevailed across the region, represented by both the Left and the Right.[24] This brought in its wake a desire to curb the excesses of authoritarian regimes and champion democratic ones.[25]

In summary,

> in the first half of the twentieth century, Monsoon Asia saw the largest and most wide spread uprising against the dominion of Occidental imperial powers that the world had seen before or since. Thereafter there were extensive attempts to work out some deep-seated revolutionary impulses to the full, so as to create much more 'modern' political systems and much more equitable and efficiently structured social orders.[26]

It should not be overlooked that Korea's pursuit of the same objectives, which saw the rebuttal of *Oriental* imperialism in the shape of Japan, was all part and parcel of a common trend which despite varying ideological stimuli, distinctive national responses and different transitory consequences, had by the twenty-first century a common component – national independence.

What is true of Monsoon Asia is more or less true of the whole of Asia – a term that took a while to 'settle'. It should never be forgotten that 'Asia as a political entity, suitable for unified treatment, had its origin in Europe. It had little meaning for the people of Asia itself until well on in the nineteenth century.'[27] It was only well into the twentieth century that Europeans began to subdivide Asia in relation to itself. Categories appeared: 'Central (Soviet); South (the Indian subcontinent and its appendages); South-East (Burma, Malaysia, Indonesia); and East (predominantly China and Japan)'.[28] These were far from hard-and-fast categories. It has been remarked, incidentally, that if Europeans tended to impose on Asia a unity not recognized nor appreciated by its diverse inhabitants, then in truth, Asians have tended to attribute to Europeans a singleness of purpose not always acceptable to them. It does scant justice to political conflict between Europeans in Asia itself or to confrontations between western philosophies and religions there.

The European colonial period began in earnest when 'the Industrial Revolution intensified the demand for raw materials and new materials, and the "colonial" phase of European intrusion into Asia followed close on its heels'.[29] In reality, this colonial period was relatively brief, but in all sorts of ways its impact was lasting. This is certainly true of the influence of modern sport. Initially a part of the extensive 'imperial baggage' and for the use of the imperialist, it came to have other uses – not least as a means of attempted control over the morals and minds of the 'native' in the interests of political stability, religious proselytism and ethnocentric moralism.[30] When these uses had served their purpose and Europeans retreated from imperial ambitions and lost some enthusiasm for control and conversion in the face of increasingly nationalistic communities, the sport of *homo ludens imperiosus* (and it was mostly *his* at the time) remained and thrived, widely adopted, sometimes adapted and increasingly enjoyed. The globalization of modern sport was the outcome. Sport is now arguably the most universal representation of a modern global popular culture. Globalization – while not an inexorable force for total homogenization – is emphatically a source of greater homogenization. Globalization came essentially in three phases: imperialism, nationalism and consumerism.

It is not infrequently overlooked that a crucial element in the process of the globalization of sport was education. It was the triumph of western theories and practices of education, not least the essentially English phenomenon of athleticism[31] that dominated England's late Victorian and Edwardian private schools for the privileged, which initially facilitated, not exclusively but extensively, the global spread of modern sport – a cultural revolution with heavily political and associated emotional reverberations which grow louder by the decade.[32]

From these reverberations Asia was not immune. In the post-imperial period, essentially after the Second World War, as the political, national and personal confidence of the European in Asia was hugely reduced, with the rise of nationalism came sport for national image, prestige and status. In addition, the collective Asian response to decades of European and American 'front running' came in the form of Pan-Asianism – going it alone as a region apart and distinct from the too often all-pervasive western presence – and thus the growth of the Asian Games. Asia, however, was not to escape the ubiquitous westerner quite so easily. In pursuit of global status, western manifestations such as the Olympic Games and the FIFA World Cup draw Asians and others to them as magnets draw iron filings. To beat the world it is necessary to join the world; to humiliate the former colonialist it is necessary to engage and defeat him; to cut a figure with your own 'local' nations it is necessary not only to defeat them but those in the still largely economically, militarily and culturally dominant West.

Tolstoy in *War and Peace* wrote: 'If the purpose of history is the description of the flux of humanity and peoples, the first question to be answered … will be: What is the power that moves nations?'[33] This quotation appeared recently in Niall Ferguson's *The Cash Nexus: Money and Power in the Modern World, 1700–2000*, and Ferguson comments sagely that if in physics, power is measured only in watts, in history it is measured in many different units.[34] Without a doubt, one unit of measurement in the modern world is the capacity to win medals, break records and defeat the best in the world's sports arenas and on the world's sports fields. For Asians and others, it provides powerfully evidence of an elitism that breeds confidence, redefines superiority, pays off old imperial scores and establishes post-imperial ways of looking at the world.

It has been claimed with total justification that 'the spread of consumer products and related values was one of the key developments in twentieth century history'.[35] Three significant phenomena spring to mind:

> the spread of British sports in the late nineteenth century [and the spread of American sports mostly in the twentieth] supplementing or displacing traditional games in many parts of the world; the development of Hollywood as an international entertainment centre; and the recent global success of American based fast-food chains, supplementing and challenging traditional eating habits in many areas.[36]

In fact, all three manifestations come together in sport in the twenty-first century in the form of a global consumer culture – profit-driven, media-controlled and entertainment-orientated. This is a culture with an international symbolic language – tracks, fields, arenas, medals, cups – even more widespread than the English language.[37]

No Asian nation has successfully resisted, or indeed has wished to resist on any permanent basis, this new 'imperialism' from the West. The global consumer culture has proved alluringly seductive – and modern sport is close to, if not at, its centre. Global success through sport sustains politicians, enriches entrepreneurs, deifies performers and intoxicates the masses. Even the fundamentalist Islamic states have failed to curb fully its 'immoralities'. Others simply enjoy it, profit from it and seek power through it.

Writing of the evolution of political culture in Europe from the late seventeenth to the late eighteenth centuries, J.C.W. Blanning has remarked that along side the old culture, centred on the courts and monarchical authority, there arose a 'public sphere' in which private individuals came together to form a whole greater than the sum of the parts. These individuals through the exchange of ideas created a cultural actor – the public – that came to dominate European culture over time.[38] This is a paradigm of value in any consideration of modern sport in the twenty-first century. There is sufficient in Blanning's insight to allow light to be shed on the evolution of modern sport from royal and aristocratic patronage, to middle-class absorption and control, to a public domination centred increasingly on 'bread and circuses' titillation.

Thus it is, in Asia and elsewhere, that past western political impositions have given way to present western cultural offerings: 'The triumph of Western leisure and consumer culture constitutes one of the great stories of cultural contact'[39] in the twenty-first century.

Yet this is not the whole truth. Complexity is the commonplace of humanity. From Asia have come sports that have been embraced by the West, in particular martial arts and polo. Furthermore, in Asia nations have taken western sports by the scruff of the neck and reshaped them in their own image – the best examples are perhaps cricket and baseball – and, of course, this reshaping has been part and parcel of other cultural adjustments. For example, the 1980s craze in Japan for American-style game shows possessed its own special twist: 'Losing contestants were elaborately shamed, subjected to ridicule to highlight their failure to live up to group norms – thus serving *Japanese* cultural goals in ways that would seem harsh to more individualistic Americans.'[40] Equally interesting, 'McDonalds triumphed widely, but it also adapted ... for Japan it developed a burger with Fesiyaki sauce (McTeriyaki)'.[41] Recently it has produced Indian-type burgers in Britain in the wake of the appetite for Indian recipes.

It is also sensible to note these cautionary words written several decades ago:

> Modern institutions are being developed in many places through imitations of non Western models ... but also ... because developments associated with modernization came about in non Western countries through internal changes for the most part and not primarily through a direct transfer of cultural patterns.[42]

Such changes embrace responses to indigenous needs and cultural resources, including 'business mentalities, specialized occupational roles and centralized nation-states with standing armies'.[43] Thus 'modernization may be endogenous as well as exogenous, and congruent with tradition as well as discontinuous'.[44] And, of course, continuity and change are part of the human condition and in the process of change, not to mention continuity, 'cultural elements, both endogenous and exogenous, may be partially learned, incorrectly learned, or transformed accidentally or deliberately in the learning'.[45]

In short, both globally induced cultural uniformity and diversity are curiously complex manifestations. Even surface commonality born of westernization may harbour beneath the veneer differences conceived for a multiplicity of local reasons and gestating due to a variety of local causes.

Prologue 9

Increasingly, of course, in the wake of growing prosperity, leisure and international self-confidence, the East now teaches the West 'how to play'. Enter China on the world sports stage – not yet fully centre stage. If, as has been predicted on occasion, the centre of the commercial world in the twenty-second century will be South-East Asia, then it is not beyond the bounds of probability that the centre of world sport will be there also – with techniques, refinements and performances that will mirror the earlier shift in an 'industrial revolution' from West to East characteristic of the twentieth century.

For all this appropriate subtlety of perspective, however, in the last two centuries modern sport, easily recognized as such, has spread from the West across the globe – its common elements widely obvious, and as obvious in Asia as in other parts of the world. To adopt the language of genetics, Asia is witness to 'a double helix' – sport and success in modern sport as indicators of a thoroughly modern society. This volume attempts to reveal at least part, if not the whole, of this unfolding process and to reveal also how important modern sport has become to Asia – politically, economically, culturally and emotionally.

Asia then is the focus of this innovatory volume and many of the issues raised above are covered in these pages. The state of present research and the space available mean that it cannot be satisfactorily comprehensive, but it attempts to be stimulatingly exploratory.

NOTES

1. The series will shortly publish a seminal monograph by Professor Dong Jinxia of Peking University – and a former research student at Strathclyde University's International Research Centre for Sport, Socialization and Society, entitled *Women, Sport and Society in Modern China: Holding Up More than Half the Sky*. Volumes are being planned on sport in South Asia and the FIFA World Cup in Japan and Korea and on sport in modern Japan.
2. Milton W. Meyer, *Asia: A Concise History* (New York: Portman & Littlefield, 1997), p.1.
3. Ibid., p.2.
4. Ibid., p.1.
5. Ibid., p.2.
6. Ibid., p.6.
7. See *The New Encylopaedia Britannica*, 15th edn, Vol.1 (Chicago, 1997), p.129.
8. See J.A. Mangan, 'Series Editor's Foreword', in Paul Dimeo and James Mills (eds), *Soccer in South Asia: Empire, Nation, Diaspora* (London: Frank Cass, 2001), pp.xi–xiii.
9. Ibid., p.xi.
10. Ibid., p.xii.
11. Ibid., p. xiii
12. Ibid.
13. Ibid.
14. D.A. Low, *Eclipse of Empire* (Cambridge: Cambridge University Press, 1991), p.25.
15. Ibid.

16. Ibid., p.26.
17. Ibid., p.44.
18. For a detailed consideration of this complexity and of the various 'Gropings', see Low, *Eclipse*.
19. Ibid., p.46.
20. For discussion on the 'Rectifications', see Low, *Eclipse*, p.46.
21. Ibid., p.50.
22. Ibid., p.51.
23. Ibid., p.52.
24. Ibid., p.53.
25. Ibid.
26. Ibid., p.54.
27. Gordon Hewitt, *The Problems of Success: A History of the Church Missionary Society 1910–1942, Vol.II: Asia Overseas Partners* (London: SCM Press, 1977), p.1.
28. Ibid.
29. Ibid., pp.2–3.
30. See J.A. Mangan, 'Prologue: Britain's Chief Spiritual Export: Imperial Sport as Moral Metaphor, Political Symbol and Cultural Bond', in J.A. Mangan (ed.), *The Cultural Bond: Sport, Empire, Society* (London: Frank Cass, 1992).
31. See especially J.A. Mangan, *Athleticism in the Victorian and Edwardian Public School: The Emergence and Consolidation of an Educational Ideology*, second edition (London: Frank Cass, 2000) and J.A. Mangan, *The Games Ethic and Imperialism: Aspects of the Diffusion of an Ideal*, 2nd edn (London: Frank Cass, 1998).
32. In one of their more intelligibly valuable comments the authors of *Globalization and Sport* recently wrote: 'Try to imagine a major international sporting event, such as the Olympic Games or World Cup, with no comprehensive media coverage, no national flags flying, no playing of national anthems, no politicians involved in the ceremonies, no military displays, no tables comparing national standings and athletes competing ... [in] national uniforms.' See Toby Miller *et al.*, *Globalization and Sport* (London: Sage, 2001), p.2. If only they wrote so clearly as a matter of course. For unnecessary 'sociological' obfuscation, see their Conclusion.
33. Leo Tolstoy, *War and Peace* quoted in Niall Ferguson, *The Cash Nexus: Money and Power in the Modern World, 1700–2000* (London: Allen Lane, 2001), p.417.
34. Ibid.
35. Peter N. Stearns, *Cultures in Motion: Mapping Key Contacts and their Imprints in World History* (London: Yale University Press, 2001), p.108.
36. Ibid.
37. Ibid.
38. See T.C.W. Blanning, *The Culture of Power and the Power of Culture: Old Regime Europe 1680–1789* (Oxford: Oxford University Press, 2002), p.2.
39. Stearns, *Cultures in Motion*, p.111.
40. Ibid. (emphasis added).
41. Ibid.
42. See Donald N. Levine, 'The Flexibility of Traditional Culture', *Journal of Social Issues*, 24, 4 (1968), pp.129–30.
43. Ibid., p.130.
44. Ibid.
45. Ibid., p.134.

1

Imperial Origins: Christian Manliness, Moral Imperatives and Pre-Sri Lankan Playing Fields – Beginnings[1]

J.A. MANGAN

To turn Horace metaphorically on his head: 'mix a little prudence with your foolishness; it's good to be careful at the right moment.'[2] The adaptation is made with good reason. Among the more inadequate explanations of the imperial diffusion of cricket is the statement that it reached colonial outposts by way of the British Navy, the Army and entrepreneurs.[3] Almost as inadequate is the remark from the same pen that in the spread of imperial cricket, capitalism has had pretty much its own way.[4]

Both remarks can usefully be set against the following observation:

> In the dissemination of British sports and games, the social historian should not overlook religious enthusiasts and diffusionists such as Patterson, Pilkington, Pennell, Clifford Harris, A.C. Clarke, Carey Francis, Chester Macnaghten and C.W. Waddington, Cecil Wilson *and many others* who took both the gospel of Christ and the gospel of games to the most distant corners of the Empire and even beyond.[5]

The following comment on early-nineteenth-century Ceylon is also worth consideration: 'In the first three decades of British rule the one consistent agent of change was the missionary. Much more than the soldier and the administration, he was committed to the advocacy of change.'[6] In reality, the missionaries dominated the educational system until the twentieth century and their impact on society was considerable. In Ceylon the missionaries of, among others, St Joseph's College, St John's College, St Thomas's College and Wesleyan College as well as Trinity College, Kandy, first taught the young, 'middle-class'[7] Ceylonese to play cricket and thus laid the foundations among the young of a later cultural source of pleasure and pride. In fact Michael Roberts has an accurate perception of a general imperial reality when he remarks: 'Cricket was introduced into Sri Lanka by the British. ... The pioneer players were British soldiers, administrators, schoolmasters, and planters.'[8] Roberts adds that

> Cricket was part of the extracurricular activities of the English language schools at urban centers. Together with soccer, hockey, and track and field, it was widely taken up by the young men within the emerging indigenous 'middle class' of Sri Lanka.[9]

E.F.C. Ludowyk, a distinguished Ceylonese historian, has provided this gracious statement about the Christian missionary:

> Though not the most important nor the most numerous group of Europeans in Ceylon, the missionaries extended the most influence on the people of the country and left the strongest impression on the island. ... It is an open question whether the characteristic mark of missionary endeavour in Ceylon is to be found in the Christian communities left by them or in the numbers who received through their agency an education in English.[10]

With others, imperial missionaries took modern games, frequently including cricket, 'among other places to the lush tropical rain forests of Africa, the verdant islands of the Pacific, the parched plains of India and the windswept prairies of Canada'.[11] With the wealth of evidence now available, it should not be necessary to state that Christian missionary cricketers, often opposed to the cruder forms of imperial capitalism,[12] were committed to cricket's moral potential – as they saw it – and were not without diffusionary influence.[13] Few illustrate this better than Alexander Garden Fraser, Principal of Trinity College, Kandy, in Ceylon from 1904 to 1924, today a redundant icon of Edwardian imperial education, and the Christian knight errant of this and the following essay.[14]

These men had the most profound of purposes: 'manliness' achieved on the games field in order to create 'a universal Tom Brown: loyal, brave, truthful, a gentleman, and if possible, a Christian'.[15] They are now an extinct species, these Muscular Christian missionary imperialists.[16] In all seriousness, the main means of their attempted moral manliness was cricket, the game of empire: 'Cricket became the symbol par excellence of imperial solidarity and superiority epitomizing a set of consolatory moral imperatives that both exemplified and explained imperial ambition and achievement.'[17] Of no one was this more true than of A.G. Fraser.

Consideration of the colonial past has its difficulties, not least because the historian 'is bound to be struck by the range and number of factors to be considered and by the varied ways in which in different countries they can be seen to act upon each other'.[18] It has been stated, accurately if somewhat obviously, that colonization varied in its stages, and that the 'very notion of a colonial past may be seen as most misleading. It leads one to imagine a clear distinction between the before of colonialism and the after of independence, seen as two sharply contrasting periods separated by the moment of decolonization.'[19] In reality, it must not be imagined that post-colonization has always meant a complete break with the pre-colonial period.

Decolonization, in fact, can bear witness to the strengthening rather than the weakening of cultural associations. Thus the colonial past can be visible in the postcolonial present in various forms. Acculturation can result in the birth of a new culture which includes elements of the past and present. Subscription to an inflexible belief in an automatic conflict between the traditional and the modern can be naive. Reality can be a great deal more complex.

In any review of the relationship between the colonial past and the independent present, there is a level involving a balance sheet of change in the case of institutions, economy, politics, education and culture; but there is also a level related to identity, status and confidence with the result that decolonization can bring about a social psychological 'remoulding of history'.[20] Myth-making, invoked in this 'remoulding', includes providing the community with necessary heroes involving 'a selective emphasis on particular episodes or persons'.[21] The pursuit of such personal icons can represent a 'deep and thorough search for the continuing presence of the colonial past'.[22]

In this search, the influence of education in establishing emotional legacies 'hard to pin point and even harder to quantify'[23] is too often insufficiently considered; yet it is in this difficult region of the 'exploration of the inexpressible' that it is sometimes possible to discern 'the clearest, fullest picture of the deep influence of the colonial past'.[24] Often this past is continued into the present through closely woven threads of emotional as well as intellectual attitudes and behaviour spun in the impressionable years of childhood.[25] With specific reference to Sri Lanka, Ludowyk has written:

By 1900 the structure of paternal Colonial Government raised by the British in Ceylon seemed a classic example of its kind, destined to endure indefinitely. Yet in less than fifty years the rulers had deported and the structure seemed cracked from the bottom. It survived, however, and still straddles the landscape.[26]

This and the next essay deal with colonial Ceylon (now, of course, Sri Lanka) and essentially but not exclusively with cricket as part of the cultural heritage of Sri Lanka. Cricket came to Sri Lanka early, took hold and became greatly enjoyed and elegantly played. It is a colonial legacy that is a source of considerable present pleasure. In the words of one of Sri Lanka's leading cricket historians, S.S. Perera:

> Of the British exports to her far-flung colonial Empire, cricket has been a much sought after product. It has endured many changes and has been time tested. Cricket commenced in Sri Lanka well before the oldest international in the world – USA versus Canada in 1844. A notice in the *Colombo Journal* on 5 September 1832 invited 'gentlemen who may be inclined towards forming a Cricket Club' to 'meet at the Library (located in the Pettah) at 2 o'clock precisely on the 8th instant'. It is recorded that the Colombo Cricket Club was formed on 8 September 1832, and a cricket match was played shortly after. According to the rule of things the British dominated everything. So with sport – most games were exclusively European at the outset. But those of us who have profited from this enterprise in our own time can only express our thanks to these pioneers who introduced the game of cricket to the island. Today, people in all walks of life find enjoyment playing or watching cricket.[27]

It should be stated immediately that it is a source of much more: pride in national identity, status from national performance, confidence from worldwide achievements. Perera in his *Notes on Sri Lanka's Cricket Heritage* – an invaluable and readable synopsis of the growth of the game with an emphasis on the post-First World War period – places the portraits of three men in pride of place among the early pictures of Sri Lankan cricket in his gallery of Ceylon's cricket personalities: J. Brooke Bailey, who introduced cricket to Colombo Academy (now Royal College) in 1838; another member of the school staff, Ashley Walker, a Cambridge Blue who played for Yorkshire and the MCC and who was responsible for the first inter-college match between Colombo Academy

Imperial Origins – Beginnings 15

and St Thomas's College played over three afternoons (from 4.00 to 6.00 pm) in July 1879; and George Vandespar, a successful businessman who played a major role in the evolution of the game both nationally and internationally between 1884 and 1908. This and the subsequent essay will make the case for the inclusion of a fourth portrait – of the intense Christian educator A.G. Fraser. Thus three school masters are iconic representatives of early cricket in Ceylon.

D.A. Low echoes the sound words of J.L. Meige recorded earlier regarding the imperial past, this time with specific reference to Monsoon Asia:

> There is a widespread assumption that the histories of the various countries of this region are quite adequately understood in their own terms. Certainly there has been little inclination to look beyond their own borders. Whilst each country has had its own superabundance of particularities, an over-rigorous concentration upon these does seem, however, to have been at the expense of allowing for the highly significant similarities that in a range of very important respects many of them have at the same time experienced.[28]

This certainly rings true for the experience of colonial cricket. Equally soundly, Low adds that any communalities were certainly matched, if not surpassed, by idiosyncrasies that were distinctive to each of the individual countries.[29] Alexander Garden Fraser's principalship of Trinity College in Kandy, from 1904 to 1924, is undoubtedly a case in point.

The British took over parts of Ceylon from the Dutch in the late eighteenth century.[30] The Dutch controlled large areas between 1658 and 1796. The kingdom of Kandy, however, remained independent for some years. By the beginning of the nineteenth century, due to various influences, in some cases going back a considerable time, the main religions in Ceylon were Buddhism, Christianity (Catholic and Presbyterian), Islam and a 'wilder and more extravagant system of Paganism called by the Dutch the worship of the Devil' – in reality, animism.[31] The British inherited from the Dutch 'a very complete religious and educational system' reduced in efficiency by initial British administrative neglect.[32] However, early in the new century matters were improving. Plans were set in place for a scheme of 'a superior nature' for the young of the more privileged of the Ceylonese population – 'The children were to be taught English, the native languages and the "lower humanities".'[33]

This innovation was a harbinger of things to come. In 1805 the first Protestant missionaries in the period of British control arrived on the shores of Ceylon from the London Missionary Society. By the 1830s, in addition to Catholics (the Portuguese had brought Catholicism to Ceylon in 1505), among others there were Wesleyans, Methodists, and Anglicans of the Church Missionary Society (CMS).[34] In time they all had their 'superior' schools with the central aim of conversion to Christianity – there was also a government school in Colombo.[35] Through these schools eventually cricket, among other western cultural phenomena, was introduced to the indigenous youth of Ceylon, and was to prove, in time, a potent cultural possession.

The 1830s proved a watershed for the missionary. Between 1833 and 1850, there was a concerted effort by the government to transform Ceylonese society.[36] It has been remarked that

> A peculiar feature of the social policy of this period was the importance attached to religion. This was partly due to Evangelical influence (mainly through James Stephen) at the Colonial Office, and to men like Governor Stewart Mackenzie (1837–41) and a host of subordinate officials in Sri Lanka who believed in the urgency of converting the 'heathen' to Christianity; and partly to the agitation of missionary organizations for a redefinition of the relationship between Buddhism and the colonial government in the island. During his brief tenure of office as Secretary of State for the Colonies in the late 1830s, Lord Glenelg had laid it down that the conversion of the people to Christianity should be a vital aspect of state policy in Sri Lanka. His successors during this period shared this belief to a greater or lesser extent.[37]

The outcome was active state support for missionary work and state endorsement of all Christian missions.

The Church Missionary Society had arrived in Ceylon in 1818.[38] By the early 1830s it had 36 schools, three of them for girls. One of these schools was in Kandy, the former capital of the Kandy Kingdom, which was finally brought under full British control in 1818.[39] Before 1833 there was no coherent government policy on education. Government involvement was 'both slight and sporadic'.[40] The distinctive feature of this first phase of missionary activity in nineteenth-century Ceylon was 'the single handed struggle of the missionaries to build up a school system at a time when the government was disinclined to do so',[41] with the result that over the years 'they devised the guiding principles that were to govern educational development ... for decades thereafter, and from their experiments emerged the system of denominational schools which prevailed in the island for more than a century'.[42]

A further consequence was that for much of the nineteenth century, due initially to the influence of W.M.G. Colebrook,[43] who recognized 'the superiority' of missionary education and 'was not inclined to encourage the establishment of government schools in areas served by the missionary schools',[44] conversion to Christianity became the primary purpose of education.[45]

The period of British rule between 1833 and 1850 has been called an era of reform and reconstruction in 'every sphere of activity – political, economic and social'.[46] As already noted, a special aspect of this period 'was the importance attached to religion'[47] due to committed evangelists both in the Colonial Office and Ceylon and in the missionary societies. In this climate of strong views, the government in Ceylon was pressured by missionary organizations for a redefinition of the relationship between Buddhism and the island's government.[48] The outcome – namely, the severance of state support, which was to have a lasting impact, not least on Fraser in Kandy – was fierce confrontation between Buddhist and Christian in a struggle for government favour.[49] Confrontation began in earnest following 'a great "Buddhist revival" in 1862–4',[50] when Buddhist priests in the Singhalese low country attempted to bring Christian converts back to Buddhism. Christianity was attacked in lectures and tracts and the 'result was most remarkable'.[51] Many Christians did return to Buddhism. The struggle polarized Christians and Buddhists – a legacy Fraser was to inherit. It brought home, it appears, to those who called themselves Christians but were Buddhist at heart, 'the fact that Christianity and Heathenism are completely opposed to each other, and that if one were true the other must be false'.[52] The polarization thus established frequently resulted in bitter verbal warfare. The battlefield had been established upon which Fraser was to fight long and hard for the duration of his time in Ceylon.

As de Silva remarks in his *History of Sri Lanka*, the 'filtration theory' – influences filtering downwards from colonial infiltrators and agents – produced among other things an emphasis on elite education, with English as a new and prestigious 'caste mark'. In this process, as noted earlier, English education was left almost entirely to the missionaries.[53] Hand in hand with Christian educational ascendancy went the transformation of the economy from the 1840s onwards, due to the rise of a plantation economy. Speaking specifically of Ceylon, Michael Roberts has written:

> Perhaps the most significant instrument of capitalist expansion was that of the plantation. Plantation ownership was not confined to Europeans. Indigenous residents took to cash crop cultivations (especially coconut) on plantations from an early date. Indeed the presence of numerous indigenous-owned cash crop plantations is one of the ways in which Sri Lankan history diverged from that of British India. It also meant the emergence of the Western educated in significant numbers among the Sri Lankese, Moor and Tamil communities ... was facilitated and even preceded by the emergence of a capitalist class of plantation owners and merchants.[54]

The plantations went through various vicissitudes but were to bring great changes to Ceylon:

> The decade of the eighties approximately marked the beginning of the transition to twentieth-century Ceylon, even though the change did not become well-defined until the nineties. In agriculture the dependence on the single staple coffee was replaced by a more diversified cultivation. The development of the nation-building services in the nineties contrasted with the older and simpler conception of the responsibilities of Government. The Ceylonese movement for constitutional reform began at the same period.[55]

One of the more important changes was that

> Capital investment poured in to tea and rubber, which grew as large-scale industries and needed a permanent labour force. Steps were taken to settle Indian labour on the plantations. Ancillary services soon arose. Increasing export trade led to the development of the Colombo Harbour and to railway and road construction. Opportunities were created for the Ceylonese entrepreneur, and employment was plentiful for the English-educated.[56]

The consequences were of special significance for the missionary schools: an improvement in Ceylonese prosperity and the growth of a Ceylonese 'middle class'.[57] As well as enriched Ceylonese entrepreneurs and owners, another outcome of the plantation industry was a new class of lawyers and others with an English education, whose earnings went into forming the beginnings of a small middle class wedged in between the very small group of wealthy British planters and merchants and the mass of the people.[58]

The Central Province, in which Kandy is located, was extensively covered by plantations; initially these produced coffee, but after a disastrous disease affected the coffee plant,[59] they turned successfully to tea – to the advantage of Trinity College, Kandy. Prosperity brought an influx of 'middle class' Ceylonese.

Thus, in summary, hand in hand with Christian ascendancy went the transformation of the economy from the 1840s onwards due to the rise of a plantation economy. As already noted, it went through various vicissitudes but was to bring prosperity to both British and Ceylonese plantation owners. The result was that the 'eighties, approximately, marked the beginning of the transition to twentieth century Ceylon, even though the change did not become well-defined until the nineties'.[60] This transition involved diversified cultivation and a shift from reliance on the single staple, coffee. With Ceylonese professionals in the urban areas and Ceylonese planters in the rural areas, increasingly an indigenous 'middle class' was emerging that would steadily take advantage of the English-speaking 'superior schools'.[61] Then a

> rise in revenue which began in the nineties with the prosperity of tea and later rubber was accompanied by a steady growth of the expenditure on education. Concurrently the popular demand for education, and particularly English education, increased to a remarkable degree with the growing prosperity of the Ceylonese.[62]

By 1910, perhaps with an element of wishful thinking, the then Governor, Sir Henry MacCallum, wrote of the newly prosperous as well as the longer established prosperous Ceylonese:

> [It] is precisely the acquisition of European ideas and the adoption of European in preference to Ceylonese civilization that differentiates this class of Ceylonese from their countrymen … [and separates them] by a wide gulf from the majority of the native inhabitants of the Colony. Their ideas, their aspirations, their interests are distinctively their own, are all moulded upon European models, and are no longer those of the majority of their countrymen.[63]

MacCallum noted the emergence of a western-educated, Anglicized elite. Whether it was separated is open to question,[64] but its existence as a westernized elite certainly is not. A further feature of the continual surge to prosperity was the emergence of a self-made 'middle class' which began to challenge the traditional elite with increasing success:

> Although the established men were compelled to accommodate themselves to an expansion of the elite by the absorption of the new rich, the latter were very soon the dominant section in terms of numbers, wealth and education, and were in effect a new elite in which hereditary status was only one and not necessarily the more significant attribute of 'elite ranking'.[65]

The new rich, as noted earlier, helped swell the numbers in the missionary schools. Thus elite secondary education was largely a phenomenon of the later nineteenth century and almost entirely in the hands of the missionaries.[66] Indeed the 'golden age' of denominational missionary education covered the last quarter of the century and the first quarter of the next century, with the missionaries undoubtedly the determining influence in the educational expansion. More than this, with pole position in the island's education system, they acted *de facto* as a form of class segregation and consolidation.

In all this they had much in common with the English public schools of the time and, like these schools, they embraced a belief in the games field as a critical source of moral education. They also uniformly pursued Christian proselytization, admittedly within a framework of sectarian rivalry, and this in the fullness of time was to bring about a reduction in their influence as religious institutions.

One result of the predominance of the elite missionary schools was a 'disproportionate number of Christians among the elite',[67] with the further result that Christians were well ahead of the other religious groupings in both the late nineteenth and early twentieth centuries.[68] Those who had an 'English' education were relatively few but they exercised a considerable influence in society and were, among other things, 'middle class' innovators who eventually nurtured, organized and developed cricket to a position in which it came to symbolize an important element of Sri Lankan modernity.

Thus, shortly before Fraser arrived in Ceylon, the Ceylonese elite had expanded in numbers and was 'quite heterogeneous', for the simple reason 'that once members of the elite had consolidated their fortunes as such, they became members of a single class, an elite representative of but not synonymous with the capitalist class'.[69] De Silva claims that 'it was the affluence rather than education or an anglicized life style which provided a degree of homogeneity'.[70] Perhaps this is to devalue the influence of the 'cultural capital' of Anglicized, mostly missionary, education too much. And de Silva probably does. Be that as it may, what the Anglicized education did foster, among other things, was subscription to modern games, especially cricket, which in turn became a significant component of Sri Lankan 'cultural capital'.

When a Church Missionary Society group arrived in Colombo in June 1818, the Governor, Sir Robert Brownrigg, suggested that one of its members went to Kandy.[71] In 1822, land was obtained there for a CMS house and school. The school opened the following year. The Ceylonese did not take enthusiastically to missionary proselytization. Mission work in the Cotta district of the island, for example, as late as 1868 was described as 'dark and sad'.[72] Other districts had a similar story.[73] The situation in Kandy was no different from that at Cotta or indeed other places in Ceylon. Eugene Stock, a late-nineteenth-century historian of the CMS, wrote:

> The Kandyans, or Singhalese of the hill districts, are a very different people from the Singhalese of the low country; but the human heart is the same everywhere, and indifference to the Gospel was as marked among the hills as in the plains.[74]

He added: 'Conversion was hard work. Progress was desperately slow: new converts from the Buddhism of the Singhalese and the devil-worship of the Tamils were few and far between.'[75] In this atmosphere of gloom, it was recorded that 'the best work of the Mission was in the schools, which were giving a Christian education to nearly three thousand children'.[76] In 1857 the school in Kandy had something of a short-term boost. It was a relatively rare Kandyan aristocratic convert, Dunawila, who played a major part in its expansion. Its ambition was crystal clear – 'to attract the sons of the Kandyan chiefs, a class proud of their ancestry and their former feudal power'.[77] However, not many of them were 'reached'.

This state of affairs sets Fraser's later success in context. His Christian militancy, relatively speaking, was of a different order of success to earlier principals. But matters did improve somewhat shortly before his arrival. It was claimed in 1899 that 'the present Trinity College, Kandy ... has proved, and still proves, a great channel of blessing'.[78]

By 1860 there were 60 pupils, but to complete their studies for the Calcutta Matriculation Examination they were obliged to go to Colombo, St Thomas's or Royal College (then Colombo Academy) and, despite the support of Dunawila and the efforts of the missionaries, a few years later the school at Kandy closed. It was reopened in 1872 under the Revd Richard Collins, a Cambridge graduate who had been at St John's College.

The reopened school owed its existence to the rising prosperity discussed earlier and to the fact that, due to the government policy of ensuring no equal rivals to missionary institutions, it was the only regional school that taught classics, mathematics and 'correct English'. There were 139 boys by the end of the year – a handful of them boarders. Cricket, it might be noted, was played from time to time. A historian of Trinity College, Valesca L.O. Reimann, noted that

> During the breakfast interval, and generally before and after school, games were played on the compound, chiefly Prisoner's Ball and a game known as Saal. There was no school elites for cricket or football, but there were sectional clubs out of school, which played on the Esplanade or Banack Square.[79]

In short, games were informal, often unsupervised and relatively unimportant. Spasmodic cricket or football, it appears, was due to the fact that the Revd Collins was not greatly interested in sport.[80] Nevertheless, the school was otherwise anchored in English public school custom. It had a Literary Association:[81]

> The stock subjects were well thrashed out by us. The Queen of Scots and Charles I were in our opinion unjustly executed; Queen Elizabeth and Warren Hastings were on the whole entitled to our admiration. ... Byron was a greater poet than Shakespeare ... and Wellington was a better general than Napoleon.[82]

The library, which opened in 1875, possessed, for the delectation of the Ceylonese,

> works of such eminent Divines as Pearson, Paley, Simeon, etc., some theological works against the Oxford movement of Pusey, Keble and Newman and against Colenso's criticism of the Pentateuch; some twenty volumes on the modern History of Europe from the French Revolution to the restoration of the Bourbons, etc.[83]

Imperial Origins – Beginnings

While the school texts books included 'Collie's History of England and Cromwell's Geography, the unrevised edition of the public school preview and Henry's First Latin Book ... Bernard Smith's Arithmetic and the mathematical works of Dr Isaac Todhunter'.[84] When in 1872 the first prize-giving took place with the Governor, Sir W.H. Gregory, present, it began 'with a choral Evensong in the Church'; later there was 'the acting of three scenes from the "Merchant of Venice" and finally, Winchester's "Dulce Domum" was sung!'[85] It is not recorded what the Ceylonese pupils made of it all.

In 1876 the CMS Annual Report stated that 'the Kandy Collegiate School is henceforth to be denominated Trinity College, Kandy'.[86] It remains so to this day.

Collins left in 1878 and a Mr Thomas Dunn became acting principal until 1880. There were now 117 boys in the school, but only 42 boarders. In 1881 the Revd J.G. Garnett of Trinity College, Dublin, became principal. He apparently was something of a disaster. The Church Missionary School had made a great mistake in appointing him: 'He was a brilliant University man, with plenty of Missionary zeal but with no experience whatever of school management.'[87] Nevertheless, by the 1890s there were 200 boys and there was certainly an annual athletic sports day, but the athleticism or games cult of the British public school had not yet reached that part of Ceylon. The missionaries so far appointed as principals were pre-cult priests. Tennis or cricket were played and, as mentioned above, athletic events took place. However, as regards cricket 'the lack of proper accommodation and playing space ... was a great handicap to its thorough development'.[88] Fraser was to overcome that handicap in no uncertain manner.

Trinity was doomed for some years yet to maintain a precarious existence.[89] Fraser was to put things right. The religious tone of the college at this time remained, as it was to remain, pronounced, with fully three-quarters of the boys Christians. In 1889 the Revd E.J. Perry (Merchant Taylor's School and Worcester College, Oxford) became principal. He had been a master of his old school for several years. Perry was the first public-school master to become principal of Trinity. Under his leadership there were many innovations, and as a consequence 'a phenomenal increase in the number of boys'.[90] Numbers rose to 252 in 1890. In the same year Perry was shot dead by a pupil in a hunting accident. Another public-school master arrived in June 1890, the Revd H. Percy Napier Clavering, a Cambridge graduate who had been a master at Monkton Combe School near Bath. For all Perry's efforts, the school remained in debt and academic standards lagged far behind the Colombo colleges. There was one silver lining. Under Napier-Clavering, cricket was improved in the hands of the Revd J. Carter, the vice-principal, who had been at Trinity College, Cambridge, in the early moments of the growth of the games cult there.[91] Under Napier-Clavering there was a cadet corps, an old boys' association and a school magazine. Trinity was acquiring more of the trappings of a public school. In 1894, with the departure of Carter to St John's, Jaffna, as principal, the college acquired R.W. Ryde (Jesus College, Cambridge),[92] a former classics master at Monkton Combe. Cricket picked up, Royal College was beaten for the first time and college colours were now introduced: dark green, old gold and chocolate ribbons. The school's financial position improved, buildings were added, academic standards raised and in 1898 the first cricket match against St Thomas's College, Colombo, occurred. Sporting contacts with prestigious Colombo colleges now expanded. The same year a cricket area close to the dormitories was created specifically as a practice ground.

Despite all this good work, at this point in time the college regrettably, in the words of Fraser's biographer, 'fell on evil days'.[93] A sequence of six principals in four years brought problems of standards, attitudes and performance; but amidst a general decline cricket appeared to flourish when in 1901 Mr Claude Orr joined the staff: 'He had a great reputation as a cricketer, and from this time onwards the Eleven began to be much more dangerous to their opponents. They now had new blazers to "serve as an additional inducement to smartness all round".'[94] Performance as well as morale now picked up. By 1903 the college, it seems, had something to boast about. The cricket and football seasons were pronounced an 'unprecedented success'.[95] Out of the 15 cricket matches played, only one was lost – and that only by a single run, against the Wesleyan College.

Napier-Clavering had resigned in 1900 – 'he had brought [Trinity's] status from its almost elementary position to one, which was beginning to be recognized as the equal of the big Colombo colleges'.[96] However, there were clear signs that all was far from well. Calculated bullying had become a habit:

> In these days the day-boys were in mortal terror of the boarders, and the boarders used this fact to their own advantage. It was discovered that if it rained heavily and the day-boys got wet on

their way to school or did not attend school at all, the Principal would give a 'rain-holiday' for that day. Consequently when there were even slight showers, the boarders used to form up near the gate and refuse to allow any day-boy to pass until they had them thoroughly soaked. It is said that the employment of buckets of water greatly expedited matters. Many of the day-boys turned back home after this rough treatment, some even in tears. Later on the Principal would go round the classes and find more than half the boys absent or shivering in their wet clothes, and perforce pronounce the day a 'rain-holiday'. Slight showers accounted for quite a number of extra holidays.[97]

In fact, the school was failing in several ways. Discipline was lax; absenteeism was considerable; drunkenness was often only too apparent. Things were so bad that the government was now giving serious thought to closing the school.[98]

At this juncture Fraser came to Trinity as principal. He immediately 'set about getting a public school spirit into the school and ... making it a first-class school' based on sound Christian principles.[99]

The spread of modern sport – so globally significant in the long term, politically, economically, culturally and emotionally, and increasingly for the world's masses more important to their lives than religion, dance or drama – throughout the British Empire and further afield owed much to ideology. The close association between the history of ideas (and indeed idealism) and the history of modern sport is still insufficiently recognized.[100] It is of considerable significance to the modern world at several levels.[101] Fraser was an early archetypal ideologue.

Across the empire, as possibly every British schoolboy (and girl) may soon know,[102] even if regrettably some contemporary historians of sport do not appear to, it was not exclusively ship-weary sailors, bored subalterns and energetic businessmen who played a part in the diffusion of modern games. If a comprehensive awareness is ever to be achieved of the manner of the movement – into every inhabited continent of the globe, and constituting one of the major modern cultural revolutions, peacefully achieved, of recent centuries – then the Muscular Christian missionary must move to centre stage. Educationists committed to a meritorious, if arguably myopic, set of beliefs subsumed under the title Muscular Christianity had a far from unimportant role in the process.[103] One chevalier of this religious army of travelling knights errant was certainly Alexander Garden Fraser. His biographer, W.E.F. Ward, has written of Fraser that he

> Became a legendary figure in his own lifetime, and anecdotes clustered thickly round his name. He was one of the greatest missionaries of his day, a notable speaker at summer schools and student conferences. He was a great teacher, voted by a group of public-school heads to be the greatest headmaster they knew: a great fighter, and often a thorn in the flesh of officialdom: an inspiring preacher, whose sermon once moved a colonial legislature to adjourn in protest.[104]

Ward added, writing as late as 1965, that in Ceylon his name was still remembered with affection.[105]

Fraser was born in 1873 at Tillicoultry in Clackmannanshire, Scotland. His father, an ambitious son of the manse, entered the Indian Civil Service and eventually became Sir Andrew Fraser, KCSL, Lieutenant-Governor of Bengal and Moderator of the Presbyterian Church Assembly in India. Both he and his wife were devout churchgoers. This fact greatly coloured both their lives and the life of their son. It is central to an understanding of the later motives and actions of Fraser in Ceylon on and off games fields.

In 1885 Fraser was sent to Merchiston Castle School in Edinburgh, a small public school. At that time, like all such Scottish schools, it had begun to imitate and follow the educational practices of the far more famous English public schools.[106] In English public schools games, in the form of 'athleticism' as it became widely known, were fast becoming an essential part of educational theory and practice.[107]

Merchiston's rugby in Fraser's time, despite the school's relatively few pupils – fewer than 100 – was considered by its rivals to be 'the best in Scotland'.[108] Fraser was not an outstanding games player either at Merchiston or later at Oxford, but he was an enthusiast – and he remained one. He was also religious, and both tendencies came together later in Ceylon where he personified the Muscular Christian:

> In Ceylon he used to conduct a post-mortem on the previous day's match at morning assembly. He had a photographic memory, and would describe with pitiless accuracy every moment when a player held on to the ball when he ought to have passed, or committed a slovenly piece of fielding at cricket. It was not lack of skill or an error in judgement that he castigated thus publicly; it was a

mistake which seemed to him to result from a player's thinking too much of himself and too little of the team ... he had seen at Merchiston how powerful an influence games could be in a healthy school community.[109]

Fraser went to Oxford in 1891. There he joined the Oxford Inter-Collegiate Christian Union. Many were members of the Anglican Church Missionary Society and, with Fraser, belonged to the Student Volunteer Missionary Union.[110] Its ambitious slogan was 'The Evangelisation of the World in this Generation'.[111] In such a pious environment, his choice of vocation is understandable. His choice of missionary society is more surprising: he was a Scottish Presbyterian but he joined the Anglican Church Missionary Society.[112] This was the result of the influence of close Oxford friends involved in the society, and of the fact that his eventual wife, Beatrice Glass, a devout Anglican, had arranged to go as a member of the Church Missionary Society to Uganda.[113] Fraser joined the CMS and then joined his future wife in Uganda in late 1900. They were married in early 1901. Fraser became a teacher of teachers and an imperial proselytizer for modern sport. He saw to it that his African servants were well exercised: 'Mr Fraser brought out a football with him and lent it to them every day for an hour and they invite their friends to come and play.'[114] It was the shape of things to come during his time in other parts of the empire.

Fraser became committed to teaching. With an energy and enthusiasm that became familiar, and sometimes exasperating, to the CMS, in 1903 he drafted plans for a CMS Ugandan secondary school broadly along the lines of an English public school with a personal emphasis 'on character rather than cleverness'.[115] Fraser obtained a site for the school and expressed great delight at the location of the playing fields – a means, of course, of character training:

> In those days there was no real secondary education in Uganda and no boarding school for boys. I talked it over with the chiefs and they were at once eager for one. They promised a site and asked me to select one. Some of us walked far and near and soon we saw the most beautiful site for a school I have ever known. But, I was told, it was on the hill sacred and reserved for the coronation of kings only. The missionaries were sure we would not be allowed on that hill. But it was a spacious hill and the eager chiefs at once granted us a wonderful building site with a beautiful playing field included.

These in no way encroached on the part which had always been used for the coronation of the kings. The chiefs said their kings and ancestors would be proud to have part of the sacred hill so used.[116]

Fraser's blueprint became reality – King's School, Budo, complete with the obligatory period playing field, was built. However, Fraser's wife's ill health meant that in the summer of 1904 they left Uganda for London and did not return. His contribution to modern Sri Lankan culture was shortly to begin.

With his return to England Fraser 'was left standing on the beach looking for his next task'.[117] His sole desire was for work as an overseas educational missionary and an opening now occurred as principal of the CMS school in Kandy, Ceylon. As already noted, the school was founded in 1857, and as also noted earlier, in 1900 the Revd H.P. Napier-Clavering, principal for ten years, retired and the school 'fell on evil days', as the school historian observed, adding that the 'accumulated lack of continuity began to tell very seriously on the college discipline'.[118] The situation occasioned a piteous cry *de profundis* from the vice-principal, the Revd A. MacLuich, in 1903:

> The College can't go on as it is. We are sinking into an inferior, badly managed school. There is something all wrong, everything is neglected.
>
> The boys don't come to study if they don't wish to, and when their names are put down for detention for being absent, some of them refuse to go to detention. ... Every week there is a list made out of those who don't appear for their detention, and nothing is said to them. ... Boys weekly are in public houses in town on Saturday afternoon, and I so often have reported offences in vain that now I say nothing about them. Boarders stay away from class for weeks at a time with nothing the matter with them, and all the notice that is taken of this is that they are marked absent, and the roll book is never looked at.
>
> The last Saturday of last term, after having corrected my papers in the evening, I went with two of the masters for a walk round the lake, and coming back about 10.15 passed some of our boys in a drunken party. ... All our best boys leave us to go to St Thomas's, because their parents find they may do as they like here, and often the senior classes are left to themselves with no teacher.[119]

Imperial Origins – Beginnings 29

Perhaps unaware of these uncongenial circumstances, Fraser applied for and obtained the principalship. The healthy situation of Kandy in the mountainous interior was a crucial factor in view of his wife's ill health.[120] Fraser was modest in his self-assessment, and a little anxious about his qualifications:

> I am an extremely bad scholar, and would have to rub up again the very rudiments of Latin, and my Greek is confined to the New Testament and not bright at that. I am not a real student, though studentish. By that, I mean I have the taste for many intellectual studies, but have spent little time in real study.[121]

He need not have worried. Intellectual rigour was not required. What was wanted was what G.E.L. Cotton took to Marlborough to save the school there and stimulate a revolution in English middle-class education – organization, firmness, determination, commitment to success and a belief in Muscular Christianity – for reasons of both realism and idealism: it was a heavy Sisphyean rock to roll to the top of the metaphorical mountain.[122] The extent to which Fraser displayed these attributes successfully in the attempt is now to be considered.

NOTES

Grateful thanks are extended to Ok Gwang for assistance with these endnotes and for supplementary research. I should like to record my appreciation to Strathclyde University and the Carnegie Trust for Scotland for financial support for enquiries leading to the publication of this and the next essay.

1. The British East India Company conquered Sri Lanka in 1796 and called it Ceylon. This name will be used in this and the next essay for the period of British control from 1796 to 1948. Ceylon was made a crown colony in 1802.
2. What Horace actually wrote, of course, was 'Mix a little foolishness with your prudence; it's good to be silly at the right moment'. For scholars the reverse is rather better advice [Horace, *Odes*, Book 4, no.12, lines 27–8, as translated in Angela Partington (ed.), *The Oxford Dictionary of Quotations*, revised 4th edn (Oxford: Oxford University Press, 1996), p.350].
3. Wendy Varney, 'Howzat! Cricket from Empire to Globalization', *Peace Review*, 11, 4 (Dec. 1999), 557. For a similar analytical shortcoming, see Richard Cashman, *Patrons, Players and the Crowd: The Phenomenon of Indian Cricket* (New Delhi: Orient Longman, 1980). The omission of missionary educationists, in an otherwise informative coverage of promoters of the game in India, is extraordinary. Cricketers did not leap onto cricket fields full-grown; schools and schoolmasters played an important part in the introduction of cricket to the Indian subcontinent. In their schools many future adults learned their skills in adolescence. Perhaps Cashman's omission is in part due to an over-reliance on Edward Docher's *History of Indian Cricket*, which oddly begins in 1926: see Edward Docher, *History of Indian Cricket* (Delhi: Macmillan of India, 1976) in which, self-evidently, the influential late nineteenth- and early twentieth-century efforts of Muscular Christian missionaries are not covered. It is due also to the neglect of the history of Indian education in colonial and postcolonial India. For a brief discussion of the 'Etons of India' and, *inter alia*, their role in bringing cricket to the Indian

royalty, aristocracy and middle classes, see J.A. Mangan, 'Eton in India: The Careful Creation of Oriental Englishmen', in J.A. Mangan (ed.), *The Games Ethic and Imperialism* (London and Portland, OR: Frank Cass, 1998), pp.122–41. With regard to the predominance of capitalism, only recently the author of a book on cricket and the weather has pointed out that cricket commercialism in England has some way to go before maximizing professional cricket's profitability. He argues further that the twentieth century witnessed a half-hearted and inefficient attitude on the part of the game towards full commercial profitability. This situation has carried over into the twenty-first century. Capitalism has clearly not had it all its own way in the home of cricket: see Andrew Hignell, *Rain Stops Play: Cricketing Climates* (London and Portland, OR: Frank Cass, 2002).
4. Varney, 'Howzat!', 557.
5. Mangan, *The Games Ethic*, pp.174–5 (emphasis added).
6. Michael Roberts, 'Ethnicity in Riposte at a Cricket Match: The Past for the Present', *Comparative Studies in Society and History*, 1 (1985), 407.
7. The concept of 'middle class' in the specific situation of Ceylon, and later Sri Lanka, has been carefully defined by Roberts as follows: 'The term middle class is used here as it is generally used in Sri Lanka. It is an ambiguous term that includes the white-collar wage dependants as well as capitalists from among the indigenous and non-European populations. By employing this native category I attempt to avoid a class analysis; any satisfactory class analysis calls for elaborations not feasible here.' ('Ethnicity in Riposte', 408). This definition is adopted in this and the following essay. Shortage of space dictates that elaborations are not feasible here. 'Not even in the early twentieth century was there a sufficiently active, cohesive and class-conscious proletariat to bring the capitalist class together and to enforce its unity in political action. In such a contest, therefore, the concept of an "elite" is regarded as a more serviceable tool for the purposes of this study than the concept of "class"' (Michael Roberts, *Class Conflict and Elite Formation: The Rise of a Karara Elite in Sri Lanka 1500–1931* (Cambridge: Cambridge University Press, 1982), p.2. For a detailed discussion of the missionary in Ceylon in the mid-nineteenth century, which provides much fascinating information on missionary ambitions, policies and strategies, see K.M. De Silva, *Social Policy and Missionary Organizations in Ceylon 1840–1855* (London: Longman, 1965).
8. Roberts, 'Ethnicity in Riposte', 408.
9. Ibid.
10. E.F.C. Ludowyk, *The History of Modern Ceylon* (London: Weidenfeld & Nicolson, 1966), p.111.
11. Mangan, *Games Ethic*, p.18.
12. No one was more fiercely critical of exploiting imperial capitalism than Fraser. His sensational sermon on the subject at Westminster Abbey in the 1920s is discussed in the next essay.
13. See Mangan, *Games Ethic*, *passim*.
14. The author, with the support of the Carnegie Trust for Scotland, will shortly be investigating a sectarian cross-section of these men (and occasionally women) in Sri Lanka in its British colonial period as Ceylon.
15. Mangan, *Games Ethic*, p.18.
16. Capitals are used deliberately and appropriately, in my view, for both 'muscular' and 'Christian' throughout this and the next chapter.
17. See J.A. Mangan, 'Prologue: Britain's Chief Spiritual Export: Imperial Sport as Moral Metaphor, Political Symbol and Cultural Bond', in J.A. Mangan (ed.), *The Cultural Bond: Sport, Empire, Society* (London and Portland, OR: Frank Cass, 1992), p.2.
18. J.L. Meige, 'The Colonial Past in the Present', in W.H. Morris-Jones and Dennis Austin (eds), *Decolonisation and After*, Studies in Commonwealth Politics and History, No.7 (London and Portland, OR: Frank Cass, 1980), p.35.
19. Ibid., p.36.
20. Ibid., p.41.
21. Ibid., p.46.
22. Ibid., p.47.
23. Ibid.
24. Ibid.

Imperial Origins – Beginnings 31

25. Ibid.
26. Ludowyk, *Modern Ceylon*, p.124.
27. S.S. Perera, *Notes on Sri Lanka's Cricket Heritage*, item faxed to the author, p.1. Perera also provides details of both early 'colonial sahib' innovations and those of businessmen, soldiers and Ceylonese. Important though these are, the introduction of cricket to the sons of influential Ceylonese through the missionary school system was arguably more important since it ensured cricket's long-term survival and expansion. At the very last, therefore, the missionary educator requires mention in any discussion of the introduction of cricket to Ceylon. A final word must be added about S.S. Perera. He is a remarkable recorder of Ceylonese/Sri Lankan sport, and his writings will be invaluable to academics and others in the generations to come. Among numerous other works, he has published *History of a Hundred Years of Rugby Football in Sri Lanka* (Colombo: Sri Lanka Rugby Football Union, 1981).
28. D.A. Low, *Eclipse of Empire* (Cambridge: Cambridge University Press, 1991), p.22.
29. Ibid., p.23.
30. A succinct outline of the history of Sri Lanka can be founded in 'Sri Lanka', *The New Encyclopedia Britannica*, 15th edn, Vol.28, Macropedia (Chicago: Encyclopedia Britannica, 1997), pp.172–9.
31. Colvin R. de Silva, *Ceylon under British Occupation 1795–1833*, Vol.1 (Colombo: Colombo Apothecaries' Co. Ltd, 1953), p.241.
32. Ibid., p.242.
33. Ibid., p.243.
34. Ibid., p.283.
35. Ibid., p.284.
36. K.M. de Silva, *A History of Sri Lanka* (London and Berkeley, CA: Hurst and the University of California Press, 1981), p.265.
37. Ibid.
38. Ibid., p.48.
39. For a description of the slow acquisition of Ceylon by the British, see de Silva, *History of Sri Lanka*, pp.210–38.
40. Ibid., p.252.
41. Ibid., p.253.
42. Ibid.
43. W.M.G. Colebrooke was the senior member of a two-member Commission of Eastern Inquiry which was to have a great influence on British policy in Ceylon. See de Silva, *History of Sri Lanka*, p.253.
44. Ibid., p.329.
45. Ibid., p.266.
46. Ibid., p.265.
47. Ibid.
48. For the background to this pressure, see de Silva, *History of Sri Lanka*, pp.268–9.
49. Ibid., p.266.
50. See Eugene Stock, *The History of the Church Missionary Society*, Vol.1 (London: CMS, 1899), p.288. For discussion of the origins of Buddhist hostility, see Ludowyk, *Modern Ceylon*, pp.112–16. For a full discussion of the rise of Buddhist nationalism, see Kitsiri Malalgoda, *Buddhism in Sinhalese Society, 1750–1900: A Study of Religious Revival and Change* (London: University of California Press, 1976).
51. Stock, *History of the Church Missionary Society*.
52. Ibid., p.289.
53. de Silva, *History of Sri Lanka*, p.329.
54. Roberts, *Class Conflict and Elite Formation*, p.2.
55. Lennox A. Mills, *Ceylon under British Rule 1775–1948* (London: Oxford University Press, 1933), Preface.
56. 'Sri Lanka', *The New Encyclopedia Britannica*, p.178.
57. See note 6 above.
58. Roberts, *Class Conflict and Elite Formation*, p.240. For details of the beginning and development of the plantation system, see Ludowyk, *History of Modern Ceylon*, pp.76–98.

32   *Sport in Asian Society*

59. de Silva, *History of Sri Lanka*, pp.333–8.
60. Mills, *Ceylon under British Rule*, p.264.
61. de Silva, *History of Sri Lanka*, p.327. See de Silva for a fuller discussion of the relationship between the Ceylonese elite and the masses, and the receptivity of the elite to the pressure of traditional values emanating from the people themselves (p.333). Unsurprisingly, therefore, the leadership of the religious revival of the time, which had strong political associations, was largely in the hands of the confident and unconfused English-educated and wealthy.
62. Ibid.
63. Ibid., p.329.
64. Ibid.
65. Ibid., p.330.
66. Ibid.
67. Ibid., p.338.
68. Ibid.
69. Ibid.
70. Ibid.
71. Stock, *History of the Church Missionary Society*, Vol.2, p.282.
72. Ibid., p.283.
73. Ibid., p.284.
74. Ibid., p.280.
75. Ibid.
76. Ibid., p.284.
77. Ibid.
78. Velesca L.O. Reimann, *A History of Trinity College, Kandy* (Madras: Diocesan Press, 1922), p.11.
79. Ibid.
80. Collins was part of the generation of schoolmasters that pre-dated the arrival of the games cult (athleticism) in metropolitan and imperial schools. For a full discussion of the rise of athleticism, see J.A. Mangan, *Athleticism in the Victorian and Edwardian Public School: The Rise and Consolidation Educational Ideology* (London and Portland, OR: Frank Cass, 2000), *passim*.
81. Reimann, *Trinity College*, p.20. Reimann drew on a paper by one of the earliest pupils, L.E. Blazé, for this material. Blazé was a huge admirer of Fraser and left an invaluable scrapbook of his doings, now in the Rhodes House Library.
82. Ibid., p.21.
83. Ibid., p.24.
84. Ibid., p.12. Note also the following: 'It is not surprising that when the English got around to building schools in India, they followed the public school model from which most of them had sprung. Initially these were from the sons of the English only; gradually scions of the Princely States and higher-ranking Indian officials joined them. After Partition they became the haunt of Anglo-Indians and the sons of the educated, and frequently political, elite. Now they are a strange anachronism, teaching an outmoded English curriculum to a largely uninterested hotchpotch of pupils. With the rise of political gangsterism and decline of the Anglo-Indian, the association between an English education and the ruling elite is no longer automatic, and it is no longer clear exactly what purpose the schools serve. It is ironic that, because the history curriculum in the UK itself now focuses almost exclusively on the twentieth century, Indian school children are far more likely to understand the classic humour of books like *1066 and All That*.' Antony Wild, *Remains of the Raj: The British Legacy in India* (London: HarperCollins, 2001), p.226.
85. Reimann, *Trinity College*, p.52.
86. Ibid., pp.56–7.
87. Ibid., p.57.
88. Ibid., p.80.
89. Ibid., pp.94–5.
90. Ibid., p.57.
91. For a description of the rise of athleticism, see Mangan, *Athleticism*, pp.22–7.
92. Jesus College was a hotbed of athleticism at this time; see J.A. Mangan, 'Oars and the Man:

Imperial Origins – Beginnings 33

'Pleasure and Purpose in Victorian and Edwardian Cambridge', *British Journal of Sports History*, 1, 1 (1984), pp.245–71, and see also J.A. Mangan, 'Bloods, Blues and Barbarians: Some Aspects of Late Victorian Oxbridge', in M. Huggins and J.A. Mangan (eds), *Disreputable Pleasures: Less Virtuous Victorians at Play* (London and Portland, OR: Frank Cass, forthcoming).

93. The school at this time seemed to bear a strong relationship to the schools in Anthony Burgess, *Time for a Tiger* (London: Heinemann, 1968).
94. Reimann, *Trinity College*, p.89.
95. Ibid.
96. Ibid., pp.99–100.
97. Ibid., p.81.
98. W.E.F. Ward, *Fraser of Trinity and Achimota* (Accra: Ghana Universities Press, 1965), p.??.
99. Reimann, *Trinity College*, pp.99–100.
100. See J.A. Mangan, 'Epilogue: The History of Sport and the History of Ideas', in J.A. Mangan (ed.), *Radicals, Modernizers, Reformers: Middle Class Revolutionaries* (London and Portland, OR: Frank Cass, 2002).
101. Take *Sport in Asian Society* as merely one example. It embraces sport and diplomacy, politics, nationalism, gender, imperialism, regionalism, modernization and globalization among other things.
102. With sports studies a popular and growing subject in public examinations, this prognostication may be partially fulfilled.
103. There are numerous studies of Muscular Christianity. For an earlier work which deals extensively but not exclusively with the topic, see J.A. Mangan and James Walvin (eds), *Manliness and Morality: Middle Class Masculinity in Britain and America, 1800–1940* (Manchester: Manchester University Press, 1987). For one that relates it especially to modern sport and evangelism, see Tony Ladd and James A. Mathisen, *Muscular Christianity: Evangelical Protestants and the Development of American Sport* (Grand Rapids, MI: Baker Books, 1999).
104. Ward, *Fraser*, Preface.
105. Ibid. See also the final part of Chapter 2.
106. For discussions of this phenomenon, see J.A. Mangan, 'Catalyst of Change: John Guthrie Kerr and the Adaptation of an Indigenous Scottish Tradition', in J.A. Mangan (ed.), *Pleasure, Profit and Proselytism: British Culture and Sport at Home and Abroad 1700–1914* (London: Frank Cass, 1988), pp.86–104, and J.A. Mangan, 'Missionaries to the Middle Classes', in Heather Holmes (ed.), 'Institutions of Scotland: Education', *Scottish Life and Society*, Vol.11 (Edinburgh: Tuckwell Press in association with the European Ethnological Centre, 2000), pp.415-34.
107. See Mangan, *Athleticism, passim*.
108. Ward, *Fraser*, p.4.
109. Ibid., p.5.
110. The 1890s saw an increase in CMS missionary recruits. Additions (average) for 1849–61 were 17.5 per cent per annum; for 1862–72, 13 per cent per annum; for 1873–82, 20.5 per cent per annum (figures exclusive of women); for 1883–95, 30.75 per cent per annum. A feature of this increase was the growing number of university graduates: 'In the whole period from the foundation of the society to the close of 1880, there were 156 graduates, viz., 78 from Cambridge, 38 from Oxford, 32 from Dublin, one from London University, others from German Universities; besides four holding medical degrees from Scotch Universities. In the fourteen years, 1881–94, there were 170 graduates, viz., 100 from Cambridge (two medical), 24 from Oxford, 16 from Dublin (three medical), seven from Durham (three medical), six from London University (five medical), one from the Royal University of Ireland, one from Leipzig University, five with medical degrees from Scotch Universities; also ten men engaged in the field, two from the University of New Zealand and eight from Canadian Universities. So the fourteen excelled the eighteen in this respect.' Stock, *History of the Church Missionary Society*, Vol.3, pp.354–5.
111. Ward, *Fraser*, p.8.
112. Ibid.

113. In 1896 the kingdoms of Buganda, Bunyoro, Toro, Ankole and Busugo had become the British Protectorate of Uganda.
114. Ward, *Fraser*, p.17.
115. Ward, *Fraser*, pp.31–2. The famous Scottish headmaster of the period, Hely Hutchison Almond, the founding headmaster of Loretto, a public school outside Edinburgh famed for its robust pupils, stated that he wanted 'First – Character. Second – Physique. Third – Intelligence. Fourth – Manners. Fifth – Information' (Quoted in Mangan, *Athleticism*, pp.55–6). The Scottish public schools, as stated earlier, at this time imitated extensively their more famous English counterparts. For fuller details of Almond and his influence, inspired by English experience, on other Scottish schools, see Mangan, *Athleticism*, pp.57–8.
116. Ibid., p.34.
117. Ward, *Fraser*, p.34.
118. Reimann, *Trinity College*, p.80.
119. Quoted in Ward, *Fraser*, pp.36–7.
120. Ward, *Fraser*, p.46.
121. Ibid., p.38.
122. See Mangan, *Athleticism*, pp.22–8.

2

Imperial Origins: Christian Manliness, Moral Imperatives and Pre-Sri Lankan Playing Fields – Consolidation

J.A. MANGAN

Alexander Garden Fraser took up his position as Principal of Kandy College in the autumn of 1904. He had an apodictic mission:

> I am no trained educationalist. I started off with no set policy, but faced, in Trinity College, Kandy, a tragic need. I set out to follow Him who had earned the title of Saviour, the greatest teacher of all time. ... We had to train our pupils to serve ... first of all they should be ready to serve each other, then to serve the needy ... later they would be prepared to serve their people.[1]

Immediately before the first cricket match of his 'rule', against Royal College, Fraser set the Christocentric moral tone for the school. He told the boys to 'play the game' as Jesus did with the result that 'every hit the Royals made, every wicket they bowled was cheered, even the winning hit.'[2] It was hard for them, Fraser remarked, 'but they did it for Christ, the King, and for the College founded in his name'.[3] Whether or not the boys were sure of their Christological position, Fraser was certain of his. He added: 'I believe firmly that the service of Christ Jesus makes men better sportsmen and that in the East sport is a valuable aid towards making them Christian men.'[4] Like Thomas à Kempis, he believed that habit could be overcome by habit; but unlike à Kempis he believed that this could be achieved on playing fields.

With the purpose of cricket clearly set out and set down, in a later letter in 1906 to the Church Missionary Society in London, he explained his reason for introducing rugby football: 'it requires more readiness [than association football] in courage and resource'.[5] Thus the rationale for school sport was made crystal clear. Charles Kingsley and Thomas Hughes were re-created in spirit if not flesh in an island school in empire.

Fraser was to have a profound influence on Ceylonese sport. Christianity, not capitalism, was his inspiration; schoolmasters, not military men or businessmen, were his 'Christian (foot) soldiers'. In the 1906 letter he included a statement that encapsulated the essentials of his thinking on sport, education, capitalism, imperialism and nationalism, and the role of exogenous sport in imperial education:

> I have heard athletics criticised on the ground that they exercise a westernising and anti-national influence. The criticism is purely superficial. Cricket and football find a ready home in the East as in England much more so than on the Continent. There boys take to them like ducks to water and the qualities cultivated by them, loyalty, courage, *esprit de corps* and honour are not western but belong to the race. Not our games but our luxury, money and purely English system of education fight against the true development of the East and its loyalty to the crown, and much of that seems beyond our power to control.[6]

Fraser was a profound professional moralist and a sensitive amateur naturalist. Immanuel Kant's words about himself are curiously apposite: 'Two things fill the mind with ever new and increasing wonder and awe, the more often and the more seriously reflection concentrates upon them; the starry heaven above me and the moral law within me.'[7]

In a now predominately secular age of sport dominated by commercialism, profit and entertainment, with the spinning of turnstiles and the ringing of tills so often a preoccupation, it is far from easy for some today to comprehend his concern that morality was a product of play, and the games field essentially a means of moral education. However it is necessary if an appreciation of historical motive behind historical action is to be understood.

In the previous essay the state of the school immediately before Fraser's arrival was discussed. Here is Fraser's own assessment of the school when he took up the post of Principal: discipline was needed; the school was in debt; parents were behind with fees; the compound was 'hopeless'; the staff were poorly trained and badly paid; buildings were in poor repair; drains were dangerous to health; the sports ground was a mile away; no cricket matches had been won in recent memory; and the Saturday before his arrival, the cricket team was drunk after a bad defeat.[8] Fraser was only too aware that the school faced closure, that the Ceylon administration was so dismayed by the bad discipline and appalling academic standards that it was considering opening a state school. However, Fraser was given the chance to turn things around. He concentrated initially and forcefully on discipline. More than 30 years later the Ceylon *Daily Gleaner* provided a vivid description of one early event: Fraser read out the names of some 70 boys to be 'sacked' for absenteeism at a meeting of the whole school, and declared that those named, if present, were to come out immediately. Of those present not one moved. He sent for a bundle of canes and on their arrival those present and named bolted.[9] In total in 1905, '140 incorrigibles were expelled'. Average attendance rose from 60 per cent to 94 per cent. Expulsions also reduced pressure on facilities, ensured higher standards through better teaching and regular attendance and as a result raised the government grant. His reforms had only started. As he fully appreciated: 'Better finance, better discipline, better buildings and equipment, better syllabuses, better teaching – all these hang together and none will make its full contribution without the other.'[10]

Fraser now fell back on his public school experience. He appointed prefects, he sought metropolitan public school teachers and he undertook a symbolic dramatic action that underlined his subscription to Christian manliness. He acquired new land and improved the games facilities. He was to repeat the action on a much larger scale a little later. Games playing was an integral part of his educational philosophy.

And he did much else: raised funds, raised teaching standards, improved sanitation and fought his early battles against late fee-payers, religious opposition and ethnocentric prejudice. In particular, at one point he took on his Buddhist critics in a series of well-attended public lectures.[11] He introduced Sinhalese and Tamil and ordered that teaching in the lower classes was to be in the pupils' mother tongue. He was disgusted on his arrival that 'any boy who spoke in a native tongue was thrashed for it'.[12] It seemed to him 'an absurd rule' and he immediately abolished it. These actions stimulated enmity especially from the Buddhists and the Ceylon Educational Association. Buddhist attacks, on occasion, were vitriolic:

> Trinity College at Kandy is one of the hot-houses of missionary labour in Ceylon, where innocent Buddhist boys are slaughtered by means of diplomatic propaganda. Why Buddhist children, who pay for their education, should be made victims of missionary lust, is what the Buddhists are unable to understand.[13]

The attacks by the Ceylon Educational Association were scarcely less vituperative. Fraser's sin was a general drift away from English history, Latin and Greek and advanced mathematics towards Ceylon history and culture, commercial studies, science, English, Sinhalese and Tamil.[14] The response from professional colleagues in the other privileged schools,[15]

> specially to the vernacular teaching, took the form chiefly of personal abuse of the College and the Principal as an individual. They criticised the lines of work and the educational policy upheld by the College, but they were generally occupied with personal details, such as the quality of Mr Fraser's brains and the credibility of his professions. The boys, past and present, were described as 'mentally decrepit,' or 'non-progressive,' while the Principal was 'anti-native', 'bribed' and a 'conspirator', and was training his boys to be 'hewers of wood and drawers of water'.[16]

As Reimann reported in 1922, in time it all came out in the wash: 'This particular form of opposition has, of course, long since died down: many of the reforms have been adopted, and education in Ceylon has not collapsed. In fact, keen opponents have in many cases become converts.'[17] All Fraser's efforts had one end – to match the prestigious Colombian missionary schools and the government school in status, image and performance, on playing fields and in classrooms. Eventually he did better than this: he outperformed them.[18] To achieve this end, *inter alia* he created more playing fields and boarding facilities to equal those of Royal College, Wesleyan College, St Thomas's and the other Colombo schools.

The educational importance of cricket to Fraser in both character training and status pursuit is clear from the fact that the captain of the school eleven was allowed to play for the Ceylon team against a Parsee eleven visiting the island, and even more so by the fact that Mr Orr, one of his recruited teachers was permitted to play regularly for the Ceylon team. In 1905 Orr 'piled up 1,233 runs'.[19] Fraser's belief in the educational value of cricket could not have been clearer than in the following year, when an action came that exemplified Fraser's energy, determination, commitment and subscription to the role of games in the creation of Christian manliness. In the effort to create moral Trinitarians in his own mould, he achieved the astonishing creation of a new expansive cricket field of eight acres out of two hills and a valley. The scheme was considered foolhardy;[20] indeed, some thought him crazy.[21] His reaction was nonchalantly confident:

> The Army was withdrawing from much that it had been doing in Ceylon, and five minutes' walk from the school they had a large bit of land which was useless to them; it would give inferior grazing but nothing else. It consisted of two hills, one high, one low, and was V-shaped. I asked the Army if I might have it and I would pay for it what they asked. They said 'certainly' – and there was no need to pay. They gave it me freely, giving the college full title deeds.[22]

Thus Fraser acquired a piece of land described later as a cliff – 'a steep hillside descending into a valley'.[23]

This description of what happened next provides an illustration of pragmatism allied to idealism:

> I got the boys and staff to help me, and we started to dig down the big hill and throw it into the V-shaped valley. The lower hill acted as a retaining wall. I then got workmen from the villages to help, and we made an eight-acre field. The Public Works Department and other experts told us that all our soil would be washed away by the big rains, but I had seen what the Dutch did in Holland, and we made similar under-surface drains with loose stones in the field. We never had any trouble and the Australians said it was the most beautiful cricket ground they had ever seen and that the pitch was perfect.[24]

Fraser's biographer G.E.F. Ward wrote prosaically: 'Much of the work of cutting and filling and levelling was done by the boys, working swiftly and singing lustily to the accompaniment of Mr C.B. Weerasinghe's violin.'[25] Reimann wrote rather more romantically:

> The making of the new cricket-pitch began to assume gigantic proportions. It was found that after moonlight nights there was a miraculous advance on the following morning, as though gnomes or pixies had been at work in the silence of the moon. And so it was. But the gnomes were college boys in their cloths and pyjamas working swiftly and singing lustily to the accompaniment of Mr C.B. Weerasinghe's violin. Almost like Nero fiddling at night to the destruction of Rome. But this destruction of a hill was the construction of a field.[26]

Plain prose or purple patch, the outcome was the same – one of the finest cricket grounds in the island, Trinity College's famous Asigiriya cricket field.[27] Ward commented in his biography: 'What a field! ... The cliffs rise 100 feet about it, and the hill below it is 120 feet.'[28]

Fraser's innovation in time assumed mythological dimensions. As late as 1961, the Principal C.J. Oorloff paid tribute to Fraser as 'a man of principle; man of action; man of vision', and added: 'Out of an uncompromising hillside ... he carved one of the finest cricket grounds in the island.'[29]

Fraser himself gave a doctrinal explanation for this extraordinary effort and achievement in a letter about this time:

> The boy has not only a body and mind, he has a spirit ... and through school ... and sports we get to know him, with one object in view, so to present Jesus Christ to him, that he may see in Him the truest type of manhood, the One who came and lived among men, that He might draw all men to Him.[30]

About this time he offered the confident ethnocentric view that 'sports such as football and cricket have proved very valuable as character training ... such training does not denationalise ... it gives of the best which one race has to offer to the other.[31]

Such statements are a sincere record of intent; today they are hardly fashionable. To an extent, secularism and materialism have ensured their replacement. However, they are also a record of historical purpose and action. Without an understanding of their sincerity, an appreciation of their existence and an awareness of their eventual consequences, the historical record is that much poorer, and certainly incomplete.

Down the years the moral message linked to sport was well and truly hammered home. By 1922, a little before Fraser's departure from Trinity, much the same refrain appeared in the first college history as a 'mission statement':

> Trinity College, of course, realises the values of sport in a school. It breaks up cliquism and lethargy, and leads to the spread of a healthy and friendly spirit. It gives endurance, self-control, courage and manliness; and, above all, it teaches the sinking of self for the good of the whole.[32]

The term 'mission statement' in 2002 is much favoured by commerce, higher education and the civil service, but it is especially appropriate to the Christian missionary college in Kandy in the early twentieth century.

A little while after his arrival in Kandy, Fraser was diagnosed as having trypanosomiasis (sleeping sickness), contracted while in Uganda. At the time it was considered a death sentence. However, advances in medicine ensured a cure. After long treatment in England, he returned to Trinity in 1908.

While in England he demonstrated his aggressive Christian militancy[33] in the missionary field in a paper that was sent to Ceylon missionaries for comment. In summary, he argued that in Ceylon Buddhism was advancing faster than Christianity. Christianity in Ceylon was thus on the defensive. To regain the initiative, Christian pupils in Christian schools must be groomed for leadership. Undue westernisation must be avoided. Tamil and Sinhalese must be promoted and a whole system of schools created for the Ceylonese Anglican Church. These comments did not go down well with the Ceylon Church Missionary Society Conference. The reduction of the metropolitan curriculum, especially Latin and Greek, aroused resentment. The paper serves to illustrate Fraser's crusading Christianity. As already noted, he was to confront the Buddhists belligerently for the whole period of his stay in Ceylon.[34] Typical of this uncompromising confrontation and the demonstration of an emphatic *parti pris*, is an appeal for funds in 1905:

> TRINITY COLLEGE, KANDY
> Occupies a splendid position for aggressive work for Christ amongst those who profess that sad atheistical religion called Buddhism. The College has been singularly blessed in the past, and now it urgently requires land to enlarge its premises, as applicants are being turned from its doors every week.[35]

While an invalid in England, Fraser acquired two athletic masters for Trinity, the Revd A.M. Walmsley and Mr G.R. Mulgrue.[36] In January 1908 Fraser won the support of a Balliol student, N.P. Campbell – a brilliant scientist and apparently a potential Lord Kelvin.[37] Campbell[38] was to bring Fraser's Ceylonese school closer to Tyndale-Biscoe's Kashmiri School.[39] In rather different ways Fraser and Tyndale-Biscoe were to prove strikingly influential Christian imperial missionaries and also, more to the point with regard to the theme of this essay, influential disseminators of modern games within the empire.[40] However, they could not have achieved all that they did without the assistance of equally committed expatriate and indigenous Christian staff[41] – in the case of the former, with a unique set of imported Victorian and Edwardian English experiences.

Restored to health, Fraser returned to Trinity in November 1908. His influence and his energy were quickly apparent in new laboratories, classrooms, common-rooms and a boarding house (he had raised much of the money required in England), a scout movement, a communicant's union and a reorganised Sunday school.

Also on his return he recruited two new members of staff – K.J. Saunders and J.P.S. Gibson, both from Cambridge.[42] These 'varsity' and public-school 'types' were deliberately chosen by Fraser for their educational experiences and values. Much later, Fraser explained why: 'No mere walking encylopedias ... are much use. Men who as men will mould men, these are what we need.'[43] With the arrival of N.P. Campbell, simultaneously with crusading efforts on games fields now went proselytising in the slums of Kandy, an action inspired by Tyndale-Biscoe's extraordinary efforts in Srinagar.[44] Campbell established the Trinity College Union for Social Service to help those in need.[45]

No better evidence of Fraser's Christian purpose could be forthcoming than the two-pronged attempt to create boys with 'strong limbs and chivalrous spirits'[46] – strong on games fields and fit to carry out acts of compassion among the poor. The role of sport in creating such Muscular Christians is nowhere more clear than in this provocative but purposeful statement of 1915: 'Our athletics prominence can hardly be questioned, and athletics are more important here than in England by a long way, for this is a soft land with a soft people.'[47] Fraser had admirable qualities in common with Tyndale-Biscoe. Like Tyndale-Biscoe, he established a school without racial, religious or class barriers,[48] and like Tyndale-Biscoe, Fraser did not believe in 'laying himself out' to convert individual boys to Christianity; but he did believe strongly in developing a school with strong Christian principles.[49]

In pursuit of social reform and justice, as in the case of Tyndale-Biscoe, Fraser was at constant odds with those leaders of local society whom he viewed in a poor light and confronted à outrance. Ward commented:

> In the town, says one of his Ceylonese colleagues, Mr Fraser had enemies: liars and cheats and grinders of the poor feared him. He would hold them in steady gaze in the street as they passed him by, riding in their rickshaws.[50]

He incurred the animosity too, as noted briefly earlier, of pious Buddhists, who resented his Christian militancy and his school's 'strong Christian atmosphere',[51] and the resentment of British colleagues of the Educational Association of Ceylon for his drift away from classics, English history and higher mathematics towards Ceylonese history and culture, local languages, science and commercial subjects.[52] Fraser was regarded by the conservative teachers who favoured an English public-school classroom curriculum as an imperial iconoclast more interested in religion than education. Tyndale-Biscoe too was far from loved by British colleagues – too righteously pious by half![53] There can be no doubt also that Fraser was righteous as well as pugnacious, opinionated and blunt.[54] To make matters worse, he was energetic, determined and competent. Unquestionably he had an ignescent temperament. He immersed himself in heated controversy. Both his assured forceful frankness and his dynamic, persistent efficiency made him lasting enemies. It was at this time that Fraser remarked ruefully of the Ceylon press: 'I have been represented as anti-native, anti-national, occasionally as anti-Christian, and almost always as evil.'[55] However, few criticized his compassionate commitment to creating Ceylonese 'Christian' gentlemen on and off playing fields. There is something in the fact that, as Graham Greene once said of Ford Madox Ford, he had the sort of enemies a man ought to have. There was also an attractive side to Fraser – his complete lack of 'side', his youthful approachability and his warmth of personality. He once wrote of life at Trinity:

> All our champion teams come to the bungalow for dinner as a matter of course, and celebrate the winning of the inter-collegiate trophy with due feasting. But almost every day masters, prefects, and other boys come in to one meal or another – breakfast, dinner or tiffin. Also my wife has tea parties for all the classes in the school and college in turn every term. Each class comes on a day fixed with its own teacher or teachers, and a few friends to help to make the party go. Then they have games and cakes and sweets and tea – stodge and a rag, in fact – for a couple of hours or more. The invitations to the class parties are all sent in writing, each boy securing his letter and answering it as best he can ... But our entertaining is only a small part of the whole. Dormitory masters, class masters and others are always giving tête-a-tête meals, or larger parties, and we sometimes get week-end trips to the jungle

at the mid-term holiday, or longer trips in the big holidays. And so everyone gets to know everyone on easy intimate terms, and we are not divided into the master caste, the prefect caste, etc., but are all members of one college, of one community, and its future lies with us all.[56]

As early as 1910 the school had come a long way in a short time. A.L. Senior, deputising for Fraser during the principal's visit to India in 1909, sent an annual report to the CMS in London, published the following year, which includes details of a strenuous 'public school' programme of cricket, rugby, swimming, boxing, athletics, shooting, fives and racquets. Senior was quite sure in his own mind that the cricket eleven was quite up to the standard of English public school cricket.[57]

By 1910 the process of change was far from over. On his return from India the same year, Fraser introduced inter-house contests in cricket, rugby and debating, and in the same year, the Colonial Secretary, H.L. Crawford, declared at the old boys' dinner that:

> It is only under the new regime that [Trinity] has become a serious, formidable competitor to the big schools in Colombo. In former days, with a few exceptions, it seemed to take the place of a preparatory school. ... It now, in many respects, takes the lead of all schools in Ceylon. It approaches more nearly to the best type of English public school than any other public school with which I am acquainted – in its boarding establishment, in its prefect system and in many other respects...[58]

Crawford was absolutely right. An extant printed programme for the 'Annual Reunion of Old Boys of Trinity College' still exists. It is a simulacrum of that of an English public school:

Sunday, Dec. 6th: Divine Service and Sermon

Monday, Dec. 7th: Cricket – Past versus Present (8a.m.); Reception (3.45p.m.); Distribution of Prizes (4.30pm); Annual Old Boys' Dinner (8p.m.)

Tuesday, Dec. 8th: Athletic Sports (8a.m.)[59]

Fraser was now beginning to be noticed; his school was beginning to exert an influence throughout Ceylon, and this influence was soon to enter its golden age. By 1913 cricket at Trinity was more than coming into its own; it had arrived. For the first time 'Trinity tied for the island

Imperial Origins – Consolidation

cricket championship'.[60] It had taken Fraser just nine years. Before long Trinity was to dominate cricket among the prestigious Ceylonese schools. Under Fraser, rugby also advanced 'with great strides'.[61] It remained a Trinity speciality for many years. Other schools did not take to it.[62] Fraser took care that the game was well taught. He recruited a master who had come close to winning Blue at Oxford, A.C. Houlder, and was to prove 'a great acquisition to the College football'.[63]

In 1914 the college carried off the island shields 'for physical drill, shooting and boxing'.[64] In 1915 the college won the cricket championship,

> winning all the six Inter-Collegiate matches. The 120 wickets of the opponents averaged only 6.5 runs each, while Trinity's were 16.8. The poorest victory was against Wesley College and that was by five wickets. All the other matches were innings victories. ... But besides this Trinity held the Shooting Cup for the seventh time in succession since its inauguration; they won the Physical Drill shield, retained the Boxing shield, and won the Cadet Corps championship.[65]

In the same year a special sports award to spur on performers within the school was introduced by Fraser – the school Lion award. In March 18 Lions won the award for cricket, rugby, boxing, shooting, marching, military efficiency and general efficiency in sport.[66] Trinity now began a steady climb to athletic pre-eminence among the island elite schools. In this way, it played its part in consolidating modern sport, especially cricket, in Ceylonese, and later Sri Lankan, culture. His boys could compete well. In the spring of 1915, Fraser wrote to his son regarding a proposed visit by the school eleven to Australia: 'I would like them to go there to play the schools. They would make a very good show I think. Ceylon school cricket is very good ... and at present TCK is far above the average run of Ceylon Cricket.'[67] He had good cause for general as well as specific confidence. He reported to the Friends of Trinity College at the end of the year that

> We stand thus:
>
> | | |
> |---|---|
> | 1st in Cricket | 111 Colleges compete |
> | 1st in Military drill | 9 Colleges compete |
> | 1st in Physical Drill | 9 Colleges compete |
> | 1st in Rugger | 3 Colleges compete |
> | 1st in Boxing | 5 Colleges compete |
> | 1st in Running | 9 Colleges compete |
> | 1st in Exams | All Colleges compete[68] |

In fact, Trinity cricket was so far above average that the following year Trinity again won the cricket championship, and won it again in 1918. This was also the year in which the school's cadet corps 'swept the board' at the Cadet Sports at Colombo, winning 'the Soysa Cup for junior marching, the Herman Loos Cup for senior squad drill, the Challenge Cup for athletics, the Tug of War Cup, the Relay Race Cup and a multitude of prizes'.[69]

Not only this, but by 1915 Trinity had become a physically attractive school in a delightful setting. In that year, *Amicus*, Ceylon's illustrated weekly, produced a special edition about Trinity College, Kandy. The magazine noted that 'The location of Trinity is ideal – in the early morning sunlight ... its many white building form a harmonious group on the hillside with a forest background that gives shade, colour and life to the entire scene.'[70] The special edition offered a eulogistic celebration of Fraser's success. Perhaps of particular importance are the numerous photographs in *Amicus* of a pulsating school and staff and pupils in a variety of activities, which promote a kaleidoscopic visual impression of the nature of the school and the remarkable achievements of Fraser in some eight years.

By 1916 there could be little doubt that Trinity and Fraser were beginning to exert a strong influence on the development of modern sport among young Ceylonese. The motive, as a newspaper article of the time made clear, was to be located more in moral purpose than status pursuit – the creation of a strong Christian character meant more to Fraser than social image. Trinity, *Amicus* noted admiringly,

> knew the secret of teaching a boy how to be a man. It drives grit, confidence, efficiency and rectitude into the least promising boy and makes a man of him. Its special function is to build character. It seems less anxious about what to teach a boy, than about what to make of him.[71]

In fact Trinity was now setting the pace both athletically *and* academically. In the words of the same Colombo newspaper:

> Trinity was first in the Intermediate Examination, first in the Arts Scholarship Examination, first in cricket, first in physical drill, first in military drill, first in shooting, first in boxing – for the Shield remains with them – *hors de concours* in rugger, and in running equal second.[72]

The newspaper further declared that by means of the 'astonishing record of this provincial institution, [Trinity] has forced its way into the very front rank of our great public schools and means to stay thus'.[73]

Eventually Trinity's reputation both scholastically and athletically became so impressive that the college historian summed up the later years of Fraser's principalship as follows:

> There had once been the accusation that Trinity College was interested in nothing but sport. Unfortunately the Ceylon parent still does not realise the important and necessary part which sport plays in a boy's education. A school is approved or condemned according as it is successful or otherwise in examinations. ... Sport was condemned because it was believed that an athlete could not be a thinker, and in fact he could do nothing in life but win cups and prizes. ... During these years no school could afford to laugh at Trinity for her achievements in cricket, rugger, athletics and military training. But neither could they point the finger of scorn at her intellectual attainments. One year after another Trinity's examination results – the only criterion Ceylon recognises – stood equal with or surpassed those of the other Ceylon colleges.[74]

Fraser left Kandy in 1919 to chair the CMS Indian Commission on Village Education. He was to spend little time at Trinity for some four years and then was to move to West Africa at the request of the British government to become principal of Achimota College – a government-created and -financed 'public school' on the Gold Coast. The commission, conferences and meetings from 1919 took up much of his time.[75] Under its acting principal, L.J. Gaster, Trinity continued its winning ways on the cricket field. On a flying visit from England in 1921 Fraser noted with justifiable pride:

> I came back at the beginning of the cricket and athletic season, and saw the cricket eleven win all its matches and seniors win the senior inter-college challenge cup for athletics. The cricket eleven were very good indeed. ... But their good sportsmanship and good temper impressed me most. On one occasion, in a critical match, the best bat of the other college was given out lbw after he had made only about three runs. Maralande [the Trinity College captain] thought he had just tipped the ball with his bat before it hit his pads, and so he asked the umpire to let him return to the

wicket. After discussion, they agreed, and the batsman came back to make his fifty and top score.[76]

That same year Trinity won the schools cricket championship for the fifth time in eight years. Fraser had sown the seed; Gaster brought in the harvest. Trinity under Fraser was at its apogee; success had become a habit. In consequence, Trinity received high praise from no less a figure than the Governor of Ceylon, Sir William Manning, in a speech at the old boys' dinner in 1923:

> Now I am glad to see – I read it and I see it day by day in the newspapers – that Trinity College, in addition to the position which it has taken as a College for learning takes no less a place in the world of sport (applause). It takes no less a place in all those attributes of manliness, which say what we like, we cannot but admire. I myself am a keen sportsman. ... I recognise and we all recognise what we learnt in those days when we were compelled to turn out to play cricket or football – what we learnt of the lessons of self-denial and of the lessons that manly sport gives to us. A school without its sporting side is, in my opinion a school which is likely to have little spirit in it.[77]

This paean of praise was only one of set of magnificats that evening.

At the same dinner in a more humorous but no less revealing apologue, the Revd G.B. Ekanayake spoke on behalf of the other elite colleges:

> I think of Trinity sometimes as a hill-tribe which makes periodical raids on the Low Country Colleges. They swoop down upon us and carry away as their spoil our trophies, prizes, places and class lists (applause) and then the invite the victims to display three trophies as they do this evening and drink to the health of their victims (laughter).[78]

Next the Revd W.A. Stone, Warden of St Thomas's, caught perfectly Fraser's quixotism, a mixture of moral muscularity, charismatic compassion, imperial patriotism and Central Scottishness:

> The history of Trinity is the history of Mr Fraser. The boys of Trinity play cricket too well. In rugger they are without a rival. ... They have their league of prayer, village work and social service so well known to you all. Indeed, the combined effect of life at Trinity

is that of Arabian Nights, Daniel in the Lion's Den, Harry Lauder and the Battle of Waterloo.[79]

Fraser in response was all serious Christian piety dressed in spotless doctrinal livery: 'Our aim was our Lord's aim, the bringing in of the Kingdom of God.'[80] What E.F.C. Ludowyk said of the first civilian Governor of Ceylon, Frederick North, applies with equal force, slightly adapted, to Fraser: 'He had far too many notions of his own to be anything but a highly individual and eccentric English milord at a time when the species could throw off extraordinary examples.'[81] Delete 'English', substitute 'missionary' for 'milord', recall to mind Tyndale-Biscoe, and the comment fits Fraser like a glove.

A little before Fraser's final departure from Trinity in 1924, Stone, as Warden of St Thomas's, one of the oldest Colombo schools and a keen rival of Trinity, again took stock of the Fraser years at Trinity. He offered an elaborate *jeu d'esprit* that is revealing of Fraser both as a personality and principal and which deserves full consideration. He began:

> My earliest recollections of Trinity go back to a time when you were merely a College in Kandy, living a happy life, when you were, one and all, merely lovable. Those were the days when you dwelt at ease; when you afforded in cricket matches the most useful practice to the members of our eleven, and you found your greatest happiness in yielding victories to your opponents after entertaining them hospitably.

He continued:

> Then came the wizard of the North to Ceylon with his band of attendant ministers, and waving the wand he cried 'Be great!' And some boys of Trinity said: 'We are quite happy; we don't want to be great.' Then spoke the wizard those fateful words: 'You don't want to be great? Then by heaven, I'll make you great.'

Stone then demonstrated a perfect understanding of Fraser's early ambition and awareness of his fierce competitiveness, as well as a knowledge of John Bunyan:

> [T]he wizard gathered you together and pointing to the great Hill Difficulty that confronted you, said: 'Up that hill you shall go. Mark how on the lower slopes are perched what are, I believe, Colombo Colleges and Schools of parts unknown. What do they

call from the walls? 'You must not trespass here; these seats are reserved' ... up the steep height you were driven and pushed, leaving few behind in Doubting Castle, and led by a wizard you emerged at last upon the delectable mountains, where ever since you have lived in delight. And that was the Pilgrim's Progress of Trinity. In that invigorating air you have lived the strenuous life, as you have proved in every form of sport. In cricket you entertained as hospitably and sent your guests away empty of honour. Well do I remember the days when the boxing tournament was held in Colombo ... you delivered the famous knock-out that left you undisputed champions. Your Principal to-day, remarking in his report that rugger is played at Trinity while other colleges follow the other game ... Why had you no opponents? Because, if the dreadful secret must be told, you had not only vanquished every team that met you but destroyed them utterly on the field of battle.[82]

The witticisms were pointed; the compliments unmistakable; the appreciation unstinted.

Fraser received many more accolades before his departure to West Africa to create the eventually famous Achimota College. Tributes, unquestionably stimulated by the desire to be courteous, nevertheless to the open minded surely point to his extraordinary successful leadership of Trinity. A newspaper article by 'Adonis' entitled 'Fraser of Trinity Whom it is a Delight to Honour' provides a glimpse of the climate of the school under Fraser: 'it simply pulsated with life and activity'.[83] Adonis commented further on the warmth of the hospitality to guests, staff and pupils. He recalled with affection the school picnics, walks and sing-songs. He praised Fraser and his wife for their assiduous interest in all aspects of school life and commented: 'No cricket match, whether Home or Away, was complete without Mrs Fraser in the pavilion; no Rugger Match without Mr Fraser on the touchline. At home matches they were among the keenest onlookers.'[84]

There was much in the same vein in the Ceylonese press. The following is but a fragment of the whole. On 23 March 1924 the *Independent* of Ceylon, under the heading 'Fraser of Trinity To Leave Ceylon' observed that 'Trinity today leads in most things ... a factor that has raised Kandy College from the status of a village school to a power in the educational world of Ceylon.'[85] The *Ceylon Morning Leader* asserted under the heading 'Rugby of the East' that especially through the development of sport and through Social Service Mr Fraser has brought to the East and to a school of 500 boys representative of all parts of Ceylon and India but also Burma, Siam and even Uganda all that is best in the public school spirit of the west.[86]

In a later article the *Ceylon Morning Leader* included a piece, 'Civilization's Advance', which quoted Tagore, whom Fraser knew and greatly admired: 'There can be no doubt that God's choice had fallen upon the Knight Errants of the West for the service of the present age', Tagore adding that 'among those Knight Errants were Mr Fraser and his colleagues'.[87] The *Ceylon Morning Leader* also had an editorial announcing that

> the athletic triumphs of Trinity are too well known to need recapitulation. It is enough to say that there are not ... effortless triumphs but the result of hard training and Self denial ... athletics at Trinity is an excellent training for character.[88]

The strongest encomium came in *The Ceylon Sportsman*: 'Fraser of Trinity ... conceived the idea with conviction and certainty that games alone can educate boys to be manly, clean, unselfish and chivalrous.' The anonymous author went on:

> Fraser has spared no pains and brooked no interference with his scheme of development ... and he has ... in and out of season spent himself in imbuing first a real love of the game itself and through this means building up the character of the boys. ... Games form a very essential part of education at Trinity, but it is just a means to an end.[89]

The pre-Fraser years were damned with faint praise:

> Long before Mr Fraser came to Trinity there was cricket, football and teams played ... not altogether in the right spirit. The elevating moral force sport was capable of generating ... was lost sight of. These are things of the past now. 'Fraser has taught us to play the game hard and well, clean and fair.'[90]

The article concluded: 'What Arnold of Rugby has been to English public school, Fraser of Trinity in greater measure has been to Ceylon.' Such compliments did not end then. Years later it was stated that to many in Ceylon 'the title "Fraser of Trinity" sounded as natural and proper as "Arnold of Rugby" or "Sanderson of Oundle" sounded to these schools'.[91]

If it is accepted that the moment of departure demanded praise, equally it can be reasonably argued that there was much to praise. Fraser earns his place in the Perera pantheon of pre Sri-Lankan contributors to the growth of modern sport there – with its contemporary individual, cultural and social advantages.[92]

Fraser was not quickly forgotten. In 1935 the *Ceylon Daily News* had a front-page article entitled 'A Famous Principal ... The Man who Made Trinity', which included the statement that Fraser 'sought to introduce the English Public School System in an Oriental environment, and although he had his critics his faith was justified by its fruits'.[93] It was no more than the truth and memories remained sharp. As late as 1949 the *Ceylon Fortnightly Review* recorded of Trinity in Fraser's time that 'games were given due attention, and under competent coaching the cricket and football teams proved almost invincible'.[94] In a tribute to Fraser in the *Souvenir of the Seventy-Fifth Anniversary* of the college in 1947, it was observed that 'even today the name of Trinity is synonymous with that of Fraser', and this succinct evaluation was added: 'He transformed a little school in Kandy into one of the leading Colleges of the Island.'[95]

This and the previous essay do not restrict themselves merely to the early evolution of cricket in Sri Lanka. They range further afield. They link religion, sport, ideology and empire to moral ambition – however unrealistic this ambition may be in the face of human nature – and ultimately they are about a continuous historical chain still unbroken; they explore the relationship between Occident and Orient, imperialism and nationalism, cultural diffusion and assimilation.

Fraser was an ethnocentric visionary whose time has well and truly passed. He had a profound, albeit now most emphatically rejected, vision of empire – misguided but well-intentioned, benign and compassionate. It was not without merit in the short term and the long term. This vision was of a multicultural Christian empire[96] of equals[97] – caring and classless.[98] This vision adds to recent discussions and assertions. It offers a necessary subtlety. It goes without saying that Fraser was far from perfect in the pursuit of his ideal. In his rush to tolerance he could be intolerant; in his search for cooperation he could be confrontational.[99] Like Tyndale-Biscoe in Kashmir at much the same

Imperial Origins – Consolidation 53

time, he was a missionary educationist with a period belief in the games field as a source of moral instruction. He was committed to sport, team games in particular, as a means of inculcating the moral quality of 'fair play' – now arguably required more urgently than ever on professional Commonwealth cricket fields as well as the sports arenas of the 'global village'.

The purpose of this depiction of Fraser is not hagiographical nor is it exculpatory; it is an attempt to ensure balance in the imperial record. Some Christian moralists of late Victorian England eschewed a crude race, class and capitalist view of imperialism and possessed a vision of imperialism that deserves mention in the interest of the completeness of the imperial record.[100] For all their ethnocentric shortcomings, such men exerted a beneficial influence – although the extent of this influence is hard to quantify precisely. Their histories add to the complexity of the imperial experience on the part of colonizer and colonized. It has been observed that

> the imposition of the Raj, under the lens of time, was a moment out of history. A turning aside. It could not last, it was an anomaly. India lapped at it and washed over it, and submerged it for ever, like a lost city obliterated by an inevitable rise of the waters. But it retains the mystery and eerie seductiveness of lost cities, a forlorn piece of the archaeology of the human spirit, grandly – triumphantly – wrong in the wrong place.
>
> Surely, among the criticisms and excuses for their conduct, we can smile at a people who made such an unforeseen, wholehearted and dedicated mistake.[101]

It would not be unreasonable in some cases to smile with appreciation and to applaud with reason, and to acknowledge that not everything was a mistake. In 1962, the year of Fraser's death, an editorial in the supplement to the *Trinity College Magazine* commemorating his death warned against denying great men from abroad 'their rightful place in the history of the country'.[102] It is a reasonable and just caveat. E.F.C. Ludowyk in his *Modern History of Ceylon* offered this gracious evaluation of the Christian missionary in Ceylon that should provide food for thought:

> Most valuable in what came through the missionary to his pupils was in effect neither indoctrination nor familiarity with the

Christian story; it was schooling coloured by certain values derived from the teacher's own education in his homeland. What these men and women believed of course influenced their personality as teachers, but it was their character as men and women rather than their beliefs (in so far as they could be separated) which left its mark on those they taught. For all its inadequacies and misdemeanours this kind of education had most effect through the contact of the pupil with persons whose qualities of mind and character had much to give them. One can only regret that contacts such as these were available only to so few.[103]

In India the cultural aspects of decolonisation, it is claimed, deeply affect every aspect of life – institutional, ideological and aesthetic. Nevertheless, while the special relationship between India and England now matters little in politics and economics, there remains a part of Indian culture today that seems forever to be England, and that is cricket.[104] There the urge 'to cut the ties with the colonial past seems weakest'.[105] Is it so very different in Sri Lanka? In India, it is suggested, the reason is to be found in a distinction between the 'hard' and 'soft' culture forms.[106] 'Hard' forms, with linked values, meanings and practices, are difficult both to break and to transform, while 'soft' forms, by way of contrast, permit an easier separation of action from value. Cricket, it has been argued, changes the individual more easily than it is changed. One reason, it has been asserted perhaps optimistically, is that its values represent – at least traditionally – a distinctive moral perspective, a set of meanings for living. In this respect it is linked to past and present class values and a capability to 'mimic Victorian elite values'.[107]

However, at the same time, it represents 'a dialect between team spirit and nationalism and thus implicitly corrodes the bonds of empire'.[108] In conjunction with this it assists in the construction of 'a post colonial male spectatorship which charges the game with a virile nationalism' – a nationalistic 'manliness'.[109] Indeed it has been asserted that the role of cricket in the creation and consolidation of communal identity must not be underestimated;[110] with the result that '"India" had to be invented, at least for the purposes of colonial cricket'.[111] Sectional community and cultural distinctiveness had to be replaced. Cricket followed the rise of Indian nationalism. There was little explicit contact between national politicians and national cricketers, but one led to the other following on – at a distance in time from the rise of national cricket in England.[112]

In the process of the emergence of cricketing national consciousness in India, the media and language played a central role. In the 1960s, for example, multilingual radio commentary – Hindi, Tamil and Bengali as well as English – began: 'Multilingual radio commentary is probable the most important instrument in the socialization of the Indian mass audience into the subtleties of the sport.'[113] This process has been reinforced by television, books, newspapers and sports magazines. This interesting analysis has resonances for Sri Lankan cricket and culture – one which embraces both continuity and change.

Thus colonial cricket in some Commonwealth countries has been one crucial element in the shaping of postcolonial globalization.[114] In India, it has been pointed out, cricket historically has involved three major community loyalties – to religious group, to empire and to the nation.[115] In Sri Lanka, similarly, a triadic set of allegiances also emerged over time – to imperialism, to ethnic group and to nationalism. It could be reasonably argued that there was, and is, another allegiance – to social class. What is interesting about Fraser is that he attempted to promote only one loyalty – to a Christian empire.[116] Involvement in cricket for his schoolboys was a training in the 'superior' moral values of a wider Christian empire without class, colour or religious prejudice.[117] This fact, at least, has the virtue of adding a further complexity to the already complex political analyses of Asian commentators such as Arjun Appadurai on cricket and culture.

Fraser did not succeed in the long run, but his effort is an interesting footnote in the imperial story. He was one of several imperial educationists of some importance. The stories of most of the others remain to be told. This briefly is his story in Ceylon. His special significance lies in the fact that he ensured that for a time that his school – Trinity College, Kandy – was pre-eminent in sport in Ceylon and his schoolboy cricketers were celebrated on the island, with long-term consequences of significance to the Sri Lankan self-image. What can never be clear, of course, is to what extent his pupils absorbed and transmitted his moral purpose; but in this respect this essay is as much a record of imperial intent as it is a record of imperial influence. As already stated, Fraser's long-term idealism was thwarted – as a believer, an educationalist and an imperialist. The writing was on the wall early; he failed to see it. In the *Ceylon Morning Leader* in 1908, in an article critical of Fraser, it was stated that the epoch of conversion was long past and that Fraser had a pipe dream of India as 'one nation under

Christ'. A later editorial in the newspaper argued that his view demonstrated that 'ears were closed to the obtrusive clamour of the facts'.[118]

The larger story of the colonial school and community cricket in Ceylon must wait.[119] It may well prove to be no less complex than in India. Appadurai, incidentally, mentions in passing those in India responsible for the growth of cricket down the decades – British army officers, businessmen and administrators, Indian princes and cricket professionals, mostly from England and Australia. For this information he drew on Cashman. Thus, like Cashman, not to mention the regrettably more superficial Varney, he is guilty of giving insufficient attention to the missionary educationist who taught the princes, the middle classes and other sections of the India community to play the game – literally and metaphorically.[120] In view of these historical omissions, the recording of the role of Fraser and other teacher-missionaries in the history of the transmission of ideas, ideals and actions by means of playing fields in Asia is all the more necessary if complete coverage of the complexity of the Victorian colonial *ecumene* scrutinised by, for example, Appadurai himself (the term is his), if all Victorian imperial visions are to be recorded and if the subtlety of the range of Victorian imperial attitudes to race, class and colour are to be revealed.[121] The unintentional impact of such men as Fraser on the minds, emotions, enthusiasms and interests of impressionable adolescents, so superbly remembered by C.L.R. James, requires thoughtful appreciation:

> It was only long years after that I understood the limitation on spirit, vision and self-respect which was imposed on us by the fact that our masters, our curriculum, our core of morals, *everything* began from the basis that Britain was the source of all light and leading, and our business was to admire, wonder, imitate, learn; our criterion of success was to have succeeded in approaching that distant ideal – to attain it was, of course, impossible.[122]

At the same time, James, a fair man, was not wholly negative in his assessment of the game's moral impact. While he considered it a bulwark against social and political change, he also viewed it as 'a reflection on the pitch of a wider manifestation – the stylised epitome of a moral order and the metaphoric essence of a cultured civilization'.[123]

Indian princes became cricket-lovers in no small measure because of their years in the 'Etons of India'[124] – with massive consequences for the masses of modern India. The same is certainly true of Sri Lanka. Fraser educated, among others, Kandy princes.

In summary, in his time Fraser played several roles well: he was an influential imperial educator; he was a forceful member of the Church Missionary Society; he was an outspoken critic of exploitation, corruption and discrimination; he was an energetic religious evangelist; he was a successful self-publicist.[125] Of course much of what he believed in turned to ashes. His Ceylonese school eventually lost official support. Denominational schooling steadily lost government backing following the creation of Sri Lanka:

> The process of westenization among the upper and middle classes probably developed further in Ceylon than in any other Asian country. A reaction was inevitable and it was well under way by the 1930s. The Christian church and the missionary societies associated with it, found their opportunities of Evangelism restricted because of it.[126]

Thus, by the late 1930s, the bigger 'English-medium boarding schools continued to be a CMS responsibility, although they were for the most part self-supporting. They were crowded and flourishing, but from 1939 onwards they were faced with the full impact of Buddhist nationalism in Ceylon.'[127] Of course, Fraser's ideal of a Christian Empire came to nothing;[128] and the Africa he loved largely disintegrated.[129] Eventually his imperial spiritual edifice was razed and the ground ploughed over. However, he himself proved a hard rock that no friction could wear away. For all that his life ended on a descrescendo, in Asia, arguably, one contribution remains: his contribution, with others, to Sri Lankan culture in the form of cricket – a talismanic cultural gift. He helped in no small measure to establish a cultural tradition. In time, cricket was adapted to Sri Lankan purposes. Cricket is a game played in Sri Lanka with confidence, poise and skill. Sri Lankan cricket has given the nation international status and become a source of national pride. These attributes are not to be dismissed lightly. They are tangible assets to the self-confidence of a society.

In the final analysis, Fraser, like Tyndale-Biscoe, was a Victorian valiant-for-truth, and like Tyndale-Biscoe his aims were uncomplicated – hygiene, hardiness and heart in the interest of Christian compassion.[130] Some, but not all, of the dilemmas of imperialism certainly passed him by. Nevertheless, his educational achievements were remarkable. He did not simply clear the ground; he sowed the seed; he reaped the harvest; he carried off the prizes. In the final analysis, for a time he was foremost among the imperial educators who introduced, fostered and encouraged a later Sri Lankan source of national identity, pride and esteem. He epitomizes a serendipitous impact of the colonial past on the independent present; he illustrates the subtleties as well as the simplicities of some imperial endeavours; he personifies the principled ideologue. He deserves at least a footnote in the cultural history of Sri Lanka, histories of educational ideas, studies of imperial visions of empire and the records of the imperial experience.

NOTES

Grateful thanks are extended to Ok Gwang for assistance with the notes and for supplementary research.

1. Rhodes House Library (hereafter RHL), Mss Brit. Emp. S 283, Fraser (hereafter Fraser), box 1, item 3, untitled single page.
2. *Annual Letters of the Missionaries for the Year 1905* (London: CMS, 1905), p.132.
3. Ibid.
4. Ibid.
5. *Annual Letters of the Missionaries for the Year 1906* (London: CMS, 1906), p.130. Fraser added, however, that he knew nothing about association football.
6. Ibid.
7. Immanuel Kant, *Critique of Practical Reason* (New York: Maxwell Macmillan Publishing, 1993), p.2.
8. RHL, Fraser, box 12 item 2, typescript autobiography, p.2.
9. 'The Transformation of a College', *Daily Gleaner*, 22 Aug. 1938, RHL, Fraser, box 12 item 3, 33. To encourage attendance he once caned 100 boys in a single day for absenteeism (W.E.F. Ward, *Fraser of Trinity and Achimota* [Accra: Ghana Universities Press, 1965], p.41) and attendance rose to 98.15 per cent in 1906 – a record for the Island (Velesca L.O. Reimann, *A History of Trinity College, Kandy* [Madras: Diocesan Press, 1922], p.106).
10. Ward, *Fraser*, p.42.
11. Reimann, *Trinity College*, pp.131–2.
12. Ward, *Fraser*, p.49. At a Church Congress in Yarmouth in 1906, Fraser, speaking on Indian agitation, stated: 'The people ought to have their own history put in the vernacular and they should be taught their own literature. The government is bound by the dead hand of the Macaulay tradition.' RHL, Fraser AGF Scrapbook of L.E. Blazé.
13. Reimann, *Trinity College*, pp.146–7.
14. Ward, *Fraser*, p.71.
15. Ibid., pp.48–9. On the matter of indigenous languages Ward states: 'One of the most controversial things Fraser did was to introduce Sinhalese and Tamil into the school. In those days, the movement towards a renaissance of Indian and Ceylonese languages and

Imperial Origins – Consolidation

culture was in its infancy; nationalism in politics had not yet brought about nationalism in culture. Then, and long afterwards, the cry was for English and more English; a thorough mastery of English was desired as the essential key to power, and a European who made boys spend time studying Sinhalese or Tamil when they might have been reading more English was suspected of wishing to keep them back. Fraser, on the other hand, contended that the boys had a very imperfect knowledge of their own language, and that if they acquired a thorough mastery of their own Tamil or Sinhalese, it would immensely facilitate their learning of English and of all other subjects' (Ward, *Fraser*, pp.48–9). In one of his early letters to the Friends of Trinity College, Fraser reported that 'The Colombo educational Missionaries attacked me vigorously for my educational policy ... the leading men of the Anglican communion are all, I believe, adverse at present, to me.' RHL, Letter from Trinity College from Kandy, 25 (20 Nov. 1912), Fraser, box 3, item 1.
16. Reimann, *Trinity College*, p.143.
17. Ibid. Nevertheless, he remarked as late as 1921 that 'at the present moment I am getting bitterly attacked again by the Buddhist Leaders in the newspapers' and added, perhaps optimistically, 'I don't think it will do any harm for I don't think they themselves believe what they say and few others will.' See RHL, letter to the Friends of Trinity College from Kandy, 56 (1 Nov. 1921), Fraser, box 12, item 3. He deluded himself. Time was to prove him wrong. In another letter shortly afterwards, he confidently gave what he thought was the reason for the attack, stating that the Buddhist attack was because 'our work is the strongest Christian force on the Island'. See RHL, letter to the Friends of Trinity College from Kandy, 56 (5 June 1922), Fraser, box 12, item 3.
18. Some measure of merely the cricketing superiority – not to mention other sports – achieved on occasion in the eventual 'Fraser Golden Age', can be gauged from the following passage in one of his printed letters to supporters: 'We defeated the Royal (Government) College by an innings and 268 runs, and two days later our strongest rivals, the Roman Catholic College, St Joseph's, by an innings and runs. The last match against the Buddhist College, Ananda, we won by seven wickets.' RHL, letter to Prayer Helpers from Trinity College, Kandy, dated 14 Apr. 1913, p.1 Fraser, box 12, item 3. These successes were achieved despite the fact that as yet there was yet no cricket field – it was still being prepared – the time for cricket in the mountains (due to rain) was shorter than in Colombo and opportunities to play clubs were restricted by the distance of Kandy from Colombo. Evidence of superiority in several other sports is contained in the later part of this essay and the associated endnotes.
19. Reimann, *Trinity College*, p.102.
20. Ward, *Fraser*, p.50.
21. Reimann, *Trinity College*, p.120.
22. Ward, *Fraser*, p.50.
23. Reimann, *Trinity College*, p.120.
24. Ward, *Fraser*, p.63.
25. Ibid., pp.63–4.
26. Reimann, *Trinity College*, p.102.
27. The field was officially opened by His Excellency Sir Robert Chalmers in 1915.
28. Ward, *Fraser*, p.63.
29. *Annual Report of Trinity College, Kandy, 1961.*
30. Reimann, *Trinity College*, p.120. Cricket, as has been stated many times in many places, was seen as the main means of transmitting moral values by the Victorian and Edwardian imperial moralists. Belief in its moral possibilities sometimes had the most curious consequences. Of all people in post-imperial Africa, Robert Mugabe once let it be known that he 'wanted Zimbabweans to play cricket as it "civilises people and creates good gentlemen"' – see Stephen Robinson's review of *Mugabe: Power and Plunder in Zimbabwe* by Martin Meredith, *Daily Telegraph*, 2 March 2002, p.A3 (Arts and Books). Clearly Mugabe's own political followers did not get enough of it.
31. RHL, Appeal for the Extension of Trinity College, Kandy, Ceylon 1907, Fraser, box 3, item 11.

32. Ward, *Fraser*, pp.53–4.
33. At one point Fraser went so far as to give a series of well-attended public lectures refuting various accusations. This was in 1909; the newspapers reported the lectures and they were eventually published in book form (Reimann, *Trinity College*, pp.131–2.).
34. Fraser sought to Christianize Ceylon. See *An Appeal for funds urgently required by CMS College in Kandy of 1905*, RHL, Fraser, box 3, item 14. In this early appeal shortly after his arrival, there were the following statements:

> THE AIM
> We intend to make a serious effort
>   First. To train Christian in Ceylon so to preach Christ their hearers may realise He is no foreigner, but the real and true fulfilment of all that is highest in their aspirations and past.
>   Second. To make our pupils good citizens of their own land
>   (a) By carefully relating all that is taught them to the native problems and language of their own people.
>   (b) By deliberately striving to foster and encourage their sense of responsibility and readiness to act, and so working as leaders [Appeal, p.19]
> and
>   We are working to win through Eastern Christian leaders nothing less than all this rising full rich life of the East for Christ. We look to the day when they shall bring the honour and the glory of the nations unto Him, and for Him to-day, therefore, we claim the national movement [Appeal, p.22].

At the Memorial Hall in central London in 1907, Fraser spoke on 'The Responsibility of Churchmen to the Heathen World' and recommended that the national movement in India 'be captured for Christianity because it would mean the rapid evangelisation of India'. See cutting from the *Islington Daily Gazette*, 5 Nov. 1907 in RHL, AGF Scrapbook.

35. Few things better demonstrate Fraser's aggression in the interests of Christian proselytism than his long-running confrontation with the Ceylonese Buddhists. In this bitter struggle he was an ardent crusader for Christ. In his defence it must be stated that he was sorely provoked.
36. Walmsley was trained at Borough Road Teacher Training College and Cambridge University. Mulgrue was a CMS lay worker in Ceylon and an excellent cricketer, gymnast and boxer.
37. See Ward, *Fraser*, p.57.
38. Fraser wrote a warm appreciation of Campbell after his death on the Western Front in 1917, in which Campbell's social work was described in detail. There can be little doubt that he was a saintly man. Fraser, in fact, wrote of Campbell on more than one occasion. In an untitled sermon in the Rhodes House Library archives, Fraser remarked of Campbell that at Trinity 'under his leadership and inspiration we improved rice cultivation, games, drainage and dispensaries through a wide area'.
39. See J.A. Mangan, *The Games Ethic and Imperialism* (London: Frank Cass, 1998), Ch.7.
40. There were many schoolteachers who took on this responsibility. The vast majority await their recorders. For brief details of some of them, see Mangan, *The Games Ethic, passim*. It is extraordinary that they have been quite overlooked by the specialist 'sports historians' mentioned earlier in the previous essay.
41. The Ceylonese schoolmasters who worked at Trinity must not be overlooked in any appraisal of Fraser's success. Many were deeply committed Christians who played particularly important roles as native role models. It should be remembered also that for the whole period of Fraser's principalship Ceylonese masters greatly outnumbered British masters. Among these Ceylonese was A.M. Jayewarden, an outstanding teacher, who became first a pupil in 1876, then a staff member in 1881, a resident master in 1890 and finally, in 1903, Headmaster of Prince of Wales College in Ceylon. There was also E.A. de Alwis who

Imperial Origins – Consolidation

was in charge of the Cadet Corps under Fraser for over ten years. H.S. Perera produced Sinhalese textbooks for school use, organized visits to places of historical interest on the island and established a Sinhalese Literature Club. The agricultural work of the college was in the hands of P.C. Dedigama. For a number of years D.J. Jasighe, released from teaching for the purpose, built much of the college in Fraser's time. Finally, H.C. Jayersinghe was master and then bursar and served the college for 41 years.

42. Fraser favoured 'Oxbridge' graduates. In 1909, in an educational report, Fraser remarked that he had seven European staff, all from Oxford or Cambridge with the exception of Mulgrue, the athletics instructor. In addition, he had five Indian graduates, four training-college-trained teachers and 12 men who had 'more or less qualified as teachers', but 'all of them Christians'! Fraser continued to favour Oxbridge until his departure from Trinity in 1924. See the report *Universities Educational Mission in India and Ceylon, 1909* by N.H.T. [Revd Norman H. Tubbs], A.G.F. [Alexander Gordon Fraser] and C.W.W. [Revd C. West Watson], RHL, Fraser, box 3, item 15.

43. See G.A. Fraser, 'The Teacher and his Work', *The New Lanka*, 1, 3 (April 1950), 15. Fraser was at one with Tyndale-Biscoe in this regard. Both were men of action. Ivory-tower intellectualism had little appeal for them.

44. Fraser, for all the efforts of his school, remained in awe of the compassionate social work of Tyndale-Biscoe. When Fraser visited him in Srinagar in 1914, his work greatly impressed Fraser, who wrote later: 'The half has not been told. He is marvellous, and makes me ashamed of my work at TCK, simply ashamed.' See Ward, *Fraser*, p.96. In the TCK *Annual Report* for 1922, Fraser wrote: 'We owe more to Tyndale-Biscoe of Kashmir than we will ever be able to repay.' RHL, Fraser, box 3, item 44.

45. Reimann has usefully provided details of the union's work in its first year:

1. Lectures on Social Service.
2. Visiting at the Government Dispensary, taking the names and addresses of patients and seeing that they took their medicine.
3. Hospital visiting to include the circulation of tracts, pamphlets and magazines; concerts and lantern lectures – specially on the prevention of Tuberculosis.
4. Slum visiting chiefly to learn conditions.
5. Work amongst rickshaw coolies. A shelter was built in front of the College at a cost of Rs425. Ten coolies used the shelter and each paid a rental of ten cents a week, besides having partly paid the initial cost of the shelter. The condition of membership was that there would be no gambling or drinking within the shelter.
6. Work amongst opium-eaters and the blind. Two habitual opium-eaters were cured.
7. Drill and deep-breathing exercise in the vernacular schools.
8. Newspaper cuttings relating to social service work collected weekly and pinned on a large map of the world.
9. Work with the Friend-in-Need Society to investigate cases. One hundred and fifty pensioners were investigated in January alone. (Reimann, *Trinity College*, p.141.)

46. See Mangan, *Games Ethic*, p.102.
47. RHL, letter to the Friends of Trinity College, Kandy from Trinity College, 32 (10 March 1915), Fraser, box 3, item 1.
48. In 1913, for example, in a letter to his 'Prayers Helpers' he reported on school numbers, ethnic backgrounds and religious affiliations as follows:

Number on Roll, 419.
Average daily attendance, 405; or 96.7%

NATIONALITIES

English – 3; European Descendants – 73; Malays – 6; Singhalese Kandyans – 117; Singhalese Lowcountry – 125; Tamils of Ceylon – 45; Tamils of India – 26; Others – Burmese, 3; Punjaubi, 1; Gujerati, 1

RELIGIONS

Christians – Church of England, 175; Presbyterian, 5; Wesleyan, 19; Others, 13; Buddhists – 150; Hindus – 25; Mahommedans – 23; Others – 1.

In the *Trinity College Annual Report* of 1909 Fraser recorded that the school included 'Christians, Buddhists, Hindus and Mohammedans' and 'Kandyans, Tamils, Singhalese, Burghers, Moors, Madrasees and Malays' and that 'chief, merchant, lawyer and peasant mix harmoniously together'.

49. Reimann, *Trinity College*, p.120. See also Ward, *Fraser*, p.70. The objective was to penetrate Hinduism and Buddhism from within Ceylonese culture and society, especially through Ceylonese leaders from his and other schools. At a Pan-Anglican congress in 1908, Fraser announced to cheers that it was not clerks nor underlings whom educational missions wished to turn out, but national Christian teachers. See RHL, AGF Scrapbook.
50. Ward, *Fraser*, p.71.
51. Ibid., p.70.
52. Ibid., p.71.
53. Mangan, *Games Ethic*, p.188.
54. Fraser, not always but not infrequently, took stances that took little account of the views of others. Ward offers the revealing remark that Fraser often went his own way with little regard for the values of others (Ward, *Fraser*, p.158) and also states candidly that 'it is plain that Alek Fraser had a hot temper. That is putting it mildly. When he was moved to wrath he was swept by a tempest of blind fury like that of his Highland ancestors whose charge overwhelmed the redcoats at Killicrankie or Prestonpans' (ibid., p.90). At the same time, he could be humble when admonished and ready to admit, and apologise for, his intemperance; see ibid., p.90.
55. When in 1924 Fraser's name was put forward for the bishopric of Colombo, he was not elected. As Ward comments: 'While all those who know him best were devoted to Fraser – "we almost worshipped him" says one – he had many enemies.' Interestingly, 'many missionaries disliked him intensely' (ibid., p.157). The reasons are not hard to find: among them, his bluntness, his reluctance to stand on his dignity, his impetuosity – spontaneous or deliberate – and his determination to get his own way.
56. Reimann, *Trinity College*, p.154.
57. *Annual Letters of the Missionaries for the Year 1910* (London: CMS, 1910), p.495.
58. Quoted in Reimann, *Trinity College*, pp.137–8.
59. Programme of the Annual Reunion of Old Boys of Trinity College in RHL, AGF Scrapbook.
60. Ward, *Fraser*, p.94.
61. Reimann, *Trinity College*, p.138.
62. Rugby was introduced to Kingswood School, Ceylon in 1891. The headmaster, L.E. Blazé, was an old boy of Trinity and eventually a great admirer of Fraser. He wrote verse in honour of Fraser and as reported earlier, kept a large scrapbook of his reported actions and thoughts. Both verses and scrapbook are now in the Rhodes House Library. Trinity, however, was the only school to play rugby regularly until Royal College took it up in 1921.
63. Reimann, *Trinity College*, p.158.
64. Ibid., p.172.
65. Ibid., p.173.
66. Ibid., p.183.
67. Quoted in Ward, *Fraser*, p.114.
68. RHL, letter to the Friends of Trinity College from Kandy, 34 (9 Dec. 1915), Fraser, box 3, item 12. In 1925, Trinity suffered its first cricket defeat after a sequence of 27 victories.
69. Reimann, *Trinity College*, p.178.
70. See Special Edition for Trinity College, Kandy, *Amicus*, XXIII, 279 (8 Jan. 1915), RHL, Fraser, box 3, item 32.
71. Ward, *Fraser*, p.113.

Imperial Origins – Consolidation 63

72. Ibid., p.114.
73. Ibid.
74. Reimann, *Trinity College*, pp.185–6. Reimann was paying tribute to the Acting Principal, L.J. Gaster, who 'filled in' while Fraser was absent for long periods, but the inspiration was clearly Fraser's. Between 1916 and 1924 Fraser was wholly absent for three years (1916–19) and mostly absent for most of the other years. See 'TCK1904–1924. A Summary of Events', in *Rev. Alexander Garden Fraser, Principal, 1904–1924*, supplement to the *Trinity College Magazine*, 1962, RHL, Fraser, box 3, item 66 (the supplement was published at the specific request of Old Boys of Trinity). Fraser volunteered in 1916 for service on the Western Front as a chaplain. In his view, his duty was there. Apart from other injuries, he was severely gassed and was invalided out in mid-1918. He returned to Ceylon in early 1919. He received a hero's welcome: 'The entire college marched down to the railway station to meet its Principal, with the band and the Scouts and the Caret Corps, and a carriage with which he was to be drawn up the hill by the boys' (Ward, *Fraser*, p.127).
75. Indeed, Fraser once referred to himself as an 'absentee landlord' – see the TCK *Annual Report for 1923*, p.7, RHL, Fraser, box 3, item 4.
76. Ward, *Fraser*, p.152.
77. Reimann, *Trinity College*, pp.202–4.
78. Ibid. St Thomas's College was opened in 1881 by Bishop James Chapman, who arrived in Colombo in 1845 as the first appointed bishop. It was a school of the Society for the Propagation of the Christian Gospel and an Anglican institution. Revd G.B. Ekwanayake was a Sinhalese nationalist movement leader and a teacher at St Thomas's College.
79. Ibid.
80. Ibid.
81. E.F.C. Ludowyk, *The History of Modern Ceylon* (London: Weidenfeld & Nicolson, 1966), p.72.
82. Speech by the Revd W.A. Stone at the Annual Old Boys Dinner of 1924. See *Trinity College Annual Report, 1924*, RHL, Fraser, box 3, item 45.
83. RHL, Fraser, box 12, item 3, press cuttings 1908–62. Ward notes that Fraser's wife 'always scored at cricket matches travelling third class with the teams to away matches' (*Fraser*, p.161).
84. Ibid.
85. Cutting from *Independent* dated 23 March 1924, in RHL, AGF Scrapbook.
86. Cutting from *Ceylon Morning Leader*, n.d., in RHL, AGF Scrapbook.
87. Cutting from *Ceylon Morning Leader*, 7 July 1924, in RHL, AGF Scrapbook.
88. Ibid.
89. Press cutting by 'Old Hand', *Ceylon Sportsman* (Sunday edition of *Ceylon Independent*), 20 Aug. 1922, RHL, Fraser, box 12, item 3, press cuttings 1908–62.
90. Ibid.
91. *Rev. Alexander Garden Fraser, Principal* (supplement to *Trinity College Magazine*, 1962).
92. For the Pereva Pantheon, see pp.14–15 of this volume.
93. Cutting from *Ceylon Daily News*, 21 Sept. 1935 in RHL, AGF Scrapbook.
94. Cutting from *Ceylon Fortnightly Review*, RHL, Fraser, box 12, item 3, press cuttings 1902–62.
95. *Souvenir of the Seventy-Fifth Anniversary, Trinity College, Kandy, 1947*, RHL, Fraser, box 3, item 57.
96. Fraser stated in 1908 that he intended to teach the boys to love their own country and literature, and the Empire of which they formed a part. Untitled press cutting in RHL, AGF Scrapbook.
97. In a CMS leaflet, 'The Church and the Nations', Fraser wrote 'Before the gentleness of Buddhism ... the other worldliness of Hinduism, the staunchness of Confucianism, we often stand in reverence and shame. But we look to a day when they shall bring the honour and the glory of them unto Him.' (RHL, Fraser, box 11, item 3.)
98. David Cannadine, in particular, makes much of the point that the Empire was structured on

class lines, not racial lines. There were those who attempted to be different! Cannadine, incidentally, makes too little of the 'ornamentalism' of imperial playing fields as a source of imperial coherence and order, and the associated rituals and symbols of the games of the middle-class public schools that the English, for the most part, took to all parts of the empire as instruments, as they saw it, of moral superiority, social control, cultural bonding and hegemonic influence. The evidence is strong, compelling, extensive. Over the last 15 years a number of books have made this clear. Cannadine's oversight is as surprising as MacKenzie's – see note 100. As recently as early 2002 yet another writer wrote again of public-school games and their rituals and symbols as imperial agents of cohesion, with perceptivity, insight and humour; see Andrew Marshall, *The Trouser People: A Quest for the Victorian Footballer Who Made Burma Play the Empire's Game* (London: Viking, 2002). Marshall discusses the imperialist Sir George J. Scott – as fascinating a ritualistic zealot of games participation in the interest of imperial discipline as Cecil Earle Tyndale-Biscoe in Kashmir and Charles Hose in Borneo. References to Tyndale-Biscoe are to be found in this chapter. A brief reference to Charles Hose can be found in J.A. Mangan, 'Oars and the Man: Pleasure and Purpose in Victorian and Edwardian Cambridge', *British Journal of Sports History*, 1, 3 (Dec. 1984), 264 and 271. In the interests of *Pax Britannica* Hose took Cambridge rowing to the headhunters of Borneo! See David Cannadine, *Ornamentalism: How the British Saw Their Empire* (London: Penguin Press, 2001), especially Prologue and Epilogue.

99. Unquestionably, Fraser's most controversial moment occurred when he delivered a sermon at Westminster Abbey in the spring of 1924. It was highly critical of imperial capitalist exploitation. In it he attacked Lord Delamere for ignoring African and Indian political representation in East Africa and quoted from Ewart Grogan that Western contact socially, physically and morally was the death knell of native races! The sermon produced comment, some of it very critical, in the press in Britain, East Africa and Ceylon, and it upset the Colonial Office; see RHL, Fraser, box 1, item 3 and in particular, cutting from *Manchester Guardian*, 17 April 1924, p.34. The following extract from the sermon provides a flavour of the passion with which it was written: 'The world stands aghast at the earth-hunger of Europe. Imperialism in the arms of Mammon dances with unholy glee. The three witches – War Lust, Power Lust, Profit Lust – revel on the barren heath of Europe holding their orgies.' At the same time, imperial Christianity was praised: 'The salt of the true life is in the Europe still, and to it Christ yet offers life external on the basis of service.' Fraser was quite unrepentant over the political furore he caused.

100. See John M. MacKenzie, *The Victorian Vision: Inventing New Britain* (London: V&A Publications, 2001). This is a sumptuous publication but most surprisingly it provides a wholly inadequate consideration of the Victorian and Edwardian vision of those missionary teachers with a Bible in one hand and a ball in the other, who played such an important role in the global spread of modern games. It is really a surprising omission by such a perceptive imperial historian. Many of these men would have provided a lively and important dimension to the book.

101. Michael Foss, *Out of India: A Raj Childhood* (London: Michael O'Mara Books, 2001), p.93.
102. Rev. *Alexander Garden Fraser, Principal* (supplement to *Trinity College Magazine*, 1962).
103. Ludowyk, *Modern History of Ceylon*, p.116.
104. Arjun Appadurai, 'Playing with Modernity: The Decolonisation of Indian Cricket', in Arjun Appadurai and Carol Breckenridge (eds), *Public Modernity in India* (Minneapolis, MN: University of Minnesota Press, 1995), p.23.
105. Ibid.
106. Ibid., p.23.
107. Ibid.
108. Ibid., p.24.
109. Ibid.
110. Ibid.
111. Ibid.
112. Ibid.

Imperial Origins – Consolidation

113. Ibid.
114. See J.A. Mangan, 'Images for Confidential Control: Stereotypes in Imperial Discourse', in J.A. Mangan (ed.), *The Imperial Curriculum: Racial Images and Education in the Colonial Experience* (London: Routledge, 1993), pp.6–12.
115. See Appadurai, 'Playing with Modernity', p.25.
116. Fraser, 'Christian Education in Ceylon', *Church Morning Leader*, 15 Sept. 1908, in RHL, AGF Scrapbook.
117. Ibid.
118. See *Ceylon Morning Leader* cuttings, RHL, AGF Scrapbook, pp.67 and 70.
119. The author, with the support of the Carnegie Trust, will shortly undertake a survey of the Colombo schools that played a initial part in the 'rooting' of cricket in Ceylon culture.
120. See J.A. Mangan, 'Eton in India: The Careful Creation of Oriental "Englishmen"', in Mangan, *Games Ethic*, pp.122–41.
121. See note 100 above.
122. Quoted in J.A. Mangan, 'Prologue: Britain's Chief Spiritual Export: Imperial Sport as Moral Metaphor, Political Symbol and Cultural Bond', in J.A. Mangan (ed.), *The Cultural Bond: Sport, Empire, Society* (London: Frank Cass, 1992), p.8.
123. Ibid.
124. Mangan, 'Eton in India', *passim*.
125. Fraser appears to have taken virtually every opportunity to stand on a podium or mount a pulpit or write a letter to a newspaper. No better examples can be found than in his printed letters to the Friends of Trinity College. For a typical example of his frenetic momentum in this regard, see the extract from no.23 – letter from Newtonmore, Inverness-shire, dated 17 Aug. 1912:

    Sept. 24th. I take a meeting at Crossmichael, in Scotland.
    Oct. 3rd. I speak at the Church Congress on India.
    – 6th. Harrow School – to the whole School.
    – 10th. Edinburgh – to Laymen's Missionary Movement.
    – 12–13th. Week-end Conference for Laymen at Ilkley.
    – 14th. Public Luncheon given by the Lord Mayor of Birmingham.
    – 15th. Afternoon Drawing Room Meeting in the West End, London, on Theosophy; and Evening Meeting in East End, at Bermondsey.
    – 17th. I speak at the C.E.MS. Annual Meeting at Leeds.
    – 18th. A Laymen's Conference.
    – 19–20th. At Oxford; on the 20th, address Indian Students there.

    There is an element of self-advertisement in these letters, perhaps best caught in letter no.21, from Oxford in 1912: 'My engagements ... are as follows: Friday, 17th, and Monday, 19th a party of Laymen at Bournemouth. I have to speak on Friday night; then on Monday, 20th I speak at 4.30 to the young Indians resident in London, at a club in the Strand. On Tuesday 21st, I speak twice in London: in the morning at the Religious Trust Society's address, and in the evening to the West and Meeting. On Wednesday, I address Rugby School. On Thursday, 23rd the Assemblies of the Established and United Free Churches of Scotland. Also speaking at the Missionary Breakfast at the United Free Church on the same morning. On ... 25th, 1st, 8th and 15th June I have meetings for undergraduates in the evening in my rooms at Oxford. On the 30th I have a meeting in London among businessmen and on the 31st a meeting in Oxford. On Monday, the 3rd, a meeting at a ladies college in Oxford' etc.

126. Gordon Hewitt, *The Problems of Success: A History of the Church Missionary Society 1910–1942*, Vol. II: *Asia – Overseas Partners* (London: SCM Press, 1977), p.167.
127. Ibid., p.180. For more complete details of what this meant for the missionary schools in the 1940s, see Hewitt, *Problems of Success*, pp.183–5 and for brief details of Trinity in the mid-twentieth century, see pp.185–9. In 1951 Trinity College became an independent school. It is flourishing in the twenty-first century.

128. In the school appeal for funds in 1907, Fraser wrote: 'Vast responsibilities and possibilities are before us. Should we shirk them and ignore them to others will they be committed. Life might then seem easier, yet the glory would have departed. But if we rise to our God-given opportunity, then, fellow-workers with Him, we shall hasten the coming of the Kingdom of the Saviour of the World, and shall fulfil the glorious responsibility of Empire bequeathed to us by our fathers.'
129. For details of Fraser's affection for Africa and his devoted work at Achimota, see Ward, *Fraser*, Chs 10–13.
130. See Mangan, *Games Ethic*, p.189.

3
Celestials in Touch: Sport and the Chinese in Colonial Singapore

N.G. APLIN and QUEK JIN JONG

I

The Singapore Cricket Club, once a symbol of imperial dominance, and the Singapore Recreation Club, the traditional home of Eurasian sportsmen, share a stretch of grass that simultaneously links and divides them. The *padang* extends its reach,[1] somewhat defiantly in the face of modern expansion, between the Supreme Court on St Andrew's Road and Esplanade Park on the far side of Connaught Drive, down where the waves used to lap against the beach. Identified as an enduring landmark, the *padang* has strong symbolic meaning, particularly when considering its function as a site for connecting and disconnecting people. Revisiting Singapore in 1935, the former British agent Sir Robert Bruce Lockhart hit the mark with his observation:

> Here on the right was the old 'padang' with the British Singapore Cricket Club at one end and the Eurasian Recreation Club at the other, a striking symbol of the British attitude towards the colour question and of the fact that the field of sport is the one place where British and Eurasians meet as equals.[2]

Today this meeting place still witnesses the ultimate imperial sporting transgression – the occasional solitary individual ambling in reflective mood across the rope, then moving unerringly past deep extra cover, between third man and the slips, and out past fine leg to the shade of the *angsanas* beyond. This is no subtle field readjustment. This is taking a short cut to dinner at the Satay Club. Oblivious of the possibility of intrusion, one reality glides ghostlike through the boundary of another. This essay examines these transitory connections and the relations of dominance and interdependence between the 'colonizing' British and the 'intervening' Chinese in the period up to the Second World War.

Without discarding totally the involvement of the indigenous 'colonized' Malays, the migrant 'Klings' or Indians, the Eurasians, and other smaller groups that comprised this colonial city, the focus here is on the interface between 'imperialists' and 'celestials' – side by side but segregated.

II

Singapore has always been a plural society, but the sons of various constellations of the 'Celestial Empire' represent the most numerous and the most highly motivated migrants. Driven out by, or escaping from, the turmoil and deprivation of the decaying Qing Dynasty in China, migrants from many dialect groups came to Singapore. The Chinese accounted for 56 per cent of the population of Singapore by 1871 and 75 per cent by 1931.[3] Yet the Chinese cannot be represented as a homogeneous group of settlers. The Straits-born Chinese, who had settled around the region for generations before the early nineteenth century, had assimilated many characteristics of Malay culture. Being somewhat removed from China, they were familiar with the British style of trading and empire-building, and thus amenable to the *laissez-faire* approach of the British. The China-born settlers were much more unpredictable and difficult to accommodate. The presence of clans, dialect groups and secret societies – known as *kongsi* or *hoey* – served to create a varied pattern of humanity.[4] Many Chinese sought to escape, at least temporarily, from the life of extreme hardship that prevailed in China. The clear goal for these predominantly male workers was always to return to China with sufficient material wealth to escape poverty and to establish themselves and their families more securely.

There were strata or tiers in the Chinese community: at the top were the wealthy *towkay*s, then the traders, shopkeepers and artisans, and last and most numerous were the coolies. *Laukheh*s (old hands) helped to cultivate an organizational system based on loyalty. Traditional martial-arts skills to ensure compliance may have been one applied sporting practice that *samseng*s (fighting men) used to deal out justice or retribution. One further distinctive characteristic concerned the gender balance among the Chinese: men outnumbered women by as much as 12 to one in 1850, approximately four to one in 1901, and even 1.7 to one in 1931.[5] The general environment was one of work, disorder, instability, prostitution and often violence. The 1850s and the 1870s were particularly turbulent, with riots between the main dialect groups – the

*Hokkien*s and the *Teochew*s.⁶ In this context it is understandable that sport existed only for a tiny minority; perhaps an adjunct for the *towkay* and his sons. The mass of workers, as well as the traders and shopkeepers, had no time for sport in the Western sense:

> In Singapore John Chinaman is both master and man: he is capital and labour: and the shops and warehouses are for the most part owned by sons of the Celestial Empire. The Chinese seem to be always working or eating, smoking or sleeping – but never playing.⁷

The British and other Europeans, who accounted for two per cent of the population in 1871 and only 1.5 per cent in 1931, created their own small replica of society at 'home'. They brought a strong work ethic, games for recreation, a dedication to exercise and a respect for sporting and, by implication, team skills. The Chinese countered this love of athleticism with their own devotion to education and the life of business.⁸ The sports experiences of the majority of the Chinese migrants were very limited and a cause of continual British concern.⁹ The inflow of people interested in capitalizing materially on the development of a new settlement quickly created a polyglot society. Singapore therefore evolved into a highly materialistic society with a pluralistic structure.¹⁰

The earliest sporting activities provide a picture of limited active participation and segregation of the racial groups. The pioneer settlement of Singapore had few sports facilities for its expanding population. Most sports were privately arranged and reserved for the higher echelons of a rough but dynamic society. In the earliest days, life was fundamentally hard and threatening. The perception of what constituted sport, therefore, also included tiger-shooting in the forests and the plantations. It represented not just an opportunity to escape from the drudgery of commercial business, but was also an important means of preserving the lives of workers.

British sport was an unknown quantity to most of the population. If it was a mystery and a source of either disdain or wonder to the Asian people, it was a panacea and the object of devotion to the Europeans. However, some activities were accessible to the wider population and designed specifically to provide entertainment via the incentive of token rewards for successful participation. At the New Year Sea and Land Sports, the first large-scale sporting event to be introduced, there was a carnival atmosphere and fun-fair types of activity. Inaugurated in 1839, and probably a development of the New Year Sea-Sports which had been introduced in 1834, they were held on the *padang*. Festivities included races and games such as horse-racing, wrestling, eating ship's biscuits, running, ducking for coins in molasses, greasy-boom walking, tug-of-war, sack races, three-legged races and even a goose hunt or pig race, which 'amused the local bystanders beyond all bounds and elicited uncontrolled bursts of laughter on all sides', according to one contemporary chronicler. These demonstrations of spontaneous frivolity were amusing and entertaining but in time there was a sense of exploitation. A feeling grew that the indigenous and migrant population was being manipulated more for the amusement of young civil service cadets or mercantile assistants than for the basic enjoyment of the local participants.[11] The sailing that took place, however, was more serious.[12]

The basic pattern of events remained unchanged until the turn of the century. The motivation for these sports however, did change with time. Initially the day was set apart by the mercantile community to amuse the 'natives'. However, by the 1870s, there were separate programmes for Europeans and 'natives' alike. The award of monetary prizes, and presumably opportunities to bet, were reasons why the sports became so popular and attracted large numbers of spectators.[13] Gradually the amusements of the native population and migrants were subordinated to the competitive sports and entertainments of the Europeans and the military. There was now a need for more rigorous exercise and less frivolity.[14]

Organized sport in the form of games became the preserve of a tiny imperial minority, who had their own imperial aims. Formalizing and segregating sport was a good way of achieving two contrasting objectives. First, activities restricted to an elite few would uphold the prestige of the ruling colonialists.[15] In this way respect accorded to the imperial minority by the Asian population would be translated into deference, discipline and therefore increased productivity. Second, in the protected confines of a club it was possible for the male-dominated colonial society to let its hair down, to suspend the constraints of everyday rules and to experience a temporary sense of liberation. This escape to the seclusion of the club, while beneficial to the Europeans, was a useful reminder to the rest of the population, of course, that apparently immutable divisions existed within the society.

The imperial system ensured that the British dictated the official pattern of life. The system of law, the economy, class and gender status, and the language that provided the official means of communication

Sport and Colonial Singapore   71

with the Colonial Office in London were all shaped by values inherent in the British way of doing things. This meant that some elements of the lifestyle adopted by the rapidly expanding population were British and for the British, in the main. Non-Europeans were excluded from the private arrangements of the Cricket Club or the Swimming Club, and so they had to create their own alternatives or imitations of their colonial masters.

A wide range of responses to colonial dominance emerged. Resistance to, avoidance of, tolerance towards and acceptance of the British system of sport were all demonstrated by some or other of the people who flooded into the island during the nineteenth century. Some demonstrated indifference, but some aspired to be accepted more fully and therefore sought to emulate the Europeans. The resistance came largely from the burgeoning migrant Chinese population. It was largely passive, as sport essentially did not exist for them as an option in life. Those who did imitate British tastes in sport were also the ones who adopted the whole spectrum of empire-building values and beliefs associated with all social and economic activities.

The development of organized games and horse racing brought the focus of attention first to the Esplanade and then to the racecourse. The first cricket match, a sure sign of incipient colonialism, was held on the Esplanade before 1837. The sport of kings arrived shortly after, when in 1842 the Singapore Sporting Club was founded to promote horse racing – and trading. Horses were very important as a means of transport and as a source of recreation and entertainment. The racecourse itself was originally a wide stretch of swampland – an area that was also dedicated to rifle practice. The Sporting Club became the first institution to promote Western sport.[16] Significantly, the constitution of the Sporting Club also permitted the involvement in club events of the more wealthy Chinese, who might also own racers.[17] Young horses, called 'griffins', were brought in from Java, Australia, China and Burma. Riders and trainers likewise made their way to the Sporting Club from all around the region. Links with other imperial bastions were forged. Racing events held in Calcutta were attractive to the owners of some of the better horses. Men of material wealth or social standing, including Chinese *towkays*, dictated the scale and nature of the activities. The only people with regular opportunities to participate actively were the Europeans and the wealthy Chinese. Seasonal race meetings organized by the Sporting Club featured the 'Governor's Cup', the 'Celestial Plate' or the 'Singapore St Leger'. In Hong Kong, Manila and Saigon the pattern was similar. The wealthier and more influential Chinese, such as Hoo Ah Kay (better known as Whampoa), became involved through ownership of horses. Iron Duke – Whampoa's own favourite racer in 1869 – was entered in seven races during a three-day 'autumn' festival. Vanitas – a horse owned by Tan Boo Liat – won the Viceroy's Cup in Calcutta and reportedly earned $100,000 for his owner.

III

Influential citizens and officials decided who should be included within the convivial confines of the early clubs. They created their own rules and administered their own events. For many individuals the motivation for involvement in sport lay in its ability to ease the passage of time in what could be a claustrophobic environment. The tedium and monotony of existence in the nineteenth-century colony sorely tested the patience and stimulated the creativity of European settlers in Singapore.

There was a fundamental difference in the respective approaches of the British and Chinese to exercise. For those Chinese who had been educated in China, the emphasis was on physical activities, which developed a sense of harmonious, coherent, cohesive and essentially non-competitive movement.[18] The British placed a far greater value on exercise as a means of aggressive personal and social development. They were keen to promote vigorous physical contact and the competitiveness of team games. The Straits-born Chinese, notably those who had accumulated considerable wealth, either attempted to emulate the British by adopting similar values and practices associated with sport or they discounted these activities entirely to pursue other forms of self-enhancement or social relaxation. Among those who imitated the British, the activities that were adopted did not correspond exactly, as the Chinese avoided any excessive body contact typical, for example, of rugby.

Certain key events were to change the nature of society in Singapore during the second half of the nineteenth century. The extinction of the East India Company in 1858, and in consequence the transfer of the Straits Settlements to the Colonial Office in London, occurred in April 1867. This, combined with the opening of the Suez Canal two years later, served to accelerate economic growth, and new wealth helped to create a new social environment which in turn helped to nurture the growth of organized sports and pastimes.

From 1867, Singapore flourished as an entrepôt centrally located on the main trading routes that linked China and the East with Europe and North America. However, if the day-to-day governing of the island rested with the British, it was the Chinese who proved to be the 'bone and sinew' of both Malaya and Singapore. As the one-time Governor of the Straits Settlements, Sir Frank Swettenham reflected, Singapore's progress rested on the twin pillars of British capital and Chinese endeavour. The relationship between the British and the Chinese was often mutually beneficial. Chinese and British were often drawn together by their sense of adventurousness, their partiality to gambling, a collective work ethic, and an ability to provide what the other might be lacking – the possession of power associated with the British for the Chinese and the ability to make financial profit associated with the Chinese for the British. Sport was to benefit from this mutually useful relationship.[19]

IV

After the arrival of Raffles, it took ten years for the first sporting club to be established in Singapore. In time private clubs became the main location for sport, although the surrounding natural environment did provide some scope for recreation. Sailing, normally a means for local trading, could be adapted into a competitive form during the time devoted to leisure. The rainforest and the jungle were not sensible places for frivolous recreation, unless it took the form of snipe shooting close to the boundaries of the town. Tigers lurked in the jungle, so shooting parties were organized with particular care and concern for safety. The first organization devoted exclusively to games was the Billiard Club.[20] Its short-lived existence was attributed to the excessive temperance of its Scottish members. Not surprisingly, the initiative to establish recreation was slow, as the colony had a very small population and the main priorities were to construct a viable port with trading facilities, complemented by formal institutions for regulating and controlling business. Nevertheless, the question of exercise was a pressing issue, with many European settlers, anxious not to be weakened by a strange and sapping environment, reserving the very early hours of the morning for walking before the heat and humidity enveloped the island.[21] Thus fortified, they were able to ward off the perils of disease and debilitation.

In 1836 a fives court was built, representing the first sport-specific facility to be enjoyed.[22] Much pride was taken in the introduction of such English sports, even though they may not always have appeared to be best suited to the climate. The adoption of English school sports, in particular team games, was one of the trademarks of the male colonial settler. This reflected enthusiastic subscription to the pastimes of adolescence. Social life was too often boring and dull, especially in a mostly male-dominated society; thus it was only common sense to recreate the pastimes of 'home'.[23] Participation was restricted to the privileged few European males. These were the early signs of ethnocentric elitism and the establishment of a distinctive caste.[24]

The Esplanade became best known for the establishment of the Singapore Cricket Club, founded in 1852. There were few active players early on, so it was difficult to field a full eleven on a regular basis. There was a need for imaginative and creative selection procedures. Teams were selected on the basis of nationality, marital status, employment, nationality and age. Cricket fixtures also involved teams from the Singapore Cricket Club itself, the legal profession and the Civil Service, the Singapore Voluntary Artillery and Officers of the Garrison. It must have been sheer delight for the cricketing purists to entertain a visiting team from the region or beyond.

Cricket, naturally, became the most significant sporting symbol of perceived imperial superiority. It was identifiable but not easily understood. The sacred domain of the privileged few rested a mere stone's throw from the busy river and the grim-faced coolies who toiled in sweltering heat from dawn to dusk. However, there were the odd amusing moments for them, for example when a portly gentleman was struck on the head by a cricket ball while passing the Esplanade in his carriage.[25]

However, the esoteric nature of the game, which still confounds most foreign visitors to Singapore, remained a mystery for the majority. They were not to be willingly enlightened. The 'flannelled fools' reserved most of the action for themselves. The Singapore Cricket Club became synonymous with snobbery. Asians were kept at the boundary until a more welcoming generation took over in the 1880s, at which stage the Straits Chinese also decided it would enhance their standing in colonial society to pursue a path to the pitch.

As elsewhere, the presence of the military contributed to the development of sport in Singapore. Regiments undertaking garrison duties and crews from visiting Royal Navy ships played their part, particularly in team games such as soccer and rugby. The East Kent Regiment of Foot – known as the 'Buffs' – and the Inniskillings – known as the 'Skins' – were typical in their involvement and were active supporters of the annual sports that were held on the Esplanade.[26] The amateur standards of the gentlemen officers was not always reflected in the actions of proletarian Tommy Atkins, however. The players in league and cup matches were not averse to fixing the result between themselves if it meant that they could gain additional time off military duties, with full pay, under the pretext of important replays. Repeated draws in competitions were commonplace.

Officers, troops and the children of the military had an occasional advantage over the higher ranks of civil servants and administrators. Their contact with the Asian population was often more down-to-earth. Consequently, some were even able to learn from the Malays how to kick a ball with bare feet.[27] These games with the poorer local people were in marked contrast to the festivities for the prosperous Europeans and wealthy migrants. Fort Canning, perched on the hill a kilometre behind the Esplanade, was the location for sightseeing and the 'gay' festivities organized by the officers of the garrison. It could not have been more divorced from the warrens in China Town to the south, where the poor were rapidly occupying all the available spaces. The self-indulgent antics of the high and mighty could not have been more different from the struggles for survival of the lowly coolies.[28] Of all the symbols of colonial ascendancy, perhaps the languid immersion of European womanhood in the social balm of conviviality contrasts most dramatically with the image of the coolie rickshaw-puller or the dockside worker straining to earn enough to pay for rice. Yet not all of the fair sex were inactive. Some were satisfied with polite conversation, bezique or piquet, but the majority were driven by boredom to emulate their husbands in more strenuous activities.[29] The issue of the importance of regular exercise and the importance of vigorous sport produced a contentious public and private concern about how much exercise to take, which activities were appropriate and what time of the day was best for physical exertion for both male and female colonialist.[30]

By 1881 the population of Singapore was approximately 138,000.[31] A critical mass of participants now existed for sport to expand rapidly. Lawn tennis championships were first contested at the Singapore Cricket Club in 1875, while the Recreation Club for Eurasians was formed in 1883 at the other end of the Esplanade. European ladies, who were excluded from the Singapore Cricket Club, had their own domain for lawn tennis by 1884. Association football was introduced in 1889 and a golf club was located inside the racecourse in 1891. This period marked the entry of the Chinese into competitive sport. They soon made their mark.

V

The Chinese section of the population was responsible for important initiatives in sport between 1885 and 1905. The Straits Chinese Recreation Club was formed in 1885. The *Straits Times* gave it strong support:

> We are glad to learn that the Straits-born Chinese having started a club called the 'Straits Chinese Recreation Club', for the purpose of playing Lawn Tennis, Cricket and practising English athletic sports. The Government has cordially encouraged the movement and supported the Club's application to the Municipal Commissioners for the use of Hong Lim Green, which the Commissioners have readily granted. This is the first club adopting English sports ever established by our Chinese friends, and is therefore a new departure for which they should be highly commended; for hitherto the amusements and recreation of the Chinese young men have been of a rather objectionable nature and it is possible that this club will prove the nucleus of a network of Tennis and Cricket Clubs among the Chinese youth of the Straits. We are sure that the Singapore Cricket Club will be only too glad to give the Chinese youth instruction in the intricacies of Cricket and tennis, so that these games may be played in all their integrity.[32]

At the official opening Tso Ping Lung, the Chinese Consul, reflected on the golden opportunity, as yet unattainable in China, that presented itself to members to develop modern sport as a complement to academic education. He said:

> Whilst in China, I am sorry to say, no play whatever is allowed to students in the school. Those who study too hard very often suffer from consumption or other diseases merely on account of not having

sufficient exercise. It is a pity that they do not understand what the proverb says: 'All work and no play makes Jack a dull boy.'[33]

The members of the Straits Chinese Recreation Club became the advocates of participation in physical activity among their own people, but like the British they also catered to other sections of the population. Events organized and run by the members, some on a large scale and involving other ethnic groups, were introduced to the sporting calendar, particularly around the time of the Chinese New Year. In style, most of these events were clearly based on the earlier British model. The Chinese New Year Sports were organized by the Straits Chinese Football Association and were almost a replica of the sports arranged by the Singapore Cricket Club, not just in the range of activities, the decorations – just like Lilly [sic] Bridge at 'home' – but even down to the segregation of 'native' and 'Chinese' events.[34] Two important Chinese associations soon appeared. The Straits Chinese National Football Association was founded in 1894, and the Chinese Swimming Club was founded under the name of the Tanjong Katong Swimming Party in 1905.

As the Straits Chinese became increasingly involved in physical activities – albeit adopting a smaller-scale approach than the British – there arose some interesting alternative philosophies. The 'athleticism' propounded by the British and, to a lesser degree, the Straits Chinese was now confronted by an alternative utilitarian approach to the necessity for physical exercise. The gradual decline of the Chinese Empire after the Opium Wars of the 1840s, the Tai Ping Rebellion of the 1850s and 1860s, the humiliation of defeat by Japan in 1895 and the Boxer Rebellion at the turn of the century brought an overwhelming despondency to China. Radical thinkers plotted the reform of an ailing empire. There was a similar reaction on the part of the Chinese in Singapore. There was an attempt at reform inspired by the period tenets of an English education, sometimes grudgingly made available by the imperialist. The need to enhance female education was a major concern of Lim Boon Keng (1869–1957) and Song Ong Siang (1871–1941), who published their ideas in the *Straits Chinese Magazine* in 1897. The removal of the 'queue' (long pigtail) was one symbol of reform that was widely advocated. There was an unexpected bonus for the athlete. High jumpers could now excel without the fear of dislodging the bar with their queue.[35]

Imitation of the British did not necessarily mean a denial of Chinese heritage among the Straits-born. Despite their open emulation of things

British, there remained an underlying resistance to adopting, exclusively, *all* things British. The brazen athleticism of the British, which set higher store on physical fitness than on intellectual performance, was not appreciated by the pragmatic Chinese who prized the material gains to be derived from a thorough education in business.

In 1889 the 23-year-old Lim Koon Tye read a paper to a meeting of the Presbyterian Young Men's Society on 'The Recreations of the Straits Chinese'. He appealed to Christians to take a special interest in the Straits Chinese community. He remarked: 'He who would bring about a reform in the physical, mental, and moral constitution of a Chinaman must begin that work in the Chinaman's home, and with the assistance of the Chinaman's wife and mother.' The 'physic' or physique represented an important outward representation of healthy living and exercise to the Chinese. There was now much emphasis on the need for exercise and healthy activity.[36] Perhaps as a consequence of this line of thinking, the Chinese Swimming Club was founded with the object of promoting interest among the Singapore Chinese in the 'useful art of swimming, life-saving and physical culture generally'.[37]

Up until this time women had not been active in sport. The inactivity of Straits Chinese women, in particular, was of concern. Song Ong Siang was very critical of a situation that he perceived had been of the Chinese population's own making:

> Straits-born Chinese women of that generation are often illiterate and uneducated. They are selfish, careless, lethargic and ignorant with a propensity for gambling and drinking for the sake of excitement. They are products of a system for which men are responsible.[38]

Social constraints represented a serious limitation on the physical improvement of women, particularly when custom prohibited even 'walking out', something which would have been clearly beneficial. Referring again to the Straits-born Chinese women, known as *nyonyas*, Ong expounded on the value of exercise:

> We must not neglect their physical training. It is not necessary for them to indulge in violent forms of exercise, such as cricket or football, but they can develop their muscles in gymnastic exercises, which will induce gracefulness in their figure, as well as give strength and grit to their muscles. They ought to be taken out of the house as often as possible for a walk and for a blow of fresh air,

especially in the morning, and live an open and more open-air life. These and other forms of exercise would keep them in good health, and drive away that unhealthy paleness, which is seen on the features of so many Chinese girls, and fit them to perform more satisfactorily their duties of maternity, and enable them to preserve their youthful appearance for a longer space of time.[39]

Comparisons drawn between the low activity levels of Chinese women ('indolent and garrulous nyonyas' especially) and the high levels of European women highlighted the new concern of Straits Chinese readers. Letters to the editor of the *Straits Times* usually bemoaned the general lack of awareness of 'exercise as one of the primary essentials of life' but also urged caution as to the intensity of activity:

> While the Europeans indulge in too many sports (healthy and magnificent no doubt to the male, but at what cost to the conformity with the true meaning of real beauty in womanhood, – gentle, soft, supple and bashful – I mean of course such mannish sports as are being participated in public by some European ladies as hockey, cycling, horse-riding, and even weight-lifting, jiujitsu, and other kindred games), while one people I say go to extremes in their modes of life and in their ways, habits and customs, the Chinese and other Asiatics exclude such sports to a ridiculous extent as to entirely debar themselves from taking up heath giving exercises which, by their simple nature, can be taken by them privately in their own homes, and in their own private rooms where no one can intrude upon their privacy.[40]

It was not until after the First World War that Chinese girls benefited from any form of structured physical activity in schools, and even then it was on a relatively limited scale. The *laissez-faire* attitude of government towards education in general resulted in the slow development of physical education in all schools, and notably in schools where teaching was based on the Chinese language. The intentions seemed sound. Those games and activities adopted were usually based on the English system of team games, house competitions and leagues. However, initiatives by the various schools to develop a lifelong attachment to rigorous exercise were represented more by word than by deed. In effect, the Chinese schools were left to their own devices. In reality, physical education for the Chinese-educated pupils was often an expression of Chinese revisionism and communal identity.[41] Mass callisthenics were advocated as a replacement for military-style drill in China and this trend reached Singapore: a shift to physical culture, or *tiyu*, signalled the rejection of earlier military-oriented exercise, or *tichao*.

Some school principals in Singapore were more active in organizing physical education and sport than others, and very often girls' schools took the lead. Nanyang Girls' High School, set up in 1917, initially as a co-educational school, was typical of such Chinese institutions in that the physical education teachers came from China and coached the girls in volleyball and basketball – games associated with the American sports introduced to China by the YMCA. Sport at Nanyang Girls' High prospered with the arrival of both male and female teachers from China. A combined sports day with Chung Hwa and Hwa Chiau girls' schools was introduced in October 1922 and later became the Chinese Schools Combined Sports Day. In 1931, as nationalistic feelings rose in China, six athletes from the school even represented the Malayan Chinese at the Chinese National Games.[42] There was a definite increase in interest in sport particularly in the larger and better endowed Chinese girls' schools during this period. Keeping in touch with the rapid progress of sportswomen in China at that time provided an important stimulus. The visits of touring basketball teams underlined the change of attitude towards female sport as an acceptable activity and an accepted form of competition.[43] One visit of a team to South-East Asia was described graphically by Bruce Lockhart in his own memoirs of his time spent in Singapore in 1935:[44]

> After dancing a slow waltz with another Chinese professional partner, I left the hall, and presently I found myself before a turnstile in the side of a high wooden wall. It looked like the entrance to a football ground. A notice intimated that the champion team of the Shanghai Tung Ah Girls School was playing a side of Singapore men at basketball. I paid fifty cents for a stand seat and went inside.
>
> The arena, surrounded by stands, was lit by powerful electric arc lights. The place was packed to capacity with Chinese. In the middle the two teams were practising. The Chinese girls dressed in white shirts and the shortest of black shorts, and with sturdy, muscular thighs showing almost up to their buttocks, were the finest physical specimens that I have seen outside of Nazi Germany. Perched on a stand, a cinema operator was filming the

scene with monotonous persistency. In the arena itself was an army of reporters and cameramen. Presently out came a young Chinese in cricket shirt and white trousers. With his closely cut hair and his horn-rimmed spectacles he looked like a medical student. He was the referee and, as such, fully conscious of his importance. He examined the ball carefully while the girls and men did some physical jerks to loosen their muscles. The camera men fired a last battery as they left the arena. The umpire looked at his watch and blew his whistle, and to shrieks of encouragement from the stand the game started.

I have seen less fuss and less ceremony at an English Cup Final or at the biggest American baseball game. The skill of the players thrilled me. Their speed was only less marvellous than their accuracy. The Shanghai girls won easily. They would have beaten any team in Europe. Although they thrashed the local favourites, they were cheered tumultuously by the Chinese spectators. To me, who in the days of my Malayan career had hardly ever seen a Chinese woman outside of the coolie or the easy virtue class, here was a change indeed.

Bruce Lockhart's personal impressions of Chinese sport in Singapore in 1935 pinpointed some of the major changes that had taken place. The gradual emancipation of Chinese women had given them freedom to travel, to participate in sport, and to keep in touch with trends and fashions around the world.[45] However, outsiders' perceptions of Asian women did not change as quickly as the reality. Europeans and Americans were slow to keep up with the rate of change that was embracing Singapore and the East.[46] Liberation was not without its problems. A dilemma existed for the Straits Chinese. Many had been educated in the English system and they had been both exposed to the revolution in sport and welcomed its liberation. But at the same time, they were still influenced by the more conservative values of their parents, which were associated with a Confucian background of female restraint.[47]

VI

The rise and fall of the world economy during the inter-war period naturally had a direct impact on sport. Increasing wealth resulted in the introduction and nurturing of new sports and greater accessibility to different types of activity. With more people becoming active, standards of performance improved and generally participation reflected a buoyant view of life. The ways in which sport was portrayed within society also expanded, and with this expansion came new concerns and issues that had to be dealt with. The inter-war years heralded a major leap forward for the Chinese in Singapore. Inter-club competitions flourished. In Singapore and up-country in Malaya, during the 1920s and 1930s, the whole community was seized by an intense enthusiasm for sport. Gone were the days when the Europeans were the only community to play games and thus swept the board and won the medals at athletics; gone were the days when Orientals gathered on the touchline to roar with laughter at the antics of Occidentals in the scrum.

Sport had come of age in Singapore, with the result that by 1936 R.H.C. Laverton, a journalist with the *Straits Times*, was to report that the Asian male – whether Chinese, Indian, Malay or any other nationality – had played an important part in the sport of Singapore. Apparently, these men had learnt to play the game in the ethical as well as the technical sense, and they had also learnt that a healthy body signified a healthier, cleaner and more straightforward outlook on life.[48] It should be noted that there was no mention of women in his report. Despite the success of visiting basketball teams, there was no real infrastructure to support the increasing participation of women in sport. Equal access and equal opportunity in sport were found only in schools. This was the outcome of an Oriental mind-set that still prevails in the minds of some Singaporeans today.

In the late 1920s male progress in sport had become dramatic and the British recognized that remarkable steps had been taken by the Chinese. Across a wide range of British sports, the Chinese now made an impression and successfully challenged the superiority of the men from Britain and the dominions. Association football, which was acknowledged as the national game well before independence in 1965, was the first team game to really catch on with the Asian population in the region. It represented an important catalyst for 'Celestial' engagement in sport. Fortunately, football avoided association with segregated private clubs and was also a favourite of garrison troops and naval ratings. The combined role of the military in establishing interest in competitive football was crucial. The game represented a down-to-earth pastime to be enjoyed as much for its physicality as for the opportunity to gamble. These characteristics appealed to the military as much as they did to the Chinese. The Malaya Cup, a competition involving inter-state and -colony matches, and including both rugby and association codes of football was a magnet for Asian players. Inspired by the visit of HMS *Malaya* in 1921, the inter-state rivalry that emerged in association football through the Malaya Cup and its successor, the Malaysia Cup, existed until 1994, when Singapore withdrew its team and established its own professional league.

In addition, the Singapore Football League had been established in 1904, while inter-state games had occurred sporadically from 1901. The Chinese were involved in both. The local population also established their own league and there were many hard-fought games between the Malays and the Chinese. Not only were Chinese teams and clubs affiliated to the state and Settlements associations, but they also formed their own Malayan Chinese Football Association.[49] Furthermore, the exchange of visits between Malayan (mainly Chinese) teams and teams from China and Hong Kong, which began in the late 1920s, became one of the main features of soccer in the region. The Chinese were considered among the most skilful and enthusiastic footballers. They experienced a very successful period against both the civilian and the military sides in the late 1920s.

By 1929 it could be stated that not even in China itself had the Chinese aptitude for sport been better illustrated than in Malaya. Participation increased to the extent that the Chinese and the Malays gradually monopolized state representative matches. The Chinese began to beat the Europeans regularly at their own games. The Chinese were able to win both the Singapore Football Cup and the Singapore League even against military opposition.[50] It was thus with a sense of both puzzled disbelief and some dismay that the director of education during the inter-war years, Sir Richard O. Winstedt, stated in 1938 that the greatest imperial influences on Malaya had been football and the cinema.[51]

Without exaggeration, it can be argued that the diffusion of sports such as football throughout the Malayan peninsula actually served to define and produce a common identity that extended beyond political boundaries. Although administrative boundaries existed, the social and racial strands of existence, of course, were tightly interwoven. Singapore, as one of three ports comprising the Straits Settlements, enjoyed such a close association with the Federated and Unfederated States of Malaya that the whole conglomeration was usually referred to as Malaya.[52] Football was a common pleasure and a common link between the various political units.

However, if it brought unity, it also brought disunity – a not unknown occurrence. Passions associated with football produced problems, and progress in the game was not without controversy. In 1936 the Singapore Amateur Football Association felt obliged to declare 20 members of the local Malay football club 'professionals' and banned them from playing. Furthermore, the association disqualified the president and honorary treasurer of the club from holding office in amateur football – the former permanently, the latter for five years. The trouble arose over a tour to Java in 1933. Payments were made to players by the organizers, a practice which was held to have contravened the laws of amateurism. For years there had been allegations of 'shamateurism' in Malayan football, and this was the first case in which there had been a full investigation.[53] Two years later, in 1935, there was a similar incident that shook the foundations of British amateur values. An unauthorized visit of a Singapore football team to Saigon led to the Council of the Singapore Amateur Football Association declaring five locals to be 'professionals' and taking action against them which was to keep them out of amateur soccer for up to three years.[54]

With the economic boom came the less pleasant aspects of a widening involvement in sport. An enduring element of life in Singapore was the propensity of men and women alike to gamble. This was nurtured with the spread of sport and access to racecourse and spectator events. Betting represented a unifying bond between the many peoples of Singapore – the British included.[55] Any impression that all the Singaporean world was swinging a racket or at the beach was inaccurate. Passive involvement in sport through betting was more appealing and was indeed deep-seated.[56] Races were held in Malaya every week and millions of dollars were spent. Racing seemed to have grown out of all proportion to the size of the population and wealth of the country. The poorer people more often than not were the losers.[57]

Makepeace, Brooke and Braddell, who devoted considerable space to the escapades of the followers of the turf in their record of sport in Singapore during its first hundred years, made little of the negative side of betting that went hand in hand with the racing.[58] Being a member of the Racing Club automatically bestowed the privilege of betting; however, there was an increasing outcry when it was discovered that these members were also placing bets for friends and business acquaintances. The money generated by the turf during the inter-war years was so considerable that racing assumed the mantle of the third industry of Malaya – behind tin mining and rubber. For some time there was a campaign against racecourse betting, which was perceived as evil among those who indulged excessively. In representing gambling as 'in the Asiatic blood' and accusing the Chinese of 'a lack of proportion', the British neatly deflected the blame away from themselves, yet simultaneously were happy to exact a betting tax on supporters of Malaya's other industry. This taxing of the returns on betting, incidentally, was a bone of contention particularly during the years of the Depression.[59]

Betting on sporting events was not confined to the devotees of the turf but was also part and parcel of Singapore football. There were many discussions concerning the evils of encouraging the poorest people to gamble with their paltry earnings. By the 1930s betting had reached embarrassing proportions. The British authorities argued that there had been no confirmed instance of players being 'got at'. The danger, however, was obvious, especially when bets running into four figures were being laid on some of the matches. Furthermore, hooliganism had also emerged as a soccer problem. With laconic British understatement, the authorities argued merely there had been instances of disorderliness among the crowds, the size of which had been increasing.[60] The simple fact was that, as in Britain, there was a benign indifference towards those spectators who were predominantly from the labouring classes, and for whom the football match represented one of the few opportunities to be entertained and to socialize. Their vigorous pleasures, as long as they did not get too out of hand, were to be tolerated in everyone's interest.

For the better Chinese players, there existed increasing opportunities to gain wider experience. Chinese football players from Singapore had the opportunity to team up with countrymen from the Malayan peninsula. The resulting Malayan Chinese soccer team undertook sanctioned tours to Hong Kong, with the return visits creating much interest. Although news from England featured regularly in the English-language press, it was clear that the affections of the Chinese were still directed towards the motherland – an empire that was suffering the ravages of conflict with Japan. The strongest expression of attachment to China occurred during a visit to Singapore by the All-China soccer team in 1936. Comparisons were made with the scenes at the very first English Cup Final played at Wembley in 1923. The crowd were said to have swarmed all over the pitch at the Anson Road Stadium after the China Olympic team defeated Singapore's Malaya Cup XI. The attendance at the game constituted a record for any football match played in Malaya up until that time, with an official figure of 'just over 26,000' in a stadium designed to hold 10,000.[61]

Other sports eventually to play a significant role in Chinese life in Singapore included tennis, boxing, swimming and athletics. For the man in the street, football was the national game, but for the well-off lawn tennis was the game. Tennis had arrived in Singapore very rapidly after the formalization of the game in England. It spread quickly through the well-to-do suburban areas of Singapore. A proliferation of grass tennis courts and croquet lawns resulted.[62] Tennis was initially considered a 'niminy-piminy' game in Singapore – in other words, a game for women and unathletic men. Real men played cricket. Later, however, it was to provide a keenly competitive activity for the privileged. The absence of European men from the competitive scene provided the Chinese with an opportunity to excel, which they took and even sustained when European men finally decided tennis was acceptable. In the mid-1870s and 1880s the Singapore Championships were held on a quarterly basis among the privileged. The game took its place as a multiracial activity in Singapore only after 1921, when the Malayan Championships were first instituted. By 1929 tennis was considered by many to be the national game, and there were eight affiliated clubs.[63] Singapore was a biennial host of the annual Malayan Championships; many players from other states made their homes on the island and made their names as players at the Singapore Cricket Club. Tennis was to become truly multicultural and multinational. Eventually the Malayan and local state championships were successful in attracting participants from six racial groups – Europeans, Malays, Chinese, Eurasians, Japanese and Indians. The first winner of the Malayan Championship was a Japanese player, S. Nakamura, who defeated the best European players with apparent ease. Then the Chinese took over. First Khoo Hooi Hye, then Lim Bong Soo proved superior to European opposition. Male Chinese lawn tennis players successfully ousted the Japanese and the Europeans from the championships within five years of its creation.

Khoo Hooi Hye was the Singapore title-holder from 1925 to 1929 and Malayan champion four times during the same period. He spent much of his time in China playing in tournaments and won the singles event at the Far Eastern Olympic Games at Shanghai in 1927. Lim Bong Soo had two claims to fame: the first as a successor to Khoo Hooi Hye as the leading tennis player in the 1930s, the second as the victim of a series of personally demeaning and discriminatory descriptions by writers in the monthly journal *British Malaya*. 'Diminutive', 'midget player', 'tiny left-hander' and 'our clever little left-hander' were typical epithets used at the time to describe Lim. The two clubmates also played on the China coast, and later appeared in Shanghai, Peiping and Tientsin, winning most of their games against the best players. Such was their success that their possible selection for China's Davis Cup team was suggested.[64]

Tennis was much more a social event and spectator sport for the privileged. Exhibition games were featured regularly on the tennis calendar. Two of the best lady players in the world, Miss Akhurst (ranked third in the world, behind only Helen Wills and Senorita de Alvarez) and Miss Bickerton from Australia graced the tennis scene in 1928.[65] The French stars Cochet, Brugnon, Landry and Rodel gave enthusiasts a treat in 1930, while Japan's top player Harada and his young compatriot Satoh, who were on their way to Europe for Davis Cup matches, also played exhibition games.[66] Dorothy Round gave impetus to the women's game when she played in Singapore in 1935.

Among the other sports that came to appeal equally to the European and the Asian was boxing, although it did not emerge as early as tennis and its source of encouragement shifted from the relatively ordered confines of private arenas to the greater mayhem and disorder of the streets. Its development as an amateur pastime originated after the First World War, with the professional form emerging strongly during the early 1920s. The sport appealed particularly to the Chinese and the Eurasian sectors of the population. The coverage of boxing in the newspapers of the time supports the reasonable assumption that it was a major spectator sport underpinned, not surprisingly, by betting. Its popularity led to the establishment of a Boxing Association in 1929 and a Board of Control in 1932 to monitor matters inside and outside the ring. By the mid-1920s local professional boxers were travelling abroad to Manila, Batavia, Saigon and cities in Australia in order to make their fortunes. Battling Key, a Chinese light-weight, was for years the idol of the Chinese crowds, and in his heyday attracted an immense following.[67]

Athletics, which enjoyed popularity within the elite private clubs and the civil service, gradually secured a position of favour among the middle range of clerical and administrative workers. Participation, triggered by the Straits Chinese Recreation Club, grew strongly during the 1920s and 1930s among the Chinese who capitalized on social and cultural connections with Nationalist China. National athletic meetings had started in China as early as 1911, but it was only after the First World War that a regular pattern of events emerged that included women participants.[68] The establishment in China of the Far East Olympic Games added further impetus to the development of athletics in Singapore, as it provided an opportunity for a few talented individuals to test themselves abroad. The All-China Games and the Far Eastern Olympics drew competitors from Malaya, the Philippines as well as from cities in China. An elaborate system of competition starting with school meetings all the way up to regional championships provided an attraction both for men and women.[69] The strength of the connection that existed between Singapore and China can be illustrated best by a brief glimpse of the experiences of Goh Chye Hin, who was an athlete in China and later became one of the foremost promoters of sport in Singapore.

Goh was born in Singapore in 1905. His family came originally from the Nan Ann district in Fukien (later Fujian) Province in China. He received his primary-school education at Tao Nan School in Singapore and his middle-school education at the Chip Bee High School, Fukien. He obtained a degree from the business department of Amoy University (Xiamen). During his schooldays he showed remarkable ability in all types of sports, being particularly talented as a sprinter and a games player. He was selected to represent China at the eighth Far Eastern Olympic Games, which were held in Shanghai in 1927, and later he was one of the delegates from Fukien Province to the fourth Chinese National Sports Meet in 1930. Basketball and volleyball were apparently not very popular in Singapore at that time as there were no courts. However, through his encouragement the Chinese in Singapore gradually developed an interest in these games. Goh was one of the most energetic promoters of the first Malayan Chinese Sports Meet, which was held in Singapore in 1931. He led the Malayan Chinese contingent to the Chinese National Sports Meet in Shanghai in 1931 and 1935. In 1937 he was elected vice-chairman of the Singapore Chinese Amateur Athletic Federation, an organization sponsored by all the sports communities in Singapore, and two years later he became chairman.[70] He was an inspirational innovator and contributor to Chinese sport in Singapore.

The growth of athletics was also stimulated by military forces of the British Empire. The build-up of troops in the East during the 1930s was a response to tension and conflict involving China and Japan, and this had a direct impact on the competitiveness of many sports. The Singapore Chinese Amateur Athletic Association and the Police Sports Association – often represented by Sikhs – were leading contenders on the athletic scene, but they were almost outnumbered by sportsmen from the incoming regiments. In order to reduce the likelihood of dominance by the British, steps were taken to divide the armed forces into their component services. A combined team in 1936 would have included athletes from the Inniskilling Fusiliers, the Royal Artillery, the Royal Air Force and the Middlesex Royal Engineers Regiment.

Sport was certainly a tool that reinforced the national identity of the Singapore section of the Chinese diaspora. The Olympic movement was significant in this regard for Chinese looking to China. Local 'Olympiads' starting in 1931 featured the Malayan Chinese. They were organized on a biennial rather than a four-yearly basis. The fourth Olympiad, held at Jalan Besar Stadium in Singapore, featured a remarkable display of allegiance. The 800 athletes and officials from the Malaya peninsula bowed three times before the portrait of the father of the Chinese Republic, Dr Sun Yat-Sen, during the opening ceremony.

Unsurprisingly, therefore, barely six weeks after the tumultuous reception for the All-China soccer team at Anson Road, it was the turn of the Chinese Olympic team on its way to Berlin to enjoy demonstrations of national solidarity. The delegation comprised track and field athletes, boxers, a cyclist, weightlifters, basketball players and swimmers:

> Chinese republican flags waved by hundreds of hands were part of a scene of great enthusiasm at the Singapore Wharf on July 2, when the liner *Conte Verde* berthed with the main body of China's star athletes on board bound for the Olympic Games in Berlin. A bright yellow silken banner inscribed with Chinese characters 'Bring Glory to China Abroad' subscribed by the Overseas Chinese was unfurled when the liner hove into sight and the crowd shouted greetings from the wharfside. Dr Philip K.C. Tyau, Consul-General at Singapore, and Mrs Tyau were among the first to rush aboard. The athletes, grouped in teams, were mustered on deck and almost overwhelmed by the reception. There are 76 athletes

and 42 officials on the *Conte Verde*. One of the most popular members is pretty 19 year-old Miss Yeung Sau-King, Hong Kong and China champion swimmer who is called the 'Chinese Venus'. Miss Yeung is the only girl swimmer and one of five girl athletes among them and has recorded good times in the 100 metres backstroke and 400 metres freestyle.[71]

Not all sports in Singapore were primarily competitive in nature or generated such adulation. Recreational pursuits such as swimming appealed particularly to the European section and to the upper echelons of the Chinese population. The coastline to the east of the city has always represented a popular recreational area. At one time largely inaccessible except by boat, it was certainly a stretch of the coast much prized as a location for a weekend home; Tanjong Katong was, and continues to be, home to the main swimming clubs. The Europeans in 1894 and the Straits Chinese in 1905 staked their claims to sections of the idyllic waterfront. Escape from the drudgery of work and an opportunity to socialize were the main incentives. Swimming and tennis were to share a common characteristic particularly during the 1930s. They were the sports in which the Chinese competitively came to dominate the Europeans. In the Chinese Swimming Club, initially called in 1905 the Tanjong Katong Swimming Party, there grew a passion first for fun, relaxation and exercise – and then for competition. Initially, as with the Singapore Swimming Club, it was only for men. Water polo became a popular team game and an important source of pride and achievement for the Chinese.[72] An unbeaten record against the European Swimming Club extended until 1932. It was lost only because of a misunderstanding over new rules.[73] Nevertheless, the Chinese Swimming Club was good enough to shock the Japanese Olympic team returning from Berlin by winning a water polo match 9–5.[74]

VIII

Today Singapore is recognized as a great commercial centre with first-world economic status – a 'tiger' of the East. This status has been most obviously created by the dynamic efforts of ambitious individuals and determined groups of settlers and immigrants. The foundations of success are located in the efforts and energy of important individuals and groups of people. The commercial success that now emanates from within its sea-lined borders is a testimony to the endeavours of successive generations of highly motivated, disciplined and materially driven people.

However, for all its ability to impress itself on the world of business, manufacturing and commerce, Singapore has never created a firm foundation for sport. A critical weakness in the development of sport and other physical activity in Singapore, and one that became more apparent as the population increased earlier in the twentieth century, was the lack of space and facilities. As the growth of population spiralled upwards and sport became a more enticing activity, the old facilities for sport in Singapore no longer sufficed. Space for sport was urgently required.[75] The *padang*s were overworked because of a widespread interest in games. There was a regrettable shortage of areas for physical culturists, club athletes and children alike. Unfortunately, during colonial times sport was not seen as an important government priority. Legislative councils were happy for the traditional amateur/volunteer approach to prevail. While the elite could be guaranteed their convivial gatherings, the ordinary enthusiast had fewer options.

Before independence, political commentators were quick to seize on the limitations of space afforded to the youth of Singapore. It was argued that physical activity was a sound antidote to revolutionary impulses that might be generated among the discontented poor during the periods of economic depression. Idle hands were dangerous, and if young impressionable people could be directed towards wholesome physical activities, then there was less danger of subversion. To provide the appropriate facilities that permitted general interest in sport, it was necessary to encourage government administrators to commit funds to the provision of facilities. Thus sport could be enlisted in the fight against the worldwide spread of Communism.[76]

There was a response to such arguments. Nevertheless, the construction of new facilities did not really keep pace with the formation of new sports associations. A new municipal sports ground was built at Jalan Besar in 1930, to take the place of the Malaya Borneo Exhibition Stadium on Anson Road, which was due for demolition.[77] The new Singapore Swimming Club pool, built in 1931 and fenced off from the sea, was said to be one of the largest in the world.[78] But these two innovations were limited in their ability to satisfy the wide range of needs of the population as a whole.

Singapore is a small island – from coast to coast at the widest point the distance is the same as the length of a marathon race. The population has always been relatively small, yet more important than absolute numbers has been the erratic yet dramatic rate of demographic increase over the years, which at one time led to dangerously high population densities in the city itself. The lack of open spaces and the heat and humidity of the tropical latitudes have never provided a truly ideal location for sport. Even the marine environment does not provide ideal year-round sailing conditions. Furthermore, at no stage during the year does Singapore benefit from long evenings, when a twilight of temperate proportions could offer a welcome extension to the active day.

Other, more human, reasons for Singapore's limited success are to be found in the beliefs of the different dominant groups within the society as it has developed since 1819. In a country that expanded its population dramatically through migration – as late as 1931 64 per cent of the population was foreign-born – and created a predominantly urban environment, the people as a whole have until recently found it difficult to come fully to terms with sport as an intrinsically vibrant cultural activity that can help to define the identity of the nation. Migrants are invariably preoccupied with survival.

For many years the pursuit of sport tended to reinforce the divisions that existed between the two most influential groups in Singapore – the British and the Chinese. As a colony that was officially administered by the British but effectively economically controlled by the Chinese, Singapore was always a two-headed horse. The British continually failed to acknowledge that the rapidly increasing population – notably the Chinese – should be provided with more extensive opportunities to participate in recreational activities. For many years the migrant groups were perceived as transient only and therefore not requiring permanent facilities. Perhaps the British did not care too much as long as their own privileges were preserved. The Chinese, for their part, looked after themselves in their own ways. They either sought to emulate the British when it was expedient or possible, or turned their back on Singapore and focused on the emerging interest in, and successes of, sport in China.

Early segregation set the pattern. Initiated by the British, but accepted and desired by the Chinese up to a point, the division imposed by the British was not designed to help facilitate the growth of a nation by means of sport; the sport that evolved was an adjunct to colonial life, with the term 'colonial' signifying temporary status. The British only adopted sport as a means of reinforcing their association with Britain, never with Singapore. The Chinese did not seize on the chance to strengthen a new national identity linked permanently with Singapore. Too often they were concerned with their association with China. The British thought wistfully of 'home' when they played tennis on balmy evenings; the Chinese were drawn to events in China for their nostalgic moments. National allegiance during the inter-war years was associated with the struggle for power in China. Singapore was not really a place thought of as 'home'. Finally, if the British were concerned with encouraging the Chinese to adopt sport to ensure control of their imperial possessions, the Chinese used sport to maintain traditional links with China.

In summary, before 1939 a loose symbiotic relationship existed between the British and the Chinese as far as sport was concerned. Entertainment, education, emulation, exercise and emancipation all figured in the symbiosis. But in the final analysis, the sport of both the British and the Chinese – and the other racial groups in Singapore – was not based on an intended or an actual shared national identity.

Today, as the government steers its people along the path of nation-building, as Peter Horton argues so convincingly elsewhere in this volume, the relationship between sport and society is one of more elaborate interdependencies and trade-offs. Sport has been integrated more successfully into the lives of the population, and yet there remain demarcations, notably in terms of the value attached to activities and the access afforded to limited resources. The main thrust of policies involving sport focus on the contribution to a healthy lifestyle that is made by regular participation in physical activities. A healthy lifestyle is seen as an important predeterminant of productivity and social progress. There is a delicate balancing act between sets of competing ideals, and in the case of sport it has been tilted strongly in one particular direction. The promotion of education – always a characteristic associated with the Chinese – as a path to employment is a familiar motivation that was recognized in the colonial period. The provision of opportunities for personal expression in the form of play is a new issue that still confounds most of the people.

ACKNOWLEDGEMENT

The authors would like to thank Professor J.A. Mangan for his editorial assistance with this contribution.

NOTES

1. The *padang*, also known as the Plain or the Esplanade, has been the traditional home of many recreational pursuits in Singapore. It represents a meeting place for cultures, a parade ground, a playing field, a stage for politicians, a site for National Day parades, an icon for Japanese tourists and a symbol of British cultural imperialism.
2. R. Bruce Lockhart, *Return to Malaya* (London: Putnam, 1936), p.81.
3. Saw Swee Hock, *Singapore Population in Transition* (Philadelphia, PA: University of Pennsylvania Press, 1999), p.57.
4. The secret societies provided protection and mutual aid, in particular to the poor and destitute *sinkheh*s or newly arrived workers.
5. Saw Swee Hock, *The Population of Singapore* (Singapore: Institute of South East Asian Studies, 1999), p.50.
6. E. Lee, *The British as Rulers: Governing Multiracial Singapore* (Singapore: Singapore University Press, 1991), pp.35–8.
7. F. Riley, 'A Trip round the World: Being Jottings made on a Tour from London to Liverpool via Africa, Asia, Australia and America', in G. Bastin (ed.), *Travellers' Singapore: An Anthology* (Singapore: Oxford University Press, 1994), p.160.
8. This is fully and well discussed in J.A. Mangan, *Athleticism in the Victorian and Edwardian Public School* (London and Portland, OR: Frank Cass, 2000) and its extension into empire is equally well dealt with in J.A. Mangan, *The Games Ethic and Imperialism* (London and Portland, OR: Frank Cass, 1998).
9. S.M. Middlebrook, 'Pioneers of Chinese Reform in Malaya', *The Straits Times Annual*, 1941, p.87. 'In 1904, Mr Choo Kia Peng made an appeal for more recreation amongst the Chinese. He pointed out that the Chinese paid little attention to physical exercise and that the only national sports were boat-racing at the time of the Dragon Boat festival in the fifth moon, kite flying during the Autumn festival, and archery on foot or on horseback.'
10. C.M. Turnbull, *A History of Singapore: 1819–1988* (Singapore: Oxford University Press, 1996), p.31.
11. Charles Burton Buckley, *An Anecdotal History of Old Times in Singapore* (Kuala Lumpur: University of Malaya Press, 1902, reprinted 1965), p.781.
12. See C.A. Gibson-Hill, 'New Year Sea Sports', *The Straits Times Annual* (Singapore: Straits Times, 1953), pp.34–8.
13. *Singapore Free Press*, 3 Jan. 1839.
14. *The Straits Times*, Overland Summary, 14 Jan. 1865, p.1: 'On each recurrence of this holiday, a motley crowd of Malays, Klings, Chinese, and other Native races gather on the public Esplanade, and are there entertained by a series of competitions among themselves at athletic and other feats for the various money prizes which the Europeans give. It is a mercenary affair on the part of the Natives, and a somewhat absurd and tiresome spectacle to the European. It was a very dismal day this year, and the sports were somewhat in keeping.'
15. J.G. Butcher, 'European Teams and the Selangor Football League', in *The British in Malaya, 1880–1941* (Kuala Lumpur: University of Malaya Press, 1979), p.117.
16. W. Makepeace, G.E. Brooke and R.St J. Braddell (eds), *One Hundred Years of Singapore*, 2 vols. (Singapore: Oxford University Press, 1991), p.348. In a preface to the Singapore Sporting Club Rules of 1896 the following account is given of the origin of the club: 'The Singapore Sporting Club was founded in 1842, with the object of encouraging the importation and improvement of horses in the Colony by giving away prizes.'
17. Song Ong Siang, *One Hundred Years' History of the Chinese in Singapore* (Kuala Lumpur: University of Malaya Press, 1922, reprinted 1967), pp.154–5: 'For the Spring Race meeting held in April 1869 the Chinese merchants presented the "Confucius" Cup, value $250 – which was

won by Capt. Moysey's "Bismarck." The first race-meeting was in 1843, and for the first twenty-five years or so racing was confined to gentlemen riders exclusively. The first record of any interest taken by Chinese in this form of sport was the ball given in May 1861 during Race Week by Mr Tan Kim Seng. In 1867 Mr. Cheang Hong Lim presented a cup, which was called by his name, and at several race-meetings in later years the 'Cheang Hong Lim' Cup was one of the prizes competed for. Nor did the Chinese merchants confine themselves to that one effort already mentioned, for at the Autumn Race meeting of 1869 they came forward again and presented the "Celestial Plate." Mr Tan Keng Swee (son of Mr Tan Seng Poh) was the first Chinese to own race-horses, and his horse won the Maharajah of Johore's Cup at the Spring meeting in 1879.'

18. Fan Hong, *Footbinding, Feminism and Freedom: The Liberation of Women's Bodies in Modern China* (London and Portland, OR: Frank Cass, 1997), p.20.
19. Turnbull, *History of Singapore*, p.39.
20. Buckley, *Anecdotal History of Old Times*, pp.206–7.
21. Ibid., p.207.
22. Fives is a game similar to squash, but one which uses the hand instead of a racket to hit the ball against the walls of the court. It had its origins in the publics schools of England.
23. I. Sharp, *The Singapore Cricket Club: Established 1852*, 2nd edn (Singapore: The Singapore Cricket Club, 1993), pp.13–17.
24. *The Straits Times*, 17 Aug. 1861, p.1: 'The old English sports and pastimes preserve their vitality, even in this distant and tropical part of the world. We are to have two race meetings a year: a few days since we had occasion to notice the first of a series of friendly scratch matches at Cricket, and today we describe a capital match at Fives. The Fives court was founded in 1835, and has been an "institution" and a valuable one, ever since. As a sport, after the fatigue and confinement of office hours, it is unsurpassed, and has at the same time the advantage of not requiring the players to stand in the sun, no small recommendation in this climate. We are the healthiest community in the East, and attribute no small share to our activity and love of outdoor sports, so that, long life we say to Fives and Cricket, and other exercises that make us so.'
25. *The Straits Times*, 28 Sept. 1872.
26. *Daily Times*, 3 Jan. 1882.
27. F. Stephen Clark, 'Pulau Brani', *British Malaya*, 5, 4 (1930), 119–21: 'It was rather surprising how the Malays took up football. Their notions of the game were sometimes hazy, but they played with great enthusiasm, and often with skill. They were swift and strong, and, although they never wore boots or any form of foot covering, they kicked with great force. This was a source of great wonder to many of the whites, but it is easy enough to understand. The feet of these people are hardened by sun and rocks, and they use them in many ways: a Malay can pick up a coin with his toes, and he can give one a painful nip (this was one of their favourite practical jokes). When they kicked a ball, they simply curled the toes in, much as one would clench one's fist to punch. I did a little of this myself. I never wore shoes, except on ceremonial occasions, and my feet became like leather, so that I could scramble over sharp rocks in my bare feet without feeling anything. I also learned to pick up coins with my toes, and I have often kicked a football with my bare feet in the way, that the Malays do. I really believe that one can give a more powerful kick with the toes bent under in this way.'
28. *The Straits Budget*, 12 Feb. 1895, p.3: 'But the most attractive and remarkable event was that open to the animal kingdom – dogs, horses, and elephants excluded. It was appropriately called a "menagerie race" for when the competitors arrived on the scene of action the collection of miscellaneous creatures at the starting post reminded us of nothing else than a menagerie. There were about half-a-dozen monkeys of as many shapes, sizes and colours, who evidently took a lively and mischievous interest in the proceedings. We thought we heard one young ape telling a severe looking black brother to make the pace hot at the start while another seemed to be encouraging him to "go for the duck." The duck certainly looked excited, the hens were evidently undecided whether it was a tea fight or a laying match, the goose patronised the rest of the company, the jackdaw, the cat, and the young black goat were eager to get out of it as quickly as possible. When the word was given, the monkeys were off like winking and three came past the post to collar the prizes. Nothing else really finished. The goose was too sedate, the duck to excited, the hens too indifferent to the issue, and the cat too nervous.'

29. See M. Shennan, *Out in the Midday Sun: The British in Malaya 1880–1960* (John Murray: London, 2000), pp.58–9, also H. Romney, 'Ladies at the Butts', *The Straits Times Annual* (Singapore, 1956), pp.66–7.
30. *The Straits Budget*, 6 Feb. 1894, p.12.
31. Saw Swee Hock, *Population of Singapore*, p.10.
32. *The Straits Times*, 14 Jan. 1885, p.2.
33. Song Ong Siang, *One Hundred Years' History*, pp.226–7.
34. *The Straits Budget*, 13 Feb. 1894, p.4.
35. J. Kolatch, *Sport: Politics and Ideology of China* (New York: Jonathan David, 1972), pp.12–13.
36. See 'Physical Religion', *Straits Chinese Magazine*, 1 (1897), 8–10, and 'Chinese Athleticism', *Straits Chinese Magazine*, 1 (1897), 29.
37. Song Ong Siang, *One Hundred Years' History*, pp.380–1.
38. Song Ong Siang, 'The Position of Chinese Women', *Straits Chinese Magazine*, 1 (1897), 17.
39. Ibid., 22–3.
40. See *The Straits Times*, 29 May 1912, p.3; and *The Straits Times*, 6 June 1912, p.4.
41. E. Teo Hoe Aik, 'A History of Physical Education in Singapore Since 1819' (unpublished Ph.D. thesis, Nanyang Technological University, 2001), Ch.2.
42. *Nanyang in Celebration* (Singapore: Nanyang Girls' School, 1997), pp.28–30: 'Be it athletics, basketball or volleyball, Nanyang was the name that resounded incessantly in the Malayan Chinese sporting events. In 1931, the school took part in the inaugural Singapore-Chinese sports meet and Singapore-Chinese basketball league, sweeping the women's athletics, basketball and volleyball titles. Nanyang's prowess in the sporting arena was further attested by the Malayan-Chinese sports association's recommendation of Principal Liu as leader of the delegation of sportswomen sent to the National Games in China. Of the participants, six were Nanyang girls.'
43. Hong, *Footbinding, Feminism and Freedom*, p.272.
44. Bruce Lockhart, *Return to Malaya*, p.144, refers to the Shanghai Tung Ah school team as playing at the New World complex, whereas Fan Hong writes of the Liangjiang women's team including Singapore in an extensive tour which began in the Philippines, and then went on to include Burma, Vietnam, and Malaya. Two separate tours perhaps.
45. See Hong, *Footbinding, Feminism and Freedom*, *passim*.
46. Cheah Cheong Lin, 'Boy Meets Girl: Straits Chinese Youth and its Elders', *The Straits Times Annual* (Singapore: Straits Times, 1938), p.149: 'There are still people in Europe and America who persist in picturing the Chinese girl as toddling about on tiny bound feet. They will be surprised to learn that Chinese girls are taking as much interest in sports as Western maidens. Swimming is a sport they love, and they are keenly competing with their brothers in it, as in tennis, badminton, volleyball and hockey, and also in cycling and motoring. They are equally at home in the field and track games. The "lily feet" of old China have given way to fleeting feet, and shyness to agility and suppleness.'
47. '"Straits-Born", The British in Us: A Colonial Paradox', *The Straits Times Annual* (Singapore Straits Times, 1940), p.169: 'In sport, the British in us has conquered our Chinese apathy towards exertion. Our youth are aquatic aces, badminton champions, athletes, footballers, and we are proud of them. Once the Chinese in us would frown upon our girls revealing their comely figures in swimming suits. Once too, we thought that sweating was only for coolies, but now we sweat ourselves in our efforts to keep fit – our girls to keep slim. Health is more important than wealth, we declare.'
48. R.H.C. Laverton, 'Malaya becomes Sport-minded', *The Straits Times Annual* (Singapore: Straits Times, 1936), pp.104–7.
49. *British Malaya*, 3, 6 (1928), 149–50.
50. H.L. Hopkin, 'A Malayan Sporting Causerie', *British Malaya*, 4, 7 (1929), 207–11.
51. Sir R. Winstedt, 'Singapore, Past and Present: Zest for Education', *British Malaya*, 12, 11 (1938), 27.
52. Bruce Lockhart, *Return to Malaya*, pp.91–2, provides a description of the administrative set-up of British Malaya as it was in 1935. This enumerates the various states and settlements and asserts that, at that time, a single name sufficed to identify the region. 'The Straits Settlements are composed of the four settlements of Singapore, Penang, Malacca, and Labuan. The Straits

Settlements, administered as a Crown Colony, have a population of over a million. The Federated Malaya States comprise the four States of Perak, Selangor, Negri Sembilan, and Pahang. They have had British advisers for the last sixty years, were federated in 1895, and were administered, in practice if not in theory, from the Federal capital of Kuala Lumpur in Selangor. The population is one million seven hundred thousand. The Unfederated States are composed of the States of Johore, Kelantan, Trenganu and Perlis in the Peninsula and of Brunei in Borneo. The population is just over one million six hundred thousand. The Governor of the Straits Settlements is also the High Commissioner for the Malay States. His dual capacity involves an inevitable, if only partial, centralisation of Government in Singapore. The Straits Settlements, the Federated Malay States and the Unfederated Malay States are known as Malaya.'

53. *British Malaya*, 9, 1 (1934), 216.
54. *The Straits Budget*, 9 April 1936, p.32.
55. See E. Lee, 'The Problem of Gambling', in *The British as Rulers*, pp.117–33.
56. G.T. Hare, 'The Game of Chap-Ji-Ki', *Journal of the Straits Branch of the Royal Asiatic Society*, 31 (1898), 63–71: 'Gambling is perhaps the commonest form of amusement known to the Chinese. Its speculative character, its prospects of loss or profit, appeal irresistibly to his genius. Out-door sports have little attraction for him. A wild kick at the flying shuttle cock, a languid dallying with a struggling kite is quite enough for him; when heavy physical exertion is indulged in, he sure there is some utilitarian object in view – a prize in the gymnastic ring or perhaps honours in the military school. From the Chinese point of view, as with us, gambling (whether it be in the form of cards, dominoes, fan-tan, or dice) is *per se* no vice. It is only the abuse and misuse of gambling that, to a Chinese mind, constitutes an offence. One's length of days here, is to his mind, but a long game where the cards are always changing. Gambling seems to clear his mind and brace his nerves. It is training ground to him for the real gamble of life.'
57. Shennan, *Out in the Midday Sun*, pp.121–6: 'Horse racing also had its keen European following, and was massively popular with the Chinese (though most of the horses and jockeys came from Australia). Race week drew crowds to the racecourses at Penang, Kuala Lumpur and Ipoh, but it was the magnificent new course at Bukit Timah in Singapore which attracted the largest numbers, with its modern stand and tote. Some judged it the finest in the East, race meetings being regarded as social occasions and fashion parades almost as much as sporting events.'
58. Makepeace, Brooke and Braddell, *One Hundred Years of Singapore*.
59. *British Malaya*, 5, 2 (1930), 39.
60. *British Malaya*, 3, 4 (1928), 95.
61. *The Straits Budget*, 21 May 1936, p.12.
62. N. Edwards, *The Singapore House and Residential Life* (Singapore: Oxford University Press, 1991), p.101. 'As in England and India, recreation in Singapore was an important part of the suburban ideal. Attitudes to recreation were brought to Singapore by the British, both directly and indirectly via India, as part of the general transfer of cultural ideas between Europe and South East Asia. In both India and Singapore, English attitudes were adopted and adapted to colonial circumstances and often extended to influence the recreational habits of the indigenous population.'
63. The affiliated clubs were the SCC, the Tanglin Club, the Garrison Lawn Tennis Association, the Dutch Club, the Straits Chinese Recreation Club, the Singapore Recreation Club, the YMCA and the Singapore Japanese Club.
64. *British Malaya*, 4, 8 (1929), 250.
65. *British Malaya*, 3, 8 (1928), 202.
66. *British Malaya*, 4, 12 (1930), 380.
67. *British Malaya*, 1, 10 (1927), 272.
68. Hong, *Footbinding, Feminism and Freedom*, p.263.
69. *British Malaya*, 10, 4 (1935), 98.
70. V. Sim, *Biographies of Prominent Chinese in Singapore* (Singapore: Nan Kok Publications, 1950), p.66.
71. 'Singapore's Warm Welcome to Olympic Team', *The Straits Budget*, 9 July 1936.
72. *Singapore Chinese Swimming Club: 88 Years and Beyond* (Singapore: Singapore Chinese Swimming Club, 1998), pp.50–51: 'Swimming, both as recreation and competitive sport, was

growing in popularity. At that time [the 1920s] the Physical Director of the YMCA was Mr J.W. Jefferson. A keen swimmer, he demonstrated the newly developed crawl stroke to the Chinese Swimming Club members who took to it like the proverbial duck to water. Jefferson taught the lifeguards and members of the Club's water polo team and it was at his instigation that a water polo league was formed with three main clubs as the nucleus – the Chinese Swimming Club, the Tiger Swimming Club, which broke away from the Chinese Swimming Club and was sponsored by the Aw family of the Tiger Balm fame, located at Pasir Panjang across West Coast Road, opposite Haw Par Villa, and the all-European Singapore Swimming Club at Tanjong Rhu. Swimming and water polo still took place in the open sea at high tide. According to the late Teo Siew Sun, "We played in the sea with goal posts stuck in the sand at each end of the pitch. The sea was rough with strong current to swim against."'

73. 'Water Polo: Chinese Lose to Europeans for First Time', *Malayan Sports Pictorial*, 3 (1932), 40: 'The excellent record of the Chinese Swimming Club of not being beaten at water polo by the Singapore (European) Swimming Club ever since the Clubs began to play against one another a long time ago, was broken on May 8 when in the new swimming pool of the SSC, the Chinese lost an exciting game by four goals to three.'
74. Khoo Kay Kim, 'The Historical Development of Sports in Malaysia', in Horst Überhorst (ed.), *Geschichte der Liebesübungen* (Bartels and Wernitz Sportverlag, 1989), p.695.
75. Brenda Yeoh, *Contesting Space: Power Relations and the Urban Built Environment in Colonial Singapore* (Singapore: Oxford University Press, 1996), p.165.
76. *The Straits Times*, 1 June 1927, p.8.
77. *British Malaya*, 4, 10 (1930), 298.
78. *Singapore Swimming Club: First 100 Years* (Singapore: YTJ Total Communications, 1994), p.29.

4

'Sportsmanship' – English Inspiration and Japanese Response: F. W. Strange and Chiyosaburo Takeda

IKUO ABE and J.A. MANGAN

F.W. STRANGE AND HIS 'SPORTSMANSHIP'

'Manliness' was a concern of early and late English Victorians, among others. For the early Victorians it manifested in seriousness, self-denial and rectitude, while for the late Victorians, it was realized in robustness, perseverance and stoicism.

In *The Games Ethic and Imperialism* there occurs this passage:

> In the guise of educator, many late-Victorian and Edwardian imperial missionaries and some administrators from public school and ancient university, and sometimes from more humble institutions, clung tenaciously to these later values and with sincerity and self-confidence took the means of acquiring those precious instrumental commodities to, among other places, the lush tropical rain forests of Africa, the verdant islands of the Pacific, the parched plains of India and the windswept prairies of Canada. Whatever the aims of other missionaries from the diverse sects and organizations which attempted to spread the Christian message, their first purpose was to create a universal Tom Brown: loyal, brave, truthful, a gentleman and, if at all possible, a Christian.[1]

These men travelled well beyond the Empire. They were not all clerics; they did not all wear the distinguishing 'dog-collar'. Nevertheless they were all in their way moral missionaries. One of them reached Japan. His name was Frederick William Strange (1853–89), who became a teacher at the Tokyo *Daigaku Yobimon*.[2] He was educated at University College School in London, a well-known English public school of the period, from 1867 to 1868. Interestingly, it was at precisely the same time that

Kikuchi Dairoku, who later became the President of Tokyo University and subsequently the Japanese Minister of Education, was there as one of the students sent by the Tokugawa Shogunate. These men certainly met in Japan later. It seems reasonable to believe that their first encounter was in the school.[3] In 1883 Strange organized the first *Undoukai* (athletics meeting) for the students of the *Yobimon* and Tokyo University. One of his most devoted students, Chiyosaburo Takeda, later recalled what Strange told the students and the staff a few days before the meeting:

> The aim of exercise is not only to discipline the animal spirit of the human being, but also to cultivate the intelligence and morality of man. Exercise is not an aim but an instrument. The aim of the training of the body does not solely rest upon the preservation of health or longevity, but it does reside in more than that; the moral training of the playing field evokes human qualities far more than the disciplines of the class room.[4]

Here was a moralist in intention.

Strange was also responsible for setting up the university rowing club, *Sokagumi*, between 1883 and 1884, as well as putting in place the *Undokai* (a governing body for students' sports activities) in 1885. Thus, for the privileged students at these elite Japanese institutions, he was an iconic 'sportsman', but he was more – he was the personification of 'sportsmanship'. Certainly, he was a sportsman. There are reports on his sporting feats in the *Japan Weekly Mail*, a contemporary newspaper for foreign residents in Japan.[5] He took part in cricket, baseball, athletics and rowing in the late 1870s. Most of these activities were organized within the circle of foreign residents in Yokohama. However, he wished to involve Japanese youth. He had his reasons.

At the first *Undokai* for the students of *Yobimon* and Tokyo University, Strange presented copies of his *Outdoor Games*, which he had published before the meeting, as prizes to the winners of the events. In *Outdoor Games* he remarked that an association over many years with Japanese boys 'has convinced me that games suitable for the playground are almost if not quite unknown to the youth of Japan. This may be, and most probably is the reason, why school-boys in this country make so little use of the playground.'[6] This did not please him. He considered that 'Japanese students take sufficient mental exercise, but they do not take enough physical exercise'.[7] Strange called for balance:

There are two kinds of exercise, Mental Exercise and Physical Exercise. Scholastic education is mental exercise, thought directed to any object is mental exercise; gymnastics and all kinds of outdoor games constitute physical exercise. In ancient times the Greek doctors and philosophers believed that mental and physical exercises went together.[8]

Calling on Asclepiades,[9] a Greek physician, Strange pointed out that this influential Greek had stressed the positive relationship between exercise and health: 'Health could be preserved by physical exercise alone, he also said that if good health were lost, it could be restored by physical exercise.'[10] Thus Strange strongly preached the value of exercise for the body. He was adamant in its advocacy: 'What is one man's food, is another's poison. But the following is a good general rule: an hour of exercise to every pound of food.'[11]

He made his mark in Japan with his book. He was awarded a decoration by the Meiji government in 1888, 'for the publication of *Outdoor Games*'.[12] He died a year later. His obituary in the *Japan Weekly Mail* described his specific impact on Japan:

During the last six or seven years of his career, he devoted himself to the task of encouraging a love of athletic sports and out-door exercise among the students of Tokyo University and its Principal Schools, with results of *permanent value* to the nation.[13]

His devotion to 'athletic sports and outdoor exercise' and his subscription to 'sportsmanship', in particular, greatly influenced an early student mentioned earlier, Chiyosaburo Takeda, who took part in the first school and university athletics meeting in Tokyo. Strange became a lifelong inspiration. Takeda recalled in later life that Strange 'introduced us aquatic and athletic sports and genuinely English sportsmanship. Hence he was a founding father of our country's exercise.'[14] Strange, as activist and moralist, became an icon, an 'idol of sportsmanship', among his Japanese students, especially Takeda.

Chiyosaburo Takeda was born in Yanagawa near Kyushu in 1867. He was the second son of Michio Takeda, who was a retainer of the Yanagawa clan.[15] He went to the *Yobimon* of Tokyo University in 1883, where he first met Strange. After his graduation from the university in 1889, he became an administrative official in the Meiji government. Subsequently he was employed in the Akita prefecture (1899), the

Yamaguchi prefecture (1902), the Yamanashi prefecture (1905) and the Aomori prefecture (1908). He became the vice-president of the Japan Amateur Athletic Association in 1913, which was the governing body of all the Japanese amateur sports associations during the Meiji, Taisho and Showa eras.[16] Later he was the headmaster of the Higher Commercial School in Osaka. In these various roles he exerted considerable influence. He died in 1932, leaving behind an account of Strange, his model for manhood, and a lasting respect and admiration for his 'sportsmanship'.

Strange's 'sportsmanship' was mostly expressed in deeds and largely unexpressed in words. His 'sportsmanship', therefore, was put into words for the Japanese by Takeda. Takeda's article on Strange, in *Athletics*, a leading magazine on physical education and sport of the period, strongly conveys the flavour of Strange's 'sportsmanship'. Takeda listed eight requirements of 'sportsmanship':

(1) Be punctual;
(2) Fight with all your might, and be a good loser;
(3) Fight fairly;
(4) Obey your umpire and his decision, and 'don't dispute the umpire';
(5) Enjoy the games, enjoy the skill of play, and learn it from your superior opponent;
(6) The prize should be only a memento. Don't show off your performance before the public in order to get the prize;
(7) Thrift must be the principal creed. Be an amateur;
(8) 'Be your own master; be your own champion. Do what is right; do what is just. Above all, do what is noble.'[17]

Takeda added: 'Regarding the spirit of exercise, English "sportsmanship" is equivalent to the qualities of the *bushi* [samurai].'[18] This was an important statement in an age of imperialism. For Takeda, English sportsmanship made good sense. This 'English Sportsmanship' was, in Takedo's view, to inspire, instruct and motivate Japanese youth – physically, morally and politically. For Takedo impressive 'English sportsmanship' went hand in hand with impressive English Imperialism.

YUGISHO: POPULAR RECIPIENTS OF 'SPORTSMANSHIP'

There was a lengthy time lag between Takeda's encounter with Strange and his memories of Strange's 'sportsmanship' as expressed in his article of nearly 35 years later. Nevertheless, the speedy influence of Strange's 'sportsmanship' on Japan can be gauged from other earlier sources. These sources provide a wider picture of Strange's impact on the Japanese and their reception to his physical and moral exhortations. After the publication of *Outdoor Games*, many books of a similar kind appeared. They were called collectively *Yugisho* (the book of games), and most were for pupils of elementary schools.[19] In these books, good health is the outcome of games. The authors, however, did not rely wholly on western practices. In *Shinsen Shogaku Taiiku Zensho* (1884), Eisaku Yusa quoted an old Chinese proverb, *gokin no tawamure*, which advocates the preservation of health by imitating the play of five kinds of animals: 'Elementary school pupils,' he wrote, 'are forced to study hard from an early age. They lack sufficient exercise and could easily become ill. Following the maxim *gokin no tawamure*, they should play and perform gymnastics every day in order to improve their health.'[20]

A recognition of children's appetite for games is evident in many *Yugisho*. A.T. Van Casteel in *Taiso oyobi Kogai Yugi* (1879) considered a liking for games as instinctive in a child: he referred to 'the child's native taste for exercise, games and gymnastics'.[21] There was a wider appreciation of the connection between instinct and purpose. In the foreword to *Seiyo Kogai Yugiho* (1885), Hisashi Terao laid stress on the pleasure children took from games which 'induce the child to do exercise for health'.[22] Gendo Tsuboi and Morinari Tanaka, for their part, regarded the essential functions of games for children as 'refreshment of mind and promotion of vigorous character'.[23] In the foreword to Ryo Higuchi's *Futsu Yugiho* (1887), Mingo Ohi argued that 'as childhood is the early stage of life when physical and mental growth is most vigorous, we have to give to children whatever they want', and he looked upon *yugi* (games) as 'natural gymnastics'.[24] In Seto's *Shin shiki Kogai Yugijutsu* (1888), cheerfulness and briskness, most often drawn out by play and games, are considered typical of 'the innate character of a child'.[25]

Games were also considered as means for the moral training of the child. Tei Nishimura took an interest in the English and American 'national' games like cricket and baseball, and was struck by their aim of producing *esprit de corps* and 'nationalism'.[26] The morality of games playing was articulated by Seto: 'Happiness in one's life is realized through games which not only bring the unconscious observance of rules and friendship but also cultivate the spirit of patriotism, courage and perseverance.'[27] Moral qualities through games are more fully enumerated by Shukichi Yoshida in his *Shinsen Danjo Yugiho* (1893). He wrote that a boy can learn from games such moral qualities as fair play, observance of the rules, decision-making, self-reliance, perseverance, magnanimity, self-belief, kindness, philanthropy, prudence, compassion, decency and loyalty.[28]

Despite the fulsome praise for games in these books, the facilities and resources for games remained poorly developed throughout the 1880s. Most *Yugisho* for elementary schools, therefore, advised teachers on playing modifications according to the conditions. The length of pitches, the rules and the equipment had to be flexible. Some *Yugisho* such as Tsuboi's *Kogai Yugiho* actually suggested new games using flags or banners.[29] Thus the modification of western games and the creation of new games by Japanese educators were common in early *Yugisho*. But western games retained their popularity even in adverse circumstances. This was due to the previous shortage of children's indigenous games. Some authors regretted this paucity of traditional children's games. In *Seiyo Danjo Yugiho* (1887), Tora Uryu, for example, noted that traditional games for children were in short supply. His main reason for translating the English *Boy's Own Book* was due to the fact that 'there were not many child's games in Japan which refresh the spirit and make the body healthy except *hanetsuki* [battledore and shuttlecock], *temari* [handball], *komakurabe* [spinning top], *takoage* [flying kite], *gitchou* [a kind of hockey] and *kemari* [a kind of football]'. In Uryu's opinion, games and study were to be regarded as 'two wheels of a vehicle, following the Occidental manner where to play was no less important than to learn'.[30]

The past had other drawbacks other than a shortage of games, in the view of some authors. Shimomura considered traditional games such as *komakurabe*, *hanetsuki* and *takoage* as 'too childish'.[31] In Taneie Tojo's *Jido Taiiku Yugiho* (1888), the reasons for teaching modern games, and his corresponding instructions for playing these games, are precise. His advice represents the contemporary view of games: friendship is most important in contending groups, and any strife caused by victory or defeat must be avoided; the final decision rests with the leader; the leader should be picked from senior boys with expertise; a player's turn should be decided by the *janken* (the toss), and the division of sides should also be made by the *janken*; players who breach rules should be excluded from the game; a long duration of the same game should be avoided; the best players should be awarded with cups or badges and praised.[32]

In 1886 regulations for Elementary School Order, Secondary School Order, Imperial University Order and Normal School Order were issued. This was the year when physical education was institutionalized in elementary and secondary schools. The rash of *Yugisho* publications during the mid-1880s reflects this institutionalization. *Yugi* reached virtually all Japanese children through compulsory national physical education. Many schoolchildren now were introduced to modern games for the first time. There occurred a sort of 'play movement'. More than this, the introduction of *Yugi* into schools was fundamental for the diffusion of 'sportsmanship'. In fact *Yugi* was also the educational, social and cultural source for modern sport. Thus in Japan, Strange's *Outdoor Games* not only gave impetus to modern physical education, it helped to initiate a modern 'play-movement', aided the assimilation of the modern concept of 'sportsmanship' and contributed to the spread of modern sport.

UNDOKAI: THE EMERGENCE OF HYBRID 'SPORTSMANSHIP'

Strange died suddenly in July 1889. His emphatically English 'sportsmanship' gradually evolved into a hybrid 'sportsmanship' in Japanese higher educational institutions. The thrust came from *Undokai*, the earliest Japanese monthly journal advocating modern sport. Both games and gymnastics programmes for higher education and secondary students were published in the journal between July 1897 and April 1900. Most of *Undokai*'s editors were associated with Tokyo University. The aim of the journal was to establish communication among athletes in higher education and secondary institutions and to promote sports both theoretically and practically.[33]

In the inaugural number of *Undokai*, one editor argued the case for the importance of physical education with specific reference to Herbert Spencer's philosophical triad 'education, intellectual, moral and physical'.[34] Although the editor agreed with Spencer that mind, body and morality were the essential elements for the education of the individual, nevertheless he stated, we intend to attach special importance to physical education, and to encourage it as far as possible. We resolve to spread the lively and soul-stirring *undo-yugi* [exercises, sports and games] among the young. We will change the evil air of effeminacy prevailing among them, [and] aim to produce a manly and sturdy nation that deserves our future successors.[35]

Here we move beyond Strange but not beyond an English initiative for games.[36] Another editor attacked the poor behaviour of athletes and spectators who certainly 'never deserve to be samurai', and requested that 'both athletes and spectators behave in as manly a way as samurai do and ... never disgrace the name of Japanese youth'.[37] Asahi, a *nom de plume*, claimed that the value of 'exercise' lay in something more than physical strength. The value of exercise rested on 'courage, endurance, open-heartedness, fairness, magnanimity, composure'. He added that 'what we call exercise must include ... *bu* [martial spirit] and fortitude'.[38] He was well aware of Darwinian 'racial amelioration' which might produce a strong race and he was of the view that exercise was the major means by which the physical strength and mental faculties of the Japanese would be improved.[39] He espoused social Darwinian competition. However, in the setting of Japanese 'sportsmanship' there was an odd contradiction in his position. It reflected an addictive Anglophilia. He regarded pleasurable amateurism as important: 'Exercise for youth must be amusement. The professional practice of exercise and its pleasures would not evoke the real spirit of exercise but bring evil. Exercise must be performed by the amateur.'[40] This concern with enjoyment, as will be made clear below, was not typical of Japanese imperialists who embraced athleticism.

Not all Japanese were anglophiles. Okujiro Nishinouchi, in the same inaugural number of *Undokai*, exhorted his readers to revive *Bushido*. He felt that western civilization had brought effeminacy to Japan: 'The cause of today's evil is attributed to the decline of *Bushido*. Ergo, our urgent business is to revive *Bushido*, to raise morale and to encourage the "samurai spirit".' He proposed the 'Japanisation' of western sport. According to him, there were two kinds of *Bujutsu* (martial arts) – the old and the new. The old *Bujutsu* of genuinely Japanese origin included activities such as *gekiken* (kendo), *judo*, *kisha* (archery) and *yuei* (swimming), while the new *Bujutsu* consisted of activities of western origin such as gymnastics, baseball, rowing and the like. He had little time for the latter:

Theirs are nothing but the low arts which ... attract people's curiosity. Consequently, theirs have only forms without god, and theirs are merely childish games. On the contrary, ours append morality to skilful pursuits, work in harmony with God, possess both moral education and physical education.

However, he did concede that western sport had some, if inferior, qualities. That is the reason he graced it with the title 'new *Bujutsu*'.[41] It is apparent from the words of Nishinouchi that militarism was raising its head in Japan in the second half of the nineteenth century. This is clear also from other contributions to the journal.

A later number of *Undokai* reproduced a speech by Shoichi Toyama, who was a teacher in the Principal High School in Tokyo. In 1899 he gave a lecture entitled 'Our Duty' to his pupils. First, he defended the *raison d'être* of physical education from the social Darwinian perspective. Next, from the social organic point of view, he underlined the need for devotion to parents, society, nation and emperor: 'Without making your body strong and improving your intellectual and moral abilities,' he said, 'you cannot perform your duty to parents, to our monarch and to our state as well as to our society.'[42] In an earlier article in *Undokai* in 1897, the connection of exercise to militarism and the Emperor system (*Tenno-sei*) was made quite explicit. The contributor, like Nishinouchi, was more in favour of the old than of the new *bujutsu*. Though he valued modern sport, he maintained that the Japanese *bujutsu* was the matchless instrument for moulding the national spirit: 'Japanese *bujutsu* is our original exercise,' he wrote, 'which, down the ages, has ensured numerous feats, rendered good service to the state, and inspired the people. ... It has also produced our heroes who have given His Majesty the Emperor peace of mind and resolved the difficulties of all classes of our nation and achieved the great enterprise of the peace and security of the nation.'[43]

Kikuchi Dairoku, who quite possibly, as mentioned earlier, had known Strange at University College School in London in 1867 and was now the influential President of Tokyo Imperial University, gave a lecture entitled *Undo no Seishin* ('The Spirit of Exercise') to the students in November 1898, which was later published in *Undokai*. The Meiji government had sent Dairoku to England again to study from 1870 to 1878. It was his second period of study abroad. He went again to University College School for a couple of years and then to St John's College, Cambridge. Thus he was present in England at the time of the consolidation of public-school and university athleticism.[44] He joined the 'East Fives Court Club' of University College School in 1872 and took part in the fives championships in 1873.[45] St John's College at this time had established its boating fame by way of its 'Lady Margaret Boat Club' which supplied many Blues to the Cambridge boat for the already famed Varsity Boat Race. Dairoku was thus immersed in the culture of athleticism that was rampant in English universities and schools. He was arguably the only Japanese who was fully competent enough at that time to deliver a knowledgeable lecture on English 'sportsmanship'. In his 'Spirit of Exercise', he described five characteristics of Englishmen: 'manliness', 'pluck', 'fair play', 'magnanimity and generosity' and 'order'. He explained that 'manliness is a quality which ensures that one behaves in a manly way. One who stands in the arena should never be a coward'.[46] 'If we translate English "pluck" into Japanese', Dairoku stated, 'it becomes *futo-no-seishin* (indomitable spirit), meaning one who bears up well under all difficult circumstances'. He continued:

> It is easy for one to be arrogant when one is victorious. However, defeat is inevitable in competition. What is difficult therefore is to behave in a dignified manner when one is defeated and to be 'a good loser'. They say that the English never 'give up', and it is the reason why the English eventually win. Things must be like this here ... arrogance in victory and cowardice in defeat is bad for the nation.[47]

Dairoku illustrated the English spirit of pluck to his audience by referring to the fact that 'Strange, an English teacher, who had contributed most to the university's athletics meetings always demonstrated the spirit of rowing right up to the end'.[48] Dairoku then defined fair play as 'the spirit of impartiality, and the rejection of the use of despicable means'.[49] He castigated the attitude of winning at all cost. He believed that 'without the spirit of fair play, a nation would not be great', and asserted that an athletics meeting provided a fine opportunity to develop this spirit in the nation's disposition or character.[50] He further argued that 'magnanimity and generosity' revealed a healthy spirit of broad-mindedness. When defeated, one should never abuse the winner and never inflict harm on his opponent by way of revenge. He should show nobility by rising above victory or defeat and as in *bujutsu* should begin and end the game with a dignified bow.[51] 'Order' was essential, he stated. It was always necessary to keep the rules, observe discipline and obey the referee. In his conclusion, Dairoku referred to *bushi-kishitsu* (the samurai spirit). According to him, 'the characteristics of fair play are consistent with the samurai-spirit for which our ancestors are held in high regard. From ancient times, the real and ideal samurai have possessed these characters.'[52] In short, English 'character' was equivalent to the Japanese 'samurai-spirit'.

In this illuminating lecture by an influential Japanese educationist familiar with period middle-class English values in schools and universities, there are visible signs of the early steps towards the blending of the values of the Occident and the Orient.

Japanese observers noted the power of western societies, found merit in an imperial Englishman's perceived stoicism, endurance and determination, and considered these imported cultural manifestations of value to an oriental culture struggling to find an identity that was self-reliant but of necessity leaned on an occidental culture that seemed at that moment pre-eminently powerful. Pride required both Japanese assimilation and adaptation. Dignity demanded an association of perceived past Japanese virtues with perceived present English virtues.

In April of the following year, Koji Kinoshita, the Chancellor of Kyoto University, addressed the students on the occasion of the first athletics meeting of the university. He treated it initially as a minor occasion: 'Originally, the athletics meeting was not important to the university. However minor it may be, once we decided to hold it as a university event we had to set an example and to carry it off well.'[53] His muted approach was due to the fact that although 'exercise' was an indispensable necessity for 'youth', the athletics meeting was 'an imported phenomenon'. While he stressed the need for the careful selection and adaptation of imported exercises, he added for good measure that 'as a seafaring nation, and as a nation with universal conscription, we have to consider what kind of exercises we select, and how we make them autochthonous'.[54] He told the students that when he had been a student at the Principal Junior High School in Tokyo, there were *gekiken*, *judo*, rowing, baseball, tennis, excursion and athletics. It was his view of that of the sports of western origin only *taiko-undo* (athletics) merited practice by the *Yamato-minzoku* (sons of Yamato).[55] There was a military reason. It lay in the fact that athletics was 'an efficacious training for bivouac and night-work as well as mind and body'.[56] He especially prized running because Japan was respected in the West 'for her hard running army' and 'running is the speciality of the

Yamato-minzoku'. Moreover, he claimed the simplicity of athletics meetings was a clear advantage:

> We do not need many events in an athletics meeting. With running alone we are able to cope with the world. We can run not only through more than 400 counties of China but also across the vast plains of Siberia. ... That is why running is adopted as the main event of an athletic meeting.[57]

Here is a direct reference to western sport as an instrument of Japanese militarism. Here is another link between Japanese respect for English sport and English imperial success as they viewed it. A modern samurai caste was to be created on the back of modern occidental cultural imports of contemporary usefulness. The import would be occidental; the product would be oriental.

Kinoshita expressed the wish that the modest athletics meeting of the university would prove to be a model for athletics meetings in junior high schools, senior high schools, normal schools and youth organizations, and it would be the 'nation's original athletics meeting'. Furthermore, he hoped it would be an annual event for the public and schools in the Kansai area. He also recommended that the winners should be awarded their 'pewter' (as at Oxford and Cambridge) and rewarded also with the conferment of banners. It was Kinoshita's hope that these athletics meetings would become the source of athletic heroes – students and locals – and that they would be a locus where fitness, discipline and nationalism would be learned.[58] With the clearest symbolic intention, he named the athletics ground *Dojo* (training hall for martial arts). Thus Kinoshita's view of the athletics meeting was directly linked to traditional, national, military and imperialistic ideas. He was anxious to adapt imported sport to his *Yamato-minzoku*. He was keen to select athletics events in accordance with apparent military efficacy, and to open the meeting to local people to prepare the young men of the area for national conscription. Finally, he advised his student athletes to hold the meeting in a simple, quiet, and orderly manner, and emphasized that it was the locus for *Shuyo* (cultivation of mind and body) rather than a 'playful, self-indulgent and convivial occasion' typical of professional displays.[59] They were to be disciplined soldier-athletes.

F.W. Strange's English 'sportsmanship' thus eventually produced a Japanese concept of 'sportsmanship' allied to Japanese interpretations of moral education, physical education, discipline, nationalism, militarism, the emperor system and social Darwinism. It was not a thousand miles from English sportsmanship in almost all of these elements, but it was eventually deliberately indigenous. The elements had in common the ambition of creating strong individuals for a strong state. Japan's imperialism was at the heart of Japanese 'sportsmanship'. English 'sportsmanship' was admired because it was perceived as the source of English imperialism.

E.H. MILES'S GAMES EDUCATION: AN INFLUENCE

Chiyosaburo Takeda's *Riron/Jikken Kyougi Undo* (Theory and Practice: Athletic Exercise) was published in 1904[60] – the year of the Russo-Japanese War.[61] He did not owe everything in it to F.W. Strange. His inspiration in part, was *The Training of the Body for Games, Athletics, Gymnastics, and Other Forms of Exercise and for Health, Growth, and Development* published in 1901 and written by Ferdinand A. Schmidt and Eustace H. Miles.[62] Takeda acknowledged in his preface that he owed his theoretical background to Schmidt and Miles as well as Strange. It would be helpful therefore to consider the impact of all three on Takeda's book with specific reference to 'sportsmanship'. The main feature of *The Training of the Body* is the contrast between Schmidt's physiological rationale for 'outdoor exercise' and Miles's educational advocacy of 'games'. As far as its English edition is concerned, the chief author of *The Training of the Body* appears to be Miles. Takeda made use of this edition. Though Takeda referred to many physiological items in Schmidt's sections, he makes little reference to Miles's support for games. It is necessary to discern the extent of which Takeda's ideology of *kyogido* was affected by Miles's advocacy of 'games'. Miles's view of the nature of education through games is summarized in the following passage:

> My object is to help people, and especially the young, to make the most they can of themselves. I wish to call the attention of all those who are in authority to what may seem to be small things, but which really are great. I do not wish simply to help the reader to success in games and exercises themselves, but to show their importance for health, to show how they affect the heart, the lungs, the digestion, the brain, and so on; and also to show *how games can be an education,* not merely in Anatomy and Physiology, which are in themselves very important subjects, and which are best learnt if one learns about interesting games and exercises, but also in the

great lessons of life, such as obedience to the right laws, practice and habit, cooperation, and so on.[63]

Here is an unequivocal moral rationale for Anglo-Saxon games.

Miles listed a variety of instrumental values for games as Anglo-Saxon exercises. These values may be arranged into two categories; physical qualities on the one hand and mental, social and moral qualities on the other. As to physical qualities, Miles wrote of 'health', the 'aesthetic advantages of health', 'a thankfulness that our bodies are so wonderfully made' and the assets of 'all-round activity'. As to mental and moral qualities, he listed among others 'independence', 'power to do good, happiness', 'all-round excellence', 'money saved and gained, and time saved', 'the control of emotion', 'persistence', 'self-control', 'regularity', 'promptitude, readiness to meet fresh conditions and emergencies', 'self-confidence', 'self-improvement', 'originality', 'observation', 'independent self-activity', 'careful accuracy', 'pluck', 'free self-movement and choice', 'specialization', 'pleasure and joy', the capacity 'to bear failure and to handle success' and 'motivation'. As for social qualities, his list included 'cooperation', 'obedience to the law', 'friendship', 'humanity', 'social intercourse', 'national and international unity', 'mutual dependence', 'helping others', 'emulation', 'competition', 'group feeling', 'democracy' and 'patriotism'. He also mentioned the importance of games for women, and of 'facing with scenery and nature'.[64] Curiously, however, there is no mention of amateurism in Miles's lists.

Miles had a view of 'national education' which included games. He criticized their contemporary international neglect:

> I have pointed out that Games are essential to the training and education of the body, the moral character, the social faculties, and even the intellect. It is high time that we realised, and that every Nation realised, how far better games are for this purpose than mere exercises ever can be.[65]

Again he left his readers in no doubt as to his subscription to the role of games in the inculcation of 'sportsmanship'. Later he returned to this point: 'I wish to expose a number of popular fallacies, especially the fallacy that a game is only a game. Many Germans (Dr Schmidt is a happy exception) are for the most part under the impression that a game is not even a game, but is merely the development of muscles; most

'Sportmanship' – English Inspiration and Japanese Response 113

English people think that it goes a little beyond this, but there are few who realise that in many respects a game may be the very finest all-round education and training which we can offer.'[66]

Miles's view of games contains the complex ingredients of ethnocentricity, nationalism, internationalism *and* militarism. He argued for games as 'Anglo-Saxon exercises' which would contribute to the implementation of national unity as well as to international harmony. At the same time games, in his view, were an excellent training for battlefields:

> Games and athletics and sport are a magnificent preparation for war, while, on the other hand, they are the great influence of the present day that is making for unity by mutual understanding and (therefore) mutual respect, while differences of language, of commercial aims, of customs, and even of dress and appearance stand in the way of this true unity.[67]

He added: 'In truth, the personal experience of numbers of separate persons may some day prove to have been and to be the greatest teaching influence in the whole world.'[68] Here is a pious Anglo-Saxon conviction that the globalization of games will bring international peace and a firm conviction that games make good soldiers. Anglo-Saxon idealism associated with internationalism was generally lacking in the Japanese understanding of the value of games. Games as military training was another matter altogether.

Miles also stressed individual and collective pleasure and joy as an outcome of education through games:

> Speaking of Education, another Fallacy must be exposed, which is disappearing indeed, but very slowly: The Fallacy that 'Education' which is *pleasant and interesting* cannot be good 'Education'. 'Discipline and Drudgery' – these are still the watchwords of many pretended 'Educators'. But, even if the 'Educators' do not go as far as this, still they have never yet realized – apparently – that most games can be made to teach some of the grandest Lessons that we wish to teach at School: it is not merely that they can made to develop qualities, for this *has* in fact been partly realised: but that they can be made the 'Object-Lessons' of such grand Principles as Co-operation, Independence, Obedience to Law and Honour, and so on; and that no other 'Object-Lessons' will be so interesting, so pleasant, so easily understood, and *therefore* so excellent, for boys,

as (let us say) an Object-Lesson on Co-operation taken from Association Football. Can anyone suggest any better means of teaching Principle?'[69]

The Japanese did not respond well to this component of Miles's philosophy. Discipline took precedence for them over delight. Thus while Miles had some impact on Takeda, Strange had a greater impact on his ideas and his ideals.

CHIYOSABURO TAKEDA'S *KYOGIDO*: CONSOLIDATION OF A JAPANESE CONCEPT OF 'SPORTSMANSHIP'

Strange was hailed in Takeda's *Riron/Jikken Kyogi Undo* as 'an initiator of our exercises' and as 'a paragon of an English gentleman'.[70] Takeda's book was dedicated to Strange, his acknowledged mentor, who encouraged exercise, rowed with his students and preached the virtues of modern sport. Takeda remembered his mentor's precise words of many years earlier:

> The reason why we respect athletics is because one competes as hard as one can and never laments the result. Winning or losing does not matter and the significance of exercise rests upon the discipline of emotion and will. The training of the body is trivial.[71]

This was Takeda's initiation into English 'sportsmanship'. He never forgot it.

Kyogi undo (athletic exercise) in Takeda's terminology meant 'those *competitive exercises* involving speed and distance such as rowing, walking, running, the long or high jump, throwing the cricket ball, the shot-put and throwing the hammer'.[72] It represented mainly those western activities which Strange had taught him. The aim of *Kyogi undo* was *shuren* (educational training). Nevertheless, in his *Riron/Jikken Kyogi Undo* Takeda attempted to go beyond Strange and to set out the significance of athletic exercise according to Herbert Spencer's framework 'education, intellectual, moral and physical'. His *kyogi undo* has the conceptual logical sequence *undo* (exercise) > *shizenteki/jinkoteki undo* (natural/artificial exercise) > *shurenteki undo* (training exercise) > *kyogi undo* (athletic exercise) – see Figures 4.1 and 4.2. Takeda saw 'natural exercise' as more fundamental and indispensable exercise for human beings, rather than 'artificial exercise' like games. For him, in a

'Sportmanship' – English Inspiration and Japanese Response

modern advanced society, 'natural exercise' was to be reconstructed as an instrument of *shuren* (training), and it was to be reshaped into the modern form of 'athletic exercise'. Athletic exercise was defined as 'the exercise of being able to decide immediately who the strongest is, among not only those who gather at one place, but also those who are foreigners and ancient peoples'.[73] The modern notion of 'athletic exercise', in short, served as an index of the capacity of nations. This definition of 'athletic exercise' implied a social Darwinian survival of the fittest as well as an imperialist metaphor for the struggles for dominance between races and nations. For this reason Takeda excluded Japanese martial arts such as *gekiken* (swordsmanship), *jujutsu* (judo) and *sumo* (wrestling) from athletic exercise, because they were 'the exercises which cannot immediately select the strongest of the participants, and cannot allow comparison with the physical faculties of ancient and foreign peoples'.[74] For Takeda, 'athletic exercise' was a modern form of competitiveness, which could ensure that a nation's physical qualities were comparable to those of the best races in an age of imperial conquest and control.

The term *kyogido* first appeared in the complete volume of *Riron/Jikken Kyogi Undo* in 1904. The essence of *kyogido* lay in the instrumentality of exercise: 'The aim of exercise is not for itself, but to achieve the greater aim, that is, the cultivation of one's intellect and will which is more important than the training of the muscles.'[75] Athletic exercise had 'the aim of producing a manlike man'.[76] According to Takeda, the essential merit of athletic exercise was its capacity to 'train the sinews, toughen the nerves, improve the intellect, and discipline the emotions'.[77] Takeda, according to his own lights, was convinced that athletic exercise was the most efficacious and indispensable means of educating a man – a belief that would have found strong resonances in the famous public schools of England in the age of the new imperialism. However instrumental his view of modern exercise, in fact, his paragons of manliness were drawn from Japanese history. He found these paragons in the students of the Edo era and of the upheaval of the Meiji Restoration,[78] who used to search for their personal mentors, travelling endlessly, enduring all weathers and bearing all hardship.[79] His inspiration was nothing more than the traditional idea of *shugyo* or *musha shugyo* – the aspiration to self-improvement and self-perfection by bearing suffering and hardship. By means of old terminology such as *shugyo* and *musha shugyo*, Takeda reinterpreted the significance of new 'athletic exercise' and asserted its modern merit: it was the modern instrument which could produce 'a man of valour and wisdom', and 'a man of virtue and righteousness'.[80] *Shugyo* equalled Darwinian struggle.

Kyogido was old wine in a new bottle. It was described by the following seven virtues: the essence of exercise; the practice of exercise; the dignity of the sportsman; the magnanimity and propriety of the sportsman; self-discipline; self-restraint and temperance; courage and audacity (see Table 4.1). The essence of exercise resides in the training of 'willpower' or spiritual strength. Physical and spiritual attributes crucial to the sportsman for Takeda consisted of strength of muscle, strength of the nerve and the possession of willpower,[81] and the will controlled the strength of muscle and nerve. In pursuit of these qualities, as already noted, modern exercise was the best. It tested control over 'the seven emotions': joy, anger, sorrow, idle ease, desire, love and hate. In short, the modern playing field or sports arena was the training ground for the formation of character. Takeda also metaphorically called these places *dojo* (training place for the martial arts), and their function *shuyo* (cultivation of the mind). Takeda, incidentally, was no philistine hearty. He stressed the need for study. As 'this world involves the competition of intellect',[82] he warned against a life of pleasure, overenthusiasm for exercise, arrogant self-display and neglect of studies: 'However ... advantageous it may be, the exercise that requires too much time to master is inappropriate for the student who wants to study properly. In this regard, baseball is too much of a good thing.'[83] He says nothing about cricket!

Takeda was keen on the 'dignity of the sportsman' – a quality that could not be acquired by professionalism. He warned against ambition, self-publicity and ostentatious display and recommended instead the virtues of amateurism – the dignified source of 'gentlemanlike performance':

> Why is the playing field so noble? Because there is found the devoted effort by the president, officials and others who cannot be manipulated by any power, because there is found a gentlemanlike performance that one is unable to buy with money.[84]

Athletic exercise, in short, must involve sportsmanship. This point of view he owed to Strange.

Regarding the 'magnanimity and propriety of the sportsman', Takeda urged English 'fair play' on his readers. Modern athletic exercise, he argued, was the source of virtues such as 'prudence, benevolence, forbearance and generosity'.[85] He was critical of then current Japanese athletic meetings. In his view, they lacked 'fair play': 'Nobody protects the justice of competition, and no one in authority teaches the youth who are vigorous but imprudent to have control over the seven emotions.'[86] He quoted a maxim of *fukasho* (a thing impossible to win, or a thing never to be beaten) from *Sun Zi*, the famous Chinese tactical treatise:

> Competition is neither quarrel nor war. Athletics is neither the contest of interests nor the struggle for power. We must compete with each other by means of our *fukasho*. We must not only make a comparison with each other but also draw a lesson from our opponents, and enjoy it. ... In quarrels or war, because the aim is victory, it might be honourable for a competent tactician to use cunning, false and foul tactics as well as practical, fair and honest ones. However, in athletics, the athlete should observe fair play from beginning to end.[87]

The one who stands in the arena should be 'a disciple of God', and set an example to others. The athlete, like the iconic samurai, should 'esteem and respect *reigi* [propriety] and *jingi* [benevolence and righteousness]. He should travel countries seeking heroes whom he might challenge, thus acquiring self-improvement and honour.'[88] Takeda's understanding of 'fair play', in short, reflected the ancient virtues such as *bushido*, *fukasho* and the Confucian virtues of *jin* (benevolence), *gi* (righteousness), *rei* (propriety), *chi* (wisdom) and *shin* (faith) as well as the 'sportsmanship' of Strange. In reality, Takeda too sought a form of Japanese 'sportsmanship' that owed something to the West and something to the East. He was a cultural synthesist.

Under 'Discipline' Takeda advocated strict obedience. Punctuality, endurance and obedience were indispensable qualities of *shugyo*. He required, however, something more:

> Many athletes know that obedience is a virtue, but few athletes comprehend its real meaning ... the observation of discipline means that they must submit absolutely to their authority without questioning any reason, right and wrong. ... It is no *shugyo* for them to obey what they can obey. They are obliged to obey on account of discipline, their willing obedience could produce a virtue of generosity and forbearance.[89]

By 'self-restraint and temperance', Takeda criticised those over-zealous athletes whom he called 'champions', stating that 'the more money they spent on their training, the more they lack the virtue of self-restraint'.[90] Reprimanding 'champions' for their self-indulgence, he recommended self-discipline, temperance and thrift to the student athletes.

'Courage and daring spirit' were needed to 'make your best': '"Fight with all your might, and never deplore the result" is probably best translated into "Make your best". Athletes should never forget this phrase unto death. The virtue of athletics is completely condensed in this phrase.'[91] This mental attitude was equivalent to Dairoku Kikuchi's 'pluck' and F.W. Strange's 'rowing right up to the end'. The virtue of athletics was completely subsumed by it. Takeda attached great importance to this quality:

> The aim of athletics is to allow comparison between two opposites and to compare the relative superiority and inferiority. Its aim is not to strive for victory. It is quite natural that you cannot defeat an athlete who is stronger than you. You do not have to feel shame. Neither do you have to bear a grudge against your rival nor insult him. [But] it is disgraceful for an athlete not to fight with all his might, and to surrender to his rival immediately seeing his superiority.[92]

Here there are clear echoes of Cyril Norwood, the famous Harrovian headmaster's exhortation to his pupils:

> 'A game is to be played for the game's sake ... no unfair advantage of any sort can ever be taken, [yet] ... within the rules no mercy is to be expected, or accepted or shown by either side; the lesson to be learnt by each individual is the subordination of self in order that he may render his best service as the member of a team in which he relies upon all the rest; and all the rest rely upon him: ... finally, never on any occasion must he show the white feather.' Norwood concluded: 'If games can be played in this spirit, they are a magnificent preparation for life.'[93]

In essence, what Takeda called *kyogido* was the required way to bring up a youth to be 'a manlike man' by means of disciplined athletic exercise. As mentioned earlier, there existed feudalistic remnants in *kyogido*, namely *bushido*, *shugyo* and Confucianism. As English 'sportsmanship' was introduced to Japan, it was grafted on to older Japanese concepts. This, in turn, reflected an ancient and modern 'social Darwinian' perspective. The world was an arena for competition, a place for the survival of the fittest and a location for the struggle for existence.

Kyogido was a modern notion of *bushido* with the modern purpose of creating a hegemonic imperial nation in imitation of the English and their empire.

It is significant that Takeda wrote another book on athletic exercise for boys, which was called *Shinshin Tanren Shonen Kyogi Undo* [Training of the Body and Mind: Boys' Athletic Exercise] and published when Japan became involved in the Russo-Japanese War (1904–5) and signed the first Korean-Japanese Agreement (1904). *Kyogido*', embracing a hybrid 'sportsmanship', became, for Takeda, the inspiration for founding the *Dai Nihon Teikoku* (the empire of Greater Japan). Takeda's imperialistic aims are conspicuous in this book: 'You know the reason why I often call you boys of the hegemonic country,' he wrote,

> because, as our *Dai Nihon Teikoku* becomes an even stronger nation of the Axis powers, I want you to rouse yourself and make ours one of the hegemonic country of the world. Boys of a hegemonic country! How happy you are to be born in this good age![94]

There was a constant thread running through the Japanese response to the English concept of 'sportsmanship' summed up in the aphorism 'imitation is the best form of flattery'. The Japanese felt humiliated by the imperialism of the West. In response, they sought to resist it, reject it, learn from it *and* imitate it. If modern 'sportsmanship' had helped make the English strong, had brought them an empire and had ensured their global pre-eminence, then the Japanese wanted both the means and the method. Some influential Japanese educationists had seen at first hand, indeed experienced, the ideology of athleticism in England and noted the claims for it by the English themselves in the production of robust imperialists. They were swayed in its favour. They brought it back to Japan and welcomed its importation into Japan by others. F.W. Strange was a welcome importer of a cultural artefact perceived to be of great value.

CONCLUSION

The modern concept of 'sportsmanship' in Japan, which was introduced by means of Strange's English 'sportsmanship', was enthusiastically welcomed by his disciple Chiyosaburo Takeda. Takeda both adopted and adapted the English concept of sportsmanship and created his own original concept of *kyogido*. Takeda graduated from the Imperial

University of Tokyo in 1889. About this time, Dairoku Kikuchi, who earlier was a schoolmate of Strange in England, became the president of *Undokai*, an alumni association of athletes at the university. At this time English athleticism in institutions such as Tokyo Imperial University and its Principal School was highly regarded. They both promoted it.

Then following the appearance of Strange's *Outdoor Games* (1883), similar books called *Yugisho* came into vogue. The educational value of modern games was now increasingly appreciated by Japanese educationists, especially with regard to moralistic, nationalist and imperial virtues. *Undokai*, a monthly sports journal, was published in 1897 under these circumstances. The concept of *kyogido* could be fomented by discourses in the journal. In it Kikuchi, who was very familiar with English athleticism, advocated English sportsmanship. In his *Spirit of Exercise* (1899), he not only recommended English manliness, pluck, fair play, magnanimity, generosity and discipline, but also maintained that these qualities were analogous to the Japanese *Bushido*. Kinoshita, the chancellor of Kyoto Imperial University, for his part contended that the reception of modern sport should be selective. From the viewpoint of *Yamato-minzoku*, he argued that specific modern sports should be selected only when of direct value to universal conscription. He was 'English', however, in so far as he warned against the showmanship and professionalism of student sport and emphasized the amateurism which would ensure the education of the self-effacing elite who could guarantee the nation's future. His promotion of 'discipline' based on ethnocentric and militaristic nationalism might have been taken from Takeda's *kyogido*. They were both working towards the same end. Meanwhile, E.H. Miles's 'games education' in his *The Training of the Body* (1901), while not without influence, seems to have influenced Takeda's *kyogido* less than the Japanese discussion of 'sportsmanship' in *Undokai*. Furthermore, Miles seemed unimpressed by amateurism, while Takeda and other Japanese stressed it. Whereas Takeda's *kyogido* advocated emulation of English sport for Japanese imperial purposes, Miles advocated English games as a means of ensuring international peace. Thus *kyogido*, while owing something to Miles, owed much more to Strange's 'sportsmanship' as interpreted in the discussions of 'sportsmanship' in *Undokai*.

Chiyosaburo Takeda's *kyogido* inevitably reflected his times and their politics. The features of *kyogido* advocated in his *Riron/Jikken Kyogi Undo* (1904) were complex. First, using the metaphor of Japanese *shugyo* that had obvious aspects of Confucianism, Takeda presented *kyogi undo* (modern athletic exercise) as an instrument for building up the character of the 'manlike man'. Confucian virtues such as *jin* (benevolence), *gi* (righteousness), *rei* (propriety), *chi* (wisdom) and *shin* (faith) were assimilated into English 'sportsmanship' smoothly and without friction. The initial inspiration for this hybrid 'sportsmanship', however, owed much to F.W. Strange.

Second, Takeda's ideal of the 'manlike man' had strong links with *Bushido*. The qualities of *Bushi*, which were composed of *chusei* (loyalty), *gisei* (self-sacrifice), *shin* (faith), *renchi* (sense of honour), *reigi* (propriety), *keppaku* (innocence), *shisso* (simplicity), *kenyaku* (thrift), *shobu* (martial spirit), *meiyo* (personal honour) and *joai* (affection), were consistent, in his view, with the aims of modern athletic exercise. Takeda argued that, by means of modern English sport, a youth could learn to observe the proprieties, to develop the feelings of benevolence and righteousness, to play fairly and with all his might, to respect his opponents, and to comply stoically with his fate.

Takeda considered that the traditional character of *Bushi* could be maintained by means of modern sport. He thought that English 'fair play' could be subsumed within *Bushido*. Due to Takeda and others, the traditional character of *Bushi* revived in adapted form with the coming of modern sport. Furthermore, he was convinced that it could be a classless phenomenon to the advantage of the whole Japanese people.

Third, *kyogido* was loosely based on Herbert Spencer's 'education, intellectual, moral, and physical'. It also owed much to English public-school mores of the period. Takeda never doubted that athletic exercise was the best educational instrument for moulding a strong nation – morally, physically and intellectually.

Fourth, *kyogido* was strongly connected with the idea of social Darwinism. Takeda regarded Japanese society since the Meiji Restoration as the locus of the struggle for survival. While one duty of students was to study, their most essential requirement was to develop powerful bodies and moral strength to prepare them for their future struggles in life. The demands of athletic exercise, in his view, were a valuable preparation for competition in modern society. As already noted, his social Darwinian attitude toward sport was somewhat different from Miles's games education, although Miles too was an obvious social Darwinian. Nevertheless, in his games education, the aspects of the 'pleasure and joy' of the game were stressed as its essential element. For Takeda, sport was not for pleasure, but a serious training (*shugyo* or *shuyo*) to an end. This was one of the reasons why Takeda got rid of games from his *kyougi undo* (athletic exercise).

Fifth, *kyogido* was associated with nationalism and imperialism. The *hakoku* (hegemonic nation) that Takeda frequently mentioned meant the hardy nation that could survive in the relentless international competition of an imperialistic era. Takeda used the term deliberately in his books, *Riron/Jikken Kyogi Undo* [Athletic Exercise, Theory and Practice] and *Shinshin Tanren Shonen Kyogi Undo* [Training of the Body and Mind: Boys' Athletic Exercise]. He looked at other Asian countries with imperialist eyes. The years in which his two books were written covered a period when Japan's imperialistic ambitions came out into the open: the Russo-Japanese War broke out in 1904, and the first Korean-Japanese Agreement was concluded in the same year. The concept of *kyogido* could never evade involvement in the imperialistic warfare.

Sixth, *kyogido* demanded unquestioning obedience. Takeda's idea of discipline, order and obedience to authority, which is best expressed in his assertion that '[athletes] have to submit themselves absolutely to authority without questioning any reasons, right and wrong' has obvious resonances for the success of the emperor system. In short, this emperor system was to embrace modern sport for its own ends by means of the 'traditional' device of *kyogido*.

Seventh, *kyogido* emphasized amateurism. Takeda's idea of 'instrumentality' hindered his understanding of the authentic amateurism that has sport as its own end and is unable to reduce itself to an instrument to other ends. Takeda's amateurism was poles apart from this idea of liberalism. He regarded amateurism as a form of *Bushido* that despised mercenary actions, prized honour, valued thrift and simplicity and produced a self-effacing patriotic elite.

Eighth, *kyogido* contained little in the way of democracy or individualism. It was authoritarian. For Miles, individualism and liberalism were fundamental principles associated with his games education. In contrast, in Takeda's *kyogido* imperial authoritarianism was the central principle.

Finally, in Takeda's *kyogido*, a sense of internationalism that transcended imperialism was absent. Whereas Miles's games education stressed the promotion of international understanding, Takeda's *kyogido* was concerned with authoritarian ethnocentric chauvinism and imperialistic hegemony.

'Sportmanship' – English Inspiration and Japanese Response   123

In *kyogido*, then, can be seen the transfer of the late nineteenth-century values of the English public school encapsulated in the term 'athleticism', suitably adapted to Japanese tradition, to ensure an imitative imperialism.

Whatever criticism there may be of Takeda, his pragmatic attitude towards modern sport was the reason for its survival in an insular country of chauvinism and ethnocentrism. He accepted modern sport without hesitation, made it part of the education of the youth of Japan and believed that through it they could become 'manlike men'. His belief in the educational functionalism of modern sport could be said to be similar in intensity to, and not hugely dissimilar in purpose from, Pierre de Coubertin's educational ideals expressed in his *L'Education Athletique* (1889). Both owed much to the athleticism of the English public schools of the period and to the associated idealism of F.W. Strange and others. It might be concluded that Takeda intuitively perceived the educational potential of Strange's 'sportsmanship' as an instrument to build Japanese character. The result was that his Confucian, half-feudalistic and traditional idealism gave birth to a hybrid concept of 'sportsmanship', namely *kyogido* – part English and part Japanese.

NOTES

1. See J.A. Mangan, *The Games Ethic and Imperialism: Aspects of the Diffusion of an Ideal* (London and Portland, OR: Frank Cass, 1998), p.18.
2. The Tokyo *Daigaku Yobimon* is one of the institutions attached to Tokyo University, which was set up in 1877. The school was renamed the *Dai'ichi Koto Chugakko* (the Principal Junior High School) in 1886, and *Dai'ichi Koto Gakko* (the Principal High School) in 1894. Tokyo Daigaku (Tokyo University), set up in 1877, also experienced several reorganizations: it became *Teikoku Daigaku* (the Imperial University) in 1866, *Tokyo Teikoku Daigaku* (Tokyo Imperial University) in 1897 and *Tokyo Daigaku* (Tokyo University) in 1949.
3. Ikuo Abe, 'Dairoku Kikuchi and F W Strange: Japanese Earliest Encounters with Athleticism', in Gertrud Pfister and Liu Yueye (eds), *Proceedings of the 3rd International ISHPES Seminar, 'Sports – the East and the West'*, Shunde, Guangdong, China, 16–22 Sept. 1996 (Sankt Augustin: Academia Verlag, 1999), pp.59–63.
4. Chiyosaburo Takeda, 'Honpo Undokai no Onjin Strange Shi wo Omou' [A Benefactor of Athletics in Japan: F.W. Strange], *Athletics*, 2, 3 (1923), 125.
5. *Japan Weekly Mail* (hereafter *JWM*), 14 May 1876. F.W. Strange was victorious in the one-mile race at the meetings of the Tokyo Amateur Athletic Association in Tokyo, May 1876. He was third in throwing cricket ball, second in hammer-throwing, second in pole-vaulting and second in a quarter-mile race. He was also second in a mile race at the meeting in the following year (*JWM*, 12 Oct. 1877). He also played in the baseball game between an affiliated team of the American fleet and the Yokohama Baseball Club (*JWM*, 5 June 1877). He rowed four as a crew member of the Yokohama Amateur Rowing Club at an autumn regatta in the same year (*JWM*, 12 Oct. 1877). He played in a cricket match between the Yokohama Cricket Club and the Yokohama Baseball Club in October 1878, and played in a football match between the Yokohama Football Club and an affiliated team of the American fleet and Tokyo in November 1878 (*JWM*, 7 Dec. 1878). His skills in cricket and rowing were highly praised in the match reports.
6. F.W. Strange, *Outdoor Games* (Daigaku Yobimon, Tokyo: Z.P. Maruya & Co., 1883), p.1.

7. Ibid., p.ii.
8. Ibid., p.i.
9. Asclepiades in the Greek Anthology (fl. 298 BC).
10. Strange, *Outdoor Games*, p.i.
11. Ibid., pp.2–3. F.W. Strange further quoted the following lines from F.L. Oswald's *Physical Education, or The Health-law of Nature* (1882): 'The beneficial effect of out-door exercise is not limited to the respiratory organs: their quickened function reacts on the nervous system, and through the nerves on the mind; true mental and physical vigour in any form can be maintained only on a liberal allowance of life-air; those who feed their lungs on miasma become strangers to that exuberant health which makes bare existence a luxury.'
12. Noboru Umetani, *Meijiki Gaikokujin Jokun Shiryo Shusei* [Original Material by the Conferment of Decorations on the Foreigners during the Meiji Era], Vol.2. (Tokyo: Shibunnkaku, 1991), pp.191–2.
13. *JWM*, 6 July 1886, p.4 (emphasis added).
14. Chiyosaburo Takeda, 'Honpo Undoukai', *Athletics*, 2, 2 (1923), 7.
15. One of the feudal clans situated in Kyushu.
16. It is thanks in large measure to Takeda, of course, that Strange is remembered and respected in Japan.
17. Takeda, 'Honpo no Undokai', 13–14.
18. Ibid., 9.
19. Ikuo Abe, 'The Japanese Reception of Modern Sport: A Modernization', *Bulletin of Institute of Health and Sport Sciences, University of Tsukuba*, 22 (1999), 73–91. See also Ikuo Abe and J.A. Mangan, 'The British Impact on Boy's Sports and Games in Japan: An Introductory Survey', *International Journal of the History of Sport*, 14, 2 (Aug. 1997), 187–99.
20. Eisaku Yusa, *Shinsen Shougaku Taiiku Zensho* [New Physical Education for Elementary Schools] (Kyoto: Ikueiya Seihoudo, 1884), pp.1–2.
21. A.T. Van Casteel, *Taiso oyobi Kogai Yugi* (Tokyo: Ministry of Education, 1879), p.1. A.T. Van Casteel was a teacher of Dutch, English, French and German hired by the Ministry of Education. He translated the *Boy's Own* and the *Girl's Own* at the ministry's request, which were respectively entitled *Taiso oyobi Kogai Yugi* (1879), and *Djlosen* (1876). His two translations of English books of games constitute the earliest *Yugisho* in Japan.
22. Yasuhiro Shimomura, *Seiyo Kogai Yugiho* [Western Outdoor Games] (Tokyo: Taiseikan, 1885), p.2. This book is a translation of Strange's *Outdoor Games*.
23. Gendo Tsuboi and Morinari Tanaka, *Kogai Yugiho* [Outdoor Games] (Tokyo, Osaka: Kinkodo, 1885), p.2.
24. Ryo Higuchi, *Futsu Yugiho* [Standard Games] (Gifu: Tanshindo, 1887), pp.1–2.
25. Koshichiro Seto, *Shinshiki Kogai Yugijutsu* [New Outdoor Games] (Tokyo: Bunendo, 1888), p.5.
26. Tsuboi and Tanaka, *Kogai Yugiho*, pp.1–2. Tei Nishimura dedicated his foreword to *Kogai Yugiho* (1885).
27. Seto, *Shinshiki Kogai Yugijutsu*, p.7.
28. Shukichi Yoshida, *Sinshen Danjo Yugiho* [New Games for Boys and Girls] (Tokyo: Tokyo Hakubunkan, 1893), pp.1–2.
29. Tsuboi and Tanaka, *Kogai Yugiho*, pp.10–12. Such examples were various kinds of races using flags or banners and scrambling for them.
30. Tora Uryu, *Seiyo Danjo Yugiho* [Western Games for Boys and Girls] (Tokyo: Fukyusha, 1887), p.3.
31. Shimomura, *Seiyo Kogai Yugiho*, pp.2–3.
32. Taneie Tojo, *Jido Taiiku Yugiho* [Physical Education and Games for Children] (Osaka: Asahido, 1888), pp.2–3.
33. *Undokai* [The Athletic World], 1, 1 (1887), 2.
34. Herbert Spencer's *Education, Intellectual, Moral and Physical* was translated into Japanese by Shinpachi Seki in 1880.
35. *Undokai* [Athletic World], I-1, 1897, p.1.
36. As already noted, manliness achieved through sport was a preoccupation of privileged English secondary schools and universities in the late nineteenth century. It was a manliness linked to nationalism, militarism and imperialism. For a fuller discussion of this point, see J.A. Mangan, 'Play Up and Play the Game: The Rhetoric of Cohesion, Identity, Patriotism and Morality', in J.A. Mangan, *Athleticism in the Victorian and Edwardian Public School: The Emergence and Consolidation

of an Educational Ideology (Cambridge: Cambridge University Press, 1981; first paperback edition – Falmer: Falmer Press, 1986; second paperback edition – London and Portland, OR: Frank Cass, 2000), pp.179–203; J.A. Mangan, 'Concepts of Duty and Prospects of Adventure: Images of Empire for Public Schoolboys', in Mangan, *The Games Ethic and Imperialism*, pp.44–70; J.A. Mangan, 'Moralists, Metaphysicians and Mythologists: The "Signifiers" of a Victorian and Edwardian Sub-culture', in Susan J. Bandy (ed.), *Coroebus Triumphs: The Alliance of Sport and the Arts* (San Diego, CA: University of San Diego Press, 1988), pp.141–62; J.A. Mangan, 'Noble Specimens of Manhood: Schoolboy Literature and the Creation of a Colonial Chivalric Code', in Jeffrey Richards (ed.), *Imperialism and Juvenile Literature* (Manchester: Manchester University Press, 1989), pp.173–94, J.A. Mangan, 'The Grit of our Forefathers: Invented Traditions, Propaganda and Imperialism', in John M. MacKenzie (ed.), *Imperialism and Popular Culture* (Manchester, Manchester University Press, 1986), pp.113–39; J.A. Mangan 'Duty unto Death', in J.A. Mangan (ed.), *Tribal Identities: Nationalism, Europe, Sport* (London and Portland, OR: Frank Cass, 1996), pp.10–38; J.A. Mangan, 'Muscular, Militaristic and Manly: The British Middle Class Hero as Moral Messenger', in Richard Holt, J.A. Mangan and Pierre Lanfranchi (eds), *European Heroes: Myth, Identity Sport* (London and Portland, OR: Frank Cass, 1996), pp.28–47; J.A. Mangan, 'Gamesfield and Battlefield: A Romantic Alliance in Verse and the Creation of Militaristic Masculinity', in John Nauright and Timothy J.L. Chandler (eds), *Making Men* (London and Portland, OR: Frank Cass, 1996), pp.141–57. For the wider cultural and educational context in which these articles and chapters are set, see Mangan, *Athleticism*; Mangan, *The Games Ethic*; but also J.A. Mangan (ed.), *Making Imperial Mentalities: Socialisation and British Imperialism* (Manchester: Manchester University Press, 1988); J.A. Mangan (ed.), *Benefits Bestowed? Education and British Imperialism* (Manchester: Manchester University Press, 1988); and J.A. Mangan (ed.), *The Imperial Curriculum: Racial Images and Education in the British Colonial Experience* (London: Routledge, 1993).
37. *Undokai*, I, 1 (1897), 2.
38. Ibid., 15.
39. Ibid., 15. Although he maintained that racial amelioration might produce a strong race, he was not in favour of mixed marriage.
40. Ibid., 15–16.
41. Ibid., 17–18.
42. *Undokai*, III, 8 (1899), 1–8, and III, 9 (1899), 1–6.
43. Ibid., 1.
44. See Mangan, *Athleticism in the Victorian and Edwardian Public School* for details of this consolidation at Oxford and in the public schools of Britain.
45. *University College School Magazine*, new series (April 1873), p.19. Concerning Dairoku Kikuchi's study abroad in England, see also Abe, *Dairoku Kikuchi*, pp.59–63.
46. *Undokai*, III, 2 (1899), 1.
47. Ibid., 1.
48. Ibid., 2.
49. Ibid.
50. Ibid.
51. Ibid.
52. Ibid., 3.
53. *Undokai*, III, 5 (1899), 1.
54. Ibid., 1.
55. *Yamato-minzoku* denotes a reactionary identity, especially popular since the Meiji Restoration in 1868.
56. *Undokai*, III, 5 (1899), 1.
57. Ibid., 3.
58. Ibid.
59. Ibid., 2.
60. *Riron/Jikken Kyogi Undo* was first published in 1903. The fuller version, in which the term *Kyogido* first appeared, was published in June 1904.
61. Edwin O. Reischauer evaluated the Russo-Japanese War in the following lines: 'The Japanese, choosing their time in February 1904, set a new pattern for modern warfare by first crippling Russian naval strength in the Far East, and then declaring war. Russia was far stronger than Japan, but suffered the disadvantage of having to fight the war at the end of a single-track railway several

thousand miles long. Her military operations were further hampered by revolutionary movements at home. The Japanese were consistently victorious, bottling up the Russians in the Liaotung Peninsula ports, which fell after costly assaults, and driving their other armies northward through Manchuria. Russia sent her European fleet from the Baltic Sea to the Far East, but the entire Japanese navy fell upon it in the straits between Japan and Korea and annihilated it. Although Russia was being soundly trounced, Japan was so exhausted that she welcomed the peace arranged in 1905, by President Theodore Roosevelt, who greatly admired Japanese efficiency and pluck.' Edwin O. Reischauer, *Japan: Past and Present* (Tokyo: Charles E. Tuttle Company, 1964), p.139.

62. Ferdinand A. Schmidt and Eustace H. Miles, *The Training of the Body for Games, Athletics, Gymnastics, and Other Forms of Exercise and for Health, Growth, and Development* (London: Swan Sonnenschein, 1901). Ferdinand Augustus Schmidt, a physiologist, was one of the leaders of German *Spiel Bewegung* and took part in the formation of *Der Zentralausschuss zur foerderung der Volks- und Jugendspiel in Deutschland* in 1891. Eustace H. Miles was a Cambridge graduate and a famous champion in tennis and rackets.
63. Ibid., p.xviii (emphasis added).
64. Ibid., pp.ix–xix, and *passim* in Chapters I and II, pp.1–72.
65. Ibid., pp.x–xi.
66. Ibid., p.xviii.
67. Ibid., p.xii.
68. Ibid., p.xix.
69. Ibid., p.47.
70. Chiyosaburo Takeda, *Riron/Jikken Kyogi Undo* [Theory and Practice, Athletic Exercise] (Tokyo: Tokyo Hakubunnkan, 1904), Preface, p.1.
71. Ibid., Preface, p.2.
72. Ibid., p.1 (emphasis added).
73. Ibid., pp.25–6.
74. Ibid., p.27.
75. Ibid., p.2.
76. Ibid., p.627.
77. Ibid., pp.604–5.
78. The Meiji Restoration in 1868 brought drastic change in Japan. It brought about the demise of the Tokugawa Shogunate and created in its place a new centralized system, It reconstructed the hegemonic, political, economic and social structures. It brought the destruction of the feudal class system, modernization, industrialization and westernization. Its purpose was to restore the supreme authority of the Emperor (*Tenno*). It broke down the *Baku-han* (Shogunate-Clan) system and deprived the samurai class (feudal retainers belonging to clans) of their fundamental bases. It gave people an expectation of democracy. It created a new class system and a new notion of a 'nation'. The ambiguity and complexity of the restoration brought a nostalgia for the samurai spirit.
79. Takeda, *Riron/Jikken Kyogi Undo*, p.606.
80. Ibid., p.607.
81. Ibid., p.127.
82. Ibid., p.612.
83. Ibid., p.613.
84. Ibid., p.615.
85. Ibid., p.617.
86. Ibid., p.618.
87. Ibid., pp.618–819. *Sun Zi* is the famous Chinese treatise on military tactics, which was written in the era of Chunqiu (770–221 BC). It was read by the Japanese warrior class with great enthusiasm during the feudal period.
88. Ibid., p.620.
89. Ibid., pp.621–2.
90. Ibid., p.624.
91. Ibid., p.625.
92. Ibid.
93. Mangan, *Athleticism*, Prologue, p.7.
94. Chiyosaburo Takeda, *Shinshin Tanren Kyogi Undo* [Training of the Body and Mind: Boys' Athletic Exercise] (Tokyo: Tokyo Hakubunkan, 1904), pp.2–3.

'Sportsmanship' – English Inspiration and Japanese Response 127

FIGURE 4.1
CATEGORICAL PHASES OF ATHLETIC EXERCISE

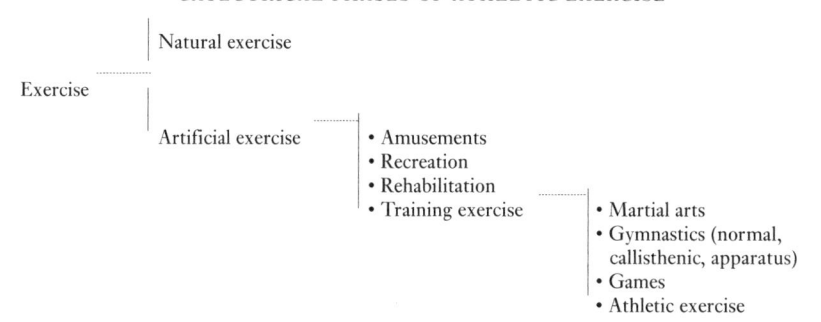

Exercise
- Natural exercise
- Artificial exercise
  - Amusements
  - Recreation
  - Rehabilitation
  - Training exercise
    - Martial arts
    - Gymnastics (normal, callisthenic, apparatus)
    - Games
    - Athletic exercise

FIGURE 4.2
THE KINDS OF ATHLETIC EXERCISE

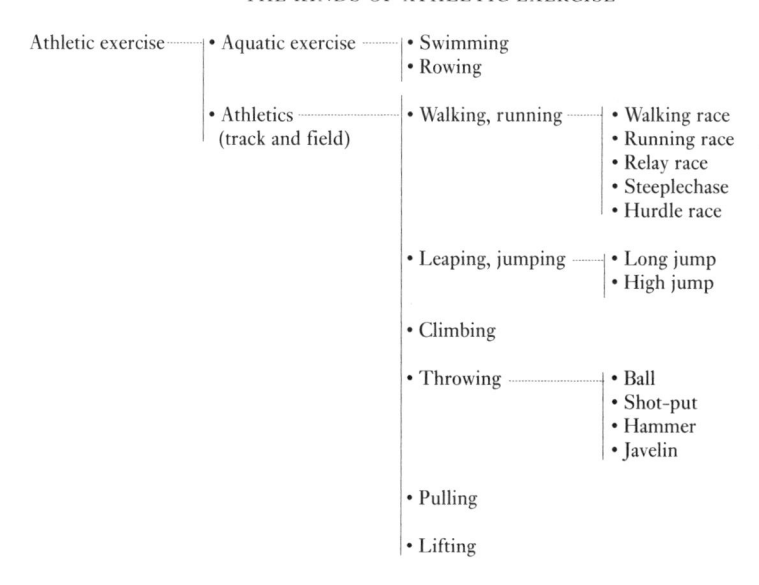

Athletic exercise
- Aquatic exercise
  - Swimming
  - Rowing
- Athletics (track and field)
  - Walking, running
    - Walking race
    - Running race
    - Relay race
    - Steeplechase
    - Hurdle race
  - Leaping, jumping
    - Long jump
    - High jump
  - Climbing
  - Throwing
    - Ball
    - Shot-put
    - Hammer
    - Javelin
  - Pulling
  - Lifting

TABLE 4.1
VIRTUES OF KYOGIDO

1. Aims of exercise (sport)
   ① Muscular training (physical strength)
   ② Training of nerves (temper)
   ③ Mental and emotional training (character)

2. Significance of exercise (sport)
   ① An instrument for disciplining the body and mind
   ② Discipline of willpower
   ③ Training in self-restraint
   ④ Training of youth
   ⑤ Preparation for hardship
   ⑥ Learning sportsmanship

3. Practice of exercise (sport)
   ① A student is not a professional
   ② Do not forget study for the sake of exercise
   ③ Walk and enhance your physical fitness
   ④ Choose your own exercise (sport) and its season
   ⑤ Improve your technique and endeavour to master it

4. Dignity of an athlete (sportsperson)
   ① There is a distinction between amateur and professional in every art
   ② Do not compete for the prize
   ③ Respect honour and righteousness
   ④ Do not compete for profit
   ⑤ Do not behave like a professional player
   ⑥ Do not compete with a professional player
   ⑦ Do not compete with a player who acts in a cowardly way
   ⑧ Do not catch 'athletic fever'

5. Magnanimity and proprieties of an athlete (sportsperson)
   ① Fair play
   ② Be alert but not guileful
   ③ Do not fall into raptures at your victory
   ④ Be a good loser
   ⑤ Respect your opponent
   ⑥ Accept your lot without complaining
   ⑦ Sport is rivalry between gentlemen and women
   ⑧ Your opponent is your master and friend
   ⑨ Observe the proprieties and be humble

6. Discipline
   ① Be punctual
   ② Obey the officials of the games
   ③ Abide by the rules
   ④ Obey the referee

7. Self-restraint and temperance
   ① Live simply and do not indulge in luxury
   ② Restrain yourself if you want to be superior to your opponent
   ③ Real liberty depends on the endurance of hardship

8. Courage and daring spirit
   ① Do your best and fight on, make your best effort

Source: Chiyosaburo Takeda, *Riron/ jikken Kyogi Undo*, 1904.

'Healthy Bodies, Healthy Minds': Sport and Society in Colonial Malaya

JANICE N. BROWNFOOT

Whatever else Britain may have contributed to the world as an imperial power, western sport was one of the most enduring achievements. The British took with them to the Empire a plethora of sports for both men and women, from football and cricket to tennis and swimming, indoor and outdoor, played on field, track, court and in water, in teams and by individuals. Malaya was no exception.[1]

Writing in Singapore in March 1908, Edwin Dingle, founder editor and publisher of the *Motor Car and Athletic Journal*, summed up a general truth:

> Wherever the Anglo-Saxon race has established itself – and that is well nigh everywhere – there it has carried its sports. The outstanding characteristic of the race is that it must find an outlet for its energies in some form of outdoor sport or exercise, and nowhere has our national games a larger proportion of votaries than in the Straits Settlements [SS] and Federated Malay States [FMS]. Colony is linked to States and State to State by sport.[2]

Twenty years later the *Malayan Sports Annual* for 1928 agreed, making the not uncommon observation that 'The secret of British success in colonisation is sometimes a matter of wonder. Part of it is certainly to be found in the games that, like trade, ever "follow the flag".'[3]

So what games had 'followed the flag' to colonial Malaya and when; what role did they play in the reputed British success there; and how were they able to achieve it? How did sport affect the local communities and how did those communities respond? This contribution considers these questions with particular reference to sport and the Asian and Eurasian populations of Malaya in the inter-war period.[4] It is not a definitive study, but reflects work in progress. Before considering in more detail what was new about the sporting innovations introduced through colonialism and the dramatic changes that resulted, an outline of Malay sports prior to the colonial period will provide a useful comparison and benchmark.

SPORT AND GAMES IN PRE-COLONIAL MALAYA

Until the introduction of the western concept of team sports, Malays[5] admired the sporting talent of individuals such as hunters (especially elite males), elephant tamers and trainers of champion cocks for cock-fighting. Malay sports requiring craft skills and manual dexterity were also popular, including kite flying (*wau*), top spinning, *sepak bola tangkis* (also known as *sepak raga* and *sepak takraw*, played with a rattan ball), finger- and arm-wrestling, *silat* (a form of self-defence) and races on bamboo stilts. Boat-racing, fishing and diving were also greatly enjoyed since Malay *kampung*s (villages) were usually located near rivers or by the sea.[6]

Malay women spent their leisure time in gentle activity, gathering seashells and flowers to string into garlands, boating and picnics on river banks. They also played *congkak*, a board game requiring skill and patience. Fundamentally, in traditional Malay games and recreations, team sports were largely unfamiliar, apart from the popular *sepak bola tangkis*.[7]

SPORT AND THE WHITE COMMUNITY

Imperialism, Health and the Importance of Sport

British colonialism in Malaya consisted of paternalistic but dominant white rule based on the aura of superiority. Imperialism, the imperial ethos and the British Empire were the creations of men mostly educated and trained in British public schools and universities. Sport, athleticism and 'muscular Christianity'[8] all played their part in the imperial culture that British men formulated during the Victorian era as essential to doing their duty, forming bonds, transmitting morality and maintaining white prestige.[9] White men from other nations – America, Australia and various European countries – similarly espoused the British philosophy.[10]

British and other white women were necessary too. But they had to fit in and play their roles as helpmates, wives and mothers and as working women (for some), exerting also a civilizing influence. In many ways they were the 'civilizing' face of colonialism and in Malaya, according to a leader in the *Straits Times* in 1911, were essential if colonization in the tropics was to continue 'without destruction of the superior race characteristics which are supposed to be possessed by the people of temperate climates'.[11]

Sport was similarly essential in helping to promote and uphold successful colonial rule, racial superiority and white solidarity: it was an integral part of imperialism. A universal belief of the British in the tropics was that regular exercise was mandatory for maintaining health and morale, as well as personal and public control. Physically energetic games were considered beneficial because they helped westerners to keep fit, build team spirit, form friendships, limit the negative effects of work, maintain white prestige, and offset any tendency to 'nerves' or mental breakdown due to alienation, isolation and loneliness. Sport enabled vital social contact amid the widely dispersed communities of the Malay Peninsula and the Borneo states. It also reputedly helped sublimate sexual urges, especially in young men. Sport, in essence, was advantageous to the individual, the group, the wider community and the Empire.[12] As Edwin Dingle writing in 1908, largely for men about men, argued:

> It is generally conceded that nothing has a more beneficial or permanent effect in the formation of character than participation in health giving sports. ... The youth is taught self-reliance and self-restraint, alertness and quickness of decision, the spirit of healthy rivalry and the more generous instincts of a true sportsman, ready to admit defeat from a better man.[13]

If sport and exercise were beneficial, indeed essential, to white men in the enervating tropical climate, then surely white women needed to participate in sport too? The issue aroused debate in Malaya which polarized between those women who argued in favour and some men, especially among medical doctors, who inveighed against. Despite the barriers white women faced, most of them played whatever games they chose.[14]

The Introduction of Western Sports in the Nineteenth Century

Western sport was introduced as soon as whites settled in Malaya, in Penang from 1786 and Singapore from 1819. Initially, horse riding and racing, driving out in horse-drawn carriages, walking and parlour games such as chess and billiards were the most popular. By the 1830s the first ball, team and field games – fives in 1836 and cricket by 1837 – had been introduced. More and more sports were introduced progressively, often soon after their innovation, adoption and development in the home country. By the latter half of the century these included croquet and rifle shooting.[15]

Initially sport was organized collectively, through groups of men and then in clubs based on British public-school models. During the 1830s and 1840s cricket enthusiasts, who met at the Hotel de l'Europe in Singapore to play cricket and then socialize over drinks, established a tradition of combining sports with social intercourse in clubs. In 1852 they set up the first sporting institution in Malaya, the Singapore Cricket Club (SCC), which over the decades offered facilities for hockey, lawn tennis and football as well as cricket, and for billiards, pool and card games in the clubhouse. The SCC quickly became a whites-only membership club, although it played against other ethnic groups too.[16]

From the late 1870s, westerners rapidly introduced modern sports to the Malay States[17] through clubs that combined sporting and social activities, the most famous being the Selangor Club in 1884 and the Lake Club in 1890, both in Kuala Lumpur (KL). Inter-state matches soon became a feature, with the first annual cricket match between Perak and Penang being played in 1884. Other European national groups in Malaya also founded their own clubs, such as the German Teutonia in 1856 and the Swiss Rifle Shooting Club in 1871. By the 1900s the Teutonia was the premier club for lawn bowls and the Swiss were leaders in rifle shooting. In the earlier twentieth century the Dutch, the French and the Americans all founded their own clubs which promoted brotherhood between their respective nationals, including through sport.[18]

From the later nineteenth century up to the Second World War, sports such as cricket, rifle shooting, golf, hockey, athletics, soccer, rugby, lawn tennis, cycling, swimming, motoring and motor racing, boxing and badminton developed in Malaya. The range of sports and games expanded as incoming westerners, male and female, brought new developments from their countries of origin, and as more facilities became available in response to growing demand. Football fields, golf courses, tennis and badminton courts and swimming pools sprang up in towns, villages, in some instances on larger rubber estates, and even in private gardens.[19]

Sport and Gender Issues in the Colonial Period

Generally, following metropolitan mores, sport was organized by men, for men, and run by committees of male members, primarily through clubs. Men thus controlled women's involvement in sport, as well as limiting their use of club facilities to specific days and certain times. Despite these restrictions, white women were rarely inspired to establish women-only sports clubs, with the notable exceptions of the Ladies Lawn Tennis Club founded in Singapore in 1884, and a couple of women's golf clubs.[20]

Nevertheless, the rules and regulations did not prevent western women from active participation in sport. By the 1890s they were playing a wide variety of games, except for cricket, soccer, rugby and polo. Opportunities also included croquet, rifle shooting, cycling, walking and swimming. Their involvement in sport became increasingly visible and by the inter-war era they were even playing in mixed-race teams or against Asian women's teams.[21] Examples from selected sports illustrate these points.

The popularity of golf – which began in the SS in 1891 – spread rapidly. By 1908 Singapore had at least four golf clubs and courses and many white women were already enthusiastic players: 'Golf is a popular pastime with many ladies in Singapore, whose energy is displayed with considerable success on the links of the Sepoy Lines Golf Club.'[22] In 1928 it was recorded that in Penang ten women had played hockey in two mixed sides and that 'their play was a surprise to many'.[23] In comparison with golf and hockey, by the earlier twentieth century, the popularity of rifle shooting among westerners was limited. Nevertheless in March 1932 a woman, Mrs L.A. Thomas, competed in the FMS Rifle Championship and came runner-up to a professional soldier, Lieutenant Laub of the Johore Volunteer Engineers.[24]

For western women the freedom to engage in sport was assisted by the advances of the women's movement in their countries of origin, notably in dress reform and women's rights. These achievements were passed on to Asian and Eurasian women and girls, informally with white women as role models and more formally through education.[25] Sport brought many innovations to local females, as it did also to Asian and Eurasian men and boys.

COLONIAL INNOVATION: SPORT, ASIANS AND EURASIANS

Introduction, Expansion and Explanation

By the early twentieth century modern sport was spreading through colonial Malaya's Asian and Eurasian communities. The development of sport among the non-white communities was intimately linked to the spread of English-language education. As government English schools, together with Protestant and Roman Catholic mission schools were opened from the 1890s, sport became an integral feature of the curricula and in due course was made compulsory (in 1932 for girls schools) by the colonial Education Department.[26]

Both boys and girls were inculcated with the value of sport to them as individuals and as members of society. In English-language schools the boys, mostly Chinese, Eurasian and Indian, learnt to play cricket and football and to enjoy sport, while also learning to play fairly by the rules. These reputed benefits they then carried with them into adult life. Asian and Eurasian girls in English-language girls schools also enjoyed similar sport training and benefits.[27]

According to the 1928 *Malayan Sports Annual*, men who continued to play games after leaving school were said to be healthier, fitter, more valuable to their employers and more morally sound. Playing sport was reputedly beneficial to the individual man and helped his productivity as an employee. The *Annual* also argued that the world needed the type of man who 'plays the game' and who understood the word 'cricket' whether applied to sport or life. By obeying the rules of sport, it emphasized, a man learnt to give and take in friendly rivalry and could then apply these lessons to life, work and his relations with others, including those from other communities.[28]

By the 1920s many Asians were in agreement with the western view that the benefits of playing sport for the individual, no matter what their ethnicity or background, included not only wholesome recreation for mind and body, but social and corporate advantages. Character building was 'a valuable incidental': 'The term "sportsmanship" is only another way of saying "gentlemanliness", and that is no matter of money or social rank, but of personal attributes found in men (and women) in all stations of life.'[29] Sport was thus equally valuable to the community, socially, ethnically and politically. In Malaya, 'where we have such a cosmopolitan population, the various racial elements in which are brought into friendly contact by no medium more effectually than that of sport'.[30]

The role of sport in bringing together the races of the British Empire in general and of Malaya in particular was recognized by various observers. As early as 1908 a writer in *The Motor Car and Athletic Journal* confirmed that the *Journal* wanted to preserve and foster sport as a cultural bond of empire. It was very necessary, he stressed, 'to encourage the sporting spirit in every way possible. ... We recognise that sport plays an important part in blending the peoples of this Empire. The competitive spirit is innate.'[31]

Throughout the earlier twentieth century Malaya was regularly described as a peaceful, multiracial society. As E. Foster-Hall (former Brigade Major of the SS Volunteer Force) commented in an article in September 1935 entitled 'My Impressions of Malaya':

> Nowhere in the wide world, I say with confidence, can people of so many races, creeds and religions be seen living together in such close proximity and such harmony. Not only do Europeans of all nationalities live in peace and harmony – though this is to be seen in many places – but there are also Eurasians, Chinese, Malays, Indians of every race and community and members of all Asiatic countries.[32]

Sport, it was firmly believed, positively assisted such community and race relations by helping to build bridges between the different ethnic groups. The 1928 *Malayan Sports Annual* laboured the point:

> Chinese, Malays, Tamils, everyone, meet on common ground at games and learn to respect each other, and the social feeling aroused in this manner is carried into everyday life. ... if we meet and come to understand and appreciate each other on the playing field we are enabled to realise how little really separates our views in more important matters, and to respect opinions sincerely held, even when they differ from our own.[33]

In these aspects, it continued, the value of sport in Malaya 'cannot be over-estimated'. Even the publication of the *Annual*, it suggested, stood 'as a material proof ... of the love of the game which is felt by so many of us in this country' whether Asian or western. Sport was multicultural.[34]

Of all the sports which could assist in forging better ethnic relations, cricket was thought to have pride of place, at least as far as men were concerned. Labelled 'the King of Games', cricket was said to be 'one of England's greatest gifts to the world' with test matches between England

and her colonies and dominions being 'among the truest bonds of Empire, cementing a solid alliance that even the fever of politics cannot disturb'.[35] An article in the Chinese-published *Malayan Sports Pictorial* in 1932 agreed and went even further, attributing to cricket a global role in helping to unite the world's nations. 'Cricket knows no creed, religion or politics,' affirmed the writer. 'A well chosen cricket team is the best possible ambassador – as good as and certainly cheaper than, any League of Nations.'[36] It is revealing that a Chinese publication should endorse the significance of cricket so strongly.

The *Malayan Sports Annual* of 1928 agreed, suggesting that of all the sports played, 'cricket is the greatest of these games. It has a grandeur and an inspiration surpassing those of even the other pastimes which Britain has spread over the whole surface of the globe – soccer and lawn tennis.'[37] Moreover, cricket was a great leveller – it did not matter whether a man was a junior clerk or a *tuan besar* (literally 'big man', i.e. boss), or what his ethnicity and background were; if he hit a century, rank and status did not count: '"On the field of sport all are equal." Such is a fine old British tradition, exemplified faithfully in cricket.'[38]

Nevertheless, sport also led to occasional resentment. One example of antagonism occurred in 1932 at a water polo game between the Singapore Swimming Club (SSC – whites) and the Singapore Chinese Swimming Club (SCSC), when 'for the first time in many years the Europeans defeated the Chinese'. The picture of each team shows the seven Europeans all wearing swimming caps and the seven Chinese bare-headed. But it was not their streamlined headgear that enabled the Europeans to win 4–3. In fact they won unfairly – the *Malayan Sports Pictorial* was grudgingly charitable in describing it as a lucky victory – because they were well aware of the new rules for water polo, while the Chinese played by the old rules and so kept getting penalized for fouls: 'And it was this big advantage that enabled the Europeans to win... [They] are to be congratulated on their success.'[39]

The more usual role of sport in helping to engender and develop more harmonious race relations was not necessarily limited to the players. One observer expressed wonderment that 'Nowhere in the world is to be seen the sight that can be seen here [in Malaya] at any golf course: Chinese, Malay, Sikh, Tamil and other South Indian caddies working in peace and harmony together'.[40]

Ethnic relations among and between their subject races, as well as Asians and westerners, were of some concern to the metropolitan and colonial governments by the inter-war period. Although sport may not have been officially defined as a policy for encouraging good race relations, it certainly played a major role at a practical and informal level. The many games played between Asians and westerners on equal terms by the 1920s can only have contributed to better understanding, although one wonders what westerners might sometimes have felt when they were defeated by Asian players to whom the modern games were such an innovation.[41]

Since it was felt that Malaya had everything to gain 'by zealously encouraging sport', it was argued that the country needed more sports grounds laid down, more sports clubs founded and more teams organized. But where, asked a writer in *The Malayan Sports Annual* for 1928, were the public spirited men to help develop sport and thereby genuinely serve their country? Many might like playing sport, but too few were willing to fund it and develop it; there was instead too much concern with making money and 'the Almighty Dollar'.[42] What Malaya needed, the writer asserted, was men who, whatever their ethnicity, 'uphold the dignity of their own race yet make real friends with those of other races – friendships based on mutual respect and cemented by cordial participation in the social and sporting activities common to all'.[43]

Although more effort could have been made to promote sport in Malaya, by the 1920s many men and women from all ethnic groups could play sport if they wanted to. The choices possible were a cause for congratulation in the 1928 *Malayan Sports Annual*: 'People of all communities in Malaya are singularly fortunate, for perhaps the fact which more than any other impresses the average young European who arrives in this country is the abundance of facilities for all games.'[44] The *Annual* continued:

> Nor is as [sic] sportsman's choice of games limited. Should he desire variety he, whether Malay, Chinese, Tamil, Eurasian or European, may play football, Association or Rugby, cricket, hockey, lawn tennis, badminton, volleyball. He may run or he may swim. The European, in addition, may ride a horse, play polo, try and reduce his handicap at golf, and join in other sporting activities.[45]

By the 1920s women and girls, western and Asian, were also playing sports from a surprisingly wide choice.[46]

Asians, Eurasians and Examples of Sports Played in the Inter-War Period

The sports that Asians and Eurasians played by the 1920s were mostly organized either by type of sport and/or by ethnic group. For example, Malays had their own clubs for individual sports such as football; separate Recreation Clubs organized sport of all kinds for Eurasians. Sport among non-whites had typically begun among the English-language educated, but by the 1930s the enthusiasm for games had spread to those educated in their own vernacular, such as Chinese and Malay.[47]

Some examples of individual sports will illustrate their popularity with and impact on Asians and Eurasians. The sports considered are the major games: soccer, cricket and athletics, symbols par excellence of imperial sport, at least for men.[48]

Association Football (Soccer)

By the end of the First World War association football – soccer – had become Malaya's national game, the most popular participator sport for men and boys. Although its popularity varied greatly in individual Malayan states and settlements, no *kampung* or district was without at least a team or two, helped by the interest and endorsement of various Malay rulers: in the 1920s the Sultan of Perak was an enthusiastic player.[49]

Awareness of and interest in soccer was due primarily to it being played in schools as part of the western educational package. By the 1920s Malaya's best footballers had learnt the game at school, playing in inter-class and inter-school matches: 'The Malayan school boy has taken enthusiastically to soccer, and already – when striving for the triumphs of the school playing field – he yearns for the day when he will represent his State in Malayan cup matches.'[50] Schoolboy football had an enthusiastic following in Selangor in the later 1920s, when the Thomson Trophy for inter-school knockout competition, was instituted in 1926. In 1939, when the Singapore Inter-School Soccer Championship competition for a cup donated by a leading Eurasian, Mr C. Clarke, was suspended, complaints were soon forthcoming. The Championship, said commentators, was necessary for students who, as the citizens of tomorrow, needed such competition to 'help promulgate better understanding, better feeling of fraternity and above all sporting spirit'.[51]

Despite its popularity, Malayan soccer went through a difficult period in the late 1920s. Although many administrative changes had been implemented in 1927, with various State and Settlement Football Associations (FAs) being either formed or re-organized and the Malayan Football Association (MFA) being inaugurated with its headquarters in KL, writing in the *Malayan Mirror*, 'CAP' concluded that 'there is no real control of the game throughout Malaya on lines approaching anything like those upon which the Associations are theoretically built'.[52]

The problems 'CAP' outlined included the varying degrees of development of the game, the lack of standardized organization, numerous irregularities and the haphazard growth of associations and leagues. Hence Selangor's League, founded in 1906, which included European, Eurasian, Chinese and Malay football clubs, was operating by 1928 as three separate divisions, each with a variety of ethnic- and occupation-based teams (e.g., United Banks, the Audit Office). From the early 1920s separate Malayan 'Exhibition Football Leagues' also existed for each ethnic group – Malays, Chinese, Tamils and Sikhs – playing on an inter-state basis. The Malayan FA had an almost impossible organizational and administrative task. Even the sizes of soccer grounds were not uniform.[53]

The quality of play and attitudes was also poor. Players and teams frequently failed to observe the rules, particularly that of being offside – 'and then they look hurt when the whistle goes!' Many players lacked real team spirit and failed to understand that 'the play's the thing', not the results. 'Soccer is only a game after all and your opponents should be real friends, not bitter enemies', advised 'Echo', writing in 1928.[54] Players also needed to learn to put their team first, rather than themselves or the crowd, a problem exacerbated by the lack of good captains: 'Real captaincy is a rare thing in Malayan football, and there is wonderful scope for it.'[55] Moreover, few competent referees were available – and by 1928 only one was an Asian, Tan Lee Wan, from Singapore.[56]

But it was not all gloom. By the 1920s football association committees were becoming multiracial with members experienced in the game. European R.G. 'Reggie' Gale, Chairman of the Selangor FA and a referee and administrator, had been one of the finest fullbacks to play in Malayan teams, while Mr M. Cumarasami, JP, the vice president, had donated the Indians Versus Ceylonese Cup. The other office bearers were European, Eurasian and Indian. Gale also used his soccer skills to introduce rigorous training for the Selangor team.[57] In 1921 the inauguration of the Malaya Cup had inspired inter-state competition. The benefits of Gale's training programme paid off for Selangor in the 1927 Malaya Cup final with their sensational 8–1 victory over Singapore. In Singapore during the same period, with numerous matches played, only three players had been disciplined – 'a fact which reflects the sporting spirit of unity amongst all nationalities represented on the SFA [Singapore Football Association]'.[58] The concept of fair play by the rules was taking root and proving advantageous.

The development of soccer among the Malays in the 1920s was regarded as particularly positive. Throughout the country Malay football clubs were 'more and more coming into their own', noted 'Fair Play' in 1928.[59] 'CAP', describing Singapore's Malay teams the same year, similarly commented: '[Malays] always attracted large crowds to the stadium not only on account of their good form but the splendid sporting spirit in which they always take the field.'[60] Moreover they had also carried a fair share of the administration burden 'which is a welcome advance'. Nevertheless, many Malay clubs, like some of their Asian and Eurasian counterparts, were being adversely affected in developing their game because they were unable to afford the costly boots and blazers needed to participate in inter-state matches.[61]

Cricket

Apart from westerners, probably the finest exponents of cricket in colonial Malaya, including the true sporting spirit, were the Eurasians. Their sports and social clubs, usually with the word 'Recreation' in the title and dotted around the SS and the Malay States, supplied some of the best players to local, state, inter-state and Malayan teams. In the late 1920s bowler F.D.C. La Brooy from Penang Recreation Club was a case in point. Eurasian schoolboys were among the first to learn cricket at school.[62] During the 1930s cricket as a game spread to many boys schools, especially the English-language and Anglo-Chinese schools.

Although cricket may have been 'synonymous with all that is straight, and fair, and honourable',[63] by the late 1920s cricket in Malaya, like soccer, was facing some significant problems. According to 'Argus', writing in 1928, Malayan cricket was suffering from poor wickets, batsmen, bowlers, fielding, team spirit and general laxness. Real cricketing progress would only occur, he concluded, when these issues were addressed.[64] One positive factor, he conceded, was inter-ethnic matches: 'The spirit is there already, and of this no more convincing proof is required than the inauguration of this most attractive annual fixture, Europeans versus Asiatics, in the FMS.'[65]

For a long time most of the players in the inter-state and Malayan teams had been westerners. In 1927, however, 'all-Malayan' teams with some Eurasian members played various matches against a visiting Australian XI and triumphed at that in KL.[66] By comparison, other ethnic groups, including the Chinese and the Indians, were far more prominent in inter-club cricket where, by the late 1920s, a noticeable feature apart from the play was 'the fine sporting spirit shown by all the teams – a spirit in full accord with the highest traditions of the great game of cricket'.[67]

A decade later, in 1939, mixed-race teams of Indian, Chinese, Eurasian and western players competed in the FMS versus the Colony championship. Some Malayan cricketers were good enough to play overseas. In 1932 the *Malayan Sports Pictorial* reported that Lall Singh, a cricketer from KL, had already had great success in England and was 'steadily making a name for himself in home cricket circles'.[68]

Athletics

Athletics is one sport which dramatically illustrates how well Asians could compete against westerners when championships were opened to them on an equal basis, even if they did not have specialized equipment. Although athletics was popular from the early years of the twentieth century among Asians and Eurasians as well as whites, the athletics championships which began in 1906 were only for white members of western clubs until 1921. Then in 1922, following agitation in the Malayan Amateur Athletics Association (AAA) committee and in the local press 'in the face of much opposition', they were opened to all comers. The effects of this revolutionary change were soon noticeable:

> The sports have advanced enormously in standard, and they now provide one of the most wholesome and enjoyable spectacles of the year. They have created a valuable bond between the different communities, and – an important point – they have justified the title of the Amateur Athletic Association of British Malaya. The Association is now truly Malayan. Before 1923 it certainly was not.[69]

With the influx of non-white athletic talent, western dominance of the championships was immediately and significantly overturned as Asians, especially Indians and Eurasians, proved just how talented they were. Between 1922 and 1928, at the annual Malayan Championship Meeting when 'the best athletes of all the States and Settlements, and of all races – European and Asiatic – meet in keen but sporting rivalry', not one of the overall champions was a westerner.[70] Nor were any of them women.

The Participation of Asian and Eurasian Women and Girls in Sports: Physical Freedom and Emancipation

Western women's educational work in colonial Malaya played a profound, indeed determining, role in bringing physical freedom to Asian and Eurasian females. Inspired by a sense of 'sisterhood' and Christian values, the English-language education provided as part of this work by females for females aimed to emancipate the whole person, body and mind. Thus physical exercise and sport were mandatory parts of the curriculum. By playing sport at school in teams and against girls of other ethnic groups, it was also felt that Asian females would learn both cooperation and competition, and interracial harmony would evolve.[71]

Dress reform was an integral part of the emancipation. Up to the 1910s traditional dress and attitudes meant mostly gentle drill and callisthenics, and prevented the girls from engaging in more lively physical exercise and games. Then, during the era of the First World War, a revolution occurred. Thus by the 1920s Chinese girls schools, established in various towns in Malaya, notably Singapore and KL, were carrying on the tradition of teaching physical exercise and sports originally introduced by white women teachers in the Anglican and Methodist Girls Schools and the convents. Even Malay vernacular girls' schools were following the trend with physical training, drill and even some team sports.[72] Hence by the 1930s badminton had become a popular sport among adult Malay women, as well as Eurasians. In 1931 Eurasian player Alice Pennefather became the first lady singles badminton champion and in 1934 Mrs Indoot of Singapore was 'the first Malay lady to take part in open competitive [badminton] games'.[73] Whether in school or in public, engaging in sport meant abandoning customary clothing.

The degree to which physical liberation, including dress reform, in relation to sport had progressed by the early 1930s is clear from photographic evidence. In 1932 the *Malayan Sports Pictorial* printed pictures of Chinese girls attired for various sports. These included the Selangor Chinese girls' basketball and volleyball teams on tour to Penang to play inter-state matches in shorts and round-necked, short-sleeved shirts, and two noted Chinese women athletes, one from Singapore, the other from Johore.[74]

Other changes had occurred too. Chinese girls' and boys' schools were now playing basketball against each other – indeed, sports offered useful means of meeting the opposite sex. In the State Lawn Tennis Tournament in Selangor in 1932 Loke Soh Yip became the first Chinese woman to play mixed-doubles tennis. So much had it become accepted for Chinese girls to play sport in public that when a fund-raiser was held at the Great World China Relief Fund in Singapore in 1932, girls from the Nanyang Physical Girls School performed an exhibition of 'Chinese Boxing' wearing shorts and round-necked, short-sleeved shirts.[75]

In 1935 the Third Malayan All Chinese Olympiad had been held (the first was in 1931), and showed 'conclusively ... the ease with which local Chinese girls have taken to sports'.[76] Recording that Asian girls playing tennis and swimming had not long before been unheard of, the writer, 'Panglima Prang', remarked that this had now changed 'and all within a period of 20 years or so'. For him this speedy freedom through sport was too much: 'Truly a remarkable and, shall I say, a too rapid change from die-hard conservatism to modern unrestricted emancipation.'[77] But he did acknowledge, with some exaggeration, the benefits sport had brought to Chinese girls: the 'anaemic, flat-chested, skinny and shy damsel of yore' had disappeared to be replaced by 'the present day product of sports and hygiene, robust, confident and well formed as a result of the healthy exercise indulged in. All for the good of the race because healthy mothers will result in healthy children.'[78]

The involvement of many Chinese girls and young women in swimming for pleasure and as a competitive sport, with photographs of them posing in swimming costumes in magazines, was one of the most remarkable changes to occur. *The Sportsman* in October 1933 had on its front cover just such a picture of two Chinese girls, one of whom was Annie Yeo. During 1933 Annie's sister Mary Yeo was 'the first Straits-born Chinese girl to win the open swimming championship of Singapore'.[79] Two years later, only 16 and still at school, Annie became the champion lady swimmer of Malaya, 'the Malayan mermaid'. 'Panglima Prang' ,who interviewed her in mid-1935, commented on the benefits which swimming gave to a woman's body. Yeo, he said, had a figure 'which, for slimness and symmetry, is the envy of her sex'.[80]

Apart from swimming and team games, cycling was the main sport that epitomized just how much Asian women had become physically liberated. Cycling had become popular with westerners in Malaya in the late nineteenth century and by the 1930s, on cheap Japanese bicycles, was much enjoyed by Malayan youth. The missionary Gertrude Owen observed:

> This might be called 'the age of the bicycle' for it is bringing freedom to the young in an astonishing way. Who has not been amazed at the sight of the young Sikh, Malay, [and] Chinese school girls on their bicycles as they dash to school.[81]

The use of bicycles and the spread of dress reform among Asian women in Malaya by 1937 led Joseph Tan, writing in *Cycling*, to comment that 'in time to come the fair sex in Malaya will out-beat the men-folks in Cycling'.[82] In fact, they were already doing so. For three successive years between 1935 and 1937, when aged between 14 and 16, Adeline Taye, Singapore's first lady cyclist, had won the Malayan Cycling Championship title and had 'astounded the cycle races fraternity by her achievements in the cycling game'.[83] In one cycling event in 1936 a Malay girl, Miss Mah, had also competed for the first time, alongside Taye.[84]

Sport, Asians and the Publication of Sports Magazines and Journals

As both players and spectators, male and female, increased significantly, so interest developed in reading about sport. During the inter-war period English-language magazines and journals, either devoted entirely to sport or with sports sections in them, began to be published by Asians for Asians. The *Malayan Sports Annual* for 1928 was one of the first. Publication every year was definitely intended, the editor wrote, because sport was now so popular that 'it is felt that there is a real demand for such a review of sporting events in Malaya'.[85] In the same year the first issue of the *Malayan Mirror*, not a sport-only publication, promised that 'a keen sportsman' would give 'accurate and critical accounts of local sporting items' because it had not been forgotten 'the fascination which Sport now holds over the people of Malaya', whether as players or spectators. The magazine specifically aimed 'to reach the Asiatic English speaking section of the people of this country'.[86]

The *Mirror* had apparently broken new ground. During the 1930s a number of English-language publications on sport, published by Asians, primarily Chinese, for a specifically Asian readership, were initiated. On

Friday, 1 August 1930, the first issue of *The Sportsman* was published in Singapore by Ong Chin Beng, C.B. Ong, on behalf of the proprietors the 'Sports Catering Syndicate'. Describing itself as 'A fortnightly pictorial publication solely dedicated to STRAITS SPORTSMEN' (at least until January 1932 when it became monthly), it was also the official organ of weightlifting in Malaya. *The Sportsman* was launched in the hope of filling 'a long felt want: The need for such a magazine ... has long been talked of.'[87]

The Sportsman's monopoly was challenged in 1932 when the *Malayan Sports Pictorial* was first published in both English and Chinese in a larger A3 size, by Lim Kok Tai (who was also the English editor) for Chinese proprietors in Singapore. Just like *The Sportsman*, the *Malayan Sports Pictorial* initiated competitions for physical culturists, male and female, whose pictures it wanted to publish to further encourage physical culture and sport, and so that both sexes could further improve themselves physically and mentally. Handsome prizes were offered.[88]

In August 1934 C.B. Ong, founder-publisher of *The Sportsman*, began another publication for an English-language educated Asian readership. Titled *Sport and Pastimes,* it was published monthly in Singapore with Ong as managing editor. The first issue contained special features on tennis, cricket, badminton, soccer, boxing and weightlifting, thus illustrating the main sports played by Asians and Eurasians (at least among men) and of most interest to readers at the time.[89]

Another example in the 1930s was the *Sports in Malaya (Review)*, also published in Singapore. The first issue of August 1939 clarified that the aim was to create for the people of Malaya 'a diversion' from the threat of war and

> to promote the sporting spirit among the people of this dominion and to give expression to the various departments of sports in this country, and help her people to expand the already vast field of both national and international games.[90]

Acknowledging the impact of westerners in arousing Asian interest in sports, the editor explained that the *Review* had 'answered the call' to assist the general progress of sports in Malaya and planned to become the national sporting organ.[91]

The final example of an English-language journal set up by Asians primarily for Asians is Syed Mohsen Alsagoff's *Super Physique*. First published in January 1939, two years later it described itself as 'The

Orient's Foremost Health, Physical Culture and Athletic Journal' and was the official organ of the Singapore Amateur Weight Lifting Federation, the governing body for weightlifting in Malaya. It printed a broad cross-section of articles to do with health improvement, body building and body maintenance, and physical culture generally.[92] Alsagoff's endeavours to build a 'League Army' of 'Mighty Manhood and Glorious Womanhood ... bound together in one big Brotherhood' was remarkable not only because it aimed to improve the health of all Malayans, but because it aimed to do this for Malaya as a *nation*, as well as developing the league globally into an international organization of like-minded, healthy, happy people.[93] Its endeavours and its publication were presumably adversely affected by the outbreak of war in 1941.

SPORT AND THE COLONIAL LEGACY

The Second World War and its aftermath brought many changes to Malaya, including the move towards independence in 1957. Developments occurred in sport too. In the later 1940s and into the 1950s, mass participation in sport, especially soccer, grew generally. But among some of the better educated, participation in competitive sport decreased. The number of sports played competitively was limited, notably to soccer, badminton, hockey and athletics. Although some Asians and Eurasians excelled and some competed at the British Empire Games and the Olympics (London in 1948 and Melbourne in 1956) they were only a handful.[94] One of them, Lloyd Valberg, a Singaporean Eurasian athlete and high jumper, illustrated the dedication essential to competitive sporting success. Having no access to professional jumping facilities, he designed a portable folding contraption in 1937 and trained without sandpits. He also had no coach: 'We were all self taught in those days.' He became an inspiration – and coach – to others.[95]

In 1950 four Chinese weightlifters did so well in the British Empire Games in Auckland, New Zealand, that they won the official championship for Malaya.[96] An Eurasian sprinter, 'Malaya's track queen of the 1950s ... the unforgettable Mary Klass' won silver at the Second Asian Games in Manila in 1954.[97] Malayan teams also participated successfully in subsequent Asian Games. In the decade after independence from colonial rule in 1957 and the subsequent formation of Malaysia in 1965, interest in both mass and competitive sport held up. In 1965 the annual Sportsman and Sportswoman Awards for outstanding achievement and sportsmanship were initiated.[98] Deputy Prime Minister Tun Razak explained the aims of the scheme: 'By encouraging sports, we are helping not only to build up our nation's youth to be good sportsmen and better Malaysians, we are also helping to achieve the task of building a harmonious, unified nation.'[99]

Yet from the late 1960s interest in, and the standard of, sports, particularly competitive, apparently declined. The popularity of weightlifting, for example, became minimal. Although a soccer-playing country since the 1890s, the best Malaysia did competitively in soccer was to win bronze at the Teheran Asian Games in 1974 and to win a place in the 1972 Munich and the 1980 Moscow Olympic Games.[100]

Writing in 1985 about the decline, Professor Khoo Kay Kim suggested that in colonial times the social elite, primarily westerners, emphasized the importance of sport so that they, together with many Asians and Eurasians, held sport 'in high esteem'. Apart from the health and social benefits, excellence in sport could open a way into the elite and perhaps into gaining a particular job or promotion. With the formation of a new, indigenous Malaysian elite, however, sports were relegated 'to a position of inconsequence', and educated Malaysians became somewhat contemptuous about the benefits and rewards of excelling at them. According to Khoo, sport was increasingly seen as primarily for mass participation in recreation, not serious competition.[101]

At various times during the last 30 or so years the Malaysian Government and others have made, with varying success, efforts to address the issue of the place of sport in the nation.[102] In 1967 a National Sport Foundation was established, 'a giant stride forward for Malaysian sport'. Its main aims were to further public participation in sport, 'a unifying influence on our diverse peoples', and to enable effective donations for its development.[103] A National Sports Council (NSC) and a Malaysian Schools Sports Council (MSSC) were also set up and, together with the Olympic Council of Malaysia (OCM), worked with the Ministry of Youth and Sport and associations for individual sports, such as football and cricket, to develop local sport.[104]

Yet sport in Malaysia remained of limited significance competitively. Malaysian participation in international competitions was limited and generally unsuccessful. Poor training, few qualified coaches, insufficient commitment, organizational weaknesses and inadequate financial and governmental support were among the explanations given.[105] During the 1980s Khoo regularly criticized negative attitudes to sport, the paucity of appropriate facilities outside the major towns, the woeful annual budget of the Sports Ministry, the lack of dedicated sports funding and the unacceptable behaviour of sporting associations' officials. In his opinion sport should have an important place in the educational system: 'There is no reason why sports cannot be considered a potential which should be nurtured,' he suggested.[106] Competitive sport brought other benefits too, he stated, arguing that 'It would not be an exaggeration to say that there is a link between "progress" (primarily in the field of technology and economics) and success in international sports.'[107]

Given such publicized concerns, in January 1988 a National Sports Policy was published emphasizing the importance of sport in helping 'achieve national development, unity and continued stability'. In outlining the wide-ranging benefits of sport to the individual, society and the nation, the policy designers illustrated just how well the sport philosophy of their former colonial rulers had been absorbed. The policy document stated: 'Sport, which serves to promote healthy competition, goodwill, tolerance, understanding and the development of physical and moral qualities, provides a conducive platform for integrating the various ethnic groups into a united nation, as well as for enhancing national prestige.'[108]

In June 1996 another important document entitled 'Standards for Sport Facilities in Malaysia' was drawn up as a set of recommendations to assist the government in achieving a more developed, prosperous nation through a healthy, active population, via proper sports planning and improved sporting facilities in urban and rural areas for both high performance and mass sport.[109] Clearly, sport was and is of ongoing importance to Malaysia and Malaysians.

CONCLUSION: THE SIGNIFICANCE OF SPORT

Sport, as promoted by the British and other whites, was a universalist ideology and practice and an early example of 'globalization' in action, which brought benefits and advantages generally and locally. Undoubtedly sport assisted in the establishment and maintenance of colonial rule and society, among widely disparate types of people, based on presumed western superiority. Yet it also helped to challenge such lifestyles and assumptions, and contributed to their downfall, especially by teaching the doctrine of equality and fair play. The western aim of introducing and inculcating the sport ethic and a belief in the benefits of physical exercise and games was broadly achieved. The effects were quite dramatic.

Although the actual numbers involved are not known, it was not only the more elite and English-educated among the local communities who were affected, but also those who were vernacular-educated and from the lower social-status groups, male and female. Malay royalty and *kampung* people, wealthy Eurasians, Chinese and Indians, as well as humble labourers, all played sport. The wide choice of games available meant many were able to find a suitable sport. It is undeniable that sport became of major importance to many Asians and Eurasians, especially in the inter-war period. It is also clear that many more were spectators than players. But whether as players or spectators, sport offered each of the Asian ethnic groups present opportunities to intermingle with and understand their colonial masters, as well as their fellow subject races. Inter-ethnic sport contributed to the breakdown of the concept of white supremacy and superiority based simply on being 'white'. Colonialism and its white rulers and participants, male and female, initiated and helped to develop a sporting culture in colonial Malaya, which has continued in postcolonial Malaysia. Sport had educational, moral and inter-ethnic effects.

The innovatory introduction of modern sports in the colonial period also had profound and lasting effects on the country's social and political dynamics. By emphasizing the importance of rules and 'playing fair', enabling inter-ethnic games and competitions, and training Asians and Eurasians in team sports and leadership, westerners assisted social harmony and helped to prepare the way for independence, albeit unwittingly. Through sport Asians and Eurasians, males and females, gained personal development, emancipation in dress, physical improvement, and changes in traditional customs and attitudes, including the adoption of the 'healthy body, healthy mind' concept. Sport also enabled them to prove that they were as good as, if not better than, their western rulers and colleagues in physical performance, sporting prowess and athletic ability.[110]

NOTES

1. Sport is defined as any physical activities or events intended to improve physical, mental and/or moral health, whether recreational or competitive. This paraphrases Roberta J. Park's definition in 'Sport, Gender and Society in a Transatlantic Victorian Perspective', in J.A.

Mangan and Roberta J. Park (eds), *From 'Fair Sex' to Feminism: Sport and the Socialization of Women in the Industrial and Post-industrial Eras* (London: Frank Cass, 1987), p.58, and J.A. Mangan, 'The Social Construction of Victorian Femininity: Emancipation, Education and Exercise', *International Journal of the History of Sport*, 6, 1 (May 1989), 1. The term 'Malaya' is used throughout this essay to cover the Straits Settlements, SS (Singapore, Penang and Malacca); the Federated Malay States, FMS (Negri Sembilan, Pahang, Perak and Selangor); the Unfederated Malay States, UFMS (Johore, Kedah, Kelantan, Perlis and Trengganu); and the Borneo States (British North Borneo – now Sabah – and Sarawak). However, only the SS and FMS are referred to specifically. The postcolonial term 'Malaysia' covers the Malay Peninsula and former Straits Settlements, except Singapore, as West Malaysia and Sarawak and Sabah as East Malaysia. Malaya was one of Britain's most economically successful colonies.
2. *Motor Car and Athletic Journal* (Singapore), I, 1 (March 1908), p.5.
3. *Malayan Sports Annual*, Kuala Lumpur (KL), First Issue, 1928, p.13. The *Annual* was published by the Commercial Press. It gives no indication of the owners or the editor, but see also note 85. This is the only issue held in the British Library.
4. A definitive, comprehensive study of sport in colonial Malaya has yet to be written. This chapter is based on a limited number of sources, primarily journals and magazines published by Asians in the inter-war period available in the holdings of the British Library in London. In 1985 historian and sports commentator Professor Khoo Kay Kim of the University of Malaya was writing a book on sport in Malaysia entitled *Public Bank's Almanac of Malaysian Sports*, said to be forthcoming. See Khoo Kay Kim, 'Sports in Malaysia: Its [sic] History', *Berita*, Public Bank, 1st Quarter 1985, p.19, held in the Library of the *New Straits Times* in KL, copy in the writer's possession. Unfortunately this book could not be located in the British Library, nor through sources in KL, and may not have been published.
5. The Malays are considered to be the indigenous inhabitants of Malaya, along with aboriginal groups on the Peninsula, such as the Orang Asli and the Sakai. In the Borneo States the indigenous groups also include the Dyaks and Muruts. The various dialect groups of Chinese and Indians have typically been regarded as immigrants. The Malays have been Muslims for centuries; many of the other indigenous groups became Christians as a result of colonialism and the impact of Christian missionaries.
6. Little has been written about any Malay sports before colonialism, with almost nothing on those of women. Sources are perfunctory, but include the *Sejarah Melayu* (Malay Annals), a translation of Raffles MS 18 with commentary by C.C. Brown in *Journal of the Malayan Branch of the Royal Asiatic Society* (hereafter *JMBRAS*), XXV, 2 and 3 (Oct. 1952), 172–3; Frank Swettenham, *The Real Malay* (London: John Lane The Bodley Head, 1900), *passim*; Anthony Reid, *South East Asia in the Age of Commerce 1450–1680*, Vol.1: 'The Lands below the Winds' (New Haven, CT, and London: Yale University Press, 1988), pp.173–96; A.H. Hill, 'Some Kelantan Games and Entertainments', *JMBRAS*, XXV, 1 (Aug. 1952), 20–34; and Khasnor Johan, *Educating the Malay Elite* (Kuala Lumpur: Pustaka Antara Sdn. Bhd., 1996), esp. p.95. The writer is also indebted to Dr Johan in Canberra, Australia and Dr Sabihah Osman of the University of Malaya in Sabah for emails with extra information, particularly on Malay women and their recreations. According to Reid ('The Lands below the Winds', pp.199–201), *Sepak bola tangkis* or *sepak raga* – literally 'kick basket' – was 'the most distinctively Southeast Asian [sport] of them all'. It was not directly competitive, but required extraordinary skill and was played all over South-East Asia. Today its international name is *sepak takraw* (a Thai word) and it has been modernized into a competitive, volleyball-like sport. Instead of rattan, materials such as leather and feathers were sometimes used to make a type of shuttlecock. Reid suggests that the similarity of this to badminton 'may help to explain the enthusiastic South-East Asian response to modern badminton'.
7. On women see author's emails with Dr Johan and Dr Osman and note 6 above. Reid's only mention of women and games is that card-playing was their most common form of gambling ('The Lands below the Winds', p.197). The modern sports that attracted Malays, notably soccer and badminton, reflected both social and cultural norms and traditions, and presumably fitted in with their interpretations of what Islam allowed. Reid comments on their passionate involvement in competitive games in the pre-colonial era (ibid., p.193). Even

Sport and Society in Colonial Malaya 151

less is known about the sports played by Chinese and Indian immigrants than about the Malays, although the Chinese were inveterate gamblers. Some information can be found in Charles Burton Buckley, *An Anecdotal History of Old Times in Singapore 1819-1867* (Kuala Lumpur and Singapore: University of Malaya Press, 1969), passim.

8. For the background to the British imperial preoccupation with sport as an instrument of Imperialism, see especially J.A. Mangan, *Athleticism in the Victorian and Edwardian Public School : The Emergence and Consolidation of an Educational Ideology* (London and Portland, OR: Frank Cass, 2000), J.A. Mangan, *The Games Ethic and Imperialism: Aspects of the Diffusion of an Ideal* (London and Portland, OR: Frank Cass, 1998) and J. A. Mangan (ed.), *Pleasure, Profit and Proselytism: British Culture and Sport at Home and Abroad 1700-1914* (London: Frank Cass, 1988). For earlier analyses see E.C. Mack, *Public Schools and British Opinion since 1860* (New York: Columbia University Press, 1941) and H.B. Gray, *The Public Schools and the Empire* (London: Williams and Norgate, 1913).

9. See J.A. Mangan, 'Prologue: Britain's Chief Spiritual Export: Imperial Sport as Moral Metaphor, Political Symbol and Cultural Bond', in J.A. Mangan (ed.), *The Cultural Bond: Sport, Empire, Society* (London: Frank Cass, 1992), pp.1–10. *The Cultural Bond* comprehensively provides the reasons for sport as part of the 'cultural baggage' of the British imperialist. See also John Mackenzie, *Imperialism and Popular Culture* (Manchester: Manchester University Press, 1986). The nature of British imperialism is discussed in Philip Mason, *Patterns of Dominance* (London: Oxford University Press, 1970), esp. pp.10–12 and J.A. Mangan, 'Introduction: imperialism, history and education', in J.A. Mangan (ed.), *Benefits Bestowed? Education and British Imperialism* (Manchester: Manchester University Press, 1988), pp.1–22, esp. Part I, pp.1–3.

10. In this chapter the terms 'white' and 'western/er' are used interchangeably as generic descriptions/titles for the British, American, Australian and European nationals resident in colonial Malaya. This is in preference to using 'European' (except where this appears in quotes or is specifically appropriate), primarily because it is not an all-encompassing term. Although other nationalities, such as the Japanese, would now be included as 'westerners', they were not regarded as such prior to the Second World War.

11. *Straits Times*, 4 March 1911. The reputed civilizing influence of white women in the British Empire is argued or considered in various sources, historical and contemporary. See in particular: Mrs Ellice Hopkins, *The Power of Womanhood, or Mothers and Sons* (London: Wells, Gardner, Drayton, 1899); Dorothy Cator, *Everyday Life Among the Headhunters and Other Experiences from East to West* (London: Longmans Green & Co., 1905); Janice N. Brownfoot, 'Memsahibs in Colonial Malaya: A Study of European Wives in a British Colony and Protectorate, 1900–1940', in Hilary Callan and Shirley Ardener (eds), *The Incorporated Wife* (London: Croom Helm, 1984), pp.186–210; Janice N. Brownfoot, 'Sisters Under the Skin: Imperialism and the Emancipation of Women in Malaya, *c*.1891–1941', in J.A. Mangan (ed.), *Making Imperial Mentalities: Socialisation and British Imperialism* (Manchester: Manchester University Press, 1990), pp.46–73; Helen Callaway, *Gender, Culture and Empire: European Women in Colonial Nigeria* (London: Macmillan, 1987); Claudia Knapman, *White Women in Fiji, 1835–1930: The Ruin of Empire?* (Sydney: Allen and Unwin, 1986).

12. Mangan, *Athleticism in the Victorian and Edwardian Public School*; Mangan, *The Games Ethic and Imperialism*, Mangan, *Pleasure, Profit and Proselytism*; Mangan, *The Cultural Bond*; Mackenzie, *Imperialism*. On the role of sport in colonial Malaya, see Janice N. Brownfoot, 'White Female Society in Colonial Malaya, 1891–1941' (Ph.D. thesis, University of Strathclyde, forthcoming); Janice N. Brownfoot, 'Emancipation, Exercise and Imperialism: Girls and the Games Ethic in Colonial Malaya', in Mangan, *The Cultural Bond*, also published in *International Journal of the History of Sport*, 7, 1 (May 1990), 61–84; John G. Butcher, *The British in Malaya 1880–1941: The Social History of a European Community in Colonial South East Asia* (Kuala Lumpur: Oxford University Press, 1979), esp. ch.4.

13. *Motor Car and Athletic Journal*, March 1908, p.5.

14. Brownfoot, 'Memsahibs', *passim*; Brownfoot, 'White Female Society', ch.4; Butcher, *The British in Malaya*, esp. ch.4; and Mrs Ada S. Ballin, 'Introduction', in Howard Spicer, *Sports for Girls* (London: Melrose, 1900). On sport and women in Britain and America during the same period, see ibid.; Mangan and Park, *From 'Fair Sex' to Feminism*; Kathleen E.

McCrone, *Sport and the Physical Emancipation of Women 1870–1914* (London: Routledge, 1988), esp. ch.7.
15. Walter Makepeace, Gilbert E. Brooke and Roland St J. Braddell, *One Hundred Years of Singapore*, 2 vols (London: John Murray, 1921), chapter on 'A Century of Sport'; and Khoo Kay Kim, 'Sportsmen in the Days of Yore', 4 June 1985, article held in the library of the *New Straits Times* (Kuala Lumpur), photocopy in the writer's possession. See also Buckley, *An Anecdotal History*, pp.304, 314, 378, 389, 566 and *passim*, and Elisabeth C.F. Alt, 'Some Memories of Elisabeth C.F. Alt 1847–1864', pp.1–64, ANU Library, Canberra, MS413. For both Malaya and the Far East in general, see George Woodcock, *The British in the Far East* (London: Weidenfeld & Nicolson, 1969), pp.190–96.
16. Anonymous, 'The Singapore Cricket Club, Its Inception and Growth', *The Motor Car and Athletics Journal*, March 1908, pp.11–13, and Alan E. Moreira, *The Malaya Sports Record* (Kuala Lumpur: Huxley, Palmer & Co., 1923), pp.1–2.
17. The Malay states began to come under formal British protection following the signing of the Pangkor Engagement in January 1874 which formalized British political involvement. See Barbara Watson and Leonard Y. Andaya, *A History of Malaysia* (London: Macmillan, 1982), pp.154–6 and ch.5.
18. On clubs see Brownfoot 'White Female Society', ch.4; Butcher, *The British in Malaya*, *passim*; D.J.M. Tate, *The Lake Club 1890–1990* (Singapore: Oxford University Press, 1990) and H. Schweizer, 'One Hundred Years of the Swiss Club of Singapore and the Swiss Community 1871–1971', unpublished MSS, copy held privately in Favre Leuba Swiss Watches Company, Singapore.
19. Brownfoot, 'White Female Society', ch.4, Butcher, *The British in Malaya*, *passim*; A. Wright and H.A. Cartwright, *Twentieth Century Impressions of British Malaya* (London: Lloyds, 1908), *passim*; Moreira, *Malaya Sports Record*, *passim*, and also note 15. When motoring first came to Malaya from the 1890s, it was seen as a recreational activity, if not a sport. Motor racing along public roads (not on specially constructed tracks) came later. Boxing and weightlifting were also introduced, but were of limited popularity among whites, as is clear from information in the magazines used for this chapter. Malaya's daily papers at the time, such as the *Straits Times*, *Malay Mail* and *Pinang Gazette*, included numerous and regular reports of sporting events and leisure activities.
20. Women-only clubs, and the role and participation of women in clubs are discussed in Brownfoot, 'White Female Society', ch.4 and Brownfoot, 'Memsahibs', p.199. See also Butcher, *The British in Malaya*, *passim*.
21. Brownfoot, 'White Female Society', ch.4 and Brownfoot, 'Memsahibs', p.199.
22. *Motor Car and Athletic Journal*, March 1908, p.20.
23. *Malayan Sports Annual*, 1928, p.23.
24. *Malayan Sports Pictorial*, 2 (April 1932), p.55.
25. For a discussion of these aspects see: Brownfoot, 'Memsahibs', *passim*; Brownfoot, 'White Female Society', various chapters; Brownfoot, 'Sisters Under the Skin', *passim*; and Brownfoot, 'Girls and the Games Ethic in Colonial Malaya', *International Journal of the History of Sport*, May 1990.
26. A few English-language schools were founded and administered by the colonial government, mainly for boys. Khoo Kay Kim mentions numbers of them in 'Sportsmen in the Days of Yore', pp.31 and 32. The Malay College, Kuala Kangsar was a notable example: for a revealing discussion of the college, its aims and English-language education for Malays, see Johan, *Educating the Malay Elite*, and Khasnor Johan, *The Emergence of the Modern Malay Administrative Elite* (Singapore: Oxford University Press, 1984). Other schools, for boys and girls, were set up and run by missionaries, especially American Methodist Episcopalians, and French and Irish nuns and priests. British Anglicans were involved in such education to a much lesser degree: the Church Missionary Society, for instance, was not active in Malaya. On the importance of sport in schools during the colonial period, see also Khoo Kay Kim, 'A Re-think If We Are to Succeed Policies and Strategies in Competitive Sports', *New Straits Times*, 22 Jan. 1987. On girls' schools, see Brownfoot, 'Girls and the Games Ethic' which includes various missionary sources and references, such as Mabel Marsh, 'The New Freedom and Athletics in Girls' Schools', *Malaysia Message*, 40, 11 (Nov. 1930). On convents

see Buckley, *An Annecdotal History*, ch.XXI; Lily Kong, Low Soon Ai and Jacqueline Yip, *Convent Chronicles* (Singapore: Armour Publishing, 1994), *passim*.
27. *Malayan Sports Annual*, 1928, p.12. For a discussion of girls schools and missionary women, see Brownfoot, 'Sisters Under the Skin', *passim*, and Brownfoot, 'Girls and the Games Ethic', pp.63–9.
28. *Malayan Sports Annual*, 1928, pp.12, 19–20.
29. Ibid., p.12.
30. Ibid.
31. *Motor Car and Athletic Journal*, 1908, p.8. See also Mangan, *The Cultural Bond*.
32. *Malayan Standard*, I, 4, 2 Sept. 1935, p.3.
33. *Malayan Sports Annual*, 1928, pp.20 and 12.
34. Ibid., p.20. Numerous examples can be found in the journals (including those used for this essay) and the newspapers of the period of players from different ethnic groups playing against each other in both single- and mixed-race teams, and competing against each other in championship matches and tournaments. To give one indoor example: at the Malayan Ping Pong Championships held in Singapore in 1932 Chinese, Japanese, Malays and an Indian team competed. See *Malayan Sports Pictorial*, 3 (1932), p.40.
35. 'Argus', 'Cricket in Malaya. Are we progressing?', *Malayan Sports Annual*, 1928, p.13.
36. *Malayan Sports Pictorial*, 2 (April 1932), p.19.
37. *Malayan Sports Annual*, 1928, p.13.
38. Ibid.
39. *Malayan Sports Pictorial*, 3 (1932), pp.15 and 40. It can only be speculated as to why the Chinese did not know about the new rules and who should have told them.
40. E. Foster Hall, 'My Impressions', *Malayan Standard*, 2 Sept. 1935, p.3.
41. The subject of ethnic relations is discussed in the writer's forthcoming thesis. It became of increasing concern throughout the 1920s and 1930s. Sport could be both a benefit and a disadvantage in promoting better inter-ethnic relations.
42. *Malayan Sports Annual*, 1928, p.12.
43. Ibid., p.11. The *Annual* gave role model examples of both westerner John Huggins, 'a sporting civil servant', and Asian Yap Kon Fah of the Selangor Chinese Recreation Club (SCRC), soccer goalkeeper in the 1920s and sportsman, who could 'be held up as an excellent example for the younger generation of players to follow'. See pp.11 and 41
44. Ibid., p.19.
45. Ibid. The writer was not strictly accurate in recording some sports as being for whites only. Various Asians, especially aristocratic Malays, also rode horses and played polo. See Moreira, *Malaya Sports Record*, pp.137–40. The writer similarly failed to mention sports for women and girls.
46. This is clear from the various reports and articles in the journals and magazines quoted. See also Brownfoot, 'Girls and the Games Ethic', *passim* and Brownfoot, 'Sisters Under the Skin', p.58.
47. See Moreira, *Malaya Sports Record*, *passim*; Johan, *Educating the Malay Elite*; and Myrna Braga-Blake, *Singapore Eurasians Memories and Hopes* (Singapore: Times Editions, 1992), as well as the various Asian published, English-language journals and magazines used for this chapter for evidence of these developments.
48. The examples of sports chosen are snapshots only of certain key aspects, not detailed descriptions, and use evidence from both the Malay Peninsula and Singapore. Owing to limited space, information on other relevant sports which Asians and Eurasians played, and at which many excelled, could not be included. Among them were tennis, boxing, weightlifting, swimming, cycling and physical culture.
49. Moreira, *Malaya Sports Record*, p.59. Moreira points out that it was also the largest spectator sport and could attract thousands. Ibid. Hence, more space has been given to soccer here because of its wide popularity among all ethnic groups as both a player and a spectator sport.
50. *Malayan Sports Annual*, 1928, p.39. The Malaya Cup had been inaugurated in 1921 following the donation of a silver cup by the captain and crew of the battleship *Malaya*. Moreira, *The Malaya Sports Record*, pp.63–4, 118–21. Soccer players were often multi-skilled in sports: Wan Puteh, one of the top Malay footballers in the 1930s was also 'a great athlete': *Sports and Pastimes* (Singapore), I, 1 (Aug. 1934), p.24.

51. Information on the Thomson Trophy from ibid., pp.39–40. Singapore Championship information from *Sports in Malaya (Review)*, I, 1 (Aug. 1939), pp.19–20. Conrad H. Clarke, well known in sporting circles throughout Malaya, donated numerous trophies and cups to Asian and Eurasian clubs and institutions, and for a wide range of sports, including soccer. See ibid., pp.15, 17; *Sports and Pastimes*, III, 5 (18 Dec. 1936), p.1, and Braga-Blake, *Singapore Eurasians*, p.139, who writes that for Clarke 'promotion of sports transcended all existing ethnic barriers in the colony'.
52. *Malayan Mirror*, I, 1 (May 1928), p.20.
53. Ibid. and *Malayan Sports Annual*, 1928, pp.43–4, 31. Throughout Malaya teams of different ethnic groups regularly played against each other. In the 1932 season of the First Division Singapore Soccer League, these included Chinese, 'Indo–Ceylonese', European and Malay: *Malayan Sports Pictorial*, 2 (1931), p.10.
54. Ibid., pp.32, 35
55. Ibid., p.32, 33. See also pp.31, 45.
56. Ibid., p.45.
57. Ibid., pp.31, 38.
58. Ibid., p.38, with quote from *Malayan Mirror*, May 1928, pp.21 and see p.20 also.
59. *Malayan Sports Annual*, 1928, p.22.
60. *Malayan Mirror*, May 1928, p.21.
61. Quote from Ibid. On costs of football see 'Fair Play', *Malayan Sports Annual*, 1928, p.22.
62. *Malayan Sports Annual*, 1928, p.22.
63. *Malayan Sports Pictorial*, 2 (April 1932), p.19.
64. 'Cricket in Malaya', *Malayan Sports Annual*, 1928, p.15.
65. Ibid.
66. 'Short Slip', 'The Australian Visit: Some Reflections', *Malayan Sports Annual*, 1928, pp.16–18. It was the Australians' only defeat. Braga-Blake, *Singapore Eurasians*, p.144.
67. *Malayan Sports Annual*, 1928, p.42.
68. *Malayan Sports Pictorial*, 3 (1932), p.40. Britain was typically referred to as 'home'.
69. 'W.A.W', 'Athletics in Malaya Remarkable Progress', *Malayan Sports Annual*, 1928, pp.25–7 (the quote is from p.26); Moreira, *The Malaya Sports Record*, pp.101–10: and Braga-Blake, *Singapore Eurasians*, pp.139–140. No championships were held between 1914 and 1919 because of the First World War. Whether the AAA was 'truly Malayan' in gender is not yet known: no women athletes' names have yet been found for the inter-war period in the records consulted for this essay.
70. 'W.A.W.', 'Athletics in Malaya', pp.26 and p.27; Moreira, *The Malaya Sports Record*, chapter on athletics, *passim*, and photograph of Eurasian H.C. Mills, champion athlete of Malaya 1922, facing p.101; Braga-Blake, *Singapore Eurasians* , pp.139–40.
71. Brownfoot, 'Girls and the Games Ethic', pp.63–9, and Brownfoot, 'Sisters Under the Skin', pp.49–54.
72. Brownfoot, 'Girls and the Games Ethic', pp.70–75. It is worth mentioning that white women also experienced a revolution in dress partly as a result of the First World War, but based also on earlier movements for dress reform, linked to developments in sport, among other factors. See, for example, Jihang Park, 'Sport, Dress Reform and the Emancipation of Women in Victorian England: A Reappraisal', *International Journal of the History of Sport*, 6, 1 (May 1989), 10–30, and McCrone, *Sport and the Physical Emancipation of English Women*.
73. Braga-Blake, *Singapore Eurasians* , p.146; *Sports and Pastimes*, Aug. 1934, pp.19 and 27.
74. *Malayan Sports Pictorial*, 2 (1932), pp.30, 31, 35, 37.
75. *Malayan Sports Pictorial*, 3 (1932), pp.7–8, 19, 22.
76. *Malayan Standard*, I, 3, 19 Aug. 1935, p.9; *Sports and Pastimes*, II, 1 (Aug. 1935), p.1.
77. *Malayan Standard*, I, 3, 19 Aug. 1935, p.9.
78. Ibid.
79. *Sports and Pastimes*, Aug. 1934, p.40; *The Sportsman* (Singapore), VI, 10 (Oct. 1933).
80. *Malayan Standard*, I, 4, 2 Sept. 1935, pp.6 and p.25.
81. Gertrude Owen, MBE, 'Aspirations of the Malayan Girl', *St Andrews Outlook*, 84 (April 1936), pp.36–7.

82. *Cycling*, I, 1 (Aug. 1937), 15; comments on 'rational dress' on p.10. See also Brownfoot, 'Girls and the Games Ethic', pp.71–2.
83. *Cycling*, I, 1 (Aug. 1937), 15.
84. *Sports and Pastimes*, II, 12 July 1936, p.4.
85. *Malayan Sports Annual*, 1928, Foreword. The *Annual* was dedicated to His Highness, HH the Sultan of Selangor, see the front page.
86. *Malayan Mirror*, May 1928, Editorial, p.1. 'Asiatics' rather than 'Asians' was the generic term commonly used in the inter-war period.
87. *The Sportsman*, I, 1 (1 Aug. 1930), cover and p.1. The magazine is available in the British Library up to Volume X, 4 (May 1937), but is incomplete. Although set up and run by Chinese, by October 1933 some of the editorial staff appeared, at least by their names, to have been either western or Eurasian.
88. *Malayan Sports Pictorial*: only issues 2 and 3, published in 1932, are extant in the British Library. On physical culturalists see issue 3 editorial.
89. *Sports and Pastimes*, I, 1 (Aug. 1934), p.1. A very professional-looking magazine, it carried lots of advertisements to assist with its funding, but the copy was not exclusively on either sport or pastimes. The last number available in the British Library is Vol.III, 5 (Dec. 1936), the front page of which shows it clearly meant to continue publication. This issue covered boxing and weightlifting more than any other sport.
90. *Sports in Malaya (Review)*, I, 1 (Aug. 1939), 'Foreword by the Editor', p.1.
91. Ibid. What happened to the publication is not known as this is the only copy held in the British Library.
92. *Super Physique*, 1, 1 (Jan 1939) to 3, 9 and 10 (Sept.–Oct. 1941). Quote from 3, 1 and 2 (Jan.–Feb. 1941), front cover.
93. Information, advertisements, competition details and a 'Contact Page for Leaguers' appeared in each issue. See for example an advertisement to 'join the Super Physique League Army' in *Super Physique*, 2, 1 (Jan.–Feb. 1940), p.6. Alsagoff, a talented self-publicist, must be admired for his innovative efforts on behalf of physical culture and health improvement in Malaya.
94. Randhir Singh, 'Did You Know', *New Straits Times* (hereafter *NST*), 17 Sept. 1984, quoting Khoo Kay Kim; Braga-Blake, *Singapore Eurasians*, p.140.
95. Braga-Blake, *Singapore Eurasians*, p.140, which reveals that Valberg came eighth in the high jump at the 1948 Olympics.
96. Singh, 'Did You Know', *NST*, 17 Sept. 1984.
97. Braga-Blake, *Singapore Eurasians*, p.141
98. 'Pinnacle of Sporting Achievement – The National Sports Awards', National Sport Foundation, 1967, p.27, document held in *New Straits Times* Library, KL, photocopy in the author's possession. On Malaysia's competitive sporting achievements in the 1950s and 1960s, see National Sport Foundation, 'A Decade of Sports in Malaysia', pp.24–6.
99. Ibid., p.27.
100. Singh, 'Did You Know', *NST*, 17 Sept. 1984, quoting Khoo Kay Kim.
101. Khoo Kay Kim, 'Sportsmen in the Days of Yore', p.32. See also Braga-Blake, *Singapore Eurasians*, p.138, on the importance of cricket for giving admission to 'higher social circles' and of sporting ability for job appointments in the colonial period.
102. This conclusion is derived from various sources, including Peter Martinez, 'Ministers in Sport: Hamzah to the Defence', *New Straits Times*, 23 May 1979; Syed Nadzri, 'Sports Officials Get the Rap from Prof Khoo', *New Straits Times*, 16 Dec. 1983; 'Government Assistance Needed to Boost Sports', *The Star*, 13 Jan. 1987; and Khoo Kay Kim, 'A Re-Think If We Are to Succeed: Policies and Strategies in Competitive Sports', *New Straits Times*, 22 Jan. 1987, together with various documents including National Sport Foundation, 1967, and Standards for Sports Facilities in Malaysia, June 1996. See below. The degree of support of and enthusiasm for sport generally appears to have depended partly on the attitudes of individual government ministers concerning its importance.
103. National Sport Foundation, 1967, quotes from p.7. The Foundation's establishment was informed by Australian and New Zealand experience and it anticipated raising money from commercial and private organizations and individuals. Its initial funding was by tobacco company Rothmans of Pall Mall.

104. Evidence from various sources, including Martinez, 'Ministers in Sport'; National Sport Foundation, 'A Decade of Sports in Malaysia', p.24; Khoo, 'A Re-think'.
105. Martinez, 'Ministers in Sport'; Syed Nadzri, 'Sports Officials Get the Rap'; *The Star*, 'Government Assistance Needed'; Khoo, 'A Re-think'; 'Stand Up for Yourself' and 'Sports Conference Policy Resolutions', *NST*, 22 Jan. 1987.
106. Ibid., as in note 105. Quote is from *The Star*, 'Government Assistance Needed'.
107. Khoo, 'A Re-think'. To help develop sport, especially competitively, Khoo also suggested that a Sport Institute be set up.
108. National Sports Policy, January 1988, p.1, document held in *New Straits Times* Library, KL, photocopy in the author's possession. See also 'Stand Up for Yourself' and 'Sports Conference Policy Resolutions'.
109. Standards for Sports Facilities in Malaysia, *c.* June 1996, document held in *New Straits Times* Library, KL, photocopy in the author's possession. This document defines 'high performance sport' as 'competitive sports' organized under international rules and conditions, and 'mass sport' as 'sports and physical recreational activities' for all, at any age, based on individual capability and aimed at greater participation rather than competition (p.3).
110. For evidence of points made in the conclusion, see in particular Johan, *Educating the Malay Elite*, *passim*, and *The Emergence of the Modern Malay Administrative Elite*, *passim*; Braga-Blake, *Singapore Eurasians*, esp. p.138.

6

Cricket in Colonial India: The Bombay Pentangular, 1892–1946

BORIA MAJUMDAR

I

This essay charts the relationship between cricket and an emerging urban society in India in the first half of the twentieth century through an analysis of the Bombay Pentangular cricket tournament. The foremost tournament in pre-partition India, the Bombay Pentangular, controlled by the communal gymkhanas[1] in the city, had its inception in the Presidency matches of the 1890s.[2] These matches were initially played between the Europeans and the Parsees. In course of time, the Pentangular tournament came into existence, with the inclusion of the Hindus in 1907, the Muslims in 1912 and the 'Rest', comprising mainly Christians and Anglo-Indians in 1937. Despite considerable opposition, the tournament continued until the 1940s, to be finally abolished in January 1946.[3] The eventual discontinuance, as existing historiography would tell us, was the outcome of prolonged agitation against the communal organization of the tournament. However, beneath this politically correct rhetoric, aligned with the broader vision of a secular nation state, may be found deeper politico-economic factors, which played a significant role in guiding the course of the anti-Pentangular movement. The influence of these forces of commercialization, bureaucratization and professionalism, components of a heightened urban consciousness in Bombay/Indian society of the early twentieth century remains obscure in any study of sport in the Indian context.

It needs to be stated at the outset that leisure and its significance has been a much-neglected arena in historical analysis. It is only recently, as Peter Bailey has argued, that it has been viewed in its own light, as a significant element of social experience, the history of which is of particular importance in the broader exercise of reconstructing the kind of lives led by ordinary people in the past.[4] A similar claim can be made for sport. For instance, as Hobsbawm has argued, sport has only recently been perceived as one of the most important social practices of Europe in the late nineteenth and early twentieth centuries.[5] While historical matters of far less importance have had their recorders and commentators and their conferences and literature, historians have taken a very long time to appreciate the relevance of sport. This discrepancy is all the more pronounced for erstwhile colonies like India.

In India, 'sport', as Ram Guha rightly points out, should be 'viewed as a relational idiom, a sphere of activity which expresses in concentrated form, the values, prejudices, divisions and unifying symbols of society'.[6] Cricket, he contends in his essay on the history of the sport in colonial Bombay, 'helps to understand the fissures and tensions of a deeply divided society ... and provides valuable insights into the history of modern India, in particular about the histories of race, caste and religion in the country'.[7] While Guha's assertions are largely true, he too, like most historians of the sport, has often assumed in conformity with the ideals of play that cricket, a 'gentlemanly' sport, could only serve to remedy social ills. The existing historiography of Indian cricket has portrayed the game in chaste terms, as being a social unifier cutting across class boundaries, a civilizing agent and a cultural bond striving to overcome communal divisions.[8] Anything 'national', it is assumed in the Indian context, should be free of the vices of communalism.[9] The communal organization of the game in Bombay, it followed, was an obstacle in the path of an emerging secular nation. This assumption has given birth to the view that the Pentangular was abolished because of its communal organization, which went against the ideals of a secular Indian nation. The following passage bears testimony to this argument:

> I can only view sport in its national setting and would have time for sport only if it led to greater national well being – national health and, what is far more important in India to day, national character. This is no mere platitude and is more than a truism. Communalism is indisputably the bane of Indian political life and, for that matter, of Indian national life. It would follow therefore, even as two and two is four that communal cricket is opposed to national cricket.[10]

I would, however, argue that, much more than communal antagonism, it was the diverse forces shaping the face of Bombay society of the 1930s and 1940s that influenced the course of the game's evolution, aspects of analysis neglected in existing historiography. It is recorded that in 1924, when the Muslims won the Pentangular tournament, the Hindus joined them in their victory celebrations.[11] This, it needs to be stated, was despite the strained relations between the two communities after the failure of the joint non-cooperation/Khilafat agitation. Muslim representation in the Indian National Congress had reached dismal proportions after Gandhi called off the non-co-operation agitation in 1922,[12] with severe communal discord culminating in riots and arson. In an ambience of growing communal contrariety in the country, Mohammed Ali Jinnah had praised the brotherly feeling that was manifested between the two communities on the sporting field of the Pentangular (then the Quadrangular) in 1924. These facts make it clear that a social history of cricket in India cannot be written simply in terms of the overarching concerns of Indian historical scholarship on sport, nationalism and communalism. This argument is strengthened further by the following eyewitness account of the 1944 Pentangular by Vasant Raiji – the final of the 1944 tournament was a closely contested match between the Hindus and the Muslims, in which the Muslims won with less than five minutes of the match remaining:

> Unprecedented scenes of jubilation followed. Ibrahim, the hero and architect of the Muslim victory (he had carried his bat for 137) was chaired by the supporters and carried shoulder high all the way to the pavilion. Never before had the Brabourne stadium witnessed a match so thrilling and exciting as this. Communalism was nowhere in evidence and everyone, including the Hindus, cheered the Muslim team at the end of the match. Merchant, the Hindu captain, went to the Muslim dressing room and hugged Mushtaq Ali warmly with the words, 'Well played Muslims, you deserved to win. It would have been a sad day for cricket if you had lost.'[13]

This essay attempts to retrieve the wider context within which the dynamics of the game evolved and operated, through a study of the Bombay Pentangular tournament. Much more than clashes between imperialism and nationalism, between communalism and secularism, cricket has to be understood in terms of the practices of everyday life in Indian society. The emergence of salaried middle-class professionals with an investment in leisure, increased leisure opportunities for workers with newly structured hours of work and the growth of a commercial culture in colonial India shaped the fortunes of our *de facto*[14] national sport. Yet historians attempting to study the history of the game have failed to transcend the overarching nationalist/communal historiographical paradigm. It is my objective to fill this lacuna in existing historiography by going beyond the assumptions and prejudices that have moulded it, and studying leisure as a part of regular urban existence in colonial India.

The Pentangular tournament was central to the urban life of Bombay in the 1930s and 1940s, as is evident from the extensive coverage it received in contemporary newspapers and journals.[15] Such investment in leisure was, of course, not restricted to cricket and horse racing; boat racing and basketball also became increasingly popular in Bombay society at this period. The sporting clientele came from a wide cross-section of society and were not restricted to the middle or the working classes:

> In a relatively poor neighbourhood like Nagpada, the sporting facilities offered by clubs like the Mastan YMCA and the Nagpada Neighbourhood house were rare and seized upon. People realised that keeping their children on the basketball courts meant that they would be off the street and less susceptible to the various malevolent temptations on offer.[16]

Like sport, other forms of leisure such as the cinema, recent researches indicate,[17] also acquired a mass following in Bombay in the 1920s and 1930s.[18] It is in terms of the dynamics of such a society, where leisure was in the process of becoming structured, that the anti-Pentangular movement needs to be analyzed.

An analysis of this movement helps demonstrate the centrality of sport in colonial India's socio-economic and political life, despite a typically Indian antipathy to recognizing the truth of the matter and categorizing it as mere 'leisure' or an 'entertainment' pursuit. The following sections of this essay, by undertaking an analysis of the significance of sport as a viable 'profession' in colonial India, and its worth as a commercial enterprise, raise fundamental questions regarding the understanding of leisure in the Indian context. This study also intervenes in existing historical debates on communalism by bringing into its ambit this very important arena of Indian social life. Contrary to the conventional understanding of the impact of communalism, cricket in India, as I see it, benefited from its communal/sectarian organization.[19]

However, before proceeding to analyze the agitation against the Pentangular, it is essential to take into account the social and economic changes taking place in Bombay society between the 1910s and 1940s – factors that, I will demonstrate, shaped the course of the protests against the tournament from the 1930s.

II

Following the plague of 1896 Bombay underwent fundamental structural transformation. The panic created by disease and overcrowding in a period marked by great political uncertainties convinced the colonial government and the city elite of the need to revamp urban spaces in order to make them safer and more governable. Through the early decades of the twentieth century Bombay grew from a cluster of distinct localities into an industrial megalopolis. Above all, the changes in the first three decades of the century inculcated a set of cultural and social attitudes among the inhabitants of Bombay that were to control the city's fortunes in times to come.

Simultaneously, communitarian bonds were strengthened in the city, as is evident from the nature of the caste-based cooperative housing movement, the communal organization of sports and the rules governing the use of civic amenities. This period also witnessed a significant improvement in transportation facilities, one that was complemented by an improving system of telecommunication and a surge in the spread of civic amenities.[20]

The improvement in systems of communication may be related to the geographical expansion of the city. With the development of the suburbs, from where people regularly commuted to the city for work, an improved system of transportation became necessary. Likewise, concern resulting from the toll taken by the plague led to an improvement in systems of sanitation and sewerage. Facilities for education and recreation also improved significantly, in an atmosphere of heightened consciousness regarding social welfare. Tanks deemed to be health hazards were filled in as part of welfare programmes of the Bombay Improvement Trust, and were often converted into sites for recreation. The basketball club in Mastan Talao, which still survives, is one of the enduring products of this initiative.[21]

Such transformation of the face of urban Bombay fostered the rise of a number of socially mobile groups in the city from the second decade of the twentieth century. Unlike in other regions of colonial India, the growth of Indian entrepreneurial initiative in Bombay led to an unprecedented commercial expansion. People from surrounding regions converged on Bombay in search of livelihood, resulting in the emergence of Bombay as the nerve-centre of economic activity in the country from the early decades of the twentieth century.

An analysis of the population of Bombay in this period shows that there were critical shifts between the late nineteenth and early twentieth centuries. For the first time since the plague, which had led to a sharp drop, the population of Bombay rose steeply in the first decade of the twentieth century. Between 1901 and 1904, an average of 83,650 people were entering the city annually. In 1904 approximately 215,682 people entered Bombay, followed by 332,436 people in 1905 and 101,185 in 1906.[22] Large-scale migration from the neighbouring regions to the city made housing a serious problem in Bombay.

The expansion of the city, together with large-scale immigration, was responsible for a significant transformation in prevalent social codes. Multi-caste social gatherings such as religious festivals, as well as schools and colleges, where students of all castes mixed freely, became commonplace in the city from the early years of the twentieth century. Nevertheless, community life remained an important consideration in the life of the inhabitants of Bombay. This explains the communal organization of sport, often arising out of an effort to foster and establish links with one's communal group. It was the novel experience of living in rented rooms in the unfamiliar landscape of the city, together with the unaccustomed rigours of office work and notions of a loss of caste and kin ties, that fostered the growth of communal organization of sport.

As is the case in other cities elsewhere in the world, the anonymity of urban living generated widespread anxieties among the inhabitants of Bombay. The growing investment in leisure in the early decades of the twentieth century may, therefore, be regarded as an important aspect of the endeavour on the part of the common man to acclimatize with his new surroundings.

The establishment of a bureaucratized work ethic accompanied the changing face of Bombay. Offices and commercial institutions came to be characterized by salaried employment, and gave birth to a new class of professionals. Having to accustom himself to the work ethic of the office, the salaried professional now came to be regulated by a code of discipline hitherto unknown. He was now accountable to the institution that employed him, displacing earlier modes of accountability to the family or community. The 1920s, therefore, saw the growing familiarity of the inhabitants of Bombay with a new disciplined commercial work culture and the growth of a meritocracy. Leisure was an arena where an identity based on merit could be established.

This changing face of Bombay brought with it an improved standard of living for the inhabitants of the city. Working hours in most factories were limited to ten hours a day, with compulsory holidays on weekends. The demand for skilled labour in the factories was high, and with supply being fairly low in the 1920s, workers were able to negotiate favourable wages. Fixed hours of work and favourable wages led to increased investment in leisure activities. This explains the growing popularity in the 1920s of the cinema,[23] the theatre, music shows and sport.

After a lull in Bombay sporting activity between 1915 and 1920,[24] sports emerged as an arena of mass spectacle in the 1920s. The growing popularity of sports is manifest in the unprecedented coverage of the Bombay Pentangular in the pages of leading dailies such as the *Bombay Chronicle* and *The Times of India*. Newspapers and magazines devoted more space to sports photographs than to those of any other category.[25] All kinds of sporting activity grew in popularity but people were especially attracted to the Derby and the Pentangular, as shown by their coverage in the mass media. The renewed popularity of the Pentangular was an established fact by the late 1920s, as the *Bombay Chronicle* of 28 November 1929 demonstrates. In it we read that 'The two weeks of the Pentangular were the climax of the cricket (and social) season, when the finest talents of India battled one another on the maidan.'[26] As the competition approached in November 1929 the city, it was argued, was swept by a furious epidemic. 'In London you have the Poppy Day, New Year's Eve, the Varsity Boat Race, Epsom, the Test matches. But in Bombay you go on working and clubbing and grubbing the whole year round except in this week.'[27] This popularity was further heightened in the 1930s with the initiation of running radio commentary on the matches, when 'office goers, eager for news, thronged hotels and other public places where receivers had been installed'.[28] However, even before the days of radio,

> You could hear reactions of the spectators in the corridors of Hornby Road, you could feel that great things were happening, that offices were denuded of clerks, especially in the afternoon and in rickety old rooms, whose access is through dark staircases amidst

ancient files and briefs, there came the muffled voices of ten thousand spectators, a call from afar, which made work impossible and narrowed Bombay to that sunny green spot, where our heroes were making hearts beat pit-a-pat.[29]

The rising fortunes of Bombay claimed the attentions of the rich and famous of the country. Princes and moneyed men, wishing to carve out a niche for themselves in the social circles of this emerging megalopolis, began dabbling in the local politics of the city. The Bawla murder case was an indication of the extent to which the city had become embroiled in the politics of the princely states of the region.[30] Some of these men, failing to secure a toehold in the city, became the bitterest detractors of those who did, often opposing significant events of the city's public life.

The burgeoning of the city of Bombay discussed above, and its growing significance in the social, economic and political life of the country, I will argue in the following sections of this chapter, had much to do with the strong protests against established structures of leisure in the city. Leisure activities in Bombay, the Pentangular being the best case in point, were commercially viable unlike in other parts of the country. This made them the envy of rival competitive interests. The rise of concerted protests against the Pentangular, therefore, has to be located against the wider canvas of the dynamics of urban life, and the analysis obliges one to rethink the dominant paradigms of the existing historiography of Indian cricket.

III

In Bombay, the first group to have taken to cricket were the Parsees.[31] They started playing cricket in the mid-nineteenth century when a British schoolteacher, Boswell, introduced the game to Parsee boys in a Bombay school.[32]

The first Parsee Cricket Club was the Oriental Cricket Club established in 1848.[33] Its closure a couple of years later was followed by the establishment of the Zorastrian Club in 1850, followed by the Mars Club in 1860, the Spartan Club in 1865 and the Young Zorastrian Cricket Club in 1867.[34] The first four clubs did not survive long and the Young Zorastrian Cricket Club was the lone survivor into the twentieth century.[35] In 1872, the Elphinstone Cricket Club was founded and initiated the practice of tours all round the country. In the late 1880s several other Parsee cricket clubs were established, though only a handful of them, such as the John Bright Cricket Club, Persian Cricket Club and Naoroz Cricket Club, survived. By 1910 the number of the Parsee clubs had increased considerably leading to the introduction of an inter-Parsee club tournament called the Shapur Spencer Cricket Challenge Cup. The Elphinstone, Baronet, Young Zorastrian, Sassanian, Marine Liberal, John Bright, Naoroz, Esplanade Liberals, Dadar Parsee Colony, Parsee Engineers, Prince Rising Star, Parsee Venus, Lancelot and Parsee Cyclists all took part in this tournament.[36]

Following the Parsees, the Hindus started playing cricket, partly in a spirit of competitive communalism, for in Bombay they were long-standing business rivals of the Parsees. The first Hindu cricket club, the Bombay Union, was established in 1866.[37] Whereas Parsee clubs often derived their nomenclature from localities in the city, Hindu cricketers tended to be grouped on the lines of caste and religion of origin. This is evident from the names of their clubs established in the latter part of the nineteenth century: the Gowd Saraswat Cricket Club, Kshatriya Cricket Club, Gujarati Cricket club, Maratha Cricket Club and Telegu Young Cricketers.[38] In course of time the Hindus too, in the manner of the Parsees, started their own cricket tournament, the Purshottam Hindu Cricket Challenge Shield tournament in 1912, with the declared intention of fostering Hindu cricket talent in the region. Initially it was played during the monsoons on a league basis. Later it was thrown open to members of all communities.[39]

The Muslims came to cricket late. It was in the 1880s that they first established cricket clubs of their own.[40] These were later amalgamated to form the Islam Gymkhana in 1892. Muslim cricket was pioneered by M.B. Lukmani and B.A. Lukmani together with the Tyabjees, men of standing in the educational and public life of the Muslim community.[41]

Together with the principal communities of the city, other smaller groups also started their own cricket clubs, namely the Mangalorian Catholic Cricket Club (for emigrés from the southern port city of Mangalore), the Instituto Luso Indian Cricket Club (for those coming from Portuguese-ruled Goa) and the Bombay Jewish Cricket Club.[42]

During his tenure as governor of Bombay between 1890 and 1895, Lord Harris used reclaimed land on the seafront of the back bay to allot plots to the cricket clubs of the Hindus, the Muslims and the Parsees. The plots were authorized by the government on 12 September 1892, for a meagre annual rent of 12 rupees.[43] This simultaneous allocation to the three communities had the dual effect of placing them on equal terms with the European members of the Bombay Gymkhana and preventing unpleasantness between the communities themselves.[44]

From the very beginning, therefore, cricket in Bombay was organized along communal lines. a form of organization that often resulted in ill feeling among the rival communities, as is evident from a description in the *Indian Social Reformer* of 1906: 'The Hindu boys played in *dhotis*, without shoes or boots, bowled under-hand and made all the mistakes of novices. Parsee players, far more advanced by then, ridiculed the Hindus for their dress and style of play.'[45] This episode, the *Indian Social Reformer* states, resulted in the generation of bad blood between the two communities.[46]

Despite such manifestations of the disruptive potential of the sport's communal organization, it was only from the 1930s that protests started in earnest against this communal organization. Further, the protests were exclusively directed against the Bombay Pentangular and ignored other tournaments organized on communal lines in the city itself, the rest of the province and in other parts of the country. It may be mentioned here that the popularity of the Pentangular and its commercial success had spawned a series of tournaments along similar lines from the second decade of the twentieth century.[47] The Sind Quadrangular, later renamed the Karachi Pentangular, had started in 1916; a Central Provinces pentangular had started in the 1920s; a triangular had started in Delhi in 1937; in Lahore also there was a similar communal competition.[48]

Some historians have tried to explain the delayed nature of the anti-Pentangular movement by suggesting that it was in the 1920s and 1930s that the socially disruptive potential of the communal Pentangular was perceived.[49] This argument follows from Gyan Pandey's contention that it was only from the 1920s that people began to think of a united Indian nation. Prior to this period, as Pandey states,

> the nation of Indians were visualised as a composite body, consisting of several communities, each with its own history and culture and its own special contribution to make to the common nationality. India and the emerging Indian nation was conceived of as a collection of communities: – Hindu + Muslim + Christian + Parsi + Sikh, and so on.[50]

Sometime around the 1920s this perception was transformed and India came to be seen as a nation, and not merely a body of motley individuals

Cricket in Colonial India, 1892–1946

or communities. This change, viewed by Pandey as fundamental, has been regarded as crucial in influencing contemporary notions of the disruptive potential of communalism in the country.

Empirical data, however, show that the sporting world was already aware of the harmful effects of communalism by the 1890s. Shapoorji Sorabjee Bengali, India's first cricket historian, had already referred to the potential dangers of communalism in the last decade of the nineteenth century in the following words: 'To expect all political difference to disappear or all available self-interest to be foregone on the institution of cricket relations is to live in a fool's paradise.'[51]

B.R. Kagal expresses a similar sentiment in his memories of the Pentangular. He argued that the consequences of communally organized club cricket in Bombay in the first two decades of the twentieth century were far from satisfactory. The crowd was always guided by divisive communal sentiments and there were cases when the police had to intervene to maintain law and order:

> I have recollections, as a small boy, of having witnessed more than one scene of this kind from the pavilion of one of the leading Gymkhanas. Of course, it must be admitted that the participants in these 'melees' came mostly from the 'mavali' or the 'goonda' class but that did not prevent more respectable classes of people getting occasionally mixed up either by accident or even through indiscreet and misplaced enthusiasm. No wonder parents forcibly kept boys away from matches, which should have proved, in most cases, a source of valuable cricket education.
>
> Looking back nearly 35 years, I distinctly recollect thoughts and reactions which I would be ashamed to own up [to] publicly at present. Worse still, I remember vividly how on returning home after some of these all absorbing contests, small boys would join groups of elders carrying on heated discussion on even slight incidents which almost always ended in the denunciation of the communal traits and failings of those teams that opposed the group's favourite or communal team. It was not unusual, in the first decade of the century, to find a couple of lathis stored in the kit bag, along with the gear, as a matter of pure precaution. At least that used to be the explanation invariably advanced in answer to child like and innocent curiosity by he young enthusiastic cricketer proceeding to the 'maidan'. What was unfortunate, was the

mistrust and the sense of insecurity that was evident from these most sincere explanations; and this while proceeding for a friendly sporting encounter, for a game and for recreation.[52]

Kagal goes on to say that the state of things improved somewhat from the beginning of the second decade of the century. The reason, according to him, was the proliferation of cricket at the college and university levels. The same players who played together for their college or university fought it out for their respective communities in the Pentangular. The existing camaraderie between these players had a steadying influence on the communal encounters. In the absence of malice among the players, communal passions among the audience too came to be tempered. Friends from college or university adhered to the gentlemanly norms of the game, diffusing the spirit of animosity and hatred among the crowd.

The above recorded observations and analyses of contemporaries make it clear that the reasons behind the delayed protest against the Pentangular cannot be sought in a retarded comprehension of the impact of communalism. Rather it has to be analyzed with reference to the emergence of Bombay as the leading commercial centre of the country, with a concentration of capital resources. The commercial viability and glamour associated with the Pentangular, missing from the other tournaments played in the country, made it an object of envy to rival sporting bodies. Princely figures like the Maharjkumar of Vizianagram (Vizzy), who wielded great power in the cricketing circles of the country but who had no place in the Bombay tournament, soon emerged as detractors of the Pentangular. Also significant was the growing commercial viability of the sport that had, by the 1930s, made the Bombay tournament an object of envy to other cricket associations, including the Board of Control for Cricket in India. Finally, the growing viability of cricket as a career option, one that intensified after the launching of the *Times of India* Shield in 1931, played its part in making the Pentangular the site for a show of defiance on the part of the players towards their erstwhile princely patrons. These factors taken together contributed to the launching of the crusade against the Pentangular in the 1930s.

It was from the late 1920s, particularly after the establishment of the Board of Control for Cricket in India in 1928 and the establishment of the Ranji Trophy in 1934 under the aegis of the board,[53] that the movement against the Pentangular gathered momentum. Echoing the sentiments of the anti-Pentangular movement, the *Bombay Chronicle* of 27 November 1935 stated: 'Communal tournaments were, perhaps, necessary at a certain stage in the history of Indian cricket. Scarcely conducive to the growth of healthy nationalism, it is time they were given a decent burial.'[54] Its sports editor, J.C. Maitra, consistently wrote in support of the Ranji Trophy and against the continuation of the Pentangular.[55] Echoing similar sentiments, Berry Sarbadhikary argued:

> Communal cricket must go by the board and be buried – five fathoms deep. That is as things stand to day. There might not have been, at the outset, anything 'communal' about communal cricket in the accepted sense of the word as Anthony S. De. Mello submitted when the controversy had been raging fiercely and fully a few years ago. There may not be anything communal about it even to day so far as the players and spectators are concerned as has been laboriously claimed with the aid of a whole heap of evidence. But the fact remains that once the controversy gathered the fierceness and the momentum it did, once communal cricket was dissected and decried or patched up and praised by politicians or cricketers, by the press and the public in the manner it was done, communal cricket became communal straightaway. Only communal cricket is basically wrong and although synonymous with the cream of Indian cricket once, it has now outlived its usefulness, to say nothing of its being not indispensable to Indian cricket any more.[56]

While these men were conscientious objectors to communal cricket, others like the Maharjkumar of Vizianagram and the Maharaja of Patiala, influential members of the Board of Control and the state cricket associations used similar rhetoric to conceal ulterior motives in their crusade against the Pentangular.

IV

The movement against the abolition of the Pentangular reached its zenith with Gandhi's pronouncement against the tournament on 7 December 1940.[57] Close scrutiny, however, reveals that the Mahatma's verdict had been selectively publicized by the opposing lobby to suit its ends. This becomes evident from an analysis of the entire text of the Mahatma's plea, which is never referred to in its entirety in existing historiography. On being met by a select delegation of the Hindu Gymkhana at Wardha, the Mahatma had remarked:

> Numerous enquiries have been made as to my opinion on the proposed Pentangular cricket match in Bombay advertised to be played on the 14th. I have just been made aware of the movement to stop the match. I understand this as a mark of grief over the arrests and imprisonments of the *satyagrahis*, more especially the recent arrest of leaders.[58]

He went on to add:

> I would discountenance such amusements at a time when the whole of the thinking world should be in mourning over a war that is threatening the stable life of Europe and its civilisation and which bids to overwhelm Asia. ... And holding this view I naturally welcome the movement for stopping the forthcoming match from the narrow standpoint I have mentioned above.[59]

It was only after this statement that he went on to condemn the communal nature of the tournament, a denunciation often quoted in existing historiography.[60] Even the headline in the *Bombay Chronicle* that reported the Mahatma's stand read: 'No Festival when world in mourning', and it was only in a sub-heading that it was stated 'Communal code in sport condemned'.[61]

Despite the Mahatma's declaration of his disapproval of the competition, there were no signs of declining interest in the Pentangular matches. The very next day after Gandhi had issued his statement, the *Times of India* reported:

> With Bombay's great annual cricket festival only a few days ahead the Pentangular fever is at its height, a height that has rarely been attained before. Large crowds watched all the three trial matches played over the weekend. ... Although rumours had been set afoot that there would be a serious attempt made by a large procession of students to compel the authorities to abandon the trial more than 500 enthusiasts gathered on Saturday afternoon for the start, and the number was almost doubled the next day.[62]

In a similar vein, when a resolution was tabled at the Hindu Gymkhana calling for a withdrawal from the tournament, it had the support of only 70 members of the Gymkhana. The members in favour of the resolution were less than ten per cent of the total membership of the Gymkhana, which stood at 900.

Though this resolution was eventually passed by a small margin of 37 votes (280–243), particularly as a mark of regard for Gandhi's pronouncement against the tournament, it generated serious ill feeling among the members themselves. A prominent member of the Gymkhana, who had supported the resolution, stated later that the managing committee of the Gymkhana had been unwise in deciding to seek Gandhi's opinion on the subject. He went on to state that once they had done so it was their duty to abide by it without question and not go against it, for that would have been a mark of disrespect towards the Mahatma.[63]

However, Gandhi's stand did provoke considerable opposition from most of the small Hindu cricket clubs of Bombay. It was pointed out that many of these clubs, which barely managed to eke out an existence on the profits accruing from the Pentangular, had already invested their meagre capital in securing seats at the Brabourne Stadium, the venue for the tournament. In the event of the withdrawal of the Hindus from the competition, interest was expected to wane to such an extent as to make the sale of tickets impossible, and would bring in its wake ruin for these clubs. This, it was argued, would be unfair in view of the wholehearted support accorded by the Hindus and Hindu clubs, both in Bombay and in the *mofussil*, to the Hindu Gymkhana in times of crisis.[64] These clubs emphasized that the Hindu Gymkhana should not overlook the fact that it was a Hindu representative XI that was expected to participate in the Pentangular and not a Hindu Gymkhana team. Accordingly, it was regarded inconceivable that any drastic action could be implemented on the decision of the 900-odd members of the Hindu Gymkhana alone. A decision that was expected to affect thousands of Hindus, it was agreed, was expected to take into account their interests and opinion.

V

Within a couple of weeks of Gandhi's pronouncement against the Pentangular, the Maharajkumar of Vizianagram, who wielded considerable power in the Board of Control, declared:

> Mahatma Gandhi has expressed unequivocally on communal cricket. He gave it as his considered opinion that communalism carried into the domain of sport is no happy augury for human growth. It is high time that we gave Pentangular cricket the burial it always deserved.[65]

He was supported by the Jam of Nawanagar and the Maharaja of Patiala, who went on to assert that no Nawanagar or Patiala player would be available for any match conducted on communal lines. Cricketers employed by these princes, it was expected, would not have the audacity to defy their orders, as defiance would have rendered them jobless. Such lobbying against the Bombay Pentangular brings into sharp focus the covert agenda behind the anti-Pentangular movement.

Suspicions regarding the motives of the patrician lobby acquire potency in the light of the fact that only the commercially successful Bombay Pentangular had been singled out to bear the brunt of their wrath, when similar 'communal' tournaments continued to be played in Sind, the Central Provinces, Nagpur and Berar.[66] Significantly, it was around this time that the Congress government in Bombay converted swimming baths in the city into communal ones with separate bathing times for Hindus, Muslims and Parsees.[67] The absence of protest against this action of the Congress government makes it evident that the motives of the protesters, though couched in the politically correct idiom of secularism, were rooted in other considerations.

The opposition of the aristocrats was also fuelled by their disapproval of a growing professionalism in cricket, through which the sport was emerging as a viable career option independent of princely patronage. This was in keeping with the new individualistic work culture and commercial ethic of Bombay. P.N. Polishwalla highlighted a concern with professionalism in the *Indian Cricket Annual* of 1933:

> The next question, which is of vital importance, is that of 'professionalism'. This is an honest living and should be fondly encouraged like other arts. Even if a certain portion of these poor cricketers is getting ready for this profession, India would be doing some duty to sport in general and cricket in particular. We must devise means of regularly encouraging this class of cricketers and in order to do this we must help the would be professionals in such a manner as to change their aspect completely; to effect such a change we must place them into absolutely new surroundings and on a sound footing. Now if we were to spend only rupees one lac throughout India in establishing cricket clubs for professionals on the scale of 'Faulkner's school of London', we shall with the help of two or three professionals in course of a few years be not only maintaining large numbers of honest professional players, enjoying

the fruits of their own labour but also uplifting the standard of the game in the country.[68]

He goes on to say that it was regrettable that despite the growing interest in games in the country, there were no sporting journals and illustrated weeklies. Such journals and magazines, he believed, had contributed to improvement of team games like cricket and soccer in England.

This dearth of sporting literature, lamented by Polishwalla, is striking because cricket was being played by a large number of upwardly mobile and educated Indians, and their numbers were on the rise. Even when attempts were made to launch ventures to generate sport literature they met with little success. In 1929, an attempt was made to start a fortnightly journal in Bombay, but this initiative collapsed after a brief spell of a year and a half. A similar effort was made in Karachi in 1930 where a monthly sporting magazine was started, but folded within a year for lack of monetary support.[69]

The growing concern with professionalism in sport, however, soon began to yield desired results. In 1934, the Cricket Club of India started *Indian Cricket*, a monthly magazine, which continued till 1939.[70] It was followed by the *Indian Cricket Annual*,[71] *Crickinia* and other periodicals.[72]

In Bombay, the launching of the *Times of India* Challenge Shield in 1931 stimulated an already growing professionalism in cricket. This tournament, as Richard Cashman argues, attracted very large crowds. In the absence of any gate fee, thousands thronged to the grounds to watch the stars in action. A large crowd ensured good publicity for the companies taking part, a fact that made them look upon the tournament as an important event in their social calendar. Crowds often ranged between 5,000 and 10,000, numbers any company would consider a good turnout in the 1930s. The *Times* Shield began in 1930 with 24 teams from business houses, colleges and 'public services' taking part. It was a knockout affair and the matches were played in the monsoon months. The scale of participation soon improved and by the 1940s the *Times* Shield attracted the best talents of the city. D.D. Hindlekar, India's leading wicket-keeper, played for the Bombay Port Trust in the late 1930s, L.P. Jai played for Imperial Bank, P. Summerhayes for Burmah Shell and D.R. Havewalla for the BB and CI Railway. Though there were no special privileges for the cricketers in the early years of patronage, they received salaries comparable to those of college graduates, irrespective of whether they had graduated or not.[73] Corporate patronage, it needs to be stated, existed in Bombay cricket even before the *Times* Shield. Pioneers in this regard were the BB and CI Railway in the 1920s. The BB and CI Railway (now Western Railway) played a significant role in the development of a professional structure in cricket by giving jobs to a number of cricketers, especially those who had displayed their talents in the Quadrangular.[74] The determining role in the proliferation of professional cricket was, however, played by the Bombay Pentangular. The players who took part in the Pentangular realized that a victory in the tournament would give them considerable media coverage and publicity. The Pentangular tournament, they realized, was the arena where they could reap the highest economic rewards for their sporting prowess, and become cynosures of public attention in the process. This element of economic gain was stimulated by the presence of corporate patronage, which though still in its infancy was making its presence felt in Indian cricket. The launch of the *Times* Shield and the commercial endorsements made by leading Indian cricketers from the late 1930s bear testimony to the point.[75] Even lesser known stars had started endorsing consumer items as early as the late 1930s.[76]

Prowess shown on the sporting field of the Pentangular, it was also realized, would enable players to break away from princely control. In November 1940 Wazir Ali, the captain of the Muslim team, issued a press statement claiming that 'the tournament is not in the least antinational and will and must go on in the interests of Indian cricket'.[77] In November 1941 C.K. Nayadu issued the following statement in retaliation against the pronouncements of Vizzy and the Maharaja of Patiala:

> There is no valid reason why the Pentangular tournament in Bombay should be stopped. On the contrary it is absolutely essential that it should be run in its present form if we do not want to see the funeral of Indian cricket.[78]

He concluded by stating:

> the Pentangular provides a fortnight of first class cricket and is in my opinion the greatest cricket tournament in the world. It would indeed be a pity and the certain death of Indian cricket if the Pentangular were abolished at the present time when Indian players have so little opportunity of playing first class cricket.[79]

Vijay Merchant, Vijay Hazare, C.S. Nayadu and Mushtaq Ali, all cricketers of repute, expressed similar views with regard to the tournament.

The anti-Pentangular movement, therefore, emerged as the arena of contest between the princes and the players, both seeking to dominate the game and enjoy the advantages such dominance brought in its wake. This rivalry, an age-old phenomenon in Indian cricket, had reached its height in the 1930s. At a time when the political influence of the princes was on the wane, their efforts to retain social ascendancy led them to indulge in desperate attempts to reinforce their control over sport. The strong arm of the Maharajas was palpable in the 1936 tour of England, when the best player, Lala Amarnath, was forced to return on grounds of 'indiscipline'.[80] On the same tour, Shunte Banerjee of Bengal was deprived of a Test berth for defying an order of the captain, the Maharaja of Vizianagram, and refusing to abuse C.K. Nayadu at the breakfast table. Baqa Jilani, who carried out the order, earned for himself a maiden Test cap.[81]

The commercial potential of the Pentangular also affected relations between the sporting gymkhanas, the organizers of the Pentangular. During the 1937 tournament, there was severe disagreement between them over the allocation of seats in the Brabourne Stadium. The Cricket Club of India (CCI), which owned the Brabourne Stadium, had allotted an equal number of seats to all the participating gymkhanas, alienating the Hindu Gymkhana, which, having membership much larger than its Muslim, Parsee and Catholic counterparts, preferred an allocation on the basis of the membership strength of each gymkhana. This preference was influenced by the realization that a larger share of seats would inevitably bring in its wake a larger share of revenue from gate receipts. As the CCI and the other gymkhanas did not agree to their proposal, the Hindus decided not to field a team in the competition in 1937.[82]

The dispute over the radio commentary of the Pentangular also demonstrates the commercial potential of the tournament. The radio commentary on the Pentangular was banned and replaced with commentary on the less popular Ranji Trophy. This ban had vital commercial significance, evident from the concern expressed by the All India Radio merchants against it:[83]

> The trade views this development with deepest concern. The trade is in the best position to judge the great interest taken all over India

in these running commentaries of Bombay's famous cricket festival and views with apprehension a move that gravely affects its business.[84]

Consequently they urged a fresh review of the entire situation, stating:

> There is still ample time to arrange for the famous broadcasts and thus make available to the public of India the commentaries that are the most looked forward to radio events of the year by every class, community or creed.[85]

Even the *Bombay Chronicle*, which was arguably the most vocal against the communal Pentangular, was unable to discount its commercial potential. Despite branding the people who attended the Pentangular as alcoholics, who were so much used to it that they were drawn to it as a drunkard is drawn to the pub,[86] the *Chronicle* gives us ample reason to place it in a similar category. On 23 December 1940, when the anti-Pentangular movement was gathering momentum, the *Chronicle* reported Pentangular matches on the front page under the heading 'Rest to meet Muslims in Final'. The Ranji Trophy, which was also being played in the city, was relegated to the sports page.[87] This differential priority given to the Pentangular was clearly due to its commercial potential, arising from its mass appeal.

The growing awareness of the commercial potential of the game impressed upon cricket patrons in other regions that it was the success of the Pentangular that lay behind Bombay's designation as the home of Indian cricket. The privilege enjoyed by the Bombay Cricket Association as the organizers of the most popular cricket tournament in the country soon made it the object of envy of competing sporting interests. Hostility towards Bombay had become stronger after the establishment of the Board of Control for Cricket in the country in 1928. The board, cash-strapped since its inception,[88] though supposedly the arbiters of the fortunes of the game in India, soon realized that real power was concentrated in the hands of the Bombay Cricket Association. The Ranji Trophy, organized on a provincial basis from 1934, was not half as popular as the Pentangular. In its crusade against the Pentangular, the board had the support of most other cricket associations in the country, which were opposed to the hegemony of Bombay.

The argument advanced by the board and its allies was that the Bombay public, brought up in a sectarian atmosphere, preferred cricket organized on communal lines only. During the Pentangular matches the stadium was often packed to capacity, while the 1935 Ranji Trophy final attracted a mere 1,000 spectators a day. In 1944 the number increased to 4,000, which was still way behind the 25,000 attendances at the Pentangular. This, it was argued, was reflective of an unhealthy attitude to the game. In comparison, people in less sophisticated centres, it was argued, had learnt to enjoy cricket even played without communal influence:

> If Bombay and Madras were to play a championship match in Calcutta today, a capacity crowd would, I know attend it. Madras, I believe, would do equally well for a Bombay and Bengal encounter at Madras. But not so in the home of Indian cricket! That is the pity.[89]

This faction also held that though the economic stability of the Pentangular owed much to the patronage of the inhabitants of Bombay, there were other factors that were often overlooked by the cricket administrators of the city. It was argued that the 'large body of headliners from outside Bombay have provided the bill of fare',[90] implying that the popularity of the Bombay tournament owed much to its all-India character. Had leading cricketers from all round the country refused to take part in the Pentangular, public support for the tournament would surely have dwindled. It was also argued that the 'days were over when Bombay alone could stage the show', largely because of the public support for the game in the city and the presence of the spacious Brabourne Stadium. It was also alleged that Bombay was failing in its duties as the richest member of the board, and that it ought to have helped the board much more than it usually did. After the Bombay–Holkar final for the Ranji Trophy at Bombay in 1945, which had leading Indian and international stars in action, Bombay had presented the board with a cheque of Rs1,500 only, which amounted to a mere 15 per cent of the net profits. For the cash-strapped board, charged with the duty of developing and promoting the game in the entire country, this was a meagre sum. Resentment was further fuelled because the communal gymkhnas, also enjoying financial stability, did nothing to promote the game in the rest of the country:

> And yet, despite the profits that it raked in annually from the Quadrangular, Bombay had done little to encourage or establish the game in Western India generally. Poona especially felt

aggrieved, alleging that the wealthy Hindu Gymkhana in Bombay drew upon and exploited its best players, Deodhar and S.S. Joshi for example, without ever paying a moment's attention to the cricket needs of Poona and the rest of the Presidency.[91]

VI

The opposition against Bombay reached a climax when the United Provinces Cricket Association passed the following resolution in 1942:

> It is felt on all hands that the time has come when concerted action should be taken to rid the country of the canker of communal cricket as it tends to retard unity and good fellowship in the country. Is it not deplorable for Hindus to play against their Muslim brethren and vice versa? The cream of Indian cricketers participate in the Pentangular and these players belong to the various provinces which are affiliated to the Board of Control as the Governing body. The Board, as constituted with these affiliating units, should come to a decision by which a player who participates in communal cricket shall not, for the rest of his cricketing career, be eligible to play for his own province or his country in any official match that may be staged or any tournament that is run under the auspices of the Provincial Association concerned or the Board.[92]

This resolution marked the beginning of a concerted campaign against the Pentangular, culminating with the government threatening to intervene if the Pentangular committee continued with the tournament. The board, which had favourable relations with the government, ensured that its protests against the Pentangular had official sanction, and this was significant in the eventual closure of the competition in 1946. Such protests however, had very little impact on the popularity of the Pentangular tournament. A *Times of India* report affirms this:

> There appears to be no doubt as to the popularity of this season's cricket festival. Youthful picketers resumed their efforts to dissuade enthusiasts from entering the Brabourne Stadium, but they were good humouredly ignored and an even bigger crowd than on the previous morning greeted the rival teams on the commencement of play, a crowd steadily increasing until it was

somewhat in the vicinity of the twenty thousand mark during the afternoon.[93]

Unable to contend with the growing popularity of the Pentangular, the Board had been forced to call an extraordinary general meeting in January 1942 to obtain the support of cricket associations countrywide for banning the Pentangular. At the general meeting the following resolution was tabled:

> The Board considers that time has come when concerted action should be taken to rid the country of the canker of communal cricket as it tends to retard unity of good fellowship in the country, and as the first step in that direction it views with strong disfavour any tournament or match being played on communal lines and calls upon its affiliated associations to co-operate in this respect and take all necessary steps to stop such matches and tournaments.[94]

This resolution understandably provoked serious opposition from the representative of the Bombay Cricket Association. H.N. Contractor, representing Bombay, retorted that the Bombay Pentangular organized by the communal gymkhanas under the aegis of the Bombay Cricket Association was an autonomous tournament and the board had no power to interfere with its internal management. He asserted that the guiding principles of the board precluded it from tampering with the conduct of any tournament run independently, especially one that had been in existence since long before the board had been formed. He pointed out that the main tenet of the board's resolution was political, being directed exclusively against the commercially successful Bombay Pentangular.[95]

Following the above response, P. Gupta of Bengal, representing the interests of the board, moved the following amendment:

> The Board of Control for Cricket in India, on a matter of principle and in the larger interests of the country deplores any cricket festival or tournament and all matches run on lines, which may, or are likely to, lead to unhealthy communal rivalry. The Board resolves to appoint a sub-committee to formulate schemes for an alternate tournament for its consideration, and adoption if necessary.[96]

At this Contractor again expressed doubt as to whether the board had the authority to interfere with the activities of a provincial association, in whatever capacity it may be. He went on to state that if the board forcibly enforced the resolution, it would lead to a parting of ways between the board and the Bombay Cricket Association.[97] This assertion clearly shows the confidence of the Bombay Cricket Association, which was in no way dependent on the board for its well-being. Contradicting the main tenets of the resolution, that communal cricket generated communal antagonism, Contractor narrated his experience of the 1936 Quadrangular. This tournament was played at a time when Bombay was experiencing bitter communal riots. Despite such strife in the city, the then Quadrangular did not cause a single unpleasant incident. On the contrary, the tournament had helped to cement amity between the members of the two communities and had 'ameliorated the estranged feelings by smoothing the hot atmosphere and had actually ended the serious riots'.[98]

In the face of opposition, Dr Subbaraon, the president of the board, announced his decision to resign if the resolution was not passed. He also justified the actions of the princes, who, he felt, had had the nation's interests in mind when they had banned players from taking part in the communal Pentangular.[99]

As a rift between the board and the Bombay Cricket Association loomed large, Pankaj Gupta of the Bengal Gynkhana appealed to the Bombay Cricket Association not to oppose the board. The board's decision, whether good or bad, was to be obeyed by all regional associations in the country.[100] Despite his plea, the representatives of the Bombay Cricket Association were relentless and emphatic that the board was doing a grave wrong. Failing to impose their decision on the Bombay Cricket Association, the board finally decided to withdraw the resolution and appoint a subcommittee to deliberate on the question of communal cricket.[101]

This committee, after much deliberation on the issue, argued in the next meeting of the board on 15 March 1942 that the controlling body was empowered to take any step deemed necessary to discontinue the holding of any tournament by any member association within its jurisdiction. It asked the member associations responsible for the management of communal tournaments to put an immediate stop to them, failing which the board would be forced to intervene. At the same time, however, fearing that the Bombay Cricket Association might decide to break away from the control of the board, the subcommittee was forced to make concessions, contradicting its own stand in the process:

The structure of Bombay and Sind cricket being on communal lines, this sub committee further considers that relaxation of the principle set forth above may be made in case of Bombay, Sind or any other association in order to follow the principle that there should be no interference normally in the internal administration of any member association, provided the tournament concerned is confined to players in the area of the association concerned on the lines of the rules of the Sind Pentangular.[102]

Despite such concessions, Contractor expressed dissent, arguing that the more the board tried to legislate on matters beyond its jurisdiction and interfere in the internal affairs of a provincial body, the more difficult it would become for the board to retain its position. The Bombay Cricket Association, he asserted, had never intervened in the affairs of the communal gymkhanas that controlled the running of the Pentangular.

Representing Sind, Sohrab Mehta echoed similar sentiments, arguing that if the board had no objection to communal cricket being played by players of a certain area, there was no reason why the Bombay Pentangular tournament should be subjected to criticism.[103]

The conflict between the board and the BCA did not abate, eventually resulting in the withdrawal of Bombay from the National Championships in November 1942. Bombay's refusal to participate provoked a hostile reaction in most quarters of the country because most of the other associations, less favourably financially endowed than Bombay, had consented to participate in the championships. The chief reason behind Bombay's refusal to participate as reported by the *Times of India* was fear of serious financial loss.[104] This decision had the support of the players: Vijay Merchant, captain of the Bombay team, was the chief advocate behind the move to stay away from the national championships, a decision that may have resulted in his suspension by the board: 'Merchant laid great stress on the danger of wrecking and it was even put to the managing committee that players themselves were against the idea of Bombay's participation.'[105]

It is possible to read into this decision an attempt by the players to take on the might of the board. Aggrieved at the board's attempts to thwart the Pentangular, the players had consciously decided to boycott the national championships organized by the board. Their attempts were largely successful, as the following statement by K.S. Ranga Rao, the honorary secretary of the board, reveals:

The recommendations of the Bombay Cricket Association to abandon the Ranji Trophy for this year has been circulated to all associations for their views and a majority of them have expressed themselves in favour of holding the all India championships as usual.

It is needless for the Board to stress how important the Ranji Trophy is for the furtherance of cricket in India, in view of its all India character. I am directed by the President of the Board to request such associations as have expressed their inability to participate in this years championships to reconsider their decision and to extend their full co-operation and support as hitherto in the successful conduct of the championships.[106]

VII

As mentioned at the start of this essay, the anti-Pentangular movement can only be meaningfully analyzed if viewed against the wider politico-economic canvas of the state. One cannot read a straightforward narrative of the rise, spread and flowering of anti-communal sentiment in Bombay, which eventually resulted in the stoppage of the Pentangular. The existing historiography seeking to explain the tournament's closure reads very much like a simple narrative of transposition where the intricacies of the history of the game and its immediate context are lost. The analysis of the anti-Pentangular movement clearly reflects that, behind the projected ideal of secularism, vested politico-economic motives were at work. The rhetoric of secularism was a facade that masked rabid commercial considerations. The empty stands at the Ranji Trophy matches, contrasting starkly with attendances at the Pentangular matches, made the board, patrons of the former, envious of the communal gymkhanas and the Bombay Cricket Association, benefactors of the latter. The BCCI and the princely patrons did their utmost to curb the mass appeal of the Pentangular, characterizing it as a barrier in the path of the evolution and burgeoning of the national movement. This effort, rooted in financial and social concerns (assertion of patrician control over the players), was a complete failure, as may be gleaned from the disappointment expressed over the lack of public support for the Ranji Trophy, even after the Pentangular was stopped in January 1946.[107]

The anti-Pentangular movement raises fundamental questions about the persisting myth of cricket being a gentleman's game. The very inception of the game in Bombay, as discussed above, was rooted in commercial rivalry between the Parsees and the Hindus, the two dominant Indian business communities. The analysis brings to the fore the central role played by the forces of urbanization and commerce in the evolution of the game in the subcontinent and challenges some of the fundamental paradigms of existing historiography. Growing professionalism in sport, it may be argued, led to the forging of an unnatural alliance between the princely/nationalist lobby, groups antipathetic to each other in normal circumstances. The princes, firm loyalists of the Raj and hence severe critics of the nationalist agenda, tried to make use of the appeal of the Mahatma to champion their crusade against the commercially successful Pentangular. The anti-Pentangular movement, proof enough of the social and commercial potential of cricket in the early twentieth century, challenges the hypothesis that commercialization of the sport was a phenomenon of the 1970s. While the degree of commercialization has certainly increased manifold since the 1970s, it was certainly because of its commercial potential that cricket was being perceived as a viable career option by men from the middle and working classes from the 1930s.

By focusing on an analysis of the anti-Pentangular movement, I have tried to shift attention from studies centring on the communal Pentangular and its ramifications to the world of the professional, and to the role played by commerce and an emerging urban public sphere, in the development of Indian cricket. This shift is significant, since emphasis on these forces of urbanization and commercialization, forces shaping the day-to-day life of the individual, leads to a reification of the culture-economy antinomy. By focusing on these processes, my effort has been to highlight the impact of capitalism and related social forces, such as urbanization and commercialization, on Indian cricket – though, at the same time, divorcing this study from normative expectations derived from European historical experience.

The above analysis of the anti-Pentangular movement illustrates how Indian cricket readjusted itself under the influence of the forces of urbanization, monetization and commercialization. It provides insights into the processes whereby an emerging urban public sphere influenced trajectories of leisure in the country, issues governing their administration and the relationship between the cricketer and his erstwhile patron.

The analysis advanced in this essay goes against the grain of existing literature on Indian cricket. Established trends in Indian cricket writing have, by and large, neglected the influence of the forces of capitalism on pre-1971 Indian cricket. The above analysis makes room for the argument that cricket was already being perceived as a potent commercial force from the third decade of the twentieth century, as the reaction of the players to the anti-Pentangular movement that influenced the economic fortunes of sub-continental cricket demonstrates.

The object of the analysis set out in this chapter has been to demonstrate the importance of sport in Indian socio-political and economic life, at the same time trying to highlight that the history of the game was always subject to influences from beyond the sporting arena. A history of Indian cricket, I have tried to argue, only makes sense when we take into account its social and commercial context, read in terms of power equations governing the day-to-day administration of public life in the country.

NOTES

I would like to thank Dr David Washbrook, my supervisor, without whose help, guidance and inspiration this essay could not have been written. Sharmistha Gooptu has found time from her own work to go through earlier drafts of this paper. Anandji Dossa, Vasant Raiji, K.N. Prabhu and Theo Braganza in Mumbai have been most helpful, tolerating my unfair demands and giving me time as and when I asked them.

1. An Indian term for clubs. In pre-partition India such clubs were community-based and cricket was organized along communitarian lines. Cricket in pre-partition Bombay was dominated by these gymkhanas, which were, in most cases, financially stable, on account of the immense popularity of the Bombay Pentangular tournament that they organized.
2. By the 1890s the Parsees of Bombay had acquired considerable cricketing prowess and had no difficulty defeating the Europeans of the city. This led to a proposal that they should henceforth play a combined European team, comprising the best European talent in the Presidency. With encouragement from Lord Harris, Governor of Bombay between 1890 and 1895, these matches were started in 1892. In the first year however, the match was washed away because of rain and fire engines had to be brought to dry the ground, which led the match becoming known as the fire engine match.
3. Initially the Pentangular was played in the monsoon months of July and August. It was shifted to the winter months in 1918. The tournament continued to be played in the last months of the year till 1944. In 1945 the tournament could not be held in December and was played in January. It was discontinued thereafter.
4. Peter Bailey, *Leisure and Class in Victorian England* (1978), p.1, quoted in J.A. Mangan (ed.), *Pleasure, Profit and Proselytism: British Culture and Sport at Home and Abroad, 1700–1914* (London: Frank Cass, 1988), p.1
5. Eric Hobsbawm and Terence Ranger (eds), *The Invention of Tradition* (London: Cambridge University Press, 1992), quoted in Mangan, *Pleasure, Profit and Proselytism*, p.1
6. Ramchandra Guha, 'Cricket and Politics in Colonial India', *Past and Present*, 161 (Nov. 1998), 157.
7. Ibid. For similar views see J.A. Mangan (ed.), *The Cultural Bond: Sport, Empire, Society* (London and Portland, OR: Frank Cass, 1992).
8. All hitherto published works on Indian cricket have portrayed the game in these terms: Ramchandra Guha, 'Cricket and Politics in Colonial India', Edward Docker, *History of Indian Cricket* (Delhi: Macmillan, 1976); Richard Cashman, *Patrons, Players and the Crowd* (Calcutta: Orient Longman, 1979); Mario Rodrigues, 'Calcutta', *The Statesman*, 1 Nov. 1997.

9. In the Indian context, communalism refers to the animosity between two communities, the Hindus and the Muslims. Communalism has been an important subject of study in Indian history, and was one of the most important factors that brought about the division of the nation into two independent states, India and Pakistan in 1947.
10. Berry Sarbadhikary, *Indian Cricket Uncovered* (Calcutta: Illustrated News, 1945), pp.60–61.
11. Ramchandra Guha, 'Cricket and Politics in Colonial India', pp.186–7.
12. When Gandhi called off the non-co-operation agitation in 1922, Hindu–Muslim relations in the country underwent a setback, leading to a drastic fall in the Muslim membership of the Indian National Congress.
13. Vasant Raiji and Mohandas Menon, *The Story of the Bombay Tournament: From Presidency to Pentangulars* (Mumbai: Ernest Publications, 2000), p.93.
14. While hockey is India's *de jure* national sport cricket far outstrips in popularity all other sports played in the country, rightfully earning for itself the epithet of the country's *de facto* national sport.
15. The anti-Pentangular movement was perhaps one of the most widely reported events in Bombay in the 1930s and 1940s. Contemporary newspapers – *The Times of India, Bombay Chronicle* and *Bombay Sentinel* – often reported the Pentangular matches on their front pages while sports magazines such as *Indian Cricket, Crickinia* and *The Indian Cricket Annual* carried detailed reports of the raging debate on the Pentangular.
16. Nikhil Rao, 'Hoops, Hunger and the City: Mumbai's Basketball Scene', *The Man's World* (Mumbai: March 2001).
17. This becomes clear from the figures of annual importation of film into India between 1922–23 and 1927–28. There was a steady increase in the quantity of imported film, which rose from 7310,429 feet in 1922–23 to 19,668,648 feet in 1927–28. The number of silent films produced in India in the 1920s also supports this argument. The number rose from 27 in 1920 to 201 in 1931. Report of the Indian Cinematograph Committee, 1927–28; quoted in Prabal Bagchi, 'Pattern of Film Business in the Silent Era in India (1896–1931) with special reference to Bengal' (RTP thesis submitted as part of the programme in the Centre for Studies in Social Sciences, Calcutta, 1991–92).
18. This is evident from the huge amount of money collected as entertainment tax in 1929–30. In this year Rs787,000 was collected under this head. Proceedings of the Government of Bombay, Finance Department (1932), IOLR, P/11909, p.187.
19. At the root of Bombay's hegemonic position in Indian cricket lay the popularity of the Pentangular tournament that was organized along communal lines. Other regions of the country with equally rich cricketing traditions had to gradually give way to Bombay, primarily because of the commercially viable nature of the game in the city. At the root of this viability lay the popularity of the communal Pentangular. The competitive spirit in the Pentangular matches was also responsible for the rise of many Indian stars in the 1930s and 1940s. Eyewitness accounts reveal that this tournament greatly stimulated interest in the game in pre-partition India.
20. Kaushik Bhaumik, 'The Emergence of the Bombay Film Industry, 1913–36' (Unpublished D.Phil. thesis, University of Oxford, 2002).
21. Nikhil Rao, 'Hoops, Hunger and the City'.
22. Proceedings of the Government of Bombay, General Department, IOLR, P/7746, Letter no.333, 1 Feb. 1907, p.187.
23. In view of the growing popularity of cinema, the state governments started to tap the money earned by cinema-houses as a major source of revenue from the 1920s. This move was started by Bengal in 1922 and adopted by Bombay in 1923. Prabal Bagchi, 'Pattern of Film Business'.
24. Sporting activity was affected by a series of factors. The impact of the First World War and the non-co-operation movement under Gandhi, together with poor organization in the sporting realm, contributed to a reduced interest in sport between 1915 and 1920.
25. This is evident from an analysis of photographs in leading dailies published in Bombay in the 1920s and 1930s. Photographs of players in action are available from this period onwards. This trend was largely responsible for sportsmen's emergence as household names in Bombay by the 1930s.
26. *Bombay Chronicle*, 28 Nov. 1929.

27. *Bombay Chronicle*, 28 Nov. 1929.
28. *Bombay Sentinel*, 23 Nov. 1937.
29. Rustam Vakeel, *The Joys of Cricket*; quoted in *Bombay Chronicle*, 2 Dec. 1934.
30. Contemporary newspapers are replete with accounts describing the visits of the various princes to Bombay. These princes, as is often described, had business initiatives in Bombay. With Bombay becoming the economic nerve-centre of the country, native princes such as the Maharajkumar of Vizianagram (Vizzy) tried their best to establish a toehold in the city.
31. Ramchandra Guha, 'Cricket and Politics in Colonial India'; Docker, *History of Indian Cricket*; Cashman, *Patrons, Players and the Crowd*; Mihir Bose, *A History of Indian Cricket* (London: Andre Deutsch, 1990).
32. Meher Homji, 'A Century of Parsee Cricket', in Meher Homji (ed.), *Parsi Cricket Centenary 1886–1986* (Mumbai, 1986), p.45.
33. S.K. Roy, *Bombay Pentangular* (Calcutta, 1945), p.85.
34. Young Zorastrian Cricket Club, 125 years' celebration souvenir (Mumbai, 1992), p.7.
35. Meher Homji, 'A Century of Parsee Cricket', p.45; Young Zorastrian Cricket Club, p.7.
36. Vasant Raiji, 'Pioneers of Indian Cricket', in Boria Majumdar (ed.), *Vasant Raiji on Indian Cricket* (Mumbai: Marine Sports, 2002).
37. Ramchandra Guha, 'Cricket and Politics in Colonial India', p.159.
38. Ibid.
39. The Purshottam Shield Cricket Tournament is the oldest cricket tournament organized by the Hindu Gymkhana. As well as this tournament, the Hindu Gymkhana also organizes the Talim Shield Cricket Tournament, the Police Invitation Cricket Tournament, the A.F.S. Talyarkhan Tournament and the Young Comrade Shield Cricket Tournament: *P.J. Hindu Gymkhana Centenary Souvenir 1894–1994* (Mumbai, 1994).
40. The first Mohammedan cricket club was established in 1883 at Parade Ground, now Cross Maidan, in Bombay. Anandji Dossa, 'Peep into Past on Glorious Chapter', in *Islam Gymkhana Centenary Souvenir* (Mumbai, 1990)
41. Ibid.
42. M.E. Pavri, *Parsi Cricket* (Bombay: J.B. Marzban and Company, 1901); J.M. Framjee Patel, *Stray Thoughts on Indian Cricket* (Bombay: Times Press, 1905).
43. Anandji Dossa, 'Peep into Past'.
44. In view of Harris's contribution to the cause of Indian cricket, the Harris Shield Cricket Tournament for schools was started in Bombay in 1893. This is the oldest surviving cricket tournament in India. Oil portraits of Lord Harris are also found in the headquarters of the Hindu, Islam and Parsee gymkhanas in Bombay.
45. 'Hindu Cricket', *The Indian Social Reformer*, 1906, p.292.
46. Ibid.
47. Ramchandra Guha, 'Cricket and Politics in Colonial India', p.163.
48. Ibid.
49. Prashant Kidambi, 'A History of the Bombay Pentangular Tournament' (Unpublished essay, JNU, 1992), p.30.
50. Gyanendra Pandey, *The Construction of Communalism in Colonial North India* (Delhi: Oxford University Press, 1990), p.210.
51. Shapoorjee Sorabjee, *A Chronicle of Cricket Amongst Parsees and The Struggle: Polo versus Cricket* (Bombay, 1897), p.123.
52. B.R. Kagal, 'Communal Cricket', in M.H. Maqsood (ed.), *Who's Who in Indian Cricket* (Delhi, 1940), pp.24–32.
53. Docker, *History of Indian Cricket*.
54. *Bombay Chronicle*, 27 Nov. 1935. For similar views see *Statesman*, 2 Dec. 1935; Berry Sarbadhikary, *Indian Cricket Uncovered*.
55. J.C. Maitra continued to write against the communal Pentangular in his columns through the 1940s. When the tournament was eventually terminated, he expressed hope that its place would be successfully taken by a zonal Pentangular. Records, however, reveal that the Pentangular could not be matched in popularity by any other tournament in pre-partition India.
56. Berry Sarbadhikary, *Indian Cricket Uncovered*, pp.60–61.
57. *Bombay Chronicle*, 7 Dec. 1940.

58. Ibid.
59. Ibid.
60. All major tracts on Indian cricket have referred to this assertion by the Mahatma: Ramchandra Guha, 'Cricket and Politics in Colonial India'; Docker, *History of Indian Cricket*; Cashman, *Patrons, Players and the Crowd*.
61. Front-page headline, *Bombay Chronicle*, 7 Dec. 1940.
62. *Times of India*, 10 Dec. 1940. It is striking to note that the mounting of opposition to the Pentangular was accompanied by a simultaneous rise in the popularity of the tournament. Eyewitness accounts reveal that the stadium was packed to capacity in all matches of the Pentangular.
63. *Times of India*, 16 Dec. 1940.
64. *Times Of India*, 14 Dec. 1940.
65. *Bombay Chronicle*, 19 Dec. 1940.
66. *Bombay Chronicle*, 29 Oct. 1946.
67. *Bombay Chronicle*, 1 Dec. 1941. Abdullah Brelvi referred to this fact in a public address. Curiously enough while he spoke of making a stand against the communal menace by banning the Pentangular, his own paper, the *Bombay Chronicle*, made no effort to boycott it.
68. P.N. Polishwalla, *The Sun Never Sets on Cricket* (Bombay, 1933), pp.6–7.
69. Ibid.
70. One of the foremost cricket journals in pre-Independence India, it carried detailed accounts of various tournaments played in the country, accounts of foreign tours, as well as items on other sports. It was discontinued in 1939.
71. The *Indian Cricket Annual* was first published by S.K. Gurunathan. Modelled on the *Wisden Almanac*, it continues to be the best handbook on Indian cricket. Published by Kasturi and Sons, it was initially priced at three rupees.
72. A short-lived annual on Indian cricket. Published for five years in the 1940s. Edited by Muni Lal, it carried detailed reports on the meetings of the Board of Control, giving an insight into the controversies plaguing the game.
73. Cashman, *Patrons, Players and the Crowd*, p.51.
74. Ibid., p.50.
75. The earliest endorsements made by the cricketers were for tea, oil and medicinal tonics. See *Indian Cricket*, passim, 1934–38; Roy, *Bombay Pentangular*. The star status of the players was firmly in place by the early 1950s; see for example a promotional campaign by the *Illustrated Weekly of India*, which offered subscribers a free poster of their favourite cricketer with every issue of the magazine.
76. Shute Banerjee, who had toured England with the Indian team in 1936 but had not played in any of the Test Matches, was endorsing products from the late 1930s. He played his first official test towards the end of his career, in 1948–9.
77. Ramchandra Guha, 'Cricket and Politics in Colonial India', p.183.
78. *Bombay Chronicle*, 13 Nov. 1941.
79. Ibid.
80. For a detailed analysis of the controversy see Anandabazar Patrika, Calcutta, July 1936.
81. Raju Mukherji, 'A History of Bengal Cricket' (Unpublished MS).
82. The dispute was settled the following year after the Hindu Gymkhana were allotted an additional 500 seats. This ensured significant returns from gate receipts, and ensured the gymkhana financial stability. The CCI's role in the dispute is understandable. The CCI, facing a huge debt of over Rs1,900,000 was looking to the Pentangular tournament as a potential source of income. It was initially decided to allot 14,000 seats to the gymkhanas for a payment of two rupees per seat. However, it was soon realized that that the gymkhanas were selling the tickets at much higher rates. This realization made the club determined not to increase the number of seats allotted to each gymkhana. Vasant Raiji and Mohandas Menon, *The Story of the Bombay Tournament: From Presidency to Pentangulars* (Mumbai: Ernest Publications, 2000), pp.75–6.
83. *Bombay Chronicle*, 16 Dec. 1940.
84. Ibid.
85. Ibid.

86. *Bombay Chronicle*, 15 Nov. 1944.
87. *Bombay Chronicle*, 23 Dec. 1940.
88. Even as late as the mid-1940s, the finances of the board were very bad. In the 1930s, the board had no funds and the Ranji Trophy was faced with the possibility of abandonment. It was the Pentangular committee that helped alleviate this crisis by donating 10,000 rupees to the board. Under President Subbaraon and Secretary K.S. Ranga Rao, the finances of the board improved somewhat and it had a balance of Rs100,000 in 1946: *Times Of India*, 30 July 1946.
89. Berry Sarbadhikary, *Indian Cricket Uncovered*, p.79. For similar views see comments of Berry Sarbadhikary under pseudonym 'Extra Cover' in the *Statesman* of the 1940s.
90. Ibid., p.79.
91. Docker, *History of Indian Cricket*, p.24.
92. Berry Sarbadhikary, *Indian Cricket Uncovered*, pp.71–2.
93. *Times Of India*, 23 Nov. 1943.
94. Proceedings of the Extra-Ordinary General Meeting of the Board held on 22 Jan. 1942, with Dr Subbaraon as the chair. The resolution was tabled by Mansur Alam, representative of the United Provinces Cricket Association. The resolution was originally in two parts, but the second, calling for the imposition of a penalty upon players who participated in communal tournaments, was eventually dropped: Muni Lal (ed.), *The Crickinia: 1942–43* (Lahore, 1943), pp.65–6.
95. Contractor declared that the resolution was *ultra vires* as there was no clause in rule 2 of the board's constitution that empowered it to interfere in the internal affairs of a provincial association: ibid., p.66.
96. A second amendment was moved by R.S. Ranga Rao, representing the Madras Cricket Association. Like the first, it wanted the question of the continuance or discontinuance of the Pentangular to be examined by a subcommittee appointed by the board, in which the Bombay and United Provinces cricket associations would be adequately represented.
97. Ibid., pp.67–8.
98. Ibid.
99. Dr Subbaraon went on to say that it was a matter of pleasure to note that the princes had become national-minded and were trying to do away with communalism in every branch of life. This, he thought, would help in laying the foundation of a free India.
100. He went on to add that his amendment had not been viewed in the right spirit. He urged the members to study the difference between the original resolution and the amendment before voting.
101. This was a victory for the Bombay Cricket Association. The board was forced to persuade Mansur Alam and Pankaj Gupta to withdraw their amendments in the face of tremendous opposition from the members of the Bombay Cricket Association.
102. Proceedings of the Communal Cricket Sub-Committee, in *The Crickinia: 1942–43*, pp.76–8.
103. Ibid., pp.83–4.
104. *Times of India*, 23 Nov. 1942; the same report goes on to state that even after a Bombay sportsman had offered to make up for the losses suffered by the Bombay Cricket Association, it refused to participate in the national championships.
105. Ibid. Merchant's stand assumes great significance in view of his statements issued in favour of the Pentangular a couple of years later. He was forthright in declaring that of all the cricket tournaments held in Bombay, the Pentangular was the only source of income to the cricket organization in the city. Responding to the criticism that it fostered communal ill-feeling, he referred to his experiences after the 1936 tournament. He went on to state: 'It may come as a very great surprise to you when I tell you that during the ten days the Quadrangular was played, not a single incident took place in the whole of Bombay, and immediately after the tournament was over the communal riot subsided.' It is no surprise, therefore, that Merchant was fully supportive of the Bombay Cricket Association in its tussle against the Board.
106. *Times of India*, 16 Nov. 1942.
107. *Bombay Chronicle*, 5 Nov. 1946. To remedy the apathy, Maitra suggested, in his columns in the *Bombay Chronicle*, that ministers and leading citizens of Bombay should attend the matches of the zonal tournament to restore confidence among the public.

Sport in China: Conflict between Tradition and Modernity, 1840s to 1930s

FAN HONG and TAN HUA

Modern sport in China is not an indigenous product. It was a foreign import and developed in a hot-house of modernization. Modern sport came to China as an element of Western culture and accompanied by military force, which directly challenged Chinese traditional culture and patriotism. This provoked conflict and confrontation between radicals and conservatives in Chinese society between the 1840s and the 1930s. Consequently, an important debate (*Tu yang zhi zheng*[1]) occurred in the 1930s. The focus of the debate was on whether China should reject or accept Western sport – an alien culture. Many politicians, educationists and physical educationists took part in the debate. Thanks to the debate, modern physical education and sport was finally established in China as a part of Chinese modern culture. This chapter will analyse the process of the cultural diffusion of sport in modern China. The development of modern sport and the modernization of China proceeded side by side. The modernization of China provided a suitable climate for the growth of modern sport and the development of modern sport stimulated the process of modernization of Chinese society at the turn of the twentieth century. It was a reciprocal relationship.

TRADITION: CONFUCIANISM AND TRADITIONAL SPORT

The Opium War with the British in 1840 was a watershed in modern Chinese history.[2] Before the Opium War China was a feudal society with a rural culture that century after century centred itself on patriarchal power and filial piety. It relied on trust, fidelity, fear of losing face and time-honoured rules of civilized conduct. All these concepts were later highlighted, standardized and exalted by Confucius and his followers through a set of precepts known as Confucianism.[3] For nearly 2,000 years, as a philosophy of life at every level,[4] Confucianism provided the political, social and moral foundation to Chinese culture.[5] It sustained an inflexible social hierarchy and ensured a static social structure.[6]

However, Confucianism was based on an autarkic family-based agricultural economy that honoured and safeguarded patriarchal power. It was not wholly negative in impact. In the early stages of its existence, it advanced the economic development of China and contributed to the creation of positive social values maintaining both the stability and living standards of the autarkic family.[7] Nevertheless, in time, it became a reactionary force that was ritualized and bureaucratized by rulers to serve as a means of maintaining the status quo. It ran directly counter to modern ideals of liberty and equality. As a result, the progress of the whole nation was halted for centuries. Gradually people became less energetic, less enterprising and less innovative and eventually the vigour of the nation was affected.[8] Interestingly, the change of form and emphasis in traditional Chinese physical activities nicely illustrates this cultural deterioration. From the moment that Confucianism came into being, it permeated the whole of Chinese society, reinforced existing social values and emphasized the concept of hierarchy – with deleterious results. Chinese traditional sports also lost some of their original competitive spirit and forms.

For instance, sports of an originally competitive nature, such as archery and *chuju*, lost their competitive nature through the influence of centuries of Confucianism. Archery was once a highly competitive contest with well-established rules and regulations, but it declined into a highly ritualized 'archery ceremony',[9] with complicated ceremonial procedures. The social status rather than the performance of the participants was stressed. Distinctive bows, arrows and accompanying music were strictly allocated according to the social status of the participants.[10] Another example of the impact of Confucian ethics on traditional Chinese sport involves *chuju*, classical Chinese football. It was originally an aggressive competitive game, played by two opposing sides with two goals.[11] Due to its competitiveness, it had been adopted and greatly favoured by military mandarins to train soldiers in order to improve their physiques and cultivate their fighting spirit during the Han (206 BC–220 AD) and Tang (618–907 AD) dynasties. However, as time passed, two goals merged into one in the Song (960–1279 AD) and Yuan (1260–1368 AD) dynasties.[12] Vigorous competition was replaced by a much gentler phenomenon: less competitive and primarily exhibitive. Grace and harmony of movement were given priority.[13] Chinese polo, competitive and popular both in and out of court in the Tang Dynasty, simply disappeared.[14]

However, there was an exception: *wushu*. *Wushu* is the Chinese term usually translated as 'martial arts' or 'gongfu' or 'kung fu' in the West. *Wu* is associated with warfare; *shu* with the skill, way or methods of doing an activity. As a term, *wushu* covers the Chinese martial traditions of a wide variety of martially inspired practices. Its entire offensive and defensive repertoire was based upon the fighting methods of certain animals and adapted to form the basis of a martial-arts system. Many of the *wushu* systems were based upon just five animals – the tiger, crane, dragon. leopard and snake. Each animal style stresses a particular element: the crane exemplifies balance; the dragon, spirit and agility; the leopard, strength; the tiger, power; and the snake, the ability to strike at vital points of the body.[15] As Chinese society came to place more and more emphasis on warfare, weapons such as the sword, spear or knife were employed. Martial arts became more complicated in terms of system and methods, and they were a specialized profession for many.

Long years of turmoil had taught the Chinese to rely on martial arts as a security measure. Those who possessed the most advanced system felt that they had an advantage in protecting their empire, clan and family. Therefore the fighting systems that evolved were highly secretive and taught only to selected individuals and groups according to their linguistic, social and, especially, philosophical bonds.[16] As a product of the feudal society, martial arts were closely linked to feudal culture. The ethical code of martial arts required absolute loyalty and obedience of students to masters, of sons to fathers and of wives to husbands. These bonds may be seen as the essence of martial-arts culture and the essence of feudal culture. These imperatives formed the foundation of monarchical despotism and social inequality and divided people into rigid status groups with different rights and duties. For example, the top priority for martial-arts masters was to maintain their particular style by passing it from generation to generation through the male line: fathers passed their martial arts skills on to their sons and kept these skills secret from their daughters, who would marry outside the family and might divulge the secrets to competititors.[17] The organizational system had tribal characteristics. Each tribe had its own rules and martial-arts style. Tribes had close relationships with powerful warlords in modern China, for example, the leader of the Nationalist Party, Chiang Kai-shek, had good relationship with powerful tribes in Shanghai. This helped to raise him to power in the late 1920s.[18] Finally, martial arts played a very important role in the famous Boxer Rebellion[19] in 1900 and, therefore, won support from both conservatives and patriots in modern China.[20]

MODERNITY – BEGINNINGS: WESTERNIZATION AND WESTERN EXERCISE, 1861–94

The military confrontation with the British opium traders and troops brought China face to face with a strange people and culture. This fact now gradually influenced the development of the country and created an immediate crisis and acute instability for the Chinese establishment. However, foreign invasion also brought opportunities for the progressive forces in the country to take action against the ruling class and dated Confucian ethics.

Some progressive Qing bureaucrats now began to appreciate the extent of the crisis the nation was facing. They united and planned the reform of Chinese culture, economy and politics. To this end they launched a movement known as 'Westernization' (*Yangwu yundong* – 1861–94).[21] The movement had two objectives: the purchase of Western weaponry to strengthen national defence in conjunction with the introduction of Western machinery and technology to industrialize the country; and the revival of traditional Chinese Confucian culture. These measures were aimed at saving the declining Qing Empire.

Inevitably, however, with Western modern equipment and technology came Western influences, which were at odds with Confucian ethics. Western missionaries, educationists, merchants and sailors flooded into the Chinese ports. Western-style buildings arose in large cities and harbour towns. Telegraph offices and foreign banks were introduced. Translations of Western books flourished. The government even felt the need to send students abroad to study and began to show a degree of tolerance for Western ideas.[22] Thus this period not only saw the introduction of Western merchandise and technology but also witnessed an influx of Western cultural institutions, such as missionary education, military training and physical culture, the last of which was greatly favoured by the government. Sensibly, it believed that military power was the bulwark of the empire, and in addition that mass military physical exercises that stressed unity and discipline helped maintain a unified regime. As a result, these exercises, borrowed from the successful Western forces, spread rapidly and widely all over China.

This military-orientated physical exercise was known as *tichao* – gymnastics. It provided most of the physical training that was available in Chinese schools during this period. The fundamental purpose of the physical exercise programme was to make boys into good soldiers. Marching, saluting and military terminology were stressed in imitation of a military camp. This tradition of military drill held a strong position of influence for the greater part of the last 20 years of the nineteenth century and should not be overlooked.[23] Western military exercises as a contribution to military success won the approval and support of the Chinese authorities because they were significant instruments of political control. However, they created a climate of acceptability for Western practices.[24]

Germination occured mostly in Western-style schools and academies established during this period, for example, in the North Western Navy Academy (founded in 1881), the Tianjin Weaponry Engineering College (1885), the Guangdong Navy Academy (1887), the Fuzhou Shipbuilding Institute (1866), the Tianjin Telegraph School (1880), the Shanghai Telegraph School (1882), the South Western Navy Academy (1890), the Hubei Weaponry Engineering College (1895) and the Nanjing Army Academy (1895).[25] In these schools, Western military exercises were taught as a major subject and physical education was a compulsory course. The physical education curriculum in the North Western Navy Academy included fencing, boxing, football, high jump, long jump, swimming, skating and gymnastics.[26] In 1872, the Qing government selected 120 young boys to be sent to the United States to study as part of the national self-strengthening programme.[27] On return from abroad after seven to nine years' study, they became major advocates for Western ideas, technology and physical activity.[28]

The Westernization Movement, then, was an opportunity for the feudal government to absorb new ideas. As part of the process Western exercises, together with Western science and technology, were introduced, for the first time, into China. From now on these exercises were part of the Chinese cultural domain.

CONTINUITY:
SOCIAL REFORM AND MODERN SPORT, 1894–1911

China's Westernization Movement came to a halt when China was defeated in the first Sino-Japanese War (1894–95).[29] The dream of restoring China's power and strength through the Westernization Movement was shattered. If the defeat by the Western powers came as a shock, the defeat by its small neighbour Japan brought nothing but utter humiliation to the Chinese. For Japan had been regarded until then by the Chinese as a cultural colony, whose modernization had been recently completed through its Meiji Restoration, launched only in 1868.[30]

The defeat had immediate and extensive repercussions at home and caused Chinese progressives to review the progress of their own efforts at westernization. They found that their attempt to modernize China was nothing more than building castles in the air. Foreign ideas and practices could not simply be raised on China's traditional cultural foundations. They realized that if China wanted to grow strong in order to catch up with the developments of the Western world, major changes to its political system and its culture, including reforms of moral, intellectual and physical institutions and the introduction of a new educational system, were all essential. These ideas were simply too much for a minor reform to accommodate. There would have to be a major revolution. Many Chinese intellectuals, therefore, now demanded radical reconstruction. Thus in 1898, another movement, known as the One Hundred-Day Reform (*Bairi weixin*) or the Constitutional Reform Movement (*Wuxu bianfa*),[31] was launched with the aim of bringing the Western democratic ideal and political system to China.[32]

The reformers persuaded Emperor Guangxu to issue edicts calling for the creation of a political advisory council, the abolition of sinecures in the bureaucracy, the promotion of industry and commerce and the creation of a national school system that would include Western learning in the curriculum. The reform movement endorsed many Western cultural institutions – among them Western exercise.[33] The leaders of the movement, as others of the Qing government before them, considered that Western military exercises and Western physical exercise programmes were conducive to boosting their revolutionary ideas, which they saw as embodied, to some extent, in Western military exercise which produced energy, developed fitness, stamina and strength and created self-reliance. Yan Fu (1853–1921), a leader of the movement and a scholar newly returned from England, who translated Thomas Huxley's book *Evolution and Ethics* into Chinese, pointed out in an essay entitled 'On Strength'[34] that Darwin's evolutionary theories and Spencer's sociological writing had implications for transforming and strengthening society. Above all, there was a need to strengthen people's bodies. Therefore Chinese culture, which ignored the value of a strong body, needed to be changed. To reform China, stated Yan, it was crucial to develop strength through (Western) exercise. His was far from being a lone voice. Kang Youwei (1858–1927), another leader of the movement, wrote a memorandum to the Qing government recommending the abolition of traditional Chinese military training and examinations and the creation of Western-style military schools throughout China to train Chinese soldiers and students.[35] Thus the idea of saving the country, in part, by promoting Western patterns of physical exercise came into being.[36] The leaders cherished the hope that cultural reform, in turn and in time, would bring about a change in political institutions. However, a hostile conservative reaction, headed by the Empress-dowager Cixi, led to the arrest of the leading reformers, the crushing of the movement, and the placing of Guangxu under house arrest.[37]

However, even the Empress-dowager Cixi herself, a couple of years later in 1905, having vaguely realized the weaknesses of the Chinese educational system and in a desperate attempt to secure the survival of the dynasty, launched a series of educational reforms. These included the abolition of the traditional imperial civil service examination system based on the Confucian classics, its replacement by a national system of modern schools and the encouragement of study abroad, particularly in Japan, which was regarded as an inspirational example of Asiatic modernization.

For the first time in its long feudal history, China's government was brought into the whirlpool of modern world politics and, among other things, made to re-evaluate its educational policy. The reforms brought significant changes to Chinese society, especially the abolition of the imperial civil service examination of some 1,300 years' standing and the establishment of a new educational system of modern schooling in 1905.[38]

Western ideals and methods of education were now introduced into schools. These included physical exercise, gymnastics and modern games, which were prescribed by the Qing government. In 1903 the government stipulated two or three hours per week of physical exercise for upper and lower elementary schools.[39] Subsequently, physical education was made a required course in middle schools, higher schools, lower normal schools and lower agricultural schools.[40] The time allotted for gymnastics and physical exercise in schools was raised to four hours per week.[41]

Gymnastics still held pride of place in the formal curriculum but other kinds of Western exercise, such as basketball, baseball, volleyball, tennis and track and field events gradually and increasingly attracted people's attention. The first modern sport club found in China was the Canton Rowing Club in 1837. The British organized football matches in Hong Kong in 1897 and football then spread from Hong Kong to the mainland to places like Shanghai, Nanjing and Beijing. The first Chinese football association was founded in Hong Kong in 1908. Baseball was brought to China by Chinese students on their return from Yale University in 1887. Basketball came to China through the YMCA in Tianjin in 1896.[42] Progressives saw in these activities the embodiment of a new spirit that could revitalize the dying empire. Traditional Chinese exercises – martial arts – inevitably associated with traditional Chinese culture, were now neglected and were excluded from the curriculum of modern schools. Western physical activities began to move from the margin to the centre of the cultural stage, especially in large cities, which were becoming locations of the developing westernized culture. From now on, the rapid expansion of modern Western exercises, sports and games and the decline of traditional Chinese activities went hand in hand.

Reports in newspapers and periodicals in the early years of the twentieth century provide clear evidence of the new fashion. The first report of a basketball game appeared in the *Tientsin Bulletin* of the municipal YMCA on 11 January 1896: 'A game of basketball will be played this afternoon. All young men interested in athletics are welcome to join the game at 4 pm.'[43] Basketball soon spread to other schools and became the most popular ball game in China.[44] In addition football matches between some Chinese college teams, such as Hsieh Ho and Huiwen, and Western legation guards' teams became a regular event.[45] Athletics were organized both in missionary schools and government schools. By 1908 athletics meetings were held frequently in Tianjin, Beijing, Shanghai, Fuzhou and at least ten other cities. The earliest events include Baodin (1904), Beijing (1905), Chengdu (1905) and Nanjing (1907).[46]

Newspapers of the period reported the First National Athletics Meeting held in 1910, which contributed greatly to Chinese interest in modern sports. This was held from 18 to 22 October, and was the first modern sports event at the national level. The activities included many of the recently introduced Western sports and games, such as athletics, tennis, football and basketball. Each day, on average, some 40,000 spectators attended. Interest was intense. The *North Herald* reported that 'The First National Athletic Meet in China bids fair to leave as significant a mark on the country as the meeting of the National Assembly in Peking.'[47] The *Association Men* remarked about the same time that

> China is getting athletic. This event tells us that the Chinese youth is awakening. ... Many schools and other organizations are eager to get involved in physical training activities. All this will mean an improvement of the physique of young China.[48]

An amusing sidelight to this national meeting, which nicely illustrates the conflict between modern Western culture and traditional Chinese culture in China in those years, is offered by the case of Sun Baoqing, a high-jumper from Tianjin. Sun had performed poorly in the opening round, because his long queue (pigtail) constantly knocked the bar off its stands. He was so angry that the same evening, without a second thought, he cut off his long queue – the source of his identity, according to Manchu law.[49] He came back the next day to become high-jump champion of China.[50] His action was more than a symbolic gesture. Involvement in Western physical activities was the mere tip of a revolutionary iceberg – large, powerful and inexorable.

THE REPUBLICAN ERA:
NEW CULTURE AND NEW SPORT, 1911–40

The radicals and revolutionaries overthrew the Qing government in 1911 and, finally and irrevocably, ended the feudal social system which had dominated China for thousands of years. The Republic was established after the Revolution. China began to change from a feudal to a modern social system. In order to create a new culture for the new society, in 1915 some intellectuals embraced anarchy, nationalism or socialism and started a campaign called the 'New Culture Movement' (*Xinwenhua yundong*). Western concepts, especially 'science' and 'democracy', became the weapons with which they attacked China's still influential feudal culture – Confucianism, which, in their eyes, was the major obstacle on the road to modernity. They wanted to see China revive and become strong and powerful again. They saw the weaknesses of traditional Chinese culture and wanted it reformed through westernization. By studying Western philosophical works and observing European and American societies, they came to the conclusion that the vigour which had accounted for the advance of the Western powers resided in the strong individual development of mind *and* body. Physical exercise, physical education and sport now once again attracted attention – this time from those of the New Culture and May Fourth Movements in the Republic.[51]

In October 1915, Chen Duxiu (1880–1942) published an influential article entitled 'The Aim of Today's Education', advocating 'animalism'. It was social Darwinism – Chinese-style. From the viewpoint of evolution, he declared, the human species is a animal which can only survive if strong. Modern education, therefore, should teach the young generation of *both* sexes how to survive, physically and mentally.[52] He criticized feudal education, which had educated the brain not the body. Youth had become feeble. The Chinese race had joined the lower order of the human species. Some time later in 'On the Problems of Physical Education for Youth' in *Xin qingnian* [*New Youth*], Chen laid stress on the significance of participation in physical exercise.[53] The evolutionary ball kept rolling. In 1915 the Second Far Eastern Championship Games took place in Shanghai, and Wang Zhenting,[54] the chairman of the games committee, wrote an article after the games proclaiming that sport was the foundation of a self-reliant nation.[55]

A major player now entered this 'evolutionary' game. In June 1917 Mao Zedong (1893–1976) published his essay 'A Study of Physical Education' in *Xin qingnian*. For the first time Mao expressed his views on the subject. First, he defined physical education as a tool to develop physical health. Second, he asserted that of the three elements of education – moral training, intellectual development and physical well-being – the last was the most important. A healthy body was the basis of moral and intellectual development. Third, Mao asserted that with regard to physical deterioration external causes were to be distinguished from internal causes. Physical fitness must be based on a positive mind; people must want to be healthy before they can be. Fourth, Mao revealed a completely dismissive attitude towards traditional cultural exercises, regarding them as unscientific remnants of feudal values. He argued that modern exercises educated people to be tough, to struggle, to deny defeat, to be strong and to be self-reliant. He criticized traditional educationists' negative attitude to physical education and many people's lack of awareness of its importance. Finally, in a telling phrase with later resonances, as we shall see, he declared that to participate in exercise was to participate in revolution.[56]

Mao Zedong was not unique in his era. Lu Xun (1881–1936), one of the greatest thinkers and writers in modern China, also strongly disapproved of traditional Chinese sports and regarded them as unscientific and a remnant of feudal culture.[57] These men supported modern sport and in advocating it they hoped to push aside feudal tradition.[58]

The Republican government responded to the call for reformation of the physical education system by the progressives. On 1 November 1922, the Ministry of Education issued 'The Decree of the Reformation of the School System'.[59] This new school system drew heavily on American educational ideas. John Dewey's pragmatic education now dominated Chinese schools. Both the traditional Chinese education system and the regimented Japanese school system were anathema to the ideologues of a developing democratic society. The result was a complete transformation of Chinese education. The new school system emphasized that education must suit the needs of social evolution and pay attention to developing individualism in pupils. In 1923 the new curriculum was issued and published in the *Jiaoyu zazhi* (*Education Journal*). According to the new curriculum, military gymnastics in schools were abolished and the previous course title of 'gymnastics' became 'physical education and sport'. This course now included ball games, athletics, gymnastics, physiology and hygiene. The new system also made it clear that male and female had the same right to participate in education, physical education and sport.[60] This decree was another important milestone in Chinese sports history.

While an enlarged programme of physical education was now part of the reformed education system in China, there were considerable differences of opinion about the types and amounts of exercise appropriate for boys and girls, and there was an extended debate regarding the degree of compulsion and time to be devoted to it.[61] Nevertheless, one to two hours of exercise a day had now become common and male and female students took part in modern sports activities, such as basketball, volleyball, tennis, athletics and swimming.[62]

These developments urgently required professional physical educationists.[63] New specialist physical education colleges, therefore, were opened to train teachers of physical education – for example, the Dongya [East-Asian] Women's Physical Education Institute (1916), the Dongya Physical Education Institute (1918), the Zhejiang Women's Physical Education Institute (1920), the Shanghai Liangjiang Women's Physical Education College (1920), the Zhongsan Physical Education Institute (1923), the Physical Education Department of Dongbei University (1929) and the Physical Education Department of Chongqing University (1936). These were physical education institutes with one- to four-year courses.[64] The students learned several subjects, including Chinese language and literature, English, history, education, psychology, physiology, gymnastics, athletics, dance, games and swimming.[65]

Provincial sports meetings had emerged at the beginning of the twentieth century, such as Hunan in 1905, Sichuan in 1905, Canton in 1908 and Fujian in 1912. There were five regional sports associations (North, South, East, West and Central) in China in 1915. Each region included several provinces and was responsible for organizing its own athletics competitions. For example, the North China Regional Association held ten sports meetings from 1913 to 1934. The Central Region had six sports meetings from 1923 to 1936. Some international competitions also took place: for example, Hong Kong Nanhua Football Club beat the Australian team in Melbourne in 1923; the Chinese Universities football team visited New Zealand in 1924; the Chinese table tennis team visited Japan in 1927; the annual Shanghai International Football Championships took place between 1908 and 1937 and China, England, Scotland, Russia and Portugal competed against each other; the annual Tianjin International Basketball Championships took place between 1925 and 1937, and participants included missionary schools, modern Chinese schools, the YMCA and American, British and Italian armies residing in Tianjin. Those annual sporting competitions became popular events in the cities and attracted a lot of spectators.[66]

In order to unify China's sports competitions in 1924 a non-governmental national sports organization, the China National Amateur Athletic Federation (*Zhonghua quanguo yeyu tiyu xiejinhui*), was founded in Nanjing. The aim of the federation was to supervise and organize all national and international athletic competitions. It was also the official national representative body in all international athletic organizations, such as the IOC.[67] Under the leadership of the federation, national games took place four times between 1924 and 1948. Chinese athletes took part in the Far Eastern Championship Games four times and the Olympic Games three times between 1932 and 1948.[68] All the sports events came completely out of the Olympic mould. The pattern of organization was copied from the Olympics, and the rules and regulations were copied from Western competitions. There were two reasons for this. First, initially most of the games were organized by YMCA sports secretaries – for example, the first Chinese National Games were organized by M.J. Exner, the secretary of Shanghai YMCA. The referees spoke English and even the rules and regulations of competitions were written in English.[69] Second, traditional Chinese sports could not be used in these newly established sports events. Therefore modern sport and the Olympic Games readily furnished Chinese sports with both forms and rules.

It was this complete imitation that provided a solid foundation for the development of modern Chinese sport. Hence this period saw the advancement from a traditional to a modern sports system. Modern sports events not only replaced traditional activities such as martial arts, but also displaced the recently introduced Western military exercises, which were increasingly regarded by the then progressives as a hindrance to personal development and a symbol of conformity to feudal culture.[70]

In December 1927 a National Physical Education and Sports Committee was established under the Nationalist government's Education Ministry. It was the first time that the Chinese had an national governmental body to supervise exercise throughout the country. To promote exercise, the government issued the Law of Sport for Citizens on 16 April 1929. It was the first sports law in Chinese history. It laid a foundation for the systematic organization of exercise throughout Nationalist China, and stated that:

> Boys and girls must take part in physical education and sport. ... They should participate in physical activity in which scientific sports methods are applied. ... The aim of physical education and sport is to develop men's and women's bodies for the good of the country.[71]

Four months later, the 'Curriculum of Middle Schools and Primary Schools' was issued by the Education Ministry. It stated that physical education and sport were compulsory. There was a revision between 1931 and 1932, but most of it remained. Primary-school pupils were to have 150–180 minutes of physical education classes in their timetable, and middle-school pupils 85–135 minutes. In addition, they had to have some activities after school. Activities in and after classes were almost all modern forms, including gymnastics, athletics, dance, mountain climbing, football, basketball, volleyball and tennis.[72]

REFORMATION: MARTIAL ARTS

Martial-arts societies remained considerably unchanged in the new republic, especially those that had close relationships with big tribes and influential warlords. However, a reformation of martial arts did start in the 1920s. Under constant attack from radicals and progressives, influenced by the philosophies and practices of modern sport, some open-minded martial artists such as Zhang Zijiang (1882–1969), Wang Ziping (1887–1937) and Tang Hao (1897–1959) absorbed modern sports ideas and modified martial arts practices.[73] Gradually the traditional martial arts system, teaching contents and methods started to change. Jingwu Sports Society (*Jingwu tiyuhui*) may be used as an example. It was founded in 1910 in Shanghai as a martial-arts society. It developed during the 1920s and became a national and international martial-arts organization. By the end of 1929 it had 57 branches, both in China and overseas, with 400,000 members. Martial arts and modern sports, such as tennnis, basketball, football and athletics, were taught and practised within the society. Members also learned Chinese and English. Its slogan was 'Reform traditional martial arts with modern sciences and use them to train strong bodies for China'. Sun Yat-sen (1866–1925), the 'Father of the Republic', called it the 'spirit of Jingwu' and hoped it would spread throughout China.[74]

Meanwhile some other modern Chinese martial-arts societies were established in big cities like Beijing, Tianjin, Chengdu and Changsha. They were regional or national organizations and tried to avoid a traditional tribal identity.[75] Their aim was to reform martial arts and bring them into mainstream physical education. In 1915 the Beijing Sports Society proposed that the Education Ministry should add martial arts to the curricula of primary and middle schools. It stated that martial arts should have the same status as gymnastics and other modern sports in schools. The ministry approved the proposal and stated that 'From

1915 every school should add Chinese traditional martial arts to its physical education curriculum'.[76] However, according to a national survey of 40 schools conducted in 1924 by the Beijing Sports Society, of these schools 37.5 per cent had martial arts in their curriculum, 35 per cent only practised them after school and 27.5 per cent had no martial arts at all.[77] In the 'Curriculum of Middle Schools and Primary Schools' issued by the Education Ministry in 1929 and revised in 1931 and 1932, as mentioned above, *Taijiquan*, a traditional martial art, was modified as *Taijichao*, a slow-movement gymnastics, and was the only Chinese exercise for primary schools pupils.[78] In general, modern sport dominated Chinese sports fields and arenas.

DEBATE: TRADITION OR MODERNITY?

Modern sport, which represented modern Western industrial civilization, and Chinese traditional culture, which embodied the feudal patriarchal system, were constantly in conflict in the late nineteenth and early twentieth centuries. Eventually an open discussion started when the Japanese invaded Manchuria in September 1931. The puppet regime called Manchuguo was established in 1932. The Japanese made the deposed Qing Emperor Pu Yi 'chief executive' of the government. The national humiliation made some educationists and physical educationists question the modern physical education system and methods. They argued that the failure to resist the Japanese invasion had proved that the modern physical education and sports system had failed to produce strong men to defend China. The editor of *Dagong Bao* [*Dagong Daily*] stated:

> Since the Japanese invasion people have started to question our current modern physical education system. They felt that the Chinese should have our own sports principles and practices. We should not just copy Western sport. Modern sport is just entertainment. It has been used in the West to release young people's energy and keep them away from politics. ... Modern sport does not suit a China that is in crisis and needs strong men to defend it.[79]

In 1932 China sent its first athlete, Liu Changchun, a national sprint champion, to the Olympics. After a 20-day sea journey, Liu arrived in Los Angeles. He was exhausted and failed in his first run. This result angered the Chinese and produced resentment towards modern sport. The *Dagong Daily* commented:

> The Chinese should wake up from their dreams. Western sport is for rich countries, not for China. We have learned to play modern sports for many years. Now let's see what results have we got? Nothing! Except we have produced thousands of Chinese students who wear foreign clothes, speak foreign languages and play foreign games. ... We must ask the government to listen to us now that we must break away from Western sport and promote Chinese traditional sport! Chinese people should be content to be Chinese. We do not need the Olympics and other foreign competitions, like the Far Eastern Championship Games. Let Liu to be the last one who participates in the Olympics. ... We Chinese should use our traditional physical exercise to keep fit and to train Chinese men to be strong soldiers for the sake of China.[80]

At the same time the Nationalist government was planning a special conference in Nanjing to discuss the problems and the future of Chinese physical education and sport and to draft 'The Implementation of Physical Education and Sport Among Chinese Citizens'. The government was open to suggestions. The call for the rejection of modern sport by the *Dagong Daily* certainly lit a fuse. Chinese sports history's famous debate, tradition versus modernity (*Tu yang zhi zheng*), began. The debate focused on which sport suited China: traditonal Chinese martial arts or modern Western sport. The debate lasted for five years and ended at the beginning of the Second World War.

In support of the *Dagong Daily*, Zhang Zhijiang,[81] the head of the National Institute of Martial Arts, argued on 11 August:

> The symbol of traditional Chinese sport is martial arts. We can use it to train both strong bodies and spirit and build our national identity. People with strong bodies and strong patriotic feeling can resist any invaders. ... Unlike modern sport, it is also economical and easy for the masses to learn and practise.[82]

On 17 August Xie Shiyan,[83] who had been educated in Japan and was a professor at Beijing Normal University, published an article in *Tiyu zhoubao* [*Sport Weekly*] in response to the *Dagong Daily*. Xie Shiyan argued that Western sport was not just entertainment. It had cultural and political values and meanings. It had been sufficient to train strong bodies in Europe, America and Japan. The failure of Liu at the Los Angeles Olympics was not the fault of Western sport. The Chinese would not abandon eating because one man had choked! Xie Shiyan went on:

> There are no national boundaries in culture, let alone in physical education. If the ideas and practices of physical education are good for people, we should adopt them no matter if they are foreign or native. ... With regard to martial arts we have to exam them with scientific eyes. They contain feudal elements and should be reformed according to modern physiology, psychology, education and sports scientific methods.[84]

On 20 August, Wu Yunrui, who was educated in the United States and was a professor at Beijing Normal University and member of the Education Ministry's National Physical Education and Sport Committee,[85] published an article entitled 'My View on the Problems of Sport in the Future' in *Tianjin tiyu zhoubao* [*Tianjin Sports Weekly*] in support of Xie. He argued that martial arts had trained warriors in the past and now it was time for modern sport to train soldiers for modern wars. We should choose suitable methods to meet the requirements of modern society.[86]

Three days later the *Dagong Daily* responded to Wu in an editorial. It argued that China and the West had different cultures and social systems, therefore their philosophy and methods of physical education and sport were different. Chinese martial arts best suited the Chinese. This traditional activity both trained young men to be soldiers and produced a healthy nation.[87]

Bi Bo, an educationist, then published an article entitled 'My Views on Traditional Sport – Martial Arts' in *Tianjin yuekan* [*Tianjin Monthly*] in August. He argued that attitudes towards martial arts on both sides were wrong. Martial arts as a great cultural tradition of China should be inherited by the young generation. They could play an important role in modern times. However, martial arts should be reformed with modern sciences. Their contents and teaching methods should be changed.[88]

In the heat of the debate, on 16 August, the National Conference of Physical Education and Sport opened in Nanjing. The debate became the major topic of the conference. On the same day the *Dagong Daily* published another editorial entitled 'Comment on the National Conference of Physical Education and Sport', proposing that the imitation of Western physical education and sport could not meet the needs of the nation. Physical education should not just focus on training a few excellent players to show off to other countries. In the future, martial arts should replace modern sport in schools. Modern sport could be used only as occasional substitute.[89]

There were heated discussions at the conference. In the end the conference reached a compromise: both Western sport and Chinese martial arts would be components in Chinese schools. However, martial arts could only be used when they were reformed by modern science. The conference declared:

> There are no national boundaries in culture. All physical activities, which are not against the laws of science and fit the nature of human beings, should be encouraged regardless of national boundaries. They should not be considered as good or bad just because they came from foreign countries. In order to ensure a bright future for Chinese physical education and sport, our people should have positive attitudes towards Western and Chinese sports no matter whether they are new or old, native or foreign.[90]

During the conference the National Physical Education and Sport Committee also produced 'The Implementation of Physical Education and Sport among Chinese Citizens'. This document stated that martial arts should become an element in school curricula and should also be included in some sports meetings. However, Western sport was now dominant.[91] The reason for this, by and large, was that the majority of members of the committee were 'returned students' (*Liuxuesheng*) from Europe and America. Over recent decades, they had been the major architects and promoters of modern physical education and sport in China.

However, the debate did not end at the conference. For the next five years influential people such as Wang Shijie, the Minister of Education, Jiang Weiqiao, the general secretary of the Education Ministry, Shao Rugan, the editor of *Qinfen Sports Monthly*, and Professors Yuan Dunli, Fang Wanbang, Wang Jianwu, Chen Dengke, Dong Shouyi and Ma Liang, were all involved in arguments for and against tradition and modernity.[92]

The debate ended in 1937 when the Japanese took control of the Marco Polo Bridge near Beijing. The fighting that followed this action marked the beginning of open hostilities between China and Japan and it was the first battle of the Second World War. Faced with a national crisis, 'saving the nation through physical exercise' once again became a loud and widespread slogan, and a combination of Western military exercise, modern sport and Chinese martial arts now became the favoured model for the Chinese. As Professor Wang Fudan[93] has pointed out, 'traditional or modern is no longer a issue now'.[94]

CONCLUSION

Between the 1840s and the 1930s radical change, which originated largely in pressure and influences from the West, characterized China. The change not only provoked strong resistance from the ruling regime but also from fellow-travellers – diehard Confucians. Disenchantment with the ethics of these fundamentalists and their contribution to political, economic and cultural decline stimulated criticism and confrontation. The consequences were internal cultural conflicts provoked by Western cultural diffusion, including a new conceptualization of physicality and the practice of modern sport. The substantial replacement of traditional sport was slow but inexorable. The promotion of modern sport was steady and successful. A direct consequence was that modern sport became a major part of modern Chinese culture and a new physical culture embracing both the traditional and the contemporary was born. This saga of the evolution of Western sport in modern China has proved the wisdom of Laoze, the founder of Taoism, who once said: 'The way to control the new is to go along with it and to master it through adaptation.'

NOTES

We wish to thank Tsai Chung-Tzu for her assistance with the notes.

1. This essay employs the Pinyin system, which is used in the PRC, for the translation of Chinese names, except some references that are originally written in Wade-Giles romanization system, which was used in Nationalist China before 1949 and is still used in Taiwan.
2. The Opium War (1839–42) fought between Britain and China was triggered by the British outcry against Qing government's ban of British opium. Between 1840 and 1841 British forces threatened major Chinese cities and the Yangzi delta city of Nanjing, the Qing government was forced to sign the 1842 'Treaty of Nanking'. At long last, China's door, having been closed for centuries, was forced open by the British. This event marked the beginning of China's modern history. Jian Bozhan (ed.), *Zhongguoshi gangyao* [History of China], Vol.4 (Beijing: Remin chubanshe [People's Press], 1982), pp.1–10; Hu Sheng, *Cong yapian zhanzheng dao wusi yundong* [From the Opium War to the May Fourth Movement] (Shanghai: Shanghai remin chubanshe [Shanghai People's Press], 1982), pp.33–82; K.S. Latourette, *The Chinese: Their History and Culture* (New York: Macmillan, 1964), p.302.

3. D.H. Smith, *Confucians* (London: Temple Smith, 1973), pp.72–3; J. Berthrong, 'Sages and Immortals: Chinese Religions', in *The World's Religions* (London: Lion Publishing, 1982), pp.246–51.
4. Berthrong, 'Sages and Immortals', p.245; J. Needham, *Within the Four Seas* (London: Allen & Unwin, 1969), p.63.
5. Smith, *Confucians*, p.158.
6. K. Jaywardena, *Feminism and Nationalism in the Third World* (London: Zed, 1987), p.170.
7. E. Croll, *Feminism and Socialism in China* (London: Routledge & Kegan Paul, 1978), p.22.
8. Feng Gesheng, 'Jun guomin pian – yuanyin yu tipo zhe' [On Military Exercise – Weak Bodies Cause the Weakness of the Nation], *Xinmin congbao* [Journal of New People], 1, 3, 7, 11 (1902), *passim*; Liang Qichao, 'Xin min shao-lun shang wu' [New People – On Promotion of Military Exercise], *Xinmin congbao*, 1 (1903), 7–14.
9. Zhou Xikuan *et al.*, *Zhongguo guodai tiyu shi* [Physical Education and Sport History of Ancient China] (Chengdu: Sichuan guji chubanshe, 1986), p.57.
10. Ibid.
11. Gong Shixun, 'Shilun handai zhuqiu' [On Chinese Football in the Han Dynasty], *Tiyu weishi* [Journal of Sports Culture and History], 1 (1989), 44–55.
12. Tang Hao (ed.), *Zhongguo tiyu chankao zhiliao ji* [Chinese Sport History Record], Vol.1 (Beijing: Renmin tiyu chubanshe [People's Sports Press], 1958), p.48.
13. Qiao Keqin and Guan Wenmin, *Zhongguo tiyu shixiang shi* [Chinese Physical Culture History] (Lanzhou: Gansu minzu chubanshe [Gansu Minorities Press], 1993), pp.98, 140.
14. Sui Peiyie, 'Tangdai maqiu' [History of Chinese Polo], *Chengdu tiyu xuebao* [Journal of Chengdu Institute of Physical Education], 3 (1985), 31–6; see also his MA thesis 'Lun maqiu de qiyuan he fazhan' [On the Origin and Development of Chinese Polo], Chengdu tiyu xueyuan [Chengdu Physical Education Institute], 1985.
15. Peter Lewis, *The Martial Arts* (London: Apple Press, 1988), pp.2–3.
16. David Levinson and Karen Christenson (eds), *Encyclopedia of World Sport* (Santa Barbara, CA: ABC-Clio, 1996), p.1198.
17. Karen Christenson *et al.* (eds), *International Encyclopaedia of Women and Sport* (New York: Macmillan Reference USA, 2001), p.1289.
18. Mu Kewei (ed.), *Minguo shida bangzhu* [Top Ten Tribes in the Republic of China] (Beijing: Zhongguo weiji chubanshe, 1995), pp.263–6.
19. It was an anti-Christian, anti-foreign peasant uprising. It originated in northern Shandong and ended with the siege of the foreign legation in Beijing. Participants were mostly poor peasants who practised a type of martial arts that gave the name 'boxer' to the movement.
20. Chinese Society for History of Physical Education and Sport (hereafter CSHPES) (ed.), *Zhongguo jindai tiyu shi* [Modern Chinese Sports History] (Beijing: Beijing tiyu xueyuan chubanshe, 1989), pp.135–7.
21. The 'Westernization movement' was also known as the Self-strengthening Movement or the Restoration Movement. It was advocated by a group of the Qing government's highly placed prominent officials. The essence of the movement was to learn from foreigners, then equal them and finally surpass them. The movement did not, however, envisage a consistent programme of modernization, since it was intended to leave the semi-feudal political and economic structure intact. For further details about this movement, see J.D. Spence, *The Search for Modern China* (London: Hutchinson, 1990), pp.197, 225; W. Rodzinski, *The Walled Kingdom: A History of China from 2000BC to the Present* (London: Fontana Paperbacks, 1984), pp.210–11; Jian Bozhan, *Zhongguoshi gangyao* [History of China], Vol.4, pp.44–9.
22. Latourette, *The Chinese: Their History and Culture*, p. 302.
23. Su Jinchen, 'Junguomin tiyu zhi yingxiang' [Influence of Military Drill on Chinese Physical Education], *Tiyu wenshi*, 3 (1987), 55–8.
24. Other kinds of Western exercise, such as basketball, baseball, volleyball, tennis and athletics were ignored by the Qing government and received little official attention, though they existed in missionary schools and through the YMCA and YWCA in some large cities. Western military exercises were the dominant form of exercise in this period in China.
25. CSHPES, *Zhongguo jindai tiyu shi* [Modern Chinese Sports History], pp.54–5.

26. Wang Anpo, '63 lian qian de tiyu huodong' [Sporting Activities 63 Years Ago], in Tang Hao, *Zhongguo tiyu chankao zhiliao ji* [Chinese Sport History Record], Vol.3, pp.121-3.
27. CSHPES, *Zhongguo jindai tiyu shi*, p.56.
28. Ibid.
29. The war between China and Japan was declared on 1 August 1894. China was routed on both land and sea, and was forced to sign the humiliating Treaty of Shimonoseki on 7 April 1895. The treaty stipulated a huge indemnity of 230 million taels, the opening of Chongqing, Suzhou, Hangzhou and Shaxi to trade, the right of Japanese nationals to engage in manufacturing in China, and the ceding of Taiwan and Liuqiu Islands. The treaty signalled a new stage in China's decline towards colonial status.
30. For a discussion of the Meiji Restoration see J.P. Lehmann, *The Image of Japan: From Feudal Isolation to World Power* (London: George Allen & Unwin, 1978); Daikichi Irokawa, *The Culture of the Meijin Period*, trans. M.B. Jansen (Princeton, NJ: Princeton University Press, 1970); G.M. Backmann, *The Modernization of China and Japan* (New York: Harper and Row, 1962).
31. L. Heren *et al.*, *China's Three Thousand Years: The Story of a Great Civilization* (London: Times Newspapers Ltd., 1973), p.172.
32. Rodzinski, *The Walled Kingdom*, p.242.
33. Qiao and Guan, *Zhongguo tiyu shixiang shi* [Chinese Physical Culture History], pp.168–76.
34. Yan Fu, 'Yuan qiang' [On Strength], in *Huoguan yansi congshu* [Collected Works of Yan Fu], Vol.3 (1895, p.3).
35. Kang Youwei, 'Qing tingzhi gong ma shi wu shi gaishe pinxiao zhe' [Memorandum: Requesting a Ban on Traditional Military Training and the Establishment of a Modern Military Academy], in Kang Youwei, *Wuxu zougao* [Memorial in 1898] (1898), pp.8–11.
36. CSHPES, *Zhongguo jindai tiyu shi*, p.62.
37. Jian Bozhan, *Zhongguoshi gangyao* [History of China], pp.91–2.
38. The following statistics illustrate a sharp increase in the provision of modern schools at this time:

Year	1907	1912
No. of Schools	37,888	87,272
No. of Students	1,024,988	2,933,387

    See Chen Jinpan, *Zhongguo jindai jiaoyushi* [History of Modern Chinese Education] (Beijing: Renmin jiaoyu chubanshe, 1978), pp.70, 167–8.
39. See 'Zhouding xiaoxuetang zhangcheng 1903' [Authorized Imperial Primary School Act, 1903], 'Zhouding zhongxuetang zhangcheng 1903' [Authorized Imperial Middle School Act, 1903], and 'Zhouding youji shifan xuetang zhangcheng 1903' [Authorized Imperial Normal College Act, 1903], in Chengdu tiyu xueyuan tiyushi yanjiushuo [Chengdu Sports History Research Institute] (hereafter CSHI) (ed.), *Zhongguo jindai tiyushi zhiliao ji* [Modern Chinese Sport History Reference] (Chengdu: Sichuan jiaoyu chubanshe, 1988), pp.138–44, 157–61.
40. See 'Xuebu biantong xuetang xinzhang zhi yiwen' [On the Authorized Imperial Acts], *Shi bao* [*Times*], 18 May 1909.
41. See 'Xuebu zhouqing biantong zudeng xiaoxue gangcheng zhe' [Authorized Imperial School Act, 1909], *Jiaoyu zazhi* [Education Journal], 5 (1909).
42. Fan Hong, *Footbinding, Feminism and Freedom* (London and Portland, OR: Frank Cass, 1996), p.263.
43. *Tientsin Bulletin*, 3 (1896).
44. Wang Daping and Fan Hong, *Tiyu shihua* [History of Sport] (Beijing: Kepu chubanshe [Science Press], 1990), p.46.
45. For further details see the 'Report of YMCA, Beijing, 1907–1908', a copy of which can be found in the Historical Library of the YMCA, New York City. See also CSHPES, *Zhongguo jindai tiyu shi*, p.64.
46. 'Jinshi daxuetang kai diyichi yundonghui gao laibin wei' [Report of the First Sports Meeting of Beijing University], *Sichuan xuebao* [Journal of Sichuan Education], 3 (1905); 'Baoding shifan xuetang diyiqi yundonghui' [Report of the First Baoding College Sports Meeting],

Chengdu ribao [Chengdu Daily], 19 Sept. 1904; 'Sichuan sheng diyichi yundonghui zhangcheng' [Rules of the First Sichuang Provincial Sports Meeting], *Sichuan xuebao*, 19 (1905); 'Nanjing diyichi xuexiao lianhe yundonghui' [First Nanjing Colleges' Sports Meeting], in Tang Hao, *Zhongguo tiyu chankao zhiliao ji*, Vol.2, pp.72–3.
47. *The North Herald*, 23 Oct. 1910.
48. *Association Men*, Beijing, 4 (1910). *Association Men* was a journal of the YMCA.
49. Manchu men's hairstyle consisted of a high shaved forehead and a long braid down the back. Originally it was developed to keep long hair out of the face in battle. By Manchu degree issued by Dorgon in 1645, all Chinese men had to adopt this hairstyle or risk execution. Cutting the queue braid was regarded as a act of defiance against the Qing government.
50. Wu Chi-kang, 'The Influence of the YMCA on the Development of Physical Education in China' (Unpublished Ph.D. thesis, University of Michigan, 1959), pp.123–7.
51. They were intellectual, social and political reformation movements covering the years 1915 to 1921. See Fan Hong, *Footbinding, Feminism and Freedom*, pp.119–22.
52. Chen Duxiu, 'Jinri zi jiaoyu fangzheng' [Aim of Today's Education], *Qingnian zazhi* [Journal of Youth], 2 (1915).
53. Chen Duxiu, 'Qinnian tiyu wenti' [On the Problems of Physical Education for Youth], *Xin qingnian* [*New Youth*], 1 (1920), 3–4. In this article Chen advocated physical exercise for youth, but he disapproved of competitive sport.
54. Wang Zhenting (1882–1961), educated in the United States, was a major figure in the YMCA in China and later became a key figure in Chinese politics and sports. He was the Foreign Minister of the Guomindang government. He supported the development of modern physical education and sport in China and was the first Chinese representative on the IOC.
55. Wang Zhenting, 'Direchi yuandong yundonguhoi zi gangyan' [My View on the Second Far Eastern Championship Games], *Jinbu* [Progress], 3 (1915).
56. Mao Zedong, 'Tiyu zhi yanjiu' [A Study on Physical Education and Exercise], *Xin qingnian* [New Youth], 4 (1917), 5–12.
57. Lu Xun, 'Shuigan lu' [My View], *Xin qingnian*, 5 (1918), 5–6; 'Quanshu yu quanfei' [On Traditional Martial Arts], *Xin qingnian*, 6 (1919), 9–10; Fan Hong, *Footbinding, Feminism and Freedom*, p.7.
58. Fan Hong, *Footbinding, Feminism and Freedom*, p.14.
59. CSHPES, *Zhongguo jindai tiyu shi*, pp.117–18.
60. Ibid.
61. Hao Gengsheng, 'Shinian lai woguo zi tiyu, 1917–1927' [On the Development of Physical Education in China, 1917–27], *Tiyu* [Sport], 2 (1927), 2–3.
62. Yang Zhikang, 'Wusi xin wenhua yundong he nuzi tiyu de fazan' [May Fourth Movement and Chinese Women's Emancipation]', in CSHPES, *Lunwen ji* [Selected Works], Vol.3 (Beijing: Beijing tiyu xueyuan chubanshe, 1986), p.96.
63. Hao Gengshen, 'Shinian lai woguo zi tiyu', 5.
64. See 'Tiyu shizhi zi peiyang' [On Physical Educationists' Training], *Di re ci zhongguo jiaoyu nianjian* [Second Yearbook of Chinese Education] (Nanking, 1948), p.1320; also see CSHI, *Zhongguo jindai tiyushi zhiliao ji* [Modern Chinese Sport History Reference], p.285.
65. CSHI, *Zhongguo jindai tiyushi zhiliao ji*, pp.308, 313, 317–21.
66. CSHPES, *Zhongguo jindai tiyu shi*, p.157.
67. There is some misunderstanding and confusion about the formation of Chinese national athletic associations in Jonathan Kolatch's book *Sport, Politics and Ideology in China* (New York: Jonathan David Publishers, 1971), pp.18–19. It is necessary to explain briefly here the process of the formation of the national athletic association. In 1915 there were five regional sports associations (North, South, East, West and Central) founded in China. In the spring of 1919 the representatives of North, South and East China appointed a committee to draft a provisional constitution for a national athletic organization. The fruit of this was the formation of *Zhonghua yieyu yundong lianhehui* [China Amateur Athletic Union], which was formally founded on 3 April 1922 in Beijing (the first preparatory meeting was on 4 June 1921 in Shanghai). There were nine members on the executive committee; three of them were foreigners (YMCA physical directors). In 1924, influenced by the May Fourth Movement, in an anti-imperialist atmosphere, the China Amateur Athletic Union was

abolished. The Chinese founded their own national athletic assocation called *Zhonghua quanguo tiyu xiejinhui* [China National Amateur Athletic Federation] on 5 July 1924 in Nanjing. There were nine members on the exeutive committee, all Chinese. This association and the Physical Education Committee of the Ministry of Education were the two major national bodies in charge of the development of physical education and sport in the Nationalist area. For details see Shen Shiliang , 'Zhonghua quanguo tiyu xiejinhui shi' [History of the China National Amateur Athletic Federation], *Tiyu jikan* [Physical Education Quarterly], Jan. 1935, 10–13. The author was a director and executive member of the federation from 1924 to 1935. See also CSHPES, *Zhongguo jindai tiyu shi*, pp.161–3; Zhang Gong, 'Zhonghua yieyu yundong lianhehui jieti yu heshi?' [When Did the China Ameteur Athletic Union Disappear?], *Tiyu wenshi*, 4 (1991), 48–9; Zhang Tianbai, 'Zhonghua quanguo tiyu xiejinhui choubei chenli shi mo' [History of the Founding of the China National Amateur Athletic Federation], *Tiyu wenshi*, 6 (1990), 30–33. See also Fan Hong, *Footbinding, Feminism and Freedom*, pp.267 and 283.
68. CSHPES, *Zhongguo jindai tiyu shi*, pp.260–62.
69. Wang and Fan, *Tiyu shihua* [History of Sport], p. 211.
70. Huang Xin, 'Xuexiao yinfuo feizhi bincao?' [Should Schools Abolish Military Drill?], *Changsa tiyu zhoubao* [Changsa Sports Weekly], 46 (1919), 3–9; Chang Baocen, 'Xuexiao yinfuo feizhi bincao?' [Should Schools Abolish Military Drill?], *Changsa tiyu zhoubao* [Changsa Sports Weekly], Feb. 1920, 1–5; see also Fan Hong, 'The Olympic Movement in China: Ideals, Realities and Ambitions', *Culture, Sport, Society*, 1 (1998), 151.
71. 'Guomin tiyu fa' [Law for Sports for Citizens], 16 April 1929, in *Diyichi Zhongguo jiaoyu nianjian* [First Chinese Educational Annual Book] (Nanking, 1933), pp.897–9; see also Fan Hong, *Footbinding, Feminism and Freedom*, p.231.
72. CSHPES, *Zhongguo jindai tiyu shi*, pp.193–8.
73. Ibid., pp.293–5.
74. Wang and Fan, *Tiyu shihua*, p.201; CSHPES, *Zhongguo jindai tiyu shi*, pp.270–73.
75. CSHPES, *Zhongguo jindai tiyu shi*, p.139.
76. Ibid., p.138.
77. Ibid., p.139.
78. Ibid., pp.194–6.
79. Editor, 'Jinhuo guomin zhi tiyu wenti' [Problems of Our Sports in the Future], *Dagong Bao* [Dagong Daily], 7 Aug. 1932.
80. Ibid.
81. Zhang Zhijiang (1882–1966), a retired general, established the National Institute of National Martial Arts in 1933 and was the head of the institute.
82. Zhang Zhijiang, 'Gei Dagong Bao de yifen xin' [A Letter to Dagong Daily], *Da Gong Bao*, 11 Aug. 1932.
83. No birth and death information is available on Xie Shiyan.
84. Xie Siyan, 'Ping Dagong Bao qiri shelun' [Comments on the *Dagong Daily* Editorial on 7 August], *Tiyu zhoubao* [Sports Weekly], 17 Aug. 1932, pp.1–3.
85. Wu Yunrui (1892–1976) obtained his master's degree in education at Columbia University, New York. After he returned to China he was professor and director in PE departments at several universities in China. He was a member of the National Physical Education and Sport Committee of the Education Ministry. After 1949 he became director of the PE department at Nanjing University and then the principal of Shanghai Institute of Physical Education.
86. Wu Yunrui, 'Jinhuo zhi guomin tiyu wenti zhi wojian' [My Views on the Problems of Sport in the Future], *Tianjin tiyu zhoubao*, 20 Aug. 1932.
87. Editorial, 'Zailun jinhou guomin zhi tiyu weiti' [On the Problems of our Sports Again], *Dagong Bao*, 23 Aug. 1932.
88. Bi Bo, 'Lun Zhongguo chuantong tiyu: Wushu' [On Traditional Chinese Sport: Martial Arts], *Tianjin yuekan*, Aug. 1932, 6–7.
89. Editorial, 'Yu Guomin tiyu dahui shangque' [To Discuss with the National Conference of Physical Education and Sport], *Dagong Bao*, 17 Aug. 1932.
90. 'Guomin tiyu dahui xuanyan' [Declaration of the National Conference of Physical Education], *Chen Bao*, 22 Aug. 1932.

91. 'Guomin tiyu sishi fan'an' [Implementation of Physical Education and Sport among Chinese Citizens], in *Jiaoyu nianjian* (Nanking, 1933), pp.897–901.
92. For details of those influential people's biographies and their articles see CSHPES, *Zhongguo jindai tiyu shi, passim*; Guojia tiwei tiyu wenshi gongzhuo weiyuanhui [Commission of Sports History of the Sports Ministry] (ed.), *Zhongguo jindai tiyu wenxuan* [Collection of Essays on Modern Chinese Sport] (Beijing: Renmin tiyu chubanshe, 1992). During this period articles such as Wu Yunri, 'Tiyu zhi guojie wenti' [On Chinese Exercise and Western Exercise], *Jiaoyu Congkan* [Education Journal], June (1935), 1–7; Tang Hao, 'Benjie quanguo yundonghui guocui zhuyizhe biaoyan gei women kan de Zhongguo wusu jinji de jiatao [On Performance and Traditional Exercise at the National Games], *Guosu sheng* [Voice of Traditional Exercise], Oct. (1935), 1–3; Fan Zhenxing, 'Wu duiyi guosu de shoujian' [A Personal View of Traditional Exercise], *Tiyu zazhi* [Journal of Sport] (1935), 252–60; Cheng Dengke, 'Women yingfuo tichang Zhongguo de minzhu tiyu' [Shall We Promote Chinese Traditional Exercise?], *Qinfen tiyu zhoukan* [Qinfen Sport Weekly], 1 (1936); Wang Jiawu, 'Fuxing minzhu yu tichang minzhu tiyu' [On Restoration the Nation and Promotion of the Traditional Exercise], *Qin Fen tiyu zhoukan*, 4 (1937), 275–7, appeared in national journals and newspapers.
93. Wang Fudan (1900–75), Chinese physical educationist, graduated from Dongnan University, majoring in physical education. He was the director and professor at Shanghai University and supervisor of Shanghai City Stadium in the 1930s.
94. Wang Fudan, 'Guanyu tiyu de jige wenti' [On Several Issues in Physical Education and Sport], *Tiyu* [Physical Education], 2 (1937), 3–5.

8

Ideology, Politics, Power: Korean Sport – Transformation, 1945–92

HA NAM-GIL and J.A. MANGAN

The growth of modern sport in Asia varied self-evidently with the pace of evolution of the 'sports movements' in the individual countries. The Asian nations' participation in the Olympic Games reveals, at merely one level, very different rates of progress. According to the *Guinness Olympics Fact Book*, during the 40-year period from the first Olympic Games (held in 1896 in Athens) to the eleventh (held in 1936 in Berlin), only two Asian countries won medals – India and Japan. And in the longer period up to the fourteenth Olympics (held in 1948 in London) only four Asian countries won medals – India, Japan, Korea and Iran.[1]

While the first South Asian country to win an Olympic medal was India, the country that led the way more ostentatiously in the assimilation of modern sport in South-East Asia was Japan. This is reflected in the fact that at the tenth Olympic Games (held in 1932 in Los Angeles) Japan took fifth place in the medal count (seven gold medals, seven silver and four bronze).[2] Then in 1964 Japan became the first Asian country to host the Olympics (the eighteenth Olympic Games). China, its huge neighbour, first entered the Olympics in 1932 with only one athlete, but at the fourteenth Olympic Games in 1948 presented 33 athletes. However, throughout this 12-year period it did not win a single medal.[3] This surely reflected domestic political circumstances.

The purpose of this contribution is to describe and then analyse the evolution of modern sport in one Asian nation – Korea[4] – in relation to the nation's post-war political, economic, cultural and social development. Korea demonstrates that modern sport, politics, economics, culture and society are intrinsically linked, in varying degrees, of course, at various movements in a nation's history, and that in the case of Korea modern sport was essentially the consequence of its political priorities.

Among Asian countries, the post-war development of Korean sport was unique. It was politically driven, resourced and endorsed and it was the direct product of anti-Communist, not Communist, ideological purpose. It was a phenomenon of the middle of the second half of the twentieth century – the time of Korea's 'Political Leap Forward' in modern sport. Progress, as in the case of China at the end of the twentieth century, was exceptional. This period of rapid change, its causes, its consequences and its political, economic, cultural and social stimuli will be our concern below. First, however, it will be illuminating to simply describe the progress of modern sport from 1945 to 1992; then to relate this period to the crucial years of the Political Leap Forward and to examine the associated political, economic, cultural and social factors. All played their part.

Restriction of the timescale to between 1945 to 1992 is for several reasons. First, while modern sport was introduced into Korea in the late nineteenth century and spread initially due to the influence of English and American missionaries,[5] there then followed the harsh and inhibiting period of Japanese colonialism. Consequently Korea did not take its place on the world sporting stage until after the Second World War. Second, the history of the halting progress of Korean sport before 1945 has already been discussed by the authors elsewhere.[6] Third, after the Second World War Korean sport was closely linked to political priorities, purposes and personnel, and this association continued until the Sixth Republic (1988–92). Thus Korea furnished a fascinating illustration of a 'marriage' between politics and sport that greatly advanced the status, success and popularity of the latter. This has not been revealed until now to an international audience.

IMMEDIATE POST-WAR KOREAN SPORT

Korean sport during the first half of the twentieth century grew out of nationalism, but from 1910 until 1945 the Japanese colonial government in Korea controlled sport and suppressed much of its growth.[7] As a result, organized sport was unable to flourish. Then, because of the Korean War of the 1950s, Korea afterwards was in ruins. Political chaos, social instability and economic destitution were the order of the day. This made it quite impossible for Korean sport to prosper. However, in the 1960s it did prosper – greatly – and by the 1980s had attracted the attention of the world. Arguably, there are at least two models that can be usefully employed in any attempt to explain the progress of modern sport in the 'global village'. The first embraces politically stable, socially advanced and economically prosperous nations that steadily establish first a system of elite sport, then general sport and then professional sport – not, of course, in simple linear progression. The reality is more complicated. Then there are the nations in which political ideology thrusts forward modern sport for its own ends and with its own rationalizations and with the extensive use of national resources. Korean sport in the latter half of the twentieth century clearly fits the second model.

THE KOREAN EDUCATIONAL SYSTEM

The key to Korean sport in the second half of the twentieth century was the school playground. Until the 1950s, remnants of Japanese imperialist education still survived. After the Korean War, because of the division of Korea and the cold war between the Soviet Union and the United States, South Korean schools stressed anti-Communism and national defence. As a result, physical education was more like military training. However, in the 1960s there was a dramatic change. With the 'Military Revolution'[8] of 16 May 1961, the Park Chung-hee regime (May 1961 to October 1979) was established. The rise to power of Park Chung-hee heralded great advances in the areas of economics, education, society – and sport.

After Park Chung-hee took over the reins of power, the catchphrase in Korean education was 'education linked to nationality', and the task of education was 'to provide for the hard-working' and 'to foster the healthy'.[9] These slogans revealed a determination to establish a work ethic and to develop an associated physical and mental toughness. Thus physical education came centre stage politically. All kinds of sports activities were recognized as important educational measures. The school physical education policy of the Park Chung-hee regime, which was at its height in the 1970s, had two purposes – to develop general physical fitness and to cultivate outstanding athletes – both in the interests of the nation.

Park Chung-hee's regime did not stop at exhortations, slogans and visionary policies. It took concrete measures and pursued practical actions. In pursuit of the general physical fitness of the young, there were: the School Health Law;[10] the School Physical Examination Law;

the Physical Fitness Badge System; and the School Physical Education Facilities Standards Order.[11] The Physical Fitness Badge System will serve to illustrate the commitment of the regime. It was introduced in 1970 in all middle and high schools throughout the country.[12] Later, a points system for performance was added, both to the secondary school entrance examination (1972) and the university entrance examination (1973).[13] Physical training was now compulsory for all Korean youth in high school and university. The School Sports Movement was introduced at the same time. The government encouraged schools to raise their level of physical education. One outcome was that school sport was divided into internal and inter-school sports programmes. Representative systems were also introduced at local, regional and national levels to stimulate and cultivate outstanding athletes. These included the School Banner Support System and the National Youth Games.[14] These became the means for the expansion of a Korean sports elite from the 1960s onwards.

The School Banner Support System was a national sports strategy that encouraged all elementary, middle, and high schools to choose a sporting event appropriate to their particular geographic or social situation and then, if possible, select and train the outstanding athletes in that event. This strategy was implemented in a highly systematic way. Outstanding athletes were 'uncovered' and went forward to inter-school competitions. A variety of scholarships and incentives were awarded to the successful. School and regional authorities provided the fullest support for exceptional athletes.

The newly established National Youth Games, like the School Banner Support System, clearly symbolized the serious intention of the government to raise the fitness of the nation in the cause of self-defence and self reliance, and to promote a confident image of South Korea to the world. The first National Youth Games[15] were held in 1972, and have been held every subsequent year.[16] The purposes of these games are encapsulated in the slogan for the Games provided by the Korean Sports Council, 'A Strong Body, a Strong Mind and a Strong Country'. The goals of the KSC were set down as follows:

> to provide basic sports to growing boys and girls and instil in them a competitive attitude, to construct the foundations for the revitalization of school physical education, the grassroots expansion of the sports population, the promotion of lifetime

sport, and the improvement of international competitiveness through the early discovery of outstanding athletes.[17]

The Ministry of Education and the Korean Sports Council during the Park Chung-hee regime went a long way to achieve their goals. The Youth Games were the apex of school sports endeavour. They became the catalyst for energizing schools and played a subsequent role in the popularization of sport and the discovery and development of outstanding athletes. Those athletes revealed by the Youth Games won automatic selection for entry into middle school, high school and university and in this way a coherent system for the progressive support, improvement and motivation of young athletes was built into the educational system. As a result, the performances of the Korean sports elite improved sharply.

The innovations began in earnest under the Park Chung-hee regime continued during the Fourth Republic (October 1972–October 1979), and the Fifth Republic (March 1981–March 1988) of the Chun Doo-hwan regime and the Sixth Republic (February 1988–February 1993) of the Roh Tae-woo regime. The efforts of these various regimes culminatively saw Korea host the twenty-fourth Olympic Games and the tenth Asian Games. These stupendous achievements produced a greatly increased general interest in sport. This led to a further expansion of school sport. Furthermore, from 1980 onwards the government actively encouraged participation in sport at home and abroad.[18] With political endorsement, government resources, an effective strategy, public support and an enthusiastic education system, in less than 50 years a revolution in sport in schools occurred – in the interests of national defence, national self-reliance and national visibility.

SPORT IN SOCIETY

In the second half of the twentieth century, then, modern sport became part and parcel of school and society. Up until the 1950s the social situation in Korea was one in which organized sport was unable to develop. Modern sport was first introduced into Korea in the 1890s, as noted earlier, largely through the YMCA centres, from which it spread steadily to both schools and society.[19] However, from 1910 to 1945, the period during which Japan ruled Korea, Korean sport was heavily regulated and largely suppressed and an independent sports system could not prosper.[20] Modern sport under civil leadership began only after the liberation from Japanese imperialist rule in 1945. On 17 August 1945, the Choseon Sports Society, which had earlier been disbanded by the Japanese imperialists, was re-established. In 1947 Korea joined the International Olympic Committee and in 1948 officially participated in its first Olympics (the fourteenth Olympic Games in London). In the 1950s, in spite of the political and social instability and the economic destitution that followed the Korean War, modern sport, under the aegis of the Korean Sports Council, slowly made progress. Korea gradually began to distinguish itself in international events such as table tennis, soccer, boxing, weightlifting and judo. Nevertheless, from 1945 to 1960 the social situation in Korea was not stable enough to support a modern sporting culture. The people's interest in sport was not great. There were more pressing priorities. Thus, only a handful of athletes met international standards. However, as mentioned earlier, in the 1960s with strong government support, sport for the people entered a new and very active phase.

In 1961, the revolutionary government of Park Chung-hee called for a national revival and demonstrated a strong and committed leadership to this end. Sport was not excluded.[21] During the 18 years and five months in which he was in power, Park Chung-hee simultaneously promoted an 'elite sports policy' and a 'popular sports policy'. In the 1980s these policies, as stated above, were inherited by the Chun Doo-hwan and Roh Tae-woo regimes. Excellent results were obtained.

The 'social sports revolution' of the 1960s to the 1980s had several distinctive characteristics. First, it was government-led. From the 1960s onwards, the government enacted laws and regulations to ensure the popularization of sport and the creation of a sports elite and crucially ensured financial support for the 'revolution'. As is clear from Table 1, and as has been noted earlier, government policies aiming at accelerating the growth of modern sport began after Park Chung-hee arrived on the political scene in 1961. In June of 1961 his government implemented a People's Educational Policy that included 'developing healthy bodies and strong minds', on the back of the slogan 'Physical Fitness is National Strength'. Then various policies for promoting sport were put in place by means of the 1962 Peoples' Physical Fitness and Sports Promotion Law. One noted element was the promotion of a national gymnastics system.[22] It would not be an exaggeration to say that modern Korean sport in the second half of the twentieth century was built on the

TABLE 8.1
AN ABBREVIATED HISTORY OF THE KOREAN SPORT MOVEMENT

1945	Reorganization of Choseon Sports Society. Establishment of 12 athletic organizations (Nov.). 20th National Games inaugurated.
1947	Formally entered International Olympic Committee (June).
1948	First Korean participation in Olympics (14th Games in London) (July). Choseon Sports Society renamed the Korean Sports Association (Sept.).[a]
1952	Formally entered Asian Games Federation (July).
1955	Inaugural publication of *Physical Education and Sports*, the Korean Journal of Physical Education and Sports (Feb.).
1960	First Korean participation in the Davis Cup (tennis) preliminaries (April).
1961	Military Revolutionary Government decides to provide government support for the budget of the Korean Sports Council. ·Headquarters for the People's Reconstruction Movement of the Revolutionary Government adopts slogan 'Fitness is National Strength' and takes action to popularize 'People's Gymnastics'.
1962	Law promoting physical education and sport is promulgated 17 Sept. (Statute No. 1146). 15·Oct. is designated National Sports Day. ·Last week of each month established as National Sports Week.
1963	Jangchung Gymnasium opened. Gymnasiums built in each city and each seat of provincial government.
1966	Construction on Taenung Athletic Village completed (15 Jan.). Korean Sports Council Hall opened (area of 8,340 square yards).
1968	Government plan to unify sports organizations promulgated. Three corporate bodies – the Korean Sports Council, the Korean Olympic Committee and the Korean School Sports Association – are integrated into the Korean Sports Council (March).
1974	Korean Sports Council decides on Lifelong Annuity System for medal winners in Olympic Games, the World Athletic Championships, the Asian Games and the Asian Athletic Championships (Dec.).
1976	First Korean gold medal in the Olympic Games (Chong-mo Yang, in freestyle wrestling at 21st Olympic Games, Montreal).
1979	Jamsil Sports Centre opened (18 April), a large-scale international-standard sports facility with one floor under ground and three floors above ground.
1981	The Korean Physical Education and Sports Promotion Foundation implements an injury insurance system (March). General Meeting of International Olympic Committee decides Seoul will host 1988 Olympics (Sept). General Meeting of Asian Games Federation decides on Seoul to host 10th Asian Games in 1986 (26 Nov).
1982	Ministry of Sports inaugurated – first Minister of Sports, Roh Tae-woo (March). ·Curtain rises on Korean Professional Baseball League (27 March).
1983	First professional *Ssireum* (Korean Traditional Wrestling) championship held (April).
1984	Armed Forces Athletic Corps established (Jan). ·Roh Tae-woo appointed president of Korean Sports Council (Oct).
1985	1988 Marksmanship Training Team for National Marksmanship Team established (June).
1986	1986 Asian Games 'Sports Science Learning Convention' held (Sept). 10th Asian Games held in Seoul (20 Sept. – 5 Oct.).
1988	1988 Seoul Olympics 'Sports Science Learning Convention' held (Sept).·24th Olympics held in Seoul.
1989	The National Sports Promotion Foundation inaugurated (April). Life Sports Departments established in local autonomous government administrative organizations.
1991	The National Sports Council of Sports for All founded (Feb.).

Note: [a] The early name (in English) of the Korean Sports Council was the Korean Amateur Sports Association. It was later changed to the Korean Sports Council.

Source: Hak-rae Lee, chronological table in *The One-Hundred Year History of Korean Sports* (Seoul: Korean Academy of Physical Education, 2000), pp.685–762.

foundations of Park Chung-hee's personal philosophy and strength of will. In a real sense, he was the 'father of modern sport' in 'modern' Korea. Most of the laws enacted to promote sport are concentrated in the 18 years when Park Chung-hee was in power. Even the idea of winning the 1988 Seoul Olympics for Korea originated during his regime.[23] As mentioned earlier, his innovations were taken up enthusiastically by the Chun Doo-hwan and Roh Tae-woo regimes, with the result that continuous progress was made and Korea took its place among those advanced nations of South-East Asia with advanced sports systems. This continuity is set out in diagrammatic form in Table 8.1.

Second, Korean sport evolved around a sports elite. It was certainly simultaneously promoted both as a popular sports movement and elite sports movement. However, the government initially laid emphasis on the establishment of a sports elite, so popular sport really got off the ground only after the successful creation of this elite. The Physical Education and Sports Promotion Law of 17 September 1962, which is often credited with having brought about the most revolutionary change in the history of Korean sport, explicitly stated as its goals enhancing the peoples' physical fitness, fostering healthy minds and providing for a contented life for the people through popular sport.[24] The specific details of this law included various measures to promote sport in general: the designation of a National Sports Day (15 October every year), the creation of a 'sports week' (the last week of each month), measures to advance local sport,[25] the training of sports coaches, the establishment of sports facilities[26] and so on. However, in spite of Herculean efforts by the government and sports organizations, there were limits to the success of the promotion of popular sport. Specifically during the 1960s and 1970s, the basic fact was that the economic condition of Korean society did not allow the public to take part in the sport available. There was simply insufficient leisure time.[27] Earning a living preoccupied people. There was the further fact that there remained a shortage of swimming pools, gymnasiums and other facilities. Accordingly, Korean popular sport did not gain great momentum until the 1980s. In contrast, however, elite sport demonstrated remarkable progress. As can be seen in Table 8.1, from the 1960s onwards the government introduced institutions to enhance the skills of outstanding athletes, provided extensive training facilities and increased financial support for promising athletes. By way of example, gymnasiums for specialist gymnasts were erected in all cities, the Taenung Athletic Village was set up in 1966 for the exclusive training use of national team members and later a decision was taken to set up a lifelong annuity system for medal-winners in major international events. In addition, the Physical Education and Sports Promotion Law implemented in 1962 included not only measures for popular sport but also provisions for the cultivation of elite sport, including the requirement that all places of employment designated by the president had to develop at least one sports team with its own coach;[28] that all government or local self-governing organizations were to provide assistance with living expenses for outstanding athletes; and that all national enterprises or enterprises designated by the government were to employ promising athletes of exceptional athletic ability.[29] Government support for elite sport became even more extensive in the 1980s. The People's Physical Education and Sports Promotion Law of 1962, revised in 1971, was revised further in 1982. The stated goal of the first Physical Education and Sports Promotion Law of September 1962, as mentioned earlier, was 'to improve general physical fitness, develop healthy minds and promote a contented life for the people'.[30] But the goal of the revised Physical Education and Sports Promotion Law of 31 December 1982 added the strategy of 'enhancing national prestige through sport'.[31] This inclusion officially expressed the intention of the government to foster elite sport in the interests of national prestige. Elite sport was now to be favoured over popular sport in the interests of national glory.

Thus, in essence, Korean sport in general expanded during the period from the 1960s to the 1980s, but this was especially true of elite sport. This is obvious from the achievements of Korean athletes in international events. For example, as can be seen in Table 8.2, the record of Korean athletes participating in the Olympics during the period from the 1960s to the 1980s reveals increasing success. The Korean marathon runner Kee-chung Son (better known as Kitei Son) had won a famous gold medal in the 1936 Berlin Olympics, but he participated as a Japanese national. Korea officially participated in its first Olympics as a nation at the fourteenth Olympics in London (1948). It obtained its first gold medal at the 1976 Montreal Games, when Yang Jung-mo won a gold medal in the freestyle wrestling. In the 1980s, however, Korea was placed in the top ten medal winning countries. The promotion of the elite sport in the two previous decades was clearly paying dividends. As was pointed out earlier, during the 40 years from the first Olympic Games in Athens, until the eleventh games in Berlin, only two Asian countries won medals – India and Japan.[32] Furthermore, the only two Asian countries to earn gold medals were also India and Japan. Of all the South Asian countries in terms of medals, Japan impressed most. In the tenth Olympic Games in Los Angeles (1932), Japan ranked fifth in medals won behind the United States, Italy, France and Sweden, with a total of seven gold, seven silver and four bronze.[33] As already stated, in 1964 Japan was the first Asian country to host an Olympics (the eighteenth Games). Up until the 1960s the Korean Olympic medal tally remained behind Japan, but also behind that of India, Iran and Pakistan. In the 1980s, however, there was a startling change. There was now a direct correlation between political will, created infrastructure, available resources and Korean medal success.

In summary, the Korean 'sports revolution' had the following characteristics: after the end of the Second World War a private sports organization, the Korean Sports Council, took charge of Korean sport but achieved little. During the 1960s, in the wake of a new president with a military background, the government designed and implemented a new sports policy. Korean sport shot ahead in a remarkably short time.

TABLE 8.2
OLYMPIC MEDAL RESULTS AT THE (SUMMER) OLYMPIC GAMES

No.	Year	City	Participants/ Events	G	S	B	Rank	Comments
10	1932	Los Angeles	3/2	0	0	0	–	Participated as Japanese nationals
11	1936	Berlin	7/3	1	0	1	–	
14	1948	London	67/7	0	0	2	24	First official participation
15	1952	Helsinki	43/6	0	0	2	33	
16	1956	Melbourne	57/6	0	1	1	23	
17	1960	Rome	75/8	0	0	0	34	
18	1964	Tokyo	224/15	0	2	1	27	First held in Asia
19	1968	Mexico City	74/10	0	1	1	32	
20	1972	Munich	68/8	0	1	0	33	First North Korean participation
21	1976	Montreal	72/5	1	1	4	19	First gold, Chong-mo Yang
22	1980	Moscow						Did not participate
23	1984	Los Angeles	284/19	6	6	7	10	
24	1988	Seoul	644/23	12	10	11	4	Second held in Asia
25	1992	Barcelona	350/24	12	5	12	7	

Source: Ch'oi Jong-sam, *Cheyouksa* [History of Physical Education] (Seoul: Pokyong Munhwa Publishing, 1995), p.476.

The reasons are beyond dispute. First, Korea successfully created an 'educational sports system' in conjunction with a 'social sports movement', with the latter growing out of the former. Second, Korean sport was promoted by both non-governmental and governmental organizations, but the state took a pronounced and emphatic lead over time and provided continuous backing over several regimes. In short, there was continuity of endorsement. Third, Korea effectively developed both elite and popular sports systems and the success of elite sport served to open the door to popular sport. Thus, in a period of some 30 years Korean sport underwent a revolutionary change; it had been transformed. There could hardly be a better example of the powerful influence of politics in modern sport.

THE IDEOLOGICAL BACKGROUND TO MODERN KOREAN SPORT

While the growth of sport in modern nations is linked to political, social, cultural and economic circumstances, the driving force behind this growth is not infrequently ideological. This is certainly the case in Korea. Korean sport was the outcome of state agencies playing a far greater role than private agencies during a period of authoritarian rule and sustained political, economic and cultural transformation. Behind this state authoritarianism was a nationalistic ideology – a social Darwinian belief in the need to ensure national survival in the future after the humiliations of colonization and the traumas of civil war.

SOCIETY AND SPORT DURING SYNGMAN RHEE REGIME, 1945–60

Throughout the first part of the twentieth century Korea had a history of repeated ill fortune. Korea fell under brutal Japanese colonial rule in 1910 and was not delivered from it until 1945. Subsequently the country experienced a horrific civil war and was divided into North and South Korea, with Communism and democracy in confrontation across the thirty-eighth parallel. Soviet troops were above the border; American troops were below it. South Korea was an American satrapy. The American military authorities wielded supreme command over politics, the economy and education, and by supporting the establishment of a newly independent democratic government[34] 'tried to check the influence of the Soviet Union on the Korean peninsula and establish a pro-American government'.[35] In 1948, three years after the American military government had been established, a legal and independent government was set up through democratic elections.[36] This was the First Republic (1948–60) of the Syngman Lee regime. The regime held onto power for 12 years, but as a result of a gradual deterioration into a corrupt and dictatorial authority collapsed with the People's Revolution of April 1960.[37]

After the liberation from Japanese colonial rule in 1945, Korean sport faced a new phase under private non-governmental leadership. The American military authorities established a Department of Physical Education and Sport in the Ministry of Education that was responsible for both a school and a social sports policy. The Choseon Sports Society that had been disbanded by the Japanese in 1938 was now re-established.[38] A variety of sports organizations were re-organized and the National Games were created. In addition, in 1947 Korea officially became a member of the International Olympic Committee, and in 1948 Korea participated in its first Olympics, the (Summer) Olympic Games in London. With the establishment of the new government on 15 August 1948, the Choseon Sports Society changed its name to the Korean Sports Council and modern sport was gradually introduced to the whole nation. But as a result of the Korean War breaking out on 25 June 1950, the new foundations of Korean sports culture collapsed. All the sports records of the Korean Sports Council were lost; Korean athletes were unable to participate in the First Asian Games and youth was mobilized for war.

The bald fact is that the Syngman Lee regime during its time in power (1948–60) never established a clear sports policy, and state support and sponsorship were insufficient. As can be seen in Table 8.1, the Syngman Lee administration left few signs of any concrete involvement in sport at governmental level, and as can be seen in Table 8.2, the record of the Korean team at the 1960 Olympics Games in Rome suggests that elite Korean sport had withered in the latter half of the 1950s. After the Korean War began, the Syngman Lee regime was obsessed with using the fear of Communism to purge opponents and so maintain its authoritarian rule. As a result, it was unable to provide a clear vision of national progress. One consequence was that the social conditions necessary for the development of sport were lacking. Then after the Korean War, the Korean economy entered a dark age, with the national economy maintained by the United Nations and the American economic aid system. Korea relied on the UN Korea Relief Administration, and American FOA for everything from basic foodstuffs to the many supplies needed for restoration after the war.[39] The 72 per cent of the post-war population living on farms became impoverished and the 28 per cent living in cities became mostly destitute.[40] Understandably in these circumstances, from 1945 to 1960 the government was not interested in the promotion of sport. It had other pressing priorities – feeding, housing and educating a destitute nation – and the population itself was concerned with basic survival. Furthermore, if this was not enough, the political situation in Korea was not stable enough for sport to become popular.

SOCIETY AND SPORT DURING THE PARK CHUNG-HEE REGIME, 1961–79

The 1960s saw the dawn of modern Korean sport. Pronounced change in Korean sport dates from 1961, and the force behind this change was the Park Chung-hee regime. After the Syngman Lee regime collapsed on 26 April 1960, a cabinet system of government was adopted, and in August the Second Republic was born with Yoon Bo-seon as president and Jang Myon as prime minister.[41] But the Second Republic did not last long. This democratic government under Jang Myon brought social chaos, with conflicting demands being made by different social classes and unabated street demonstrations. The Jang Myon government came under severe criticism for this state of affairs. Government incompetence and social unrest provided the justification for a military *coup d'état*. On 16 May 1961, Major-General Park Chung-hee led a successful coup – the '16 May Revolution', formed a military government and took power. He served as the fifth, sixth and seventh president in the Third Republic, which began in December 1963, and as the eighth and ninth president in the Fourth Republic, which began in December 1972. In all, he ruled some 18 years until he was assassinated on 26 October 1979 by Kim Jae-kyu, Minister of the Korean Central Intelligence Agency.[42] A sea change in the history of modern Korean sport began at the same moment as the Park Chung-hee regime took office. Modern Korean sport and Korean military rule were closely connected.

As has already been confirmed in Table 8.1, all major developments in modern Korean sport are concentrated in the period from the early

1960s to the late 1970s – the period when Park Chung-hee was in power. In short, modern Korean sport, in a real sense, may be said to have begun with the Park Chung-hee regime. Korean society during the 1960s was far from being a stable and prosperous society in which non-governmental sports organizations could take the lead with confidence and success. As is shown in Table 8.3, the gross national product per capita in Korea in 1960 was a mere US$78, and even in 1980 it had reached only US$1,597. It was difficult, indeed impossible, for sport under the aegis of non-governmental organizations to succeed in such conditions of deprivation. Only the national government could successfully move modern sport forward. Support now came from the new regime.

Popular evaluation of the Park Chung-hee regime polarized after it collapsed. One view was of Park Chung-hee as a great man, the saviour of modern Korea, who had brought about an economic miracle that freed the country from poverty. The other painted him as a military dictator who set back the advance of Korean democracy. (Of course, they are not mutually exclusive.) As a result, the military government that he brought about on 16 May 1960 has been referred to as both an advantageous '*coup d'état*' and a disadvantageous 'military revolution'. In academia, assessments of the significance of Park Chung-hee have differed from scholar to scholar, but there has tended to be the same polarization. Assessments in the foreign press have also revealed polarization. For example, on 27 October 1979, the day after Park Chung-hee died, Henry Scott Stokes, in a special to the *New York Times*, wrote:

> His enemies called him a corrupt and ruthless dictator who stifled dissent, eliminated opponents and created a police state nurtured in fear and repression. His loyalists called him a tough, pragmatic patriot who preserved his nation from Communism and wrought a national economic miracle with his iron will. In the more than 18 years since he seized power in a coup, President Park Chung-hee, with the blessing of the United States, dominated and revolutionized virtually every aspect of life for the 38 million people of South Korea, stunting political institutions while lifting industry, business and the standard of living to unparalleled levels for a developing nation.[43]

Park Chung-hee was certainly a dictator and in some things he was a benign dictator. He forced through beneficial change that was substantial. Among other things, he was the author of a 'Korean sports revolution'. Nearly all of the laws promoting sport, to rehearse the point again for emphasis, were enacted during Park Chung-hee's rule – even the plan to attract the 1988 Olympics to Seoul was his inspiration.[44] Because of this, it would not be an exaggeration to state that understanding Park Chung-hee provides a shortcut to understanding the causes of Korean sport's astounding progress in the latter half of the twentieth century. Accordingly, if Park Chung-hee's beliefs, his pronouncements concerning sport and his actions in power are examined, they reveal the potent source of a progression in sport as political. It is as simple as that.

Park Chung-hee's strenuous personal involvement in the post-1960s sports revolution is closely related to his individual disposition. He was himself a distinguished sportsman and, in addition, an admirer of the martial mentality. He was born on 30 September 1917 in Kumi City, Northern Gyeongsang Province. After he completed middle school, he attended a teacher training college and became a teacher. Later he entered a military academy and became an army officer.[45] He was athletic, intelligent and artistic, and he performed well on sports fields. Not only were his school grades excellent, he also had artistic talents. He showed great interest in poetry, painting, musical composition, calligraphy and piano playing.[46] Over and above this, his playing of the Korean flute was considered of professional standard.[47] As a student physically he was initially quite weak but he strengthened himself by devoting himself to sword training (*Geomdo*).[48] As an adult he immersed himself in horsemanship, archery, swimming, golf, hunting and tennis. At all these activities he excelled. Once in power, he wanted a nation of sportsmen – the requirement, in his view, for a self-reliant nation – economically and militarily.[49]

Park Chung-hee was out of the mainstream of Korean traditional culture. As mentioned earlier, he attached great importance to the martial frame of mind. Admiration for the scholarly and denigration of the martial was part of traditional Korean society. For centuries of the Choson Dynasty (1392–1910) the unaggressive philosophy of the Chinese neo-Confucian philosopher Chu Hsi was revered. As a result, there was more than a tendency to look down on physical activity; and in Korean history there was an equal tendency for many rulers to ignore the worth of folk games and sports.[50] Park Chung-hee made full amends. He was the most militaristic of all the men of power in the modern history of Korea. He was convinced that a martial spirit could serve as a source of regeneration. He saw the political value of sport as an extension of the political value of the martial spirit. On 30 June 1966, in his opening address on the occasion of the inauguration of the Korean Hall of Physical Education, he stated that 'when we look at our history, the periods when our race flourished and developed were the same periods when the martial arts were revered and the people were physically strong.'[51] On 5 October 1967, at the forty-eighth National Games, he claimed that the 'short cut to the reunification of the nation was an increase in national strength, and an increase in national strength began with an increase in physical fitness'.[52] As a military officer who became president, he was certain in his own mind that the martial arts and sport could improve physical fitness and general morale and thus both directly and indirectly the defence of the nation.

Park Chung-hee's leadership of the popular sports movement was based on his 'Healthy People Policy'.[53] During his years in power he continually stressed the need to cultivate a national character that possessed strong morale linked to physical health.[54] The Korean dictionary definition of a 'healthy people' is given as a 'sound people'.[55] Park Chung-hee's Healthy People Policy was aimed ultimately at creating a socially prosperous and strong nation. The policy was to foster a 'sound Korean people' to this end. In this context, sport was a means, in his view, of cultivating strong bodies and healthy minds. This is clear again and again from his speeches. At the first National Student Games in May 1966, he declared:

> The rise and fall of a nation and the increase and decrease in its national strength depends on the physical fitness of a people. The physical fitness of a people is assessed on the basis of the strength and spirit of its youth. Twenty years from now, how much our motherland will change, and how much it will develop, depends on how strong and sound the bodies and minds of our young students are. At present we are pressing to mobilize all our national resources so as to establish a self-reliant economy. More than anything, the realization of this historical task demands robust bodies and minds as well as an independent and self-reliant national spirit that these bodies and minds will create, and it also

demands the spirit of unity and perseverance that is cultivated through sport.[56]

Park Chung-hee's speeches provide many examples of such rhetoric. In his speech at the opening ceremony of the National Games on 12 September 1968, for example, he declared:

> Physical fitness is the foundation of national strength. We must not forget for even a moment that cultivating a strong and fit people and making sport an everyday part of people's lives will provide the vitality necessary for the task of modernizing the Motherland.[57]

There can be absolutely no doubt that Park Chung-hee's ideological conviction that the 'key to the development of the nation ... was the character of the people' was, for him, the source of 'a pan-national sports movement in pursuit of the cultivation of progressive and vibrant nation'.[58]

There was yet more to Park Chung-hee's ideological convictions concerning the health of the mind and body – the reunification of Korea. In the process of pursuing modernization, the intention of the Park Chung-hee regime was to create once more a unified, and this time strong, nation. Park Chung-hee's popular sports movement had nationalism as an ideological foundation. Here was a post-war nationalist movement with the aim of putting an end to foreign domination, ending internal discord and re-establishing a united country[59] with sport as the cement of the national edifice, national consciousness and national unity.[60] However, there is yet another aspect to his espousal of sport. In terms of self-interest, Park Chung-hee hoped by promoting sport to secure legitimacy for his regime and win popular support for his military rule. Nevertheless, there was far more than simply self-interest in his ideology, strategy and action. This is clear from the historical awareness displayed in his writings.[61] He was acutely sensitive of the rivalry among the powerful nations of the world with their bitterly opposed political ideologies and the putative consequences for sucked-in nations. His ambitious intention was to pursue maximum autonomy in these circumstances.[62] Consequently, during his regime, the ideology of self-sufficient and successful nationalism pervaded every aspect of life. To make the point one more time, sport was one means – an important means – of attaining this objective. Generally speaking, in order to maintain its sovereignty, a nation is faced with several basic tasks: political security, social order, material prosperity and mass patriotism.[63] These were the fundamental tasks of the Park Chung-hee government.[64] The Korean sports movement was linked to them all. Arguably, above all else it was linked to nationalism, youth and the future. At the opening ceremony of the National Student Games of 1965, Park Chung-hee stated: 'Whenever a country strives to restore and revive its people the cry from youth for national progress and rebirth is heard. Witness Ancient Greece, witness modern Germany and witness the unified Silla Dynasty from our own history.'[65] The later references in the speech to the nationalistic gymnastics movement (*Turnbewegung*) of Germany and to the *Hwarangdo*[66] movement of the ancient Silla Dynasty – both militaristic in their emphasis – are revealing. Undoubtedly he thought of his national sports movement as a militaristic nationalist movement; he considered the sound physical fitness and high morale of the people achieved through a mass national sports system as the foundation of a new Korea, modern, strong and self-reliant; and he viewed elite athletes sent off to participate in international games and tournaments as warriors symbolizing the vitality, self-respect and self-confidence of the nation.

An understanding of the twentieth-century history of Korea, then, provides an understanding of the politicization of sport under Park Chung-hee. His knowledge of this history ensured that he lost no time in developing his national sports movement after his military revolution succeeded in 1961. Various innovations have already been mentioned earlier under the umbrella slogan 'Physical Fitness is National Strength', and there were more, including exemption from military service for outstanding athletes. Implementation of these policies left no doubt that the government would now actively intervene in sport in the interest of the well-being of the nation. He returned to this theme time and again. Early in his regime, he declared:

> During the last two years, the revolutionary government, within the restrictions of time and conditions placed on it, has, on the one hand, enacted and enforced laws promoting physical education and sport and expanded and strengthened governmental sports organizations, while on the other hand it has reaped the rewards of devoting itself to unprecedented efforts developing the sports of this country by securing international exchanges and cultivating outstanding athletes. I am sincerely happy about this, and believe that it is a proud achievement of the revolutionary government.[67]

Again:

> The development of this country's sport can be said to be a very important enterprise that aims at enhancing the wholesomeness of the everyday life of the people and, going one step further, at enhancing the respect and national prestige of our people abroad. The government has replaced the formalistic and makeshift physical education and sports policies of the past, promoted an active and long-term development policy, increased the physical fitness of the people and cultivated a more wholesome spirit so as to provide for a better social life.[68]

Finally:

> It is not necessary to repeat that the influence of the sport of today contributes much to the enhancement in the level of the physical fitness of a country. Furthermore, we know full well how important the role sport has been in enhancing the national prestige and international reputation of a country. ... We must know that our athletes going abroad to participate in international games and achieving splendid records have achieved more than hundreds of our foreign diplomats spending large budgets ever have.[69]

These excerpts reveal just how far he was committed to sport as a political tool, and how far he was prepared to pour resources into the sports systems, popular and elite. They reveal also how much he valued outstanding athletes as civil 'ambassadors' who enhanced the nation's reputation abroad. From the moment he came to power in 1961 until his death in 1979, Park Chung-hee endlessly repeated mantras similar to the extracts above. His commitment to cultivating outstanding athletes and generally fostering strong bodies never wavered.[70] Modern Korean sport, as a consequence, was the outcome of well-meaning political despotism.

SOCIETY AND SPORT DURING THE CHUN DOO-HWAN AND ROH TAE-WOO REGIMES, 1980–92

If the evolution of modern Korean sport is compared to the four seasons, then the 1960s was the spring when the seeds were sown, the 1970s was the summer when the roots took firm hold and the 1980s and 1990s were the autumn when the fruits ripened.

The sports policies of the Park Chung-hee regime in the spring and summer of Korean sport were inherited by the Chun Doo-hwan regime (March 1981–February 1988) of the Fifth Republic and the Roh Tae-woo regime (February 1988–February 1993) of the Sixth Republic. One thing in the autumn of Korean sport common to all three men was their military and athletic background. They were all military officers fond of sport. If Park Chung-hee left a legacy of great achievements associated with Korean sport, the same can be said, to a lesser extent, of Chun Doo-hwan and Roh Tae-woo. Chun Doo-hwan, who seized the reins of power through a *coup d'état* in 1979, continued the sports policies that Park Chung-hee had set in train. In fact, he showed a deep interest in them. Roh Tae-woo, a central figure in the Chun Doo-hwan regime, became Minister of State for Sport. He thus played a key role in Korean sport in the Chun Doo-hwan regime, which witnessed the national hosting of the Seoul Olympic Games. He then followed Chun Doo-hwan as president.

Major sports initiatives in which the Chun Doo-hwan and Roh Tae-woo regimes showed particularly strong interest included the winning and hosting of the Olympic and Asian Games – significant symbols of Korea's entry onto the world sporting stage. After Chun Doo-hwan was inaugurated as president in 1981, he began, with Roh Tae-woo, his partner in the *coup d'état* that brought him to power, to bring to realization the aim of bringing the twenty-fourth Olympic Games to Seoul that had been set by the Park Chung-hee regime in 1979.[71] On 10 August 1981, at the 'Policy Meeting to Attract the Olympics', Roh Tae-woo, who at the time was the Minister of State for Political Affairs, stressed the need to develop a nationwide strategy to win the Olympics for Korea. He formed a 'Committee for the Movement to Attract the Olympics' consisting of people from all walks of life and on 30 September 1981, the bid to host the twenty-fourth Games in Seoul was successful. This success in attracting the Olympics to Seoul was followed by an attempt to secure the 1986 tenth Asian Games. This too was successful. The plans to bring both the Olympics and the Asian Games to Korea had been announced simultaneously on 8 October 1979.[72]

The act of bringing both the Olympic Games and the Asian Games to Korea greatly accelerated the forward momentum of elite sport in Korea. In 1982 Chun Doo-hwan established a Ministry of Sports within the Central Intelligence Agency Administrative Organization and he named Roh Tae-woo as the first Minister of Sport. Chun Doo-hwan devoted much of his energy to sports promotion policies including the preparations for the Olympics and Asian Games, the cultivation of outstanding athletes and the training of capable coaches. Now followed strenuous efforts to locate more outstanding young athletes,[73] to strengthen the capacity of the Sports Science Research Centre, to establish university sports science annexes, to create a national military athletic corps and to work to attract various international events to Korea[74] (see Table 8.1). The results were strikingly apparent at the twenty-fourth Olympic Games held in Seoul in 1988. Even taking into consideration the advantage resulting from the fact that the games were held on home territory, Korea ranked an astounding fourth in the medal count, out of 160 countries.[75] This result graphically demonstrated the 'Political Leap Forward' of elite sport, under three military-led authoritarian regimes.

The Chun Doo-hwan and Roh Tae-woo regimes did not neglect popular sport. They poured resources into a 'Sport for All' programme. This had been promoted under the Park Chung-hee regime, but, as noted, little progress had been made because of a shortage of facilities and a general lack of interest among the public. But in the latter half of the 1980s, in line with the increase in economic growth, public interest in sport grew rapidly and the government responded with an equally rapid provision of resources, facilities and equipment. The encouragement of professional sport provides an excellent illustration. Before 1980 the only professional sports in Korea were boxing and golf. But in the 1980s Korea saw the emergence of professional baseball (1982), professional soccer (1983) and professional traditional Korean wrestling (*Ssireum*) (1983) A new era of professional sport opened.[76] After successfully hosting the 1988 Olympic Games, the Roh Tae-woo regime of the Sixth Republic devoted even greater attention to popular sport than before. The Three Year Comprehensive Plan for the Revitalization of the People's Lifetime Sports, also referred to as the 'Hodori Plan',[77] was launched. In order to further this scheme, the People's Lifetime Sports Association, a nationwide organization, was established. Within the framework of rapid economic development, popular sport flourished and by the 1990s a popular sports era had began in Korea.

Korean sport in the 1980s was a success story. Three reasons stand out: first, the foundations laid by the sports promotion policies of the Park Chung-hee regime throughout the 1960s and 1970s; second, significant social change brought about by economic growth; and third, the sustained influence of political power.

It is time to say something about social change and economic transformation in the Korea of the 1960s, 1970s and 1980s. As can be seen in Table 8.3b, during the years from 1960 onwards, such was the success of the economic development achieved that by 1997 the Korean economy, as measured by gross domestic product, had risen to eleventh in the world.[78] The structure of society changed very rapidly. In the process of the transformation from an agricultural to an industrial nation, the urban population increased markedly. The population ratios of cities to countryside rose from 43.7 per cent in 1961 to 55.3 per cent in 1970, 71.6 per cent in 1980 and 84.5 per cent in 1990.[79] Economic development and changes in social structure ensured public interest in, and opportunities for, sport. In short, and unsurprisingly, the Korean popular sports movement in the 1980s was, in part, a product of change in both social and economic structures – but for the most part, the result of political power, interest and support. In essence, therefore, an awareness of Korean politics is crucial to an understanding of the evolution of Korean sport in the second half of the twentieth century. It is also the case that its history was the history of individual initiative as much as institutional reform. The two went hand in hand, of course, but the former pushed the latter along. Ideology, politics and personality meshed into a moment of rapid innovation.

Park Chung-hee planned to remain in power indefinitely. As a result,

TABLE 8.3a
KOREAN ECONOMIC GROWTH, 1965–95

Year	1965–70	1971–80	1981–90	1995
Growth Rate (%)	10.4	9.1	9.5	8.9

Source: http://www.koreascope.org/sub/linex3-a.htm.

TABLE 8.3b
CHANGES IN KOREAN PER-CAPITA GROSS NATIONAL PRODUCT (US$)

Year	1960	1970	1980	1990	1995
Per-capita GNP	US$79	US$253	US$1,597	US$5,883	US$10,037

Source: http://www.koreascope.org/sub/linex3-a.htm.

Korean Sport – Transformation, 1945–92 235

he was fiercely opposed by those of democratic persuasion; but he managed to hold on to power until 26 October 1979, when he was assassinated by his own subordinate, the director of the Central Intelligence Agency, Jae-kyu Kim. Now the Korean people hoped for a new democratic era – without avail. Recent Korean political history was repeated. On 12 December 1979, powerful military leaders including Major General Chun Doo-hwan, head of the Army Security Command, Roh Tae-woo and Ho-yong Chong launched another successful *coup d'état*. Under martial law declared in September 1980, Chun Doo-hwan became the eleventh president (1 September 1980–2 March 1981) and then the twelfth president (3 March 1981–24 February 1988) of Korea. During this time many people lost their lives. Many students and civilians who demonstrated in opposition to military government were killed, and many intellectuals, politicians and journalists purged. Nevertheless, the Korean democracy movement grew in strength after Chun Doo-hwan came to power. After nationwide democratic protests in 1985, Chun Doo-hwan and his successor Roh Tae-woo accepted the people's so-called '29 June Proclamation',[80] which 'called for constitutional reform producing the direct election of the president'. However, just before the 1987 election of the president, the two opposition candidates who had led the democracy movement, Kim Young-sam and Kim Dae-jung, fell out; Roh Tae-woo took advantage of the confusion, won the election and became the thirteenth president of Korea with only 36.6 per cent of the votes cast. Korea had yet another military leader.

In history dictatorships have frequently used sport as a medium of political socialization.[81] In recent times in Europe there have been Benito Mussolini and Adolf Hitler, to mention only the more notorious dictators. More recently, elsewhere in the world, the South American military dictators of Brazil and Argentina in the 1970s used sport as a medium of social control.[82] A similar phenomenon characterized Korean society during the 1980s, and in the wake of this phenomenon came the flowering of modern sport. Sport made a great leap forward in the 1980s on the back of political despotism. Politicians furthered, encouraged and developed Korean sport for both altruistic and ulterior purposes. As already noted, the Fourth Republic came into existence through a *coup d'état*. Whatever its nationalistic idealism, and the visions of its leader, it was an illegal government lacking the backing of the people. Accordingly, the new regime attempted the classical strategy using sport as a means of distracting the people's interest from politics and winning their support:

> In conjunction with harsh policies aimed at 'social and political purification…' and the passing of endless laws ensuring tight control, once the regime felt secure it used blatant mass bribes to curry favour with the people including free colour television sets and at the same time the liberalization of the uniforms and hair lengths of middle and high school students, and ending of the night-time curfew. At the same time it made a huge effort to bring the 1986 Asian Games and the 1988 Olympics to Korea posing as the champion of Korean nationalism, the source of a new international recognition and the means of raising the image of the Korean nation. [83]

Of course, as mentioned already, the plan to secure the bid for the twenty-fourth Olympics for Seoul had been the brainchild of the Park Chung-hee regime – but had seemingly been stillborn with the death of Park Chung-hee. However, on his inauguration as president, Chun Doo-hwan resuscitated the apparently lifeless corpse.[84] He declared: 'We can not change without good reason something that was already decided on by a previous president and publicly announced both in Korea and abroad, but we must not shrink through defeatism from attempting to promote this historic enterprise.'[85] Were his intentions altruistic? As a politician who had seized power, he certainly needed something to win over the hearts and minds of the nation; attracting the Olympics was a dazzling way of achieving this. After securing the Olympic Games, the Chun Doo-hwan regime pleaded for the setting aside of all political dissent until after they had been held. His opponents responded with the argument that the Olympics would be used by the dictatorship in the same manner that the Nazis used the 1936 Olympics in Berlin[86] – as a political showpiece. A YMCA report at the time stated bluntly that the Olympics enterprise was a ruse by the military dictatorship to turn the attention of the Korean people away from internal politics and to smother social confrontation in national pride at worldwide attention.[87] In his book *The One-Hundred Year History of Korean Sport*, published in 2000, the historian Lee Hak-rae wrote that the Fifth Republic, faced with a crisis of legitimacy, thought up the scheme to host the Seoul Olympics in an attempt to overcome this disadvantage,[88] to overcome the instability the regime faced, to prevent dissidents from concentrating

Korean Sport – Transformation, 1945–92

their energies on political reform and to separate the common people from the democratic movement.

The use of sport as a distraction was not limited to the plan to secure the Olympic and Asian Games. The Chun Doo-hwan regime mounted a popular culture offensive involving, among other things, mass sport. After the Fifth Republic had secured the Olympics it began to promote sport on a large scale. There followed the expansion of professional sports, a rapid augmentation in the numbers and hours of sports broadcasts and an increase in newspapers' sports pages. The promotion was only partially successful. In 1980 per-capita GNP was only US$1,597 and sports facilities were poor. Nevertheless, the motivation was clear. Lee Hak-rae wrote of the time that:

> the Chun Doo-hwan regime, as a means of maintaining military rule that had turned away from any ardent desire for democracy, needed to create an epochal system to avert the attention of the people, and planned to use the professionalization of sports as one part of this artifice.[89]

It seemed to know what it was doing. Professional sport grew faster than expected and a government-controlled press that worked to stifle the interest of the people in politics certainly helped paralyse general political involvement. Television was a potent instrument of government seduction. Television sports broadcasts greatly increased. In September 1981, for example, the sports broadcasts of the three main television stations accounted for only eight per cent of total broadcast time, but by June 1984 this had grown to almost 25 per cent.[90] Significantly, in the light of what has been written above, in the middle of the 1980s the phrase 'A Sports Republic' appeared. It brought ridicule down on the regime and it left very few in any doubt as to the ulterior motives that lay behind the strong government action. Nevertheless, there were positive as well as negative consequences of this interest. This must be frankly recognized. The military regimes, whatever their unpalatable politics and blatant actions, successfully promoted the rapid development of modern Korean sport. They have left a legacy of advantage to the nation at least in this regard. Both causes and consequences are, of course, complex. Nevertheless, Korean sport during the 1960s and 1970s, promoted by Park Chung-hee and then during the 1980s pushed by the Chun Doo-hwan and Roh Tae-woo regimes, provides a fascinating illustration of the influence of politics on modern sport.

CONCLUSION

The process by which modern sport was introduced into, and spread throughout, the different countries of South-East Asia is complicated and as yet insufficiently recorded. This chapter has concentrated on Korean sport in the second half of the twentieth century. This later evolution is even less well covered.

The phases after the Second World War reveal specific characteristics which can be summarized as rapid expansion, government control and initially an elitist emphasis. An extensive system of modern sport was created in roughly a 30-year period, from the 1960s until the late 1980s. Until the 1960s sport was the responsibility of the private Korean Sports Association, a relatively passive and conservative body that had little impact. However, with the government taking control of sport in the 1960s it was all very different. The government simultaneously promoted a 'school sports movement', a 'social sports movement', a 'popular sports movement' and an 'elite sports movement'. Until the middle of the 1980s government interest and investment were directed towards elite sports for reasons of national image abroad and impecuniousness at home. In modern Korea elite sport did not develop out of popular sport; popular sport developed out of elite sport.

The decisive agent in the successful advance of modern sport was the government. Underpinning its success, of course, was massive social change including urbanization, industrialization and economic progress. The modernization of Korean sport – a nationwide movement – owed much to the military regimes of Park Chung-hee, Chun Doo-hwan and Roh Tae-woo. In particular, Park Chung-hee, a Korean icon, initiated the Korean 'sports revolution'. He was himself an all-round sportsman and he energetically promoted Korean sport at every level with a primarily nationalist intention – the creation of a healthy, strong, secure people. He is 'the Father of Modern Korean Sport'. The military dictators Chun Doo-hwan and Roh Tae-woo inherited Park Chung-hee's policies and the 1980s saw the high point of the evolutionary saga – the winning of the 1986 Asian Games and the 1988 Olympics. Korea had arrived on the world's sports stage.

Finally, the similarities between the growth of modern sport in Korea and China might be usefully noted. Sport in both nations had ideological foundations arising out of political imperatives and political despotism.

Here, however, the similarities end and for a very good reason. In China sport was seen as a bulwark *of* Communism; in Korea sport was seen as a bulwark *against* Communism.

NOTES

Appreciative thanks are extended to Ok Gwang for assistance with the notes.

1. Stan Greenberg, *The Guinness Olympics Fact Book* (London: Guinness Publishing, 1991), pp.12–44.
2. Ibid., p.36.
3. Hai Ren, 'China and the Olympic Movement', in James Riordan and Robin Jones (eds), *Sports and Physical Education in China* (London: E. & F.N. Spon, 1999), pp.204–5.
4. In all instances in the text, unless used in a pre-Korean War context, the terms 'Korea' and 'Korean' refer to South Korea.
5. See Ha Nam-Gil and J.A. Mangan, 'A Curious Conjunction – Sport, Religion, and Nationalism: Christianity and the Modern History of Korea', *International Journal of the History of Sport*, 11, 3 (Dec. 1994), 329–54.
6. J.A. Mangan and Ha Nam-Gil, 'Confucianism, Imperialism, Nationalism: Modern Sport, Ideology and Korean Culture', *European Sports History Review*, 3 (2001), 49–76.
7. Tong-sup Oh, Ha Nam-Gil and Sam-hyon Chong, *Cheyouksa* [History of World Physical Education] (Seoul: Hyong-sol Publishing, 2001), pp.456–60.
8. In Korea there is a difference of opinion between conservatives and liberals over how to interpret the phrase *Gunsa Jeongbyeon* – 'militarily achieved political change'. Conservatives often interpret it as 'revolution', liberals as '*coup d'état*'. Here this phrase is translated as 'revolution', but, in fact, in this chapter, depending on the content being explained, it can be understood as either the former or the latter.
9. Central Alliance of Association of Korean Mothers, *HanKook Kyoyouk 30nyeonsa* [Thirty-Year History of Korean Education] (Seoul: Publications Division of the Central Alliance of Association of Korean Mothers, 1977), p.52.
10. Statute No.1928, 30 April 1967. From Yi-hyok Han, *Cheyouksa* [History of Physical Education] (Seoul: Taegeun Publications, 1998), p.322.
11. Presidential Order No.4398, 4 Dec. 1969. This order set standards for the maintenance of all athletic fields and school facilities used for student physical education and sports activities. Yi-hyok Han, *Cheyouksa*, p.322.
12. Ibid., p.324.
13. Myong-ryol Cho *et al.*, *Cheyouksa* [History of Physical Education] (Seoul: Hyong-sol Publishing, 1997), p.381.
14. Hak-rae Lee and Chong-hee Kim, 'The Political Ideology of the Park Chung-hee Regime and Sports Nationalism', *Journal of Korean Physical Education*, 38, 1 (March 1999), p.32.
15. See the Korean Sports Council Hompage at http://www.sports.or.kr/.
16. For the 29th Youth Games held in 2000, 17 events were included for elementary school students and 28 events were included for middle-school students. Elementary school student events included track and field, swimming, soccer, baseball, tennis, soft tennis, basketball, volleyball, table tennis, handball, wrestling, judo, archery, gymnastics, badminton, *taekwondo* and roller-skating. Middle-school student events included track and field, swimming, soccer, tennis, soft tennis, basketball, volleyball, table tennis, handball, rugby, cycling, boxing, wrestling, weightlifting, judo, traditional sword, archery, marksmanship, gymnastics, hockey, fencing, badminton, *taekwondo*, roller skating and canoeing. See the Korean Sports Council Homepage at http://www.sports.or.kr/.
17. Korean Sports Council Homepage at http://www.sports.or.kr/.
18. Yi-hyok Han, *Cheyouska*, p.326.
19. See Ha Nam-Gil and J.A. Mangan, 'A Curious Conjunction', pp.329–54.

20. As one link in its imperialist policy, Japan suppressed and put Korean sports activities under surveillance. In 1938 even Korea's all-inclusive sports organization, the Choseon Sports Society, was forcefully disbanded. For details see Mangan and Ha Nam-Gil, 'Confucianism, Imperialism, Nationalism'.
21. Hak-rae Lee, *HanKook Geundae Cheyouksa* [Research on the History of Modern Korean Physical Education] (Seoul: Jisiksanup Publishing, 1990), p.223.
22. Ibid., p.224.
23. The Park Chung-hee regime decided on the plan to secure a bid for the twenty-fourth Olympics in Seoul on 21 September 1979. Park Chung-hee died on 26 October 1979. Myong-ryol Cho, *Cheyouksa*, p.386.
24. People's Physical Education and Sports Promotion Law and Enforcement Law (17 June 1962), Chapter 1, Article 1, Hyeon-sung Na, *Hackgyo Cheyouk Kwanri* [Administration of School Physical Education] (Seoul: Mun-chon Publishing, 1975), p.19.
25. Specifics included the requirements that 1) local autonomous government organizations held athletic games at least once a year or supported sports organizations in holding such games and 2) local autonomous government organizations held worker athletic games at least once a year. Physical Education Promotion Law, Article 8, Kyu-dong Lee, *Cheyouk Haengjung* [Physical Education Administration] (Seoul: Kyohak Research, 1986), p.256.
26. In accordance with directives of the president, national and local autonomous government organizations were to build, maintain and pay for athletic fields, gymnasiums, swimming pools and other facilities as determined by the president. Physical Education Promotion Law, Article 12, Kyu-dong Lee, *Cheyouk Haengjung*, p.256.
27. With 27–53 per cent of the population suffering under conditions of poverty, sport was unable to become a popular form of leisure. In 1965, 53 per cent of the total population lived in poverty; in 1970, 28 per cent, and in 1978 27 per cent. Keum-chan Bae *et al.*, *1970nyeondae Hankook Junhangieui jungchi-Sahwoi Byeondong* [Socio-Political Changes in the Republic of Korea in the Early 1970s] (Baiksan Seodang Publishing, 1999), p.140.
28. Enforcement Orders for the Physical Education and Sports Promotion Law, Article 10, Formation of Sports Teams in Places of Employment, Kyu-dong Lee, *Cheyouk Haengjung*, p.256.
29. Ibid., p.256.
30. People's Physical Education Promotion Law and Enforcement Orders (17 June 1962), Chapter 1, Article 1 (Goals), Hyeon-sung Na, *Hackgyo Cheyouk Kwanri*, p.19.
31. People's Sports Promotion Law, 31 Dec. 1982, Article 1, Kyu-dong Lee, *Cheyouk Haengjung*, p.255.
32. Greenberg, *The Guinness Olympics Fact Book*, pp.12–40.
33. Ibid., p.36.
34. Ibid., p.40.
35. Jang-jib Ch'oi (ed.), *Hankook Hyeondaesa I* [Modern Korean History I] (Seoul: Yolum Publishing, n.d.), p.181.
36. Ki-baek Lee, *Hankooksa Shinron* [New Korean History] (Seoul: Iljogak, 1993), p.474.
37. This People's Revolution broke out on 19 May 1960, under the leadership of students. This revolution, which opposed the corruption and authoritarianism of Syngman Rhee regime, is on record as the first revolution in Korean history which successful overthrew an oppressive government. As a result of this uprising, Syngman Rhee resigned his presidency on 28 May 1960, went into exile in Hawaii (USA). See Lee Ki-baek, *Hankooksa Shinron*, p.485.
38. On 5 September 1945, the Choseon Friends of Sport Association was formally organized (committee chairman, Lee Sang-baek) and on 26 November 1945, the forerunner of the Korean Sports Council, the Choseon Sports Society was inaugurated (eleventh president, Yoh Woon-hyong). From *One-Hundred Years of Korean Physical Education*, compiled by the Compilation Committee for One-Hundred Years of Korean Physical Education (1988), p.226.
39. Kang Man-gil, *Hankook Hyeondaesa* [Modern Korean History] (Seoul: ChangjakGwa Bipeong Publishing, 1985), p.233.
40. Kim In-kol *et al.*, *Hankook Hyeondaesa Kangeui* [Lectures on History of Modern Korea] (Seoul: Dolbegae, 1998), p.192.
41. Ibid., p.527.

42. Ibid., pp.515–46.
43. Henry Scott Stroke, 'He Ran Korea, Down to the Last Detail', *New York Times*, 27 Oct. 1979.
44. The plan to bring the 1988 Olympics to Seoul was announced in October 1979. The person who drew up this plan at the time was Jong-gyu Kim, the chairman of the Korean Olympic Committee. Jong-gyu Kim had been the long-time head of Park Chung-hee's Secret Service. He began his plan to draw the Olympics to Seoul after close talks with Park Chung-hee. See Kwang-hon Ko, *Sportswa Jungchi* [Sport and Politics] (Seoul: Pureun Namoo Publishing, 1988), pp.93–9.
45. Park Chung-hee, 'Naeui Sonyeon Sijol' [My Youth], *Choson Monthly* (May 1984), p.84.
46. Representative songs that he composed included the '*Saemaeul Norae* [New Village Song] and *Naeui Jokook* [My Motherland].
47. An Kwang-jae, *Park Chung-hee Daetongryeong Jungi* [Biography of President Park Chung-hee] (Seoul: Daeil Bookstore, 1980), pp.97–8.
48. Oh Hyo-jin, 'Daetongryeongeui Dongchansaengdeul' [Old Boys of the President], *Choson Monthly* (May 1984), p.144–5.
49. 'A Simple Yet Powerful Leader – President Park Chung-hee as Seen by Foreign and Domestic Reporters', *New Books of Koryo, Fifth Collection* (Seoul: Kwangmyong Publishing, 1967), pp.55–66.
50. Mangan and Ha Nam-Gil, 'Confucianism, Imperialism, Nationalism'.
51. Office of the Secretariat of Information (comp.), *Collection of Speeches by President Park Chung-hee, First Collection* (Seoul: Dong-A Publishing, 1967), p.248.
52. Chong Jae-kyong, *Park Chung-hee Shilki* [Authentic Records of Park Chung-hee] – *Extractions of a Lifetime's Achievements* (Seoul: Jibmundang, 1994), p.241.
53. Hak-rae Lee and Jong-hui Kim, 'The Political Ideology', 30; Yi-hyok Han, *Cheyouksa*, p.326.
54. Han Yi-hyok, *Cheyouksa*, p.326.
55. Woon Pyong Language Research Center (comp.), *The Grand Dictionary of the Korean Language* (Seoul: Kumsong Publishing, 1995), p.111.
56. *Collection of Speeches by President Park Chung-hee, First Collection*, p.193.
57. Ibid., pp.263–4.
58. Ibid., p.270.
59. Jong-hui Kim, 'Park Chung-hee Jungkwoneui Jungchiynyeomkwa Cheyouk Jungchaeke kwanha Yeonku' [Research on the Political Ideology and Sports Policy of the Park Chung-hee Regime] (Ph.D. thesis, Hanyang University, 1999), p.142.
60. Hak-rae Lee and Jong-hui Kim, 'The Political Ideology', 337.
61. Chong Jae-kyong, *Hanminjok Jungheung Sasang* [Restoration of the Korean People: President Park Chung-hee's Political Philosophy] (Seoul: Silla Publishing, 1979), p.81. Examples of works by Park Chung-hee clearly revealed that his beliefs include *Woori Minjokeui Nagal Gil* [Road our People Must Follow] (Seoul: Dong-A Publishing, 1962); *Kookga Hwyoknyeongkwa guerigo Na* [Nation, Revolution, and I] (Seoul: Hangmoon, 1962); *Minjokeui joryeok* [Latent Energy of the People] (Songru: Kwangmyong Publishing, 1971); and *Minjok Jungheungeui Gil* [Road to the Revival of the People] (Seoul: Kwangmyong Publishing, 1978).
62. Se-joong Kim, 'The Ruling Ideology of Park Chung-hee and Nationalism', in Yu Byong-yong et al. (eds), *Hankook Hyeondaesawa Minjokjueui* [Modern Korean History and Nationalism] (Seoul: Jibmuntang, 1996), pp.129–130.
63. James N. Danzinger, *Understanding the Political World* (New York: Longman, 1991), p.309.
64. Yu Byong-yong, *Hankook Hyeondaesawa Minjokjueui*, pp.131–40.
65. *Collection of Speeches by President Park Chung-hee, First Collection*, p.194.
66. For details see Ha Nam-Gil and J.A. Mangan, 'The Knights of Korea: Hwarangdo, Miltarism and Nationalism', *International Journal of the History of Sport*, 15, 2 (Aug. 1998), 77–102.
67. *Collection of Speeches by President Park Chung-hee, First Collection*, p.539 (Expression of Gratitude on 4 October 1963, at National Games).
68. Ibid., p.88 (Second Physical Education and Sports Awards Ceremony on 27 April 1964).
69. Ibid., p.248 (Remarks made at the Opening Ceremony for the Korean Sports Council Hall on 30 June 1966).
70. Hak-rae Lee and Jong-hui Kim, 'The Political Ideology', 210
71. The plan to attract the 24th Olympic Games to Seoul was promulgated on 8 October 1979,

just before Park Chung-hee's death. With Park Chung-hee's death on 26 October 1979, the plan to draw the Olympics to Korea had to be tabled. Hak-rae Lee, *The One-Hundred Year History of Korean Sports* (Seoul: Korean Academy of Physical Education, 2000), pp.535–6.
72. Ibid., p.540.
73. At the time, after a physical fitness test was required nationwide of all students, 4,359 athletes were chosen. Ministry of Sports and Youth, *Administrative History of the Ministry of Sports and Youth* (1992), pp.90–91.
74. By 1990 sports science research centres had been established in some 35 universities starting with Seoul University. Hak-rae Lee, *The One-Hundred Year History*, p.480.
75. Cho Myong-ryol, *Cheyouksa*, p.388.
76. Hak-rae Lee, *The One-Hundred Year History*, pp.501–8.
77. Hodori was the mascot for the 24th Olympic Games in Seoul. The goals of the Hodori Plan were to realize a healthy people and a social welfare society to accelerate social development by utilizing the stored energy of the people and to cultivate a healthy youth through wholesome leisure. Ministry of Sports and Youth, *Administrative History*, p.166.
78. http://www.koreascope.org/sub/linex3-a.htm
79. Dong-se Cha, Kwang-suk Kim and Dwight H. Perkins (eds), *The Korean Economy 1945–1995: Performance and Vision for the 21st Century* (Seoul: Korea Development Institute, 1997), p.75.
80. On 29 June 1987, Roh Tae-woo, who was then head of the government party, accepted the citizen's demands in a special proclamation submitted as a means of bringing the difficult social situation under control. These demands included the direct election of the president and the pardon of and reinstatement of political rights for Kim Dae-jung.
81. Richard C. Helmes, *Ideology and Social Control in Canadian Sport: A Theoretical Review, Sport in Sociocultural Process* (Dubuque, IA: Erown Company Publishers), p.207.
82. Lee Eun-hee, 'Jabonjueuiwa Hyeondae Sport' [Capitalism and Modern Sports], *Soksun*, 4 (1985), 197; Ko Kwang-hon, *Sportswa Jungchi* [Sports and Politics] (Seoul: Pureun Namoo Publishing, 1988), p.99.
83. Kim In-gol, *Hankook Hyeondaesa Kangeui*, p.386.
84. Ibid., p.388.
85. Seoul Olympic Organizing Committee, *Outline for the 24th Olympic Games* (1989), p.34.
86. Kwang-hon Ko, *Sportswa Jungchi*, p.111.
87. YMCA Issues Research Committee, *Dangsindeuleui Chukje* [Your Festival] (Seoul: Minjung Publishing, 1988), p.50.
88. Hak-rae Lee, *The One-Hundred Year History*, p.547.
89. Ibid., p.502.
90. Kwang-hon Ko, *Sportswa Jungchi*, p.149.

9

Shackling the Lion:
Sport in Independent Singapore

PETER A. HORTON

Singapore's history as an independent state is dominated by a political ideology, an 'attitude to freedom',[1] a single political party, the People's Action Party (PAP) and a single politician, Lee Kuan Yew. The crown colony of Singapore[2] had, since British settlement in 1819, become a centre for trade and commerce in South-East Asia. Its geographical location on the trade routes between East and West, its free-trade policy and the stability afforded by British rule provided the ideal situation for the industry and enterprise of its multiethnic population to turn the tiny island-state into the leading trading centre in the region.[3] The period of occupation by the Japanese from 1942 to the end of the war in 1945 was a tortuous period for all Singaporeans, but seemed only to steel the people in their pursuit of prosperity. Singapore separated from Malaya in 1946, largely because of the communal division between the Chinese and the Malays.[4] The journey to full independence for Singapore was not a simple or indeed painless one;[5] Britain had bequeathed independence to Malaya in 1957 but, clearly considering the geopolitical and economic importance of Singapore, stalled in such a move for the island-colony. Singapore gained partial independence from the British Empire in 1963; full independence and its awesome responsibility came soon, however. The British had encouraged the leaders of the Malayan government to embrace Singapore into a new Federation of Malaysian states including the previously British-ruled territories of Sabah, Sarawak, and Brunei.[6] However, as Vasil suggests, 'separation was inevitable'.[7] The Malaysians feared the emergence of a Chinese-dominated federation while the PAP felt insecure and did not trust the Malaysians. Singapore also had an identity culturally, politically and socially disparate from that of Malaysia. Already its uniqueness was evident.

Formed in 1954, the PAP first gained power in Singapore in 1959 when the British introduced internal self-government. The party was an alliance between social democrats and pro-Communists and was replete with ideological differences. All factions, however, were united in their anti-colonial sentiments. The dual threats of ethnic chauvinism and Communist support clearly put the party at odds with the British and the dominance of the Chinese caused insurmountable concerns for the Malaysian leader Tunku Abdul Rahman.[8]

The Labour Front, a pro-labour socialist party, formed the first elected 'internal' government of Singapore, led in 1955 by David Marshall. Attempts at forming a coalition with the PAP had failed. Following David Marshall's term of only 17 months as chief minister, his successor Lim Yew Hock immediately became embroiled in student and union riots in October 1956; he crushed opposition almost as soon as it emerged. This proved to be a fatal mistake for the Labour Front and Lim, who as Chua says, was 'reduced, in local parlance, to representation as a "running dog" of colonialism'.[9] The way was thus left open for the PAP to assume leadership of the anti-colonial movement. In addition, they had astutely avoided alienating the British by not asserting an openly anti-British position. Lee Kuan Yew and the PAP had cleverly captured the support of the Chinese-educated and largely 'economically discontented and Communist-infiltrated electorate'[10] by adopting a 'pragmatic socialist ideology'[11] steeped in ideological hegemony that was to characterize future PAP governments.

Britain offered Singapore quasi-independence (all policy-making except defence and foreign affairs) and, in the general elections of 1959, the PAP was swept into power, winning 43 of the 51 seats. Having gained the loyalty of the moderate unionists by taking office conditional upon gaining the release, from detention, of the left-wing union leaders detained after the riots of 1956, Lee Kuan Yew immediately finessed all potential opposition from the right. Fortuitously, as it turned out, intra-party clashes began to emerge as Lee and his cabinet began to assert an authoritarian control; soon the pro-Communists became alienated and in 1961 they left the government to form their own political party, the Barisan Sosialis. Though losing a significant level of popular support as well as some sitting members, the split gave the PAP leaders, Lee Kuan Yew, Toh Chin Chye, Goh Keng Swee and S. Rajaratnam, the opportunity and power to institute a 'homogenous organisation both in political as well as organisational terms'.[12] The PAP under Lee Kuan Yew was now rid of the internal constraints that would have prevented it from undertaking the journey to a viable independence using its inimitable 'approach'.[13] It now had to regain the support of the people and absolute control of government. Lee set in stone the nature of the social and cultural transformation he thought was necessary to assure a viable future for the new nation that he believed was to be won in 'a battle of ideals and ideas', not with 'bullets and bayonets'.[14]

Shrewd policies that unified the people, addressed their real concerns regarding housing, employment and education and that maintained the neophyte nation's drive to industrialization restored the party's popular support. This, plus the massive endorsement for the government's position in the referendum on the merger with the Malaysian Federation, all combined to vindicate the party's perception of the reality of Singapore and with it its leaders' disposition to adopt a system of limited democratic rights and freedoms. Rajaratnam confirmed the PAP's stance in his interview with Raj Vasil in 1983:

> We did not have so much a plan as an approach, an attitude to freedom. Freedom is an abstraction. Freedom for what? Once you start translating freedom to specifics, there have to be limits. On that we are very clear. And the limits had to be based on specific conditions and problems obtaining in a country at a given time. We made a statement to ourselves that we will not win and take over. ... You can argue in terms of principles, abstractions, that it is wrong, but principles carried to the point where people suffer cannot be allowed. We can defend the limitations and even to this day we maintain them.[15]

Thus the same political party that had for years decried their imperial masters for their repression of personal freedom and liberty adopted an 'approach' which unequivocally justified the use of what, at best, could be said to be a 'limited' notion of democracy. The task naturally was not simple or painless; the PAP had after all campaigned long and hard for 'independence through merger with Malaya'. After the initial and painful attempts to merge with equity and honour for the Chinese-dominated Singaporeans, the PAP and particularly Lee Kuan Yew had to reinvent themselves with respect to the fundamental principle of governance to be adopted. They had still to ensure that the underpinning state ideology remained intact; it was still to 'be a multiracial, non-Communist, non-aligned, and democratic socialist state'.[16]

Sport featured early in the PAP's efforts to reduce sectional communalism. The communal nature of sports clubs in Singapore, which had persisted in an unofficially sanctioned manner throughout the colonial era, was seen to be so divisive that once independence was achieved in 1965 such structures and inter-communal contests were banned. Clubs such as the Tanglin Club and the Singapore Cricket Club, once the preserve of the expatriate British, were required to have a specific percentage of local members. Sport was to be an agent of social engineering in the creation of the new nation, and since independence, the government has pragmatically used the institution of sport in this way in its nation-building endeavours.[17] In 1965, as Singapore was moving to independence, racial disharmony had surfaced in intense and violent clashes on the sports field. The government viewed this as an impediment to their efforts of achieving unity and harmony in this multiracially structured state. The communal-based clubs were considered to 'lead to fragmentation of a migrant people into racial groups each falsely believing in racial superiority of its kind'.[18] To ameliorate the threat of further racial unrest, which erupted during the early 1960s, the Lee government virtually banned the racial exclusivity of the premier clubs and the communal nature of the ordinary sports clubs. Lau Teng Chuan remarks that this represented one of the first incursions of the government of the sovereign-state of Singapore into sport:

> Despite being placed low in priority among the Government's objectives in social reforms, sports were thus given a role in breaking down communalism and its dangers. Communal clubs were advised to open their doors to encourage a wider multiracial membership. Even the traditional and conservative Cricket Club and the Tanglin Club responded. Sports are for everyone regardless of race, creed, or religion. In schools, equal opportunities are given to all children to play games, which before tended to be the sports of Chinese schools, Malay schools and English schools.[19]

The PAP not only was intent on gaining and retaining power in independent Singapore but also wanted to 'establish a viable polity'[20] by constructing a prosperous, stable and significant political entity. To achieve this it had to unite a population that was a composite of heterogeneous races and cultures, held together previously by the common pursuit of economic survival and the overarching control of their colonial masters. An empathetic authoritarian decision-making style was chosen deliberately to undertake the daunting tasks that faced the government in its initial years. No aspect of economic, political and social activity, including sport, was to be left to chance. Thirty years later Lee Kuan Yew justified this authoritarian approach:

> I say without the slightest remorse that we would not be here, would not have made the economic progress if we had not intervened in every personal matter – who your neighbour is, how you live, the noise you make, how you spit or what language you use.[21]

All decisions that concerned national development, whether pertaining to the most dramatic issues of foreign policy or nation economic management or the seemingly more mundane aspects of social development involving, say, sport or the arts were to be considered and reactions and responses planned. Lee Kuan Yew created a political and essentially social environment where citizens, commerce and industry became compliantly immersed in the hegemonic process because it was and still is in their best interests, as present living, educational and social standards indicate. Chan suggests that Lee Kuan Yew's genius was that he

> ensured that in the pursuit of a political objective, events were so structured that there was very few alternative choices of policies [sic] available which seemed to fit the circumstances, and the seemingly inevitable option that should be or could be adopted was the one he favoured.[22]

Both an understanding and an acceptance of the nature, effectiveness and appropriateness of the political domain of Singapore emerges with a contextual knowledge of the country, its people and their aspirations. The outcomes of the past three decades of PAP rule could be characterized by rolling out their successful achievements.[23] However, their greatest achievement is undoubtedly the fact that the party has so competently created a hegemony where the values of the party have been completely internalized by the people. Critics enviously eye the economic, social and, above all, educational achievements of this dynamic state. Its budgetary surplus is by most standards awesome, yet they marginalize this 'success' by citing the draconian nature of the authoritarian government's policies.[24] However, Singapore's political stability, economic success, standards of law and order, particularly with regard to its zero-tolerance of drug crimes, its suitability as a business and shipping centre and phenomenal public housing schemes constantly receive acclaim. Singapore's national development undoubtedly came as a consequence of the high 'value consensus' between the political leaders and the people as well as the PAP's ability to offset the expected 'progressive decline of its penetration and embeddedness in the social consciousness of the population'.[25]

The nature of Singapore's limited form of democracy can, according to Vasil, be acclaimed as being 'singularly successful in producing the national development it had deliberately designed to produce'.[26] How does one categorize or demonstrate the extent of social development in Singapore? Typically, naive criticism extends no further than the level of home ownership (albeit in terms of public housing estates), the magnificence of Changi airport, the container port, the excellent zoo and of course the wonderful shopping/dining potential that the city offers tourists. Singapore can, however, boast many other outstanding achievements that can be justifiably held aloft to illustrate its meteoric rate of social and cultural development.[27] Such social dimensions as education, at all levels, health care and medical research, law and order, public transport, housing and the arts can all provide examples of the nature of the government's achievements in social development. No aspect of the lives of Singaporeans escapes the purview of policy. A domain so centrally significant as physical activity and most certainly sport has not.

SPORT, NATION-BUILDING AND SINGAPORE

The linkages between sport and national identity are fundamental and grounded in sport's symbolic power. Each ideological or political system that enlists sport as a means of cultural imposition does so from its contextual ideological position.[28] Sport was once considered an entity that could be extracted from an analysis of a particular society like some 'homogenous cultural universal for the purposes of cross-cultural comparison'.[29] However, sport is not a singular form or abstraction that can be treated with such simplicity. Not only is 'sport' complex; so are the myriad social, cultural and geographical situations in which it is found. A single sport or game such as association football (soccer) can be played under uniform rules but has a different reality and meaning in each country. Even though the forces of globalization are striving to create a uniform global soccer subculture, the game can still be seen in many different cultural forms throughout the world. The twentieth century saw sport, certainly among the first great agents of globalization, adopted by all manner of rival proselytizing political ideologies. As J.A. Mangan suggests, 'all ... powerful ideologies in the twentieth century adopted sport, used sport and promoted sport within their representative cultures, often dressing it in the most florid rhetoric'.[30] The ideological leaders of Singapore, initially in their efforts to traverse the white water of decolonization, and subsequently on their way to creating the hegemony that brought the nation to developed-nation status, kept a firm policy grip on all dimensions of physical activity. Over the 40-plus years of PAP rule, the underlying philosophy of sport policy has ranged from eugenics to excellence. At all times the government has pragmatically directed and promoted the nation's play, its fitness programmes and its sport. It has also very purposely enlisted aspects to achieve specific fundamental political goals such as communal integration and racial harmony, productivity through better health and fitness, national defence and nationalism.

At the time of 'full' independence the PAP had adopted the totally revised goal of creating a sense of nationalism that was indicative of a viable, non-communal, multiracial nation able to stand alone and chart its own destiny. This represented a statist notion of nationalism[31] that saw national identity as being the 'direct product of the overriding political ethos of the nation-state'.[32] Consistent with the statist view of the nature of nationalism, the PAP had to unite the people, diverse as they were, by 'inventing traditions' and creating a shared sense of community and mission to support the revised version of the new nation.[33] Sport proved to be a fertile field for policy in this quest.

Sport in Singapore, as it was in all British Imperial territories, was one of the most enduring features of the British cultural imperialism.[34] In terms of this analysis it is ironic that Singapore's greatest individual sporting achievement, an Olympic Silver medal, was won by Tan Howe Liang in the lightweight weightlifting event at the Rome Olympics in 1960, five years before independence. Competing for Singapore, Tan Howe Liang had also lifted at the Melbourne Olympics in 1956, but under the flag of Malaya. Indeed, after his efforts in Rome he was still acclaimed by the Singapore press as 'the first Malayan in history to win an Olympic award'.[35] Tan's heroic achievement occurred in an era of no government funding. He competed, as he said, when 'there were no facilities, no sponsor. You buy your *makan* [food], find your job.'[36] Tan Howe Liang received little acclaim and melted into obscurity. Following the policy paradigm shift in the late 1990s, the pursuit of sporting excellence and the creation of national sporting icons became more prominent features of PAP policy. It was only then that Tan Howe Liang gained the public recognition he had deserved for so long. In 1999 the quest to enhance Singapore's sporting mythology further prior to the 2000 Sydney Olympic Games intensified, Tan Howe Liang was honoured with an award, presented by the Prime Minister, Goh Chok Tong, for being voted second amongst Singapore's sporting greats of all time. The winner was the champion badminton player Wong Peng Soon, who won three All-England Badminton Championships in the early 1950s, also well before independence.

FIRST-GENERATION PAP, LEE KUAN YEW AND SPORT

As Singapore moved to independence, its sports culture understandably reflected the cultural imposition of the British Empire. However, the influence and effect of the cultural imperialism of the British, though highly effective, was not absolute. Certainly, the games played and the prevalent ethos of sport were driven by the dominant British games culture, but this was not the sole or most influential force at work:

> [T]he imperialism of the British was not the only cultural force imposing itself upon the colony of Singapore, nor was it *the* most influential. It has been demonstrated that the numerically dominant ethnic group, the Chinese, also exerted a tremendous and enduring influence upon the diffusion of sport in Singapore. This influence was carried along by a powerful parallel cultural imperialism that proved to be an effective figurational force that facilitated the creolization of the British model of sport and the establishment of the template of Singapore's very idiosyncratic sports culture.[37]

In the new nation of Singapore in sport, as in all aspects of social activity, the overarching influence was in fact not so much that of the Chinese but of a single Chinese person, Lee Kuan Yew. In the absence of tangible resources, Lee Kuan Yew recognized that the people were in fact the 'country's precious asset'.[38] Developing or newly industrializing nations that have few or no resources, as Singapore had at independence, will by necessity base their economic development upon labour-intensive manufacturing or service industries.[39] Thus, the people must be fit, healthy and sensible to be productive. Though fully cognizant of elite sport's potential for nation-building, Lee Kuan Yew adopted policies that were underpinned by eugenic philosophy.[40] Even at the opening of the National (sports) Stadium in 1973, in what amounts to a most lucid (modern) appreciation of the politico-economic significance of sport, the Prime Minister promoted a 'sport for life' message rather than an elitist one:

> There are no national benefits from gold medallists for smaller countries. ... For the superpowers with large populations superiority in sports is national propaganda to persuade other people of the superiority of their competing political systems. But it is foolish and wasteful for the smaller countries to do it. Singapore's best return is to generate healthy, vigorous exercise for the population, young and old enhancing the valuable qualities it has – a keen, bright, educated people who will lead better and more satisfying lives if they are fit and healthy.[41]

This represented an unabashed authoritarian call for support for the political notion of sport that sought to produce a healthy and productive labour force. The question could be asked: why build a 55,000-seat sports stadium, at the cost of S$50 million,[42] at such a critical stage in the nation's development when you are not promoting elite sport? The building of the National Stadium, the reclamation of the surrounding land and the building of the vast park setting and car parks had a purpose that went far beyond the running track and football field it contained. The project initially represented a boon to employment and the subsequent circulation of revenue. Second, and most importantly in political terms, it stood as a symbol of the nation's emerging sophistication and development. Lee Kuan Yew's speech at the opening was a convoluted statement of apparently paradoxical reflections on sport. It demonstrated the extent of the underlying instrumental rationality that has pervaded all aspects of the PAP's control of social life in Singapore, which infiltrates, as Chua says, 'extensively and intrusively into [all] spheres of social and political life',[43] including quite evidently sport. Lee Kuan Yew stands at the opening of the nation's greatest (certainly most expensive) elite sporting facility and yet refers to the pursuit of sporting excellence as 'foolish and wasteful'.[44] Why would the great man feel he could reflect upon sport thus? He could because he totally understood the attitude and perception of the majority of the Chinese Singaporeans. He knew of their entrenched, almost genetic, view of sport as 'wasteful' with there being no merit in play, only in work.[45] He knew that for the Chinese, particularly after suffering at the hands of the

Japanese during the occupation, the accumulation of wealth and a 'full rice bowl' were their priorities. Thus it could be surmised that to promote such endeavours would be seen by Lee Kuan Yew as having, at that moment in history, little political value. It may be naively deduced that he viewed sport as having no value; not so – he had simply decided that at that time 'sport' was of a more functional value to Singapore. It could be far more productive to use it than to revere it or worship its stars: 'as a social investment, fully and properly *used*, it can be made a great asset'.[46] Lee Kuan Yew looked on sport dispassionately and considered all aspects – the wins, the losses, the rivalry, the passion, pragmatically, all had their purpose. He believed that, 'given leadership', elite sporting success had the potential to make people not only watch sport but also take part.[47] He had predicted the malaise of modernized Singaporean society – the sedentary lifestyle, 'the artificial city life'[48] – and extolled the worth of 'wholesome exercise and recreation'[49] to offset the moral sins that 'passive entertainment … television, cinemas, floor-shows and exhibitions'[50] engendered. This seemingly naive 'call to arms' was received well in Singapore, so complete was the acceptance of the PAP's ideology. The populace complies because it has accepted the underpinning logic of the party's pragmatism, which it has, as its overriding goal, the nation's, and thus the *people*'s, continuous economic growth, for this is no corrupt authoritarian power.[51]

Writing in 2000, Lee Kuan Yew reaffirmed his positive perception of sport as a means for socialization. Despite the fervent calls for international sporting success by the newly formed Committee of Sporting Singapore (the government's task force for sporting advancement), the senior minister still retains his realistically pragmatic attitude to sport. In discussing the government's monumental task in overcoming the largely Chinese population's entrenched loathing for military service, he also reflected upon the need to change their attitude to physical activity.

> People must admire military valour. As Keng Swee [the Defence Minister] said in sorrow, 'The Spartan approach to life does not come about naturally in a community that lives by buying and selling.' I had to get people to change their attitudes. We also had to improve the physical condition of our young by getting them to participate in sports and physical activity of all kinds, and to develop a taste for adventure and strenuous, thrilling activities that

were not without danger to themselves. We need institutions, well organized, well staffed, and well directed to follow up the exhortations and stirring speeches. The prime responsibility was that of the Ministry of Education. Only if we changed people's thinking and attitudes could we raise a large citizen army like Switzerland's or Israel's.[52]

Lee Kuan Yew repeated a traditional saying that demonstrates the mindset of Chinese parents towards what was viewed as a wasteful use of their sons' lives: 'Every Chinese parent knew the saying *hao han bu dang bing, hao tie bu da ding* (a good lad does not become a soldier, good steel does not become nails).'[53] This notion is still prevalent in modern Singapore and in fact is seen as contributing to the rising levels of emigration by Singapore nationals as a growing educated affluent middle class emerged towards the end of the twentieth century. This could be viewed as one of the problems resulting from 'the excesses of success'.[54]

1960 saw the establishment of the Singapore Sports Council (SSC), heralded by the minister in charge, Inche Othman Wok, as being a 'sports factory' that would 'turn out champions of the future'.[55] Throughout his opening address, Inche Othman Wok claimed that with the establishment of this 'factory machinery'[56] all was now ready for the nation to commence 'production, systematically converting raw material into probables, probables into possibles and possibles into potential champions in every sports arena in the world'.[57] Inche Othman's speech overflowed with such rhetoric. He even used wartime metaphors to stress how important he viewed the Sports Council's emergence: 'For all our sports associations and sportsmen [sic], today is surely a kind of D-Day as we launch our long awaited Singapore Sports Council.'[58] There can be no doubt as to how the first cabinet of the PAP government viewed its interventionist stance on elite sport:

> Sport is politics. To put it more specifically, sport is international politics. When one of our sportsmen [sic] gains a gold medal, the credit goes not only to him but to his country as well. It is therefore right and proper that the country, the community, the fellow-citizens of the sportsmen, should do their bit and give as much help as possible to the sportsmen whose victories they share. For a new nation like ours it is all the more important all of us work closely together and strive to give every aid to our sportsmen.[59]

At the opening of the Festival of Sport (*Pesta Sukan*) on 29 July 1965, during the political and social turmoil immediately before the separation from Malaysia, Lee Kuan Yew conceded that he viewed sport as political. He said: 'Sport is politics – very much politics in a very international way. And sport, I am sorry to say, is also very internal politics.'[60] Here he was embracing sport in an attempt to placate Malaysian concerns over communalism. He said that apart from all the historical and geopolitical assets Singapore had, sport was a major social force: 'Sport militates towards a non-communal, multi-religious, multilingual approach to life.'[61]

Lee Kuan Yew, as noted earlier, regarded the fitness of people to be of major importance if Singapore was to survive. He constantly introduced sport and the need for both fitness and 'ruggedness' into survivalist statements during the early years of nationhood. Oon suggests that 'Lee Kuan Yew was instrumental in creating a nation-wide awareness of the importance of physical fitness'.[62] At the opening of the *Pesta Sukan* in 1965, the Prime Minister stated that the festival was a 'lesson that every citizen must keep himself [*sic*] fit if he wants to lead an effective life'.[63] This comment typified the Prime Minister's paternalistic demands on his 'people' (the Chinese) to be fit, healthy, robust and rugged; a set of expressions he used constantly to admonish Singaporeans.[64] A central feature of the government's preoccupation with fitness and a sense of ruggedness was the obvious necessity for its national servicemen to have these qualities. Lee Kuan Yew's exhortations to create a rugged nation were in essence directed at the Chinese and in particular the better educated middle class who traditionally regarded physical exertion with disdain. Lee was continually concerned that 'his' people should be physically fit, active and as rugged as the Malay and Indian sections of the community.[65]

A fitness drive started in May 1967 with the launch of a physical fitness test programme in the schools of Singapore. From level four of primary school, pupils were to be tested twice a year on a battery of five activities. Teo suggests that the physical fitness campaign and constant calls for a rugged society represented an attempt to create 'an idealised national psyche'[66] with physical fitness as a major 'dimension of the official appeal to cultivate a cultural and spiritual disposition of toughness and resilience amongst Singaporeans'.[67] In March 1969 the government launched the National Fitness Exercises (NFX), centred on a set of basic callisthenic exercises, similar to the Canadian 5BX programme. Much research and many demonstrations, ministerial pronouncements and publicity events followed the launch. The rhetoric and intensity of the campaign was incredible: daily radio and television broadcasts promoted this rather bland routine; thousands of leaflets and booklets were published; even gramophone records were made.[68] The idea was to have the NFX done in factories, schools, at home and in the community centres. Within three years, however 'nobody was following these exercises'.[69] Various reasons have been suggested for the demise of this rather boring programme – its broadcast time, the limited set of exercises, its intensiveness, even that perhaps Singaporeans had expected something more.

The Singapore Sports Council (SSC) was born on 1 October 1973, following the amalgamation of the National Sports Promotion Board and the National Stadium Corporation.[70] The SSC had a wide-ranging brief and, as a statutory government body, it was the government's mouthpiece as well as its arms and legs in the implementation of all sport and recreation-related policy. The SSC's main thrust for the first 20 years of its existence was the implementation and expansion of the 'Sport for All' programme. This was despite its links with all elite national sporting associations and the National Olympic Council. Today its mission remains 'the education and involvement of the masses in the regular participation of wholesome forms of physical activity'.[71]

The 'Sport for All' policy was unashamedly nationalistic: building fit and healthy individuals, who in turn were to build a fit and healthy nation.[72] The policy material propagated by the SSC, though admitting 'there is also room for sporting excellence',[73] stressed that community sport was seen as *the* vehicle for building community spirit and for creating a cohesive society. The policy patently reflected the government's paternalistic concern for its 'children'. To make the point yet again, the policy was seen by Lee Kuan Yew to be a valuable aid in the production of 'a keen, educated people who will lead better and more satisfying lives if they are fit and healthy'.[74] A pyramid model was used to represent the scheme at work, with the masses at the bottom providing the broad base from which those with talent 'could with some assistance from national sports associations, commit themselves to higher levels of competition and achievement'.[75] The SSC sold this concept as attractive since it 'offers a place to everyone according to his [sic] interest and ability'.[76]

The ease with which Singaporeans willingly comply and actively engage in mass sporting events is indicative of the extent to which the PAP has successfully projected an internalization of the common ideology. The government, through the SSC, has continuously promoted events such as the National Walk/Jog, the National Swim, the National Cycle, the Great Singapore Workout and the Family Sports Programme. In schools there is ACES Day where 'all children exercise simultaneously'. It should be perfectly clear by now that the SSC instituted this form of mass participation to 'encourage Singaporeans to participate and develop an awareness of the importance of sports and physical fitness'.[77] Such events attract an amazing response and the commemorative T-shirts or caps are proudly worn throughout the following year. These mass events engender a surprisingly high level of enthusiastic support and an appropriately high-ranking minister always leads them; in recent years the statuesque frame of Prime Minister Goh Chok Tong has invariably led the way. At these events Goh Chok Tong is often supported by the Minister for Community Development (which now officially embraces sport in its portfolio), Abdullah Tarmugi, and the head of the SSC, Ng Ser Miang.

In its first ten years the Singapore Sports Council exerted an omniscient control over the fitness, recreation, and leisure activities of Singaporeans. Today no aspect of sport from the elite to the most mundane recreational activity is beyond the purview of the SSC. Indeed, a marked change has occurred since the earliest days of independence, when the installation of several senior cabinet ministers as titular heads of prominent sports associations caused concern. Desmond Oon, having been personally involved in elite sport as a member of the national tennis team, reflected that there was, initially, a widespread fear that 'the presence of Government men and top politicians had made sports observers and followers at that time wonder whether the Government would take over control of all matters relating to sport, in the country'.[78] The level of control, provision and intervention in sport, recreation and fitness activities has been so profound that it is now taken for granted. As with the economy, employment, education and housing, the central control of sport has precipitated higher performance expectations and can now be linked to the other 'excesses of success' that Chua outlined with respect to the social and economic successes the nation has experienced in its first 30 years of existence.[79]

To promote sport the communalism of pre-independence Singaporean sport was replaced by an artificially constructed tribalism that was generated by inter-constituency sport competitions which were based upon the Housing Development Board housing estates. In the decade 1972–82 there were 75 constituencies divided up into seven zones, and each constituency had a formally constituted proprietary sports club (CSC). The first inter-constituency competition was initiated by the SSC in 1972 with a soccer competition. By 1983, the programme had grown to embrace badminton, table tennis, *sepak takraw*,[80] volleyball, netball, seven-a-side soccer, six-a-side hockey, squash and swimming.[81] The constituency sports programme was far too imposing and socially significant to be allowed to proceed unshackled. A member of parliament, naturally, led each constituency and each politician assumed a very high profile in the activity of their various teams. It was, and still is, a very important platform for the members of parliament, but for the team members, coaches and administrators involvement was seen as an aspect of their voluntary social activity, whose ethos has been enthusiastically inculcated by the government.

The government's emphasis, throughout this period, was still very much on the Sport for All programme. Soon, however, the 'accent on sports excellence ... [began] to find a voice all its own – a far cry from the days when efforts to groom champions had to be less than concerted'.[82]

A major legacy of the government's initial emphasis on its grass-roots policy was the tremendous sporting and recreational facilities that were built, including the National Stadium, the Singapore Indoor Stadium, the Delta Hockey complex and the Toa Payoh Swimming complex. The government has also constructed synthetic (Tartan) athletic tracks at centres such as the National Stadium, at the old National Institute of Education in Bukit Timah and in the Queenstown Stadium as well as at numerous schools, junior colleges and polytechnics. When the Singapore government endorses policies that seek to change behaviour or that promote an aspect of social activity, there are no half measures; the people are left in no doubt as to the government's intentions.[83] Surely such efforts are indicative of an administration that has seriously considered the future needs of the elite track and field athlete? They are, of course, also evidence of the ideological use of sport to enhance a sense of nationalism. As with most dimensions of social activity, the development of new facilities and their use were measured, planned and, as always, held in check – shackled, even. Some such as Cronin believe that there are two ideologies at work when nations strive to harness the nationalistic symbolism of sport for international prominence: first, that of 'aspiring and new nations'[84] using the international sporting arena to herald their arrival on the world stage, and second, that of 'established nations so that they may demonstrate their strength and prowess'.[85] However, neither description fitted Singapore as it pushed forward onto the world stage as an independent nation. He further suggests that the political linkages between 'sport and nationalism are of central importance to struggling and marginalized states'.[86] Certainly, the linkages were evident but unlike many third world nations, the pursuit of gold medals was never initially part of Singapore's aim. The leaders diverted the attention of the public to the more pragmatic and productive outcomes of physical activity.

SPORT EXCELLENCE: GOH CHOK TONG LOOSENS THE SHACKLES

Since Goh Chok Tong became Prime Minister in 1990, the direction of sporting policy has changed, as has the nature of the discourse of sport used by leading politicians. Prime Minister Goh Chok Tong, in his 'message' in the SSC publication commemorating its twenty-fifth year, maintains the traditional party line but now he adds an emphatic call for international sporting success:

> A fit people makes a rugged nation [sic]. Being fit is not just about muscles, speed and stamina. It is also about determination, discipline and dedication. These attributes make for mental toughness. They help us to overcome unexpected adversities like the present challenges posed by the regional economic crisis and political uncertainty. Sports and physical fitness activities thus have a national dimension. ... The contribution of sports to nation building and national pride is far-reaching. When Singapore athletes win medals at international sports competitions, they bring immense pride and joy to our people. Sporting victories foster national joy and pride.[87]

The pursuit of sports excellence as a seriously endorsed government policy sprang into life with the instigation of Sports Excellence 2000 (SPEX 2000) in 1993. Singapore under Lee Kuan Yew's leadership had become a developed industrialized nation, its productivity and burgeoning gross national product (GNP) resulting from the politically stable environment and the compliant and industrious workforce. However, its level of sports production (especially with regard to elite sporting success) did not match its high level of industrial production. The correlation between GNP and success in international sport, using Olympic medals as a measure, is usually quite high.[88] The 'lion' as yet had not been unleashed, but in the 1990s, the political merits of a sophisticated and internationally competitive and visible sporting image had become more acceptable to the nation's leaders. It was now time to make a 'serious' (which in Singapore means funded) attempt to promote sport as another domain from which the people could gain national pride. Achieving sporting success was no longer politically superfluous or to be left to chance. The new policies reflected very direct and orchestrated political attempts to change the whole perception of sport in Singapore. A lot had changed in 25 years of nationhood. The people by any standards had become affluent, highly educated and extremely materialistic, and they were now to be pushed along by the demands of a government quest for an athletocracy.[89] Elite sport, though watched more and more on television, had never been considered as being of economic value and was thus not a worthwhile pursuit for the majority.[90] However, things began to change with the launch of SPEX 2000 and particularly with the attachment of an impressive array of monetary incentives to performance in the Million Dollar Award Programme (MAP), with a $1 million prize for an Olympic Gold medal, the most impressive prize and a SEA Games Gold medal being worth a 'mere' $10,000. The new athlete support systems, overseas sporting scholarships and the creation of two new divisions in the SSC, the Sports Excellence and the Market Development divisions have also unashamedly oozed elitist aspirations.[91] The biggest impact of the policy shift was perhaps the total turnaround in the nature of political discussion of sport. Once people began to hear from their leaders the virtues of elitist sport, then they began to accept the message, and sport became a worthy as well as possibly profitable pursuit with a new status. SPEX 2000 was launched in the official magazine of the SSC, *Sports*, in 1994. In an article entitled 'The Dawn of a New Era for Singapore Sports – Sports Excellence 2000 – Winning for Singapore' the author looked to the forthcoming Sydney Olympic Games and fantasized:

> Thousands of miles away, in a small island republic, millions sitting transfixed in front of their TV screens burst into spontaneous celebration that spills over into the streets. As the athlete stands on the winners' rostrum, singing his heart out to the strains of 'Majulah Singapura' [the national anthem], tears of joy are seen pouring down his cheeks. Is this a mere pipedream? Not so, if SPEX 2000 has its way. ... In the boldest initiative yet, the Ministry

of Community Development (MCD) and the Singapore Sports Council (SSC) have jointly launched Sports Excellence 2000 – or its catchy acronym SPEX 2000 – a strategic blueprint that will propel Singapore into the legion of sporting bigwigs.[92]

SPEX 2000 AND THE LION'S PURSE

The new policy contained no subtle shift but an emphatic shift in direction in pursuit of sporting excellence. In Singapore 'money speaks'; the almost indecent recourse to monetary incentives, and certainly the advertisement in an extremely flagrant manner of the pecuniary side of the government's new sports excellence programmes, was indicative of the government's seriousness in its elitist ambitions. SPEX 2000 immediately became synonymous with its $10 million annual budget. Headlines and news broadcasts at this time seemed to stress nothing but this.[93] In its magazine *Sports*, the SSC outlined the actual make-up of the funding. The most interesting feature perhaps was that direct government funding was to be $4 million per year and Singapore Pools (the government-owned and -administered national gambling organization) was also to contribute $4 million, with the shortfall being made up by corporate sponsors. The major sums, which in essence were both government funding, represented a quadruple increase in elite sport funding.[94] At all times pragmatic, the SSC decided that it would apportion the 'lion's share'[95] of these funds to a set of sports which it felt would maximize the chances of producing champions.[96] The SSC, using unassailable logic, decided 'after much deliberation'[97] upon two sets of sports, seven 'core sports' and seven 'merit sports', with the most of funding and weighting being given to the core sports. Interestingly, the prioritization of the sports was established not just on past records and successes, the quality of the sport's administration and player base, but also with reference to the fact that that the athletes should not be at a 'disadvantage where physique is concerned'.[98]

The launch of SPEX 2000 was supported by two direct-grant schemes for athletes in the various core and merit sports; these were the Sport Excellence Assistance Programme (SEAP) and the Sport Excellence Assistance Programme for Schools (SEAPS) for student athletes.[99] The Sports Aid Fund had continued to grow through the 1980s and, by 1990, the fund had accumulated over $6 million from corporate and government sponsorship.[100] The gradual relaxation of the government's restraint on calls for elite sports funding began in 1985. In an article headed 'Excellence in Sport Career Comes First', the recommendations of Desmond Oon, who had been sponsored by the government to undertake his doctoral work at the University of Queensland in the 1980s, were announced in 1985, calling for a dramatic rethinking of government policy towards elite sport.[101] Oon looked at the changes he considered had to be made to produce 'international winners'.[102] His vision called for 'Revamping the educational system on American lines; changing parental attitudes; promoting sports as a career; developing an awareness of sports and its values'.[103] The article, evidently sanctioned by the government, also carried comments from athletes and sporting administrators calling for more funding, more sympathy from employers and, most significantly, a change in the mindset of parents of aspiring athletes, to shake off the shackles of economic and academic obsession.

In response to these and other (tolerated) calls, Dr Tan Eng Liang, the chairman of the SSC, dismissed suggestions that their recent surveys were nothing but statistical exercises. He announced that athletes would have some monetary assistance, but ruled out full professionalism, saying: 'That's definitely out, we cannot pay our sportsmen [sic] salaries to do nothing but train.'[104] The loosening of the shackles continued, however, and by 1987 the chairman announced that as the 'kitty' was fuller, athletes could now be helped more generously. This had followed a call by E.W. Barker, the Minister for Law and president of the SSC, for sports organizations to go for gold rather than just take part.[105] The launch of SPEX 2000 was another calculated and well-orchestrated step in the process of establishing a supportive environment for elite sports excellence in Singapore. SPEX 2000 was to complement the 'Sport for All' philosophy that had prevailed since independence; it was not going to subsume it. Thus, the government through the agency of the SSC, the National Olympic Committee, the Ministry of Education, the Ministry of Defence and the various national sports associations 'aimed to embed sports in the bedrock of Singapore society so as to stimulate national pride and unity whilst it was to add a new dimension to Singapore's development as a nation'.[106]

OTHER CATS – SOME FIT, SOME NOT SO TRIM

Sport had now become not only part of the rhetoric of nationalism in Singapore but also a feature of the portrayal of its image internationally.

Yet, as is to be expected, the 'lion' was not to run free or alone; it was always to be accompanied by some of its more domesticated cousins. Through the 1990s and into the twenty-first century, the twin thrusts forward for sports excellence and, axiomatically, 'sport for all' ran in tandem with the attempts of the government to improve the health standards of the nation. The 1991 report of the Review Committee on National Health Policies, entitled 'Healthy Family – Healthy Nation', painted a bleak picture of the state of the nation's health and called for major efforts to reduce obesity levels, increase activity levels and decrease the level of smoking. As McNeill points out this would 'not only make for a more productive workforce ... but would [lead] to a better quality of life for all Singaporeans'.[107] As the twin sports policies emerged in the 1990s, so the National Healthy Lifestyle Campaign was launched in 1992. The problem of obesity levels in children was (and still is) of major concern for the Ministry of Health; thus, in 1992, in collaboration with the Ministries of Education and Defence, the Trim and Fit (TAF) programme was introduced in all Singapore schools. This draconian weight-reduction programme involved all children from seven to 18 years being weighed and their height being measured and a pronouncement of their 'healthy-weight' status being declared: they were defined 'excessively overweight, overweight, normal weight, under weight [or] excessively under weight'.[108] The underlying motive and instrumental rationality of the scheme can be applauded. However, the fact that schools were ranked according to their levels of the percentage of obese students provoked concern. Such an emphasis, the constant close scrutiny of physical education inspectors and the fact that the findings were published, saw school physical education programmes dominated by fitness and weight-reduction activities to the detriment of the physical education and sports activities. The willing compliance of the physical educators of Singapore with this and the testing for the National Physical Fitness Award (NAPFA),[109] against which schools are also ranked, is a measure of the power and extent of the government's ideological control.

The pragmatism of PAP policy-making was again evident in 1996 with the launch of the 'Sports for Life' programme which had been designed to 'make sports more attractive, accessible and most of all, fun for all Singaporeans'.[110] Since 1992 the government had been concerned with the participation levels in physical activity, and by 1996 it was recognized that not only had the world of sport changed, so too had the nature of its clientele. The message had to be repackaged to accommodate the 'new strata of socio-economic groups and diverse needs, tastes and aspirations'[111] of Singapore. It was recognized that Singaporeans now lived more 'sophisticated lives'[112] and had a far wider range of social and recreational options available to them. However, there was now another fast approaching concern that had emerged from 'a joint-survey by the National University of Singapore and the Institute of Policy Studies'[113] that forecast that within 21 years (by 2017) Singapore's elderly population would double.[114] The policy statements for the first time mentioned the need to 'keep up with changing demographics of Singapore's society'.[115] At the launch of the 'Sport for Life' programme, Prime Minister Goh Chok Tong and the Chairman of the SSC, Ng Ser Miang, both rather softly encouraged all Singaporeans to become competent in at least one sport. Goh Chok Tong's tone and the manner in which he embraced sport as a central element of the 'projected culture of the future as an integral, even core, behaviour of a mature and gracious society',[116] demonstrated that sport had become a descriptor of an ideal citizen and society:

> My idea of an all-rounded Singaporean is one who is well-educated, cultivated, sporty, caring and gracious. Such a Singaporean reads widely, enjoys music and the arts, sings or plays at least one musical instrument, is active in sports and cares for his fellow citizens. Most of us are not such a complete person ... but everyone can be competent in at least one sport.[117]

The notion of the 'Sports for Life' programmes adding value to the lives of every Singaporean in the cultural as well as the physical sense significantly elevated the status of sport in Singaporean society. The extent of government spending on the Sport for Life initiatives certainly suggested this, with the government contributing $9 million annually up to 2000 and $12 million thereafter, notwithstanding a further $250 million promised to build four new sports facilities by 2010.[118]

THE SPORTS MINISTRY ARRIVES

As Singapore's athletes and sports officials hurtled towards the year 2000, elite sport and the government's high level of involvement continued at a rapid pace. Athletic endeavour and the pursuit of dreams were acceptable and, for the government, most palatable fare. What better achievement than conquering the greatest physical challenge on Earth, Mount

Everest? On 25 May 1998, after their first attempt had failed, the Singapore team represented by Edwin Siew and Khoo Swee Chiow, supported by a group of Sherpa guides, reached the summit and planted the national flag. The fact that both of these heroes were Malaysian-born permanent residents of Singapore, not citizens, was a thorny issue, the matter even being reflected upon at length by the Prime Minister in his National Day speech in 1998. 'Singapore gave them the opportunity. It was a Singapore team that put the flag on the summit; it was a Singapore effort, a Singapore achievement.'[119] The programme had not been directly funded by the government; indeed, it had taken the group four years to raise the necessary financial support. However, the project was far too important to be allowed to fail. The attempt received scientific, logistical and, of course, indirect funding from the government albeit through the Sports Council and the government-owned national telecommunications provider Singtel. When the team leader David Lim and his team returned to Changi airport they were personally ushered from the arrival lounge by a jubilant Minister of State for Defence, Matthias Yao Chih. This in itself demonstrates the nuances of the relationship of physical endeavour to the realpolitik of Singapore. The Prime Minister and the nation's President feted the Everest-conquering team; indeed it was 'Flag Before Self ... a personal triumph but ... also a national high'.[120] The climbers had become the 'Bravehearts'[121] of the nation and their example was used immediately to goad Singaporeans into considering sporting endeavour as a valid form of actualization and, as is so typical of the nation, the current economic exigencies were somehow woven into the fabric of the rhetoric:

> With the spectacular economic progress that Asia has made over the recent years, the gap between East and West will gradually narrow as more and more money is being pumped into achieving sporting success. This is the general trend notwithstanding the present Asian economic downturn. ... Where Singapore is concerned, the lack of talent and will rather than money seems to be the problem. The number of Singaporeans willing to sacrifice the comforts of life for sporting fame is very small indeed. Lack of commitment and dedication etc seems to be another bugbear. The lesson from the recent Mount Everest success is very clear. If more Singaporeans, particularly the gifted ones, are prepared to dedicate themselves to

win for themselves and Singapore there are enough resources under SPEX 2000 for them to scale the highest peaks of sports.[122]

1 April 2000 marked the official birth of a Sports Ministry in Singapore. The Ministry of Community Development, led by Abdullah Tarmugi, so long the advocate of sport in Singapore, became the Ministry of Community Development and Sport. The political significance of the placement in this ministry is obvious; sport had now been elevated to a central position in the culture of this wonderfully textured young nation.

The government has moved the goal posts for sports excellence in Singapore. Sydney has come and gone and the government has now re-worked SPEX 2000 into SPEX 21. It has carried the targets of SPEX 2000 over and added other challenges to its quest for international sporting success. It has not only set the target of a gold medal in sailing at the Beijing 2008 Olympic Games; it has also sought to resurrect past glories in badminton by setting the target of finals places in the Thomas Cup by 2012. Most ambitious of all is 'Goal 2010', which is to qualify for the World Cup soccer finals in that year. This challenge came directly from the Prime Minister's admiration for the French team's World Cup victory in 1998. Goh Chok Tong boldly aired this challenge at the 1998 National Day Rally speech; the choice of such a setting is indicative of the new regard the PAP government now has for elite sport and its potential as an agent of nationalism, patriotism and productivity.[123] A year later, on the same stage, Goh Chok Tong reiterated his recurring plea for Singaporeans to embrace sport: 'Earning money is not the sole objective to life or education. A community of any quality should have a wide range of skills and interests. Its members should take part and excel in sports.'[124] In what was a very paternal 'end of year report', the Prime Minister reflected upon topics ranging from the catastrophic consequences of regional and global economic crises to the somewhat bizarre analysis of the quality of the language used in a popular locally produced television situation comedy. He also revisited a long-term aim of his – to make 'Singapore ... a fun place to live'.[125] It can be deduced that the government was concerned that the people, armed with an ever-increasing level of surplus income and time were perhaps in need of excitement: 'People laugh at us for promoting fun so seriously. But having fun is important. If Singapore is a dull, boring place, not only will talent not want to come here, but even Singaporeans will begin to feel restless.'[126] It would seem that the view of Norbert Elias and Eric Dunning that societies are 'inherently unexciting'[127] and that sport now serves to sate society's 'need for excitement' had been internalized by the Singapore government's policy analysts.

In September 2000, when the gaze of the world was fixed on Sydney and the Olympic Games, Singapore was taking a further step to assure the future of sport in the island state. A 'high-powered committee',[128] the Committee on Sporting Singapore (CoSS), was established with the function of steering the future course of sport in Singapore. At a 'tea session' to honour the nation's Olympic and Paralympic teams before they departed for Sydney, Abdullah Tarmugi, Minister for Community Development and Sports, announced the formation of the committee and its intended mission to develop a 'blueprint for the development of sports in Singapore'.[129]

The importance of the committee was indicative of the intention of the government to get the 'right' answers from the committee; but first the 'right' questions had to be asked. CoSS, headed by Tarmugi, included two other cabinet ministers, Teo Chee Hean (Minister for Education and Second Minister for Defence), sitting in his capacity as president of the Singapore National Olympic Council and Mah Bow Tan (Minister for National Development) as an adviser, in his role of president of the Football Association of Singapore. The deputy chairman of the committee was Associate Professor Ho Peng Kee (Minister for State for Home Affairs and Law) who was, incidentally, deputy president of the Singapore Football Association. The committee's infrastructure included four subcommittees that were to investigate four of the five key strategies the government considered critical to 'moving sport forward'.[130] Thus the 'right' questions *were* going to be asked. Each subcommittee was headed by a major figure in the PAP machinery.[131] This committee was indeed high-powered. It is also interesting to note that the government had recognized the tremendous opportunities that existed in the very lucrative sports industry. The charismatic business leader-cum-SSC chairman and South-East Asia's only IOC delegate, Ng Ser Miang, heading this sub-committee, was to bring an element of entrepreneurialism to the discussions.

After five months of deliberation, CoSS came up with a set of preliminary recommendations. In an unusually open gesture, the committee called a forum of over 700 stakeholders in sport that included athletes, coaches, parents, school principals, teachers, sports officials and sponsors to review CoSS's initial pronouncements. All speakers from CoSS, and particularly 'all four ministers made it plain the government was serious about promoting sports'.[132] The recommendations included several new projects and initiatives, such as the establishment of a sports school and a 'new' National Stadium. For some of the elder statesmen, this must have evoked a sense of *déjà vu*, as these were two of the original ideas that the National Sports Promotion Board of Singapore had considered in the 1960s. However, the major thrusts of these initial findings concerned what have come to be known as the 'three pillars' of the foundation of the future of sport in Singapore: encouraging people to take part in sports; the production of excellence: and the promotion of a thriving sports industry. Evidently Ng Ser Miang had argued his case well.

The final report of CoSS was delivered in July 2001 and the report was officially accepted by the Prime Minister as he opened a splendid new $54 million Sports and Fitness Centre. The report and its recommendations, emanating from not only the 'high-powered' committee but from the comments and input of the 'stakeholders', was a far more plausible document than previous sport policy outpourings such as SPEX 2000. There is a sense that the 'people' did have an element of ownership of its contents and the level of jingoism was a little more realistic than in the past. However, the funding levels and expansiveness of the projects were, as always, hyperbolic. The government, through its Sports Ministry, set aside $500 million to be spent over five years in the three-pronged attack to promote sport in Singapore. Six targets were identified and 40 strategies were outlined to achieve them.[133] The sports fraternity had expected a revolution; however, CoSS delivered a somewhat conservative and strangely restrained set of proposals. The recommendations clearly had been influenced by a very knowledgeable group of sport aficionados as well as the 'high-powered' politicians.[134]

NEW LION, NEW SHACKLES?

The new policies for sport development in Singapore embrace vast spending, the dream of becoming a 'top ten' Asian sporting nation by 2010 and a hope to have 50 per cent of the population actively involved in sport by 2005.[135] The sentiments behind these goals are still paternalistic. Prime Minister Goh has now, however, introduced a new dimension to the government's view of sport: 'it makes us a more rounded and resilient people. ... It will bring our people together and open new paths of success beyond academic pursuit.'[136] The view that sport is worthy, valid and equal to other avenues of endeavour is apparent; he considers the nation's obligation to sports excellence is to 'aim high'[137] and that those who wish to pursue the dream should not only be committed but should also receive the 'right support'.[138] The support is to be embedded in the concept of 'Team Singapore' outlined in the CoSS report as being 'the heart of the new world of sports we are embarking upon'.[139] Team Singapore is to be the 'emblematic'[140] symbol of the new sports movement in Singapore. Deputy Prime Minister Tony Tan defined it thus:

> Team Singapore is, at the core, the spirit of cooperation and national pride in all our efforts. Such cooperations must involve committed athletes, professionally run national sports associations, skilled professionals such as coaches and officials, spirited fans, committed parents, enlightened schools, a supportive private sector and an engaged government.[141]

Has there ever been a doubt that the Singapore government is 'engaged'? The government now wants the average citizen to incorporate active sports 'as part of a lifelong necessity'[142] and as Tony Tan has intimated that all aspects will now be part of the government's purview. It could be suggested that now we have a new lion in Singapore – sport – and a whole new system of shackles. In fact these shackles are now made of stronger steel, for as a society grows more serious so too does the cultural importance of sport.[143]

Sport, physical activity and recreation have clearly been central elements in the government's intervention in the politico-social development of Singapore, and germane to this has been the impact of the Chinese majority.[144] By virtue of demographics, the ethnic Chinese majority has dominated all social change in Singapore.[145] The dominant political ideology and subsequent hegemony has been significantly influenced by Confucianism and the paternalistic authoritarianism it begets. In fact, it is this that has allowed the PAP to maintain its hold on power. Consistent with the pragmatic view that if a government is performing effectively – and for all Singaporeans that means if it is making progress and improving the opportunities for amassing more wealth – then do not rock the boat.[146] Singapore's limited democracy may not conform, as Vasil says, 'to the accepted democratic norms and values, but it is difficult to deny that the system has worked well and has produced remarkable national development'.[147] Unequivocally this is true of sport, physical activity and associated health levels, but so far they have no Olympic gold; so what? They have a prosperous, educated, content and healthy people and a modern and well-endowed, if somewhat crowded, island home which sits comparatively like a beacon in a region rife with turmoil. The constant overview of the social domain, including the 'lion' of sport, by the government has evoked criticism and the retort that Singapore is a 'nanny state'[148] not only for the frequency of the 'do-good' campaigns but also for the nature of the paternalistic authoritarian nature of the polity. However, leaving the last word to Lee Kuan Yew, as is appropriate, it could very well be that they will have the 'last laugh'.[149] He maintained that without the draconian policies and controls, Singapore 'would have been a grosser, ruder, cruder society. … It made Singapore a more pleasant place to live in. If this is a "nanny state", I am proud to have fostered one.'[150]

NOTES

I extend my thanks to Lim Lai Kaun, James Cook University who gave me access to much of the primary data used in this essay, she has also been invaluable as a sounding board and proofreader extraordinaire.

1. S. Rajaratnam, personal interview, Singapore, Sept. 1983. In R. Vasil, *Governing Singapore: Democracy and National Development* (Sydney: Allen & Unwin, 2000), p.7.
2. 'Singapore' evolved from the Malay construct, 'Singapura', the name that had previously been used to describe the island of Temasek upon which Stamford Raffles landed in 1819. Temasek was a meagre outpost of the declining empire of the Sultan of Johore that at the time of Raffles's arrival was under the aegis of the Temenggong Abdur Rahman. The main village settlement, according to legend, was built upon site of the legendary settlement of Singapura, which literally means 'Lion City'; ironically, no lions, only tigers, existed on the island. The author's attraction to the figurative use of the term 'lion' stems obviously from the noble status and power of the beast and the fact that in recent years sporting teams representing Singapore, most notably their football team, have been anointed with the epithet. The island nation's sport has in this instance been bestowed, somewhat cynically, with the same title, the potential, power and significance of the realm of sport have always been recognized in independent Singapore, but the 'beast' as yet has never been let out of its cage unshackled.
3. Vasil, *Governing Singapore*, p.7.
4. See C.M. Turnbull, *A History of Singapore 1819–1988* (Singapore: Oxford University Press, 2nd edn 1988), pp.216–50.
5. Accepting independence, Lee Kuan Yew demonstrated his personal feelings by publicly weeping. He had fought long and hard for Singapore to become a member state of the federation; however, he was perhaps more motivated politically than personally. He was born in Singapore, whereas the majority of his Cabinet had been born and bred in Malaya.
6. Brunei did not enter the enlarged Federation of Malay States when it was formed in 1963.
7. Vasil, *Governing Singapore*, p.3.
8. B-H. Chua, *Communitarian Ideology and Democracy in Singapore* (London: Routledge, 1995), p.9.
9. Ibid., p.13.
10. K.W. Yeo and A. Lau, 'From Colonialism to Independence, 1945–1965', in E.C.T. Chew and E. Lee (eds), *A History of Singapore* (London: Oxford University Press, 1991), p.148.
11. Ibid.
12. Vasil, *Governing Singapore*, p.7.

13. Rajaratnam, personal interview, Singapore, Sept. 1983, in Vasil, *Governing Singapore*, p.7.
14. Lee Kuan Yew, 'The Battle for Merger', in *Towards Socialism*, Vol.5, Ministry of Culture Series of 12 Talks delivered between 13 Sept. and 9 Oct. 1961 (Singapore: Government Printing Office, 1962), pp.10–11.
15. Rajaratnam, personal interview, Singapore, Sept. 1983. Vasil, *Governing Singapore*, p.7.
16. Lee Kuan Yew, *Parliamentary Debates*, Vol.4, Cols.5–6 (Singapore: Government Printer, 1965).
17. Lau Teng Chuan, 'The Origin and Development of Sports for All in Singapore', Paper presented at International Conference on the History of Sports and Physical Education in the Pacific Region, University of Otago, Nov. 1978, pp.1–3.
18. Ibid., p.3.
19. Ibid.
20. Vasil, *Governing Singapore*, p.14.
21. Lee Kuan Yew, *The Economist*, 22 Nov. 1986, cited in Vasil, *Governing Singapore*, p.51.
22. Chan Heng Chee, 'Political Developments, 1965–1979', in Chew and Lee, *A History of Singapore*, pp.178–9.
23. In his National Day speech in 2000, PM Goh Chok Tong stated that the average per capita income in Singapore was now S$40, 000, while economic growth for the first six months in 2000 had been estimated at 8.8 per cent. The final annual figure for 2000 was later published as 9.9 per cent (Goh Chok Tong, National Day Speech cited in *Straits Times*, 9 Aug. 2000). The next year Singapore was ranked second in terms of competitiveness, third in economic performance and first in governmental efficiency (Professor Stephane Garelli, Director, the International Institute of Management [IMD], World Competitiveness Yearbook 2001, Switzerland).
24. See 'Singapore Survey: Lee's creation and legacy', *The Economist*, 22 Nov. 1986, pp.3–22.
25. Chua, *Communitarian Ideology*, pp.3–4.
26. Vasil, *Governing Singapore*, p.233.
27. For an outstanding overview of such changes in social life in Singapore since they gained self-government in 1959 see Chua Ben-Huat, 'The Business of Living: Transformation of Everyday Life' in Chua, *Communitarian Ideology*, pp.77–100.
28. J.M. Hoberman, *Sport and Political Ideology* (Austin, TX: University of Texas Press, 1984), p.7.
29. Jennifer Hargreaves, 'Theorising Sport: An Introduction', in idem (ed.), *Sport, Culture and Ideology* (London: Routledge, 1982), p.2.
30. J.A. Mangan, 'Epilogue: Post-Imperialism, Sport, Globalization', in J.A. Mangan (ed.), *The European Sports History Review*, Vol.3: *Europe, Sport, World: Shaping Global Societies* (London and Portland, OR: Frank Cass, 2001), p.268.
31. See B. Moore, *The Social Origins of Dictatorship and Democracy* (London: Allen Lane, 1967).
32. M. Cronin, *Sport and Nationalism in Ireland: Gaelic Games, Soccer and Irish Identity since 1884* (Dublin: Four Courts Press, 1999), p.27.
33. E. Hobsbawn and T. Ranger, 'The Invention of Tradition', in ibid.
34. P.A. Horton, 'Complex Creolization: The Evolution of Modern Sport in Singapore', in Mangan, *Europe, Sport, World*, p.77.
35. N. Siebel, 'The Man Who Hated to Lose', *The Straits Times*, 10 Sept. 1960, p.12.
36. Tan How Liang, cited in 'Back to the Games for Strongman', *The Straits Times Interactive*, 5 Aug. 2000.
37. Horton, 'Complex Creolization', p.98.
38. Lee Kuan Yew, *From Third World to First: The Singapore Story 1965–2000* (New York: HarperCollins, 2000), p.135.
39. Lee Kuan Yew, *From Third World to First*, p.51.
40. P.A. Horton, 'Olympism in the Asia-Pacific Region: A Question of Naviety or Pragmatism?', *Culture, Sport, Society*, 1, 1 (1998), 178.
41. Lee Kuan Yew, reported by R. Chandran and L. Fong, in 'Our goal in Sports: Mr. Lee', *The Sunday Times* (Singapore), 22 July 1973, p.1.
42. Ibid., p.6.
43. Chua, *Communitarian Ideology*, p.66.
44. Lee Kuan Yew, reported by Chandran and Fong in 'Our Goal in Sports', p.1.
45. See Horton, 'Complex Creolization', for an analysis of the role and impact of the Chinese in the emergence and development of the sporting culture of Singapore. It is shown that though the residual sports culture of the British was an enduring feature of their rule, the Chinese also exerted a tremendous and lasting influence upon the evolution of sport in pre-independence Singapore.
46. Lee Kuan Yew, reported by Chandran and Fong, in 'Our Goal in Sports', p.6.

47. Ibid.
48. Ibid.
49. Ibid.
50. Ibid.
51. For an excellent critical analysis of the pragmatism of the PAP governments of Singapore, see Chapter 3 in Chua, *Communitarian Ideology*, pp.57–78.
52. Lee Kuan Yew, *From Third World to First*, p.18.
53. Ibid., p.17.
54. Chua, *Communitarian Ideology*, pp.116–19.
55. E. Frida, 'Sports Factory is Set Up', *The Straits Times*, 15 Sept. 1960, p.13.
56. Inche Othman Wok, reported in ibid.
57. Ibid.
58. Ibid.
59. Ibid.
60. Lee Kuan Yew, reported in *The Straits Times*, 29 July 1965, p.22.
61. Ibid.
62. D. Oon, 'Government Involvement in Sport in Singapore' (Unpublished Ph.D. thesis, University of Queensland, 1984), p.128.
63. Lee Kuan Yew, in the programme of the Festival Sports 1965, p.5.
64. Lee Kuan Yew continually embraced such sentiments. Oon, in his splendid doctoral thesis, points to speeches in December 1965, September 1966, July 1967 and November 1967 to justify his belief that Lee Kuan Yew instigated the drive for national fitness through the 'Sport for All' campaign towards the end of the 1960s and early 1970s.
65. Lee Kuan Yew, *From Third World to First*, p.12. During the Japanese Occupation, there was significant support from ethnic Singaporean Indians for the Japanese-inspired Indian National Army. The INA had come about as a feature of the Indian Independence League, some 200 of whom had actually taken part in a diversionary operation before the actual Japanese invasion of Singapore in 1942 (M.K Durrani, *The Sixth Column* [London: Cassell, 1955], p.74, quoted in Turnbull, *A History of Singapore*, p.209). During the occupation some Indians (Sikhs mostly) and Malays acted as police and watchmen for the Japanese. Many of them, along with former members of the Indian National Army, were slaughtered when the Japanese surrendered in 1945. The whole question of the position and role of the Malaysian armed forces in Singapore was highly vexatious; they had been stationed there as a part of the Anglo-Malaysian Defence Force, and the position of the Malay members of Singapore's own rather meagre armed forces immediately became an issue at the time of separation. Today Malays are only allowed limited positions even within the National Service ranks, and indeed in 1988 Brigadier General Lee Hsien Loong (Lee Kuan Yew's son) admitted that Singapore Malays had been 'kept out of the Singapore air force, navy and some sections of the army' (cited in Vasil, *Governing Singapore*, p.33).
66. E. Teo, 'A History of Physical Education in Singapore since 1819' (Unpublished research paper, Nanyang Technological University, Singapore, January 1998), p.183.
67. Ibid.
68. Oon, 'Government Involvement in Sport', pp.131–42.
69. *New Nation*, 12 Oct. 1972, cited in Oon, 'Government Involvement in Sport', p.141; Teo, 'A History of Physical Education', p.184, suggests that the mass callisthenics that still occur in the morning before school in some Singaporean schools are a legacy of this long-forgotten national fitness campaign.
70. C.J. Chua, *On Track: 21 Years of the Singapore Sports Council* (Singapore: SSC Publication by Times Editions, 1994), p.15.
71. Singapore Sports Council, *The First Ten Years* (Singapore: Singapore Sports Council, 1983), p.11.
72. Chua, *On Track*, p.16.
73. Ibid., p.17.
74. Lee Kuan Yew, opening speech of the National Stadium, 21 July 1973, in Chua, *On Track*, p.16.
75. Singapore Sports Council, *The First Ten Years*, p.16.
76. Ibid. The unintentional use of the gender-specific language indicates that perhaps sport was still, at this stage, not quite for 'all'.
77. Singapore Sports Council, *The First Ten Years*, p.17.
78. Oon, 'Government Involvement in Sport', p.159.
79. Chua, *On Track*, pp.116–19.
80. *Sepak takraw* is a net sport played between teams of three. The game is rather like volleyball

played over a lower net, with a woven rattan ball that can be propelled by any part of the anatomy except the arms. The play is characterized by a swirling and flashing of legs and bodies; the athleticism and flexibility of the players is amazing. The sport evolved from the traditional Malay game of *sepak raga*, which was a game that simply involved a circle of players keeping the ball in the air for as long as possible. Typically, a formalized institutional form of the game emerged on the Malay peninsular during the colonial period.
81. Chua, *On Track*, pp.28–9.
82. Ibid., p.20.
83. The implementation of the (still ongoing) Master Plan of Sports Facilities begun in 1976 with projects such as the refurbished constituency sports clubs, the fitness stations dotted around the HDB estates, the numerous swimming complexes, athletics tracks and football fields. All are indicative of the energy with which 'sport' policies are pursued. Many of the major sporting facilities were built when Singapore hosted the South-East Asian Peninsular Games (SEAP) in 1973 and the South-East Asian Games (SEA) in 1983 and 1993. The pragmatism of the PAP government was evident as it accepted hosting the 1973 SEAP Games at a time when, economically speaking, it might have been considered a somewhat extravagant gesture; however, it was deemed a diplomatic necessity and one that would gain the new nation considerable international prestige. Hosting the games, which incidentally cost the government S$2,299,900 (Oon, 'Government Involvement in Sport', pp.390–91) produced some tangible ongoing outcomes; the games village, accommodation for the 1,500 competitors, was built as part of the developing new town of Toa Payoh. Four large 25-storey apartment blocks were built adjacent to the games' swimming complex, which subsequently became the recreational centre of the new suburb (ibid.). The government also set aside the then massive sum of S$610,500 for the full team's pre-games training and preparation (Letter from the Permanent Secretary, the Ministry of Social Affairs to the Secretary of the SEAP Games Training Sub-Committee, 6 March 1973, in Oon, 'Government Involvement in Sport', p.391).
84. Cronin, *Sport and Nationalism in Ireland*, p.62.
85. Ibid.
86. Ibid., p.63.
87. Goh Chok Tong, *A Nation at Play: 25 Years of the Singapore Sports Council* (Singapore: SSC by Times Editions, 1998), p.8.
88. B. Rigauer, 'Sport and the Economy: A Developmental Perspective', in E. Dunning, J. Maguire and R. Pearton (eds), *The Sports Process: A Comparative Developmental Approach* (Champaign, IL: Human Kinetics, 1993), p.283.
89. The generation of young Singaporeans, particularly the Chinese, born in the late 1960s and 1970s had, as a direct consequence of the government's expressed ideological stance, internalized the notion of sport as having a low economic value. Everything, particularly for the middle-class Chinese, was focused on the achievement of the 'five Cs': cash, credit card, car, condominium and country club membership. These were only attainable through academic excellence, qualifications and a subsequent occupation.
90. Horton, 'Complex Creolization', pp.85–6.
91. In addition to these developments, the Sports Medicine, Fitness and Research Centre that had been in operation at the National Stadium since 1973, when basically it was a physiotherapeutic centre, had grown significantly by 1983. It boasted a full-time staff of ten, made up of two trained sports medicine physicians, a sports physiotherapist, two nurses, one laboratory technician, a clerk, two fitness instructors and a general hand, and its functions were the prevention, treatment and rehabilitation of sports-induced injuries and conditions. They also very pragmatically conducted extended medical and physical fitness examinations and assessments (EMPFEA), so even in what would have been a sport-specific facility the SSC ascribed a general 'healthist' function to the centre. The EMPFEAs involved blood tests, urine analysis and other simple tests that assessed obesity levels, muscle strength and flexibility and aerobic fitness in a series of what would now be considered unreliable tests. The centre's elite sport-specific function was also enhanced with the inclusion of a sports psychologist, a biomechanist as well as an exercise physiologist. The then School of Physical Education at Nanyang Technological University led by Dr Quek Jin Jong (the Dean) had also increased the level, intensity and quality of its research in all areas of human movement study. By far the greatest recipient of direct government funding, however, was the area of sports science and particularly the discipline of exercise physiology, which was boosted by an injection of several million dollars throughout the 1990s.

92. SSC, *Sports*, 22, 1 (Jan. 1994), 5.
93. See 'SSC Launches $10m Excellence Scheme', *The Straits Times*, 7 Dec. 1983; 'SSC Approves $640, 000 for Training; Competition Abroad', *The Straits Times*, 24 Dec. 1993; '$893,940 ... Sports Excellence Boost for Nine Teams and 266 Athletes', *The Straits Times*, 31 Jan. 1994; and 'Wanted: $10m a Year for Sports Excellence 2000 Plan', *Business Times*, 7 Dec. 1993.
94. In reality the actual breakdown of the funding for SPEX 2000 was not excessive in comparison with such sporting giants as the USA or even lesser powers such as Australia. However, it must always be remembered that this was a nation with a population of just over 3 million and with what must be said was a very mediocre record in international sport, though regionally it had done well, winning 50 gold medals in the Singapore-hosted SEA Games in 1993. This wonderful tally and the general sense of national euphoria that was engendered by the performances of the athletes and organizers alike were major contributive factors leading to emergence of SPEX 2000. In 1994 the $10 million for SPEX 2000 was allocated accordingly: manpower costs, $0.5m; scholarships, $0.33m; loss of income scheme, $0.5m; miscellaneous, $0.87m; sports association funding, $1.15m; training schemes, $1.18m; athlete grants (SEAP and SEAPS), $1.6m; overseas training/competitions, $1.7m; and finally the 'acquisition of foreign coaches and the upgrading of local ones', $2.17m. The fourfold increase in funding of over $10 million dollars per year up to the Sydney Olympics failed to achieve a single medallist; the closest an athlete came to a medal was the ex-PRC national Jin Jun Hong, who came fourth in the women's table tennis.
95. SSC, *Sports*, 22,1 (Jan. 1994), 5.
96. Ibid.
97. Ibid.
98. Ibid., 6. The sports chosen as 'core sports' were badminton, soccer, swimming and water polo, table tennis, tenpin bowling, track and field athletics and yachting, with the 'merit sports' being bodybuilding, hockey, sepak takraw, squash, taekwondo and wushu. Both lists include sports generally not considered to be mainstream, while sepak takraw is virtually only played on the South-East Asian peninsula. It would be very hard to justify the inclusion of bodybuilding as a sport let alone as a sport of merit. Later, drugs scandals brought the 'sport' into disrepute and it was dropped from the programme a year later.
99. The SEAP programme had in fact been in existence for over 20 years in the form of the Sports Aid Fund, which had given amounts ranging from $1,000 to $10,000 to individual athletes depending on their training needs (A. Johnson, 'Fund Splashes Out', *Sunday Times*, 28 April 1985).
100. P. Khoo, 'Almost $6 million in Sports Aid Fund', *The Straits Times*, 5 Jan. 1990.
101. 'Excellence in Sport: "Career comes first"', *The Singapore Monitor*, 9 March 1985, p.27.
102. Ibid.
103. Ibid.
104. Tan Eng Liang, reported in 'No Breadline Blues', *The Straits Times*, 26 Feb. 1985.
105. Mahmood Gaznazi, 'SSC to Provide Increased Aid for Some Sports', *The Straits Times*, 27 Oct. 1987.
106. M.C. McNeill, 'Sport Specialisation in a Singapore Secondary School: A Case for Legitimisation' (Unpublished doctoral thesis, Loughborough University, 1999), p.29.
107. Ibid., p.31.
108. Ministry of Education, *The Trim and Fit (TAF) School Handbook* (Singapore, 1992).
109. The National Fitness Test has been held twice a year from 1967 to 1970 and once a year since. The battery of tests and the norms were revised in 1974 and again in 1992 to coordinate with the launch of the Trim and Fit Programme. By 1997 published figures from the Ministry of Education indicate that there has been an annual decrease in obesity levels of 0.5 per cent and an annual increase in the passing rate of the NAPFA of 3.5 per cent. See Peter Tan, 'Trim and Fit Programme [TAF] in Singapore Schools', in *Proceedings of the AIESEP World Conference* (Singapore: SPE, 1997), pp.416–23.
110. SSC, *Sports*, 24, 9 (Nov./Dec. 1996), 7.
111. Ibid., 9–10.
112. Ibid., 9.
113. Ibid., 10.
114. Ibid.
115. Ibid.
116. Goh Chok Tong, *The Straits Times*, 30 Nov. 1996

117. Ibid.
118. SSC, *Sports*, 24, 9 (Nov./Dec. 1996), 3.
119. Goh Chok Tong, National Day Speech, *The Straits Times*, 28 Aug. 1998, p.51.
120. SSC, *Sports*, 26, 6 (July 1998), 4–6.
121. Ibid.
122. Ibid., editorial, 2. This editorial comment from the mouthpiece of the government's administrative arm of sport in Singapore can be read as being a direct government policy statement.
123. Goh Chok Tong, 1998 National Day Speech, Singapore Government Press Release, Aug. 1998.
124. Goh Chok Tong, 1999 National Day Speech, Singapore Government Press Release, Aug. 1999.
125. Ibid.
126. Ibid.
127. N. Elias and E. Dunning, *Quest for Excitement: Sport and Leisure in the Civilizing Process* (Oxford: Blackwell, 1986), pp.63–90.
128. Chan Tse Chueen, *The Straits Times*, 7 Sept. 2000, p.63.
129. Ibid.
130. Ibid.
131. The areas were: 'Strengthening the National Sports Associations' – Alex Chan Council, member of the SSC: 'Enhancing the Support Infrastructure' – Lim Soon Hoon, permanent secretary of the Ministry of Community Development; 'Developing the Sports Industry' – Ng Ser Miang, chairman of SSC and IOC delegate; and 'Promoting Sports for All' – Ong Keng Yong, chief executive of the People's Association. The committee as a whole was to consider the final issue, adopting a 'Team Singapore approach' (Chan Tse Chueen, 'Plans to Reverse Negative Perception of Sport', *The Straits Times Interactive*, 25 Feb. 2001). The balance of the committee was made up of 17 very senior representatives of various major stakeholder-groups in Singapore sport.
132. Chan Tse Chueen, 'Plans to Reverse Negative Perception'.
133. 'At a Glance: The Recommendations', *The Straits Times Interactive*, 2 July 2001.
134. A full outline of the Report of the Committee on Sporting Singapore can be found in 'At a Glance: The Recommendations', *The Straits Times Interactive*. It looks at recommendations on: creating a sturdy sports culture, the development of a new environment of sport, making the NSAs effective, a Sports for All Master Plan, Sports Excellence and Selling Sports Singapore.
135. 'S'Pore Sport Targets Top-10 Spot in Asia', *The Straits Times Interactive*, 1 July 2001.
136. Goh Chok Tong, cited in ibid.
137. Ibid.
138. Ibid.
139. 'CoSS Report – Last Word: Team Singapore', *The Straits Times Interactive*, 1 July 2001.
140. Ibid.
141. Ibid.
142. CoSS Report, 'The Vision', *The Straits Times Interactive*, 1 July 2001.
143. Elias and Dunning, *Quest for Excitement*, pp.63–90.
144. See Horton, 'Complex Creolization', *passim*.
145. Ibid.
146. Vasil, *Governing Singapore*, p.248.
147. Ibid., p.249.
148. Such allegations often surfaced in Singapore from foreign correspondents working for such newspapers as the *New York Herald Tribune* and the *Asia Wall Street Journal*. Lee Kuan Yew summed up their criticism by suggesting that in Singapore they had 'no big scandals of corruption or grave wrongdoings to report. Instead, they reported on the fervour and frequency of these "do good" campaigns, ridiculing Singapore as a "nanny state"'. See Lee Kuan Yew, *From Third World to First*, p.183.
149. Lee Kuan Yew, ibid.
150. Ibid., p.184.

10

The Juggernaut of Globalization: Sport and Modernization in Iran

H.E. CHEHABI

IRAN IN ASIA

It is often forgotten that Asia has not only an East, a South-East, a South and a Centre, but also a West. Contrary to Westerners, who often seem to consider the 'Middle East' to be a continent rather than merely a Eurocentric geopolitical term, Iranians have always considered their country to be part of Asia. Although, for obvious geographic reasons, the main non-European power to be emulated by Iranian modernizers in the nineteenth and early twentieth centuries was the Ottoman Empire,[1] a few did propose to consider Japan as a model.[2] The Japanese victory over Russia in the war of 1904–5 gave a big impetus to reform in Iran. Since Asia's only constitutional power had defeated Europe's only absolutist power, the event was interpreted as proving the superiority of constitutional government.[3] The lesson was learnt not only in Russia but also in Iran, and after the Russian Revolution of 1905 Iran inaugurated in 1906 the series of Asian revolutions that reached the Ottoman Empire in 1908 and China in 1911.[4]

What facilitated Iranians' sense of belonging to a community of destiny with the rest of Asia was the fact that, like China, Japan and Siam, Iran was never formally colonized by European powers although, like China, it faced imperialist pressures from Russia and Britain. One important consequence of the continued sovereignty of Iran was the preponderant role native elites played in the modernization of the nation. Their main goal was not the attainment of independence, but narrowing the military, economic and cultural gap that separated Iran from the dominant West and rendered it vulnerable to imperialism, political interference in its domestic affairs and economic exploitation. Until the Islamic revolution of 1979, these modernizing elites sought to achieve their goal by emulating the West. Europeans were present in Iran and affected modernization, but they had only ancillary functions as missionaries, diplomats, businessmen and government advisers. Modern sports were introduced to Iran by both these resident foreigners and Iranians who had spent some time in Europe.

After the achievement of independence by most Afro-Asian nations in the 1960s, Iranians gradually came to internalize the idea that they belonged to a region called the 'Middle East', but with the manifold unresolved international conflicts in this area, chiefly the Arab-Israeli dispute, 'Asia' remains meaningful as a regional frame of reference one level below the global system. Iran has thus taken great interest in the Asian Games right from the outset, and participates actively in Asian championships and Asian cups.[5]

TRADITIONAL SPORTS IN IRAN

Iran's athletic traditions reflect its location and geography. The horse was first domesticated on the steppes of Central Asia, on whose southwestern edge the Iranian plateau begins; the two areas have always interacted culturally. Classical authors paid tribute to the equestrian skills of the 'Persians', as the Greeks called Iranians,[6] and the English language preserves this homage in the expression 'Parthian shot'.[7] The game of polo is widely admitted to have originated in Iran.[8]

A more popular sport, and the one in which Iran has gained the highest number of international medals, is wrestling. Traditional Iranian wrestling is similar to the styles practised in Turkey and India in that it admits ground action, and in pre-modern times champions of different national and ethnic backgrounds, called *pahlavāns*, used to travel widely in a vast region that stretched from North Africa to Central Asia and from the Balkans to Bengal.[9] Wrestlers formed a guild whose head was a court official, and exercised in gymnasia called *zurkhāneh* ('house of strength'), which still exist in most cities and towns although, due to the introduction of modern freestyle and Greco-Roman wrestling, athletes no longer wrestle in them.[10] These traditional gymnasia evince fascinating parallels with the Indian *akhara*,[11] but the exact nature of the relationship remains a mystery.[12]

In addition to these national traditions, Iran's mountainous terrain has favoured the emergence of countless regional and local games and contests, in particular wrestling styles, most of which are engaged in at harvest-time, weddings or other communal celebrations. What the vast

Sport and Modernization in Iran

majority of the national, regional, and local games and contests have in common is that they involve only men. This made physical education for women a major item on the agenda of modernizers, who faced daunting obstacles in a country whose Islamic culture mandated (albeit to various degrees in different regions) veiling and gender segregation.

THE INTRODUCTION OF WESTERN SPORT

The introduction of Western sport in Iran is not well documented. At the *Dār al-fonun*, the first modern school, founded in 1851, the European officers on the teaching staff made their Iranian pupils exercise regularly, for which purpose the school's theatre was transformed into a gymnasium. After 1915 a German-educated military officer by the name of Gerānmāyeh introduced Friedrich Ludwig Jahn's gymnastics into the Iranian army.[13]

Physical education was also an important part of the curriculum of the American School (later Alborz College), which was founded by Presbyterian missionaries. In a conscious effort to inculcate the value of cooperative effort, insufficiently fostered by traditional Iranian *zurkhāneh* exercises, the director of the school, Dr Samuel Jordan, concentrated on ball games. Students had to take up pick and shovel to help build the school's football field.[14]

If there is one figure who can be credited with striving to introduce Western sport into Iran, this man was Mir-Mehdi Varzandeh. Varzandeh studied physical education in Belgium and spent some time in Istanbul before coming back to Iran some time towards the end of the First World War. When he returned to Iran, he was first made fun of for having gone abroad to study physical education, but established the seriousness of his expertise with the help of physicians who referred patients to him for massage. He taught physical education in French schools in Tehran, and there attracted the attention of Ministry of Education officials who created a permanent position for him as physical education teacher in state schools. It is typical of the modernists' mindset in those days that Varzandeh wanted to import Western sport wholesale; there is no reference to Iran's indigenous physical education in his writings.[15]

Varzandeh propagated the introduction of physical education into school curricula. Attempts to do so went back to the constitutional period, but it was only in 1919 that the system of gymnastics developed by Per Henrik Ling in Sweden was officially adopted for Iranian schools.[16] A British observer, however, noted that the exercises he witnessed at the Anglo-Iranian Oil Company's primary school in Ahvaz, whose curriculum conformed to 'the scheme of the Persian Minister of Education', were 'compounded of Russian and German methods of physical training, and ... characterized by great rapidity of execution'.[17] On 5 September 1927 the Iranian parliament passed a law authorizing the Ministry of Education to introduce compulsory daily physical education in public schools.[18]

It seems that the clergy and religious opinion opposed the measure. Callisthenics, called 'Swedish sport', was the main form taken by physical education, but it struck traditional people as frivolous because it resembled dancing. In his memoirs the (conservative) prime minister, Mehdi-Qoli Hedāyat, wrote that far too much attention was being paid to physical education in schools, especially girls' schools. Sports uniforms reduce girls' sense of shame, he wrote, adding that he did not 'know what girls' foot races do for their education'.[19]

Competitive Western games were introduced to Iran either by Iranians returning from Europe or by Iranians who had daily contact with Europeans living in Iran. Football, which is today Iran's most popular sport, reached the country through three conduits of modernization: the military, the oil industry and missionary schools. As elsewhere in the world, British expatriates played a major role in the introduction of football to Iran.[20] In the oil cities of southern Iran, employees of the Anglo-Iranian Oil Company played the game as Iranians watched. Soon some Iranians began replacing individual players on British teams, until Iranians formed their own teams. These young Iranian football players met some hostility from their social environment for partaking in the games of the 'infidels', and at times they were beaten up or pelted with stones. Elsewhere in the south of Iran, football was introduced by the British officers of the South Persia Rifles (a military force that existed between 1916 and 1921) to the Iranian troops they commanded, who spread it among the population. Football became a symbol of modernization and began enjoying state support after the First World War. In 1919 two British residents of Tehran founded a football association which soon came under Iranian control and, after many name changes, became the Iranian Football Federation that later joined FIFA. Other British citizens too played their part in the spread of modern sport.[21]

In 1925 a military man, Reza Pahlavi (1877–1944), overthrew the reigning dynasty and in early 1926 crowned himself Shah, founding a new dynasty that would last until the Islamic revolution of 1979. Reza Shah was an ardent nationalist, and wished to carry out the modernists' agenda for emancipating Iran using authoritarian methods. Having been disappointed by the troubles and instability following the constitutional revolution of 1906, much of the modern middle class acquiesced in the new dictatorship. Improving public health ranked high on the agenda of the regime, and, as elsewhere in the world, physical education and sport were deemed to be conducive to creating a healthier nation.[22]

In the spring of 1934 a number of Iranian statesmen and educators founded the National Physical Education Association. From the outset, the association placed itself under the patronage of the Crown Prince, who was then studying at a boarding school in Switzerland. Later that year a recent graduate of Columbia University, Thomas R. Gibson, was employed by the association to organize Iranian sports. Gibson stayed until 1938 and also reorganized scouting in Iran.[23] He set up competitions between school teams, mostly in football, and also systematically sent coaches to the provinces to propagate modern sport. The educationist Isā Sadiq relates that in the beginning the public was so indifferent to spectator sports that the Physical Education Association had to resort to serving free tea and sweets to lure people to the football games.[24]

In 1936 sport received a new impetus, as in May of that year the Crown Prince returned to Iran. During the five years he had spent in Switzerland, Mohammad-Reza Pahlavi had been a much better athlete than scholar, and became the captain of his school's football and tennis teams.[25] Upon returning to Iran he took a personal interest in sport. In 1939 the first national championships were organized in a number of modern disciplines, such as athletics, football and swimming.

As we noted earlier, Iran has an indigenous athletic tradition, the *zurkhāneh*. Until the constitutional revolution of 1906 the court had patronized this tradition, but with the passing of the *ancien régime* and the subsequent triumph of westernizing modernists, the traditional athletic culture was neglected both by the state and by the elites. Things changed in 1934 when the Pahlavi state celebrated the millennium of the birth of the poet Ferdowsi. Ferdowsi is the author of Iran's national epic, the *Book of Kings* (*Shāhnāmeh*), and arguably the reviver of the Persian language. Chanting verses from the *Book of Kings* accompanies the exercises of the *zurkhāneh* – which meant that this traditional institution could be harnessed for the ideological purposes of the state, which promoted Iranian nationalism. Henceforth the exercises performed in the *zurkhāneh* became known as 'ancient sport', and it became conventional wisdom that they originated in the Iranians' secret resistance activities against the Arab invaders of the seventh century CE, although their earliest mention is in the seventeenth century. In 1953, a leading practitioner of 'ancient sports', Sha'bān Ja'fari, was instrumental in the CIA-backed *coup d'état* that ousted Prime Minister Mohammad Mossadegh, and for this service he was made the head of the traditional athletics establishment.[26] Every year, on such occasions as the Shah's birthday, he would lead hundreds of athletes in synchronized exercises at Tehran's main stadium.

Traditionally the exercises of the *zurkhāneh* had prepared athletes for wrestling. Beginning in the 1940s, international freestyle and Greco-Roman wrestling replaced the wrestling of the *zurkhāneh*, and Iranian wrestlers gained many medals at the world championships and Olympic Games. By the late 1960s, however, football began to overshadow wrestling. A number of games against Israeli teams, which the Iranian teams won,[27] added to the popularity of football, which, as in so many other countries, became a national obsession. Tehran had two major teams, Tāj and Persepolis, and the rivalry between the two ('the blues' and 'the reds', respectively) dominated Iranian fandom before the revolution.

The first to introduce physical education for girls were Christian missionaries in the nineteenth century, who included it in their schools' curricula. However, since these schools catered mostly to Iran's non-Muslim minorities their impact remained limited. The few Muslim women who graduated from these schools were among the first Iranians to demand access to physical education for all women. In 1911, a woman who had graduated 20 years earlier from one of these schools, Badr al-Dojā Khānom, complained in a graduation address that because of veiling Iranian women had been deprived of sports, for which reason most of them were weak and unhealthy.[28] In the 1910s physical education for women became part of the modernists' agenda for reforming and regenerating Iranian society. In the 1930s physical education became compulsory in public girls' schools, and in 1935 the new state-sponsored Ladies' Centre (*Kānun-e Banovān*) made the development of physical education programmes for women one of its main goals. In 1939 the first national championships were held in athletics and swimming.

Conservatives opposed women's sport and girls' physical education, mostly because the wearing of sportswear in view of men violates the traditional Islamic dress code (*hijāb*), which requires that a woman cover her body with the exception of her face, hands, and feet in the presence of unrelated men. However, under the rule of the Pahlavi dynasty, which sought to westernize Iranian life, an ever increasing number of women belonging to the non-devout upper and middle classes became involved in many sports. Female members of the imperial family acted as patrons of the state-sponsored Women's Sport Organization of Iran.

In the 1970s one new element came to enrich Iran's sports scene, and that was East Asian martial arts. Here the impetus came from a nephew of the Shah's, Prince Shahryar Shafiq, an accomplished athlete who introduced martial arts to the armed forces, but the great popularity of Chinese kung fu films also played a role.

Beginning in the mid-1960s, an increasing number of Iranians contested the westernizing policies of Shah Mohammad-Reza Pahlavi (1919–80). At the same time the Shah's regime became increasingly dictatorial and heavy-handed. Given the impossibility of expressing opposition to the regime in the political arena, religious opponents of the regime gained greater popularity, and they found a leader in a senior cleric, Ayatollah Ruhollāh Khomeini (1901–89). By the late 1970s, even secular opponents of the Shah were willing to cooperate with the Islamic opposition, and the alliance of the two resulted in a revolution that swept away the old elite, and with it the westernizing policies that the state had pursued for over half a century.[29] 'Authenticity' became the new goal of all cultural policies.

Like revolutionaries elsewhere in the world, the Iranian revolutionaries, both leftist and Islamic, had an ascetic streak that viewed many of the Pahlavi state's cultural policies as designed to divert the people from more serious matters;[30] the alleged support for football was seen in this light. Religious circles, in addition, deemed the official promotion of women's sport as an effort to weaken public morality in that it exposed insufficiently covered women to the public gaze.

SPORT IN THE ISLAMIC REPUBLIC OF IRAN

It is safe to say that sport has not featured very high on the agenda of the Islamic regime. Islamism is ambivalent about sport, as it recognizes the importance of keeping fit while frowning on the entertainment side of sport.[31] This created a problem for state television in the early years of the new regime, for after purging most entertainment programmes, deemed immoral by the puritanical standards of the new power-holders, sport and nature were the only remaining non-religious and non-political subjects. The new regulations on veiling ruled out broadcasting women's events (on which more below), but even showing male athletes was objectionable to traditionalists because female viewers would see insufficiently covered men. After much back and forth between the television authorities and conservative clergy, the matter was referred to Khomeini himself, who ruled in 1988 that it was permissible to broadcast and watch sports programmes provided viewers watched without lust.[32] In 1993 a third television channel was set up which broadcast mainly sport.

The new authorities' attitude to various disciplines varied. Shortly after the revolution chess, boxing and kung fu were forbidden, the first because traditionally Islamic jurisprudence considered it conducive to gambling, the latter two because they inflict physical harm, which is contrary to divine law. However, karate and taekwondo were encouraged, to the point that training facilities were occasionally provided in mosques. Equestrian sports caused the new regime a dilemma: on the one hand polo and show jumping were elite sports and therefore frowned upon by the populist revolutionaries; on the other hand horse races were one of only two sports mentioned in Islamic jurisprudence, which even allowed betting on the outcome – the only exception made to the prohibition of gambling. Horse races had an added political dimension, in that they were particularly popular among the Turkomans in Iran's north-east; to outlaw them might have given separatists an additional grievance point. In the end, the 'popular' dimension of these races was discovered, and they have been going on ever since, as have other equestrian sports for both men and women. Tennis, too, was seen as an elite sport and therefore not worthy of state support.[33]

The *zurkhāneh* tradition presented a different problem for the new regime. In the eyes of many revolutionaries, traditional athletics were discredited because of the propagandistic use the old regime had made of them, but it was also the case that the *zurkhāneh* was the most authentically Iranian sporting tradition, and one that appealed mainly to traditional non-elite sectors of society, precisely those that had supported the Islamic revolution. In the end it was decided to legitimize the *zurkhāneh* by emphasizing its Islamic dimension as opposed to the nationalist dimension stressed under the Shah. To broaden its appeal to younger people, an attempt was made to turn it into a 'sport'. Age groups were introduced, as were standard rules and regulations that would make objective judging possible, and competitions were held at all levels. The inclusion of children and adolescents necessitated the introduction of T-shirts, which represented the intrusion of an alien, Western element into an environment in which the athletes' bare-chestedness had represented the irrelevance of outside status distinctions. The large number of men participating in the competitions meant that events had to be staged in modern sports halls rather than in the traditional gymnasium with its religious aura, which desacralized the events at a time when, in theory, its Islamic dimension was to be emphasized. Finally, the determination of rankings on the basis of objective and quantitative criteria ended the system of seniority whereby an athlete would pass from one rank to the higher based on the assessment of his elders.[34]

Parallel to the attempt to repopularize the *zurkhāneh*, much attention was paid in the early years of the Islamic republic to local folk games whose revival had been begun in the 1970s. Iranian television produced 65 documentaries,[35] and exhibitions took place during the *Fajr* Games, an annual international sports festival commemorating the victory of the revolution.[36] But by the late 1980s interest in these local games fizzled out.

The one modern sport that resonated with Iran's traditions was freestyle wrestling, and the new authorities favoured it openly; it is commonly referred to as the nation's first sport. The state appropriated the figure of Gholāmrezā Takhti (1930–68), the legendary wrestling champion of the 1950s and 1960s who had been an opponent of the Shah,[37] and, presenting him as a precursor of the Islamic revolution, named many sports facilities around the country after him. The victory of the heavyweight wrestler Ali-Rezā Soleimāni over the American Bruce Baumgartner at the 1989 World Championships in Martigny (Switzerland), which gave the Iranian a gold medal, was an adrenalin shot for the sport, and state funding for it increased. In 1998 a *Khāneh-*

ye koshti (house of wrestling) was inaugurated in Tehran. It includes training facilities, dormitories, a traditional tea-house, a library, a museum and a research institute.[38] The international governing body of wrestling, FILA, declared it one of four international centres for the sport at the time of Iran's hosting of the World Championships in September 1998 – the first time Iran had hosted a world championship since the revolution. But all the official attention paid to the sport could not hide the fact that it was no longer the nation's most popular sport. Football had taken that place. The revolutionaries' call for more 'authenticity' had not prevented a British import with hardly a century of history in Iran from taking the place of an indigenous tradition that was over a thousand years old.

The revolution, and especially the consolidation of clerical power in 1981, disorganized Iranian sporting life. The war against Iraq (1980–88) limited the resources the state could devote to non-essential activities such as sport. All private clubs were nationalized and the national football league was dissolved. The demise of many football clubs led to the growth of improvised neighbourhood games, called *gol kuchak*, 'little goal'. The popularity of these games in the city quarters that formed the social bases of the new regime worried the new men in power, who would have preferred to see youngsters in the mosques rather than on the playing fields. Major football games presented difficulties for the regime. In a country from which most public entertainment had been banished, attending football matches was one of the few remaining leisure activities for young men. However, if the regime tried to stop football, it would antagonize precisely the popular classes on whose support it depended most. The result was constant attempts in the press to contrast traditional Iranian values of chivalry with the commercialization, exploitation and hooliganism that characterize sports in the corrupt West. The horrendous prices paid for top players by professional clubs were presented as an example of misplaced priorities in the West.

After Khomeini died in 1989 his successors cautiously tried to liberalize the country. The revolutionary decade (1979–89) had brought Iranians war, turmoil and deprivation; most Iranians were tired of them and aspired to a better life. In the early 1990s some of Iran's leaders began to realize that the post-revolutionary policy of frowning on all forms of entertainment was self-defeating, as it gave rise to illicit practices, chief among them drug abuse, that were far more objectionable than the ones outlawed. One of the results of this was a greater emphasis on sport. The head of the physical education organization admitted that the state's takeover of sports clubs after the revolution had inflicted great damage on sport. At a press conference he said that 'all over the world sports is the people's own business, the people's own participation matters a lot, and the regime has come to this conclusion too'. He then expressed the hope that with the help of new legislation the private sector would invest in sports facilities.[39] In 1989 the national football league was started again, and it was named *Lig-e Āzādegān* (veterans' league) after the POWs who had returned from Iraqi camps.[40]

The summer of 1993 was a turning point in Iranian sport, as official policy changed as a result of a number of victories by Iranian athletes abroad. In football, Iran reached the second round of the qualifying games for the 1994 World Cup; in Greco-Roman wrestling the Iranian team won the world championship of the deaf; and in freestyle wrestling the Iranian team was placed first in the junior championships. Finally, in the first World Ex-Service Wheelchair and Amputee Games held in Aylesbury, England Iran won 35 gold, 22 silver and four bronze medals – a reflection of the devastating impact of the Iran-Iraq War on Iran's youth. Receiving the victorious disabled athletes, Khomeini's successor as Iranian head of state, Ayatollah Khāmeneh'i, made a major statement on sports policy. Five years earlier he had extolled traditional athletics, claiming that as a young man he had been active in the ancient sports section of a club in Mashhad that offered both Western and ancient sports;[41] now he said that while it was incumbent upon all to practise a sport, this could be achieved only if Iran had professional and champion athletes in the arenas of the world, as they brought honour and respect to Iran and its Islamic revolution.

The travails of men's sport after the revolution paled in comparison with the damage done to women's sport. In the first months after the revolution, women's sports competitions continued as normal, although they met with increasingly shrill opposition from Islamists. The principle of women's sport was not at issue; rather it was the presence of men on the fields that was objected to, for it exposed insufficiently covered women to their gaze. For this reason, women's competitions were discontinued until further notice in 1981, the year veiling became obligatory in Iran. Ayatollah Beheshti, one of the founding fathers of the new regime, said that he hoped adequate sports facilities could be provided for both brothers and sisters, but they would have to be strictly separated, as a 'mixed sports environment is not acceptable to our Islamic ethics and order'.[42] Gradually separate facilities were provided and women resumed their competitions. The main sports auditorium reserved for women was renamed *Sālon-e Hejāb*, 'Veil Auditorium', and the name of the street on which it was located was changed to *Khiābān-e Hejāb*, Veil Street.[43] In recreational sports that are practised in a mixed environment, segregation became the norm. Early on in the revolution the beaches of the Caspian Sea had been sexually segregated, but with the ski slopes north of Tehran something interesting happened that shows that social custom and its evolution is at least as important as ideology. In Lashkarak, a village that has been a ski resort for decades, mixed skiing continued, as the local villagers had got used to it. In Dizin, however, whose ski slopes had been opened only a few years before the revolution, the local authorities in charge of upholding Islamic morality insisted on dividing the slopes in two so as to separate male and female skiers.[44]

In the mid-1980s, possibilities for women to practise sport were so limited that the weekly women's journal *Zan-e ruz* ran a series of articles criticizing the situation. Matters changed for the better following Khomeini's death, when Ali-Akbar Hāshemi Rafsanjāni acceded to the presidency in 1989. His daughter, Fā'ezeh Hāshemi, took a personal interest in women's sport and, in a pattern reminiscent of the nepotism of the monarchy, she became the head of the women's sport organization and a vice-president of the National Iranian Olympic Committee and set out to revive women's sport. The war with Iraq having ended, the state was able to allocate more money for women's sport, and sports halls and swimming pools were set aside for women. At these facilities, women compete according to international rules and standards, but men are not allowed to be present. Women in Iran now participate in 25 different disciplines including such individual sports as handball, tennis, karate and equestrian and team sports such as basketball and hockey. Programmes are also available for disabled women athletes.[45] The ban on men in sports halls has led to a dramatic increase in woman coaches and referees. In addition, many more traditional women who would have avoided a mixed environment now feel comfortable pursuing their athletic interests.

To study the modalities of Muslim women's participation in sport, Hāshemi convened the First Islamic Countries' Sports Solidarity

Congress for Women in Tehran in October 1991. President Rafsanjāni gave the keynote speech and said that sport was an inevitable necessity for women, who needed it to be healthy, cheerful and joyful, and to fill their leisure time.[46] The congress led to the founding of an organization that held 'Islamic Countries' Women Sports Solidarity Games' in 1993 and 1997 and has become the major women's sports organization in the Muslim world. At these games women from predominantly Muslim countries competed in the total absence of men. The segregation of men and women on the playing fields has been maintained to this day, but to send a signal to the world that women were active nonetheless, at the Olympic Games in Atlanta Iran's flag was carried by the sole woman on the team, a target shooter.[47]

In the parliamentary elections of 1996 the followers of President Rafsanjāni for the first time openly challenged the clerical social conservatives. Their slate of candidates in Tehran was headed by the president's daughter, whose credentials included her leadership in matters of sports policy. She had advocated the right of women to ride bicycles in public and set aside a path for them in Tehran's Chitgar Park. Conservatives seized on this to criticize her. And so in the spring of 1996, while the economic situation and the US embargo on trade with Iran were on everybody's minds, women's bicycling became a hot issue in Iranian politics. Vigilantes arrived in Chitgar Park and beat up its administrator, even though cyclists were properly dressed.[48] In the parliamentary elections of 2000, Fāezeh Hāshemi failed to be re-elected, but women's sport has acquired a momentum of its own.

THE IMPACT OF INTERNATIONAL COMPETITION

Beginning with the 1948 Olympic Games in London, Iran began sending official teams to international events such as the Olympic Games and Asian Games, and to world championships. In 1974 Iran for the first time hosted the Asian Games. Only one year after the quadrupling of oil prices had made it rich, the Iranian government wanted to use the event to enhance the country's international profile. If successful, the games might presage the Olympic Games, the hosting of which in 1964 had consecrated Japan's membership in the rich countries' club. In 1978 the Iranian national football team qualified for the first time for the finals of the World Cup in Argentina, but was eliminated after the first round. A few months later the revolution put an end to most international participation.

Western models of sport served as a rationalization for the drastic reduction of Iran's participation in international events. It was argued that athletes from rich countries were pampered and had optimal training facilities, which gave them an automatic advantage over Third World amateurs. Their victories, moreover, would serve to undermine the self-esteem of Third World people and enhance the prestige of those who exploited them, namely the rich industrial countries. It was therefore preferable not to play the game. Ideological qualms were not the only reason for keeping a low international profile, however. The turnover of officials in the sports and physical education bureaucracy after the revolution was very high, and veteran administrators with international experience had been purged, leaving Iranian sport hopelessly disorganized. Worse, a considerable number of athletes, including some Olympic medallists, used their trips abroad to defect, some to opposition groups. Finally, given the financial corruption of organized sport and the difficulties of foreign travel while the war with Iraq consumed much of Iran's foreign currency reserves, all sorts of people accompanied Iranian teams abroad with the sole aim of exporting a few rugs or importing European goods into Iran. As for the Olympic Games, the Islamic Republic's foreign policy motto of 'neither East nor West' was a convenient excuse to boycott both the 1980 games in Moscow and the 1984 games in Los Angeles.

On the few occasions in the 1980s that Iranian athletes did venture abroad, they were made to spread the message of the revolution. Speaking to a number of athletes bound for the Asian Games on 21 July 1983, Khomeini pointed out that since ancient times athletes had been mindful of God and Imam Ali, and expressed the hope that they would become champions and succeed to export the revolution in all its meanings. Turning to a sportsman who had lost both legs and an arm in the war against Iraq, Khomeini said that he was proud of men like him and hoped that God would give him two wings in his afterlife so that he could fly around paradise.[49] Sports functionaries responded by holding congregational prayers and chanting anti-imperialist slogans in public. Competing against the United States and Israel at international meetings was problematic, since Iranian foreign policy was implacably hostile to these states. After some initial hesitation and a public spat between the Foreign Ministry and the physical education authorities over Iranians wrestling Americans at the 1985 World Freestyle Championships in Budapest,[50] Iranian athletes were allowed to compete against Americans but not against Israelis, in line with an often-repeated statement that Iran harboured no enmity towards the American people.

The only discipline in which Iran could still field world-class competitors was wrestling. Since the countries that dominated that sport in the 1980s were the United States and the Soviet Union, the propaganda value of international medals became apparent. In 1986 a newspaper article stated that 'gaining medals in international arenas can help us attain our goals, i.e. exporting the Islamic revolution'.[51] President Khāmeneh'i qualified this return to the international playing fields in early 1988 when he stated: 'With some countries we do not even want to meet on the sports arenas, like Israel and South Africa. We don't like them, we consider them false peoples.'[52] But a book of traditions from the Prophet (*hadith*) that are relevant to sport stated that in today's world international understanding and peace were promoted by sports contacts with other countries.[53] Iran participated in the 1988 and 1992 Olympic Games, although the games were criticized in the press. The country's main sports weekly, *Keihān-e varzeshi*, kept denouncing the inequality of the international system, in which rich countries could afford to train their athletes according to the latest scientific methods and Third World athletes were decoration to highlight the superiority of the winners. Nonetheless, victories by Iranian sportsmen were eagerly awaited and used to boost national pride.

The most politically charged discipline in contemporary Iran is football. Beginning in the 1980s, riots and scuffles often broke out after major soccer matches. The government interpreted them as counter-revolutionary, but it is likely more often than not that soccer violence just resulted from the presence in a small area of tens of thousands of young men. In the beginning the press waxed indignant about the behaviour of Iranian fans and called it a remnant of decadent Western culture imposed on pre-revolutionary Iran by imperialism, but football fever could not be controlled and by the early 1990s the state relented. Television began covering major events, even the 1994 World Cup in the United States, and efforts were made to rebuild the national team.

Iran's qualification for the finals of the 1998 World Cup in France, obtained in November 1997, was greeted with unprecedented public jubilation. Iranians used the more liberal atmosphere ushered in by recently elected President Mohammad Khātami to proclaim their desire to be part of international society, as symbolized by the World Cup, in which 32 nations participated. They turned the celebrations into demonstrations of support for Khātami, whose liberal policies were (and are) resisted by conservative hardliners. When Iran and the United States ended up in the same group for the first-round matches, an ideal setting was provided for demonstrating a new spirit in United States–Iranian relations, which had been severed on the diplomatic level after the seizure of US hostages in November 1979.

The interval between Iran's qualification for the World Cup and the game with the United States on 21 June 1998 was marked by intense politically charged infighting among Iran's sport functionaries. In the end the followers of President Khātami emerged victorious, and before going to France the national team's spokesmen proclaimed that they would surprise the world. Far from antagonizing their hosts by displaying revolutionary zeal and looks, the Iranian players vowed to present the world with a new image of their country. They came to the grounds well groomed and clean-shaven,[54] and presented their counterparts with a bouquet of flowers before each game. The US-Iran game had been built up as a grudge match by Western media, but American and Iranian officials had instructed players to be courteous and FIFA, the world governing body of football, had declared 21 June 'Fair Play Day'. When the big moment came, the two teams exchanged gifts and eschewed the customary pre-game team photos in favour of a joint one with the 22 players intermingled. The two teams jointly received the FIFA Fair Play Award on 1 February 1999.[55]

The Iranian team did not make it beyond the first round, but many Iranian players found employment with European teams, resulting in European football becoming even more closely followed in Iran. In 2001 the Iranian team came close to qualifying for the 2002 World Cup finals in Japan and Korea, but on 19 October that year it lost against tiny Bahrain. After this game thousands of young people poured into the streets of Tehran, and this time their frustration did result in anti-government demonstrations.

CONCLUSION

Looking back at twentieth-century Iran one cannot help but note the continuities in the development of Iranian sport. To be sure, the Islamic revolution of 1979 affected society deeply. The victorious Islamic revolutionaries attempted a cultural revolution that would eliminate foreign influence and restore a measure of authenticity to national life. For a decade or so the pre-revolutionary patterns of sports activities were indeed disrupted, but by the 1990s, traditional sports (like those practised in the *zurkhāneh*) and modern sport with traditional roots (wrestling) were eclipsed by such foreign imports as football and taekwondo. The adoption of Western sport continues. In 1997 the first national cricket championships were held, although it must be added that the game was imported from neighbouring Pakistan. In 1998 women's football was introduced.

In some ways the revolution actually intensified trends that were already apparent in the 1960s and 1970s. A culture of competition has gained hold of society, which means that at the grass-roots level the number of athletically active people may be higher today than before the revolution, although no systematic data are available.[56]

A final lesson to be drawn is that sport, and in particular football, need not be the ruling elite's instrument for controlling the population. The revolutionaries, both Islamist and leftist, had criticized the Shah's regime for using football fever as an 'opiate' of the people. The intricate connection between football fandom and reformist politics that appeared in the wake of the national team's 1997 qualification for the World Cup finals shows the limits of this line of analysis, as stadiums have emerged as foci of dissent and international events, such as the football World Cup, the Olympic Games and the Asian Games, allow Iranians to be part of a global society that is viewed with profound suspicion by many of the founders of the Islamic Republic.[57] Judging by the passions of young Iranians, it would seem that the juggernaut of globalization cannot be stopped by Islamic fundamentalism.

NOTES

1. Anja Pistor-Hatam, *Iran und die Reformbewegung im osmanischen Reich: Persische Staatsmänner, Reisende und Oppositionelle unter dem Einfluß der Tanzimat* (Berlin: Klaus Schwarz, 1992).
2. See Anja Pistor-Hatam, 'Progress and Civilization in Nineteenth-Century Japan: The Far Eastern State as a Model for Modernization', *Iranian Studies*, XIX (1996), 11–126; and Roxane Haag-Higuchi, 'A Topos and Its Dissolution: Japan in Some 20th Century Iranian Texts', *Iranian Studies*, XIX (1996), 71–84. In the end, however, physical and cultural distance stood in the way of any direct influence of the Japanese exemplar on Iran.
3. Hashem Rajabzadeh, 'Russo-Japanese War as Told by Iranians', *Annals of Japan Association for Middle East Studies*, III (1988).
4. Nader Sohrabi, 'Historicizing Revolutions: Constitutional Revolutions in the Ottoman Empire, Iran, and Russia, 1905–1908', *American Journal of Sociology*, C (1995), 1383–447.

5. Bizhan Ru'inpur, *Irān dar bāzihā-ye Āsiā'i* [Iran in the Asian Games] (Tehran: Keyhan, 1377/1998).
6. For a discussion of what the ancient Greeks had to say about the physical education of Iranian elites, see Wolfgang Knauth, 'Die sportlichen Qualifikationen der altiranischen Fürsten', *Stadion*, II (1976).
7. Persians were, like Parthians and Medes, a subgroup of Iranians. Iranians have always called their country 'Iran', a word which is etymologically related to 'Aryan' and 'Ireland'. Following the Greeks, Europeans continued calling Iran 'Persia', but in 1936 the Iranian government requested that the country be officially known as Iran outside the country as well. The aim was to demonstrate a break with a more subservient past – three years before, for similar reasons, the Siamese changed the name of their country to 'Thailand'.
8. See Chehabi and Guttmann's contribution later in this volume.
9. See Marius Canard, 'La lutte chez les arabes', in *Le cinquantenaire de la Faculté des lettres d'Alger (1881–1931)* (Algiers: Société Historique Algérienne, 1932).
10. For description of the traditional world of the house of strength see A. Reza Arasteh, *Man and Society in Iran* (Leiden: E.J. Brill, 1964), pp.29–35; and Sayyed Mohammad Ali Jamalzadeh, *Isfahan is Half the World: Memories of a Persian Boyhood*, trans. W.L. Heston (Princeton, NJ: Princeton University Press, 1983), chapter 3, 'The World of Chivalry and Manliness', pp.170–200.
11. See Joseph S. Alter, *The Wrestler's Body: Identity and Ideology in North India* (Berkeley, CA: University of California Press, 1992).
12. For the most thorough effort to date to analyse the parallels between *zurkhāneh* and *akhara*, see Philippe Rochard, 'Le "sport antique" des zurkhâne de Téhéran. Formes et significations d'une pratique contemporaine' (Ph.D. thesis, Université Aix-Marseille I, 2000).
13. Abolfazl Sadri, *Tārikh-e varzesh* (Tehran: Vezārat-e Farhang, 1961), pp.138–40.
14. Arthur C. Boyce, 'Alborz College of Tehran and Dr Samuel Martin Jordan, Founder and President', in Ali Pasha Saleh (ed.), *Cultural Ties between Iran and the United States* (Tehran, 1976), pp.193–4 and 198.
15. The details of his life are contained in a brief autobiographical note published in the official organ of the ministry of education. *Ta 'lim va tarbiat*, I, 6 (Shahrivar 1304/Aug.–Sept. 1925), 33–8.
16. *Dānesh-e varzesh*, II, 13 (Bahman 1367/Jan.–Feb. 1989), 43. On Ling see Carl Diem, *Weltgeschichte des Sports und der Leibeserziehungen* (Stuttgart: Cotta, 1967), pp.793–5, and Jan Lindroth, 'The History of Ling Gymnastics in Sweden: A Research Survey', *Stadion*, XIX–XX (1993–94). On Ling's reception in Iran see M.M.T.T., 'Ling: shā'er va varzeshkār 1776–1839' [Ling: Poet and Sportsman, 1776–1839], *Āmuzesh va parvaresh*, X, 2 (Ordibehesht 1319/April–May 1940), 15–16, 58.
17. J.W. Williamson, *In a Persian Oil Field* (London: Ernest Benn Limited, 1927), p.152.
18. For the text of the law see *Ta 'lim va tarbiat*, III, 7–8 (Mehr-Ābān 306/Sept.– Nov. 1927), 1.
19. Mehdi-Qoli Hedāyat Mokhber al-Saltaneh, *Khāterāt va khatarāt* [Reminiscences and Dangers] (Tehran: Rangin, 1950), p.625n. Cf. the opinion of the director-general of the Ministry of Education in 1934 that physical education prepared boys for work and soldiery and girls for services at home (housework). Dr Valiollāh Khān Nasr, 'Tarbiat-e badani' [Physical Education], *Ta 'lim va tarbiat*, IV, 5 (Mordād 1313/July–Aug. 1934), p.257.
20. Allen Guttmann, *Games and Empires: Modern Sports and Cultural Imperialism* (New York: Columbia University Press, 1994), pp.41–70. See also J.A. Mangan, *The Games Ethic and Imperialism: Aspects of the Diffusion of an Ideal* (London and Portland, OR: Frank Cass, 1998).
21. In particular, Clifford Harris, who taught at the Stuart Memorial College, Isfahan – a Christian school run on English public school lines. Harris was a powerful, gentle and saintly 'giant' and a keen sportsman, who played a major part in the sport of the school. He died of typhus when still a young man, and shortly before his death he cleared the football field of snow to allow his boys to play. See Mangan, *Games Ethic and Imperialism*, p.224.
22. Cyrus Schayegh, 'Sport, Health, and the Iranian Modern Middle Class, 1920s and 1930s', *Iranian Studies*, XXXV, 3–4 (2002).
23. A discussion of scouting is beyond the scope of this chapter. Suffice it to say that it was introduced in Iran in 1925, but not actively encouraged by the state until 1934. In 1935 scouting

became an obligatory subject in schools, but met with religiously motivated opposition. In 1935 there were 9,000 boy scouts and 1,000 girl scouts in Iran. The movement was weakened after Reza Shah's departure in 1941, and regained significance only after its organization was separated from sports in the early 1950s. For a history see Firouz Daghigh-Nia, 'Die Entwicklung des Pfadfindertums im Iran und seine jugendfördernde Bedeutung' (Unpublished diploma thesis, Deutsche Sporthochschule, Cologne, 1968–69).
24. Isā Sadiq, *Yādegār-e 'omr: khāterāti az sargozasht* [Memoirs], Vol.2 (Tehran: Dehkhodā, 1975), p.172.
25. Gérard de Villiers, *L'Irresistible ascension de Mohammad Reza Shah d'Iran* (Paris: Plon, 1975), pp.69–70.
26. On the coup see Mark Gasiorowski, 'The 1953 *Coup d'Etat* in Iran', *International Journal for Middle East Studies*, XIX (1987), and Ervand Abrahamian, 'The 1953 Coup in Iran', *Science & Society*, LXV, 2 (Summer 2001).
27. For details see H.E. Chehabi, 'Jews and Sport in Modern Iran', in Homa Sarshar and Houman Sarshar (eds), *The History of Contemporary Iranian Jews* (Beverly Hills, CA: Center for Iranian Jewish Oral History, 2001), pp.3–24.
28. *Irān-e Now*, 3 (1 July 1911), 3, as quoted in Afsaneh Najmabadi, 'Veiled Discourse – Unveiled Bodies', *Feminist Studies*, XIX (1993), 509.
29. The literature on the Islamic revolution is vast. For two excellent studies see Shaul Bakhash, *The Reign of the Ayatollahs: Iran and the Islamic Revolution* (New York: Basic Books, 1984), and Mohsen Milani, *The Making of Iran's Revolution: From Monarchy to Islamic Republic* (Boulder, CO: Westview, 1988).
30. See Bruce Mazlish, *The Revolutionary Ascetic: Evolution of a Political Type* (New York: McGraw-Hill, 1976).
31. See Youcef Fatès, *Sport et Tiers Monde* (Paris: Presses Universitaires de France, 1994), pp.100–18.
32. Khomeini merely acknowledged what is known but not commonly talked about in the West. See Allen Guttmann, *The Erotic in Sport* (New York: Columbia University Press, 1996).
33. On the travails of one of Iran's top tennis players see Rudolph Chelmiski, 'Les bouffon des courts', *Sélection*, Nov. 1999, 80–87.
34. On the changes in the *zurkhāneh* tradition see Philippe Rochard, 'The Identities of the Iranian Zurkhāneh', *Iranian Studies*, XXXV, 3–4 (2002).
35. *Dānesh-e varzesh*, 4, 38 (Tir/July–Aug. 1991), 6.
36. On Iran's regional games and contests see Gholan Hosein Malek-Mohammadi, *Varzeshhā-ye sonnati, bumi va mahalli* [Traditional, native, and local sports] (Tehran: National Olympic Committee of the Islamic Republic of Iran, 1986).
37. For a detailed analysis see H.E. Chehabi, 'Sport and Politics in Iran: The Legend of Gholamreza Takhti', *International Journal of the History of Sport*, XII (Dec. 1995).
38. *Resālat* 19 Khordād 1377/9 June 1998, 14.
39. *Dānesh-e varzesh*, 5, 54 (Shahrivar 1371/Aug.–Sept. 1992), 29.
40. Ludwig Paul, 'Der iranische Spitzenfußball und seine sozialen und politischen Dimensionen', *Sozial- und Zeitgeschichte des Sports*, XII, 2 (1998), 77–8.
41. *Dānesh va varzesh*, 1, 3 (Esfand 1366/Feb.–March 1988), 14.
42. 'Nazarāt-e shahid Doktor Beheshti dar khosus-e varzesh', *Ettelā'āt-e haftegi*, 15 July 1981, 55.
43. It is off Peasant Boulevard, formerly Elizabeth II Boulevard!
44. Personal communication from an avid skier.
45. For more details see *The International Encyclopedia of Women and Sport* (New York: Macmillan, 2001), s.v. 'Iran', pp.586–7.
46. *Dānesh-e varzesh*, 4, 43 (Āzar 1370/Nov.–Dec. 1991), 3.
47. Andrew Longmore, 'Iran lifts veil on women's sporting life', *Times*, 22 July 1996, p.31.
48. Frank Herrmann, 'Radlerinnen sind den Mullahs ein Graus', *Hamburger Abendblatt*, 7 May 1996, p.2. It is interesting to note that a century earlier, the proper attire of woman cyclists had been quite a controversial issue in Europe as well. See Nancy Bradfield, 'Cycling in the 1890s', *Costume*, VI (1972).
49. *Sahifeh-ye nur*, Vol.18 (Tehran: Ministry of Islamic Guidance, 1986), p.125.
50. *Jomhuri-ye eslāmi*, 15 Oct. 1985, p.2; 16 Oct. 1985, p.2; 21 Oct. 1985, p.11.

51. *Ettelā'āt*, 26 May 1986, p.10.
52. *Dānesh-e varzesh*, 1, 3 (Esfand 1366/Feb.–March 1988), 14.
53. Seyyed Rezā Taqavi, *Chehel hadith: varzesh* [Forty Hadith: Sports] (Tehran: Islamic Propaganda Organization, 1992), p.14.
54. N[awid] K[ermani], 'Gut rasiert', *Frankfurter Allgemeine Zeitung*, 11 July 1998, p.32.
55. For details see H.E. Chehabi, 'US-Iranian Sports Diplomacy', *Diplomacy and Statecraft*, XII,1 (March 2001).
56. This is analyzed in Fariba Adelkhah, *Being Modern in Iran*, trans. Jonathan Derrick (London: Hurst & Company, 1999), Chapter 6, 'Looking after Number One: A Competitive Society', pp.139–74.
57. See Christian Bromberger, 'Troisième mi-temps pour le football iranien', *Le Monde diplomatique*, April 1998; Christian Bromberger, 'Le football en Iran', *Sociétés & Représentations* (Dec. 1998); Paul, 'Der iranische Spitzenfußball'; Marcus Gerhardt, 'Sport and Civil Society in Iran', in Eric Hoogland (ed.), *Twenty Years of Islamic Revolution: Political and Social Transformation in Iran since 1979* (Syracuse, NY: Syracuse University Press, 2002), pp.36–55.

Pancasila: Sport and the Building of Indonesia – Ambitions and Obstacles

IAIN ADAMS

Indonesia is the largest archipelago in the world. There are possibly 17,000 islands (13,667 is a commonly cited figure), of which about 6,000 are inhabited. These islands are strung along 5,000 kilometres of the equator, north of Australia and south of mainland Asia. Less than a fifth of the area of Indonesia is land. Indonesians often refer to their country as *Tanah Air* (land and water). Indonesia is divided into 27 provinces. There are still important local leaders such as the Sushunan of Surakarta, the Pangeran of Mangkunegara and the Sultan of Yogyakarta. The power of these leaders is very limited today.

Indonesia is the fourth most populous nation in the world, after China, India and the US, with a population of over 215 million. The island of Java is one of the most densely populated areas on earth, with over 100 million people. About 83 per cent of the people live in rural areas and over half of the population are under 20 years of age. This population comprises 366 known ethnic groups with unique cultural identities. At least 669 languages and dialects are used. The national language, *Bahasa Indonesia*, is unknown to many and is the second or third language of many others. Local languages are still of prime importance. All the great religions are present in Indonesia as well as many more local ones.

Europeans have influenced the area since the sixteenth century, with Portuguese, Spanish, Dutch and British traders operating in the area. The Dutch eventually achieved hegemony of Java and loose control over other areas of the archipelago through the Dutch East Indies Company. This company basically governed until Napoleon conquered the Netherlands. The Dutch East Indies Company licences were revoked and the government assumed colonial responsibility. The defeat of Napoleon saw Indonesia fall back into the hands of the Dutch, a position that remained until the Japanese occupied the area in 1942. The defeat of the

Japanese led the Dutch to attempt to re-establish their colonial power. However, fierce fighting occurred between the Dutch and nationalist forces and the Dutch eventually recognized the sovereignty of Indonesia. The Dutch East Indies formally ceased to exist on 27 December 1949 and the Republic of Indonesia was proclaimed.[1] The Republic of Indonesia became a member of the United Nations in 1950.

PANCASILA

Ahmed Sukarno first described *Pancasila* in a speech in June 1945 that 'might well be considered the most important speech in modern Indonesian history'.[2] *Pancasila* is a word of Sanskrit origin that means five principles. Sukarno presented the five principles as nationalism, humanitarianism/internationalism, democracy, social justice and monotheism. The speech recognized the plurality of the inhabitants of the proposed new nation and appealed for consensus to hold the disparate ethnic, religious and lingual groups together. *Pancasila* was proposed as a system of life for the state and society and was adopted as the ideological and philosophical basis of the new republic. The philosophy of *Pancasila* was reinforced by the selection of *Bhinneka Tunggal Ika* ('unity in diversity') as the national motto. This was a phrase coined by the poet Mpu Tantular in the fourteenth century and appears on the national coat of arms.

NATIONALISM

Movements against foreign intervention can be traced back to the seventeenth century. However, these did not envisage Indonesia in the modern sense and were centred on local independence. Even in the 1880s there were over 80 local leaders in Java who retained a measure of authority under Dutch suzerainty. The Dutch often enlisted their help against each other when insurrection occurred. It is probable that the modern concept of Indonesia evolved in intellectual circles in Amsterdam and Indonesia in the late nineteenth century. This concept probably accelerated and nascent independence movements born as a result of the Dutch colonial 'ethical policy' that was inspired by a speech of Queen Wilhelmina in 1901.[3] The first nationalist political party genuinely to gain widespread popular support was *Sarekat Islam*. The Dutch did not suppress this movement possibly because it was open and constitutional and therefore its activities were easy to track. This movement had about two million members by 1918.

There was sufficient ferment in the early twentieth century for the Dutch, in November 1918, to promise independence at an indeterminate future date. There were widespread mass demonstrations against colonialism in the early 1920s and Sukarno emerged as one of the leaders. He realized that the disparate groups had to work together to stand any chance of lasting success. He identified the concept of nationalism as the keystone that might hold disparate Islamic, Communist, ethnic and tribal groups together.

Steps towards independence were achieved during the Japanese occupation. The Japanese allowed civil administration to be placed in Indonesian hands as Allied victories stretched their resources. The Japanese agreed to Indonesian independence on 9 August 1945. This was to be granted on 24 August 1945. However, on 15 August the Japanese surrendered to the allies and agreed to hand back the former colonies to the Dutch.

Sukarno had begun to install mechanisms to develop national unity and integration even before independence was achieved in 1949. He had persuaded the Japanese to allow the red/white flag of the independence movement to be flown and *Indonesia Raya* to be adopted as the national anthem. He had managed to have *Bahasa Indonesia*, based on Malay, accepted as the official language of the Indonesian Nationalist Party in 1927. This was ultimately adopted as the national language and is now taught to all children. Sukarno introduced a constitution that was applied to the areas under nationalist control in 1945, the same year that he had publicized the concept of *Pancasila*.

The youth of the Dutch East Indies made up a large percentage of the membership of the early independence movement. Many of the groups targeted youth and sought ways to influence them. This led to the concepts of independence and nationalism being inculcated through local sports clubs. These clubs became centres of opposition to Dutch rule during the colonial period. In some ways the independence and nationalistic fervour of Indonesian youth was kindled through sport.

The nationalist government recognized the potential in sport to influence the nationalist movement and an early priority was the development of a coherent policy. Sports leaders from around Indonesia were called to the Hadiprojo Convention Hall in Surakarta in 1946. They approved the formation of the Indonesian Sports Association, *Persatuan*

Olahraga Republik Indonesia (PORI).[4] PORI was to be based in Yogyakarta, which was in a nationalist controlled region.

It was decided that a national sports week, *Pekan Olahraga Nasional* (PON) could have beneficial affects on the movement towards independence and nationhood. This would provide an opportunity to bring spectators and athletes from the different areas together in friendly competition and celebrate nationhood rather in the style of early Soviet *Spartakiad*s. It may have also been aimed at developing an affection for the idea of an independent Indonesia among those people who were not convinced about total separation from the Dutch or the evolution of a large pluralist state rather than a number of small homogenous ones. The first PON was held from 8 to 12 September 1948 in Surakarta. About 400 athletes participated and around 40,000 spectators attended every day. It was opened by the president and watched by United Nations representatives as well as other foreign dignitaries. PORI arranged to stage another PON in October 1951. PON II was organized in Jakarta, but provincial teams rather than district teams participated. This created teams from larger geographical areas, and hence they were of a more diverse ethnic, religious and linguistic mix. It was hoped that this would help an emotional attachment develop between the different peoples of the provinces. This move also had the effect of raising performance levels. A third PON was organized in Medan, Sumatra, in 1953. This was important in that it was the first to be held outside Java, and the new facilities demonstrated the government's commitment to development across the country. This commitment to the development of sports facilities around Indonesia was continued, with PON IV being held in a new sports stadium in Ujung Pandang, South Sulawesi, in 1957. Financial pressures on the new nation were becoming very severe by 1960 but sport, at local and national level, was judged to be of sufficient importance to continue to enjoy government support. Economic restrictions were applied to PON V held in Bandung, Java, in 1961, leading it to become known as 'small PON'. Athletes stayed in family homes scattered around the city to save money. Financial strictures continued to haunt the PON series and PON VII, held in Surabaya, Java, in 1969 is now known as 'money PON' because athletes had to pay to watch events other than those in which they were competing.

One of the reasons why the leaders backed the idea of the PON was that, if it were successful, it would demonstrate to the outside world that an independent Indonesia would be a peaceful and secure state interested in the welfare of its citizens. This was a reason why so many international representatives were invited to the games. At the same time there was a belief that involvement in international sport would reinforce the legitimacy of Indonesia as a nation state. The Olympic Games of 1948 provided an immediate opportunity for the country to obtain recognition and prestige on the international scene. Many governments have become involved in international sport for similar reasons.[5] A further benefit of international competition was that the diverse people would hopefully develop a common interest in supporting the national team and develop an emotional unity through that support.

An attempt was made to organize a team for the forthcoming London Olympiad, but PORI was unable to complete arrangements in time. However, it is doubtful that the International Olympic Committee (IOC) would have accepted an application because Indonesia was not internationally recognized as a country at the time and had no recognized Olympic committee. However, Indonesia was being discussed at the United Nations after the Soviet Union had formally raised the question of its sovereignty in 1946, and the tide of international opinion was turning against colonialism.

The Indonesians believed that PON had been successful in lifting the prestige of Indonesia at an international level. This added to the support for a second PON. The next opportunity to participate in the international arena was the inaugural Asian Games in New Delhi in 1951. Athletics championships were organized in Bandung in December 1950 to select a team for the games. The selected athletes then attended a special training camp at Bandung. The athletes acquitted themselves well at the Asian Games: several Indonesian records were set and several bronze medals won. The football team, who were knocked out by the eventual winners, India, accompanied the athletics team.

An Olympic Committee, *Komite Olympiade Republik Indonesia* (KORI), was established to help prepare for the fifteenth Olympiad in Helsinki in 1952. Three athletes were sent, one competing in swimming, one in weightlifting and one in the high jump. By 1954 elite sport was more established and more individuals were competing in the sports that featured in international competitions. Facilities were improving and coaching opportunities were becoming more widespread. Indonesia participated at the second Asian Games in Manila in 1954 with a significantly larger team than in previous international games. Over 100 athletes were sent in seven sports. Indonesia participated in six sports at the Melbourne Olympiad in 1956 and received international publicity when its football team drew 0–0 with the favourites Russia in the semi-final. They lost the replay.

Governments often view the hosting of major international sports events as a greater opportunity to achieve international recognition as a developed country than merely participating.[6] The administrators of sport in Indonesia believed that they had accumulated sufficient experience from attending Olympic and Asian Games to host a major event in Indonesia. They successfully bid for badminton's Thomas Cup in 1961 and have been regular hosts since; they have also hosted the women's equivalent, the Uber Cup.[7] Their first attempt to host a multi-sport event was bid for the fourth Asian Games that were scheduled to be held in 1962. Their success was announced when the team was participating in the third Asian Games in Tokyo in 1958. To prepare for the Asian Games, a special administrative team accompanied the athletes to the 1960 Olympics in Rome to study how to host multi-sport events.

The financial outlay necessary to host a major multi-sport event such as the Asian Games led to the Indonesians seeking foreign aid to establish the facilities. The Soviet Union was asked for assistance and a substantial grant was forthcoming to fund facility construction. This new sports facility was known initially as the *Bung Karno* Sports Complex and was one of the most modern in the world at the time. It has been continually expanded and its name was later changed to the Senayan Sports Complex. Indonesia has hosted other international events since the Asian Games. These have included the South-East Asian Games (SEA Games) in 1979, 1987 and 1997. The success of these events encouraged the government to bid for the 2008 Olympics for Jakarta.

Success in major international sporting events relies on expertise in the sports that are emphasized on these occasions. This has meant Western sports rather than the sports that reflect the local traditions and values of Indonesia. The SEA Games do feature sports of specific regional interest, such as *sepak takraw* which is a rattan ball game resembling three-a-side badminton using the feet. *Sepak takraw* is popular throughout the ASEAN region, although different versions occur.[8] The Indonesian government had realized the need for the development of Western sports and PORI was charged with developing various sporting disciplines at its initial meeting in 1946. Possibly, it was further felt that traditional sports emphasized local and tribal identity rather than a pan-Indonesian identity and therefore that nationalism could be reinforced if interest and support could be developed for internationally supported sports.

The Western sports of football and badminton had already been established in the Dutch East Indies. In 1930 there were two national governing bodies (NGBs) of football. *Persatuan Sepakbola Seluruh Indonesia* (PSSI), a nationalist organization, was formed in 1930 in Yogyakarta to replace seven regional organizations. Another NGB, the Netherlands Indies FA (NIVU), represented six regions and was supported by the Dutch administration. The NIVU selected the representational team, the Dutch Indies.[9] This team qualified for the 1938 World Cup in France and were defeated in the first round; Indonesia has been unable to reach the final rounds since. The two NGBs continued operating until Indonesian independence, the PSSI becoming the sole NGB of football in 1949. In 1951 the PSSI joined FIFA and launched a national championship. The same year marked its international debut with a national team participating in the Asian Games at New Delhi. A semi-professional league was started in 1981 and *Liga Indonesia* was formed in 1994–95. Today, there are over 6,600 clubs and 1.6 million players. There has been disquiet in recent years, at private and government levels, that football has not been achieving its potential and a variety of measures have been put in place to improve the reputation of Indonesian football on the international scene.[10]

Badminton is the national sport of Indonesia; the NGB (PBSI) was established in Bandung in 1951.[11] When the government of Indonesia decided to participate in international sport, badminton was termed *Anak Mas*, the 'golden child'. It has lived up to these expectations. The gold, silver and bronze medals were won in the men's singles, gold in the women's singles and gold in women's doubles at Barcelona in 1992, when badminton was introduced to the Olympics. Indonesia received widespread publicity when the two individual gold medallists, Alan Budikusuma and Susi Susanti, were married shortly after the games. Indonesia has maintained its powerful presence in badminton at the Olympic Games since its introduction, winning three more medals in both 1996 and 2000. In 1989 Indonesia founded a mixed world team championship, the Sudirman Cup. The inaugural event was held in Indonesia and won by the hosts. This cup was named for Dick Sudirman who is known as the father of Indonesian badminton.[12] He was a long-serving member of the International Badminton Federation council and founder of the PBSI, serving as president for 22 years.

Football has developed a national following in Indonesia, although this seems to be focused on supporting local clubs rather than the national team. Crowd behaviour at *Liga* games may lead to the conclusion that football is not developing mutual admiration and affection between the regions. However, badminton has truly achieved nationwide standing as the national sport. The joy accompanying Thomas Cup victories is widespread, whatever the origin of the Indonesian players.

HUMANITARIANISM/INTERNATIONALISM

Sukarno realized that his vision of one united country was reliant upon the equal promotion of the welfare of all of its citizens. Everybody should be free from physical and spiritual oppression and treated with due regard to their dignity as one of God's creatures. This consciousness of the plurality of Indonesia and the need to avoid feelings of superiority on the grounds of ethnicity, ancestry or colour led Sukarno to condemn all forms of colonialism in the 1945 Constitution.

The 1950s and 1960s were a time of major dissolution of colonies and some of the newly independent countries felt left out by the First World and Second World and defined themselves as rising nations of the Third World. Sukarno began to see himself as a leader of the Third World, which consisted of over 100 countries, and called a conference of the Non-aligned Movement in Bandung in 1955. This conference stressed neutrality in the cold war and recognized Communism as a new form of colonialism. This was a success for Sukarno, as various Communist movements had been causing problems within Indonesia from its establishment. Sukarno saw the award of the 1962 Asian Games to Indonesia as an opportunity to demonstrate his freedom from European influences and his philosophical credentials to lead the Third World. The IOC had developed a policy of supporting regional games, such as the Pan-American Games and the Asian Games, and expected them to occur under similar philosophical circumstances as the Olympics themselves. The IOC was still heavily bound by Western traditions despite the increasing number of developing-country members.

One aspect of this Western philosophy was that sport should be free from politics. The perilous economic situation of Indonesia led Sukarno to seek succour from a variety of sources. His decision to bar Israel and Taiwan from the Asian Games was possibly a blatant attempt to increase economic support from Arab nations and China. Israel was seen to be a

Western country denying rights to Arabs within its sphere of influence, and Taiwan was viewed as an outpost of American capitalism. China supported Indonesia as China maintained a 'political posture of open confrontation with the International Olympic Committee over the "one China" concept'.[13] The IOC threatened to expel Indonesia from the Olympic movement and Sukarno responded by withdrawing from the IOC and attacking it as an imperialist organization. He saw this disagreement as an opportunity to further his cause as the natural leader of the developing nations. An Indonesian spokesman expressed the Foreign Minister's view 'that sports cannot be separated from politics. Therefore let us work for a sports organization on the basis of politics.'[14] A new organization was established with the specific goal of advocacy for the sporting interests of the Third World and other non-aligned countries. This organization was called the Games of the Newly Emerging Forces (GANEFO) and one of its aims was to run multi-sport games on a regular two-year cycle. China fully supported GANEFO having left the IOC over the 'one China' issue, but the Soviet Union did not immediately join GANEFO, possibly because of the 'shop window' that the Olympics offered. However, the Soviet Union later joined to prevent China increasing its influence with the newly emerging states.

The GANEFO games opened in October 1963 and provided a second major international spectacle for the Senayan Sports Complex. The games continued for 12 days and provided exceptional international prestige for Indonesia among the developing nations and a well-publicized medium for expressing foreign policy. Sukarno also used GANEFO to apply pressure to Malaysia. Western Malaysia, Indonesia's northern neighbour, had undergone a gradual and relatively peaceful transition to independence. However in the 1950s, other ex-European colonies in the area were choosing to federate with Western Malaysia. Sukarno viewed this development as neocolonialism and began activities against the developing state. Malaysia federated as an independent state in 1963, despite the opposition of Indonesia and the Philippines. The United Nations censured Indonesia for its military forays into Malaysia, leading Indonesia to leave the United Nations when Malaysia joined in 1964. Indonesia entered into an anti-imperialist alliance with China the following year. This evolving struggle was an added incentive to Sukarno to found GANEFO.[15]

The refusal to allow Israel and Taiwan to compete in the Asian Games in Jakarta had potential repercussions for the 1964 Tokyo Olympics. The

IOC announced that GANEFO participants would not be allowed to participate in Tokyo and this was supported by both the IAAF and FINA. This was a very threatening situation for the Japanese because other Third World countries threatened to boycott the games in support of GANEFO. Eventually negotiations between the disputing parties led to the GANEFO countries not selecting athletes for the Olympiad who had participated in Jakarta. North Korea was the only country that refused to compromise and boycotted the Olympics.

A second GANEFO games was organized after a meeting in Beijing in 1965. This was scheduled for Cairo, with an alternative venue of Beijing. However, days after the meeting, a failed coup (the G30S coup) led to Sukarno being replaced by General Suharto. This change of leadership resulted in a move away from non-aligned and developing-country leadership aspirations and a move towards mainstream international politics. Suharto rejoined the United Nations in 1966, reformed the Indonesian Olympic Committee in 1967 and rejoined the Olympic fold in time for the Mexico Olympiad in 1968.

Suharto, like Sukarno, believed in the influence of sport in international circles and remained in GANEFO. Internationalism, the pursuit of peace and friendship among countries, had been one of the aims of GANEFO. He tried to moderate its strident anti-Western attitude as he moved to rejoin mainstream international sport. He had decided that one of the causes of Indonesia's economic problems was the inefficiency of its economic system and inefficient exploitation of its natural resources. In order to improve the situation, he decided to open up the country to Western investment and management systems. Suharto chose a middle path with sport: a team was prepared for the second GANEFO games and the fifth Asian Games in Bangkok. The economic situation in Cairo had meant that the Egyptians could not afford to host the GANEFO games and the Cultural Revolution caused too much chaos for the Chinese to organize the games. This resulted in the games being moved to Phnom Phenh in Kampuchea.

Suharto moved towards rapprochement with Malaysia and joined the SEA Games movement that is sanctioned by the Olympic Council of Asia. Among the stated aims of the SEA Games is the promotion of cooperation, understanding and relations among the member countries. The SEA Games have provided opportunities for leaders of the ten member countries to talk and provide a public impression of the togetherness of the region. Indonesia suggested that the member countries cooperate to improve sporting performance. It was envisaged that each country would develop a centre of excellence to be shared by athletes from all of the member countries. Indonesia offered to develop a centre of excellence for badminton. This suggestion was enthusiastically received but nothing came of the idea. However, following the poor performance of athletes at the most recent games, SEA Games delegates are negotiating the resurrection of ASEAN-wide centres of excellence.

At the national level, stressing the importance of all local cultures and their traditions within the national framework supported the humanitarianism of *Pancasila*. The enormous size of Indonesia and the island nature of the country, coupled with significant mountain ranges and huge tracts of dense jungle, have led to the development and survival of a large variety of different activities especially in such areas as Irian Jaya and Kalimantan. The modernization and westernization of Indonesia threatened to undermine traditional values; therefore the government decided to actively support traditional cultures through folk activities. The government centred its support through the Directorate of Non-Formal Education, Youth and Sport within the Ministry of Education and Culture.

Indonesia has a plethora of traditional sport activities: many are restricted to a small isolated geographical area while some are widespread across the country and indeed the region. *Pasola* is an activity restricted to one small area; cock fighting is common across the country; and varieties of *sepak takraw* are widespread across the ASEAN region.

Pasola is an annual ritual war between two villages in Sumba in which several hundred mounted warriors attack each other with spears on a ceremonial battlefield obstructed by burial mounds. The horses are ridden in intersecting circular paths to represent the orbits of celestial bodies and spears are flung at close range where the circles intersect. The spirits are only satisfied by spilled blood or death and in the past the warriors intentionally missed narrowly, relying on nicks and cuts to appease the spirits. The government decreed that the warriors had to use blunted spears and the army are present to check. This has led the warriors to aim at the throat and temple as the spilling of blood is less likely with the blunted spears, and therefore death is needed to appease the spirits. Survival depends on the riding skills and reactions of the warriors. The warriors offer their lives to the gods if they are killed.

There are many varieties of martial art forms that have evolved across the country. *Sisemba* is a kicking sport from Tanatoraja and *pentjak* is a self-defence form with musical accompaniment. *Pentjak* has a variety of forms across the country. Traditional archery is common throughout Indonesia, with bamboo bows and arrows used against straw pigeon targets on poles. The first Olympic medal won by Indonesia was a women's team silver in archery at Seoul in 1988.[16]

'Marching' is a widespread sport, particularly in urban areas. This is a team sport with points being awarded for smartness and teamwork as well as completing the required distance. Teams wear uniforms, often shorts and matching T-shirts, and compete in different divisions. The distances marched depends upon the division in which a team competes.

One of the best known of the traditional activities is *kerapan sapi*, the colourful bull-racing of Madura. Plough-teams of two bulls race over the length of a rice paddy. This event has spread from the island of Madura to East Java and the district and regency heats in August lead to the finals in September. Today's bulls are specially bred for racing and are never used for ploughing; the ploughs pulled would not survive a day in the paddies. However, the winning team achieves great status and an early defeat in the district rounds is accompanied by a severe loss of 'face' for the owner.

The encouragement of traditional sports, through the Directorate of Non-Formal Education, Youth and Sport, is an acknowledgement of the importance of these activities. It recognizes the educational value of these activities in transferring and maintaining local culture and reinforcing social identity.[17] Involvement can help ensure a sense of continuity and belonging. However, to many people the support of traditional cultures through *Pancasila* is a means of transition to modern society through subterfuge. Gradually, over a number of years, traditional cultures would be influenced by outside forces to become an amalgam of traditional and modern society. Traditional society would then be slowly replaced by modern society.[18] The roots of this process are seen to be monotheism, the introduction of a common language, common laws, common money and loyalty to one common ruler and nation. This idea is acceptable to most Javanese because they dominate parliament and the administration and, therefore, Javanese ways have dominated when things are done across the country. However, this has meant that many people in the outer areas of Indonesia feel that Javanese culture is taking over and they are becoming a colony of Java.

DEMOCRACY

The pluralism of the prospective new nation led Sukarno to propose government through representative democracy or mutual consent. He realized that consensus would have to be reached and the best method would possibly be through the deliberations of elected representatives. He had espoused the Western notion of parties representing different interests in 1945. However, 170 different parties fought the 1955 election, and Sukarno was irritated by the confusion the parties brought to the country. He recognized the failure of this system in such a diverse country and the continuous problems it brought about. He was also becoming more aware of the limitations being placed upon him by the restrictions on his position as president. He therefore pronounced a new system based on a slightly different interpretation of representative democracy as described by *Pancasila*. The new system was 'guided democracy' or 'leadership according to the current environment'. Western nations and many Indonesians were worried that this signalled a reduction in liberal democracy and a further increase in centralization. The continuous economic pressure on Indonesia had led to a marked decline in the infrastructure of the nation and a worsening of living standards for a large number of people. This led to a notable increase in support for the Communists and the likelihood of a Communist victory in the next election.

A wave of military-led insurrections occurred in diverse locations, including Central Sumatra, North Sumatra, Sulawesi and South Sumatra. These were put down by military loyal to Sukarno, but Muslim and Communist-led disturbances occurred into the 1960s. According to Challis,[19] the internal situation, allied to Sukarno's foreign policy, particularly with regard to Malaysia, was of sufficient worry to the Americans and British that they engineered a coup supporting the more Western-capitalist-sympathetic General Suharto.[20] The coup was designed to be blamed on the Communists or on the military. The G30S coup of 1 October 1965 led to Suharto taking control and an elimination of many of the Communists in Indonesia, perhaps more than a million being killed by the late 1960s.[21] Suharto rescheduled Indonesia's massive debt and encouraged investment by foreign and domestic companies; Sukarno had basically kept the colonial economy in place using the export of raw materials as a foundation.

The Suharto years were marked by a steady decline in the power of the political parties and an increase in the powers of the president and the military. Sections of the economy were kept under government/military control and other sections opened to market forces. Suharto oversaw a change of strategy towards development through economic growth. This was based on Western capitalism with industrialization, scientific progress and technical innovation. This view received strong support from organizations such as the World Bank. However, Suharto's policies did not foster 'a profound sense of Indonesian-ness'.[22] Local communities watched their environment become ravaged by industries such as logging and oil and saw no economic benefit as the revenues disappeared to Jakarta. The attempts to modernize through development may have been more successful if corruption had not removed so much money from the system. Relatives and friends of Suharto and the military dominated much of the market economy. Cronyism and nepotism were rife and a Javanese 'mafia' controlled most of the country's administration. Even education was not safe from economic corruption. This is illustrated on a small scale by the inappropriate sites selected for World Bank-upgraded elementary PE teacher education schools, *sekolah guru olahraga* (SGO). The sites seemed to be selected for the benefit of local administrators rather than education. For example, one is sited across a bay from the town and students have to take small sailing-boat ferries to and from it, with resulting problems in bad weather; one is located next to the local power station that generates power from jet engines; and another was built in an area of known dry wells so that the head teacher had to ferry water every day in his car.[23]

Enormous profits have been made in Indonesia through the global marketplace. International brands of clothing and shoes are made in 'sweatshops' where the workers have not benefited from any 'trickle down' of profits. The steady increase in average income has hidden the widening gap between the middle and lower classes. Many areas have 40 per cent of their population living in poverty. The steadily increasing dissatisfaction among the masses was exacerbated by the financial crisis of the Tiger economies of Asia in 1997–98. Large-scale devaluations of Indonesia's rupiah were followed by over 3,500 disturbances nationwide that left over 1,000 dead and led over 150,000 to flee the country. Suharto resigned on 21 May 1998.[24]

Suharto's resignation has been followed by a period of confusion as his allies battled reformists. The reformists have attempted to decentralize power and even allowed a referendum on independence in East Timor. Independence received 78 per cent of the vote; this led to renewed struggles by dissatisfied groups across Indonesia and renewed vigour from the army to suppress them. Eight of Indonesia's 27 provinces were aflame by August 2000. In 2001 the government, under President Wahid, continued its reforming ideas of increasing parliamentary power at the expense of the president and decentralizing certain powers to the provinces.

The changes in the administrative and controlling structures of Indonesia have emphasized the government's and the people's belief in the power and importance of sport. This is reflected in the need to control its operation. Sukarno ensured that PORI was set up before the country was established and that national sports events, such as PON, occurred. The attraction of international competition led to the establishment of an Olympic Committee (KONI) in 1952 but the need to coordinate and oversee sporting development saw PORI and KONI merged into one, the National Olympic Committee of Indonesia (KOI). The prestige of hosting the Asian Games in 1962 led Sukarno to stipulate that the Asian Games Council of Indonesia would control all sports activities in Indonesia (President's Decree 79, 1961). This was portrayed as a means of quality control, although some opponents of the regime intimated a widening of government control. Decree 79 included activities such as first aid training, government translation facilities, city guides and referee and judge training.

The arguments with the IOC over the 1962 Asian Games led the Indonesian Olympic Committee (KOI) to be disbanded and replaced by a new Ministry of Sport, *Dewan Olahraga Republik Indonesia* (DORI). DORI's major role was to coordinate preparations for the new GANEFO games. However, the remit of DORI was extremely wide, ranging from international competition to all physical activities in the educational system. It was also responsible for sport research and medicine, the construction and maintenance of sports facilities and the development of sports industries including the importation of sports equipment. This range of responsibilities resulted in DORI being able to set up special committees with wide-ranging powers, *Komando Gerakan Olahraga*. These were formed for special projects. The government provided DORI with all the support it could by mobilizing all forces and funds available. These changes reflected government interests and aspirations rather than those of the people. Many athletes competing at the GANEFO games would probably have preferred to be at Tokyo in 1964.

Sport was severely disrupted in 1965 by the overthrow of Sukarno after the G30S coup. A PON was cancelled for the first time (PON VI), despite all arrangements having been completed. The foreign and economic policy changes that occurred in the wake of the coup led to DORI being dissolved and a new National Sports Council of Indonesia, *Komite Olahraga Nasional Indonesia* (KONI), was established in December 1966.

The establishment of KONI simplified the structure of sport, as it assumed responsibility for all elite sport and also represented Indonesia at the Asian Games Federation and the IOC. KONI also assumed all responsibility for the planning and participation of teams in the Asian Games and the Olympics. Today KONI acts as an adviser and coordinator for all the NGBs, who are responsible for their own programmes, and has branches in all regions of Indonesia; all NGBs belong to KONI. However, KONI is a heavily centralized body that tends to cascade information and policies downwards rather than disseminating information upwards. It has been responsible for enacting government policy that sometimes seems to be more foreign-policy-driven than providing what the people want. KONI encouraged the development of the competitive form of *sepak takraw* rather than *sepakraga*, the previously more common cooperative game. Similarly *pencak silat* is being promoted through the national curriculum in schools at the expense of more local forms of martial arts. KONI has also brought in modifications to sport through regulations. As has been noted earlier, armed soldiers attend the annual *pasola* event to ensure that only blunt spears are used, despite the increased risk of death these have brought. There are instances of these soldiers beating up participants if they feel the event is becoming too dangerous. Also the soldiers have been known to imply the inferiority of the local culture to their own.[25]

SOCIAL JUSTICE

Sukarno called for the equitable spread of welfare across the entire nation with the *Pancasila* philosophy. He called for the protection of the weak and emphasized the need to provide opportunities that were fair, safe and relevant to the needs of the people. He believed that everybody should work according to his or her abilities and fields of achievement.

The government doctrine of social justice through protection of the weak and respect for the cultural and economic needs of all was undermined within a year of independence. The government started a resettlement programme in 1950 that continued into the 1990s. People from the densely populated areas of Java and Bali were moved to less populated areas such as Kalimantan and Irian Jaya. The resettled population were often moved in military ships and provided with only basic agricultural implements and seed. Many were ex-military and most were Muslim. They formed the foundations of armed pro-Indonesian gangs when local populations demonstrated for local rights. These settlers were placed on 'unsettled' land, a concept that demonstrated a complete lack of understanding of the traditional lifestyles in Kalimantan and Irian Jaya. This brought clashes between Muslim Javanese settlers and indigenous people.

Javanese plots began to be seen in all aspects of development organized by central government. For example, the government demanded a common design for the SGO teacher education schools improvement project funded by the World Bank. This design featured a mosque. In 1988 the headmaster of one SGO was furious at this waste of money because the SGO was in a Christian community with very few Muslims, and those few regarded sport as un-Islamic – therefore Muslims were unlikely to become SGO students. This was the first occasion that the World Bank PE technical specialist had come across the concept of the 'Javanese Empire'.[26] However, by 2000, Muslim immigration into Ambon from Flores and Java had radically changed the demography of the island and the Muslim majority entered a state of virtual warfare with the Christians, particularly the Chinese Christians.

Sukarno saw education as a major tool to be used to develop social justice. The Dutch 'ethical policy' had resulted in improvements in education, health care, communications, irrigation and the general infrastructure of the area. Locally established Islamic and Hindu religious education centres had been established in the sixteenth century. The Portuguese, Spanish and Dutch had introduced European-type schools into some areas before the Dutch government assumed responsibility for education in 1848. This led to the setting up of a variety of schools and a number of teacher-training institutions in the nineteenth century. The education system in parts of Indonesia resembled that of the Netherlands by the beginning of the Second World War. However, education was neither compulsory nor widespread.[27] A number of different types of school had been founded by the time independence was achieved. The new government of Indonesia was faced with the difficult task of establishing an educational system that would reflect and inculcate the new national philosophy. A Ministry of Education was set up to meet the challenges.

A nationwide school system had been instituted by the 1970s. This is based upon four levels: one year of kindergarten, six years of elementary schools, three years of junior high school and three years of high school. In 1984 all organizations were required to adopt the *Pancasila* as their guiding ideology. This included the schools and sport NGBs. In the same year education became compulsory for children aged between seven and 12. However, despite a significant increase in the number of children attending school by the 1990s, a large number still did not attend due to shortages of schools, teachers and transport. This is especially true in the more remote areas of the country. The Indonesian government has constructed thousands of new primary schools over the last 20 years with many being in the more remote areas. These are often supplied by air. There are also missionary schools mainly funded through the US or the Netherlands, many of which are also supplied by air through the Missionary Aviation Fellowship.

Sport and physical education had not been prioritized under the Dutch because the subject received little attention in the Netherlands. Where it did exist, it was modelled on the Swedish system and carried out by military or ex-military personnel. The military character of any existing physical activity in the schools was re-emphasized and expanded under the Japanese occupation as the Japanese required Indonesian manpower.

The 1950 Education Act stipulated that PE should be offered in all schools and it must aim to develop a harmonization of physical and mental development and create physically and mentally healthy people. Also, the act recognized that it was not sufficient to simply offer PE and sport within the allocated school hours. The Ministry of Education sponsored a conference on physical education in 1957 and a PE council, *Madjelis Pendidikan Djasmani*, was established. This council was very active until it was subsumed under Decree 79 in the run-up to the Asian Games of 1961. Many of its proposals had been hindered by a chronic lack of finance and resources. The responsibility for PE was moved to DORI in 1964. This political move meant that 'sports, and consequently physical education, became more and more a tool to be manipulated for

Sport and the Building of Indonesia 313

the purposes of national and foreign policy'.[28] This merging of PE and sport has led to the word *olahraga* being used for both in the educational system. In general usage the term *olahraga* has an educational connotation. Further political changes resulted in the demise of DORI and the establishment of a Directorate-General for Sports as a subdivision of the Ministry of Education and Culture. In 1968 the Directorate-General for Sports was expanded to include youth. The frequent changing of responsibility for *olahraga* has resulted in just as frequent changes in aims and objectives for the subject as it is adapted to reflect the political priorities of the day. In 1980 the objectives centred on meeting the psychological, physiological, sociological and cultural needs of the child and developing a harmonious individual.[29]

The methods of achieving the aims of *olahraga* were left, to a large extent, to the *Kanwil*, the provincial Offices of the Ministry of Education and Culture. However, a much more centralized curriculum was implemented in the early 1980s. This new programme was more detailed. The *olahraga* programme for elementary schools, *sekolah dasar* (SDs), aimed to promote harmonious physical, spiritual, mental and social growth and development; to develop the basic skills of movement; to inculcate positive values and attitudes; and to develop the knowledge and habits necessary for a healthy life.[30] These aims reflect one of the original aims of education in developing a consensus of values across the land. The new curriculum was to be based on athletics, gymnastics, swimming, games and *pancak silat*. The required minimum per week is three periods of *olahraga* for all schoolchildren. Health education is included in this total. A survey of schools in 1987 found that the national curriculum in *olahraga* was less rigorously used, or more liberally interpreted; the further away a school was from Jakarta. This led to recommendations for the establishment of a *Pusat Pengembangan dan Pentaran Guru* (P3G), a National Teacher Education Development Centre for PE.[31]

The new national curriculum reflected the continuous move towards centralization in Indonesia and away from the needs of people in the outer areas of the country. It was noted that some of the activities in the national curriculum were inappropriate in some locations. For example, many schools in urban areas have no access to open spaces for football, volleyball or basketball. Any space available to urban schools has normally been dedicated to classrooms due to the burgeoning population. One school in Rantepao in the north central uplands of South Sulawesi had its small playing space taken over by the town market as houses intruded on the old market.[32] Some PE lessons, such as athletics, take place in the street outside the school in one SD in Malang.[33] Competition for space is intense even in rural areas as food production is a high priority. Some schools do have play areas large enough for volleyball and basketball, but very few have sufficient space for football, which the government is keen to support due to its high international profile. Many village SDs in remote rainforest areas have no access to suitable land for football or water facilities for formal swimming classes. Rivers are common in many areas, but the local wildlife often makes the risk of swimming lessons unacceptable. The culture in some areas does not accept competitive games and yet the option to use local non-competitive activities was removed.[34]

The government attitude towards *olahraga* has resulted in consistent attempts to expand and 'upgrade' the subject. This has included projects sponsored by UNESCO and the World Bank. However, the investment in facilities, teachers and equipment has not been sufficient to meet the aspirations for education.

Teachers of *Olahraga* (*guru Olahraga*) in elementary schools are graduates of specialist elementary PE teacher education high schools (SGOs). There are 55 of these spread throughout Indonesia and ten were significantly upgraded in a World Bank five-year project that involved supplying new buildings (including sports halls), equipment and in-service training to SGO staff on methods of teaching the elementary school curriculum.[35] Secondary teachers are prepared through *olahraga* departments attached to universities. These teachers are normally taught over four years to degree level and master's and doctorate programmes are available at some of the universities. Teachers are posted to schools by central government on completion of their training. This can lead to teachers being assigned to schools outside their area and being limited in their capacity to interact with students. For example, teachers may not know the local language and the student's (and the teacher's) capacity in *Bahasa Indonesia* may be limited.[36]

One of the major weaknesses of Indonesian sport has been the lack of competitive sport in the schools. School-age competitions are based on occasional festivals and sports days, often organized by local clubs and organizations. Often PE teachers would like to organize extracurricular activities but do not have the time. The low pay of teachers means that most have to have at least two jobs. Some NGBs operate national championships in their sports for the school-age groups and children can progress from local tournaments to regional, and then national, competitions. However, the lack of formal school sport has led to a narrow base for the performance pyramid.

MONOTHEISM

Indonesia is the world's largest Muslim nation, with 87 per cent of the population being Muslim. Christians are the next largest group with approximately seven per cent of the population. Buddhists and Hindus form large minorities and there are a variety of other religious practices, ranging from animism to ancestor worship.

Some Muslims had theological problems with the introduction of *Pancasila*, as they believed they were being asked to place *Pancasila* above their religion. Muslim leaders prevailed on Sukarno to have the order of principles changed and for monotheism to be the first principle of *Pancasila*. This did not satisfy many of the more fundamentalist groups who wanted Indonesia to be founded on the *shariah*. As early as 1950 an Islamic revolt tried to overthrow the central government and establish a Muslim state. *Pancasila* is acceptable to other Muslims because they see it as a method of converting people of other 'mistaken' religions to Islam with eventual progression to a more Islamic state. Non-Muslims are wary of *Pancasila* because it does seem to be leading to a Muslim state. This is because the Javanese dominate administration and Islam is the dominant religion in Java.

Christian and Chinese individuals and groups found themselves to be the target of Muslim unrest from the foundation of Indonesia. Continuous confrontations between Muslims, Christians and Chinese have been marked by attacks on churches, Christian schools and homes. Problems have continued to the present day. In 1995 Christians burnt down homes and shops of Muslims in Deli and in 1996 there were anti-Christian riots in Java. In 1997 the Association of Muslim Intellectuals called for ethnic Chinese to be banned from some economic activities to prevent racial tensions.[37] The effective Ministry of Information ensured that very few incidents were reported.[38] Many fundamentalist Muslims around the world have rejected the Western concept of sport and have made sport, and sometimes athletes, ideological or even terrorist targets. The widespread nature of Muslim unrest would seem to indicate that the possibility of sport being targeted is high, but no incidents have been reported.

REFLECTIONS

The nationalist concept of establishing one nation from the diverse lands and people of the Dutch East Indies was very ambitious. The success in achieving nationhood removed the artificial colonial boundaries and replaced them with artificial Indonesian boundaries that ignored ethnic and geographical realities. The solution to the problems of such a diverse ethnic, religious and linguistic population was thought to be *Pancasila*; Suharto summed this up by claiming 'what we should do is to have these differences blend us together in perfect harmony like the beautiful spectrum of the rainbow'.[39] Unfortunately *Pancasila* means different things to different people.

Sport has been actively used to instil and develop some of the principles of *Pancasila*. Undoubtedly, sport has stimulated national pride and national consciousness, particularly in the case of badminton. It has also helped achieve a measure of social justice through interesting people in education programmes and has improved health through activity and the development of awareness of health issues. Sustaining traditional activities has supported humanitarianism, and sport has been used to support visions of internationalism. Sport does not seem to have been used to target monotheism. No traces of the equivalent of 'muscular Christianity' are evident although sport occurs in missionary schools. The lack of progress in achieving democracy can be traced to some extent through the history of sport administration.

The 1965 G30S coup event may, in time, turn out to have been a 'focusing event' for Indonesian sport.[40] A 'focusing event' can help determine the course of sports policy in a significant way and give policy-making momentum. Sport was moving away from the international mainstream before the attempted coup and was being used as a definite tool for creating a major role for Indonesia in the leadership of the Third World. This was being accompanied by an apparent move, in the West's eyes, towards the major Communist nations and against Western interests. The extent of this was such that 50 USA Peace Corps volunteers working in sport and PE were deported and the US suspended aid.

After the coup Suharto swiftly moved sport back into the mainstream by rejoining the IOC and joining the SEA Games group. The movement of Indonesia into a Western-style economy, albeit a corrupt one, has allowed sport to develop as an industry. Today there are specialist sports papers and magazines, commercialized gambling, international-standard sports clubs and facilities, companies specializing in sports law, internet retailers of sports equipment and a notorious sports goods manufacturing base. The 2000 Olympics was the most successful yet, with gold and silver medals in badminton and silver and bronze medals in women's weightlifting. Sport is still heavily centralized and the government still believes in the efficacy of sport to achieve desirable outcomes. This has led to the maintenance of heavy subsidization for sport and hence its availability to a greater number of people. The government has supported the NGBs and sports clubs across the country through facilities, equipment and manpower. Part of the government funding for sport is provided by the state gambling commission, the Totalizator.

In many ways Indonesia can be judged to be a classic example of the use of sport in developing countries. Sport has been used for nation-building, the integration of disparate cultures, the improvement of health, the reinforcement of cultural identity and the obtaining of international recognition.[41] Political leaders have seized opportunities to be associated with sport.

However, sport cannot succeed in building a nation in the face of overwhelming economic and social difficulties. The fragility of Indonesia seems to reflect the trend of collapse in multicultural, multilingual and multi-ethnic countries in recent years. This is exemplified by the Soviet Union, Czechoslovakia and Yugoslavia. Success seems to have involved the selection of a national culture and language; examples are France, Italy and Germany. *Pancasila*, supported by sport, seems to have failed and it is possible that the sight of East Timorese athletes marching as independent Olympic athletes at the Olympics in Sydney is a forerunner of things to come. How long before East Timor, Aceh, Sumatra and Irian Jaya have their own flag, anthem and motto and sports teams?

NOTES

1. H. Soetjipto, W.A. Karamoy and M.S. Wuryani, *Indonesia: An Official Handbook* (Jakarta: Department of Information, Directorate of Foreign Service Information Services, 1995).
2. R. Challis, *Shadow of a Revolution: Indonesia and the Generals* (Stroud: Sutton Publishing, 2001), p.22.
3. P. Carey, *To Struggle for Freedom: Indonesia Yesterday, East Timor Today*, online at http://www.insideindonesia.org/edit49/carey.htm.
4. Most of the information in this article was obtained during the author's sojourn as the National Consultant in Sport Education during 1987 and 1988. Dr 'Pak Edo' Rahantoknam of the Physical Education Department of IKIP Jakarta was a tireless partner responsible for translating presentations, seminars, workshops and papers when the author's *Bahasa Indonesia* collapsed with ineptitude.

5. J. Coakley, *Sport in Society: Issues and Controversies* (Boston, MA: McGraw-Hill, 7th edn 2001), pp.389–90.
6. Ibid., pp.391–2.
7. The Thomas cup is officially known as 'The International Badminton Championship Challenge Cup'. It is the men's world team championship and held every two years. It was inaugurated in 1948–49 and Indonesia has won it 12 times, more than any other nation. Sir George Thomas, the President of the International Badminton Federation in 1948, donated the cup (see http://www.intbadfed.org/tcup.html).
8. S. Ross, 'Indigenous Games of Indonesia: Preservation of Local Culture', *International Journal of Physical Education*, XXVII, 3 (1990), 32.
9. Senayan Indonesia Football Website, http://senayan.8k.com/About/aboutfai.html.
10. Ibid.
11. http://www.bpkpenabur.or.id.
12. http://www.intbadfed.org/sud.html.
13. G. Rizak, 'Sport in the People's Republic of China', in E.A. Wagner (ed.), *Sport in Asia and Africa: A Comparative Handbook* (London: Greenwood Press, 1989), p.114.
14. D.B. Kanin, *A Political History of the Olympic Games* (Boulder, CO: Westview Press, 1981), p.85.
15. J. Kotlatch, *Sport, Politics and Ideology in China* (New York: Jonathon David, 1972).
16. 'Pak Edo' Rahantoknam was the national women's archery coach as well as being the author's partner and a full-time professor at IKIP Jakarta in 1987–88.
17. Ross, 'Indigenous Games', 29–31.
18. K. Heinemann, 'Sport in Developing Countries' in E.G. Dunning, J.A. Maguire and R.E. Pearton (eds), *The Sports Process* (Champaign, IL: Human Kinetics, 1993) pp.139–50.
19. Challis, *Shadow of a Revolution*.
20. Ibid.
21. Ibid., pp.104–13.
22. Ibid., p.228.
23. I. Adams, *Interim Report: Physical Education* (Jakarta: Direktorat Pendidikan Guru dan Tanaga Teknis, 1987).
24. Challis, *Shadow of a Revolution*, pp.201–5.
25. L. Blair with L. Blair, *Ring of Fire* (London: Bantam Press, 1988), pp.218–27.
26. Adams, *Interim Report*.
27. N.J. Moolenijzer and Sieswanpo, 'Physical Education in Indonesia', in W. Johnson (ed.), *PE Around the World* (Indianapolis, IN: Phi Epsilon Kappa Fraternity, 1971) pp.35–48.
28. Ibid., p.40.
29. N.J. Moolenijzer and Sieswanpo, 'Sport and Physical Education in Indonesia', in W. Johnson (ed.), *Sport and Physical Education Around the World* (Champaign, IL: Stipes, 1980), pp.314–38, 325.
30. I. Adams, *Final Report of the Element 'A' Technical Specialist in Physical Education in Physical Education, Second Indonesia-IBRD Teacher Training Project* (Jakarta: Direktorat Pendidikan Guru dan Tanaga Teknis, 1988), p.4.
31. M.B. Haslam, *Indonesia/SUNY Technical Assistance Program: Implementation and Completion Report* (Albany, NY: State University of New York at Albany, 1990).
32. Adams, *Interim Report*.
33. Ibid.
34. Ibid.
35. Haslam, *Indonesia/SUNY Technical Assistance Program*.
36. Adams, *Interim Report*.
37. *Jakarta Post*, 24 Oct. 1997.
38. Challis, *Shadow of a Revolution*, pp.134–8.
39. www.i2.co.id/travel/pancasila.asp.
40. L. Chalip, 'Policy Analysis in Sport Management', *Journal of Sport Management*, IX (1995), 1–13.
41. J. Coghlan, 'Towards More Equal Opportunities in Sport and Physical Education – Issues, Problems and Programmes in Developing Countries', in R. Chappell and J. Coghlan (eds), *Developing Countries and Sport for All: Some Thoughts on the Problems and Issues* (Uxbridge: Department of Sport Science, Brunel University, 1997).

12

Communist China: Sport, Politics and Diplomacy[1]

FAN HONG and XIONG XIAOZHENG

Politics and diplomacy are among the oldest of human activities.[2] Politics may be briefly defined as matters concerning the state or its government, or public affairs generally.[3] Diplomacy is the management of international relations.[4] Once people started to live together in groups, diversities in culture, religion, ideology, economy and social system resulted. Global diversity is thus a universal feature and political and diplomatic activities are two means of creating and accommodating conflict resulting from this diversity.[5] Both involve disagreements and the resolution of those disagreements. The essence of many political and diplomatic situations remain that of conflict and the resolution of conflict.[6] Military confrontation and summit conferences are, of course, two ways of solving conflicts. However, sport can also be a powerful means of achieving and perpetuating both confrontation and conflict resolution.

This is clearly demonstrated in the history of sport in Communist China since its birth in 1949. This chapter will examine the relationship between sport, politics and diplomacy in Communist China by means of some important landmark events: the joining and breaking with the International Olympic Committee (IOC) in the 1950s; the involvement with the GANEFO in the 1960s; and the 'ping-pong diplomacy' of the 1970s. The events clearly demonstrate that as long as conflict continues in the world, politics, diplomacy and sport will be inseparable.

THE JOINING AND BREAKING WITH THE IOC

The relationship between China and the IOC goes back to the year 1915 when the IOC invited China to attend the Olympic Games.[7] In 1921 Wang Cheng-ting (Wang Zhengting), Foreign Minister in the Chinese government, became a member of the IOC. In 1931 the IOC accepted the China National Amateur Athletic Federation (*Zhonghua quanguo yeyu tiyu xiejinhui*) as an official member of the IOC governing all Olympic activities in China.[8] Kung Xiang-xi (Kong Xiangxi), Minister of Finance in the Nationalist government, and Tung Shao-yi (Dong Shouyi), an influential physical educationist, became members of the IOC in 1939 and 1947 respectively. From 1928 to 1948 China sent delegations either to watch or participate in five successive Olympic Games.[9]

In 1949 the Communists won the Civil War and controlled all China except Taiwan, to which the Nationalist government had fled. The Nationalists remained there as the Republic of China. They took with them the China National Amateur Athletic Federation and two of three IOC members.

On the mainland the Communists established the People's Republic of China (PRC) and in 1950 established their own All-China Sports Federation (*Zhonghu quanguo tiyu zonghui*). The Communists claimed that only they represented all of China, and thus the All-China Sports Federation represented the whole of China in sports matters. However, both federations were affiliated with the corresponding international federations, which in turn sought recognition from the IOC.

On 28 February 1951 in Beijing, the Foreign Ministry informed the All-China Sports Federation that Finland would like to invite Chinese athletes to participate in the fifteenth Olympic Games in May 1952 in Helsinki.[10] Two months later, on 18 April, the Sports Federation responded to the Foreign Ministry. It said:

> It is good news that the Finnish government has invited Chinese athletes to participate in the Olympic Games. However, before the games we must set up an affiliated Olympic Committee in China, and we should join the world Olympic organization. At present the All-China Sports Federation is not fully aware of the principles, structures and activities of this world sport organization. We also do not know the attitude of the Soviet Union to this Olympic Games, so we would like to know more about the above-mentioned matters before we decide if we will go or not.[11]

No decision was taken during 1951.[12]

At the beginning of 1952 the ambassador of the Soviet Union in Beijing paid an official visit to the Sports Federation. He informed the

PRC that the Soviet Union was going to participate in the summer Olympics for the first time. He wanted to know if the PRC would go so that the Soviet Union would be able to construct a suitable policy towards the IOC.[13]

The early 1950s were the height of the cold war. In Europe the Berlin blockade failed, a separate West German state was formed, the city of Berlin was split into two sectors – East and West – and the NATO alliance was consolidated. In Asia the Chinese Communists had already achieved power and established the PRC with recognition from the Soviet Union. The Nationalists had set up a government in exile in Taiwan with recognition from the United States and the United Nations. The Korean War broke out, with the Chinese and Soviets on one side and the Americans and the United Nations on the other. The world had been broadly split into two camps, the capitalists and the Communists. The Soviet ambassador's visit clearly conveyed the message that participation in the Olympic Games was not a sporting issue but a political matter. It was another manifestation of the cold war.[14] Feng Wenbin, the president of the All-China Sports Federation, reported to Prime Minister Zhou Enlai on 2 February. He proposed that the PRC should join the IOC in the form of the All-China Sports Federation and participate in the Olympics with the Soviet Union. Three days later the Prime Minister approved his proposal.[15] Feng sent a letter to the deputy-mayor of Helsinki and the secretariat of the IOC. It read:

> The All-China Sports Federation, in accordance with the history of the Chinese participation in the Olympic Games in the past, has decided to join the IOC and will send athletes to participate in the Helsinki Olympic Games. The All-China Sport Federation is the only sports organization which represents the PRC. No other organizations do, including Chinese Taiwan. Thus Taiwan cannot be allowed to attend the IOC sessions or the Olympic Games. We know that the IOC session will be held in Oslo on 15 February, and our representatives will be there.[16]

On 15 February 1952 Sheng Zhibai, secretary of the PRC embassy to Sweden represented Communist China at the IOC session. He emphasized that Taiwan could not represent China at the meeting.[17] It was reported that he spoke 'politics rather than sport' and irritated all the delegates. As a result nothing came of his visit.[18] The Nationalist government in Taiwan also had representatives at the meeting. They insisted that the sports body, which was recognized in 1931 by the IOC, still existed in Taiwan and that it was the formally approved representative of China.

The IOC now faced an acute political problem: who should represent China, the Nationalists or the Communists? There was no simple answer. Sigfrid Edstrom, the president of the IOC, and Avery Brundage, the vice-president, recognized that China's participation had become a very difficult political matter.[19] The Soviets came to the rescue. The Soviet Olympic Committee advised Communist China that it was better to change the All-China Sports Federation into a Chinese Olympic Committee and to apply for membership first, then attend the Olympic Games. Prime Minister Zhou responded to the suggestion on 23 March. He informed the All-China Sports Federation that:

> 1. The most important point is that we can only join the IOC and have an official relationship with it when Taiwan is dismissed and rejected by the IOC. 2. We cannot change the official name of the All-China Sports Federation, but we can give this organization a new name, the Chinese Olympic Committee, for the purpose of communication with the IOC.[20]

In May, Rong Gaotang, the vice-chairman of the Sports Federation, sent a letter to the Hungarian ambassador to China who wanted to know if the PRC would take part in the fifteenth Olympic Games. Rong stated:

> We sent a telegram to the IOC on 5 February, which pointed out that China has changed to the People's Republic and that the former China National Amateur Athletic Federation has become the All-China Sport Federation. Therefore, the All-China Sports Federation is the only legal representative of China in the IOC and other international sports organizations. Sports organizations from Taiwan cannot represent China. The IOC should expel the Taiwan members. We have decided to continue our membership of the IOC and will take part in the fifteenth Olympic Games. We have also sent telegrams to the international federations for athletics, football, swimming, cycling and basketball. To date we have received responses from the international federations for swimming, football and athletics. The International Federation of Swimming has agreed to recognize the All-China Sports Federation, but the international federations of football and athletics would like to

consider the matter for a while. Now the matter of whether China will participate in the Olympic Games depends on the IOC.[21]

Under pressure from both the Nationalists and the Communists, on 11 June Edstrom, the IOC president, told Taiwan not to attend the fifteenth Helsinki Olympic Games. A few days later, on 16 June, the IOC also informed the All-China Sports Federation that 'Because of the confused situation in China, no athletes from the PRC are allowed to participate in the Olympic Games until the situation is cleared up'.[22]

The 'two Chinas' issue was discussed at the forty-seventh IOC session in Lausanne. Beijing and Taiwan were both invited. The IOC suggested that both sides should be invited to the games. However, Beijing and Taiwan responded to the congress with equally inflexible attitudes: Beijing would not go to the games unless Taiwan was expelled,[23] and Taiwan 'could not compete with Communist bandits on the same sports field'.[24] Taiwan immediately withdrew from the Games in protest.

The Helsinki Olympic Games started on 19 July, but Beijing received an official invitation only on the previous day. One week later, on 25 July, a delegation consisting of 40 members from Communist China appeared in Helsinki. On 29 July the five-red-stars flag of the People's Republic was raised at the Olympic village. Although the PRC had missed most of the competitions, Prime Minister Zhou stated that it was a great victory simply to raise the national flag at the Olympic Games, whether the PRC could compete in the events or not.[25] It meant that the Communist China had won an important political battle.

However, the battle did not end with Helsinki. At the 1953 Mexico City session, in view of the lack of information on the athletics situation in China, the IOC, in frustration, asked its Soviet members to check on the PRC and to report back at the Athens session in May 1954. This was done and a favourable report was produced. It stated that the PRC Olympic Committee conformed to all IOC rules. There were no Nationalist Chinese IOC members at the session to rebut the report, although before the session Brundage had privately urged that the exiled members, Wang and Kung, attend. Only the President of the Taiwan Olympic Committee was present, and his report was regarded by the IOC as politically biased because he was not an IOC member.[26]

The IOC finally chose to recognize both committees by a vote of 23 to 21.[27] In this way they followed the political fashion of the day. Their ruling, for all intents and purposes, recognized two separate states: Beijing-China and Taiwan-China. To that extent they did not compromise their rules, for the rules stated that there could be only one committee per country. By recognizing two committees they recognized two countries. The IOC, although its principles were allegedly apolitical, plunged right into the heart of politics. However, the IOC had no other choice. In its view, it could no longer exclude a nation of 600 million people in Communist China, while it would be unfair to exclude 8 million people in Taiwan. The best solution was to recognize both, as the world did elsewhere in the cases of West and East Germany and South and North Korea.[28] The IOC hoped that the situation between Beijing and Taiwan would settle down. It was a vain hope.

Taiwan immediately denounced the arrangement. The president of the Taiwan Olympic Committee complained to Brundage that it was an unfair decision. Brundage replied:

> Don't forget that according to the Olympic charter the Olympic Games assemble amateurs of all nations, no discrimination being allowed on ground of color, religion or politics. When the Red Chinese made an application and agreed to respect the Olympic rules, it was difficult to exclude them. Don't forget, also, that if Dr Wang and Dr Kung [IOC members from Nationalist China] had been in attendance as I had urged, the score would have been different.[29]

Beijing also refused to accept the IOC solution. In June 1955, at the IOC session in Paris, Beijing pointed out that it was against the Olympic Charter and illegal to incorporate Taiwan, a regional sport organization, into the IOC, and requested that Taiwan's membership should be annulled. Brundage, who had become president of the IOC in 1952, rejected the request of Beijing and argued: 'Sport has nothing to do with politics.'[30] In IOC eyes, the PRC always exploited political issues rather than involve itself in apolitical sport. Brundage later recalled that he 'had not yet met a sportsman from Red China with whom I could discuss athletic matters, but only diplomatic representatives'.[31]

With the sixteenth Olympic Games approaching, Beijing sent an open invitation on 1 September 1956 to athletes from Taiwan, Hong Kong and Macao to attend the qualifying competitions in mainland China. The mainland would guarantee their safety and cover all their expenses.[32] Taiwan sent a protest to the IOC claiming that 'Beijing is

Communist China: Sport, Politics and Diplomacy 325

playing politics.'[33] The IOC informed the PRC: 'The IOC would like to know your opinion on this matter since this protest will be discussed at the IOC Melbourne session.'[34]

In response to the request, on 22 October Rong Gaotang, now the vice-president and general secretary of the Chinese Olympic Committee, held a press conference in Beijing. He stressed:

> Taiwan is a province of China. Taiwan sports organizations should be under the leadership of the Chinese Olympic Committee. Item 24 of the Olympic Charter rules that within one country, there is only one Olympic Committee that organizes activities according to the Olympic Charter and the Olympic Ideal. The IOC should not accept the protest from Taiwan.[35]

The PRC also sent a protest to the IOC stating that if Taiwan went to the Games Communist China would withdraw.

The IOC ignored both protests as pure politics.[36] 'Beijing-China' and 'Taiwan-China' were both used in the documents of the organizing committee of the games. The national flags of Beijing and Taiwan both flew in the streets of Melbourne. On 29 October, as the Taiwan Chinese delegation arrived in the city, the PRC flag was accidentally raised. The Taiwan Chinese dragged the flag down to the cheers of the crowd that had gathered.[37] After this incident, on 6 November, the Chinese Olympic Committee officially declared that the PRC would not participate in the 1956 games despite the fact that the qualifying events for it had taken place on 7 October.[38] More than 1,400 athletes from 27 provinces, cities and autonomous regions had attended the preparatory athletics, swimming, weightlifting, basketball, football, gymnastics and shooting competitions; 92 athletes had been selected for the PRC delegation and were waiting to go to the Olympics.

From 1957 to 1958 there were still some written exchanges between Brundage and Tung Shao-yi, the IOC member who remained on the mainland after 1949. There was every reason to believe that Beijing still intended to participate in the 1960 games if the Taiwan issue was resolved. However, the IOC did not have any intention of expelling the Taiwan committee from the Olympic movement. Brundage tried to reason with Beijing: it was better for two committees to coexist, he argued, and he repeated that political issues were not the province of the IOC. However, his observation complicated rather than simplified the issue. On 8 January 1958 he sent a letter to Tung: 'There is an independent government ... Taiwan, [which] had been part of Japan, not of China, local Taiwanese are neither Chinese nor Japanese.'[39] Tung, who under instructions from the mainland Chinese government constantly raised political issues at IOC meetings and in correspondence with it, used this opportunity to teach Brundage some basic historical facts:

> Taiwan has always been part of China from ancient times; this is a historical fact that no one can change. Although Taiwan had been occupied by Japan between 1895 and 1945, it was returned to China after World War Two according to the Declaration of Cairo and Bocitan Bulletin. ... Among the eight million Taiwan population, more than 90 per cent are migrants from the mainland. Their migration was begun several hundreds years earlier than your ancestors to America.[40]

Tung stated that it was Brundage who had introduced politics into the matter by his continued insistence on two committees. Finally, in a letter dated 19 August 1958, Tung accused Brundage of being a 'faithful menial of US imperialists. ... A man like you ... has no qualifications whatsoever to be IOC President. ... I will no longer cooperate with you or have any connection with the IOC while it is under your domination.'[41] With this brutal statement the PRC withdrew from membership of the IOC.

The IOC might have had its own reasons to compromise on the situation by acknowledging two committees. However, the Communists had fought hard to win the Civil War and to become the master of their own house. They wanted to be recognized by the world. Sport was one of the best stages on which they could display their new identity. Beijing decided to tell the world who was master of China. In 1958 Beijing announced that the PRC would refuse to cooperate with any organization or personnel that recognized 'two Chinas'. PRC sports associations therefore withdrew from eight international sports federations, including football, athletics, weightlifting, swimming, basketball, shooting, cycling, wrestling and the Asian Table Tennis Federation.[42] Marshal He Long, the Sports Minister, stated confidently:

> We must stick to our principles and stances. We also cannot do anything harmful to the interests of the country. China is a great Communist country, I believe there will be a day when they will

invite us back to the international sports family. China has one-fourth of the world population, and no one can ignore it.[43]

However, Communist China had to pay a high price for its political action. It was excluded from most sports organizations. Athletes now mainly competed with East European countries. The situation got worse when the PRC split with the Soviet Union in the early 1960s and the exchanges between the PRC and East Europeans stopped. Communist China now felt totally isolated, politically, economically and culturally, from both the capitalist and Communist worlds. It desperately tried to seek new friends among the countries of the Third World. The opportunity came in 1962 during the Asian Games.

GANEFO I AND THE ASIAN GANEFO

The Asian Games started in 1951 under the leadership of the Asian Games Federation, which was recognized by the IOC. The games took place every four years. Taiwan was a member of the federation and participated in the Asian Games three times between 1951 and 1958. The PRC was excluded. The situation changed at the fourth Asian Games in Jakarta, Indonesia, in the summer of 1962, when President Sukarno of Indonesia looked on the games as a means to strengthen his own position among the newly emerging forces of Asia, Africa and Latin America that were 'struggling against capitalism and trying to create a new world order'.[44] Communist China was a useful ally in this endeavour. It was welcome at the Jakarta games, and the PRC used this opportunity to attempt to establish its position as a leader of the 'newly emerging forces' of the world.

On 1 March 1962 the Jakarta organizing committee sent an invitation to Taiwan. At the end of April Ho Geng-sheng (Hao Gengsheng), the representative of Taiwan and a board member of the Asian Games Federation, went to Jakarta to attend the preparation meeting. This attracted the attention of the PRC since Indonesia and China had diplomatic relations. On 31 May the embassy of the PRC in Indonesia sent a memo to the Indonesian government. It pointed out:

> The Chinese government sincerely wishes that the Asian Games held by Indonesia will be a great success. But Chinese government cannot ignore those imperialists and their followers who wanted to use the Asian Games to create 'two Chinas'. These activities will

not only harm the friendship between the PRC and Indonesia, but also harm the stand of Indonesia's fight with imperialism.[45]

In the light of the reaction of the PRC and some Arab countries, Indonesia decided not to allow Taiwan or Israel to attend the games and refused to issue visas to athletes from these two countries.[46] The IOC and the international federations of weightlifting and athletics regarded this as a political action. They claimed that the games would face the sanction of not being recognized.[47] The Indonesian government discussed this with Beijing and prepared three options: to offer delayed visas to Taiwan and Israeli athletes so as to hinder their participation; to hold a successful fourth Asian Games to impress the IOC and international sport federations so that they would recognize the games; to create a new games called the Games of the Newly Emerging Forces (GANEFO), based on the support of the PRC and other Asian, African and Latin American countries, if the IOC still would not recognize the games.[48] On 24 August 1962 the Foreign Minister of Indonesia formally announced that it would eject Taiwan and Israel from the fourth games. The IOC and the international federations immediately stated that they would not recognize the fourth Games, as they could not tolerate a sports movement whose aim was political.

After the Asian Games the IOC held an executive board meeting on the evening of 7 February 1963. It decided that the IOC would suspend the membership of the Indonesian Olympic Committee for an indeterminate period of time for not having protested against its government's discriminatory action against Taiwan and Israel.[49] The IOC stated: 'The IOC and the IFs [international federations] are completely opposed to any interference in sport on political, racial or religious grounds, and particularly any which prevents the unhindered passage of competitors and officials between their member countries.'[50]

Two days later, on 9 February, the Indonesian Sports Ministry responded:

> The exclusion of Indonesia from the Olympic Games will not harm Indonesia. On the contrary, Indonesia will now have the freedom to organize a new games without the participation of imperialists and colonists. The new games is GANEFO – the Games of the Newly Emerging Forces – Asia, Africa, Latin America and the socialist countries.[51]

The Sports Ministry also pointed out: 'It is the time that the new emerging countries should have a revolution to destroy the spirit and structure of the international sports movement which is controlled by the imperialists and colonialists.'[52] On 13 February Sukarno, the president of Indonesia, announced that Indonesia would withdraw from the IOC. It would hold a new world games: GANEFO. The announcement put the future of the IOC and the international sports federations in jeopardy. It was a direct challenge to the Olympic movement.[53]

From the beginning the PRC showed great interest in GANEFO. The government gathered experts from the foreign and sports ministries to analyse the feasibility of organizing the new games. After careful study, those experts indicated that since the Second World War, the colonial and semi-colonial countries of Asia, Africa and Latin America had become independent, but imperialist countries, which dominated the IOC, still denied their rights in international sports affairs. The new games, therefore, would attract those newly independent countries. At the same time the new games could provide a unique stage for the PRC to demonstrate its power over and influence on those countries. The PRC decided to give GANEFO its full support and the announcement was made on 2 September 1962.[54]

On 22 November a Chinese sporting delegation visited Indonesia and exchanged views on the new games. The PRC agreed to use its influence to persuade some Asian and African countries to join the games. A special research department was set up to advise Indonesia about GANEFO.[55] In April 1963 Liu Shaoqi, the Chairman of the PRC, visited Indonesia. He signed a joint declaration stating that: 'The Chinese government strongly supports President Sukarno's GANEFO proposal, and will make its best contribution to the games.'[56] It was reported that the PRC had agreed to give the Indonesians an US$18 million gift for the games and to pay the transportation costs of all the delegations at GANEFO.[57]

At the same time a preparatory conference for GANEFO was held in Jakarta. The PRC, Cambodia, Guinea, Indonesia, Iraq, Mali, Pakistan, North Vietnam, the United Arab Republic and the Soviet Union were present; Ceylon and Yugoslavia sent observers. The aim of GANEFO was agreed: GANEFO was to be 'based on the spirit of the 1955 Bandung Conference and the Olympic ideals, and was to promote the development of sport in new emerging nations and to cement friendly relations among them'.[58]

The games were political games. Sukarno strongly denounced the IOC's attitude towards politics and sport. He argued: ' Let us declare frankly that sport has something to do with politics. And Indonesia now proposes to mix sport with politics.'[59] Sukarno stated that in Indonesia sport was used to further the country's political aims, namely, world friendship and peace. For Sukarno and the PRC, the Olympic Games were but a tool of the old-established forces that engaged in discriminatory actions against Asian, African and Latin American nations. Now these discriminated nations were going to use GANEFO as a tool to oppose the old-established forces.[60] The PRC stated in October 1962 that GANEFO would help develop sport in Asia and Africa and combat the 'forces of imperialism and sports organizations manipulated by imperialist countries'.[61]

With the joint effort of some Asian, African and Latin American countries, in November 1963 the first GANEFO took place in Jakarta. More than 2,200 athletes and officials from 48 countries and regions, including France, Italy, the Netherlands, Belgium, Finland and the Soviet Union, attended the games. Most of the participating states did not send official teams for fear of being barred from the Olympic Games. In general only athletes of less than Olympic calibre were sent. The PRC sent a delegation of 238 athletes, coaches and officials, won 66 gold medals, 56 silver and 46 bronze and broke two world records.[62] For the first time since the isolation from the Olympic Games and international competitions since the late 1950s, athletes from Communist China had an opportunity to show the world their talents.

After the games, a GANEFO Congress was held in Jakarta. A council consisting of 36 member countries was established during the congress, which proposed that GANEFO continental committees should be set up in Asia, Africa, Europe, America and Australasia, and the 36 member countries should have their own national GANEFO committees.[63]

GANEFO was a clear attempt to compete with the Olympic Games. More importantly, according to its stated purpose, GANEFO was to unite the new emerging forces and to emphasize their presence on the world scene. The PRC was behind the success of GANEFO. Its political, financial and organizational support made the games happen. In return, GANEFO provided a stage for Chinese athletes to show off their talents and for the Communists to reveal the new image of China.

GANEFO II was scheduled to take place in Cairo in 1967, with Beijing as an alternative site. However, this was not enough for Beijing.

Communist China: Sport, Politics and Diplomacy

The PRC had ensured the success of the GANEFO and grasped the opportunity to expand its influence through sport in Asia. In September 1965 the second session of the council of GANEFO was held in Beijing, with 39 delegations present.[64] A GANEFO Asian Committee was formed. Beijing played a major role in its formation and a Chinese became the chairman of the executive committee of the GANEFO Asian Committee. A proposal for an Asian GANEFO was approved and it was to take place in Cambodia in 1966. It was designed as an alternative games and was strategically timed to take place at the same time as the Olympic-sanctioned Asian Games in 1962.

The Asian GANEFO was underwritten in large measure by the PRC. In addition to financial support, the Chinese helped to build a sports stadium with 50,000 seats as well as other facilities, and to train 300 referees for the games in five months. The games took place from 25 November to 6 December 1966 – virtually simultaneously with the fifth Asian Games taking place in Bangkok, where the PRC was excluded and Taiwan included. The Asian GANEFO was a great success. There were 17 countries and regions and more than 2,000 athletes participating. Chinese athletes competed in 18 sports events and won 113 gold medals, 59 silver and 36 bronze, breaking two world records.[65] The PRC established itself as a sporting superpower as well as the leader of the 'new emerging forces' in Asia.

The existence of the GANEFO had posed a real threat to the IOC, especially in the Third World. Brundage, the President of the IOC, voiced this fear in a letter to the Marquess of Exeter, the President of the International Amateur Athletic Federation, the most important and influential international federation, with regard to the 'Africa Games' proposed by some African countries. He wrote:

> If we want to hold the Olympic world together we must not let these 37 countries be led into the GANEFO camp, which may easily happen. Peking, China is very active now in Africa, and Congo Brazzaville has recently received from it a $20,000,000 loan. The Egyptians are organizing the second GANEFO Games in Cairo in 1967 ... the Indonesian Embassy in Switzerland is inviting the National Federations and the Swiss NOC [National Olympic Committee] to the reception on the anniversary of the First GANEFO Games. This is probably also taking place in other places. The Arab countries and a few others are sympathetic. ...

We ... will probably drive them all into the receptive arms of the GANEFO crowd if we are not most careful.[66]

The GANEFO movement intended to divide and fragment the Olympic movement, to emphasize the political realities of the new world structure, and to dramatize the political ambitions of the new and non-aligned states. At the same time, GANEFO was a product of East-West estrangement as it existed in the early 1960s. By the time of GANEFO, the Sino-Soviet split had taken place, halving the Communist camp and creating three power blocs – the United States and Western Europe, the Soviet Union and Eastern Europe, and the PRC – each striving for the support of the non-aligned emerging states. The Soviet Union provided some financial support[67] and participated in GANEFO but not enough to jeopardize its stature in the Olympic movement. The PRC was GANEFO's main supporter.

GANEFO played a major part in establishing the status of Communist China in the world through sport. Before 1960 Constantin Andrianov, the Soviet IOC member, had consistently referred to the Chinese question in order to pressure the IOC to expel Taiwan, but after the PRC split with Soviet Union during the 1960s he was conspicuously silent over Chinese involvement. Chinese Communists now had to fight their own battles. GANEFO certainly provided the best stage for the PRC to project its image, to extend its influence and enable it to compete with the other two power blocs: the Soviet Union and East Europe, and the United States and the West Europe. The PRC established its leadership in the Third World through GANEFO. However, GANEFO was approaching the end of its existence. Egypt announced it could not hold GANEFO II in 1966 for financial reasons. The PRC was entering the turmoil of the Cultural Revolution and had no intention of supporting the Egyptian initiative. GANEFO died quietly. It was not until the early 1970s, when Communist China wanted to escape its isolation from the international community, that competitive sport was brought back to the political centre stage and served as a means of diplomatic communication. 'Ping-pong diplomacy' was the strategy used to open up new diplomatic channels between East and West.

THE ERA OF PING-PONG DIPLOMACY

The Great Proletarian Cultural Revolution started in 1966 and ended with the death of Chairman Mao Zedong in 1976. It was one of the greatest political and social upheavals in modern history. The goal of the Cultural Revolution was to re-establish the ideological purity of Communism threatened by revisionists and capitalists over the previous 18 years, and to recreate unpolluted Mao Zedong thought.[68] It was believed that by using mass political action and revolutionary ideology, the Maoists could achieve their revolutionary goal *and* further socio-economic development. In fact, the outcome was a chaotic and violent political upheaval, accompanied by ferocious ideological debate, that engulfed the whole country.

He Long, the Sports Minister, was criticized and jailed. He died in prison in 1975. More than 1,000 administrators and coaches from the Sports Ministry were sent to the countryside to do physical labour. The training system broke down. Sports schools closed. Sports competitions vanished. Chinese teams stopped touring abroad. The table tennis team that won 15 medals at the 1965 world championships disappeared and missed the 1967 and 1969 championships. The Chinese delegation that was preparing for GANEFO II in Cairo was disbanded without any explanation.

The situation changed due to the urgent need to establish better Sino-American relations. The frontier clash with Soviet troops on Zhenbao (Damansky) Island in the Ussuri River in March 1969 aroused concern in Beijing that Moscow was going to escalate what had hitherto been a series of minor confrontations. There were subsequently a series of clashes on the north-western frontier, a particularly serious one occurring in Xinjiang in August. Rumours began to emanate from Eastern European sources that the Soviet Union was sounding out its allies about a 'surgical strike' against Chinese nuclear weapons installations.[69]

The question for the PRC leadership was how to achieve national security in these new circumstances. The lesson learned by Mao and Premier Zhou from the clash of 1969 was that the armed forces probably would be incapable of defending the PRC effectively if the Soviet Union were to launch a major attack. Good relations with Washington, however, could undermine the calculations of the Soviet leadership as to the impunity with which they could attack the PRC.[70] By 1970 the idea of reopening some avenues of contact with the United States was in Mao's mind.[71]

In January 1970, at the Warsaw Pact, the PRC broke away from the routine patter of angry exchanges over the status of Taiwan and mentioned the possibility of having future talks 'at a higher level through other channels acceptable to both sides'. Coincidentally an American statement at the same meeting suggested that the United States might 'be prepared to consider sending a representative to Peking for direct discussions with your officials'.[72] On 1 December, Chinese National Day, Chairman Mao invited Edgar Snow, an American journalist and author of *Red Star Over China* (1938), to stand beside him on the reviewing platform at celebrations in Beijing of the twenty-first anniversary of the founding of the PRC. Unfortunately no one in the US government realized that this was a signal for rapprochement.[73]

The Chinese had to find another channel. The opportunity arrived at the thirty-first World Table Tennis Championships held in Japan from 25 January to 3 February 1971. The chairman of the Japanese Table Tennis Association, the organizer of the championships, came to Beijing and invited the PRC to attend.[74] Premier Zhou asked Mao for instructions. Mao responded: 'Our team should go, even if there is danger of death. ... However, our athletes should not be afraid of death and hardship.'[75] He set out the principles of participation for the Chinese team: friendship first, competition second.[76]

The Chinese team went and acted on the following instructions: 'If you meet the US team do not initiate communication, but do not refuse to communicate. If you compete with the US team, do not exchange flags, but shake hands instead.'[77] During the meeting American and Chinese players became friends. When the Americans knew that the Chinese had invited delegations from Britain, Australia, Canada, Colombia and Nigeria to visit China after the championships, the chairman of the American Table Tennis Association asked whether they could visit China too. Mao agreed.[78] The gesture was overt and clear. The opportunity was too good to let go. Within days, the era of 'ping-pong diplomacy' was declared to be at hand. On 14 April 1971 the US table tennis players were received by Premier Zhou Enlai at the People's Hall, Beijing. He said: 'You have opened a new chapter in the relations of the American and Chinese people. I am confident that this new beginning of our friendship will certainly meet with majority support of our two peoples. We welcome you.'[79] The Americans immediately invited the Chinese team to the United States. Without hesitation this time Zhou gave a positive response.[80]

Thus the diplomatic door was opened unexpectedly by table tennis. On 11 July 1971 Henry Kissinger, President Nixon's national security adviser, travelled to Beijing to meet with Zhou and plan the details of a visit by Nixon. On 15 July the public announcement of a presidential visit was made on radio and television by Nixon himself in California.[81] On 25 October the PRC took up China's seat at the United Nations.[82] On 21 February 1972 President Nixon and Chairman Mao met in Beijing.[83] Seven days later a 'joint communiqué' was issued in Shanghai. This document marked a major policy shift for both countries. The *People's Daily* proudly announced that China had now come back to the international family.[84] Nixon commented that the agreement of 1972 had built a bridge across 16,000 miles and 22 years of hostility and had changed the world.[85] Sport had played a significant role in bringing the two nations together and provided the opportunity for Communist China's global realignment. The moment marked a turning point in foreign relations of the PRC.[86] Wu Shaozu, Sports Minister from 1989 to 2000, wrote: 'The Chinese have learned from ping-pong diplomacy that sport and politics are inseparable. ... Athletes have shouldered heavy responsibilities. They are our political ambassadors.'[87]

'Ping-pong diplomacy' changed not only the status of the nation but also the fate of the cadres of the Sports Ministry. After the victory of 'ping-pong diplomacy' sport became increasingly important, since it could help effectively to break down international barriers and to establish and promote international contacts between different political systems. The Communist Party decided to restore the Sports Ministry in August 1971. Mao decided to appoint Wang Meng, a political commissar of the Beijing military region of the People's Liberation Army, as Sports Minister, and two other senior army officers as deputy ministers.[88] The whole country was still in chaos and only the Sports Ministry started to recover. The cadres were released from the countryside and came back to Beijing.[89] In May the Sports Ministry held a work conference to promote athletics training programmes and restore the training system of spare-time sports schools.[90] In 1973 the Ministry held a national conference to promote sport nationwide.[91] By the end of 1974 1,459 sports schools had been reopened. Provincial and national teams started training schedules for national and international competitions. Sports competitions took place frequently in every county, region and province. At the national level, a five events competition (basketball, volleyball, football, table tennis, badminton) took place in 1972; 19 national competitions, including the first National Student Sports Meeting took place in 1973, when more than 20,000 athletes took part and 70 athletes broke 40 national records; the third sports meeting of the People's Liberation Army and the third National Games took place in 1975, when three world records were broken.[92]

The new era required a new slogan. Thus the slogan 'Friendship first, competition second' was born. It characterized Chinese sport for over ten years. It clearly showed the inseparable relationship between sport, politics and diplomacy in China. What was the essence of the slogan? The Sports Ministry explained in 1972: 'Friendship means politics. Friendship first means politics first. We use competition to project our socialist country's new image, and to make and win friends in the world.'[93] An editorial in *Xin tiyu* [New Sport] in 1973 claimed:

> Friendship first means to put politics in command of competition. Competition only serves the purpose of politics. For our socialist China, sport is a channel to make friends. The result of competition is not important. The important thing is to win friends.[94]

In short, competition must serve the purpose of politics.[95]

Sport in specific conditions is an important political instrument. Politics can confront and replace, on occasion, sporting outcomes, such as nationalism, individualism and aggression. The promotion of sporting fraternalism is a case in point. Its purpose was twofold. First, the concept of friendship in national sport required self-control and self-discipline in the interests of political ambitions. Self-expression, self-promotion, aggression and individualism in sport were suppressed by Mao's proletarian political correctness. In fact the sports field was the place to learn collective ideals and public order. Second, sporting fraternalism played a central role in conducting inter-state relations in terms of the metaphor of friends and foes. The idea of friendship in international politics represented a seemingly sentimental pragmatism concealing calculated national interest. What is national interest? Kenneth Minogue once explained: 'It is whatever a state judges necessary to its security. ... A national interest is limited by reality.'[96] When the PRC was isolated by the Western capitalists and also faced a vast hostile military power in the Soviet Union, it stood alone. It needed to win support from socialist states and developing states in Africa, Asia and Latin America. Kenneth Minogue further stated that 'sometimes the national interest requires the dignity of a theory to sustain it'[97] – 'Friendship first, competition second' became the theory. It reflected diplomatic and strategic considerations. Ironically, sport, being evidently 'apolitical', was seen as one of the most suitable vehicles for political diplomacy. It helped to open Communist China's door to the Western world for the first time after 22 years' isolation. To some extent it laid the foundation for the 1980s' open-door policy of catching up economically with the Western capitalist world.

Sport now played a very important role in winning friends in the world. At the 1971 World Table Tennis Championships in Japan, when the PRC team failed to allow the North Korea team victory in a match, Cao Chen, who was the head of the Management Group which was in charge of sport from 1969 to 1971, was sacked.[98] In November 1971, when Beijing held the first Asia and Africa Table Tennis Friendship Competition, the athletes were instructed to lose some games to North Korea so that the Koreans could achieve second place.[99] Such incidents happened in most international games. Chinese athletes were always instructed to lose to some socialist country or other in order to strengthen political friendships. Meanwhile the PRC spent huge sums to build sports stadiums in some Third World countries including Morocco, Tanzania and Pakistan. Juan Antonio Samaranch once said: 'The best sports stadia built by the Chinese are not in China, but in Africa.'[100]

On the international stage, the PRC re-occupied its seat on the Asian Olympic Sports Committee in November 1973. Thus Communist China sent a delegation with 269 athletes to attend the seventh Asian Games in Iran in 1974.[101] From 1971 to 1976, the PRC attended 54 international competitions.[102] It also hosted the Asian Table Tennis Championships in 1972, the Asian, African and Latin American Table Tennis Invitational Tournament in 1973, the Beijing International Swimming and Diving Invitational Tournament in 1975, the Beijing International Women's Basketball Invitational Tournament and Shanghai International Table Tennis Invitational Tournament in 1976.[103]

In January 1973 Zhong Liang, editor of *Xin tiyu*, reported the achievements of 1972. He stated: 'Led by Chairman Mao's proletarian diplomatic line our international sports activities developed rapidly. In

1972 we established friendships with 79 countries through sports.'[104] In October 1974, Hong Liu, editor of *Xin tiyu*, claimed that

> through more than 300 sports activities ... we strengthened our revolutionary relationship with some socialist countries and developed new friendships with more than 100 countries. We ... had one victor: the friendship of the Third World, and one loser: imperialism and colonialism.[105]

Sport during this period clearly had political characteristics: initially as a vehicle for nation-building within the PRC. After the clash with the Soviets at the border area militant ethnic nationalism became a dominant force. 'Be prepared against war, be prepared against natural disasters, do everything for the people' and 'An entire nation in arms' and '800 million peasants are 800 million athletes and soldiers'[106] became prominent slogans. Since sport had the unique functions of promoting nationalism and training potential soldiers, the government was only too eager to demonstrate its commitment to sport. Sport was also a diplomatic means of communicating with the outside world when other formal channels failed. It helped to pave the way and to lay down stepping-stones for the 'opening-up' policy and successful economic reform, which brought Communist China fully into the international family.

CONCLUSION

Sport has proved extremely valuable as a political and diplomatic resource. As such, sport has enabled the Chinese Communists both to oppose Western imperialists and to make approaches to the same Western imperialists through a medium that benefited from its apolitical image. Sport has also been used to strengthen relations between socialist allies. In the recent past the slogan 'Friendship first competition second' served a serious diplomatic purpose. Furthermore, sport deserves credit for helping the PRC reconstruct and transform both its internal and external image for the better. Sport has thus assisted the implementation of both political and diplomatic goals. Sport in Communist China has always been, therefore, a political tool. It grew out of its infancy and reached its maturity through the 1950s' 'two Chinas' struggle, the GANEFO initiative of the 1960s and the 'ping-pong diplomacy' of the 1970s. Unquestionably, then, sport emerged as a means of implementing political and diplomatic policies in post-Mao China in the 1980s and 1990s.

Communist China: Sport, Politics and Diplomacy

NOTES

We wish to thank Tsai Chung-Tzu for her assistance with the endnotes, Professor J.A. Mangan for his helpful advice and Craig Gill for his proofreading.

1. This essay employs the Pinyin system, which is used in the PRC, for the translation of Chinese names, except some references that are originally written in Wade-Giles romanization system, which was used in Nationalist China before 1949 and still is in Taiwan.
2. Allen R. Ball and B. Guy Peters, *Modern Politics and Government* (London: Macmillan, 2000), p.1.
3. *Oxford English Reference Dictionary* (Oxford: Oxford University Press, 1996), p.1121.
4. Ibid., p.407.
5. Ball and Peters, *Modern Politics and Government*, p.31.
6. Ibid., p.28.
7. Fan Hong, 'The Olympic Movement in China: Ideals, Realities and Ambitions', *Culture, Sport, Society*, 1 (1998), 151.
8. Guan Wenmin *et al.* (eds), *Tiyu shi* [Sports History] (Beijing: Beijing gaoden jiaoyu chubanshe, 1996), p.145; Chinese Society for History of Physical Education and Sport (CSHPES) (ed.), *Zhongguo jindai tiyu shi* [Modern Chinese Sports History] (Beijing: Beijing tiyu xueyuan chubanshe, 1989), p.163.
9. Guan Wenmin, *Tiyu shi*, p.145.
10. 'Ganyu canjia dishewujie aulinpike yundonghui wanlai wenjian' [The Document about Participation in the Fifteenth Olympics], in Guojia tiyu zhongju danganguan [National Sports Bureau Archives], 68 (1952). The National Sports Bureau Archives are in A3 Anding Road, Beijing, China. Page numbers are not available in the documents from the National Sports Bureau Archives).
11. Ibid.
12. Ibid.
13. Ibid., 69 (1952).
14. Ibid.
15. Ibid.
16. 'Zhonghua quanguo tiyu zhonghui gei Herxinji fushizhang Foluankai xiansheng ho guoji auweihuei mishuchu de dianbao' [Telegram to Deputy Mayor of Helsinki and the Secretariat of the IOC], Guojia tiyu zhongju danganguan [National Sports Bureau Archives], 69 (1952).
17. Ibid., 70 (1952).
18. Otto Mayer, *A Travers les anneaux Olympiques* (Geneva: Pierre Cailler, 1960), p.208; see also R. Espy, *The Politics of the Olympic Games* (Berkeley, CA and London: University of California Press, 1979), p.36.
19. Circular, Edström to the members of Executive Commission, 10 June 1952, and letter, Brundage to Edström, 16 June 1952, Brundage Papers, Brundage Archive, University of Illinois, Box 43; Espy, *The Politics of the Olympic Games*, p.37.
20. 'Zhonghua quanguo tiyu zhonghui gei Herxinji' [Telegraph to Deputy Mayor of Helsinki], National Sports Bureau Archives, 70 (1952).
21. National Sports Bureau Archives, 59 (1952).
22. Ibid., 70 (1952).
23. Ibid.
24. Ibid.
25. Hao Keqiang, 'Zhongguo yundongyuan canjia di shiwu jie Aoyunhui de jinguo' [Chinese Athletes at the Fifteenth Olympic Games: A Recollection], *Tiyu wenshi* [Journal of Sports History and Culture], 1 (1984), 17.
26. *The New York Times*, 11 May 1954; Espy, *The Politics of the Olympic Games*, p.45.
27. 'Yiqiuwusinian guoji tiyu huodong de gongzhuo zhongjie' [Review of Work in 1954], National Sports Bureau Archives, 33 (1954).
28. Espy, *The Politics of the Olympic Games*, pp.42–3, 66–7, 82–3.
29. Brundage to Cun Sun Hoh (Taiwan committee president), 16 Sept. 1954, Brundage Papers, Box 120; Espy, *The Politics of the Olympic Games*, p.45.

30. 'Yu guoji auweihui diwushejie huiyi de laiwan wenjian ji huiyi qingkuang' [The Documents and the Relevant Meeting Reports with the 50th IOC Executive Board], National Sports Bureau Archives, 70 (1955).
31. *The New York Times*, 15 May 1954; Espy, *The Politics of the Olympic Games*, p.44.
32. 'Disheliujie auyunhuei daibiaotuan choubei gongzuo wenjian' [The Preparatory Documents of the Sixteenth Olympic Games Representatives], National Sports Bureau Archives, 128 (1956).
33. 'Disheliujie auyunhui fandui "liangge zhongguo" de douzheng wenjian' [Documents about the 'Two Chinas' Issue at the Sixteenth Olympic Games], National Sports Bureau Archives, 126 (1956).
34. 'Disheliujie auyunhui fandui "liangge zhongguo" de douzheng wenjian ji guoji auweihui diwushierjie huiyi' [52 IOC Session about the 'Two Chinas' at the Sixteenth Olympic Games], National Sports Bureau Archives, 127 (1956).
35. Ibid.
36. Minutes of the Meeting of the Executive Board of the IOC, Melbourne, 17 Nov. 1956, Brundage Papers, Box 91; Espy, *The Politics of the Olympic Games*, p.54.
37. *The New York Times*, 30 Oct. 1956; Espy, *The Politics of the Olympic Games*, p.54.
38. 'Dishiliujie auyunhui fandui "liangge zhongguo"', National Sports Bureau Archives, 126 (1956).
39. 'Yu guoji auweihuei de laiwan hanjien' [Documents Dealing with the 50th IOC Executive Board], National Sports Bureau Archives, 142 (1958).
40. Ibid.
41. Jonathan Kolatch, *Sports, Politics, and Ideology in China* (New York: Jonathan David Publishers, 1972), p.183; Espy, *The Politics of the Olympic Games*, p.63.
42. 'Guanyu tuichu guoji tiyu zhuzhi de shangminggao' [The Declaration Document of Withdrawal from International Sports Federations], National Sports Bureau Archives, 139 (1958).
43. 'Guanyu zai guoji tiyu zhuzhi zhong fandui "Liangge zhongguo" de fangan' [A Proposal Against International Sports Federations' Attitudes towards the 'Two Chinas' Issue], National Sports Bureau Archives, 137 (1958).
44. Cited in Alfried Erich Senn, *Power, Politics, and the Olympic Games* (Champaign, IL: Human Kinetics, 1999), p.128.
45. 'Diyijie xinxing liliang yundonghui gexiang gongzuo zhongjie baogao' [Working Report of the 1st GANEFO], National Sports Bureau Archives, 135 (1963).
46. Ibid.
47. Ibid.
48. 'Diyijie xinxing liliang yundonghui neibu jianbao (1–56)' [Brief Reports of the Committee of the 1st GANEFO, nos.1–56], National Sports Bureau Archives, 136 (1963).
49. Espy, *The Politics of the Olympic Games*, p.80.
50. Senn, *Power, Politics, and the Olympic Games*, p.129.
51. 'Diyijie xinxing liliang yundonghui neibu jienbao', National Sports Bureau Archives, 136 (1963).
52. Ren Dao, *Guoji tiyu zhong de xinqizhi* [The New Flag of International Sport] (Beijing: Renmin tiyu chubanshe, 1963), p.16.
53. 'Diyijie xinxing liliang yundonghui neibu jienbao', National Sports Bureau Archives, 136 (1963).
54. 'Huang Zhong yu Maladi lianhe guongbao' [Announcement by Huang Zhong and Maladi], National Sports Bureau Archives, 79 (1962).
55. Kolatch, *Sports, Politics, and Ideology in China*, p.191; Espy, *The Politics of the Olympic Games*, p.81.
56. Guojia tiwei [Chinese Sports Ministry] (ed.), *Zhongguo tiyu nianjian (jinghuaban)* [Chinese Sport Yearbook] (Beijing: Renming tiyu chubanshe, 1963), p.39.
57. Kolatch, *Sports, Politics, and Ideology in China*, p.191; Espy, *The Politics of the Olympic Games*, p.81.
58. Ibid., p.81.
59. Ibid.

60. George Modelski (ed.), *The New Emerging Forces: Documents on the Ideology of Indonesian Foreign Policy* (Department of International Relations, Australian National University, 1963), p.90; Espy, *The Politics of the Olympic Games*, p.81.
61. Kolatch, *Sports, Politics, and Ideology in China*, p.191; Espy, *The Politics of the Olympic Games*, p.81.
62. Sun Baoli, 'Yayun bianzhouqu' [The GANEFO], *Tiyu wenshi*, 5 (1990), 6.
63. Ibid., 3.
64. Those present included Albania, Arab Palestine, Bulgaria, Cambodia, Ceylon, China, Cuba, Czechoslovakia, the Dominican Republic, Finland, the German Democratic Republic, Guinea, Hungary, Indonesia, Iraq, Italy, the Democratic People's Republic of Korea, Laos, Mongolia, Pakistan, Poland, Syria, Somali, the Soviet Union, the UAR, the Democratic Republic of Vietnam, Yemen, Lebanon and the South Africa Non-Racial Olympic Committee; observers were Afghanistan, Mali, Mauritania, Nepal, Romania, Sudan, Tanzania Uganda, and Morocco. Kolatch, *Sports, Politics, and Ideology in China*, p.198; Espy, *The Politics of the Olympic Games*, p.109.
65. Sun Baoli, 'Yayun bianzhouqu', pp.8–10.
66. Brundage to Exeter, 28 Nov. 1964, Brundage Papers, Box 55; Espy, *The Politics of the Olympic Games*, p.84.
67. Ibid., p.128.
68. Ge Dajun *et al.*, *Zhonghua renmin gongheguo shi 1949–1993* [The History of the People's Republic of China 1949–93] (Beijing: Beijing shiyuan chubanshe, 1995), pp.187, 205–6.
69. Henry Kissinger, *The White House Years* (London: Weidenfeld & Nicolson and Michael Joseph, 1979), pp.687 and 696; Jonathan D. Spence, *The Search for Modern China* (London: Hutchinson, 1990), pp.628–9.
70. R. MacFarquhar (ed.), *The Politics of China, 1949–1989* (Cambridge: Cambridge University Press, 1993), p.263.
71. Richard Nixon, *The Memoirs of Richard Nixon* (New York: Grosset & Dunlap, 1978), pp.546–7.
72. Spence, *The Search for Modern China*, p.629; Kissinger, *The White House Years*, pp.687, 691, 697–8; Nixon, *Memoirs*, pp.544–7.
73. Kissinger, *The White House Years*, p.699; Nixon, *Memoirs*, p.547; Spence, *The Search for Modern China*, p.629; Qian Jiang, *Ping-Pong waijiao shimo* [The Story of the Ping-Pong Diplomacy] (Beijing: Dongfang chubanshe, 1987), p.49.
74. Wu Shaozu, 'Jinian Zhou Zhongli danceng 100 nian' [For Premier Zhou Enlai's 100th Anniversary], *Tiyu wenshi*, 1 (1998), 6–7.
75. This perception now seems extrodinary but needs to be understood in the context of the time. Cited in Wu Shaozu, 'Jinian Zhou Zhongli danceng 100 nian', 7; Qian Jiang, *Ping-Pong waijiao shimo*, p.73.
76. Wu Shaozu, 'Jinian Zhou Zhongli danceng 100 nian', 8.
77. Qian Jiang, *Ping-Pong waijiao shimo*, p.76.
78. Qian Jiang, *Ping-Pong waijiao shimo*, pp.110–27; Kissinger, *The White House Years*, pp.708–10.
79. Kissinger, *The White House Years*, p.710; Qian Jiang, *Ping-Pong waijiao shimo*, pp.154–61.
80. Kissinger, *The White House Years*, p.710; Qian Jiang, *Ping-Pong waijiao shimo*, p.159.
81. Nixon, *Memoirs*, pp.552–4; Kissinger, *The White House Years*, pp.755–60.
82. On 25 October 1971 the UN General Assembly voted 76 to 35, with 17 abstentions, to expel Taiwan and to admit the PRC as the sole government representing China. See Nixon, *Memoirs*, pp.556–7; Kissinger, *The White House Years*, pp.784–5, 755–84.
83. Nixon, *Memoirs*, pp.559–79.
84. See editorial, *People's Daily*, 26 Feb. 1972.
85. Nixon, *Memoirs*, pp.559–80.
86. Spence, *The Search for Modern China*, p.633.
87. Wu Shaozu, 'Jinian Zhou Zhongli danceng 100 nian', p.7.
88. Wang Dinghua, 'Yuanshuai zihuo you mengjiang' [Marshal and Generals], *Tiyu wenshi*, 4 (1993), 12–15.
89. Ibid., 13–14.
90. Guan Wenmin, *Tiyu shi*, p.195.

91. Guojia tiwei zhenche yanjiushi [Policy Department, Chinese Sport Ministry] (ed.), *Tiyu weijian xuanbian 1949–1981* [Selected Documents on Sports, 1949–81] (Beijing: Renmin tiyu chubanshe, 1982), pp.112–20.
92. Guan Wenmin, *Tiyu shi*, p.195.
93. Guojia tiwei dapipan zu [The Criticism Group of the Sports Ministry], 'Jianping Youyi diyi, bisai dire de fangzhen' [Comments on the Principle: Friendship First, Competition Second], *Xin tiyu* [New Sport], 3 (1972), 11–12.
94. Editor, 'Zai tiyu yundongzhong jinyibu fayang shehuizhuyi xinfengshang' [On the Further Promotion of the Socialist Morality in the Sports Movement], *Xin tiyu*, 3 (1973), 3–4.
95. See *Xin tiyu*, 1, 5, 12 (1973), *passim*.
96. Kenneth Minogue, *Politics* (Oxford: Oxford University Press, 1995), p.58.
97. Ibid., p.59.
98. Wang Dinghua, 'Yuanshuai zihuo you mengjiang', p.13.
99. Ibid., p.14.
100. Zhou Peian, 'Yuanjian de guowai tiyu sheshi' [Building Sports Facilities for Foreign Countries], in The Department of Policy, Sports Ministry (ed.), *Zhonghua tiyu sishi chun* [40 Years' Achievements of Chinese Sport] (Beijing: Renmin tiyu chubanshe, 1990), pp.145–9.
101. Bai Lei and Gu Shiquan, 'Yayun huigu' [The Brief History of the Asian Games], *Tiyu wenshi* [Journal of Sports Culture and History] 2 (1990), 2–3.
102. Source from Renmin tiyu chubanshe [People's Sports Press] (ed.), *Zhongguo yundongyuan zai guoji bisai zhong de chengjiu* [The Achievements of Chinese Athletes in the International Sports Competitions] (Beijing: Renmin tiyu chubanshe, 1983).
103. Chao Shouhe, 'Cong youyi diyi, bisai dire tanqi' [On Friendship First, Competition Second], *Tiyushi lunwen ji* [Annual Selected Work of Sports History], 8 (1991), 86; Zhang Min, 'Xin Zhongguo jinji tiyu zhenche de fazhan he tedian chutan' [Research for the Policy on Competitive Sport in New China], *Tiyu wenshi*, 2 (1991), 3–4.
104. Zhong Liang, 'Woguo guoji tiyu huodong shenli fazan de yinian' [The Successful Year of Our International Sports Activities], *Xin tiyu*, 1 (1973), 18–19.
105. Hong Liu, 'Youyu di, bisai dire fangzhen jie shuoguo' [The Principle: Friendship First, Competition Second Grows Rich Fruits], *Xin tiyu*, 9 (1974), 8–9.
106. Rao Yuan, 'Zhongguo tiyu 40 lian' [Review of 40 Years' Sport in China], *Tiyu wenshi*, 2 (1989), 8.

The Road to Modernization: Sport in Taiwan[1]

TREVOR SLACK, HSU YUAN-MIN, TSAI CHIUNG-TZU and FAN HONG

This essay examines the history of the involvement of the Taiwanese people in modern sport. It starts by looking at the origin of Taiwanese sport during the Japanese occupation (1895–1945). It then focuses on the period since 1945, a time of rapid transition within the country, and breaks the post-war years down into three phases: the early post-war years (1945–69); the foundation years (1970–84); and the developing years (1985–present).

THE PERIOD OF JAPANESE OCCUPATION (1895–1945)

From the beginning of the nineteenth century Taiwan was nominally controlled by the Chinese Ching Dynasty,[2] but in 1895, at the conclusion of the Sino-Japanese War,[3] Taiwan was ceded to the Japanese in the Ma-Kuan Treaty.[4] Over the next 50 years the population of Taiwan was under the administration of the Tokyo government. The Japanese, anxious to show Western colonialists that they too were a power to be reckoned with, treated their occupation of Taiwan as an experiment in colonial management.[5] They were hard taskmasters, but brought stability to the island. They built roads, railways and harbours, developed industry and generally improved the country's economy. They also developed cultural and educational policies. Before the Japanese takeover, education had received little attention from the central government on the Chinese mainland. There had been very little in the way of any type of provision for higher learning.[6] The Japanese opened a number of schools, but these were in part designed to destroy Chinese cultural influences on Taiwan, in that students were indoctrinated into the Japanese language, culture and traditions.

There were two types of schools for the Taiwanese: private-sector schools (*shu fang*) and public-sector schools, the latter being segregated along ethnic lines. The Japanese went to the best schools, which were called 'small schools'; the Han residents went to the 'public schools'; aboriginal people went to schools specially established for them.[7] The *shu fang*, which taught classical Chinese, were banned in 1919 as they stood in the way of the Japanization of Taiwan. Tsurumi reports physical education being taught in both types of schools.[8] Before the Japanese occupation Confucianism was the dominant culture and it shaped Taiwan as a male-dominated patriarchal society. There was no education for females. Footbinding was widely practised among girls and women.[9] When the Japanese occupied Taiwan they saw footbinding as a disgusting feudal custom and they were determined to change it. In 1898 the Governor of Taiwan advocated an anti-footbinding policy. At the same time Taiwan reformers responded to the call of anti-footbinding movements in mainland China and organized the first Natural Foot Society in 1899.[10] In 1911 a regulation was passed by the government that newborn baby girls should not have their feet bound and that girls under 20 years old with bound feet must be released from their bandages. Parents who disobeyed this regulation would be fined.[11] At the same time girls were encouraged to go to co-educational public schools. They were described as being 'as enthusiastic participants as their brothers in gymnastics, track and field, swimming, tennis, basketball, and volleyball'.[12] However, it is important to note that such opportunities were only afforded to a few. Despite the increased importance of education under the Japanese it was 1938 before there were even half as many girls in school as boys.[13]

Along with education, the Japanese also introduced sport and games to Taiwan. While the Taiwanese were initially suspicious of these strange practices they had won fairly wide acceptance among the islanders by the end of the first decade of the twentieth century. Toyotoshi reports that 'when the parents of the first Taiwanese students to attend the Japanese Language School, ... saw their children performing gymnastic exercises they were horrified. They were sure their offspring were being trained to serve as soldiers.'[14] The growth of public (state) school sports and the holding of school meetings, competitive league games and displays of physical culture worked to help change this perception.[15] Both sexes participated in sports such as track and field,[16] lawn tennis, basketball, volleyball and swimming;[17] additionally, boys played rugby, soccer, hockey and baseball.[18]

Baseball was originally introduced by newly-arrived Japanese administrators and company employees.[19] Chang Che-Wei suggests that Taiwan's first baseball team was set up in 1906[20]. The sport soon developed to become the most popular on the island. A northern Taiwanese baseball federation was formed in 1915,[21] and Sundeen suggests that 'Taiwanese children were playing organized baseball long before little league baseball was a gleam in the eye of its North America founder'.[22] By 1919 over 10,000 spectators watched an organized youth tournament in Taipei's Hsin-Kong-Yuan (New Park). The tournament expanded to include other cities and was an annual event. Each of these had a regional tournament to select representatives for an island-wide competition.[23]

Initially only the Japanese played baseball and, in the era in which they controlled the island, it was referred by its Japanese name, *yakyū* (fieldball).[24] Tsai also suggests that as a result of the Japanese influence the baseball jargon used in Taiwan (mainly by older Taiwanese) includes Japanese terms such as *pitchāt* (pitcher), *kyatchā* (catcher) and *fasutō* (first base).[25] The use of the term *yakyū* was, it is suggested, not just an indication of the Japanization of the game but also a means by which the colonial rulers created a sense of ethnic superiority. The Taiwanese people were initially not encouraged to play the game and were seen as lacking any appreciation for a sport that involved brandishing a stick at a ball.[26] However, by the 1920s the game had become less of a symbol of Japanese imperialism and Taiwanese adults and children started to participate. In 1916 the Waseda University team had visited Taiwan and were allegedly 'enthusiastically welcomed by Taiwanese'.[27] Baseball exchanges between the islanders and the Japanese became popular, and in 1931 a team from Chiayi School of Agriculture and Forestry won second place in the Pan-Japanese High School Baseball Tournament.[28] The success of the team was seen as an indication that the Taiwanese were equal to their colonial oppressors.[29]

Women appear to have had no involvement in playing baseball. In addition, our research found no details of women's involvement in competitive sport. However, as the percentage of girls in school increased to nearly 61 per cent by 1944 it is possible to speculate that the participation rates of young women in sport did increase but remained relatively small in comparison with those of boys.

A slightly more bizarre form of exercise in which women did play a role, albeit a relatively passive one, was recorded by the Japanese. It took place in the areas that are now the Pingtung villages of Chiatung, Linpien, Hsinpi and Fangliao. On the fifth day of the fifth month, the date of the annual Dragon Boat Festival, people in the area would get together and go to the fields to fight by throwing stones at each other. The men threw the stones, the women collected them. The winning side was the one that held out the longest. The rationale presented for this form of 'sport' was that at the time malaria was prevalent in the area and the sweating from the vigorous exercise rid the participants' bodies of the disease. However, in spite of any medicinal benefits, the battles could result in someone being hurt or property being damaged and consequently the Japanese enforced a ban on them, so that they gradually died out.[30]

THE EARLY POST-WAR YEARS, 1945-69

Following the Second World War Japan ceded control of Taiwan and in 1945 the island was handed back to the Chinese. The mainland Chinese from the ruling Nationalist Party, the Kuomintang (KMT), saw the Taiwanese as 'slaves' of the Japanese who would have to undergo a complete re-Sinification before being able to exercise their full political-cultural rights.[31] However, in 1949 Chiang Kai-Shek's KMT lost the war on the mainland to the Communists and fled to Taiwan; approximately 1.6 million civilian and military personnel followed him. The mainlanders essentially reconstituted the KMT in Taiwan. It was a highly centralized hierarchical party that controlled the government, the military and the security services and imposed martial law. In this period the island was in a state of devastation from the destruction of the war and the turmoil over the relocation of the KMT. Production was down and inflation was high, and in addition the US discontinued financial support to the island – although this was reinstated in 1950 after the Korean War broke out. The lack of material resources and the poor conditions on the island meant that sport was afforded a low priority. However, the government did form an unofficial 'sports association' within the educational bureau from 1954 to 1958 and from 1961 to 1973.[32] These organizations lacked funding or government support, and were very loosely structured. Their major purpose was to put together simple nationwide sports events that were mainly for students and only in the most popular events, such as track, baseball and basketball.[33] Because of a very limited budget and an inadequate number of public sporting facilities, almost all the sports events that were staged were held on school grounds. However, most school sport facilities and fields were small and so it was very difficult to stage any type of large-scale sporting event.

Internationally, Taiwan did have some success at the Asian Games but, with the exception of two athletes whom we discuss in more detail below, many of those who competed for Taiwan were actually people with Taiwanese backgrounds who resided in other countries. For example, at the second Asian Games in 1954 players for the gold-medal-winning Taiwan soccer team came from Hong Kong; at the third games, held in Tokyo in 1958, the gold-medal-winning weightlifter Wu Min-Kao was from the Philippines, and at the 1966 games held in Bangkok the Taiwanese shooter Wu Dao-Yuan, who won three gold medals and one bronze, was from the United States. Nevertheless, Taiwan did have some other successes and achieved the following results before 1960: second Asian Games (1954) – two gold, four silver, and seven bronze medals; third Asian Games (1958) – six gold, 11 silver, and 17 bronze medals.

Taiwan's involvement in the Olympics was a more complex issue. China had first participated in the Olympics in 1932 and its Olympic Committee was a member in good standing of the IOC when Chiang Kai-Shek and the Nationalist government moved to Taiwan. However, between 1947 and 1951 the officially recognized Chinese Olympic Committee address was on the Chinese mainland in Nanking. However, in this period two of the three Chinese IOC members and the committee left the mainland and settled in Taiwan, from where it still claimed jurisdiction over the whole of China. The IOC acknowledged the change of location, although it never formally voted on it, and by 1951 the Chinese National Olympic Committee was listed as being located in Taiwan. The People's Republic of China (PRC), which had no formally recognized Olympic committee, formed an All-China Sports Federation and lobbied to attend the 1952 Helsinki games. The Taiwanese, who only had one competitor, left the games as a protest over the 'illegality and impropriety' of the decision made by the IOC. However, in 1954 the IOC voted 23 to 21 to recognize the PRC Olympic Committee.[34] Through the unilateral actions of the IOC president, Avery Brundage, it also recognized Taiwan and as a result the PRC refused to compete in the 1956 games. Two years later the PRC withdrew from the Olympic organization and a number of other sporting federations.[35] Taiwan subsequently sent a team to the 1956 Melbourne Olympics.

Three years later, at the IOC meeting in Munich, two Soviet members put forward a proposal to recognize the PRC as the sole Chinese Olympic committee. After much debate Brundage announced that since Taiwan did not administer sport in China it would be taken off the IOC membership list. The US objected to what as it saw as the Communists pressuring the IOC. Subsequently Brundage explained that the earlier Munich decision had been misinterpreted and he proposed to the membership of the IOC that Taiwan be readmitted under the name 'the Olympic Committee of the Republic of China'.[36] Lord Killanin, who succeeded Brundage, took an opposite view and was keen to get both Chinas involved in the Olympics. Most IOC members sided with Brundage's position, and at the 1960 meeting in Rome the IOC voted to recognize the Republic of China Olympic Committee but stated that Taiwan had to compete at the upcoming Olympics under the name Formosa. Although there were protests from the Taiwanese, the IOC refused to change its position. As the Taiwanese team marched into the opening ceremonies under the name Formosa, the *chef de mission* Lin Hung-Tan unfurled a banner which read 'Under protest'. The Taiwanese were also denied visas for the 1962 Asian Games in Indonesia, a move that subsequently led to the IOC suspending the Indonesian Olympic Committee.[37]

Despite the problematic situation overshadowing their participation, two Taiwanese athletes who would subsequently have a significant impact on world track and field first gained prominence in this era. The first of these was Yang Chuan-Kuang (known in the West as C.K. Yang). Yang was born into an aboriginal Amei family in Taitung County. He had finished tenth in the decathlon in the 1956 Melbourne games[38] and won the gold in this event at both the 1954 and 1958 Asian Games.[39] At the 1960 Olympics he was involved in an epic battle with his UCLA teammate, the American Rafer Johnson. At the start of the final event, the 1,500 metres, Johnson needed to beat Yang by ten seconds to win the gold, but Yang's personal best in the 1,500 was 18 seconds better than Johnson's. Johnson ran a great race and broke his personal best 1,500 time by five seconds, finishing just 1.2 seconds behind Yang to win the gold. Yang won seven of the ten events but Johnson's achievements in the shot, discus, and javelin helped him accumulate a total of 58 points more than Yang.[40] Yang topped the world decathlon rankings in both 1962 and 1963, breaking the world record in the latter year.

Following his success at the Olympics, Yang worked as a coach and a consultant to athletic organizations. In 1983 he was elected to the legislature and became something of a political pawn.[41] In 1986, as well as being a legislator Yang was the head coach of the 'Chinese Taipei' track and field team at the Asian Games in Seoul. Rumours started to spread that Yang had contacted PRC officials and was about to flee to the mainland: 'The KMT government in Taipei couldn't afford the loss of face that would accompany being "deserted by a national treasure".'[42] Reporters questioned Yang but he would neither admit nor deny the claims; he was, however, seen as dissatisfied with the Taiwan government. The government mobilized efforts to get Yang to return to Taipei but he feared that with the intense anti-Communist ideology of the time, he would be unable to go abroad again if he returned. With an assurance from the Taiwanese ambassador to South Korea that he could return to Seoul, Yang flew back to Taiwan to explain matters and returned to Seoul the same day.[43] Yang was described as 'falling silent' and many questions about his actions went unanswered. Some suggestions were made that when his three-year term in the legislature was coming to an end, the KMT had given signs that it would not be nominating him again; hence the rumours of defection were made up to threaten the KMT. As expected, Yang was not nominated to run again for the legislature and he returned to his job as a coach. Chu suggests that 'Yang was like a political tool of the KMT that no longer had propaganda value after being thoroughly used ... he was maliciously cast aside'.[44]

However, Yang's political career was not over. In late 1989 he announced that he had joined the Democratic Progressive Party (DPP) and ran for the position of commissioner in his home, Taitung County. As Chu notes,

> Of course most people knew that running as a candidate from the opposition party, especially in socially conservative Taitung, his chances of being elected were extremely remote. Everyone simply regarded his candidacy as a farce. And everyone knew that honest, straightforward Yang was being intentionally used by someone again. Once more he had become a political tool of other people. The only difference was that this time it was a different political party using him.[45]

It was even suggested by one of his political backers that Yang auction off his Olympic medal to raise money for his campaign. He was defeated in the election and 'the DPP threw him away like an old shoe'.[46] Yang now changed his focus to religion and the occult, and became a medium in a temple he had established in the early 1980s.[47] In recent years he has suffered financial and health problems, and in early 2001 he was taken ill while visiting his son in the US. Unable to pay his medical bills he was assisted by the National Council on Physical Fitness and Sports, which arranged for him to receive treatment in Taiwan.[48]

The other Taiwanese athlete who would subsequently excel on the world stage and who competed for Taiwan at the 1960 Olympics was female sprinter Chi Cheng, 'the flying antelope'. Generally acknowledged as the greatest Asian female athlete of the twentieth century, Chi Cheng set a series of records, including eight world records and 23 Asian records, in 1970 alone. During the period from 1969 through to 1970 she won 153 of 154 events, including sprints, hurdles, long jump and relays. She competed at the 1960, 1964 and 1968 Olympics, winning a bronze medal in the 80 metres hurdles in 1968, the same year that she also set an Asian record in the pentathlon. Chi also won a number of 'Athlete of the Year' awards. Her achievements were particularly outstanding since at that time Taiwanese society still held very conservative opinions about women who wanted to participate in sport. Being a sportswoman implied that a woman wanted to compete with men. Women were traditionally viewed as smaller, weaker and inferior subjects, and they were oppressed in the sporting world, where men usually dominated proceedings. Hence trying to become an elite-level sportswoman was always difficult. Nevertheless, after attending university and working in the US, Chi returned to Taiwan in 1980 and continued her success. She was elected to congress and served three terms, a total of nine years. She has also held numerous prestigious positions, such as secretary-general of Taiwan's Track and Field Association, president of the Republic of China National Sports Association for the Deaf, and president of the ROC Community Healthful Life and Sports Association. Most recently she was criticized for organizing a ten-city marathon on both sides of the Straits (the area between Taiwan and China) in support of China's bid to stage the 2008 Olympics.[49]

In addition to the achievements of Yang and Chi, the other major sporting accomplishment in the early post-war years involved baseball. Despite the fact that the sport had grown popular under the Japanese, wartime bombing took its toll on Taiwan's baseball fields. From 1948 to 1968 the sport was sustained by a handful of enthusiasts incorporated as the Taiwan Baseball Association. This organization sponsored and operated tournaments for adults and children on the island's remaining four diamonds.[50] In 1968 the team from Wakayama, Japan, that had won the Little League World Series was invited to visit Taiwan for a 'friendship series'. The team from Japan played three games against the youth champions of Taiwan (albeit with a rubber ball rather than a regulation ball) and lost all three, failing to score a single run. The Japanese coaches suggested that the Taiwanese consider participating in the Little League World Series. They did, and the following year beat a team from Santa Clara to win the series.[51] Between 1969 and 1996 teams from Taiwan won a total of 17 world series championships.[52] In the lead-up to the final of the 1996 series the Taiwanese team outscored their opponents by 49 to six.[53] The continuing success of the Taiwanese was interrupted in 1997 when the Taiwan Baseball Association announced that it was not going to compete in future world series tournaments. At the time the Taiwanese programme was under investigation for some relatively minor infractions, the most significant of which being the size of the area from which it drew its players.[54] There had also previously been criticism of the Taiwanese emphasis on competition, and in 1993 the team that won the Far East regional competition was barred from the Little League World Series for suspected rule violations. Sundeen, however, suggests a different rationale for the withdrawal of the Taiwanese. He argues that in the 1970s and early 1980s, under the KMT, little league baseball played an important role in supporting a nationalistic Taiwanese identity based on a belief in reunification with the PRC[55] and on creating favourable comparisons for Taiwan. Victory in baseball presented an image that Taiwan was modern and could compete with the West; yet it also exemplified the traditional Confucian values of respect for authority and hard work. However, in recent years this view has been supplanted as the idea that Taiwan should assert its own identity as an independent entity has become more accepted. Little league baseball has also suffered as a result of the creation of professional baseball in Taiwan, which has diminished the importance of lower-level games.[56]

The success of the little league baseball players in 1968 did prompt the government to approve an Act for Training Talented Sports Personnel and Athletes by Promoting Nationwide Sports Interest.[57] This was the first complete strategy for the Taiwanese government with regard to national sporting development. The proposals covered areas such as physical education within schools, community sports, research, international sport and sports education training for teachers. Unfortunately the plan was not successful, as it had neither the personnel with power or financial support necessary for its implementation. The Department of Education failed to form any type of specialist group to manage the plan; rather responsibility for its implementation was given to staff with no specialist sports knowledge.

Generally speaking, the development of sport in this early post-war period was constrained by the general economic and political conditions on the island. There were, however, some successes, most notably by Yang Chuan-Kuang, Chi Cheng and the little league baseball players. The achievements of these athletes showed the world and the Taiwanese that their athletes could be competitive in the global sports arena.

THE FOUNDATION YEARS, 1970–84

The period 1970–84 was one of the most difficult political periods in the history of Taiwan, and this had an impact on the development of sport on the island. In 1947 Chiang Kai-Shek had been one of the original signatories of the United Nations Charter and China had received one of the permanent seats on the Security Council. When the Nationalists fled to Taiwan they continued to be recognized by the United Nations. In fact, in 1960 part of the claim to the IOC for the Taiwanese National Olympic Committee to be known as the Olympic Committee of the Republic of China was the fact that Taiwan was recognized by the United Nations as the Republic of China. However, in 1971 the United Nations recognized the PRC, expelled Taiwan from the Security Council and gave its seat to the PRC. The US started to forge links with the PRC and these culminated in President Nixon visiting the PRC in 1972, his way being paved by 'ping-pong diplomacy', the visit of a US table tennis team to China. The majority of member states shifted their recognition from Taipei to Beijing.[58] Subsequently, in 1972 and 1978 respectively, Japan and the United States broke off diplomatic relations with Taiwan. These changes impacted on Taiwan not only politically but also economically.

The Taiwanese government responded to the problems it faced as a result of its expulsion from the UN with several national construction plans to boost the economy. These included a north-south highway, an international shipping port, an electrical railway system, an international airport, nuclear power plants, iron mills, shipyards, oil refineries and several other transport and heavy industry projects. Sport would also be used both domestically and internationally to help the country's situation.

However, paralleling the actions of the UN, the IOC indicated in 1971 that the PRC would be welcomed back to the organization if it respected the Olympic rules. There was, however, no move to expel Taiwan. The PRC began to rejoin international sporting federations in order to secure the five memberships required for Olympic eligibility. This posed problems for those federations that recognized Taiwan. For example, in 1973 the US State Department wanted to send ten swimmers to the PRC. However, the Amateur Athletic Union, the governing body of swimming in the US, belonged to FINA, the international governing body of swimming. FINA did not recognize the PRC and did not allow competition against countries that were not members of its organization. Hence, if the swimmers competed in China the AAU would have no choice but to suspend them or it would be suspended by FINA – which would then mean that no American swimmers could compete internationally. The US Senate asked FINA to make an exception but it would not agree. However, the swimmers were at the end of their careers and subsequent suspension would not affect them, so they decided to visit China.[59]

In October 1973 the Asian Games Federation voted to allow the PRC to attend the 1974 games in Tehran and to expel Taiwan. The proposal, put forward by Taiwan's former colonial master Japan and Iran, met with some opposition from international federations. Also the IOC threatened to withdraw their patronage of the Asian Games, but in the end Lord Killanin's conviction that China needed to be brought back into the Olympic Games overrode any sanction.[60] Taiwan consequently missed the next four Asian Games.

By April 1975 the PRC had garnered enough international federation memberships and applied to rejoin the IOC. However, the PRC indicated that it would only join the IOC if Taiwan was expelled. There was also a suggestion made by the Romanian Alexandru Siperco at the May 1975 IOC session that the PRC's Olympic committee be recognized as the sole representative of China. If this decision was acted on it would have immediate ramifications for the upcoming Olympic Games in Montreal. Henry Hsu, a Taiwanese member who had been brought onto the IOC somewhat subversively by Avery Brundage, objected on the basis that a country could not attach conditions to its application for membership. He also argued that Taiwan was recognized by a number of countries and had been a member of the IOC for 15 years. No immediate decision was taken, but the situation was ultimately brought to a head by the Canadian government.

In 1969 the IOC was considering a bid from Canada for the 1976 Summer Olympics. As part of its normal protocols the IOC had written to the Canadian government asking if there were any laws or customs in the country that would interfere with the games and noting that free entry into Canada would have to be afforded to all teams from national Olympic committees recognized by the IOC. The Canadian secretary of state for external affairs, Mitchell Sharp, had responded that all countries would be free to enter Canada 'pursuant to normal regulations'. The IOC took the statement from the Canadian government at face value, not foreseeing any problems with entry. In 1973 the PRC was actively lobbying for recognition by the IOC and was also expressing concern to the Canadian government that it would be violating its recognition of the PRC if it allowed Taiwan to compete in the upcoming Montreal Games. Although the Canadian government protested that such actions were outside its jurisdiction, it was anxious to preserve its foreign policy successes with the PRC.[61] A meeting was held between representatives of the Canadian government and the IOC. However, as Macintosh and Hawes note,

> it subsequently became apparent that grave misunderstandings existed between Lord Killanin and Allan MacEachen, who was to take over the post of secretary of state for external affairs, regarding the substance of this crucial meeting. MacEachen would subsequently claim that Canadian officials had refused to give Killanin assurances that Taiwan would be admitted under the name Republic of China to which ... Killanin had replied that he hoped the IOC could resolve the issue before the Olympics. Killanin, on the other hand, recalled only that he had met about a year before the Montreal Olympics with Mitchell Sharp ... who had inquired about the positions of mainland China in the IOC.[62]

In April 1975 the PRC applied for admission to the IOC and its case was considered at the IOC meeting in May 1975. The Soviet Union and its allies were no longer supporting the PRC and the debate was split, with the result that the IOC decided to withhold its decision until Lord

Killanin could visit both Beijing and Taiwan. The decision posed a dilemma for the Canadian government. Taiwan was a member of the IOC, whereas China was not; yet Canada recognized the PRC but not Taiwan. By the beginning of 1976 Canada was taking steps to impose restrictions on Taiwanese boxers coming to a pre-Olympic meet if they tried to enter under the name Republic of China. It also withdrew an invitation that had previously been given to young people from Taiwan to attend the Olympic Youth Camp during the Montreal games. However, in April 1976 Donald Jamieson, the secretary of state for external affairs, approved a policy stating that Taiwan could compete provided it did so under a name other than the Republic of China and that it did not use any ROC flags, symbols or anthems.[63] The IOC had still to resolve the issue of the PRC's membership in the IOC, but it was suggested to the IOC that Taiwan participate under a name other than the Republic of China. The IOC rejected the proposal. At the end of June a further meeting between government officials and the IOC was held, but little was resolved and the IOC then went public on the issue, claiming Canada had broken its pledge about the entry of teams into Canada for the Olympics. An international uproar ensued with the possible threat of the US pulling out of the games (and hence television money being lost) or the IOC withdrawing its recognition of the games. Killanin met again with Canadian officials who noted that their government was willing to let Taiwanese athletes compete in the games, but not under the name Republic of China. Eventually, on 10 July, Killanin agreed to the Canadian demands and the IOC proposed that Taiwan compete under the Olympic flag and in the name of the IOC.[64] The Taiwanese turned down the offer and Canadian Prime Minister Pierre Trudeau capitulated on the issue of the anthem and the flag, saying the Taiwanese could fly whatever flag they wanted and play their own anthem but could not be known as the Republic of China. The Taiwanese would not accept the conditions and on 16 July 1976 they pulled out of the games.[65] They subsequently missed the 1980 Olympics.

Although Taiwan missed out on most major international competitions between 1970 and 1984, it still continued to work on developing its athletes. In 1973 the government established a sports department within the education bureau. This was an official department with its own financing and was responsible for all the nation's sport affairs. In 1974 the department published a 'five-year development plan' and in 1979 'the complete citizen's sport education plan'. This latter plan was initially decided by the central government and involved personnel in districts, cities and councils working with related departments to ensure the funding and implementation of the plan. The most important aspect of the project was to ensure that sports facilities were designed and built and to ensure that opportunities for school sports, physical education and sports for the general population were available. Programmes were also directed to national-level athletes to prepare them to compete internationally. In addition several track and field areas, stadia, gymnasia and swimming pools were built. Schools were required to offer physical education as a mandatory class. Every grade of elementary school had to have three periods of physical education in the curriculum; each grade in middle school through to college had to have two periods. Sports teachers were given the chance to learn and further their knowledge in the area. This was partially achieved through an annual conference to discuss ways to improve the sports system. The government also began to run sports clinics to counsel and educate local communities about sport; in 1983, 712 clinics were held.[66] Although there were a number of sporting organizations in Taiwan, Chi Cheng was critical of the structure of these organizations, suggesting that their presidents often stayed in office too long due to the lack of regulations governing their tenure and when they did leave there was a lack of continuity. The National Council on Physical Fitness and Sport, which will be discussed in more detail below, was set up in 1996 in part to address these problems.[67] This period in Taiwanese sport, then, was one of turmoil and relative isolation from the major international competitions. It did, however, lay the foundation for resolving some of the issues that existed between the PRC and Taiwan. It was also an era that saw increased understanding by the Taiwanese government of the value and importance of sport. This understanding would lay the foundation for the developments of the next 25 years.

THE DEVELOPING YEARS, 1985–2001

Following the 1976 Olympics the problem of the two Chinas still remained. Several IOC representatives, including the president, Lord Killanin, visited either the PRC, Taiwan or both to assess the situation. It was recognized that it was difficult to get the two sides to talk to each other and both were intent on making political capital out of the situation. However, at the April 1979 IOC meeting in Montevideo signs of a compromise began to appear.⁶⁸ João Havelange suggested that 'it would be to the glory of the Olympic movement if there could be two Chinese IOC members, one from the PRC and one from Taiwan'.⁶⁹ The mainland representative Ho Chen-liang (He Zhenliang) made the point that the PRC would not accept the title 'Chinese Olympic Committee' but would accept 'Chinese Taiwan Olympic Committee' for Taiwan. This was the first indication that the PRC was willing to allow the Taiwanese to include the word China in its title. Following an October 1979 IOC executive board meeting in Nagoya, the matter was subjected to a postal vote, which recommended that the national Olympic committee on the mainland be recognized as the Chinese Olympic Committee and be allowed to use the PRC flag and anthem. The Taiwanese Olympic committee would be called the Chinese Taipei Olympic Committee (CTOC) and would have a different flag and emblem from those currently being used. The resolution was passed and in 1981 it was reported that the flag and emblem of the COTC had been agreed upon by the IOC and Taiwan.⁷⁰ Chu suggests that the name was agreed upon by the PRC and Taiwan but for different reasons:

> Beijing thought that it suggested that Taiwan was a part of China. For Taiwan, it could translate the title 'Chinese Taipei' into the mandarin 'Chung-Hua', an abbreviation for the Chinese for ROC, thereby allowing Taiwan to use its official name at least before Chinese speakers.⁷¹

Despite this approval both countries boycotted the 1980 Games in Moscow. However, both attended the 1984 Los Angeles Games.

Although relations with the PRC remain strained even today, the resolution of the Olympic situation allowed Taiwan to start to develop its sports programmes. The economy, although subject to a number of fluctuations, also grew stronger. From 1985 to 1999 average economic growth was maintained at around 7.28 per cent and the GNP rose from US$3,993 to US$13,235. This provided a strong basis for the development of sport and the government decided to invest in this area. In 1989 it devised a Mid-Term National Sports Construction Plan. The central focus of this plan was to invest in sport programmes for schools and nationwide sporting events, to increase the availability of sports equipment and facilities and to train athletes and sports professionals.⁷² Schools began to promote sport and in 1987 136 school teams competed with each other. The government's hope was that by sponsoring sporting events among the student body it would provide a base of future athletes and also promote family interest in sport. It is important to note that sport was being developed in a climate where the primary objective of education for many Taiwanese students is to pass exams in order to increase their job prospects. For this reason there are a number of 'cramming schools' (*pu-hsi-pan*). As Gold notes, 'in the very early morning, late afternoon and evening one can see hordes of young people in school uniform grabbing snacks from fast food stalls on their way to and from [these] schools'.[73] Such an emphasis obviously limits the time that these children have for involvement in sport. However, by 1994 the number of competitive school teams had risen to 2,678.[74] The quality and number of sports facilities also improved. All of Taiwan's 23 cities, districts and counties now have their own standard gymnasium, field, swimming pool and other related sporting facilities. As a result, each takes turns sponsoring an event during the national games.[75] In 1998 a government survey reported that Taiwan had a total of 63,003 sports facilities, including 1,841 swimming pools (33.7 per cent of which are indoors), 3,524 track facilities (94.1 per cent attached to schools), 83 golf courses, 15,239 recreational parks and 2,208 gymnasiums (60.2 per cent within schools).[76] For a population of approximately 20 million people, this is a significant improvement in the quality of sports provision compared to two decades ago.[77] Improvements were also made in the training of high-performance athletes and in 1990 Taiwan built its second national sports training centre in northern Taiwan. In 1991 the National Championship Sports Medal (*kuo-kuang ti yu chiang chang*), which had been started in 1983 to reward athletes who did well in international competitions, was expanded to include coaches. Funds were also made available for training professional coaches, for try-out camps and pre-game training camps, for travel to compete in international competitions and for sports science research.[78]

One of the most significant developments concerning the development of sport in Taiwan in recent years is the creation of the National Council on Physical Fitness and Sport (NCPFS). The aim of the NCPFS is to

> foster a healthy nation based on the policy of promoting participation in sports at all levels. It will help all athletes in Taiwan who demonstrate the potential to win medals at regional and international competitions to develop their skills to the fullest. [It]

will also assist athletes in Taiwan to obtain jobs in sports-related enterprises or elsewhere so as the [*sic*] help them enjoy a decent and dignified life after they retire from the competitive arena.[79]

The NCPFS has 19 members, who are drawn from the ranks of administrators and experts in sport and represent athletic organizations, government and academia. There are currently 109 staff (which includes contract employees and maintenance personnel). The council has five departments, three offices and three committees. The departments are responsible for research and planning, sport for all, sports excellence, international issues and facilities. The offices are a secretariat, a personnel office and an accounting office. The committees are concerned with laws and regulations, administrative appeals and sports for the disabled.[80] Along with other appropriate organizations the NCPFS is involved in a range of activities to support and develop sport. These include, but are not limited to, controlling the use of banned drugs; a physical ability survey; hosting events (such as the thirty-fourth baseball World Cup, the International Council for Health, Physical Education, Recreation, Sports and Dance conference, the William Jones Cup men's basketball championship and a sports volunteers training camp), sending athletes to international competitions, recognizing successful athletes and working with business to promote sports and recreation activities.[81]

At the international level, Taiwan returned to the Olympics in 1984. Tsai Wen-Yi won a bronze medal in weightlifting and the men's baseball team also won the bronze medal. In Seoul in 1988 there were four medals for the Taiwanese in the demonstration sport of taekwondo and similarly in Barcelona five medals in taekwondo plus a silver medal in baseball. At the Atlanta Games there was a silver medal for Chen Jing in table tennis. She also won a bronze in Sydney and there were medals (a silver and a bronze) for two of the women weightlifters and a bronze for weightlifter Huang Chih-Hsiung. In 1990 Taiwan once again entered the Asian Games, winning ten silver and 21 bronze medals. In 1994 the country's medal total was 43 (seven gold), and in 1998 in Bangkok there were 77 medals (19 gold).[82]

Professional sport has also started to emerge in Taiwan. In 1990 the Chinese Baseball League was established. This was eventually made up of seven teams: the Hsiung-Ti Elephants, Wei-Chuan Dragons, San-Sang Tigers, Tung-Yi Lions, Shi-Pao Eagles, Sinon Bulls and He-Hsin Whales. However, in the 1990s baseball matches and players were directly linked to betting, which was controlled by Taiwanese gangsters. Scandals involving match-fixing and the corruption of players and coaches caused famous teams like the Wei-Chuan Dragons, San-Sang Tigers and Shi-Bao Eagles, who won the Olympic silver medal in 1992, to be disbanded.[83] Players such as Liao Min-Hsiung, the 'baseball prince', have been indicted in court and are still awaiting trial.[84] These incidents seriously damaged the reputation of baseball and the number of spectators declined rapidly.[85] People started to question the morality of professional sport in Taiwan. However, despite these problems, achievements in international sport and the growth of mass sport and fitness movements on the island suggest that there has been considerable progress in Taiwan's standing as a sporting nation.

Relations with the PRC are somewhat better than in the past and many problems have been solved. However, there is still a smouldering animosity between the two countries that continues to manifest itself in sport. A commentary written just after the Asian Women's Football Cup started in Taipei in late 2001 was highly critical of the fact that, since the Chinese attended the event, the so-called 'Olympic model' did not allow the Taiwanese to fly their national flag in their own territory.[86] Similar criticism was levelled at the IOC by both the *Taipei Times* and the *e-Taiwan News* after the decision to award the 2008 Games to Beijing.[87] Not surprisingly, both are critical of China's human rights record and the *Taipei Times* suggests that Taiwan should have fought harder against the bid, suggesting that until the PRC abandons its threat of force against Taiwan it should not have been seen as a suitable host for the Olympics. Although there have been suggestions that the Olympic flame will pass through Taiwan, there is scepticism about the motives behind such a move. The *Taiwan News* has argued that

> the Beijing authorities want the Olympic flame to pass through Taiwan for two reasons. The first is to show the outside world that it is sincere in wanting to thaw cross-strait relations and thereby win international support. Second they plan to use such a move to create the appearance that the people on both sides of the straits are Chinese and stir up identity contradictions in Taiwan.[88]

Such sentiments suggest that the conflicts that have divided the two Chinas may well continue in the future.

CONCLUSION

The road to modernization in Taiwanese sport has been and still is a rocky one. The growth of sport has been considerably influenced by the island's struggles; first with its colonial oppressor Japan and more recently with the PRC. Since the Second World War Taiwan's strategic importance, particularly in relation to the PRC, has, unfortunately for the people of the island, made it a pawn in a number of political power plays. Through the cold war years of the 1950s and 1960s Taiwan had support from the US; from the late 1970s through to the 1980s and 1990s the US turned its support to the PRC. The political support of the US has been important for Taiwan's participation in international sport. As we write, the tide is turning again somewhat. The United States has recently announced that it is targeting seven countries, including the PRC, for possible future use of nuclear weapons. One of the possible contingencies in which the US use of such weapons is envisaged is in the case of another confrontation between the PRC and Taiwan, an issue that is regarded in Beijing as a domestic matter.[89] Such potential problems, along with Communist China hosting the 2008 Olympics and Taiwanese suspicion over the way Beijing will use the Games to promote its claim over Taiwan, suggest that further modernization of Taiwanese sport will be influenced by future politics. However the people of the island remain optimistic. Their hopes for sport on the island perhaps are best expressed through the Chinese proverb *Sanchiungshuichin yiwulu, liouanhuaming you yitsun* (Where the mountains and rivers end, the beautiful village with willow trees and flowers will appear).

NOTES

1. This essay employs the Wade-Giles romanization system, which is used in Taiwan, for the translation of Chinese names, this is the case throughout, except within references that are originally written in Pinyin system, which is used in the PRC.
2. '100 Years since Treaty of Shimonoseki', online at http://www.taiwandc.org/hst-1895.htm, 1996, pp.1-4, extracted 28 Jan. 2002.
3. This war fought was between China and Japan from 1894 to 1895. It was provoked by a dispute over control of Korea. The Sino-Japanese War came to symbolize the degeneration and enfeeblement of the Ching Dynasty. It demonstrated how successful modernization had been in Japan since the Meijin Restoration as compared with what had taken place in China.
4. The Ma-Kuan Treaty was signed in April 1895, at the end of the Sino-Japanese War of 1894. China's Ching government (1644–1911) was forced to cede Taiwan to Japan 'in perpetuity'.
5. 'Taiwan History: Taiwan under the Japanese (1895–1945)', online at www.mcauley.acu/staff/andrewp/Taiwan_History_4.htm, extracted 3 Feb. 2002.
6. E.H. Epstein and Kuo Wei-Fan, 'Higher Education', in D.C. Smith (ed.), *The Confucian Continuum: Educational Modernization in Taiwan* (New York: Praeger, 1991), p.169.

7. Tsao Feng-Fu, 'Postwar Literacy Programs in Taiwan: A Critical Review in Sociolinguistic Perspective', in Huang Chun-Chieh and Tsao Feng-Fu (eds), *Postwar Taiwan in Historical Perspective* (Bethesda, MD: University Press of Maryland, 1998), pp.163–4.
8. See E.P. Tsurumi, *Japanese Colonial Education in Taiwan, 1895–1945* (Cambridge, MA: Harvard University Press, 1977), p.70.
9. See 'Shehui pianchian' [Social Change], online at http://content.edu.tw/junior/co_tw/ch_y1/grat/921/gra8_2.html; 'Fu chiao yma' [Grandmother with Bound Feet], online at http://www.content.edu.tw/87/endshow/4/contry/P-7-3-1.html, extracted 16 Feb. 2002.
10. See 'Hanyi chichiao ti yi jen Huang Yu-Chieh kuoshi' [The First Qualified Chinese Doctor Huang Yu-jieh Passaway], online at http://www.ftvn.com.tw/Topic/CaringTW/TWnotes/0726.html, extracted 16 Feb. 2002.
11. See 'Jichu chianchi (1895–1919) Taiwan yishi wenhua hsianhsiang chi chutan' [To Know the Taiwanese Costume Culture in Japanese Occupation], online at http://fashion-colour-beauty.com.tw/html/clothes-6.html, extracted 16 Feb. 2002.
12. Tsurumi, *Japanese Colonial Education*, p.220.
13. Ibid., p.221.
14. T. Toyotoshi (ed.), *Taiwan Taiiku Enkakushi* (Taihoku, 1933), p.5, cited by Tsurumi, *Japanese Colonial Education*, p.168.
15. Ibid., pp.168–9.
16. In addition a road relay race, originally the Three Lines Road Relay, now called the Road Relay Race, was first held in 1911. See http://163.29.141.191/spo.english/3-3-3.htm, extracted 3 Feb. 2002.
17. See 'Swimming Education in Pali Town', http://163.29.141.191/spo.english/3-3-3.htm for a brief description of the importance of swimming and a picture from the early 1940s of students at Taipei First Girls' High School taking part in swimming activities extracted 3 Feb. 2002.
18. Tsurumi, *Japanese Colonial Education*, p.169.
19. Hsieh Shih-Yuan, 'Taiwan Baseball: A Century-Old Love Affair', online at http://etaiwannews.com/History/2002/11/12105530406.htm, extracted 2 Feb. 2002.
20. Chang Che-Wei, 'Taiwan tdi yi tsi pangchiuchiutui chengli' [Taiwan's First Baseball Team Set up], online at http://home.pchome.com.tw/internet/s9300197/main/html/d/160.html, extracted 7 Feb. 2002.
21. Chang Che-Wei 'Peipu panghsieh chengli' [Baseball Federation Formed in Northern Taiwan], online at http://home.pchome.com.tw/internet/s9300197/main/html/d/160.html, extracted 7 Feb. 2002.
22. J.T. Sundeen, 'A Kid's Game: Little League Baseball and National Identity in Taiwan', *Journal of Sport and Social Issues*, 25 (2001), 253.
23. *Taiwan Shao Bang Shi* [History of Little League Baseball in Taiwan, part 1] (10 Aug. 1993), *Lai Shen Shui Hua Zhi Bang*, pp.68–70; and *Taiwan Shao Bang Shi* [History of Little League Baseball in Taiwan, part 2] (10 Sept. 1993), *Lai Shen Shui Hua Zhi Bang*, pp.80–82 cited by Sundeen, 'A Kid's Game', p.253.
24. Tsai Mien-Tang, 'Shadow Foe-the Legacy of Japanese Culture in Taiwan', online at http://etaiwannews.com?/History/2001/11/26/1006740731.htm, extracted Feb. 2002.
25. Ibid.
26. Hsieh, 'Taiwan Baseball'.
27. Tsurumi, *Japanese Colonial Education*, p.169.
28. Hsieh, 'Taiwan Baseball'.
29. Ibid.
30. Tai Pao-Tsun, 'Dragon Boat Festival', online at http://etaiwannews.com/History/2002/06/25/993440990.htm, extracted 4 Feb. 2002.
31. E.A. Winckler, 'Cultural Policy on Postwar Taiwan', in S. Harrell and Huang Chun-Chieh (eds), *Cultural Change in Postwar Taiwan* (Boulder, CO: Westview Press, 1994), p.30.
32. Wu Wen-Chung, *Chung Kuo Ti Yu Fa Chan Shi* [Chinese Sports Development History] (Taipei: Sanmin shuchu, 1981), p.231.
33. Chiao Yu Pu, *Di Su Chi Chunghuaminkuo chiaoyunianchian* [Fourth Issue of the Taiwanese Educational Almanac] (Taipei: Chiao Yu Pu [Department of Education], 1974), pp.1337–42.
34. W. Lyberg, *The IOC Sessions: 1894–1955* (Stockholm: National Olympic Committee of

Sweden, 1988–89), p.309, cited by D. Macintosh and M. Hawes, *Sport and Canadian Diplomacy* (Montreal and Kingston, ON: McGill-Queen's University Press, 1994), p.43.
35. Macintosh and Hawes, *Sport and Canadian Diplomacy*, p.43.
36. 'Taiwan May Rejoin Olympics', *New York Times*, 1 Aug. 1959, p.2, cited by Macintosh and Hawes, *Sport and Canadian Diplomacy*.
37. R. Espy, *The Politics of the Olympic Games* (London: University of California Press, 1979), p.80.
38. 'Medal Holders Hall–Olympic Games', online at http://wwwl.tpe-olympic.org/english2002/page03_2.htm, extracted 7 Feb. 2002.
39. 'Medal Holders Hall–Asian Games', online at http://wwwl.tpe-olympic.org/english2002/page03_2.htm, extracted 7 Feb. 2002.
40. http://www.decathlon2000.ee/english/legends;yang.htm, extracted 7 Feb. 2002.
41. Francis Huang, 'Taiwan's "Iron Man" to Return Home to Hospital', *Taipei Times*, 4 Jan. 2001, online at http://www.taipeitimes.com/news/2001/01/04/story/0000068331, extracted 2 Feb. 2002.
42. Rick Chu, 'Yang Chuan-Kuang Deserves Better', *Taipei Times*, 10 Jan. 2001, online at http://www.taipeitimes.com/news/2001/01/10/story/0000069188, extracted 2 Feb. 2002.
43. Ibid.
44. Ibid.
45. Ibid.
46. Ibid.
47. Huang, 'Taiwan's "Iron Man" to Return Home'.
48. Ibid.
49. 'Olympic Decision Hurts Taiwan', online at http://www.taipeitimes.com/news/2001/07/18/print/0000094634, extracted 2 Feb. 2002.
50. P. Carry, 'Going to Bat for Taiwan', *Sports Illustrated* (1974), 64–74.
51. Sundeen, 'A Kid's Game', 254.
52. 'Past Champions', online at http://www.littleleague.org/series/divisions/llbb/llbbhistory.htm, extracted 9 Feb. 2002.
53. Sundeen, 'A Kid's Game', 251.
54. Ibid.
55. See also Hsieh, 'Taiwan Baseball'.
56. Sundeen, 'A Kid's Game', 251–62.
57. Chiaoyupu, *Di wu tsi Chunghuaminkuo chiaoyu nianhian* [Fifth Issue of the Taiwanese Educational Almanac] (Taipei: Chiao Yu Pu [Department of Education], 1974), pp.1335–6.
58. M. Yahuda, 'The International Standing of the Republic of China on Taiwan', in D. Shambaugh (ed.), *Contemporary Taiwan* (Oxford: Clarendon Press, 1998), p.277.
59. C.R. Hill, *Olympic Politics* (Manchester: Manchester University Press, 1992), pp.43–4. See also pp.50–52.
60. Ibid., p.44.
61. Macintosh and Hawes, *Sport and Canadian Diplomacy*, p.46.
62. Ibid., p.47.
63. Ibid., p.49.
64. Ibid., p.53.
65. This account of the Taiwan situation relies heavily on Macintosh and Hawes, which contains much more detail of the actions of the Canadian government and the IOC.
66. Chiaoyupu, *Di wu tsi Chunghuaminkuo chiaoyu nianhian*, pp.1250–93.
67. Wu Pei-Shih, 'Former Olympian Discusses Challenges Facing Taiwan's Athletes', *Taipei Times*, 10 Jan. 2001, online at http://www.taipeitimes.com/news/2001/01/10/story/0000069189, extracted 6 Feb. 2002.
68. Hill, *Olympic Politics*, p.48.
69. Ibid.
70. Ibid., pp.48–9.
71. Monique Chu, 'In Games, China Sees Way to Mix Sports, Politics', *Taipei Times*, 17 July 2001.
72. *Ti liou tsi Chunghuaminkuo chiaoyu nianchian* [Sixth Issue of the Taiwanese Educational Almanac] (Taipei: Chiao Yu Pu [Department of Education], 1974), pp.1862–78.
73. T.B. Gold, 'Taiwan Society at the *Fin de Siècle*', in Shambaugh, *Contemporary Taiwan*, p.54.

74. *Ti liou tsi Chunghuaminkuo chiaoyu nianchian* [Sixth Issue of Educational Almanac], p.1890.
75. Ibid., pp.1909–22.
76. Ibid., pp.46–132.
77. The Republic of China Yearbook section on 'Sports and Recreation' does however note that a lack of facilities is a problem for the development of sport in Taiwan. See http://www.gio.gov.tw/taiwan-website/5-gp/yearbook/chpt23-6.htm, extracted 4 Feb. 2002.
78. Ibid.
79. National Council on Physical Fitness and Sports, 'Introduction', online at http://163.29.141.191/spo/english/, extracted 4 Feb. 2002.
80. More details about the roles of each of these units and the functions of the NCPFS can be found at http://163.29.141.191/spo/english/.
81. More details of the NCPFS can be found in their newsletter, which can be accessed electronically at http://163.29.141.191/spo/english/.
82.

TABLE 13.1
RESULTS OF TAIWAN'S PARTICIPATION IN THE ASIAN GAMES, 1954–98

Year	Gold	Silver	Bronze	Total	note
1954	2	4	7	13	
1958	6	11	17	34	
1962					Did not attend
1966	5	4	10	19	
1970	1	5	12	18	
1974					Did not attend
1978					Did not attend
1982					Did not attend
1986					Did not attend
1990	0	10	21	31	
1994	7	13	23	43	
1998	19	17	41	77	

TABLE 13.2
RESULTS OF TAIWAN'S PARTICIPATION IN THE OLYMPIC GAMES, 1960–2000

Year	Gold	Silver	Bronze	Total
1960	0	1 (track and field)	0	1
1968	0	0	1 (track and field)	1
1984	0	0	1 (weightlifting)	1
1988	2 (taekwando, demonstration)	0	3 (taekwendo, demonstration)	
1992	3 (taekwando, demonstration)	1 (baseball)	2 (taekwendo, demonstration)	1
1996	2 (taekwando, demonstration)	1 (table tennis)		1
2000		1 (weightlifting)	4 (2 weightlifting, 1 taekwendo and 1 table tennis)	5

Source: Chungkuo tiyu shi hsuehhui [China Sports History Association], *Chungkuo tiyu shi* [Chinese Sport History in Modern Times] (Beijing: Peiking tiyuan chupanshe [Beijing PE Institute Press], 2001).

83. Lin Yi-Chun, 'Chipang fangshui shichian chianke yichou wannian' [The Case of Corruption of Baseball Will Go Down in History as a Byword for Infamy], online at http://chemist.cycu.edu.tw/bbs_announce/D.914580867.A/D.914581080…/M.949233670. A_.htm, extracted 16 Feb. 2002.
84. 'Chipang chiantu an chichi weiliao, pangchiu wangtzi Liao Min-Hsiung pan tzaicho' [The Trail of Corruption in the Betting on Baseball Has Not Finished Yet and the Baseball Prince Liao Min-Hsiung Wishes to Come Out and Play], online at http://www.cts.com.tw/news/headlines/news20011129N15.htm, extracted 16 Feb. 2002. 'Kuo Hong-Chi – chiekouhsin erchi huanchin te hsishengche' [Kuo Hong-Chi – A Victim of Evil Environment], in *Chiumi yuanti*, online at http://palyballx.com/garden/Kou.htm, extracted 16 Feb. 2002.
85. Yang Chao, 'Meiyou hsiuhsianchuan te Taiwan chineng kanche chipang tsongken lanchu' [Taiwan, the Country without the Right of Leisure, Can only Watch the Corruption of Baseball], online at http://www.news7.comtw/weekly/old/545/article052.html, extracted 16 Feb. 2002.
86. 'Trampling on National Dignity', *e-Taiwan News*, 27 Dec. 2001, online at http://etaiwannews.com/History/2001/12/27/100915393.htm, extracted 5 Feb. 2002.
87. 'Disappointment at IOC', *e-Taiwan News*, 14 July 2001, online at http://etaiwannews.com/History/2001/11/26995081206.htm, extracted 4 Feb. 2002.
88. 'We Don't Want Beijing's Olympics', *e-Taiwan News*, 1 March 2001, online at http://etaiwannews.com/History/2001/03/01983419180.htm, extracted 5 Feb. 2002.
89. 'China Shocked to be on US Nuke Hit List', online at http://europe.cnn.com/2002/WORLD/asiapcf/east/01/12/china.nuclear/index/html, extracted 16 March 2002.

Sport in Modern India: Policies, Practices and Problems

PACKIANATHAN CHELLADURAI, D. SHANMUGANATHAN, JAIHIND JOTHIKARAN and A.S. NAGESWARAN

India is a vast country, with more than 1 billion people in a surface area of 3,288,000 square kilometres. Thus the population density is quite high at 336 people per square kilometre. Apart from the sheer size of its population, India is also characterized by great diversity in terms of religion, ethnicity, language, and culture.

Religions

Hinduism is the predominant religion, practised by nearly 80 per cent of the population, followed by Islam, practised by 11 per cent of the population. This 11 per cent actually makes it the largest single congregation of Muslims in the world. Sikhism, Buddhism, Jainism and Christianity are also practised by segments of the Indian population.[1]

Ethnicity

The Indian population is composed largely of two ethnic groups. The Indo-Aryan group accounts for 72 per cent of the population while the Dravidians constitute 25 per cent. The remaining three per cent belong to other ethnic groups.[2] The Dravidian ethnic people are found largely in the southern states of Andhra Pradesh, Karnataka, Kerala and Tamil Nadu.

Languages

There are 18 languages officially recognized by the Constitution of India. These are Assamese, Bengali, Gujarati, Hindi, Kannada, Kashmiri, Konkani, Malayalam, Manipuri, Marathi, Nepali, Oriya, Punjabi, Sanskrit, Sindhi, Tamil, Telugu and Urdu. It is suggested that as many as 1,652 dialects may be spoken in India.[3] It is a proof of the country's amazing diversity. These languages and their dialects belong to the Indo-Aryan and Dravidian families of languages. Hindi is the official language of India and English is an associate language. However, it must be noted that English is the one language spoken across the whole nation, albeit by a smaller percentage of the population. Further, inter-state governmental communications are largely carried out in English. In fact the largest English-speaking population outside the United States of America resides in India.

Most of the inter-state boundaries were drawn on a linguistic basis so that people who spoke the same language and its dialects were placed under one administration. Before independence, the British government had created provinces in such a way as to have more than one language group in each province. It was one way of enacting the 'divide and rule' policy. After independence the boundaries were redrawn to reflect the boundaries of the dominant languages. As of today, India is the largest democracy in the world and is modelled after Britain's parliamentary democracy. The Indian Union is made up of 29 states that are sufficiently autonomous in many areas.

Currency

The lowest denomination of the Indian currency is the paisa, 100 of which make up a rupee. The rupee is traded in international markets at the rate of approximately 46 rupees per US dollar. Instead of using the terminology of million and billion, the Indian governments and the people use the terminology of lakh (100,000) and crore (100 lakhs or 10,000,000).

Economic Development

India's gross national product (GNP) in 2000 was US$442.2 billion, ranking it the eleventh largest economy in the world, according to the World Bank. In comparison, South Korea ranked thirteenth and Australia ranked fifteenth.[4] The annual growth in the Indian economy was an astounding 6.9 per cent compared to less than three per cent in many developed nations such as Canada and the USA. Several United Nations reports laud the achievements of India in the agricultural, industrial, business, transport, technological and educational fields. However, the impact of the size of the economy and its annual growth is considerably diminished because of the huge population of India. Thus, the per capita GNP was only 450 US dollars, ranking it 162nd in the world. Even when converted to purchasing power parity, the per capita GNP rises to a modest sum of 2,149 US dollars with the rank of 153 in the world. Since gaining independence from British rule in 1947, India has relied heavily on state run industries and banks, resulting in self-sufficiency in several areas. In recent years, however, India has liberalized its industrial and trade policies resulting in large-scale investments by foreign corporations. The future looks very bright with the expectation that India, along with China, will be an industrial giant by the middle of this century.

INDIA'S PERFORMANCE IN INTERNATIONAL SPORT

India's performance in international sport is not consistent with its population and economic bases. For instance, at the 2000 Sydney Olympics, India was able to secure only one bronze medal, for K. Malleshwari in weightlifting. This was equal to the performance of much smaller countries such as Armenia, Barbados, Iceland, Israel, Kuwait, Macedonia, Qatar and Sri Lanka.[5] In contrast, Australia, which ranked only fifteenth in GNP, secured 16 gold, 25 silver and 17 bronze medals. At the thirteenth Asian Games, held in Bangkok in 1998, India secured seven gold, 11 silver and 17 bronze medals.[6] This placed India in ninth place behind countries like Thailand, Taiwan, Iran and North Korea. Despite this lacklustre performance in international competitions, India has done well in some sports. For instance, Indian cricketers compare very favourably with those from cricketing nations such as the UK, Australia, South Africa and the West Indies. Similarly, India can boast of some outstanding players in tennis and badminton. Vishwanathan Anand won the World Chess Championship held in Tehran in 2000. Abhinav Bindra created a world record in the air rifle event at the ISSF World Championship held in Munich in June 2000. Seema Antil won the first ever gold in the discus at the Junior World Athletics Championships.

Despite these sporadic achievements the overall image of Indian sport is not very encouraging. The failure to achieve prominence on the international scene can largely be attributed to the country's low per-capita income. Pursuit and achievement of excellence in sport is costly in terms of time, effort, dedication and monetary resources. While an individual may be willing to invest his/her personal resources of time, effort and dedication to excel in a given sport, the necessary financial resources may not be available to the average Indian. In several countries national and local governments provide funds in support of the pursuit of excellence in sport. The Indian government and its counterparts in the states also provide such funds for the promotion of sport and sporting excellence. Unfortunately, the actual amounts are meagre in relation to requirements. Such a situation is understandable when the same governments have to expend their resources and energies on issues of much greater priority, such as eliminating poverty, illiteracy and disease. The emphasis in the following pages is on the policies pursued by the government of India to promote sport and sporting excellence.

GOVERNMENT INITIATIVES TO PROMOTE SPORT

The following sections on the role of the Indian government, its policies and initiatives are drawn from websites of the Indian government and its ministries as cited in the endnotes. It was in 1954 that the government of India took its first step to promote sport by creating the All India Council of Sport (AICS). It was deemed to be an advisory body informing the government on (a) national sports policy; (b) government funding of national sport governing bodies; (c) regulation of sport governing bodies; (d) coaching of elite athletes; (e) selection of specific national teams for financial support in international competitions; (f) construction of sport facilities; and (g) selection of sportspersons for the Arjuna Award, the highest award India offers to sportspersons.[7]

National Sports Policy of 1984

The next significant policy initiative came in 1982, with the creation of a separate Ministry of Sport within the broader Ministry of Human Resource Development. Following this initiative the National Sports Policy was formulated in 1984. Further, the National Education Policy of 1986 included the National Sports Policy's emphases for application in the educational sector. In conjunction with the National Sports Policy the government also set up an apex body, the Sports Authority of India (SAI), in 1984 to promote (a) the development of coaches; (b) the training of physical education teachers; (c) participation in sport and physical activity; and (d) building infrastructure for sports. As Chelladurai and colleagues noted, 'these thrusts make eminent sense as they are designed to achieve three sufficiently distinct purposes –

pursuit of excellence, pursuit of knowledge in sport and physical activity, and pursuit of a healthy life style'.[8]

Apart from the supervisory role it played in the promotion of sport by all sectors, including state governments, and the financing of selected projects, the government of India also established two distinct government units to promote sport and physical education. The Netaji Subhas National Institute of Sport was set up in 1961, at Patiala in the state of Punjab, to train coaches in various sports including track and field. At present there are several branches that cater to the different regions of the country. The second unit is the Lakshmibai National College of Physical Education in Gwalior, in the state of Madhya Pradesh. These two institutions, oriented towards training coaches and physical education teachers, continue to serve as models for the state governments.

National Sports Policy of 2001[9]

At present sport comes under the jurisdiction of the Ministry of Youth Affairs and Sports. Noting that the National Sports Policy of 1984 was not implemented properly and that its goals were not realized, the Ministry has reformulated the National Sports Policy in 2001 to make it more concrete and to specify the measures to be undertaken and the agencies (for example, state governments, the Indian Olympic Association [IOA] and the national sports federations) to carry out these measures.

The two main objectives of the policy are to promote broad-based participation in sport (that is, mass sport) and the achievement of excellence at the national and international levels (that is, elite sport). Towards this end, sport and physical education are to become an integral part of the educational curriculum. The policy also suggests that those sports in which the country has the potential to excel would be vigorously promoted. The policy also envisages that broad-based sports would be the major responsibility of state governments. The promotion of the pursuit of excellence would be assumed by the union government and the Sports Authority of India in collaboration with the Olympic association and the national sports federations. The policy also places great emphasis on promoting participation by women and young people in rural areas. A more significant thrust of the policy is to move to include sport in the 'concurrent list' (as a joint responsibility of union and state governments) instead of leaving it to the states alone (leaving it in the state list) as it is now.

Sports Infrastructure

The 2001 National Sports Policy highlights the need for adequate sports facilities to promote both broad-based and excellence-oriented sports. It encourages local governments to maintain their existing facilities while adding to the infrastructure, and at the same time to put the available facilities to maximal use for the benefit of sportspersons. The Ministry will make efforts to provide more open land for the construction of sports facilities and to develop low-cost functional and environment-friendly designs for sports facilities so that they can be built at relatively low levels of investment.

Ranking of Sports Disciplines

In terms of promoting excellence, the National Sports Policy suggests that sports disciplines should be ranked on their potential for success, popularity and past performance in international competitions. The implication is that the higher-ranking disciplines would be supported more than the lower-ranking sports. The union government would also encourage the IOA and the state governments to place higher priority on such disciplines. The policy also advocates a scientific approach to the development of sportspersons by taking into account the genetic and geographical variations within the country when identifying and developing talent. It would also set up centres of excellence to foster and train those sportspersons identified for higher levels of performance.

Sport Governing Bodies

Another major thrust of the 2001 National Sports Policy relates to the IOA and the national sport federations. While recognizing that the IOA and the national sport federations, along with their state-level counterparts, are responsible for the management and development of sport, the National Sports Policy aims to help make these organizations more efficient and transparent in their operations. They must become result-oriented and be accountable for their actions. Accordingly, it proposes to draft model by-laws and organizational structures to be followed by the national sport federations, while respecting the Olympic Charter.

The 2001 National Sports Policy urges national sport federations to hold annual championships for all categories of participants – seniors, juniors and sub-juniors (for both men and women) at the district, state and national levels – with greater emphasis being placed on competitions for the juniors and sub-juniors. The policy also envisages the national sport federations drawing up long-term planning documents incorporating details of standards of performance, targeted levels of performance, participation in competitions at national and international levels, sports exchanges, scientific support and the holding of international competitions in India. More significantly, the policy stipulates that government support for these organizations is to be based on how well federations have carried out the plan and how well they have performed in relation to the plan.

Scientific Support

The National Sports Policy is intended to assign scientists to each sports discipline or group of disciplines to offer their expert services in terms of the various sports sciences that relate to sporting performance. The SAI and other relevant organizations will coordinate their efforts in scientific research to foster excellence in sport. In addition, attention will be paid to the training and development of coaches, referees and other officials without whose contributions the goal of excellence in sport cannot be achieved.

Financial Support

The government of India is also to offer financial incentives for sportspersons during their sporting careers and after their retirement as a form of recognition for their services to the country and as financial security (for example, insurance coverage and medical treatment). Such incentives would also motivate youth to pursue excellence in sports. The current system of reserving jobs for sportspersons will continue. Further, coaches, judges and referees will also be provided with financial incentives to improve their skills and enrich their experience. The recognition of sportspersons would also take the form of social awards and honours at the national, state and district levels.

Sport and Tourism

Although the linkage between sport and tourism has long been recognized in other countries, the National Sports Policy makes such a link for the first time in India. Recognizing the financial implications of this linkage, the government is to promote the volume of tourist traffic within the country and from abroad. Adventure sports would be a particular focus as the potential for revenue generation is great. A major effort will be undertaken to coordinate the activities of the relevant ministries/departments of the union and state governments, to draft unified policies to promote sport and tourism and to execute those plans efficiently.

Mobilization of Resources

As for resources for the promotion of sport, the National Sports Policy includes arrangements for higher budgetary provisions. In addition, to facilitate the mobilization of corporate funds for the development of sport the government may offer suitable incentives for corporations to adopt and support particular disciplines as well as sportspersons. The government, the sport federations and the corporations may enter into joint agreements to sponsor specific disciplines. The policy notes that the existing National Sports Development Fund has been created with an initial contribution from the union government. It is the intention of the government to continue the practice of exempting all contributions fully from income tax and to exert greater efforts to solicit contributions towards this fund. The government will also explore the feasibility of exempting the incomes of sport federations and sportspersons (from sources other than employers) from payment of income tax. Another significant policy statement is that the revenues stemming from broadcast rights for sporting events should be shared between the sports federation/association concerned and the broadcasting agency (whether public or private), through appropriate revenue-sharing arrangements.

Sport as a Diplomatic Tool

Finally, the policy recognizes the role that sport can play in fostering friendship and cooperation among countries in the region, through sporting exchange programmes and organized competitions:

> As a resurgent India confidently enters the New Millennium, Sports (and related activities) will be increasingly utilized as a medium for promoting cooperation and friendship in the Region, as also globally. Sports Exchange Programmes will be pursued with all friendly Nations, with emphasis, on the one hand on Advance Training for Sportspersons and Coaches, Scientific Support, the latest Research Aids and Development of Infrastructure, and earning laurels for the country, in Sports and Games, on the other.[10]

THE SPORTS AUTHORITY OF INDIA[11]

As noted, the SAI is the apex body controlling the promotion and development of sports in the nation. Also, the union minister in charge of sports chairs the governing body of the SAI. Its headquarters is located at Patiala in the Punjab. It has established six regional centres at Bangalore, Gandhinagar, Calcutta, Chandigarh, Delhi and Imphal and one sub-centre at Guwahati. In addition to training coaches, physical education teachers and sportspersons in these centres, the SAI also has two academic units. The first is the Netaji Subhas Bose National Institute of Sports at Patiala, which offers a degree/diploma programme in coaching, and conducts research and development in sport. The second unit is the Lakshmibai National College of Physical Education, with its headquarters at Gwalior and a branch at Thiruvanathapuram. In its efforts to promote sport and sporting excellence, the SAI initiates, undertakes and/or supports various projects and schemes. The more notable among them are a) sub-junior schemes to cater to those between ages eight and 17, involving schemes such as the Army Boys' Sports Companies and National Coaching Scheme; b) junior-level schemes involving the SAI Training Centres and the Special Area Games (that is, tribal areas) to train and develop children between 14 and 21 years of age; c) centres of excellence in regional SAI branches for priority disciplines.

National Sports Talent Contest Scheme

In addition, the SAI has also introduced a National Sports Talent Contest Scheme to identify genetically gifted and talented children in selected Olympic disciplines: athletics (track and field), badminton, basketball, football (soccer), gymnastics, hockey, swimming, table tennis, volleyball and wrestling. The scheme involves state governments administering a battery of tests to assess physical and psychomotor abilities to all children between eight and 12 years of age and organizing contests at local levels. Those children who excel at various competitions are to be included in this group of gifted and talented children.

Adopted Sports Schools

The scheme also envisages that those children identified as gifted and talented would be admitted to specially designated schools adopted by the SAI for scientific sports training. These 'adopted' schools would be residential and have good academic standing. They should also have the required sports facilities, such as a track, hockey and football fields, basketball and volleyball courts, and facilities for badminton, wrestling and so on. The SAI provides to each adopted school a lump-sum of Rs500,000–750,000 to create and/or improve sports facilities, and annual grant of Rs50,000 to maintain the facilities and to purchase sports equipment and books. While the SAI bears the costs of boarding, lodging, travelling and daily allowances, uniforms, books and sports kit for each student, parents are expected to bear the cost of tuition fees. There are, at present, 29 'adopted' schools, at which 1,033 trainees are undergoing training.

Training Centres

The SAI has set up 40 training centres across the nation to train sportspersons in 15 sports: athletics, archery, basketball, badminton, boxing, cycling, football, gymnastics, hockey, handball, judo, swimming, volleyball, wrestling, table tennis and weightlifting. Each training centre is designed to train sportspersons in three to four sporting disciplines. At the moment these centres train 1,760 people in the selected disciplines. The SAI pays for all recurring expenditure related to the trainees, as well as the coaches and administrative staff who run these centres.

Centres of Excellence

As an extension of the 'adopted' schools scheme for youth and training centres, the SAI has also set up centres of excellence on all six of its regional campuses. Sportspersons who have won medals or distinguished themselves at senior national-level competitions are selected for further training at these centres of excellence for nearly 200 days each year. From one perspective, these centres of excellence would be coaching camps for sportspersons at two or three of the highest levels of skills. Catering to more than one level of skill provides for continuity in emergence of highly skilled sportspersons for national representation. In the year 1999/2000, 115 sportspersons were trained at these centres of excellence in the disciplines of athletics, boxing, hockey, badminton, swimming, lawn tennis, kabaddi, table tennis and weightlifting.

Sports Academies

The SAI also facilitates the establishment of sports academies sponsored by the corporate sector. Sponsored and financially supported by a private or public corporation, a sports academy is formed to train talented sportspersons in one or more disciplines. The effort includes providing nourishing diets, proper coaching facilities and scientific support on a long-term basis. The SAI and the sports federations have jointly proposed a model for setting up such academies. In the year 2000/1, there were eight such academies:

- Hockey Academy with Air India (residential) at Delhi;
- Hockey Academy with SAIL (residential) at Rourkela for tribal players;
- Table Tennis Academy with Petroleum Sports Control Board (residential) at Ajmer;
- Handball Academy with SAIL (residential) at Bhilai;
- Volleyball Academy with Brihaspati Sports Academy at Narayanpur (MP);
- Basketball Academy with CABT at Indore;
- Rural Sports Academy for wrestling at Mungeshpur (Delhi);
- Hockey Academy with the Babu Memorial Society at Lucknow.

National Coaching Scheme

The SAI hires coaches in various disciplines and lends their services to state governments on a matching basis. These coaches are assigned to state-level and district-level coaching centres for the purpose of promoting broad-based sport (that is, mass sport). The coaches are also involved in identifying talented young people and grooming them towards excellence. Some coaches are also assigned to universities. The SAI had 1,600 coaches on its payroll during the year 2000/1. A panel of senior coaches is proposed for conducting national camps and monitoring the work and performance of coaches. In addition, incentives are provided to coaches in the form of cash awards for producing state, national and international champions.

Special Area Games

In order to tap into the talent that resides in the tribal areas of India, the Special Area Games have been founded to scout and nurture natural talent available in the tribal, inaccessible rural and coastal areas of the country.

Sports Fund for Pensions for Meritorious Sportspersons[12]

As an incentive towards higher performance in international competitions and as a reward of financial security for actual achievements, the National Sport Policy calls for a Sports Fund for Pension to Meritorious Sportspersons. The scheme would pay monthly pensions to those sportspersons who have won medals in specified international competitions (the Olympic Games, Commonwealth Games, Asian Games and world cups or world championships in selected disciplines). The rates of pensions and the standards of performance in the Olympic, Asian and Commonwealth Games are shown in Table 14.1.

TABLE 14.1
PENSION RATES FOR SPORTSPERSONS IN INDIA

No.	Performance standard	Amount in rupees
1.	Medallists at the Olympic Games	Rs2,500 per month
2.	Gold medallists in world cups or world championships in Olympic and Asian Games discipline	Rs2,500 per month
3.	Silver and bronze medallists in world cups/world championships in Olympic and Asian Games discipline	Rs2,000 per month
4.	Gold medallists in Asian Games	Rs2,000 per month
5.	Gold medallists in Commonwealth Games	Rs2,000 per month

National Welfare Fund for Sportspersons[13]

In order to help sportspersons who have been injured or incapacitated during participation in vigorous training and/or competitions, a Scheme for National Welfare Fund for Sportspersons is to be set up. The scheme would also cover those persons with outstanding performances on the international scene who have been disabled as an after-effect of their strenuous training. In addition, the fund would support sportspersons in indigent circumstances (that is, where the family income is less than Rs3,000 per month). The fund would also provide assistance in cash or kind to aspiring and talented sportspersons in their pursuit of excellence in sports. The rates of payment and the criteria are shown in Table 14.2.

TABLE 14.2
NATIONAL WELFARE FUND RATES FOR INDIAN SPORTSPERSONS

No.	Type	Criterion	Amount in rupees
1.	Lump-sum payment	Fatal injury in training for or participation in international competitions	100,000
2.	Lump-sum payment	Less than a fatal injury	40,000
3.	Monthly pension	Outstanding sportsperson permanently or indefinitely incapacitated and in indigent circumstances	2,500 per month
4.	Monthly pension	Other cases of injury and indigent circumstances	2,000
5.	Lump-sum payment to families	Outstanding sportsperson in indigent circumstances	4,000
6.	Assistant for medical treatment	Outstanding sportsperson in indigent circumstances	40,000
7.	Lump-sum assistance for sports promoters	Eminent sports commentators, coaches, umpires in indigent circumstances	10,000

Sports Scholarships[14]

Scholarships are also awarded to talented and promising boys and girls to secure nutritious diets and sports equipment for them in their pursuit of sport as a career. The scheme now provides for:

- Scholarships of Rs450 per month for sportspersons excelling at state level;
- Scholarships of Rs600 per month for sportspersons excelling at national level;
- Scholarships of Rs750 per month for sportspersons excelling at university and college-level competitions.

In addition, special scholarships for women in sport are also awarded as follows:

- Scholarships of Rs1,000 per month for senior women champions;
- Scholarships of Rs6,000 per course for women studying for diplomas in sports coaching at a SAI centre;
- Scholarships of Rs6,000 per year for three years for women studying for M.Phils/Ph.D.s in physical education.

Sports Awards[15]

In addition to financial incentives and scholarships, the government of India honours outstanding sportspersons with national awards. The following awards are highly cherished and they confer enormous social status and prestige on the recipients.

- *Rajiv Gandhi Khel Ratna Award*. This award, worth Rs300,000 in cash, and much more in terms of honour and dignity, is awarded to the most spectacular and outstanding performance in the field of sport by an individual sportsperson or a team in a year.

- *Special Awards to Medal Winners in International Sports Events*. The cash worth of these awards ranges from Rs75,000 to Rs1,500,000. They are given to sportspersons who win medals in international sporting events in disciplines included in the Olympic, Asian or Commonwealth Games as well as chess and billiards/snooker. Junior sportspersons also receive special awards for winning medals in World, Asian and Commonwealth Championships. In the year 1999/2000, 168 sportspersons received special awards.

- *Arjuna Award*. The Arjuna Award, the highest national recognition in sport, is bestowed on a sportsperson for outstanding performance during a year and the three years preceding it, and to those who have made lifetime contributions to their disciplines. The award consists of a bronze statuette of Arjuna (the hero of the Mahabaratha), a scroll of honour and a cash prize of Rs150,000. Sportspersons in a) disciplines of the Olympic, Asian or Commonwealth Games, as well as cricket; b) indigenous games; and c) sports for the handicapped are eligible for this award. To date 543 persons have received the Arjuna Award.

- *Dronacharya Award*. The Dronacharya Award is bestowed on eminent coaches of outstanding performers in international competitions. The award consists of a statuette of Guru Dronacharya, a scroll of honour and a cash prize of Rs250,000.

- *Maulana Abul Kalam Azad Trophy*. This trophy is awarded to a university for all-round performance in a year. The winning institution receives a replica of the trophy and a cash award of Rs100,000 for the purchase of sports equipment.

The foregoing description of the initiatives undertaken by the government of India through its Ministry of Youth Affairs and Sports in general, and the SAI in particular, shows how much effort and time has gone into devising projects and schemes to promote both mass and elite sport. As noted, these plans and projects are rational means to achieve the desired ends. As a blueprint for promotion of both mass and elite sport, the government of India's initiatives are comparable to those of governments in other countries.

THE NON-GOVERNMENTAL SECTOR

The well-laid plans of the government of India lose some of their impact due to poor implementation at the grassroots level. Further, government plans cannot by themselves elevate the status of sport within the country or abroad. They can only set the tone and directions for other segments of society to follow. If sport and sporting participation are to become part of the national psyche, sport governing bodies and educational institutions have to play a larger role than they do now. They are after all the conduits through which all government initiatives and support, and the benefits thereof, flow to the common people.

Sport Governing Bodies

The sport governing bodies such as the IOA, the national sport federations and the state sport associations have to carry the larger responsibility for promoting sport. There are 23 state Olympic associations and 30 national sport federations affiliated with the IOA. In a democratic society such as India, these sport governing bodies are expected to be most responsible for the promotion of sport.

There is some indication that all is not well with the sport governing bodies, as has been noted in government reports. Because they are not successful in carrying out their mandates, governments at various levels tend to impose rules to regulate their activities. Further, these sport governing bodies rely on the government for their resources instead of generating their own resources. This reliance on government grants and subsidies results in the operation of the 'golden rule' – that is, the one who has the 'gold' makes the 'rules'. This, in turn, leads to a lack of initiative and entrepreneurship, and to subservient and docile leadership within these sport governing bodies.

Even where the resources are available, the sport governing bodies apparently fail to capitalize on them. Take the case of the Board of Control for Cricket in India (BCCI). Cricket is the most popular sport in India. In fact it has been claimed that one in every two cricket fans watching a televised cricket game around the world is probably an

Indian, such is the fervour with which the Indian masses follow cricket. Such fervour has also led to the unsavoury practice of gambling followed by the involvement of bookies and players in fixing matches. As many cricket fans know, the Indian government ordered an inquiry into these malpractices. The government intelligence agency, the Central Bureau of Intelligence (CBI) unearthed considerable evidence on the existence of illegal linkages among gangster groups, bookies, players and officials. The CBI, in its report for 2001,[16] also noted the weaknesses of the sport governing body, the BCCI. It said that the BCCI was negligent in not preventing match-fixing and related malpractices. Moreover, it noted that the amounts of guarantee money received by the BCCI were 'not commensurate with India's standing in the cricketing world'. The BCCI had not provided any satisfactory explanation for consistently underselling itself in terms of guarantee money for various tournaments. Even in terms of selling advertising, there is no systematic evaluation of the market or appropriate pricing for advertising space. Further, the selection of state, regional and national teams and the appointment of coaches, managers and other officials are not always based on merit and are subject to malpractices. According to the CBI's report, the primary reason for this poor performance by the BCCI is the lack of accountability on the part of the BCCI to anyone but the administrators themselves. The report also noted that it is very hard for anyone who is not already in the clique of administrators to get into the BCCI or its counterparts in the states. This does not permit any fresh blood or ideas within the BCCI. It is not clear if this scenario of dysfunctional BCCI management as depicted by the CBI is reflective of a general pattern among sport governing bodies.

Educational Institutions

As Kamlesh, Chelladurai and Nair noted,[17] physical education and sport are rather weakly handled in educational institutions. Both union and state governments stipulate that every school and university must have adequate numbers of physical education and sports personnel based on the number of students. However, these physical education and sports personnel are not fully utilized for three significant reasons. First, in most states physical education is not a compulsory subject and thus does not have regularly scheduled classes. Second, adequate playing fields and equipment are often not available, particularly in urban schools. Finally, teachers and parents place a far greater emphasis on academic study at the expense of physical activity, sport and other leisure-time activities. If India is to become a dominant force in international sport, the educational institutions will have to place greater emphasis on sport and physical education. As guardians of young people in their formative years, they need to expose their students to quality experiences in sport and physical education.

THE FUTURE

As noted, the most serious limitation on the pursuit of excellence in sport in India is an economic one. The very low level of average family income in India cannot sustain any serious effort in this regard. Government subsidies and grants, while encouraging, cannot support all activities at the necessary level of extensive and intensive effort. The necessary support and encouragement must come from families and non-governmental agencies, such as the sport governing bodies and educational institutions. It is expected that these non-governmental institutions will be able to provide suitable levels of monetary support with the increasing economic power of India and the increasing size of the middle class, which is estimated to be around 40 per cent of the population.[18] Further, the increasing coverage of sporting events from around the world will also provide the impetus for a growing involvement in sport by young people and their families. By the same token, the corporate sector could also attempt to tap into the huge market of sport fans. An obvious way of accessing that market would be to sponsor sporting events involving Indian sportspersons. Such moves by the corporate sector could trigger further interest and involvement in sport. A final point on the future of sport in India relates to the government's suggestion about the issue of rating/ranking sport disciplines on the basis of potential and popularity. Along similar lines, the Indian sport movement may increasingly focus on those sports in which Indians are not hindered by their size (height, weight and so on). For example, competitions in boxing, wrestling, and weightlifting are organized, and winners declared, according to different classes of weight. Given the relatively smaller size of the average Indian, there is a much greater likelihood of India producing champions in the lighter weight classes than in the heavier ones. Other examples of sports where size is not the dominant factor in performance are rifle shooting, archery and gymnastics. Further, given the relatively low income of the average Indian family, it would be prudent to encourage the pursuit of excellence in those sports disciplines where it does not cost very much to participate. Middle- and long-distance running, wrestling and weightlifting are examples of sports that require minimal equipment and facilities. In the final analysis, the fundamental and deciding factor will be the desire and determination of the people to excel at international sport. As they say, 'where there is a will, there is a way'.

NOTES

1. Malayala Manorama. *Manorama Year Book 2001* (Kottayam, India: Malayala Manorama, 2001), p.629.
2. Freedom in the World, Freedom House, India (2001), online at http://www.freedomhouse.org/research/freeworld/2001/countryratings/india.htm.
3. Malayala Manorama, p.629.
4. World Bank, *World Development Report 2000/2001* (New York: Oxford University Press, 2001), p.274.
5. Sydney Olympic Games, *Sydney Games Medal Tally, 2000*, online at http://www.olympics.smh.com.au/tally.html.
6. ASIAD 98, *XIII Asian Games Results, Bangkok*, online at http://www.sadec.com/Asia98/Pages/Medil.htm.
7. P. Chelladurai, M.L. Kamlesh and U.S. Nair, 'Management of Sport in India', in *Sport Management: An International Approach* (Lausanne: International Olympic Committee, 1996), pp.69–75.
8. Ibid., p.70.
9. Government of India, *National Sports Policy 2001*, online at http://yas.nic.in/vsyas/nsp2001.htm.
10. Ibid.
11. Government of India, *Sports Authority of India*, online at http://yas.nic.in/vsyas/sai.htm
12. Government of India, *Pension Fund for Sportspersons*, online at http://yas.nic.in/vsyas/merit.htm.
13. Government of India, *Welfare Fund for Sportspersons*, online at http://yas.nic.in/vsyas/nsp2001.htm.
14. Government of India, *Sports Authority of India*, online at http://yas.nic.in/vsyas/sai.htm.
15. Ibid.
16. Government of India, *Report on Match-Fixing in Cricket*, online at http://yas.nic.in/vsyas/mfrep.htm.
17. M.L. Kamlesh, P. Chelladurai and U.S. Nair, 'National Sport Policy in India', in L. Chalip, A. Johnson and L. Stachura (eds), *National Sport Policies: An International Handbook* (Westport, CT: Greenwood Press, 1996), pp.228–30.
18. Chelladurai, Kamlesh and Nair, 'Management of Sport in India', p.74.

From Iran to All of Asia: The Origin and Diffusion of Polo

H.E. CHEHABI and ALLEN GUTTMANN

The Ball no question makes of Ayes and Noes,
But Right or Left as strikes the Player goes;
And He that toss'd Thee down into the Field,
He knows about it all – HE knows – HE knows![1]

THE ORIGINS OF POLO

In all probability polo developed from rough equestrian games played by the mounted nomadic peoples of Central Asia, both Iranian and Turkic. In Afghanistan such a game survived into the twentieth century. In its original form *buzkashi* was a dusty mêlée in which hundreds of mounted tribesmen fought over the headless carcass of a goat or a calf. The winner was the hardy rider who managed to grab the animal by the leg and drag it clear of the pack.[2] In the 1960s a tamer version of the game was developed in Afghanistan under the auspices of the National Olympic Committee,[3] but in the aftermath of the Soviet invasion of 1978 the original rough version experienced a renaissance in the refugee camps of Pakistan. In 1996 the puritanical Taliban outlawed the game in those parts of Afghanistan which they controlled. In the neighbouring regions of northern Pakistan another form of polo has survived to this day.[4] But it was further to the west, in Iran (formerly known in the West as Persia), that polo was developed into the game it is today, played with a wooden stick, *chowgān*, and a round ball, *guy*. In time the word *chowgān* came to denote the game itself.[5]

POLO IN IRAN

In ancient Iran, polo was a favourite game of kings and noblemen. But as Wolfgang Knauth shows in his study of the athletic performance of Iranian kings, the Achaemenid founders of the first Persian empire did not know the game.[6] It seems probable that polo was introduced by the Parthian dynasty (247 BCE–224 CE), which originated in north-eastern Iran (roughly Khurasan), close to the steppes of Central Asia. (Parthian equestrian prowess was admitted even by their perennial enemies the Romans.) In its later phase the Parthian state was decentralized and there occurred 'a proliferation of titles and insignia, war, hunting, polo, feasting, and the recitations of epic poetry [characteristic of] aristocratic life'.[7]

The earliest known mention of polo seems to corroborate the hypothesized Parthian origin of the game. The early seventh-century text *Kārnāmak-e Ardashir-e Pâpakān*, which records the deeds and exploits of Ardashir (r. 224–41), the third-century founder of the Sasanian dynasty (224–651 CE), we learn that Ardashir appeared at the court of his suzerain, the last Parthian King, Ardavān V (r. 212–24), and so impressed the king that he told him to accompany his sons and other princes to the polo grounds, where Ardashir proved himself better than the princes at the game.[8] His Sasanian successors were enthusiastic patrons of the game. In a brief text, probably written shortly before the end of the dynasty, the last major Sasanian ruler, Khosrow II (r. 590–628), meets a young nobleman who seeks employment at court. The young man boasts that 'on the hippodrome I am proficient in the ball game',[9] which is obviously meant as proof of his qualifications for office. The Sasanians' love of polo is also attested by the great Muslim historian Tabari (838–923), who almost certainly had access to ancient Persian sources.

In 650 Muslim Arab invaders put an end to the Sasanian empire and Iran became a part of the Muslim caliphate. Polo continued to flourish under Islam. Some 200 years after the Arab conquest, local Iranian dynasties, some of which traced their ancestry back to noble families of pre-Islamic Iran, reasserted their independence in the eastern lands of the caliphate. The rulers of these states also practised polo. It is related that one of them, the Saffarid 'Amr b. Layth (r. 879–901), who was blind in one eye, was admonished by one of his army commanders not to play polo, even though the commander himself indulged in the game. Asked by the ruler to explain, the commander replied:

> I have two eyes. If one of them should happen to be struck by the ball, I should be blinded in one eye, but one would still remain to me with which I should be able to behold the world. You have only the one eye, and if by accident the ball should hit it, you would be compelled to bid farewell to the emirate of Khurasan.[10]

Polo was obviously a dangerous game. One could lose not only one's throne (blind men were deemed unfit to rule) but also one's life. This is exactly what happened to 'Abd al-Malik (r. 954–61), a prince of the Samanid dynasty that ruled Khurasan and Transoxiana from its capital in Bukhara. 'Abd al-Malik frequently played polo, but one day he had drunk too much wine and was unable to control his horse which threw him and broke his neck.'[11] It is no surprise that the *Qābusnāmeh*, a celebrated eleventh-century manual of statecraft, ethics and good manners written by a minor Ziarid ruler in northern Iran for his son, advised the youth to play polo no more than once or twice a year and to station himself prudently at one end of the field where it was possible to avoid scrimmage and collision.[12]

The Turkic and Mongol dynasties that ruled Iran from the mid-eleventh century onwards continued the royal patronage of polo. Sultan Mahmud (r. 998–1030) played the game and one of his court poets, Farrokhi, devoted an entire poem to his game.[13] Elsewhere the poet wrote: 'There are four things for kings to do:/ To feast, hunt, play polo, and make war.'[14] For these rulers, as the mystical poet Rumi (1207–73) tells us, polo was a way to achieve proficiency in the art of warfare.[15] The great conqueror Timur (1336–1405), known in the West as Tamerlane, seems to have promoted polo as well as Islam in his domains, which extended from Russia through Iran and Central Asia to India. The Persian poet Hafiz (1320–89) drew upon Timur's knowledge of the game when he wished him luck: 'May the heads of your enemies be your polo balls.'[16] Timur is said to have done exactly what the poet suggested he do.[17]

The Safavids, who ruled for more than two centuries and created the modern Iranian state as we know it, were all ardent polo players. A poem by Mohammad Qāsem Jonābādi celebrates a polo game played by the dynasty's founder, Shah Ismail (r. 1502–24).[18] In 1540 the Venetian envoy Michele Membrè observed a game of polo in the Safavid capital of Tabriz in which the King, Shah Tahmāsh, and his brother each led a team of five players:

> The King mounts, and in the said *maidān*, that is, piazza, he gallops his horse and plays at the wooden ball with the wooden bat, galloping on his horse. He places two pillars in the said *maidān* as marks, and they play in company, his brother with four men, and the Shah with four others. So, each has his pillar to mark. So, the Shah aims to have his ball pass his pillar and his brother aims to have it pass his. And they gallop, hitting the said wooden ball, which is small, a little larger than an egg. And they ride and play in that way for two hours; and the people of the land and the soldiers, an infinite number, stand all around by the walls and in the street; and when they see the Shah, they bow their heads on the earth and say, '*Shāh, Shāh*', as I have said.[19]

The greatest of the Safavid rulers, Shah Abbās (r. 1587–1629), was himself an ardent polo player whom the English traveller Sir Anthony Sherley described at play. Sherley emphasized the game's musical accompaniment. When the king 'had taken his horse, the drums and trumpets sounded ... and ever when [he] had gotten the ball before him, the drums and trumpets would play one alarum'.[20] When Shah Abbās moved the Safavid capital to Isfahan, he gave this ancient city a new centre organized around a grand square, the *maydān*, which was used for polo; the stone goal posts still stand today. Overlooking the square was his new palace, from the balconies of which one could watch the game:

> When the King wishes it, and this is almost every evening, the game of pall-mall [polo] is played ... and whoever knows how and whoever wishes to comes out to play; and some who play well, though they may not be of high standing, the King himself often calls on to play. The King too plays, and this ... he does very well, and perhaps better than any other.[21]

In the 1670s a game in the main square was described thus:

> Their Play at the Mall is perform'd in a very great Place, at the end of which are Pillars near each other, which serve for the Ball to pass thro'. They throw the Ball in the middle of the Place, and the

Players with a Mall-stick in their Hand, gallop after it to strike it: As the Mall-stick is short, they must stoop bellow the Saddle-bow to strike it, and by the Rules of the Game, they must take their Aim galloping. They win their Match, when they have made the Ball pass between the Pillars. They play at this Game, having fifteen or twenty to a side.[22]

After the end of the Safavid dynasty the game seems to have suffered greatly from the general state of upheaval and insufficient court patronage,[23] but it was eventually reintroduced into Iran in the late nineteenth century by Major Sir Percy Sykes, who had British and Indian troops play it in Tehran and Mashhad.[24]

POLO IN PERSIAN LITERATURE AND ART

It is a tribute to the popularity of polo that its imagery entered Persian poetry soon after Persian was revived as a literary language about a millennium ago. In the *Book of Kings* (*Shāhnāmeh*), the national epic of Iran written by Hakim Abu l-Qāsem Ferdowsi (933–1021), horses and horsemanship play an important role.[25] Kings, princes and heroes are forever playing polo – even those who belong to the largely mythical origins of the Iranian state, a period that antedates the first historically attested mention of polo by many centuries and for which no archaeological, historiographic or numismatic evidence exists.[26] One famous episode describes a game played by Afrāsiyāb, king of Turan, who leads a Turanian team against an Iranian one captained by his son-in-law Siāvosh, the son of the king of Iran. In the course of this first 'international' polo competition Siāvosh first 'smote [the ball] so high that it disappeared from sight', and then struck another ball 'until it appeared to come alongside the moon'.[27]

The last ruler of Siāvosh's Kianid dynasty, Dārā (sometimes written as Dārāb), is equated in the Iranian epic tradition with the historical Darius III, the last of the Achaemenids. Both were defeated by Alexander of Macedonia (r. 336–23 BCE), except that the Iranian epic tradition turned Alexander into a son, by a Macedonian princess, of the penultimate Kianid king, making Alexander an older half-brother of Dārā and a legitimate heir to the Iranian throne, which he assumes after defeating Dārā.[28] Having thus naturalized Alexander and removed the stigma of having been an enemy of Iran, mediaeval Persian romances were free to recount his heroic exploits. These romances were based on the Greek Alexander romance, which contains an episode in which the Persian King sends Alexander a ball – the implication being that he should stick to children's games and leave warfare to adults.[29] In the Persian literary tradition this ball becomes the *guy* and *chowgān* of polo, and Alexander tells the Persian envoy that the ball symbolizes the earth and that he, Alexander, is the mallet that will send it where he wills. The story was mentioned in the history of Tabari and then became an episode in a number of Persian Alexander romances,[30] the most famous of which is the *Eskandarnāmeh* of Nezāmi Ganjavi (1140–1202).[31]

The historically attested taste of the Sasanians for polo also left traces in Persian literature. Ardashir I had a son by a daughter of Ardavān V, the last Parthian ruler. This son, Shāpur, was raised in obscurity, but he was quickly recognized by his father when he alone among the youthful polo players was bold enough to retrieve a wayward ball that had rolled beneath his father's throne. In Ferdowsi's version:

> To a slave the king said, 'Go and bring [the children's] ball here with a mallet so that I can see which of those boys will approach, boldest of the bold, lion-like, and carry off the ball under my very eyes. ... The one who does that will indubitably be my own pure son. ... The king's slave departed at his command, struck the ball and bore it ahead of him while mounted on horseback. The boys galloped after him swift as arrows but as they neared Ardashir they stopped short and remained where they stood, having failed to overtake the ball. Shâpur the Lion advanced, took possession of the ball before the father's face and carried it off, passing it to the other boys when he had gone some distance away.

Ardashir was overjoyed.[32]

Khosrow II was another Sasanian enthusiast for polo. In the poem *Khosrow and Shirin* the poet Nezāmi told how the ruler met his Armenian wife Shirin. When he came upon her and her girlfriends he was 'ignorant of their strength and courage', but when they began to play polo he marvelled to see that the girls, whose beauty reminded him of 'doves in the meadow', played the game 'likes hawks in their attacks'. When Khosrow challenged them to a game, 'now Shirin won, now the Shah'.[33]

Lyric poetry, too, used polo for its images. 'The beloved's long, curved tresses resemble, at least in the poet's eye, a polo stick which has caught the poor, spinning head of the confused lover.' To give but one example from the poet Mo'ezzi:

> For lovers the heart is like a ball and their back is curved like a polo stick,
> Because the chin [of the beloved] resembles the ball and his tresses the mallet.[34]

Polo metaphors found their way into mystical poetry. The 'highest bliss' occurred when a mystic was 'driven hither and thither by the polo stick of the beloved or of Love itself'.[35]

The centrality of polo to court life meant that it became, together with hunting, a favourite subject for Persian (and later Turkish and Indian) miniature painters, who illustrated scenes from Ferdowsi's *Shāhnāmeh* and Nezāmi's various romances.[36] This tradition is alive to this day, as any visit to an Iranian handicrafts store will prove.

POLO'S SPREAD IN THE WEST

From Iran polo spread westwards through the Byzantine Empire to its capital of Constantinople, where it may have been played as early as the fourth century. The Greek term for the game was *tzykanion* (from the Persian *chowgān*).[37] Emperor Theodosius II (r. 408–50) built a stadium in Constantinople for the game, the *tzykanisterion*. The sport was very popular among members of the imperial court and the nobility. Basil I (r. 867–86) excelled at it, and John I (r. 1235–38), Emperor of Trebizond, was fatally injured while playing in that city's *tzykanisterion*.[38] Of twelfth-century Crusaders passing through Asia Minor on their way to the Levant, the French historian Jean-Jules Jusserand wrote that 'their enemies Noureddin and Saladin loved the game quite as much as their Byzantine friends. The Crusaders took the idea of the game back to France, where it prospered only as a game played on foot.'[39] A generation later, in 1204, the French Crusaders who seized and sacked Constantinople were also enamoured of the game and carried it with them when they returned to France, where polo once again failed to take root.

After the Arab conquest of Syria and Iraq in the mid-seventh century, the Umayyad and Abbasid caliphs who ruled the Muslim world continued the Sasanian tradition of patronizing the game. Polo was played in the Umayyad capital of Damascus under the second

Umayyad caliph, Yazid I (r. 680–83), and in Baghdad during the reign of the Abbasid caliph Hārun al-Rashid (r. 786–809), the contemporary of Charlemagne who is better known to Western audiences as the presumed listener to Scheherazade's *Thousand and One Nights* (in which polo makes several appearances). Hārun al-Rashid's son Ma'mun (r. 813–33) had a polo ground constructed near his palace. In the city of Samarra, which was the Abbasid capital from 836 to 892, a large polo field can be seen to this day.[40] After the caliphs the secular rulers who succeeded them in the Arab Near East, like their contemporaries in Iran, continued playing polo, which is known in Arabic as *sawlajān*.[41] The founder of Egypt's Ayyubid dynasty, Salah al-Din (r. 1169–1193), more familiar in the West as the Crusaders' chivalrous opponent Saladdin, was a polo enthusiast, and so was the Mamluk ruler Baibar I (r. 1260–77), a man renowned for his physical prowess, who was said to have played polo in both Cairo and Damascus in a single week.[42]

In Anatolia the Seljuk and then the Ottoman Turks played the game, but it was less popular than another game played on horseback, *cirit*.[43] Polo was also known among the Kurdish population of eastern Anatolia, where it was described by Evliya Celebi in 1655:

> At either end of the arena are stone pillars. Two teams of a thousand horsemen each gather on each side, every man wielding a crooked mallet of cornel wood. In the middle of the arena they place a round wooden ball the size of a man's head. As the eight-fold band strikes up, and the beat of the drums reaches a peak, one man from each side gallops forth and tries to knock the ball past the goal post on his side. ... And so it goes on ... until [the ball] is torn into pieces. ... It is an excellent military exercise, although occasionally it turns into a real battle over the ball, and blood is shed. ... In all of Kurdistan and Iran, this is the favourite cavalry exercise.

Celebi adds that the doctors of law disapproved of polo and strictly forbade it. Their reason is intriguing: according to Celebi, the Umayyad caliph Yazid played polo with the head of the Prophet Muhammad's grandson Husayn after he, whom the Shi'ite Muslims consider their third Imam (legitimate successor of the Prophet), was martyred in Kerbala in 680 CE. This obviously did not prevent the Safavids, who made Shi'ism the official religion of Iran, from enthusiastically patronizing the game. Celebi explained, rather lamely, that 'the Persians and the Kurds are not familiar with [the story], and so they indulge in polo'.[44]

POLO'S SPREAD IN THE EAST

The Islamic conquest of the northern parts of the Indian subcontinent began in 711, and Muslim rule reached a culmination in the Mughal Empire established by Tamerlane's descendant Babur. Polo arrived with the Islamic invaders. The first sultan of Delhi, Qutbuddin Aimak (r. 1206–10) died prematurely during a polo game when he fell from and was then crushed by his horse. Emperor Akbar (r. 1556–1605), the most famous of the Mughal rulers, was, like his contemporary Shah Abbās of Iran, renowned for his polo skills and for his love of the game, which he also played at night, using luminous balls made from the wood of the palas tree. His advisor Abu l-Fazl (1551–1602) wrote a lively defence of Akbar's favourite pastime:

> Superficial observers regard the game as a mere amusement, and consider it mere play; but men of more exalted views see in it a means of learning promptitude and decision. Strong men learn, in playing the game, the art of riding; and the animals learn to perform feats of agility and to obey the reins. It tests the value of a man and strengthens bonds of friendship. Hence His Majesty is very fond of this game.[45]

Mughal literature and art, which reached their apogee in the seventeenth century, frequently depicted polo players. A number of illuminated manuscripts depict Akbar's son Jahangir (r. 1605–27) playing polo.[46] The text of one manuscript urges him to strike the ball boldly.[47] Hindu princes were not encouraged to do likewise. In fact their Muslim rulers tried to prevent Hindus from drinking and playing polo, two activities liable to make them unruly if not rebellious subjects.[48] Mughal art sometimes included female polo-players, but we cannot be sure that the scenes depicted contemporary customs; an anachronistic miniature from the court of Akbar shows us the Queen Homāi (mother of Dārā) at play.

Although historians are uncertain when polo reached China, it is a fair conjecture that it came by way of the Silk Road, one branch of which began in north-eastern Iran and reached north-western China by way of Turkistan and Tibet. It is certain that the game was quite popular throughout the Tang dynasty (618–907 CE). A wall-painting from the tomb of Li Xian (653–84) shows a game of polo in which more than 20 riders rush to gain control of the ball, but Tang-era teams were normally composed of 16 players whose strenuous efforts were accompanied by music. Archaeological evidence indicates that a large ball field was constructed in the palace grounds at Chang'an in 831. Ten of the 14 Tang emperors are known to have played polo and some were said to have made skill at polo a prerequisite for advancement in the civil service. Emperor Xiaong (r. 874–88) remarked about his own obsession with the game that he would have taken top honours if civil-service examinations were given in polo. At one point he staged a game of polo in order to determine which of four generals he should appoint to command a garrison.[49]

Emperor Ruizong (r. 684–90, 710–12) and the ladies of his court were said to have been greatly amused when some elderly courtiers, whom he had ordered to play the game, fell to the ground:

> His Majesty, who was paying a visit to his famous Pear Garden, had given orders that all officials *above* the third grade were to take part in the game; but certain eminent statesmen were worn out and aged, the consequence being that they were tumbled over on to the ground, and remained there, unable to rise, to the great amusement of the Emperor, Empress and Court ladies, who all shouted with laughter at the sight.[50]

Poor sportsmanship seems to have a long history.

Ruizong's son Xuanzong (r. 712–56) 'presided over one of the most glorious epochs in all Chinese history'. He was 'a lively patron of poetry, music, dance, and the arts'[51] – and of polo. He may well have devoted too much of his time and energy to fun and games. His ministers revolted and his son deposed him.

Polo was widely played in the Chinese army and the most skilled player of the entire dynasty may have been General Xia. During the reign of Dezong (r. 779–805) Xia is said to have placed a stack of 12 coins in the middle of the polo field and then to have struck them, at full gallop, one by one, 20 metres into the air.[52] There was a downside to the popularity of polo among military men. When the Mongols invaded China the Chinese generals were said to have been 'more competent at polo than at war'. One of them was satirized as the 'polo-stick commander'.[53]

Li Guo was among the many Tang poets who wrote about polo. In his eyes, 'the tip of the polo sticks curves like a crescent moon'.[54] Another Tang poet, Wang Jian, wrote of the somatic benefits to court ladies who had taken up polo: 'Since the ladies of the court have learned to play polo, they ride with slender hips.'[55] These women were definitely not isolated examples of female participation in the game. Many Tang statuettes show women riding and wielding polo sticks. Six of these statuettes are shown in Carl Diem's *Asiatische Reiterspiele*.

Polo continued to be played during the Song dynasty (960–1279). Women of the court, including the empress, played the game as they had during the Tang era. During this period there were also polo matches for mixed male-and-female teams and there is even a report of a game played 'in drag' by young men dressed as girls. (They rode donkeys instead of ponies.) There were also nocturnal games played by torchlight. On the whole, however, enthusiasm for polo was less intense and less widespread than it had been. Members of the court no longer rode horses and the game seems to have been 'largely limited to professional players in the army and to court entertainers'.[56]

If that was the case then Emperor Taizong (r. 976–97) was an exception. He staged a national polo tournament and participated in it as an active player. It was he who began play and resumed play after a goal was scored. Chang'an's relatively simple polo field, on which the Tang emperors had played, developed into splendid grounds. By this time it was customary to have two goals rather than one and to have the goals defended by goalkeepers. The east and west goals were bedecked with flags and each was surmounted by a golden dragon. The 'Easterners' wore yellow; the 'Westerners' wore red. Gongs were sounded to signal that a goal had been scored. To some, Taizong's enthusiasm seemed excessive. One of his advisers warned him that his participation in the game created a political problem. When his team won his subjects were shamed by the defeat; when his team lost his subjects grew haughty and forgot their place. In either event time spent in play was time not spent on his imperial duties.[57]

The Southern Song emperor Xiaozong (r. 1163–89) was also devoted to the game:

From Iran to All of Asia: The Origin and Diffusion of Polo 395

His ministers ... were unwilling that his Majesty should expose himself to danger, and handed in many memorials, to none of which any attention was paid. One day, the Emperor decided to join in the game; after playing for a short time, he lost control of his pony. The animal bolted under a verandah, the eaves of which were very low; there was a crash, and the terror-stricken attendants crowded around to help. The pony had got through, and his Majesty was left hanging by his hands to the lintel. He was at once lowered to the ground; but there was no trace of alarm on his face, and, pointing to the direction taken by the pony, he quietly gave orders for its recapture. At which point the relieved spectators cheered.[58]

Taoist priests frequently objected to the game. As early as the Tang period one of them complained that 'polo hurts the vitality of the players and it also hurts that of the horses'.[59] During the Song dynasty Confucian scholars articulated their doubts about polo: 'From the standpoint of strict Confucian morality, polo was akin to heavy drinking, gambling, popular music, licentious conduct, and other forms of immoral activity.'[60] Criticisms of this sort may have had some effect. Polo went into a decline during the Ming (1368–1644) and the Qing (1644–1911) dynasties. According the James T.C. Liu, Xiaozong was the game's last imperial enthusiast; after him, 'not a single Chinese emperor or prince has ever played polo'.[61] Despite the game's loss of popularity the most beautiful Chinese depiction of the game was executed during the Qing dynasty. It was a set of ink drawings done in 1747 by the artist Ding Yuanpeng. The drawings were not, however, contemporary. The scroll was copied by Ding Yuanpeng from pictures, now lost, painted by the better-known Song dynasty painter Li Gonglin (also known as Li Longmian; 1049–1106).[62] Li Gonglin's interest may have been in the horses rather than their riders; he was warned 'that if he continued much longer [to paint horses] he would become like a horse himself, whereupon he switched to other themes'.[63]

Korean culture has been thoroughly influenced by China and in this country a game similar to polo existed, known as *Kyuk Koo*. Used by the court to train soldiers and horses for mounted combat, games of *Kyuk Koo* were surrounded by ceremony and often attended by royalty.[64] According to James T.C. Liu, 'Korean historical records mention the ritual of polo 51 times before the time of the Mongol invasion'.[65] After the invasion the game seems to have gone into a decline.

Polo seems, however, to have been played by the Japanese of the Nara (710–94) and Heian (794–1185) periods. Whether the game arrived in Japan via Korea or directly from China is unknown, but the *Man'yōshū* an eighth-century collection of poetry, indicates that the game of *dakyū* ('strike the ball') was played by court aristocrats in Nara in 727. For the next 500 years the game was popular among the nobility. During the Heian period, when the emperor ruled from Kyoto, the imperial guards included *dakyū* among the annual events of the fifth lunar month. As power shifted from the emperor to the Fujiwara clan and then to the *shogun*s ('generals') of Kamakura, the game gradually died out. The last recorded performance at court occurred in 986. Since *dakyū* was played on foot as well as from horseback, it is not always clear whether the games played in Nara and Kyoto should be classified as polo or as a Japanese equivalent of the Native American game of lacrosse. The immense popularity of *yabusame* and other forms of mounted archery suggests, however, that *dakyū* was primarily an equestrian sport.[66]

After a long period in which references to the game were sparse or non-existent, *dakyū* was revived in the eighteenth century by Tokugawa Yoshimune (1684–1751), but the sticks resembled lacrosse sticks rather than polo mallets. The ball seems to have been hurled rather than hit. This was certainly the case when the game was performed at court, early in the twentieth century, for the amusement of British diplomats, one of whom opined that the Japanese 'set a great value on their game of *dakyū*'.[67]

By the time of *dakyū*'s revival in eighteenth-century Japan, polo had all but disappeared from the continental Asian cultures that had invented and developed the game. It survived, however, in northern India, in the Hindu Kush and in the princely state of Manipur. It is not clear whether these games, introduced in 1600,[68] were influenced by the courtly culture of the Mughals or were direct descendants of the Central Asian game.[69] Be this as it may, it was on the borderlands of Burma, in Manipur, that British soldiers were introduced to the pleasures of swinging a mallet and driving a polo ball through a goal while galloping at full speed. Tea-plantation workers from Manipur played the game and were observed, in 1854, by Lieutenant J.F. Sherer: 'Fascinated with the charms of the sport, he took to playing himself.'[70] Together with

Captain Robert Stewart, Sherer organized a polo club in 1859. Stewart's brother introduced the game in Punjab (in what is now Pakistan). By 1877 the game was popular throughout British India. An interregimental polo tournament was organized that year. British officers took the game with them when they were posted home. From Britain it spread to the rest of the world, including Iran, to which it returned in 1897.[71]

NOTES

The authors wish to thank Melissa Birch and Sunil Sharma for their help.

1. *Rubaiyat of Omar Khayyam*, trans. Edward Fitzgerald (Garden City, NY: Dolphin Books, n.d.), pp.45, 72, and 98.
2. C. Whitney Azoy, *Buzkashi: Game and Power in Afghanistan* (Philadelphia, PA: University of Pennsylvania Press, 1982).
3. For the rules see *Mosâbeqeh-ye Buzkashi* (Kabul: Government Printing Press, 1971).
4. Peter Parkes, 'Indigenous Polo and the Politics of Regional Identity in Northern Pakistan', in Jeremy MacClancy (ed.), *Sport, Identity and Ethnicity* (Oxford: Berg, 1996), pp.43–67. It is unclear whether this game is a lineal descendant of the original Central Asian game or a local adaptation of the highly ceremonial game played at the Mughal courts.
5. *Encylopaedia of Islam*, 2nd edn, s.v. 'Cawgân'. *Chawgân* is a cognate of *chub*, which means wood.
6. Wolfgang Knauth, 'Die sportlichen Qualifikationen der altiranischen Fürsten', *Stadion*, II (1976), 48.
7. Malcolm A.R. Colledge, *The Parthians* (London: Thames and Hudson, 1967), p.175.
8. Darab Dastur Peshotan Sanjana, *The Kârnâm î Artaakhshîr Pâpakân* (Bombay: Education Society's Steam Press, 1896), pp.6–7.
9. Jamshedji Maneckji Unvala, *Der Pahlavi Text 'Der König Husrav und sein Knabe'* (Vienna: Adolf Holzhaurer, 1917), p.15.
10. Kai Kā'ūs ibn Iskandar, *A Mirror for Princes: The Qābūs Nāma*, trans. Reuben Levy (London: Cresset Press, 1951), p.86. The association of polo with the Saffarids is interesting, for this dynasty was of decidedly non-noble origin, their founders' father having been a coppersmith.
11. Richard N. Frye, *Bukhara: The Medieval Achievement* (Costa Mesa, CA: Mazda, 1997), p.88.
12. Kai Kâ'ùs, *A Mirror for Princes*, p.86.
13. Annemarie Schimmel, *A Two-Colored Brocade: The Imagery of Persian Poetry* (Chapel Hill, NC: University of North Carolina Press, 1992), p.441, n2.
14. Ibid., p.286.
15. Mowlana *Jalâleddin* Rumi, *Fīhī mā fī hi*, in A.J. Arberry, *Discourses of Rumi* (London: John Murray, 1975), p.146.
16. Carl Diem, *Asiatische Reiterspiele* (Hildesheim: Olms, 2nd edn 1982), p.188.
17. J. Moray Brown, 'Polo', in Robert Weir, *Riding* (London: Longmans, Green, 1891), p.251.
18. Titled '*Guy-o-chawgān*' or '*Kārnāmah*', it has not been printed yet. D.N. Marshall, *Mughals in India: A Bibliographical Survey of Manuscripts* (London: Mansell, 1985 reprint), p.397.
19. Michele Membrè, *Mission to the Lord Sophy of Persia (1539–1542)*, trans. A.H. Morton (London: School of Oriental and African Studies, 1993), p.32. Elsewhere (p.36), Membrè

implies that polo was played during the 'Easter' or *bairam* festival. He may mean the Iranian new year: Nowruz.
20. See *The Three Brothers; or, the Travels of Sir Anthony, Sir Robert, and Sir Thomas Sherley in Persia, Russia, Turkey, Spain, etc. with Portraits* (London: Hurst, Robinson, 1825), pp.70–71 for a description of a game in his first capital Qazvin.
21. *The Journeys of Pietro della Valle the Pilgrim*, trans. George Bull (London: The Folio Society, 1989), pp.173–5.
22. Sir John Chardin, *Travels in Persia, 1673–1677* (New York: Dover, 1988), p.200.
23. Ella C. Sykes, *Persia and Its People* (London: Methuen, 1910), p.109.
24. Sir Percy Molesworth Sykes, *Ten Thousand Miles in Persia, or, Eight Years in Iran* (New York: Scribner's Sons, 1902), p.343.
25. Paul Horn, 'Roß und Reiter im Sāhnāme', *Zeitschrift der Deutschen Morgenländischen Gesellschaft*, 51, 4 (1907), 837–49.
26. Jivanji Jamshedji Modi, BA, 'The Game of Ball-Bat (Chowg n-gui) among the Ancient Persians, as Described in the Epic of Firdousi', *Journal of the Bombay Branch of the Royal Asiatic Society*, 48 (1891), 39–46.
27. Ferdowsi, *The Epic of the Kings*, trans. Reuben Levy (London: Routledge & Kegan Paul, 1977), pp.97–8. While it seems obvious that Ferdowsi anachronistically ascribed the customs of his time to mythical earlier figures, it is worth pointing out that the mythology on which the early portion of the *Shahnameh* is based originates in north-eastern Iran and Transoxiana, and that the rivalry between Iran and Turan may be an echo of the rivalry between settled and nomadic peoples of Central Asia – which is, after all, where polo originates.
28. See *Epic of the Kings*, pp.228–42. For a discussion of the 'iranization' of Alexander, see William Hanaway, 'Alexander and the Question of Iranian Identity', *Iranica Varia: Papers in Honor of Professor Ehsan Yarshater* (Leiden: E.J. Brill, 1990), pp.93–103.
29. *The Greek Alexander Romance*, trans. Richard Stoneman (Harmondworth: Penguin, 1991). Darius's letter is on pp.70–71.
30. See Minoo Sassoonian Southgate, 'A Study and a Translation of a Persian Romance of Alexander, its Place in the Tradition of Alexander Romance, and its Relation to the English Versions' (Unpublished Ph.D. thesis, New York University, 1970).
31. [Nezāmi Ganjavi], *The Sikandar nâma, e bará: or, Book of Alexander the Great*, trans. H. Wilberforce Clarke (London: W.H. Allen, 1881). The ball and mallet episode is in canto 24, pp.251–65. It is interesting to note that there is a strikingly similar scene in Shakespeare's *Henry V* (act I, scene 2), where the French ambassador presents the young English king with a set of tennis balls 'meeter for [his] spirit', explaining that he is too young to 'revel into dukedoms'. Henry's answer to the Dauphin is as defiant as Alexander's to Dārā: 'When we have match'd our rackets to these balls,/We will in France, by God's grace, play a set/Shall strike his father's crown into the hazard.' While it is highly improbable that Shakespeare was familiar with Persian romances, one may speculate that this episode echoes the one recounted in the original Greek Alexander romance, on which several medieval English Alexander romances are based.
32. *Epic of the Kings*, pp.274–5.
33. Sykes, *Ten Thousand Miles in Persia*, p.338.
34. Schimmel, *A Two-Colored Brocade*, p.284. There are more examples on the following pages.
35. Ibid., p.285. As an example of a mystical treatise steeped in polo imagery see Arifi, *Guy va chawgan, ya, Halnamah* [The Ball and Polo Stick, or, The Book of Ecstacy: A Parallel Persian-English text] (Costa Mesa, CA: Mazda, 1999).
36. For examples see Norah M. Titley, *Persian Miniature Paintings* (Austin, TX: University of Texas Press, 1982); and Norah M. Titley, *Sports and Pastimes: Scenes from Turkish, Persian, and Mughal Paintings* (London: British Library, 1979).
37. Antonio Pagliaro, 'Un gioco persiano alla corte di Bisanzio', in *Atti del V Congresso internazionale di studi bizantini, Roma, 20–26 settembre, 1936* (Rome: Tip. del Senato del dott. G. Bardi, 1939), volume 1, pp.521–4.

38. *The Oxford Dictionary of Byzantium* (New York: Oxford University Press, 1991), volume 3, p.1939, s.v. 'Sport'.
39. Jean-Jules Jusserand, *Les sports et jeux d'exercice dans l'ancienne France* (Paris: Plon, 1901), p.319. What remained was the word 'chicane', which derives from the Persian word *chowgān* and is a reminder of the mischief (chicanery) that one can cause with a polo stick!
40. Tahir Muzaffar al-Amid, *The Abbasid Architecture of Samarra in the Reign of Both al-Mu'tasim and al-Mutawakkil* (Baghdad: Al-Ma'aref Press, 1973), pp.115–17.
41. For a full discussion of polo in the mediaeval Arab world see 'Abd al-Razzāq al-Tā'i, *Al-tarbiya al-badaniya wa al-riyādiya fi al-turāth al-'Arabi al-Islāmi* (Amman: Dār al-Fikr, 1999), pp.277–91 and 'Abd al-Hamid Salāma, *Al-riyāda al-badaniya 'inda al-Arab: tārikhuh, anwā 'uhā, adabuhā* (Tunis: al-Dār al-Arabiya lil-kitāb, 1983), pp.271–80. For an excellent study in a European language see footnote 4 in Taki-eddin-Ahmed-Makrizi, *Histoire des sultans mamlouks de l'Egypte*, trans. M. Quatremère (Paris: Oriental Translation Fund of Great Britain and Ireland, 1837), pp.121–32.
42. Diem, *Asiatische Reiterspiele*, pp.173, 174, and 178.
43. Zhāleh Mottahedin, 'Chowgān dar Tārikh-e Ebn-e Bibi', *Nāmeh-ye Farhangestān*, 3, 4 (Winter 1376/1997–8), 73–80.
44. Robert Dankoff (ed. and trans.), *Evliya Celebi in Bitlis* (Leiden: Brill, 1990), pp.147–51.
45. Abu l-Fazl Allami, *The Ain-i Akbari*, trans. H. Blochmann (Delhi: New Taj Office, 1989 reprint), pp.309–10.
46. Titley, *Sports and Pastimes*, p.5
47. Diem, *Asiatische Reiterspiele*, pp.218–19.
48. Ibid., p.212.
49. James T.C. Liu, 'Polo and Cultural Change: From Tang to Sung China', *Harvard Journal of Asiatic Studies*, 45, 1 (June 1985), 207, 209.
50. Herbert A. Giles, 'Football and Polo in China', *The Nineteenth Century*, 59 (March 1906), 511; Liu, 'Polo and Cultural Change', p.208. Diem (*Asiatische Reiterspiele*, p.138) assumes that the courtiers fell from horseback, but they may simply have fallen to the ground from a standing position.
51. Howard J. Wechsler, 'Tang Dynasty', in Ainslie T. Embree (ed.), *Encyclopedia of Asian History*, 4 vols. (New York: Scribner's, 1988), 4, 68.
52. Diem, *Asiatische Reiterspiele*, p.143.
53. Liu, 'Polo and Cultural Change', p.214.
54. Diem, *Asiatische Reiterspiele*, p.145.
55. Ibid., p.146.
56. Liu, 'Polo and Cultural Change', pp.215, 219. It was during the Song dynasty, when courtiers became sedentary, that foot-binding was introduced for aristocratic women.
57. Diem, *Asiatische Reiterspiele*, pp.152–6.
58. Giles, 'Football and Polo in China', p.512.
59. Quoted in Liu, 'Polo and Cultural Change', p.208.
60. Ibid., p.218.
61. Ibid., p.222.
62. Ibid., pp.157–60.
63. Michael Sullivan, *The Arts of China* (Berkeley, CA: University of California Press, rev. edn 1977), p.159.
64. 'Korea's Tradition Weapons', online at www.turtlepress.com/myt1a.html.
65. Liu, 'Polo and Cultural Change', p.215.
66. Jörg Möller, *Spiel und Sport am japanischen Kaiserhof* (Munich: Iudicium, 1993), p.80; Iwaoka Toyoma, 'Dakyū,' in Kishino Yūzō (ed.), *Saishin supōtsudaijiten* (Tokyo: Taishūkan shoten, 1987), pp.752–6.
67. Lord Redesdale, *The Garter Mission to Japan* (London: Macmillan, 1906), p.71. An appendix to Redesdale's book (pp.269–74) gives the 'rules and manner of playing the game'.
68. Bimal J. Dev and Dilip Lahiri, *Manipur: Culture and Politics* (Delhi: Mittal Publications, 1987), p.4.

69. Parkes, 'Indigenous Polo', pp.44–5.
70. Brown, 'Polo,' p.279. A similar story is recounted in Brigadier Jack Gannon, *Before the Colours Fade* (London: J.A. Allen, 1976), pp.20–21. However, a 1891 history of polo puts the date of its first adoption by British soldiers in 1869; see Frank Milburn, *Polo: The Emperor of Games* (New York: Alfred A. Knopf, 1994), pp.34–5.
71. Sykes, *Ten Thousand Miles in Persia*, p.343.

EPILOGUE

Into the Future: Asian Sport and Globalization

FAN HONG

The year 2002 could be described as the year of Asian sport. In June the football World Cup, one of the world's most prestigious sporting events, was hosted by the Japanese and South Koreans. It was the first time that the event had been held outside Europe or the Americas. It provided high visibility. During the course of the event Asia was the focus of the world. As China participated in the World Cup, it also represented a high point in relations between Korea, Japan and China, three major North-east Asian economic powers. As Cheng Hae-moon, the Minister of the Embassy of the Republic of Korea remarked, it would 'lead to a strengthening of trilateral relations and provide a basis for further co-operation, not just in sports but also in business, trade, investment and foreign affairs'.[1]

In addition to the World Cup, in September the fourteenth Asian Games took place in Busan, South Korea. More than 43 Asian countries participated. The aim of the games was 'to promote unity and partnership among Asian countries' and the slogan 'New Asia, New Vision' set the tone for the regeneration of Asia.[2] Sport has the potential to enhance the image of Asian countries in the international sports arena and to provide an opportunity for advancing the development of Asian nations in the international community. Sport can also strengthen ties among countries in Asia and help forge a strong bond between Asia and the rest of the world.

As noted in the Prologue, Asia is the largest of the continents. Covering one-third of the land surface of the world, Asia comprises some 18,500,000 square miles. It is larger than the combined area of North and South America, and more than four times the size of Europe. Asia's physical diversity is matched by an even greater cultural and social diversity. It contains three main cultural areas, the Islamic, the Hindu-Buddhist and the Sinic. It is home to a third of the world's population.

Although there are diversities in culture and society, Asian countries have taken the same recent historical journey, from political independence to social transformation and modernity.[3] In the twentieth century Asian countries, through a triadic process of cultural continuity, assimilation of contemporary ideas and resistance to imperial power, have developed political modernity. Modern sport has played an important role in stimulating political re-assertion, a sense of regional identity and the arousal of Orientalism. The inaugural Asian Games were held in New Delhi in 1951. Their ostensible purpose was to promote sport in Asia and to unite Asian countries through sport. The games now take place every four years. The number of participating countries has increased from 11 in 1951 to 43 in 2002. Sheikh Ahmad Al-Fahad Al-Sabah, President of the Olympic Council of Asia, has claimed that 'the Asian Games … has become the greatest youth festival in Asia and possibly second to none but the Olympic Games. I am equally confident that the youth of Asia will continue to celebrate the Asian Games every four years with enthusiasm, friendship and harmony.'[4]

Asia has undergone dramatic transformation since the 1980s. It has become a centre of modernity. Colonialism is the past. Globalization is the present. Globalization, as R. Holton has argued, is a notion of 'one single world or human society, in which all regional, national, and local elements are tied together in one interdependent whole'.[5] The process of the globalization of sport characterized East Asia in the 1980s and the 1990s. Although there is diversity in the politics, ideology, culture and economic and social systems of the area, the characteristics of the process are virtually the same: change in sports systems, the involvement of the media, dependence on sponsorship and the growth of a sports industry. China and Japan offer the best examples of these phenomena.

In terms of change in sports systems, Communist China, which Trevor Slack identifies as representative of an emerging economy, has undergone a dramatic transformation and now has government policies that favour economic liberalization and the adoption of a free-market system.[6] In the 1980s, in order to catch up with Western countries economically, China adopted an 'open door' policy and began its economic reformation. The system is changing from a centrally-planned economy to a free-market system. It has shown rapid development and trade liberalization. With regard to sport, the national and regional sports organizations that were developed under previous centrally planned regimes are now expected to be more economically self-sufficient. In the mid-1990s the Chinese Sports Ministry and provincial and local sports commissions set up national and local sports management centres (*tiyu guanli zhongxin*) according to the nature of the sports, such as athletics, football and gymnastics. Each centre was an independent unit in terms of human resources and finance. These centres were expected to stand on their own feet and not rely on state support, and to turn sport into a money-making proposition.[7] At the same time private sports clubs emerged. These public and private sports organizations have become increasingly involved with, and dependent upon, sponsorship, the development of a sports goods industry, the establishment of sports lotteries, the hosting of sporting events as a means of economic regeneration and the securing of foreign direct investment in sports-related activities.[8]

In Japan since the 1980s all national projects within a coherent sport policy have stressed the importance of joining forces with the private sector. The latest Basic Plan for the Promotion of Sport (2001) explicitly suggests that the future of sports supply lies with private finance initiatives (PFIs), and opportunities have been largely expanded since the passing of the Private Finance Initiative Law in July 1999, allowing new forms of co-operation between public and private enterprises.[9] Local government enthusiastically promotes sport, for sport is considered an economic income generator because of its investment in new facilities and theme parks in the regions to improve the quality of life of the inhabitants. Local government, therefore, is forging new kinds of public-private partnerships with other beneficiaries of regional development, particularly private enterprises.[10] Change in sports systems has also taken place in South Korea, India and other emerging and market-economic Asian countries.

In terms of the involvement of the media, the desire of international organizations to conquer new markets has brought a new version of the internationalization of sport to the Asian world. US Major League Baseball, NBA basketball, NFL football and European Champions' League football are watched by millions of Asian people through their domestic media networks. In China since 1995 European Champions' League Football, English Premier League games and the Chinese first division have attracted more than 16 billion spectators per year.[11] In Japan the Japan Sky Broadcasting Company – a joint venture between

Rupert Murdoch's News Corporation and Softbank Corporation – was launched in 1997. Through this, live English Football Association Premier League games were made available to millions of Japanese.[12] Through the global network of media services, popular sports, athletes and teams together with their logos and brand names, reach audiences all over the Asian world. People are able to recognize and decipher the codes of these icons and to participate in the globalized cultural economy.[13]

In terms of dependence on sponsorship, large and small foreign and Chinese companies are coming to realize that they can promote their goods, enhance their public image, reach their target audience, achieve their marketing objectives and even motivate employees through use of skilled sponsorship. Sponsorship is 'an investment, in cash or kind, in an activity in return for access to the exploitable commercial potential associated with that activity'.[14] Sports sponsorship is the support of a sport, events, organizations or competitions by an outside body or person for the mutual benefit of both parties. With the move from a planned economy to a market economy, as in the case of China, and with the move from public sector to private sector, as in Japan, direct state funding is being reduced and sponsorship is being used to take its place. For example, at the Beijing Asian Games in 1990 Coca-Cola's sponsorship amounted to US$2.7 million; Fuji Film's sponsorship amounted to US$3 million; and Jian Li Bao's (the Chinese version of Coca-Cola) sponsorship amounted to RMB 16.5 million (US$1 = RMB8).[15] In 1993 the Shanghai Sport Council claimed that the first East Asian Games took place without state financial support. The RMB 300 million spent on the games came from sponsorship, endorsement, lotteries and advertising.[16] In 1995, when the Zhuhai Global Endurance GT Race took place, Mobil and Marlboro sponsored the multi-million dollar event.[17] In 1996 the Imperial Tobacco Company sponsored the Chinese Professional Basketball League with US$3 million. In 1999, while the Chinese government's sport organization budget was US$450 million, an additional US$200 million was raised from sponsorship. Wolfram Manzenreiter pointed out that in Japan and Korea in 2002 the 'war of the boots' would be played out. Adidas was official supplier to the Japan Football Association (JFA) and the national squad and Nike sponsored the Korean team and the KFA.[18] Other national squads had similar allegiances. This involvement of companies and sponsorships, of course, is not purely the results of the companies' love of sport; rather it is the outcome of their commercial ambitions. As a representative of British American Tobacco which manufactures the 555 cigarette brand, and sponsored the 555 Hong Kong to Beijing Rally in 1995, stated: 'The 555 Hong Kong to Beijing rally is not just the ultimate test of driver and machinery but in the age of consumerism, an opportunity to perform in a potentially huge market place.'[19]

In terms of the growth of the sports industry, transnational corporations such as Nike and Adidas use the international differences in labour costs to produce sportswear in Asian countries. In 1980 Nike negotiated with China to produce its shoes there. During the 1980s all Nike footwear was finished by foreign suppliers, with China, as well as South Korea and Taiwan, doing most of the basic manufacturing. The emergence of Nike as a major shoe manufacturer coincided with the emergence of China as a leading exporting nation, whose fundamental industrialization strategy has been the promotion of manufactured goods, concentrating particularly on low-cost labour-intensive industries. Prospects for growth in the sports industry have never been better. The Chinese Sports Ministry has asked all national, provincial and local sports commissions and organizations to adopt the effective use of marketing techniques to develop the Chinese market even more rapidly than in the past and to make it even more attractive for foreign companies' investment.[20]

Wolfram Manzenreiter and Saskia Sassen have pointed out that since the 1980s the new world economy has been characterized by the growing influence of global capital, transnational markets, a new international division of labour based on low-paid and flexible workforces, the decreasing influence of national governments over the regulation of economic processes, and time-spatial compression due to world-encompassing computer and telecommunications networks.[21] Sport has become a part of the new world economy, since sport is an international business. Against the background of this new phenomenon, the Asian Games Association, which was established in 1949, changed its name to the Olympic Council of Asia in 1986. This indicated that Asian sport has become part of global sport.

While globalization of sport drives the direction of change and makes for progress in the Asian world, some questions have to be asked. Will globalization benefit elite sport as well as grass-roots sport? Two Korean sociologists, Minseok Ahn and Chung Hongik, have pointed out that while elite sport has achieved great success in South Korea since the

1980s, grass-roots sport, school sport and community sport have been neglected.[22] The same problems exist in China, Japan and other developed and developing countries in Asia.[23]

Can national governments effectively protect local and traditional sport cultures from the negative effects of globalization? The obvious growing inequalities among elite sports clubs and athletes with regard to access to capital, mass media and sponsorship have resulted in 'bringing the state back in' as a regulator to reduce the gap between the rich and the poor in a sports world where a few gain and many lose, and to protect the heritage of traditional and local sports culture.[24]

Can the nations of the Asian world retain their distinctive cultural identities under the pressure of globalization? Asia is a continent of great civilizations. The West has yet to recognize Asian power, wealth and possibilities. Asian countries have adjusted their national, regional and local differences to the international sports community. They have also made, and still make, their own marks on the growing culture of global sport. The future of Asian sport has been expressed in the slogan of the Asian Games, 'Ever onward' – but in what direction?

NOTES

The author wishes to thank Wolfram Manzenreiter and John Horne for their invitation to the conference of Soccer Nations and Football Cultures in East Asia, which inspired some of the ideas for this essay.

1. Cheng Hae-moon, 'Speech at the Soccer Nations and Football Culture in East Asia', 21 March 2002.
2. 'The 14th Asian Games: Busan 2002: New Vision, New Asia', online at http://www.ocasia.org/asiangames/pusan.asp, accessed 13 Dec. 2001.
3. K.M. Panikkar, 'Foreword', in Jan Rome, *The Asian Century* (London: George Allen & Unwin, 1962), p.9.
4. 'The Asian Games 1951–2003', online at http://www.ocasia.org/timeline/timeline.asp, accessed 13 Dec. 2001.
5. R. Holton, *Globalization and the Nation-state* (Basingstoke: Macmillan, 1998), p.2.
6. Trevor Slack, 'Theoretical Issues in Understanding the Changing Nature of Sport Organisations in Emerging Economies: Some Examples from China', Paper presented at Soccer Nations and Football Cultures in East Asia Conference, Vienna, March 2002, p.2.
7. Fan Hong, interview with Zhang Hao, the Head of Department of Planning and Finance in Chinese Sports Ministry, 28 Aug. 2001, Beijing.
8. Slack, 'Theoretical Issues', *passim*. Fan Hong, 'Commercialisation and Sport in China: Present Situation and Future Expectations', *Journal of Sport Management*, 4 (1997), 346–9.
9. Wolfram Manzenreiter, 'Japanese Football and World Football', Paper presented at Soccer Nations and Football Cultures in East Asia Conference, Vienna, March 2002, p.18.
10. Ibid., p.19.
11. Yan Xuening, 'Zhongguo chunamei and zhiye zuqiu' [The Chinese Media and Professional Football], Paper presented at Soccer Nations and Football Cultures in East Asia Conference, Vienna, March 2002, p.3.

12. Manzenreiter, 'Japanese Football and World Football', p.9.
13. Ibid., p.9.
14. J.A. Meenaghan, 'The Role of Sponsorship in the Marketing Communications Mix', *International Journal of Advertising*, 10 (1991), 36.
15. Y. Cheng, Q. Liu and S. Li (eds), *1990 Yayunhui* [The 1990 Asian Games] (Wuhan: Wuhan chubanshe, 1990), pp.5–10, 194–8.
16. R. Liang and G. Liu (eds), *Yanyun shenghuo* [The Flame of the Asian Games] (Beijing: Zhonhguo guanbo dianshi chubanshe, 1990), p.263.
17. *South China Morning Post*, 12 Oct. 1995.
18. Manzenreiter, 'Japanese Football and World Football', p.8.
19. *South China Morning Post*, 14 Oct. 1995.
20. Jichishi [Planning and Finance Department, Ministry of Sport] (ed.), *Jiashu fazhan tiyu chanye huiyi wenjian huibian* [The Urgent Promotion and Development of Sports Business Conference] (Beijing: Guojia tiwei [Chinese Sports Ministry], 1993), p.21.
21. Saskia Sessen, *Globalisation and Its Discontent: Essays on the New Mobility of People and Money* (New York: The New Press, 1994); Manzenreiter, 'Japanese Football and World Football', p.1.
22. Fan Hong, interview with Minseok Ahn and Chung Hongik at Soccer Nations and Football Cultures in East Asia Conference, 23 March 2002.
23. Fan Hong, 'Olympic Movement in China: Ideals, Ambitions and Realities', *Culture, Sport, Society*, 1 (1999), 61; Nogawa Haruo, 'Infrastructures and Public Spending in Japanese Football', Paper presented at Soccer Nations and Football Cultures in East Asia Conference, March 2002: interview with Satoshi Shimizu, sports sociologist at University of Tsukuba, Japan, at the same conference, 23 March 2002.
24. Karen Imhof, 'Comments on Papers about Football in Japan, China and South Korea', Paper presented at Soccer Nations and Football Cultures in East Asia Conference, March 2002, p.6.

Select Bibliography

Imperial Origins: Christian Manliness, Moral Imperatives and Pre-Sri Lankan Playing Fields – Beginnings and Consolidation
J.A. MANGAN

J.A. Mangan, *Athleticism in the Victorian and Edwardian Public School: The Emergence and Consolidation of an Educational Ideology* (London: Frank Cass, 2nd edition 2000).

J.A. Mangan, *The Games Ethic and Imperialism: Aspects of the Diffusion of an Ideal* (London: Frank Cass, 2nd edition 1998).

J.A. Mangan, 'Catalyst of Change: John Guthrie Kerr and the Adaptation of an Indigenous Scottish Tradition', in J.A. Mangan (ed.), *Pleasure, Profit and Proselytism: British Culture at Home and Abroad 1700–1914* (London: Frank Cass, 1988), pp.86–104.

J.A. Mangan, 'Prologue: Britain's Chief Spiritual Export: Imperial Sport as Moral Metaphor, Political Symbol and Cultural Bond', in J.A. Mangan (ed.), *The Cultural Bond: Sport, Empire, Society* (London: Frank Cass, 1992), pp.1–10.

J.A. Mangan, 'Making Imperial Mentalities', in J.A. Mangan (ed.), *Making Imperial Mentalities: Socialisation and British Imperialism* (Manchester: Manchester University Press, 1990), pp.1–22.

J.A. Mangan, 'Ethics and Ethnocentricity: Imperial Education in British Tropical Africa', in William J. Baker and James A. Mangan (eds), *Sport in Africa: Essays in Social History* (New York: Holmes and Meier, 1987), pp.138–71.

J.A. Mangan (ed.), *'Benefits Bestowed': Education and British Imperialism* (Manchester: Manchester Univerity Press, 1990).

Valesca L.O. Reimann, *A History of Trinity College, Kandy* (Madras: Diocesan Press, 1922).

C.E. Tyndale-Biscoe, *Tyndale-Biscoe of Kashmir: An Autobiography* (London: Seeley Service, n.d.).

W.E.F. Ward, *Fraser of Trinity and Achimota* (Accra: Ghana Universities Press, 1965).

Celestials in Touch:
Sport and the Chinese in Colonial Singapore
N.G. APLIN and QUEK JIN JONG

Association of British Malaya, *British Malaya* (London: Association of British Malaya, 1926–51).

R. Bruce Lockhart, *Return to Malaya* (London: Putnam, 1936).

C.B. Buckley, *An Anecdotal History of Old Times in Singapore* (Kuala Lumpur: University of Malaya Press, 1965).

W. Makepeace, G.E. Brooke and R.St.J. Braddell (eds), *One Hundred Years of Singapore* (Singapore: Oxford University Press, 1991).

M. Shennan, *Out in the Midday Sun: The British in Malaya 1880–1960* (London: John Murray, 2000).

Song Ong Siang, *One Hundred Years' History of the Chinese in Singapore* (Singapore: University of Malaya Press, 1967).

C.M. Turnbull, *A History of Singapore: 1819–1988* (Singapore: Oxford University Press, 1996).

'Sportsmanship' – English Inspiration and Japanese Response:
F.W. Strange and Chiyosaburo Takeda
IKUO ABE and J.A. MANGAN

Ikuo Abe and J.A. Mangan, 'The British Impact on Boy's Sports and Games in Japan: An Introductory Survey', *International Journal of the History of Sport*, 14, 2 (Aug. 1997), 187–99.

Ikuo Abe, 'Dairoku Kikuchi and F W Strange: Japanese Earliest Encounters with Athleticism', in Gertrud Pfister and Liu Yueye (eds), *Proceedings of the 3rd International ISHPES Seminar, 'Sports – the East and the West'*, Shunde, Guangdong, China, 16–22 Sept. 1996 (Sankt Augustin: Academia Verlag, 1999).

J.A. Mangan, *The Games Ethic and Imperialism: Aspects of the Diffusion of an Ideal* (London and Portland, OR: Frank Cass, 1998).

Ferdinand A. Schmidt and Eustace H. Miles, *The Training of the Body for Games, Athletics, Gymnastics, and Other Forms of Exercise and for Health, Growth, and Development* (London: Swan Sonnenschein, 1901).

F.W. Strange, *Outdoor Games* (Daigaku Yobimon, Tokyo: Z.P. Maruya & Co., 1883). *Undokai* [Athletic World], 1, 1 (1887).

Chiyosaburo Takeda, *Riron/Jikken Kyogi Undo* [Theory and Practice, Athletic Exercise] (Tokyo: Tokyo Hakubunnkan, 1904).

Chiyosaburo Takeda, *Shinshin Tanren Kyogi Undo* [Training of the Body and Mind: Boys' Athletic Exercise] (Tokyo: Tokyo Hakubunkan, 1904).

Chiyosaburo Takeda, 'Honpo Undokai no Onjin Strange Shi wo Omou' [A Benefactor of Athletics in Japan: F.W. Strange], *Athletics*, 2, 3 (1923).

'Healthy Bodies, Healthy Minds': Sport and Society in Colonial Malaya
JANICE N. BROWNFOOT

Janice N. Brownfoot, 'Memsahibs in Colonial Malaya: A Study of European Wives in a British Colony and Protectorate, 1900–1940', in Hilary Callan and Shirley Ardener (eds), *The Incorporated Wife* (London: Croom Helm, 1984).

Janice N. Brownfoot, 'Emancipation, Exercise and Imperialism: Girls and the Games Ethic in Colonial Malaya', *International Journal of the History of Sport*, 7, 1 (May 1990), 61–84 (first published in J.A. Mangan, *The Cultural Bond*, q.v.).

Janice N. Brownfoot, 'Sisters Under the Skin: Imperialism and the Emancipation of Women in Malaya, c.1891–1941', in J.A. Mangan (ed.), *Making Imperial Mentalities* (Manchester: Manchester University Press, 1990).

J.A. Mangan, *Athleticism in the Victorian and Edwardian Public School: The Emergence and Consolidation of an Educational Ideology* (Cambridge: Cambridge University Press, 1981; Falmer: Falmer, 1986; and London and Portland, OR: Frank Cass, 2000).

J.A. Mangan (ed.), *The Cultural Bond* (London: Frank Cass, 1992).

J.A. Mangan and Fan Hong (eds), *Freeing the Female Body: Inspirational Icons* (London and Portland, OR: Frank Cass, 2001).

J.A. Mangan and Roberta J. Park, *From 'Fair Sex' to Feminism: Sport and the Socialization of Women in the Industrial and Post-Industrial Eras* (London: Frank Cass, 1987).

J.A. Mangan, *The Games Ethic and Imperialism: Aspects of the Diffusion of an Ideal* (London: Viking Penguin, 1986; Frank Cass, 1998).

Kathleen E. McCrone, *Sport and the Physical Emancipation of English Women 1870–1914* (London: Routledge, 1988).

Cricket in Colonial India:
The Bombay Pentangular, 1892–1946
BORIA MAJUMDAR

Berry Sarbadhikary, *Indian Cricket Uncovered* (Calcutta: Illustrated News, 1945).
Edward Docker, *History of Indian Cricket* (Delhi: Macmillan, 1976).
J.M. Framjee Patel, *Stray Thoughts on Indian Cricket* (Bombay: Times Press, 1905).
M.E. Pavri, *Parsi Cricket* (Bombay: J B Marzban and Company, 1901).
Mihir Bose, *A History of Indian Cricket* (London: Andre Deutsch, 1990).
M.H. Maqsood, *Who's Who in Indian Cricket* (Delhi, 1940).
P.N. Polishwalla, *The Sun Never Sets on Cricket* (Bombay, 1933).
Richard Cashman, *Patrons, Players and the Crowd* (Calcutta: Orient Longman, 1979).
S.K. Roy, *Bombay Pentangular* (Calcutta, Nov. 1945).
Vasant Raiji and Mohandas Menon, *The Story of the Bombay Tournament: From Presidency to Pentangulars* (Mumbai: Ernest Publications, 2000).

Sport in China:
Conflict between Tradition and Modernity, 1840s to 1930s
FAN HONG and TAN HUA

Fan Hong, *Footbinding, Feminism and Freedom* (London and Portland, OR: Frank Cass, 1996).
Chinese Society for History of Physical Education and Sport (CSHPES) (ed.), *Zhongguo jindai tiyu shi* [Modern Chinese Sports History] (Beijing: Beijing tiyu xueyuan chubanshe, 1989).
K.S. Latourette, *The Chinese: Their History and Culture* (New York: Macmillan, 1964).
W. Rodzinski, *The Walled Kingdom: A History of China from 2000BC to the Present* (London: Fontana Paperbacks, 1984).
D.H. Smith, *Confucians* (London: Temple Smith, 1973).
Zhou Xikuan et al., *Zhongguo guodai tiyu shi* [Physical Education and Sport History of Ancient China] (Chengdu: Sichuan guji chubanshe, 1986).

Ideology, Politics, Power: Korean Sport – Transformation, 1945–92
HA NAM-GIL and J.A. MANGAN

Stan Greenberg, *The Guinness Olympics Fact Book* (London: Guinness Publishing, 1991).

Hak-rae Lee and Jong-hui Kim, 'The Political Ideology of the Park Chung-hee Regime and Sports Nationalism', *Journal of Korean Physical Education*, 38, 1 (March 1999).

In-kol Kim *et al.*, *Hankook Hyeondaesa Kangeui* [Lectures on History of Modern Korea] (Seoul: Dolbegae, 1998).

J.A. Mangan and Ha Nam-Gil, 'Confucianism, Imperialism, Nationalism: Modern Sport, Ideology and Korean Culture', *European Sports History Review*, 3 (2001).

Office of the Secretariat of Information (comp.), *Collection of Speeches by President Park Chung-hee, First Collection* (Seoul: Dong-A Publishing, 1967).

Yi hyok Han, *Cheyouksa* [History of Physical Education] (Seoul: Taegeun Publications, 1998).

Shackling the Lion: Sport and Modern Singapore
PETER A. HORTON

Lee Kuan Yew, *From Third World to First: The Singapore Story 1965–2000* (New York: HarperCollins, 2000).

B-H. Chua, *Communitarian Ideology and Democracy in Singapore* (London: Routledge, 1995).

C.J. Chua, *On Track: 21 Years of the Singapore Sports Council* (Singapore: SSC Publication by Times Editions, 1994).

J A. Mangan, 'Epilogue: Post-Imperialism, Sport, Globalization', *European Sports History Review*, 3 (2001).

R. Vasil, *Governing Singapore: Democracy and National Development* (Sydney: Allen & Unwin, 2000).

K.W. Yeo and A. Lau, 'From Colonialism to Independence, 1945–1965', in E.C.T. Chew and E. Lee (eds), *A History of Singapore* (London: Oxford University Press, 1991).

The Juggernaut of Globalization: Sport and Modernization in Iran
H.E. CHEHABI

Fariba Adelkhah, trans. Jonathan Derrick, *Being Modern in Iran* (London: Hurst & Company, 1999).

Christian Bromberger, 'Troisième mi-temps pour le football iranien', *Le Monde diplomatique*, April 1998.

Christian Bromberger, 'Le football en Iran', *Sociétés & Représentations*, Dec. 1998.

Marius Canard, 'La lutte chez les arabes', in *Le cinquantenaire de la Faculté des lettres d'Alger (1881–1931)* (Algiers: Société Historique Algérienne, 1932).

H.E. Chehabi, 'Sport and Politics in Iran: The Legend of Gholamreza Takhti', *International Journal of the History of Sport*, XII (Dec. 1995).

H.E. Chehabi, 'US-Iranian Sports Diplomacy', *Diplomacy and Statecraft*, XII, 1 (March 2001).

H.E. Chehabi, 'Jews and Sport in Modern Iran', in Homa Sarshar and Houman Sarshar (eds), *The History of Contemporary Iranian Jews* (Beverly Hills, CA: Center for Iranian Jewish Oral History, 2001).

Youcef Fatès, *Sport et Tiers Monde* (Paris: Presses Universitaires de France, 1994).

Wolfgang Knauth, 'Die sportlichen Qualifikationen der altiranischen Fürsten', *Stadion*, II (1976).

Ludwig Paul, 'Der iranische Spitzenfußball und seine sozialen und politischen Dimensionen', *Sozial- und Zeitgeschichte des Sports*, XII, 2 (1998).

Philippe Rochard, 'Le "sport antique" des zurkhâne de Téhéran. Formes et significations d'une pratique contemporaine' (Ph.D. thesis, Université Aix-Marseille I, 2000).

Philippe Rochard, 'The Identities of the Iranian Zurkhāneh', *Iranian Studies*, XXX, 3–4 (2002).

Cyrus Schayegh, 'Sport, Health, and the Iranian Modern Middle Class, 1920s and 1930s', *Iranian Studies*, XXX, 3–4 (2002).

Pancasila: Sport and the Building of Indonesia – Ambitions and Obstacles
IAIN ADAMS

L. Blair with L. Blair, *Ring of Fire* (London: Bantam Press, 1988).

P. Carey, *To Struggle for Freedom: Indonesia Yesterday, East Timor Today*, online at http://www.insideindonesia.org/edit49/carey.htm.

R. Challis, *Shadow of a Revolution: Indonesia and the Generals* (Stroud: Sutton Publishing, 2001).

K. Heinemann, 'Sport in Developing Countries', in E.G. Dunning, J.A. Maguire and R.E. Pearton (eds), *The Sports Process* (Champaign, IL: Human Kinetics, 1993), pp.139–50.

N.J. Moolenijzer and Sieswanpo, 'Sport and Physical Education in Indonesia', in W. Johnson (ed.), *Sport and Physical Education Around the World* (Champaign, IL: Stipes, 1980), pp.314–38.

S. Ross, 'Indigenous Games of Indonesia: Preservation of Local Culture', *International Journal of Physical Education*, XXVII, 3 (1990), 28–34.

H. Soetjipto, W.A. Karamoy and M.S. Wuryani, *Indonesia: An Official Handbook* (Jakarta: Department of Information, Directorate of Foreign Service Information Services, 1995).

Communist China: Sport, Politics and Diplomacy
XIONG XIAOZHENG and FAN HONG

Allen R. Ball and B. Guy Peters, *Modern Politics and Government* (London: Macmillan, 2000).

R. Espy, *The Politics of the Olympic Games* (Berkeley, CA and London: University of California Press, 1979).

Qian Jiang, *Ping-Pong waijiao shimo* [The Story of the Ping-Pong Diplomacy] (Beijing: Dongfang chubanshe, 1987).

Alfried Erich Senn, *Power, Politics, and the Olympic Games* (Champaign, IL: Human Kinetics, 1999).

Jonathan D. Spence, *The Search for Modern China* (London: Hutchinson, 1990).

Guan Wenmin et al. (eds), *Tiyu shi* [Sports History] (Beijing: Beijing gaoden jiaoyu chubanshe, 1996).

The Road to Modernization: Sport in Taiwan
TREVOR SLACK, HSU YUAN-MIN, TSAI CHIUNG-TZU and FAN HONG

C.R. Hill, *Olympic Politics* (Manchester: Manchester University Press, 1992).
D. Macintosh and M. Hawes, *Sport and Canadian Diplomacy* (Montreal and Kingston, ON: McGill-Queen's University Press, 1994).
D.C. Smith (ed.), *The Confucian Continuum: Educational Modernization in Taiwan* (New York: Praeger, 1991).
J.T. Sundeen, 'A Kid's Game: Little League Baseball and National Identity in Taiwan', *Journal of Sport & Social Issues*, 25 (2001).
E.P. Tsurumi, *Japanese Colonial Education in Taiwan, 1895–1945* (Cambridge, MA: Harvard University Press, 1977).
E.A. Winckler, 'Cultural Policy on Postwar Taiwan', in S. Harrell and Huang Chun-Chieh (eds), *Cultural Change in Postwar Taiwan* (Boulder, CO: Westview Press, 1994).

Sport in Modern India: Policies, Practices and Problems
PACKIANATHAN CHELLADURAI, D. SHANMUGANATHAN, JAIHIND JOTHIKARAN and A.S. NAGESWARAN

L. Chalip, A. Johnson and L. Stachura (eds), *National Sport Policies: An International Handbook* (Westport, CT: Greenwood Press, 1996).
J.-L. Chappelet and M.-H. Roukhadzé (eds), *Sport Management: An International Approach* (Lausanne: International Olympic Committee, 1996).
M.L. Kamlesh, *Physical Education: Facts and Foundations* (Faridabad, India: P.B. Publications).
D. Macintosh and M. Hawes, *Sport and Canadian Policy* (Kingston, Ontario: McGill-Queen's University Press, 1993).
U.S. Nair, 'Government and Sport in Kerala, India', *Journal of Sport Management*, 7 (1993), 256–62.
J.E. Thoma and L. Chalip, *Sport Governance in the Global Community* (Morgantown, WV: Fitness Information Technology).

From Iran to All of Asia: The Origin and Diffusion of Polo
H.E. CHEHABI and ALLEN GUTTMANN

Carl Diem, *Asiatische Reiterspiele* (Hildesheim: Olms, 2nd edn 1982).

Ferdowsi, *The Epic of the Kings*, trans. Reuben Levy (London: Routledge & Kegan Paul, 1977).

Kai Kâ'ûs ibn Iskandar, *A Mirror for Princes: The Qâbû Nâma*, trans. Reuben Levy (London: Cresset Press, 1951).

James T.C. Liu, 'Polo and Cultural Change: From Tang to Sung China', *Harvard Journal of Asiatic Studies*, 45, 1 (June 1985).

Annemarie Schimmel, *A Two-Colored Brocade: The Imagery of Persian Poetry* (Chapel Hill, NC: University of North Carolina Press, 1992).

Sir Percy Molesworth Sykes, *Ten Thousand Miles in Persia, or, Eight Years in Iran* (New York: Scribner's Sons, 1902).

Notes on Contributors

Ikuo Abe is a professor at University of Tsukuba's Institute of Health and Sport Sciences and Chairman of the Historical Research Section of the Japanese Society of Physical Education. He has been a member of the International Olympic Committee's Olympic Study Centre in the Olympic Museum since 2000.

Iain Adams is a principal lecturer in the Department of Tourism and Leisure Management at the University of Central Lancashire. He has taught PE at primary and secondary schools, sixth-form and FE colleges and in PE teacher education programmes at universities in the USA, Jordan, Bahrain and England. He was the national consultant for sport education in Indonesia in 1987–1988.

Nick Aplin is an assistant professor in the Physical Education and Sports Science Academic Group of the National Institute of Education at Nanyang Technological University in Singapore. He is also the Head of Olympic Studies at the Singapore Olympic Academy, which is located at the university. A permanent resident of Singapore, where he has lived for 16 years, he chairs the Research and Education Section of the Women and Sport Working Group established under the auspices of the Singapore Sports Council. He is an elected council member of the Singapore Chess Federation, and his external consultancy interests include television commentary work on local and regional events for the state-owned broadcast company, Mediacorp.

Janice N. Brownfoot is a research and training consultant. Her areas of special academic interest are women and the British Empire and interethnic relations, including cross-cultural marriage, with particular reference to the Asia-Pacific region, especially Malaysia. Her forthcoming doctoral thesis is a study of the roles and influence of white females in colonial Malaya from 1891 to 1941, for which she is enrolled in the Department of Educational Studies at the University of Strathclyde, Glasgow. Her publications include a number of articles relating to her research area, as well as *The Unequal Half: A History of Women in Australia* (with Dianne Scott).

H.E. Chehabi is a professor of international relations and history at Boston University. He is the author of *Iranian Politics and Religious Modernism* (London: I.B. Tauris, 1990) and co-editor, with Alfred Stepan, of *Politics, Society, and Democracy: Comparative Studies* (Boulder, CO: Westview, 1995) and, with Juan J. Linz, of *Sultanistic Regimes* (Baltimore, MD: Johns Hopkins University Press, 1998).

P. Chelladurai is a professor in the School of Physical Activity and Educational Services at Ohio State University. He has written five books and more than 70 journal articles. He is on the editorial board of the *Journal of Sport Management* and the *European Sport Management Quarterly*.

Fan Hong is reader in the Department of Sports Sciences at De Montfort University in England. She was an editor of the *Journal of Sports Culture and History*, published by the Sports Ministry in Beijing in the 1980s. Her main research interests are in the areas of body, gender and sport with particular reference to China and Asia. Her most recent books in English are *Footbinding, Feminism and Freedom: The Liberation of Women's Bodies in Modern China* (1997) and *Freeing the Female Body: Inspirational Icons*, co-edited with J.A. Mangan (2001).

Allen Guttmann is the author of a number of books on sports history, the best known of which is *From Ritual to Record* (1978). His most recent books are *Games and Empires* (1994) and *The Erotic in Sports* (1996).

Peter Horton is a lecturer in the School of Education at James Cook University in Queensland. He has previously worked in schools and universities in Singapore, Brisbane, New South Wales and England. He has published widely in the area of sport studies, particularly in the discussion of the nature of sport cultures in post-colonial territories and upon Olympic issues. This essay is the third in a series analyzing the nature and role of sport in Singapore.

Hsu Yuan-Min holds a doctoral degree from National Taiwan Normal University. He is the director of the Sports Physics Research Committee of the National Society of Physical Education of the Republic of China. He is the author of *Postmodern Chinese Sports Competition (1910–1948)*, *Postmodern Chinese Academic Sports – A Target in Progress (1902–1949)*, *Postmodern Chinese Academic Sports – Mental Advancements (1902–1949)*, *Postmodern Chinese Intellectuals Versus the Spread of Sports Mentality (1895–1949)* and several other books in Chinese.

Jaihind Jothikaran is a senior lecturer in the Department of Physical Education of the Alagappa University, Karaikudi, Tamil Nadu, India. He is a member of the National Association of Physical Education and Sports, and a specialist in yoga.

Boria Majumdar, a Rhodes Scholar, is completing his doctorate on the social history of Indian cricket at St John's College, University of Oxford.

J.A. Mangan is Director of the International Research Centre for Sport, Socialisation and Society at the University of Strathclyde and author and editor of many books. He is founder and General Editor of the Cass series *Sport in the Global Society* and founding and Executive Academic Editor of the following Cass journals: *The International Journal of the History of Sport*; *Culture, Sport, Society*; *Soccer and Society*; and *The European Sports History Review*.

A.S. Nageswaran is a lecturer in the H.H. Rajah's College, Pudukottai, Tamil Nadu, India. He has published several articles and presented papers at national and international conferences.

Ha Nam-Gil is a professor in the College of Education, Department of Physical Education, Gyeongsang National University, Korea.

Quek Jin Jong is the principal officer of the National Institute of Education at Nanyang Technological University in Singapore. He was dean of the School of Physical Education from 1991 to 2000 and principal of the Singapore Olympic Academy from 1993 to 2000. He taught in schools for 18 years before becoming an academic. He has also served on a number of advisory and technical committees of the Singapore Sports Council since 1991 and on the Singapore National Olympic Council selection and awards committees from 1991 to 2000.

D. Shanmuganathan is sports officer and head of the Department of Sports and Physical Education of the Manonmaniam Sundraranar University, Thirunelveli, Tamil Nadu, India. He is a member of the Sports Board of the Association of Indian Universities. He has presented several papers at national and international conferences and has organized two international conferences on sports management.

Trevor Slack is professor and Canada Research Chair in Sport Management at the University of Alberta in Canada. He was formerly the editor of the *Journal of Sport Management* and is currently the editor of the *European Sport Management Quarterly*. His work has appeared in such journals as *Organization Studies*, *Journal of Sport Management*, *Journal of Management Studies* and *Human Relations*. His current work is on the changes that are occurring in sports organizations in emerging economies.

Tan Hua is a professor in the School of Physical Education at South China University in Guangzhou. He has been working for two decades at the prestigious Research Centre of Sports History at Chengdu Physical Education Institute. His recent publications include *The Olympic Movement* (1993) and *The History of Sport* (1996). He is a major contributor to the books *Modern Chinese Sports History* (1989) and *The History of Sport in the People's Republic of China 1949–1998* (1999), all in Chinese.

Tsai Chiung-Tzu is a doctoral student in the Department of Sports Sciences at De Montfort University in England. She received her BA from National Chung-Cheng University (Taiwan) and her M.Phil. from De Montfort University. Her research interests are in women's leisure with a focus on constraints from Confucian and feminist perspectives.

Xiong Xiaozheng was editor of the *Journal of Sports Culture and History* and is director of the Research Department of the China Sports Museum in Beijing. He is the general secretary of the Chinese Society for the History of Physical Education and Sport. He has written extensively on sports in China from historical and cultural perspectives. He was a major contributor to *The History of Sport of the People's Republic of China 1949–1998* (1999) and several other books in Chinese.

Index

Abbas, Shah 387
'Abd al-Malik 386
Abu l-Fazl 392
Akbar, Emperor 392
Alborz College, Iran 277
Alexander 388
All India Council of Sport (AICS) 369
All-China Games 88
All-China Sports Federation 320–22, 347
Alsagoff, Syed Mohsen 145–6, 155n93
amateurism 84, 122
'Amr b. Layth 385–6
Anand, Vishwanathan 368
Anatolia, polo 391
Anglo-Iranian Oil Company 278
Antil, Seema 368
Appadurai, Arjun 55, 56
archery, China 190
Ardashir 385, 389
Arjuna Award, India 379
Asahi 106
Asia, definition 1–2
Asian Games
    Chinese participation 327–8
    Indian participation 368
    Indonesian participation 299–300
    participating countries 402
    Taiwan participation 327–8, 347, 359, 364n82
    Indonesia (1962) 300, 302, 309, 327–8
    Korea (1986) 232–3, 236, 238
    Beijing (1990) 404
    Korea (2002) 401
association football
    amateurism laws 84
    Indonesia 301
    Iran 278, 280, 284, 289–90
    Malaya 138–40
    Singapore 82–4, 85–6, 95n27
athletic exercise, Japanese concept 114–19
athletics
    China 88, 196–7
    Japan 109–10
    Malaya 141–2
    Singapore 88–9

badminton
    Indonesia 301–2

    Sudirman Cup 301
    Thomas Cup 300, 318n17
    women's participation 142
Bailey, J. Brooke 14
Bailey, Peter 157
baseball, Taiwan 345, 350–51, 359–60
basketball, China 196
Battling Key 87
Bi Bo 205
Bindra, Abhinav 368
Blanning, J.C.W. 7
Blazé, L.E. 62n62
Bombay Pentangular cricket tournament
    157–84, 184nn2–3, 185nn15, 19, 186n62, 187n82
Boxer Rebellion 192, 208n19
boxing, Singapore 87
British American Tobacco 405
British Empire Games 146
British imperialism
    and sport 63–4n98, 129, 130–31, 148–9, 249–50
    see also England
broadcasting, international 403–4
Bruce Lockhart, Robert 67, 80–81
Brundage, Avery 322, 324–5, 331–2, 347
Buddhism, Ceylon 17, 37, 41
Bushido 106, 121
Byzantine Empire, polo 390

callisthenics 278
Campbell, N.P. 41, 42, 60n38
Canada, and International Olympic Committee 354–5
Cannadine, David 63–4n98
Cao Chen 337
Carter, J., Revd 24
Celebi, Evliya 391–2
Ceylon
    cricket 11–12, 14–15, 31n27, 38–40, 57
    language in schools 37–8, 58–9n15
    middle classes 19–20, 30n7
    missionary education 11–25, 31n27
    plantations 18–19
Chang Che-Wei 345
Chen Dengke 206
Chen Duxiu 198

Chen Jing 359
Cheoson Sports Society, Korea 218, 224, 240n38
Chi Cheng 350, 356
Chiang Kai-shek 192, 346
children's games, Japan 103–5
China
  Asian Games 327–8
  athletics 88, 196–7
  basketball 196
  Confucianism 189–92
  Cultural Revolution 333
  economic reformation 402–3
  education system 193, 195–6, 199–200, 209n38
  GANEFO 329–32
  and International Olympic Committee (IOC) 319–27, 347–8, 352–5, 356–7
  Japanese invasion 203, 206
  martial arts 191–2, 202–3
  modern sports 201–2
  New Culture Movement 197–8
  Olympic Games 213
  physical education 199–200, 201–2, 202–3
  polo 393–5
  Qing dynasty 192–7
  Republican era 197–202
  social reform 194–7
  sponsorship 404
  sports competitions 200–1
  and Taiwan 360–61
  tradition or modernity 189, 203–7
  traditional sports 189–92
  Westernization movement 192–4, 208n21
China National Amateur Athletic Federation 200–1, 210–11n67, 320
Chinese
  attitude to sport 69, 72, 76–7, 82, 94n9
  queues 77, 197, 210n49
  in Singapore 68–9, 72–93, 251–4, 268, 270n45, 272n89
Chinese Swimming Club, Singapore 77, 78
Chinese Taipei Olympic Committee (CTOC) 357
Christianity, missionairies in Ceylon 15–17, 41, 60nn34–5
chuju (Chinese football) 190–91
Chun Doo-hwan 231–7
Chung Hongik 406
Church Missionary Society
  Ceylon 16, 21
  graduate recruits 33n110
  Uganda 27–8
cinema, India 160, 185nn17, 23
Cixi, Empress-dowager 195
clothing, for women 142–3, 154n72, 281

cold war 321
Colebrook, W.M.G. 17
Collins, Richard, Revd 22
colonial period 5–6
colonialism
  and cricket 11–12, 29–30n1, 71, 135–6
  Singapore 70–71
  see also imperialism
commercial endorsements, Indian cricketers 174, 187n75
commercialization, cricket 183–4
communalism
  Indian cricket 158–60, 166–84, 185n9
  Singapore 246
Confucianism
  China 189–92
  and polo 395
consumer culture, global 7
Contractor, H.N. 179–80, 181
Crawford, H.L. 44
cricket
  Bombay Pentangular cricket tournament 157–84, 184nn2–3, 185nn15, 19, 186n62, 187n82
  Ceylon 11–12, 14–15, 24, 31n27, 38–40, 57
  and colonialism 11–12, 29–30n1, 54–5, 56, 71, 135–6
  commercialization 183–4
  India 157–84, 380–81
  Indian journals 173, 187nn70–72
  Malaya 132, 140–41
  and missionaries 11–12, 35
  moral values 40, 59n30
  professionalism 173–4, 183
  Singapore 67, 74, 132
  social significance 158
  Times of India Shield 173–4
  Trinity College, Kandy 38–40, 44–8, 59n18
Crusaders, and polo 390
cycling
  Iranian women 287
  Malayan women 143–4

Dairoku, Kikuchi 100, 107–9, 119–20
dakyû 396
Darwinism 106, 115, 121, 195, 198
de Alwis, E.A. 60–61n41
Dedigama, P.C. 60–61n41
Ding Yuanpeng 395
Dingle, Edwin 129, 131
Dong Shouyi 206
Dronacharya Award, India 379
Dutch East Indies Company 295–6

Edstrom, Sigfrid 322

education
    and missionaries 11–25
    and sport 6, 35–6
    see also schools
Egypt, polo 391
Ekwanayake, G.B., Revd 48, 63n78
England
    sportsmanship 102, 108, 119, 121
    see also British imperialism
ethnic relations, and sport 134–7
European colonialism 5–6
Everest, Mount 263–4
exercise, benefits of 101, 106, 124n11

Fang Wanbang 206
Far Eastern Championship Games 88, 201
Feng Wenbin 321
Ferdowsi, Hakim Abu l-Qâsem 279–80, 388, 398n27
Ferguson, Niall 6
fives court, Singapore 74, 95nn22, 24
football *see* association football
footbinding 344
Foster-Hall, E. 135
Fraser, Alexander Garden 12, 15, 25–9, 35–58, 62nn54–5, 63n74, 64n99, 65n125

Gale, R.G. 'Reggie' 139–40
gambling, Singapore 84–5, 97n56
Games of the Newly Emerging Forces (GANEFO) 303–4, 309–10, 328–32
Gandhi, Mahatma 169–71
Garnett, J.G., Revd 23
Gibson, Thomas R. 279
girls *see* women
globalization 5–8, 402–6
Goh Chok Tong 256, 258–60, 263, 265
Goh Chye Hin 88–9
golf, Singapore 133
Guha, Ram 158
Gupta, P. 179, 180
gymkhanas, India 157, 184n1

Harris, Clifford 292n21
Harris, Lord 165, 186n44
Harun al-Rashid 391
Hāshemi, Fā'ezeh 286
Havelange, João 357
He Long 333
Ho Geng-sheng 327
Ho Peng Kee 266
Hobsbawm, Eric 158
Hong Kong to Beijing Rally 405
Hong Liu 338
horse racing
    Iran 282

Singapore 71–2, 84–5, 94–5n17, 97n57
Hsu, Henry 353–4
Huang Chih-Hsiung 359

imperialism
    Japan 122
    Monsoon Asia 3–5
    and sport 63–4n98, 129, 130–31, 134–7, 148–9
    sportsmanship 99, 102
    see also colonialism
Inche Othman Wok 253
India
    adopted sports schools 375
    Board of Control for Cricket in India (BCCI) 176, 188n88, 380–81
    Bombay Pentangular cricket tournament 157–84, 184nn2–3, 185nn15, 19, 186n62, 187n82
    centres of excellence 375–6
    cinema 160, 185nn17, 23
    communalism and cricket 158–60, 166–84, 185n9
    cricket and colonialism 29–30n1, 54–5, 56
    cricket malpractices 380–81
    currency 367
    economic development 367–8
    educational institutions 381
    ethnicity 366
    future of sport 382
    government policies 369–79
    gymkhanas 157, 184n1
    Hindu cricket clubs 165, 170–71, 186n39
    Indian Olympic Association 371, 380
    international competitions 368–9
    languages 366–7
    Muslim cricket clubs 165, 186n40
    national coaching scheme 376
    National Sports Policy (1984) 369–70
    National Sports Policy (2001) 370–73
    National Sports Talent Contest Scheme 374
    National Welfare Fund for Sportspersons 377–8
    non-governmental sector 380–81
    Parsee cricket clubs 164–5
    pensions for sportspersons 377
    polo 396–7
    religions 366
    scholarships 378
    Special Area Games 376–7
    sports academies 376
    Sports Authority of India 374–9
    sports awards 378–9
    training centres 375
Indonesia
    Asian Games (1962) 300, 302, 309, 327–8

badminton 300, 301–2, 318n17
colonial history 295–6
democracy 307–10
education system 311–14
football 301
G30S coup (1965) 304, 307, 310, 316
humanitarianism/internationalism 302–6
Indonesian Sports Association (PORI) 297–8, 309
international competitions 299–300, 302–5
kerapan sapi 306
Ministry of Sport (DORI) 309–10
National Sports Council (KONI) 310
National Sports Week (PON) 298–9, 309–10
nationalism 296–302
Olympic Games 299–300, 316–17, 328–9
Pancasila 296, 305–6, 315–16, 317
pasola 305, 310
religion 315
social justice 310–14
teacher education schools (SGO) 308, 311, 314
traditional sports 305–6
Indoot, Mrs 142
International Olympic Committee (IOC)
and Canada 354–5
and China 319–27
and Indonesia 302–3
and Taiwan 347–8, 352–5
see also Olympic Games
internationalization, broadcasting 403–4
Iran
Asian identity 275–6
equestrian sports 282
football 278, 280, 284, 289–90
international competitions 287–90
Islamic regime 282–7
physical education 277–8
polo 276, 385–90
televised sport 282
traditional sports 276–7, 279–80
Western sport 277–81
women and sport 277, 278, 280–81, 285–7
World Cup (France, 1998) 289–90
wrestling 276, 280, 283–4
zurkhāneh 276, 279–80, 282–3
Islam, and women's sports 277, 285–7
Islamic Countries' Women Sports Solidarity Games 287
Israel, and Indonesia 302–3, 328

James, C.L.R. 56
Japan
children's games 103–5
Meiji Restoration 115, 126n78

Olympic medals 213, 222
polo 396
sports policy 403
sportsmanship 99–123
World Cup (2002) 401
Japan Sky Broadcasting Company 403
Japanese, in Taiwan 343–6
Jasighe, D.J. 60–1n41
Jayersinghe, H.C. 60–61n41
Jayewarden, A.M. 60–61n41
Jiang Weiqiao 206
Jingwu Sports Society 202
Johnson, Rafer 348
Jordan, Samuel 277
journals *see* magazines
Jusserand, Jean-Jules 390

Kagal, B.R. 167–8
Kang Youwei 195
Kee-chung Son (Kitei son) 221
Khameneh'i, Ayatollah 285, 289
Khānom, Badr al-Dojā 280
Khatami, Mohammad 289–90
Khomeni, Ayatollah Ruhollāh 281, 282–4, 288
Khoo Hooi Hye 86–7
Khoo Kay Kim 147–8
Khoo Swee Chiow 264
Killanin, Lord 354–5
Kinosita, Koji 109–10, 120
Klass, Mary 146
Knauth, Wolfgang 385
Korea
American military rule 223–4
Chun Doo-hwan regime 231–7
educational system 215–17
Healthy People Policy 228
history of sports movement 219
Hodori Plan 233, 242n77
Japanese rule 217–18
National Youth Games 216–17, 239n16
Olympic Games participation 221–2, 224
Olympic Games (Seoul, 1988) 225, 232–3, 236–7, 241n44, 242n71
Park Chung-hee regime 215–17, 218–20, 225–31, 238
People's Revolution (1960) 224, 240n37
polo 395–6
post-war sport 214–15, 223–5
Roh Tae-woo regime 231–7
socio-economic development 234
sports revolution' 218–23, 227–31
World Cup (2002) 401
Korean Sports Council 216–17, 218, 222, 224
Korean War 224–5
Kung Xiang-xi 320
kyogido 114–15, 118–19, 120–23

Lake Club, Malaya 132
Lau Teng Chuan 246
Laverton, R.H.C. 82
Lee Hak-rae 236, 237
Lee Kuan Yew 243–8, 250–54, 269n5
Li Gonglin 395
Li Guo 394
Liao Min-Hsiung 360
Lim Bong Soo 86, 87
Lim Boon Keng 77
Lim, David 264
Lim Koon Tye 78
Lim Yew Hock 244
Liu Changchun 203–4
Liu, James T.C. 395, 396
Liu Shaoqi 329
Low, D.A. 15
Lu Xun 199
Ludowyk, E.F.C. 12, 13–14, 49, 53–4

Ma Liang 206
MacCallum, Henry 19–20
McDonalds 8
MacLuich, A., Revd 28
magazines
    Indian cricket 173, 187nn70–72
    Malaya 144–6
Mah Bow Tan 266
Maitra, J.C. 169, 186n55
Malaya
    administrative set-up 96–7n52
    association football 138–40
    athletics 141–2
    colonial period 131–49
    cricket 132, 140–41
    football 83–4
    indigenous groups 130, 150n5
    post-colonial period 146–8
    pre-colonial sports 130, 150–51nn6–7
    sport and colonialism 129, 130–31, 148–9
    sports magazines 144–6
    western sports 131–2, 134–7
    women and sport 131, 133, 142–4
    see also Malaysia; Singapore
Malaya Cup 83, 138, 140, 153n50
Malayan Amateur athletics Association 141, 154n69
Malayan Chinese Football Association 83
Malayan Mirror 144
Malayan Sports Annual 144
Malayan Sports Pictorial 145
Malaysia
    and Indonesia 303
    National Sports Foundation 147, 155n103
    see also Malaya
Malleswari, K. 368

Manipur, polo 396–7
manliness, English concept of 99, 108, 124–5n36
Manning, William 48
Manzenreiter, Wolfram 405
Mao Zedong 198–9, 333–8
Marshall, David 244
martial arts
    China 191–2, 202–3
    Iran 281
    Japan 106–7
Maulana Abul Kalam Azad Trophy, India 379
media, internationalization 403–4
Mehta, Sahrab 181
Membrè, Michele 387
Merchant, Vijay 181, 188n105
Miles, Eustace H. 111–14, 120, 126n62
militarism, of games 110, 113
Minogue, Kenneth 336–7
Minseok Ahn 406
missionaries
    Ceylon 11–25, 31n27, 41
    Japan 99–100
Mugabe, Robert 59n30
Mughal Empire, polo 392
Mulgrue, G.R. 41, 60n36
Muscular Christianity 12, 25, 33n103, 42, 130

Nakamura, S. 86
Nanyang Girls' High School, Singapore 80, 96n42
Napier-Clavering, H. Percy, Revd 23–4, 28
Nayadu, C.K. 174
Ng Ser Miang 266
Nike 405
Nishimura, Tei 103
Nishinouchi, Okujiro 106–7
Nixon, Richard 335, 352
Norwood, Cyril 118

obesity, Singapore 262
Ohi, Mingo 103
Olympic Council of Asia 405
Olympic Games
    Asian participation 213
    Chinese participation 319–27
    Indian participation 368
    Indonesian participation 299–300, 316–17
    influence on China 201
    Korean participation 221–2, 224
    Taiwanese participation 359, 364n82
    Los Angeles (1932) 203–4
    Berlin (1936) 89–90
    Helsinki (1952) 320–23
    Montreal (1976) 354–5
    Seoul (1988) 227, 232–3, 236–7, 241n44, 242n71

see also International Olympic Committee (IOC)
Ong, C.B. 145
Oon, Desmond 256, 261
Opium War 189, 207n2
Owen, Gertrude 144

Pahlavi, Reza Shah 279, 281
Pancasila, Indonesia 296, 305–6, 315–16, 317
Pandey, Gyan 166–7
Park Chung-hee 215–17, 218–20, 225–31, 238
Parthians 385
Pennefather, Alice 142
People's Republic of China *see* China
Perera, H.S. 60–61n41
Perera, S.S. 14, 31n27
Perry, E.J., Revd 23
Persians 276, 292n7
  see also Iran
physical education
  China 199–200, 201–2, 202–3
  Indonesia 312–13
  Iran 277–8, 280–81
  Korea 215–17
  Singapore 254–5
'ping-pong diplomacy' 333–8, 352
plantations, Ceylon 18–19
Polishwalla, P.N. 172–3
politics, and sport 336–7
polo
  Iran 276, 385–90
  in literature and art 388–90
  origins of 384
  spread eastwards 392–7
  spread westwards 390–92
professionalism, cricket 173–4, 183

Rafsanjani, Ali-Akbar Hāshemi 286–7
Rajaratnam, S. 244, 245
Rajiv Gandhi Khel Ratna Award, India 379
Ranji Trophy, India 176–7, 182
Rao, K.S.Ranga 181
Razak, Tun 147
Reimann, Valesca L.O. 22, 39
Rhee, Syngman 224–5, 240n37
rifle shooting, Malaya 133
Roberts, Michael 12, 18
Roh Tae-woo 231–7
Rong Gaotang 322, 325
rugby, Ceylon 45, 62n62
Ruizong, Emperor 393
Russo-Japanese War 122, 125–6n61

St Thomas's Collge, Ceylon 49, 63n78
samurai, values of 106, 109

Sarbadhikary, Berry 169
Sassen, Saskia 405
Schmidt, Ferdinand A. 111, 126n62
schools
  Ceylon 11–12, 20–25
  China 193
  Korea 215–17
  Malaya 134, 152–3n26
  Singapore 80
  Taiwan 343–4
  see also education
schoolteachers, Ceylon 41, 42, 60–61nn41–2
scouting, Iran 279, 292–3n23
Selangor Club, Malaya 132
Senior, A.L. 44
sepak takraw 257, 271–2n80, 300, 310
Seto, Koshichiro 103–4
Shaʻbān Jaʻfari 280
Shāhnāmeh 388, 398n27
Shao Rugan 206
Shapoorji Sorabjee Bengali 167
Sharp, Mitchell 354
Sheng Zhibai 321
Sherer, J.F. 397
Sherley, Anthony 387
Shimomura, Yasuhiro 104
Siew, Edwin 264
Singapore
  association football 82–4, 85–6, 95n27, 138–40
  athletics 88–9
  boxing 87
  British colonialism 67–8, 92–3, 249, 250
  Chinese community 68–9, 72–93, 251–4, 268, 270n45, 272n89
  Committee on Sporting Singapore (CoSS) 266–7, 274n131
  communalism of sports clubs 246
  economic growth 247–8, 270n23
  fitness campaigns 250–58, 262–3, 273n109
  gambling 84–5, 97n56
  golf 133
  horse racing 71–2, 84–5, 94–5n17, 97n57
  independence 243–8
  Indian National Army 271n65
  lack of space 91–2
  military sports activities 74–5, 89
  name of 269n2
  'nanny state' 269, 274n148
  national identity and sport 248–50
  National Stadium 251
  New Year Sea and Land Sports 69–70
  Olympic Games 249–50
  padang 67, 94n1
  People's Action Party (PAP) 243–50
  'Sport for All' policy 250–58

'Sport for Life' campaign 262–3
sporting clubs 67, 71–2, 73–7, 246
Sports Excellence 2000 (SPEX 2000)
  258–61, 265, 273nn94, 98
sports facilities 257, 272n83
Sports Medicine, Fitness and Research
  Centre 272n91
swimming 90, 97–8n72
tennis 86–7
water polo 90, 97–8nn72–3, 136
women's sports 78–81, 96nn46–7
Singapore Amateur Football Association 84
Singapore Chinese Swimming Club 90,
  97–8n72, 136
Singapore Cricket Club 67, 74, 132, 246
Singapore Football League 83
Singapore Recreation Club 67, 75–6
Singapore Sporting Club 71–2, 84–5, 94n16
Singapore Sports Council (SSC) 253, 255–6
Sino-Japanese War 194, 209n29, 361n3
Siperco, Alexandru 353
Slack, Trevor 402
Snow, Edgar 334
soccer *see* association football
Soleimāni, Ali-Rezā 283
Song Ong Siang 77, 78
South Korea *see* Korea
South-East Asian Games (SEA) 300, 304–5
Soviet Union, and China 320–21, 332, 333–8
Spencer, Herbert 105, 114, 121
sponsorship 404–5
sport
  and education 6, 35–6
  and imperialism 63–4n98, 129, 130–31,
    148–9, 249–50
  and national identity 248–50
  and politics 336–7
social significance 157–8
Sport and Pastimes 145, 155n89
Sports Authority of India 374–9
Sports in Malaya (Review) 145
The Sportsman 145, 155n87
sportsmanship
  English concept 99, 102, 108, 119
  Japan 99–123
  Malaya 134–5
Sri Lanka *see* Ceylon
Stock, Eugene 21
Stokes, Henry Scott 226
Stone, W.A., Revd 48–9
Straits Chinese National Football Association
  77
Straits Chinese Recreation Club 76–7, 88
Strange, Frederick William 99–103, 105, 108,
  114, 119, 123n5
Subbaraon, Dr 180, 188n99

Sudirman Cup 301
Suharto, General 304, 307–8
Sukarno, Ahmed 296, 297, 302–4, 307, 329,
  330
Sun Baoqing 197
Super Physique 145–6, 155n93
Swettenham, Frank 73
swimming, Singapore 90, 97–8n72, 143

table tennis
  international championships 337
  'ping-pong diplomacy' 334–8, 352
Taiwan
  Asian Games 327–8, 347, 359, 364n82
  baseball 345, 350–51, 359–60
  and China (PRC) 346, 360–61
  Chinese Taipei Olympic Committee
    (CTOC) 357
  and International Olympic Committee
    320–27, 347–8, 352–5, 356–7
  Japanese occupation 343–6
  Kuomintang (KMT) 346
  National Council on Physical Fitness and
    Sport (NCPFS) 356, 358–9
  Olympic Games 359, 364n82
  physical education programme 355–6
  schools 343–4
  sports policy 357–60
  stone throwing 346
Taizong, Emperor 394
Takeda, Chiyosaburo 100, 101–2, 111, 114–23
Takhti, Gholāmrezā 283
Tan Eng Liang 261
Tan Howe Liang 249–50
Tan, Joseph 144
Tan, Tony 268
Tanaka, Morinari 103
Tanglin Club, Singapore 246
Tarmugi, Abdullah 266
Taye, Adeline 144
televised sport
  internationalization 403–4
  Iran 282
tennis, Singapore 86–7
Teo Chee Hean 266
Terao, Hisashi 103
Teutonia Club, Malaya 132
Thomas Cup 300, 318n17
Timur 386
Tojo, Taneie 104
Tokyo University 99–100, 123n2
Toyama, Shoichi 107
traditional sports
  China 189–92
  Indonesia 305–6
  Iran 276–7, 279–80

Trinity College, Kandy 15, 19, 21–5, 28–9, 35–58, 60–61nn41–2, 61n45, 61–2n48
Tsai Wen-Yi 359
Tso Ping Lung 76–7
Tsuboi, Gendo 103, 104
Tung Shao-yi 320, 325–6
Tyndale-Biscoe, Cecil Earle 41, 42, 61n44

Undokai 105–7
United States, and China 333–8, 352–3, 361
University College School, London 99–100, 107–8
Uryu, Tora 104

Valberg, Lloyd 146
Van Casteel, A.T. 103
Vandespar, George 15
Varzandeh, Mir-Mehdi 277
Vizianagram, Maharajkumar of 171–2

Walker, Ashley 14–15
Walmsley, A.M., Revd 41, 60n36
Wang Cheng-ting 319–20
Wang Fudan 207, 212n93
Wang Jian 394
Wang Jianwu 206
Wang Meng 335
Wang Shijie 206
Wang Zhenting 198, 210n54
Ward, W.E.F. 26, 39, 42
water polo, Singapore 90, 97–8nn72–3, 136
Whampoa (Hoo Ah Kay) 72
Winstedt, Richard O. 83
women
    Chinese in Singapore 78–81, 96n46

clothing 142–3, 154n72, 281, 285–6
cycling 143–4
Iran 277, 278, 280–81, 285–7
in Malaya 131, 133, 142–4
polo players 394
Taiwan 344, 345–6
Wong Peng Soon 250
World Cup
    France (1998) 289–90
    Japan/Korea (2002) 401
wrestling, Iran 276, 280, 283–4
Wu Dao-Yuan 347
Wu Min-Kao 347
Wu Shaozu 335
Wu Yunrui 205, 211n85
wushu 191–2

Xia, General 393
Xiaong, Emperor 393
Xiaozong, Emperor 395
Xie Shiyan 204–5
Xuanzong 393

Yan Fu 194–5
Yang Chuan-Kuang 348–50
Yeo, Annie 143
Yoshida, Shukichi 104
Yuan Duili 206
Yugisho 103–5, 120
Yusa, Eisaku 103

Zhang Zhijiang 204
Zhong Liang 337–8
Zhou Enlai 322, 323, 333–5
zurkhāneh, Iran 276, 279–80, 282–3